Education and Politics
at Harvard

Other Books by Seymour Martin Lipset

THE DIVIDED ACADEMY: PROFESSORS AND POLITICS, *with Everett C. Ladd, McGraw-Hill, 1975.*

FAILURE OF A DREAM? ESSAYS IN THE HISTORY OF AMERICAN SOCIALISM, *(ed.), with John Laslett, Anchor Doubleday, 1974.*

ACADEMICS, POLITICS, AND THE 1972 ELECTION, *with Everett C. Ladd, American Enterprise Institute for Public Policy Research, 1973.*

PROFESSORS, UNIONS, AND AMERICAN HIGHER EDUCATION, *with Everett C. Ladd, Carnegie Commission on Higher Education, 1973.*

REBELLION IN THE UNIVERSITY, *Little, Brown, 1972.*

THE POLITICS OF UNREASON: RIGHT-WING EXTREMISM IN AMERICA, 1790–1970, *with Earl Raab, Harper & Row, 1970, Torch Books paperback, 1973.*

REVOLUTION AND COUNTERREVOLUTION: CHANGE AND PERSISTENCE IN SOCIAL STRUCTURE, *Basic Books, 1968, and Anchor Doubleday, revised 1970.*

STUDENTS IN REVOLT, *(ed.), with Philip G. Altbach, Daedalus Library, Beacon Press, 1969.*

POLITICS AND THE SOCIAL SCIENCES, *(ed.), Oxford University Press, 1969.*

AGRARIAN SOCIALISM: THE COOPERATIVE COMMONWEALTH FEDERATION IN SASKATCHEWAN, *University of California Press, 1950, revised 1968.*

SOCIOLOGY AND HISTORY: METHODS, *(ed.), with Richard Hofstadter, Basic Books, 1968.*

STUDENT POLITICS, *(ed.), Basic Books, 1967.*

PARTY SYSTEMS AND VOTER ALIGNMENTS, *(ed.), with S. Rokkan, Free Press, 1967.*

THE FIRST NEW NATION: THE UNITED STATES IN HISTORICAL AND COMPARATIVE PERSPECTIVE, *Basic Books, 1963, and Anchor Doubleday, 1967.*

CLASS, STATUS AND POWER: SOCIAL STRATIFICATION IN COMPARATIVE PERSPECTIVE, *(ed.), with Reinhard Bendix, Free Press, 1966.*

ESTUDIANTES UNIVERSITARIOS Y POLITICA EN EL TERCER MUNDO, *Editorial Alfa, Montevideo, 1965.*

CULTURE AND SOCIAL CHARACTER: THE WORK OF DAVID RIESMAN REVIEWED, *(ed.), with Leo Lowenthal, Free Press, 1961.*

POLITICAL MAN: THE SOCIAL BASES OF POLITICS, *Doubleday, 1960, Anchor Doubleday, 1963.*

UNION DEMOCRACY, *with Martin Trow and James S. Coleman, Free Press, 1953, Anchor Doubleday, 1962, and Free Press paperback, 1975.*

SOCIAL MOBILITY IN INDUSTRIAL SOCIETY: A STUDY IN POLITICAL SOCIOLOGY, *with Reinhard Bendix, University of California Press, 1959.*

Other Books by David Riesman

ACADEMIC TRANSFORMATION: 17 INSTITUTIONS UNDER PRESSURE, *(ed.), with Verne Stadtman, McGraw-Hill, 1973.*

ACADEMIC VALUES AND MASS EDUCATION: THE EARLY YEARS OF OAKLAND AND MONTEITH, *with Joseph Gusfield and Zelda Gamson, Doubleday, 1970, McGraw-Hill, 1975.*

THE LONELY CROWD: A STUDY OF THE CHANGING AMERICAN CHARACTER, *with Nathan Glazer and Reuel Denney, Yale University Press, rev. ed., 1969.*

THE ACADEMIC REVOLUTION, *with Christopher Jencks, Doubleday, 1968.*

CONVERSATIONS IN JAPAN: MODERNIZATION, POLITICS, AND CULTURE, *with Evelyn Thompson Riesman, Basic Books, 1967.*

ABUNDANCE FOR WHAT? AND OTHER ESSAYS, *Doubleday, 1964.*

CONSTRAINT AND VARIETY IN AMERICAN EDUCATION, *University of Nebraska Press, 1956, rev. ed., 1965.*

FACES IN THE CROWD: INDIVIDUAL STUDIES IN CHARACTER AND POLITICS, *with Nathan Glazer, Yale University Press, rev. ed., 1964.*

INDIVIDUALISM RECONSIDERED AND OTHER ESSAYS, *Free Press, 1954.*

THORSTEIN VEBLEN: A CRITICAL INTERPRETATION, *Scribner's, 1953.*

Education and Politics at Harvard

by *Seymour Martin Lipset*
and *David Riesman*

Two Essays Prepared for
The Carnegie Commission on Higher Education

MCGRAW-HILL BOOK COMPANY
New York   St. Louis   San Francisco
Düsseldorf   Johannesburg   Kuala Lumpur   London   Mexico
Montreal   New Delhi   Panama   Paris   São Paulo
Singapore   Sydney   Tokyo   Toronto

The Carnegie Commission on Higher Education,
2150 Shattuck Avenue, Berkeley, California 94704
has sponsored preparation of this volume as
part of a continuing effort to obtain and present
significant information for public discussion.
The views expressed are those of the authors.

EDUCATION AND POLITICS AT HARVARD

This book was set in Palatino by B. Handelman Associates, Inc.
It was printed and bound by The Maple Press Company.
The designer was Elliot Epstein. The editors were
Nancy Tressel and Michael Hennelly for McGraw-Hill Book Company
and Verne A. Stadtman and Karen Seriguchi for the
Carnegie Commission on Higher Education. Audre Hanneman
edited the index. Milton J. Heiberg supervised the production.

Library of Congress Cataloging in Publication Data

Lipset, Seymour Martin.
Education and politics at Harvard.

Includes bibliographies and index.
1. Harvard University—Students. 2. College students—United States—Political activity—History.
I. Riesman, David, date II. Carnegie Commission on Higher Education. III. Title.

LD2160.L56   378.744'4   74-34137
ISBN 0-07-010114-0

1 2 3 4 5 6 7 8 9 MAMM 7 9 8 7 6 5

Contents

Foreword, ix

Part One: Political Controversies at Harvard, 1636 to 1974
by Seymour Martin Lipset

1 *Introduction*, 3

2 *The Colonial Period*, 15

Discipline and academic freedom ▪ Revolutionary politics ▪ Changes in governance

3 *From the Post-Revolution Era to the Civil War*, 47

Student indiscipline ▪ The Unitarian triumph ▪ Partisan conflicts ▪ Efforts at
reform ▪ Academic losses ▪ Renewed student rebellion ▪ Religious liberalism ▪ Politics
and meritocracy ▪ Partisanship and governance ▪ The slavery issue avoided ▪ The state of
education ▪ The end of state control

4 *The Golden Age of Eliot*, 91

Student reactions ▪ Academic freedom ▪ Reactions to Eliot's policies ▪ Social-class
differences ▪ Political activity ▪ Alumni attacks on academic freedom ▪ Student political
views and activities ▪ Religious liberalism extended ▪ Settlement work ▪ Antiwar
activity ▪ Support for academic freedom ▪ Student socialism ▪ The sources of
nonconformism ▪ Intellectual achievements ▪ Renewed dissatisfaction

5 *The Lowell Administration*, 133

World War I ▪ Postwar threats to academic freedom ▪ Racism at Harvard ▪ Anti-Semitism
and admissions quotas ▪ Political activity in the Yard ▪ The decline of scholarship

6 *The Protest of the Thirties*, 157

Faculty activism ▪ Concern for faculty quality ▪ The end of the Faculty Council ▪ External
pressures ▪ Developments in the Student Union ▪ The politics of intervention ▪ Resistance
to racism

7 *The Postwar Era*, 179

The rights of Communists under attack ▪ Threats to the economics department ▪ Cold War
pressures on scholarship ▪ Student opinions ▪ The academic culture ▪ A new
president ▪ Student reactions ▪ Liberal student attitudes

8 *The Sixties and Beyond,* 205

Activism revives ▪ SDS appears on the scene ▪ Spring riots ▪ Antiwar protest ▪ SDS plans for action ▪ The "bust" ▪ The Afro-American demands ▪ The restoration of authority ▪ Postcrisis change ▪ Change in administration ▪ The new president ▪ The issues of the calm ▪ Economics and politics again ▪ Free speech and other issues

9 *Conclusion,* 245

References to Part One, 257

Part Two: Educational Reform at Harvard College: Meritocracy and Its Adversaries
by David Riesman

Prologue, 281

1 *Edging Toward Meritocracy in the 1920s,* 293

2 *Meritocracy Triumphant,* 305

3 *Moderating Meritocracy,* 333

4 *Altered Student Climates,* 359

5 *Altered Faculty Climates,* 369

References to Part Two, 393

Index, 403

Foreword

Harvard is the preeminent institution of higher education in the United States, and Seymour Martin Lipset and David Riesman are two of the leading social scientists in the world. This volume has Harvard as its subject as seen from two vantage points: first, of its long history of intramural and extramural politics as reviewed by Lipset, and, second, of its more recent transformations in educational spirit as sensed by Riesman. This combination in a single book of two such informed and astute analysts at work on the life of such an important institution has a special history.

At the end of the 1960s, I asked David Riesman, who was then a member of the Carnegie Commission on Higher Education, to put together a volume of essays on how some major colleges and universities had coped with the political and educational vicissitudes of that decade. One of those who agreed to prepare an essay for the volume—on Harvard—was Seymour Martin Lipset. But as Professor Lipset began to study the contemporary controversies at Harvard, in which he was a participant as well as an observer, he concluded that the subject could not be understood without going back to Harvard's origins. He and Professor Riesman also soon realized that the study of Harvard, as it was at this point conceived, would take longer to complete than the schedule for the volume of essays allowed.

When it became apparent that Professor Lipset's work would not only extend beyond the deadline for the essay volume but would also produce a manuscript of greater scope and size than was originally contemplated, Professor Riesman considered some alternatives. To produce a book on institutions under pressures in the 1960s without including Harvard as a case study was out of the question. Professor Riesman first decided to fill the gap himself. He was then on leave from Harvard at the Institute for Advanced Study in Princeton and was able to make a substantial beginning on an essay based principally on his own Harvard observations as an undergraduate from 1927 to 1931, as a law student from 1931 to 1934, as a research fellow from 1934 to 1935, and as a faculty member from 1958 to the present. Because he deliberately avoided the issues of politics that he knew Professor Lipset was working on, and because he found that his own essay was becoming too long, he decided that it, too, would be unsuitable for the volume of essays he was editing. At this point, he proposed that Marshall Meyer, a sociologist at Cornell, should be asked to conduct a survey of Harvard student attitudes in the spring of 1972 and to compare them with an earlier study he had done of students in the spring of 1969. His suggestion was accepted, and Marshall Meyer's essay on this work became a part of the Carnegie Commission's volume, *Academic Transformation: Seventeen Institutions under Pressure,* which Riesman edited with the assistance of Verne Stadtman, associate director of the Commission.

Happily, the work of Professors Lipset and Riesman on Harvard was continued, with the understanding that the resulting essays would be combined for publication. The Carnegie Commission, which had been instrumental in launching their efforts, continued to give encouragement to the project. The final result is the volume at hand.

The essays here are in many respects two separate works that have their subject, Harvard University, in common.

Professor Lipset's essay is primarily historical and political. It expresses the view that politically relevant tensions are endemic to a university, and that such tensions are most intense at research universities, where there is great toleration for new ideas and where academic freedom most protects those who are inclined to be critical and engage in reform politics. Professor Lipset documents his theory with reports of wave after wave of political activity that have taken place at Harvard since 1636.

Professor Riesman's essay is more limited and impressionistic, and deals almost exclusively with educational developments in Harvard College. In particular, he is concerned with the rise of meritocratic values and the way that they have survived initiatives of the 1960s and 1970s that have tended to alter the competitive atmosphere for undergraduates.

Although the two essays are dissimilar in many ways—in length, perspective, and subject matter—they also complement each other and show us a Harvard that perhaps can only be seen with the help of writers who have spent much of their lives there. Professor Lipset's careful search for the politically significant events of Harvard's past and Professor Riesman's diligent reconstruction of its educational milieu since the

1920s have produced a most valuable book with very great relevance to the important higher education issues of our times.

Perhaps only Harvard could give rise to a volume like this one. For the story of Harvard is at the center of the general history of American higher education. Much of what has occurred there has been reflective of similar events and developments at many other schools. But, beyond this, Harvard is the oldest of all, and it has been for much of its life the leadership institution in the nation. Its political and educational innovations and conflicts, and its reactions to changing environments, have been watched more carefully than those at any other single institution. This is nearly as true today as it was when Eliot transformed Harvard, and the American university, a century ago. Somebody needs to know everything about each college and university, but only about Harvard does everybody need to know something. Lipset and Riesman make it much easier to know this something on the basis of the most careful of scholarship and the most perceptive of insights.

Clark Kerr

Chairman
Carnegie Commission
on Higher Education

February 1975

Education and Politics
at Harvard

Part One

Political Controversies at Harvard,
1636 to 1974

by Seymour Martin Lipset

1. *Introduction*

The ties between academic life and political controversy are clearly not new, although many Americans were totally surprised by the campus-based rebellion of the 1960s. As institutions linked intimately with religion in their origins in the Western world, universities often formed the main arena for religious disputation. Martin Luther found his strongest support at his University of Wittenberg and at other German universities (Moller, 1968, p. 238). Erik Erikson describes Hamlet as "the morbid young intellectual of his time, for did he not recently return from studies at Wittenberg, the hotbed of humanist corruption, his time's counterpart to Sophist Athens. . . . He is estranged from the ways of his country . . ." (Erikson, 1968, pp. 237–238). Writing of the English

ACKNOWLEDGMENTS: I am grateful to David Riesman for suggesting this volume, for wise comments and suggestions on various drafts of the essay which, in the process, grew much larger than was initially intended, and for continued insights into the problems of higher education. One could not ask for a better colleague and collaborator.

Various of my other colleagues at Harvard have provided important advice and information. These include particularly Bernard Bailyn, Daniel Bell, Nathan Glazer, Oscar Handlin, George Homans, Phyllis Keller, David Landes, Talcott Parsons, and James Q. Wilson. Colleagues elsewhere who have added much to my knowledge of problems of university life include Philip Altbach of the University of Wisconsin, Morton Keller of Brandeis University, Everett Ladd of the University of Connecticut, Clark Kerr of the Carnegie Commission on Higher Education, and Marshall Meyer of the University of California at Riverside. As will be evident to any reader of this essay, my intellectual debts to Samuel Eliot Morison, the preeminent historian of Harvard, are far greater than the references to his works can possibly indicate.

I am particularly grateful to the Carnegie Commission on Higher Education for sponsoring this work. Its completion was facilitated by a year at the Center for Advanced Study in the Behavioral Sciences, supported in part by a Guggenheim Foundation Fellowship. This work on Harvard forms a constituent part of my efforts to understand the conditions of academic and intellectual life generally, which have been supported over the years by grants from the Ford Foundation and the National Endowment for the Humanities. Related analyses of student and faculty behavior, both historically and comparatively, may be found in various other writings, most recently Lipset, 1972*a*; 1972*b*; and Ladd and Lipset, 1975.

3

Revolution of the seventeenth century, which combined religion and politics, Thomas Hobbes noted: "The core of the rebellion, as you have seen by this, and read of other rebellions, are the Universities, which nevertheless are not to be cast away, but to be better disciplined" (Hobbes, 1682, p. 74). In the United States, faculty and students at the group of small colleges of the pre-Revolutionary period were engaged in assorted disputations with religious and political authorities and ultimately were deeply involved in the movement for independence (Hofstadter, 1961, pp. 201–208). Within the first decade of the American Republic, President John Adams wrote: "I really begin to think, or rather to suspect, that learned academies, not under the immediate inspection and control of government, have disorganized the world, and are incompatible with social order" (Adams, 1853, p. 596). In czarist Russia, which had experienced a massive peasant rebellion in the late eighteenth century, Joseph de Maistre warned the czar, at the time "when the fermentation of ideas had barely begun in Russia, that the real danger to order in the country was not the peasants as such but an eventual *'Pougatchev d'universite'"* (Malia, 1961, p. 8). Universities formed significant centers of dissent in the events which led up to the Revolution of 1848, described by Namier as "The Revolution of the Intellectuals" and reaching a high point in Vienna, where the revolutionary regime was based on the "Academic Legion," largely composed of university students (Namier, 1964, p. 25; Altbach, 1969, pp. 451–474). Looking over the relationship of the scholar to politics in the Western world in 1873, Whitelaw Reid, former abolitionist leader and then editor of the New York *Tribune*, noted his political role in a series of commencement addresses at different American colleges:

Exceptional influences eliminated, the scholar is pretty sure to be opposed to the established. The universities of Germany contain the deadliest foes to the absolute authority of the Kaiser. The scholars of France prepared the way for the first Revolution, and were the most dangerous enemies of the imperial adventurer who betrayed the second. . . . While the prevailing parties in our country were progressive and radical, the temper of our colleges was to the last degree conservative. As our politics settled into the conservative tack, a fresh wind began to blow about the college seats, and literary men, at last, furnished inspiration for the splendid movement that swept slavery from the statute book. . . . Wise unrest will always be their [the scholars'] chief trait. We may set down . . . the very foremost function of the scholar in politics, *To oppose the established.*

. . . As for the scholar, the laws of his intellectual development may be trusted to fix his place. Free thought is necessarily aggressive and critical. The scholar, like the healthy redblooded young man, is an inherent, an organic, an inevitable radical. . . . And so we may set down, as a second function of the American scholar in politics, *An intellectual leadership of the radicals* (Reid, 1873, pp. 613–614).

Although many American scholars were instrumental in fostering the abolitionist movement, Reid's image of their role as leaders of the radicals was clearly an analytic projection of the inherent consequence of free (creative) thought. Across the Pacific in Meiji Japan, Arinori Mori, the minister of education in that great group of self-conscious aristocratic reformers who remade the country so as to be able to meet the West on its own terms, in establishing the government-supported university system, anticipated that scholarly institutions inevitably would become centers of critical thought. Mori noted that the lower segments of the educational system, which would teach needed skills, would also "help teach the people to be loyal to the state." But he also felt that the country required a high level of science and technology. This meant that there was a need for universities that "should be allowed sufficient freedom in the conduct of research to assure academic progress and the development of the applied sciences." Given the prospective tension between the need both to indoctrinate the masses and for "free thought" in the universities, Mori insisted that the universities, which would inevitably become centers of critical ideas, should not be in contact with the people, particularly that they should not be allowed to train teachers for the rest of the educational system. He believed they should be educated in nonscholarly teachers colleges that could "mold teachers who would assume the responsibility of educating a people both loyal to the state and militaristic in outlook" (Nagai, 1964, pp. 29–30).

In calling attention to these commentaries on the role of the university, it is not my intention to suggest that the main estates of higher education, faculty and students, are inherently in conflict with established institutions or modes of thought. It is obvious that the great majority in both strata, most of the time, have accepted the status quo. Universities are educational institutions, which implies that they are part of the social apparatus designed to transmit the existing culture, including the beliefs that help to legitimate the authority system of the society. For much of their history, universities were expected to uphold the doctrines of the religious faith to which they were linked. Faculty and students have been members of the privileged elites, and as such have had a major stake in preserving the distribution of privileges. Although as Mori noted, universities have become important centers of intellectual innovation, this was not their original purpose, often not even an auxiliary function, until relatively recent times. And even today, in the United States, in Japan, in the Soviet Union, the vast majority of institutions of higher education, although called colleges and universities, are essentially schools rather than universities, i.e., knowledge-creating centers. The school requires the faculty to be primarily involved in the transmission of skills, the indoctrination of accepted values, the preparation for life, and the development of total personality and character. In essence, therefore, the "school" components of higher education are the conservative aspects, and not surprisingly, research on the correlates of varying political orientations of American academics reveals that the more committed faculty are to teaching, as distinct from research, the more conservative their social views (Lipset, 1972*a*, pp. 273–277; Ladd & Lipset, 1975).

A relatively small proportion of the half-million college faculty in the United States are at universities that conceive of the professional role as involvement in creative scholarship. As various commentators on intellectual life have stressed, there is a strong relationship between having the capacity for innovative intellectual activity and being disposed to also reject other aspects of the established order, including politics and religion.

This emphasis on creativity is central to many definitions of the intellectual, which see intellectuality as a concern for creativity. As Robert Merton notes: persons may be considered "intellectuals *in so far* as they devote themselves to cultivating and formulating knowledge.... [I]t does not follow that every teacher or professor is an intellectual. He may or may not be depending on the actual nature of his activities" (Merton, 1968, pp. 263–264). As the reciprocal finding to that for teachers, mentioned above, the surveys of academic opinion indicate clearly that those most involved in the world of scholarship—as judged by their record of publication, allocation of work time, and presence at major research-oriented universities—are the most liberal-left and least traditionally religious of the American professoriate (Lipset, 1972*a*, pp. 243–245; Ladd & Lipset, 1975).

In the past, American academe was generally apolitical and conservative, for as long as higher education was primarily in the hands of the churches, as most of the predominantly private colleges were, instruction by the faculty could not contradict revealed, traditional truth. They basically sought to socialize new generations in the accepted system of values. Colleges, therefore, were centers of conventional thought. The secularization of the university, with the associated emphasis on original research and creativity, is a major factor associated with the American university becoming an important center of political activity in modern times.

The growing adherence to liberal-left egalitarian political values that has characterized academe should not be related solely to the linkage between scholarly innovativeness and antitraditional thought generally. Scholarship has certain guiding values, which as Merton points out have "become embodied in the university as its principal institutionalized frame" (Merton, 1968, pp. 604–605). These include skepticism about existing knowledge; the belief that no "truth"—finding, conceptual framework, overreaching paradigm—exists that can expect to endure; and universalism—treatment of all involved in the scholarly process according to impersonal criteria. These value orientations imply the need for a free society operating under the rule of law. State or church interference requiring that scholarship adhere to a party, national, or religious line, or that scholars not remain free to criticize each other, makes for bad scholarship. The stress on universalism, on functional specificity, on an achievement orientation implies also opposition to those aspects of stratified societies that limit equality of opportunity. For scholarship, trained intelligence, not family background, race, or wealth, must be the primary quality associated with rewards. Hence, as noted earlier, the more committed an academic is to research, the more likely he will oppose those aspects of the social system that appear to perpetuate inequality of opportunity.

At the same time that the commitment of the major centers of academe to the universalistic meritocratic values of science and scholarship has been growing, changes in the technological structure have increased the importance of creative scholarship for the bodies politic, social, and economic. Although scholars remain dependent on others for resources, particularly financial support, they supply services that are vitally needed, including expertise, new basic "discoveries" that help to keep their national economic and military collectivities in the vanguard, and symbolic formulations for the cultural interpretation of reality. Contributing to the increased political importance of the university, and its linkages wth political events and controversies, has been the rapid expansion of the occupational groups that are engaged in knowledge production. These changes, as well as growing numbers of persons in the higher echelons of the "service sector," have even led some to posit the beginning of a new social order, in which creative intellectuals and the university are an important, if not the major, dynamic force for social change. Daniel Bell writes of a "post-industrial" society in which theoretical knowledge becomes the principal source of social and economic development, the "matrix of innovation," and in which the scientific-technological intelligentsia gains great prominence, prestige, and power (Bell, 1973).

The greater impact of the university community on the body politic is not a function simply of increased numbers, of the vital services performed, or even of increased social prestige. Both serving to certify other elites as technically competent through their control of formal education and helping to produce the ideational and cultural resources that the various collectivities need, the culture-producing centers have been gaining in their ability to exercise great influence over the other elites, whether in government, the churches, business establishments, or the mass media. The most visible and distinguished scholars and scientists constitute important reference individuals for those who respect intellectual accomplishment (Lipset & Dobson, 1972, pp. 174–184). This process suggests a reversal of Tocqueville's description of pre-Civil War intellectuals who, finding themselves at variance with the laity, withdrew into private circles, where they supported and consoled each other. In effect, there has been a steady increase in the "linkages" between academe and the rest of society, an increase that not only gives academe more prestige and power, but necessarily subjects it to recurrent attack from those collectivities who find their interests and/or values being undermined by the ideas stemming from the campus.

On many occasions, universities have been perceived as centers of moral, religious, and ideological corruption that undermine the faith of the young and threaten the stability of the larger social order. Consequently, there are frequent efforts to repress the freedom of scholars to choose research topics, to publish freely, and to teach as they please. Tension between the university and the powers is inherent in the linkages between them. Scholars demand academic freedom—the right to totally control their professional activities, including choosing their colleagues, determining the curriculum, and evaluating their own achievements. Society, dependent on the scholars' services and respecting their contributions and intelligence, grudgingly yields. But during periods of social instability and of rapid changes in the culture and values, universities and the extramural powers are often in sharp conflict. In the United States, religious and secular powers sought to retain ultimate control through lay governing boards, which had the final legal authority to set policy, to hire, and to fire. Controversy over the boundaries of authority of the faculty and the governing boards representing the church and/or the polity has provided the manifest content of a university power struggle for over three centuries of American higher education.

This discussion of the political potentialities of the university world has focused, thus far, on the consequences of linkages between academe as a collectivity concerned with ideas, largely stemming from the role of the faculty, and other power centers in the larger society. The most publicized form of university-based politics and the most important root of political turmoil or disruption, however, has involved students. Students, rather than professors, provided the mass base and often the activist leadership for groups like the Academic Legion of Vienna in 1848 that overthrew the government; for the nineteenth-century Russian revolutionary movement; and for the massive movement against the Vietnam War in the United States, which led to the withdrawal of an incumbent president and the abandonment of direct American military involvement in Indo-China.

From Aristotle on, commentators have long noted the propensity of the young, but especially the students among them, to adhere to absolute principles; to engage in expressive forms of oppositionist activity, rather than in instrumental politics; to take risks, since they are not yet caught up in the responsibilities of career and family. Until the 1960s, however, sensitivity by governing elites to the potential political role of university students was evident only in colonial, less developed, and authoritarian nations, for it was there that students played dramatic and well-publicized roles in revolutionary movements, some of which were able to overthrow governments and social systems (Lipset, 1964b). As in more recent nationalist protests, American college students were deeply involved in the demonstrations that led up to the American Revolution (Hofstadter, 1961, p. 206). Yet C. A. Bristed, a Yale graduate of the late 1830s who also spent much time in Britain and Europe, noted that the majority of students "under any government are opposed to the spirit in which that government is administered. Hasty and imperfect as the conclusion is, it certainly does hold good of many countries." He concluded that the typical student "sees the defects in the government of his country; he exaggerates them with the ardor of youth, and takes that side which promises to remedy them, without reflecting at what cost the remedy may have to be purchased" (Bristed, 1874, p. 61). As I noted in earlier writings on student protest, many explanations have been offered for the special readiness of a segment of university youth to engage in such activities.

Some point to the inherent need of youth to find their own outlook, but clearly university students are normally much more disposed than other groups of young people to engage in protest. Students are marginal, between roles; that is, between the security and status derived from their own families and the obligation to find a status of their own. Like all marginal men, they suffer from special insecurities, and also have special capacities to see the imperfections of society. They have more freedom than other segments of youth, and adults as well, to act without concern for consequences. They are foot-loose, without economic or social obligations to restrain them, and with considerable energies to use up. Whatever outlet any particular group of them chooses to use, the ecology of the university, the easy communication among people on a campus, makes it possible for those who hold similar views to find one another. Out of their new awareness as members of an intellectual community, out of their detached and advantaged position, students are better able than most to recognize the inconsistencies around them and to afford the expressions of disaffection thus produced in them. Sometimes their horizons are limited to the institutions that are close by, the universities themselves, as in much of the nineteenth century; in periods of broad social ferment, however, the world and its problems are their oyster (Lipset, 1971, pp. 753–754).

With a few exceptions, such as the participation of students in the events that led up to the American Revolution, American student protest against the ways of their elders did not take on ideological form until the twentieth century. For the most part, the many, sometimes quite violent, controversies, involving strikes, demonstrations, bombs, and arson, were dedicated to changes within the university (Lipset, 1972b, pp. 127–146). The colleges of America sought to enforce a rigid code of discipline, insisted on attendance at chapel services, gave students little choice in the curriculum they studied, and, in spite of being small institutions by modern standards, maintained a severe barrier between faculty and students, which rarely allowed for informal, friendly relations between them. The professors were almost exclusively teachers repeating conventional knowledge and moral virtues, usually living under a relatively authoritarian system in which the power to hire, fire, and set salaries was held by the president and a board of external trustees.

This situation began to change, first at Harvard, where religious liberalism permitted a freer attitude toward independent scholarship than at schools more under the control of traditional and evangelical denominations, and through the latter part of the nineteenth century, at a number of leading private and public institutions that took on the task of fostering research and graduate study. Such developments were accompanied, as Mori anticipated, by increased tension between the innovative faculty and the powers, reflected in a growing number of academic freedom cases.

The change in the nature of higher education from emphasis on religious and secular revelation and orthodoxy to scholarly innovation helped to increase the number of those within colleges who gave voice to more liberal, anti-Establishment, and egalitarian views. And the fact that the American university became a center of critical thought meant a sharp increase in student political activism whenever events called accepted political and social institutions and doctrines into question, particularly at times when policy failures led men to question their adequacy.

The inclination of contemporary students to engage in antisystem protest, more than youth from other strata, cannot be derived only from their growing role as "apprentice scholars" and the linkage between intellectuality and avant-garde social and political orientations. The increase in the time spent in school, which now includes graduate school for many, prolongs the period of marginality, referred to above, for students who live in a society in which individuals must establish their status based on personal abilities and achievements. And though American universities have given up those extreme forms of control and discipline over the manners and morals of their undergraduates which characterized them from the founding of Harvard on, dependency remains built into the very essence of the system of higher education. The American university in particular, with its stress on frequent examinations and faculty recommendations, emphasizes the dependent relationship. In this respect it continues to resemble the high school. Hence while many aspects of the society urge undergraduates to become independent, to act as free adults, they remain in what is ultimately a situation highly controlled by older people.

Since in each generation protest is usually assertive of the fact that conditions are worse than in the past, rebellious students repeatedly argue that their particular institutions and faculty care less about them, and more often force them to take poorly taught courses that bear little relationship to what they really need or are interested in, than was true in previous epochs. Yet a variety of historical works attest to the fact that students have complained bitterly about their relations with faculty for centuries. Laurence Veysey notes that "class tension" between students and faculty has always characterized this country's educational system (Veysey, 1965, pp. 294–302).

Youth, as various students of the psychology of adolescence have noted, needs to find patterns of behavior that set it apart from the adult world, that express its independence. And increasingly, politics has become a particularly logical source of such self-expression for those on the campus. Many faculty, first in the social sciences, but in recent decades in the natural sciences as well, have become involved in politics. At most major academic centers, students are made aware that their professors are political actors in various ways. Hence, for many students who seek to express their independent identity through politics, there is need to create a student political culture which is outside, and somewhat in opposition to, that of most of the adults to whom they relate. As a result, those who are politically active often extend the political vision of their parents and faculty in the same direction (left or right), but beyond the limits set by the adults.

As is evident, neither students nor faculty direct their fire solely or even predominantly at authority in the outside world. Much of what correctly may be called political behavior has involved struggles among the estates of the university, as well as within them. Thus, as will be made abundantly evident in the main body of this work, the long history of Harvard University has included frequent, sometimes violent, battles between students and faculty. Such conflicts have reflected differences in interests and views concerning the rules governing student conduct; living conditions, including the adequacy of food; due process in discipline proceedings; grading procedures; student self-government; the extent to which colleges may act *in loco parentis*; the right of students and their publications to free speech; *lern freiheit*, the freedom of students to hear and read different views, and even to have faculty of varying persuasions; the nature and power of student self-government, and the like.

Faculty, in their struggles with students, have sought to enforce their prerogatives, in particular to retain their right to dictate the content of the curriculum, and in recent years to choose research topics and evaluate colleagues. More commonly, however, professors have been involved in fights with one another, and with organs and officers of the university over what Cotton Mather, analyzing a faculty-student alliance against a Harvard president in the late seventeenth century, described as a struggle for "preferment." For the most part, this essay on Harvard's political controversies will not concern itself with this form, which has inspired many novels dealing with campus life. More important have been the contests with governing boards and university administrations seeking to define the authority of each. Essentially, faculty have sought to win the total power held by the Fellows of the Colleges of Oxford and Cambridge to allocate resources, choose colleagues, control curriculum and student discipline, and teach and write as they please.

American college presidents, a uniquely powerful group in the international university world, have been placed in a middle position between the governing boards and external sources of financial support, the state and private donors, on one hand, and the faculty on the other (Cohen & March, 1974; Kerr, 1963). To maintain their influence and prestige, they have found it necessary to conciliate the different strata, to be perceived by each as acting in its interests during disputes. Increasingly, their authority became personal rather than institutional. The office is inherently a political one, requiring the ability to mobilize support from constituencies with divergent interests and values.

Given the conflicting role requirements of the university as the transmitter of traditional culture and as the principal source for changes in ideas, the structural bases for taking independent stances inherent in the condition of undergraduates and of the creative intellectuals at the summits of the faculty, the reliance of the university for financial support on the most powerful established elements of the external society; and not least, the overriding concerns of parents for the way in which their children are cared for and educated, it is hardly surprising that political disputation and struggle have formed a recurrent aspect of the story of higher education.

This essay on Harvard University is an effort to report on some of the most evident controversies that have formed its development since it was founded in 1636. It is an outgrowth of an attempt to write a chapter of conventional length for a book reporting on the way the crises of the 1960s affected different colleges and universities (Riesman & Stadtman, 1973). It soon became evident that the story of the sixties at Harvard, and at many other institutions as well, could not be understood as an exceptional event. Rather, Harvard, as the oldest and preeminent American university, had found itself intensely involved in almost every wave and type of controversy that has run through American higher education. If the sixties taught any lesson to those participating in American collegiate life, it is that people who do not know their own history cannot know on what road they are. Since politics, conventional and unconventional, conservative and radical, will continue in the university world as long as such institutions remain centers of free and creative thought, and since there will be more student rebellions, and faculty–administration–governing-boards struggles, an effort to report on politics at Harvard in more detail than could be developed in a brief chapter in a book dealing with many institutions seemed warranted.

In the largest sense, I have attempted to trace through the relationship of politically relevant factors, including religion, to Harvard's preeminence in American higher education. The interaction has been in both directions. On one hand, developments in the larger political and religious systems within the Massachusetts community played a decisive role in formulating the conditions that encouraged Harvard to become a major center of learning. These involved particularly the very early commitment of a "people of the book," the Puritans, to support education combined with the subsequent emergence within the Boston elite of a relatively cosmopolitan, religiously liberal outlook, which fostered a more open attitude toward intellectual innovation. Conversely, as Harvard took the road to scholarly greatness, the consequent freedom it emphasized for both faculty and students made it a center for innovative political and religious views. Although the way the story is told and the topics that are emphasized clearly reflect the values, biases, and conceptual outlook of the author, I have deliberately sought to present it in narrative fashion.[1] The reader, whether connected with Harvard or academe or not, is free to draw his own conclusions and to decide what concept of the university, of social change, or of politics it serves to favor.

---

[1]Those interested in a presentation of my personal concerns in this area may find a statement of them in the Introduction to an earlier book (Lipset, 1972*b*, pp. xiii–xxvi).

2. The Colonial Period

Harvard College, the first such institution in what was to become the United States, was founded in 1636 as the summit of the educational system of the Massachusetts Bay Colony. The Colony, created by religious refugees from England, the Calvinist Puritans, began as a closely knit theocratic society in which all institutions—church, state, and education—were closely interwoven and designed to maintain the word and the law of God. The first published discussion of Harvard in *New England's First Fruits* (1647) reveals the priorities of the settlers, many of whom were university graduates.

After God had carried us safe to *New England*, and we had builded our houses, provided necessaries for our livelihood, rear'd convenient places for God's worship, and settled the Civil Government: One of the next things we longed for, and looked after was to advance *Learning* and perpetuate it to Posterity; dreading to leave an illiterate Ministry to the Churches, when our present Ministers shall lie in the Dust (Morison, 1956, p. 31).

Both the church and the college were "established" institutions, that is, linked to and supported by the state. When the General Court (legislature) of Massachusetts passed the act establishing the College, it also provided for financial support. In prescribing a government for the new institution in 1650, it created two governing boards: (1) the Corporation, which would have primary control and would be composed of five Fellows, tutors or faculty, much as in the colleges of Oxford and Cambridge, plus the President and Treasurer, and (2) a Board of Overseers drawn from the ranks of clergy and local magistrates, who would represent the community. In establishing a bicameral form of government, the Puritan founders of Harvard compromised between the system used at the colleges of Oxford and Cambridge, of which many of the Puritans were graduates and which were totally controlled by their faculties, and the system of extramural governance by "safe persons who represented the standing civil and ecclesiastical order" as existed in the Calvinist-dominated universities in Geneva, Edinburgh, and the Netherlands (Reisner, 1931, p. 64; Herbst, 1973; Conant, 1938, pp. 315–316). The intent that the Fellows of the Corporation should be faculty was complicated by the fact that during the seventeenth century the tiny college never had more than two or three tutors, most of them very young men who rarely kept the position for more than a few years because they could not live on the low salaries and who were also available for jobs as ministers (Hoffmann, 1972, pp. 206–207). Hence the practice developed of electing "non-resident Fellows" to complete the required number of five. Given the short terms of most of the Fellows, Harvard was, in fact, run during its first half century by its Presidents, without much check from a transitory group of Fellows and an external Board of Overseers which met infrequently.

Although the early governance of Harvard was quite different in practice from that laid down in the Charter of 1650, the basic structure established at that time was to determine the way Harvard has operated through the centuries. In effect, the Fellows were given the main authority to run the school; the revisions in the Act of 1667 made clear that the Corporation could make decisions "without dependence upon the consent of the overseers," although the latter could veto and alter them (ibid., p. 198). The second provision guaranteed that representatives of the church and the community had the power to prevent the faculty from getting out of hand. This unique university constitution is, perhaps, the first example of the deliberate introduction of a system of checks and balances in the governance of an American community. Harvard has maintained a bicameral government down to the present, although a number of changes have been made in the composition of the boards and the way they are selected. Charles Eliot, who held the post of Harvard President for 40 years (1869–1909), credits the two-board system with making Harvard much more responsive to the need for change over the centuries than would have occurred under a less pluralistic structure (Eliot, 1908, pp. 49–64).

The intention of the elders of the Commonwealth to keep control over their College was strongly in evidence at the end of the first year of classes, 1638–1639. Nathaniel Eaton, the head or "Master" of the new school, was brought to public trial for acts of cruelty, particularly indiscriminate use of corporal punishment, against his "usher" (assistant) and students. Eaton's conviction and removal from office demonstrated the faith the Puritans held in reason.

[The action] set a precedent concerning Harvard discipline; namely, that the purpose of discipline was to bring the student to reason, to reform him, rather than simply to repress or punish his behavior. Clearly if repression or simple punishment were the goal, then whatever means in whatever degree that compensated for the crime would be the most desirable. ... However, if reform were the objective, then the question became more complex, for this involved a consideration not only of the rights and objectives of the master, but also the possible rights and individuality of the students as children of the elite and "Sons of the Prophets.". ... Eaton's misuse of his powers as head of the college was a lesson well-remembered by all those in the colony who were concerned with the college. Thereafter each president could expect his policies and practices regarding the students' welfare in general and student discipline in particular to be closely watched (Moore, 1972, pp. 136–137).

Involvement in religious and political disputation was inherent in Harvard's relationship with the community that it served. Given the theocratic character of the colony, and its origins in making a "great refusal" to the authority of the Church of England, it is not surprising that key figures in early Harvard history continued a pattern of conscientious objection to authority whenever authority demanded they adhere to what they considered false or immoral doctrine. Harvard's next four heads, Dunster, Chauncy, Hoar, and Oakes, had personally suffered persecution for their views in England. "Increase Mather, the first American-born president, was the son of Richard Mather, who had been suspended from his ministry in Lancashire" (Hofstadter, 1961, p. 79). Henry Dunster, the first effective President, demonstrated the obligation that Puritan morality had required of him. He embraced "what his contemporaries in New England regarded as an abominable heresy—the ... belief that infant baptism is 'unscriptural' and that, following the primitive Church practice, only adult believers should be christened." Faced with the choices of keeping silent, recanting, or resigning, Dunster resigned in 1654 (Morison, 1936c, pp. 18–19). "His successor, Charles Chauncy, fearlessly opposed the popular views on baptism and also suffered persecution" (Thayer, 1914, pp. 561–562). Chauncy found it necessary a year after taking office to put out a pamphlet answering various published attacks on higher education from fanatical Puritans who described universities as "'stews of Anti-Christ,'

'houses of lies,' that 'stink before God with the most loathsome abomination'" (Morison, 1956, p. 29). Comparable attacks from fundamentalist sources, both religious and political, would plague Harvard
throughout its history. Presidents of the school would repeatedly find it
necessary to devote considerable time and energy to defending the institution and the faculty against similar criticisms.

Leonard Hoar, the first graduate of the school to become its President, took office in 1672 with the vision of making Harvard a center of
scientific research with a "laboratory chemical for those philosophers,
that by their sense would culture their understandings," and for bota-
nists, "a large well-sheltered garden and orchard." He saw these as
means of teaching students, as these "are in our design, for the
students to spend their times of recreation in them; for readings or no-
tions only are but husky provender." And in a letter to Robert Boyle,
shortly after his inauguration, in which he reported these plans, Hoar
asked Boyle "to deign us any other advice or device, by which we may
become not only nominal but real scholars" (Morison, 1936b, pp.
400–401). Yet Hoar's presidency was a disastrous failure. He antago-
nized both students and tutors. Cotton Mather, then a student,
reported that the students *"travestie whatever he did and said with a
design to make him odious. . ."* (Eliot, 1848, pp. 22–23). Student antagonism may have stemmed from his use of harsh disciplinary methods.
The only known use of whipping a student as a form of corporal
punishment (as distinct from boxing) occurred in his administration
(Peirce, 1833, pp. 227–228; Moore, 1972, pp. 145–146). A few months
after this event, in November 1674, the entire student body left the
College.[1] Four of the Fellows had resigned even earlier, thus setting a
precedent for the students. Hoar quit early in 1675. Thus the most
scholarship-oriented of Harvard's early Presidents was forced to resign
by the combination of student and faculty revolt after three years in
office (Peirce, 1833, p. 42).

There is some indication that the tensions which undermined Hoar
were an outgrowth of the most recurrent source of academic politics, the
struggle for preferment. One of the Fellows who had resigned, Urian
Oakes, minister of the church at Cambridge, had been favored for the
presidency, before Hoar was chosen, by some connected with the
college. Some narrators of Harvard history indicate that Oakes and his
friends may have been responsible for Hoar's troubles. Cotton Mather

---

[1]A similar event had occurred in 1655 under Chauncy when "the students had departed
in protest of the switch from a three-year to a four-year residence requirement for the
bachelor's degree" (Moore, 1972, p. 150).

attributed them to "the emulation of some seeking the preferment," a description which latter-day Harvard President Josiah Quincy argued "is applicable to no one except Oakes" (Quincy, 1840, vol. 1, pp. 36–37). In his first talk as President, Oakes strongly supported the students who had undermined his predecessor, saying "it is not fair for old men, not prone to those things that youth do, to censure boys." Samuel Eliot Morison (1936*b*, pp. 420–421) was to argue that this plea "lends some credibility to the charge that . . . [the students] were instigated by him.

The tensions with students, which made Hoar's life miserable, were not solely a product of larger conflicts or encouragement from faculty and other adult sources. The young teenagers who formed Harvard's student body in the seventeenth century apparently took pleasure in disobeying conventional manners and college rules, much as did their successors in future centuries. Some indication of the continuity in the forms of generational conflict may be found in the effort of the College authorities in 1649 to inhibit "the waring of long hair after the manner of Ruffians and barbarous Indians," stating that "[we] doe declare and manifest our dislike and detestation against the waring of such long haire . . . whereby men doe deforme themselves, and offend sober and modest men, and doe corrupt good manners . . . " (Moore, 1972, p. 51).

President Chauncy, who took office in 1654, attacked long hair as "'abominable' in the sight of the Lord; suitable only for 'ruffians and swaggers and cavileers.'" These concerns of the Harvard authorities were apparently to little avail, for almost two decades later, the issue was still around. In 1672, a petition addressed to the Overseers by a number of ministers criticizing the ways of undergraduates particularly noted as an "evyl . . . long haire" (Moore, 1972, p. 52). And in line with the views of other historians, Moore suggests that the persistent concern about hair styles, linked explicitly to the customs of "barbarous Indians," may have reflected the Puritans' anxiety over the possibility of cultural degeneration in the wilderness (Moore, 1972, p. 51).

In 1659, a resolution passed by the Corporation dealt with the problem of student-police relations.

Whereas there are great complayntes of the exorbitant practices of Some students of this Colledge by their abusive wordes and accions, to the Watch [police] of this Towne. The Corporaccion accounting it their duty by all lawfull meanes to seeke the redress thereof for the future, do hereby declare to all persons whom it may concerne, That the Watch of this Towne from time to time, and at all times shall have full power of inspeccion into the manners and orders of all persons related to the Colledge, whether within or without the precincts of the said Colledge houses and lands, as by law they are impowred to act in cases within the limmitts of their Towne, any law, usage, or costome to the contrary not withstanding.

The Fellows of the Corporation stated, however, that whenever the Watchmen laid "violent hands on any of the students" within the "Colledge yard," they should inform the President or one of the Fellows (then tutors) before taking them away. They also forbade the police the right to enter any room or study in the College without permission from a College authority (Lane, 1928, pp. 359–360).

The concern of the Fellows for the protection of the legal rights of the students did not reflect any self-restraint on their own part with respect to the means used to protect their own authority. The laws of the College "declared the right of the president or tutor to 'break open any chamber or study door . . . wherein the good of the College is . . . thought to require it' " (Moore, 1972, p. 98). As punishment for the offense of blasphemy, they sentenced a student to the following sanction:

That being convicted of speaking blasphemous words concerning the H.G., he should be therefore publickly whipped before all the scholars. . . .

Sit alone by himself in the Hall uncovered at meals, during the pleasure of the President and Fellows, and be in all things obedient, doing what exercise was appointed him by the President, or else be finally expelled from the College . . . (Peirce, 1833, pp. 227–228).

Strangely, the greatest challenge to the role of Harvard as the center of theological purity in the Massachusetts colony took root under the presidency of Increase Mather (1686–1701), perhaps the most orthodox of Harvard's Presidents. During his administration, various political and intellectual battles resulted in the triumph of liberal theology. Mather, who had worked hard to secure the presidency, generally regarded as the leading clerical post in the colony, devoted little time to administering the school and remained in charge of his church in Boston. Active in politics, he also spent considerable time in London seeking to regain the autonomy of the province then under challenge by the anti-Puritanical Restorationist regime in England. During the time he was absent, the College was in the hands of two faculty Fellows, John Leverett and William Brattle, who, much more liberal theologically than Mather, introduced the students to "the best in literature and divinity, regardless of puritan prejudices" (Morison, 1936c, p. 46). They produced, in the words of a contemporary observer, a generation of "young men educated at the Colledge at Cambridge, who differ much in their principles from their parents" (Morison, 1936b, p. 535). Mather finally took note of these happenings in 1697 and demanded obedience to his will, pointing out that an orthodox college was at the heart of purity in the society (ibid., pp. 542–543). He fought with the liberal faculty and an Anglican governor, trying in vain to restore the school to conservative orthodoxy (Hofstadter, 1961, pp. 98–105).

Mather spent considerable time in efforts to change the governance system of the College. He had some short-lived victories, including a revision of the Charter eliminating the Board of Overseers, "which as a semi-political body would have included a number of Anglicans," and reorganizing the Corporation as an enlarged, predominantly nonresident group, with Fellows drawn largely from the ranks of Congregational ministers. This meant a drastic reduction in the status and power of the faculty since "From 1650 to 1692 all the Tutors were Fellows of the Corporation, though not all Fellows of the Corporation were Tutors; and it was customary to call a Tutor either Tutor or Fellow. . . . After 1692 no Tutor was necessarily a Fellow of the Corporation" (Matthews, 1925, p. cxxxiii).

In the continuing struggle over the religious views of the faculty, Mather went so far in 1699 as to insist that the Congregationalist-controlled legislature refuse to compromise with the Anglican governor on the issue of a religious test for officers of the College, even though this meant "that the College be without a charter, and consequently lose the power of granting degrees . . . " (Morison, 1936c, pp. 47–48). He, too, finally resigned rather than give in, and Harvard experienced an interregnum in which the chief executive officer for six years was a Vice-President, Samuel Willard.

Mather's effort to have Harvard governed by a single, large, predominantly nonfaculty Corporation was doomed to failure. The Anglican governor and the authorities in London who had ultimate veto power over a new charter would have none of it (Hoffmann, 1972, p. 384). By 1707, the theological liberals had a majority on the Corporation, and selected as President John Leverett, who as tutor had strongly opposed Mather's narrow views and who therefore was also welcomed by the Anglican segment of Boston's elite. The more popularly based lower house of the legislature, dominated by religious conservatives, refused to confirm Leverett's election, a right they had, since Harvard was then operating without a charter. The Royal Governor intervened and proposed the restoration of the original Charter of 1650. The General Court welcomed this, since it acknowledged their right to issue a charter without royal action, even though it also gave the Governor the power to name the five Fellows on the revived small Corporation. He appointed a predominantly liberal board composed of two tutors and three Congregationalist ministers (Hoffmann, 1972, p. 478; Morison, 1936b, pp. 551–559). The revived Board of Overseers, however, which was responsible to the General Court, was controlled by clerical conservatives (Hoffmann, 1972, p. 485).

Given the background to Leverett's assuming the presidency, it is not surprising that his administration was stormy and controversial. It witnessed a "struggle for control of the College between two factions of the Puritan community, the 'liberals' who gained the presidency with his election, and the 'conservatives' who would restore the influence of the Mathers" (ibid., p. 456).

Following the end of the war with France in 1713, the College began to expand rapidly, taking in students who had little interest in becoming divines. One result of these changes, as entries in Leverett's diary indicate, was that "the Faculty were having plenty of trouble with . . . 'riotous Actions' " of students (Morison, 1936c, p. 61). Studying in a more secularized school, the undergraduates exhibited a readiness to debate issues that undercut the very fabric of the Puritan Commonwealth. The editors of the first Harvard student publication, *The Tell Tale*, discussed among other things questions such as "Whether there be any Standard of Truth," and "Whether it be Fornication to lye with ones Sweetheart (after Contraction) before marriage" (Lane, 1909, p. 228). In essence, the students of Leverett's day were debating the relativism of morality and freedom in sex relations, not a very different set of topics from those to be discussed in the next 250 years at Harvard and other institutions. These discussions and the undisciplined behavior of the students played into the hands of Leverett's conservative opponents who saw breakdowns in both morality and adherence to authority as not unnatural consequences of the weakened structure of traditional religion within the College. This resulted in attacks on the school resembling those of later years. As Morison notes:

The controversies of his administration are readily understandable if we translate the religious conservatism or orthodoxy of his day into the "patriotic society" brand of "Americanism" that has been causing our colleges no little vexation in the last few years. As today [1936], the inevitable concessions of college authorities to the needs and tastes of post-war youth were made the occasion for a general attack on enlightenment. In 1720, important elements of New England society were, in imagination, still living in the puritan century, just as today numerous very worthy people believe in the economic and social theories of the last century, and resent the fact that it is no longer possible to live by these formulae. Then, as now, the fundamentalist elements looked with extreme disfavor on educational institutions which endeavored to prepare their alumni for the age in which they were to live and which sought to advance knowledge rather than to embalm it (Morison, 1936c, p. 63).

As in subsequent periods of change and unrest, the various elements concerned with the College seized the occasion to try to change power relationships. Leverett, who had been a victim of Increase Mather's desire to have a subservient faculty, reacted in much the same fashion now that he was President. Seemingly the role determined behavior. As strong-minded a reformer as his predecessor was a religious zealot, Leverett secured a rule from the Corporation limiting the term of the teaching staff to three years. He also joined with the nonresident members of the Corporation to again achieve Mather's objective of a predominantly nonfaculty group of Corporation Fellows. These changes meant that "Harvard would be controlled by the President assisted by a board of non-resident and usually subservient trustees" (ibid., p. 71).

The tutors of the College, in alliance with a majority of the Board of Overseers, then largely composed of orthodox Calvinist ministers, joined the issues of resident government and religious traditionalism. They held Leverett's liberal policies responsible for "extravagansas and disorders" and "dangerous tendencies" among the students. They felt that the President undermined their authority with the students by reversing disciplinary decisions made by them and remitting penalties (Hoffmann, 1972, p. 527; Moore, 1972, pp. 153–156).

Perhaps the most interesting and revealing disagreement between Nicholas Sever, the leader of the tutors, and President Leverett concerned changes in the peculiar system of student rankings used for the first century and a half of the College. Students were not listed alphabetically in their class, but rather according to a ranking system that somehow combined estimates of students' intellectual abilities and prospects, their conduct with respect to the rules, and the social status of their families (Peirce, 1833, pp. 308–309; Morison, 1932, pp. 371–431). A recent statistical analysis by P. M. G. Harris indicates conclusively that academic merit was the foremost determinant of place for most of the seventeenth century (Harris, 1971, p. 36). Sever sought to emphasize academic potential in ranking students, but Leverett insisted on stressing ancestry and family position (Hoffmann, 1972, pp. 526–527). It is difficult to evaluate the reasons for the shift. With the growth in the size and affluence of Boston and of various towns, which resulted in the evolution of a large wealthy upper class, the College authorities were under growing pressure to rank students according to family social status. Two close students of the subject, Morison and Shipton, have concluded that the large increase in the student body after the Peace of Utrecht "made any complicated system of balancing scholarly perform- ance with inherited ability very difficult to administer. At the same time, with the growth of aristocracy and a general hardening of class distinctions, the pressure of ambitious parents to have their sons ranked high" naturally increased (Morison, 1932, pp. 415–416; Shipton, 1954, pp. 258–263; Morison, 1955, p. 417).

The shift toward emphasizing family status over academic merit was favored by Leverett, who was himself of high-status origins as a grand- son of Governor Leverett and who had close social and political connec- tions with the Boston upper class, which included a growing Anglican sector and which increasingly sought to imitate English aristocratic mannerisms. The tutors, however, led by Nicholas Sever, preferred to stress intellectual ability and favored a more meritocratic ranking sys- tem, but were unable to influence Leverett (Hoffmann, 1972, pp. 572–573).

These disputes between the tutors and Leverett, backed by a majority of the Corporation, led the frustrated faculty to seek a fundamental change in authority relationships. "Provoked, if not humiliated by Leverett, disregarded if not overruled in College decisions, the tutors conceived the idea of petitioning for a place for all of them on the Cor- poration" (ibid., p. 533). They appealed in 1720 to the Board of Over- seers, controlled by the more popularly based and more religiously con- servative elements, to restore the original meaning of the Fellows of the Corporation to the resident tutors. As a group, they were quite different from the young, highly transitory staff of the mid-seventeenth century who had been unable, therefore, to exercise authority as Fellows. Tutor- ing had become a career by Leverett's time; the average age was 39. And thus, for the first time in American history, a " 'Faculty' . . . acted collec- tively in a way opposed to the 'administration' " (ibid., p. 537).

The conservative clergymen of the Overseers and their supporters in the legislature favored restoring resident (faculty) government as a way of reversing the trends that had given control of Harvard to a liberal Corporation. "The support which Sever and Welsteed's petition received among the Overseers and in the General Court is evidence that it was promoted not as an educational principle, but rather as a partisan maneuver. The conservative party was not so much concerned with the principle that a college should be governed by the teaching staff as they were desirous of eliminating Wadsworth, Colman and Appleton [the liberal nonresident Fellows] from the Corporation" (Reisner, 1931, pp. 65–66).

Since the ultimate power to determine the governance of Harvard lay with the legislature, the General Court, these disputes were also entangled with the conflicts between the more popular body, the House of the Representatives, and the British government and its representative, the Governor. The latter, as a supporter of the Anglican church and a believer in aristocratic elitism, backed Leverett's more catholic attitude toward religious teaching. Although the matter of student rankings did not become a subject for public debate, presumably the divisions about it among the extramural forces were similar to that for religion. As Peirce noted: "Leverett and the Corporation were not much in favor with the popular party, while they were esteemed and respected by the governors" (Peirce, 1833, p. 126). The popular party in the General Court, most of whom were also supporters of evangelical Calvinism, backed the proposal for faculty resident Fellows, and after much political intrigue, a compromise was reached giving "the residents a majority of the fellowships as soon as vacancies should occur." By 1725, three of the five were once again College faculty (Kirkpatrick, 1922a, p. 190).

Whatever the political forces underlying the disputes over university governance in the 1720s, the arguments made by the various parties involved include many of the points that have been debated in universities around the world down to contemporary times (Kirkpatrick, 1931, pp. 12–22, 218–246). The tutors contended that ancient university practice at Oxford and Cambridge, and at Harvard from its foundation on, was on their side. In reply, President Leverett, writing "a Subversion of the Pretensions and Scheme of the Memorialists," noted the presence of nonresident Fellows, particularly in the early years of the College. The tutors in their petition "groaned to be delivered from A foreign yoke," arguing that they were necessarily much more concerned with the well-being of the College than nonresidents who could devote little time to its activities. The reputation of the faculty was linked to the success of the College "and if anything be amiss it will be imputed to them." The nonresidents argued that it was "contrary to the light of nature, that any should have an overruling voice in making those laws by which they themselves must be governed in their office work and for which they receive salaries. . . . [To have the tutors involved in] the choosing, and upon occasion, removing all officers, and of themselves, among the rest, . . . we think must have a very harsh and ungrateful sound in everybody's ear." The tutors acknowledged the validity of the argument against their setting their own salaries, which they noted "the General Court has declared ought to be done under the direction of the Overseers."

Both sides in the dispute contended that their proposals would have a positive effect on student conduct. Supporters of nonresident government claimed that "the Corporation at a distance is of Terrour to the schollars." They also argued that since the tutors were frequently very young, their lack of experience and low status weakened their ability to enforce discipline. A tutor replied cynically that since the only qualification which seemed to recommend a tutor to the Corporation is that he be "entirely passive," they had ought to appoint even younger men to these posts. "Under these circumstances they will be very orderly and respectful to their Masters, but they will make a very awkward figure to those below them, and whom they ought to govern." The tutors argued that "the whole Instruction, constant Inspection, Government and discipline of the Students ... must be with the residents. ... [I]f the powers of the college are abroad, the Government and discipline of the College . . . will dwindle in their hands . . . and if Government and discipline be wanting in a College tis very whit as evident and certain that the Students will grow Slack and negligent in their studies. . . ." The contention was also made that a tutor "that is not of the Corporation on this account cannot have the same Credit and Authority as one that is of it. . . . And if the . . . [tutors] were admitted to the Corporation, . . . They would then have a greater reputation, and Authority in the house. . . ."

The issue of tenure was also raised by the tutors since the Corporation under Leverett's urging had changed their terms of service from *in perpetuum* to three years. The tutors argued in reply that "to have the residents kept at short allowance and in A constant dependence mainly upon the President for their places, and for the bread they eat . . . [would mean that] under these circumstances the residents will be very Orderly and respectful to their Masters, but they'll make a very awkward figure to those who know them and whom they ought to govern." In a letter to an Overseer, opposing the policy of limited terms of office, a supporter of the tutors noted that it was "contrary to the usual form of Elections (there formerly, and in all Colledges abroad) which is, in perpetuum—Now this will probably raise many needless, hurtful disputes in the Colledge, about the continuance of Fellows [the title used also for tutors], if the Fellows business is to secure their Jobbs.

They may in my opinion safely do it at the expense of the Colledge" (ibid., p. 224).

This battle was won by the tutors through their triumph in an early "academic freedom" battle involving Nicholas Sever, the leader of the fight for faculty government. Sever, who had held two three-year terms, was not reappointed by Leverett and the Corporation, then in the midst of the governance fight. In effect, he was dismissed for his activities. The Board of Overseers reversed the decision in 1722, and three years later Sever was elected as a Fellow of the Corporation. At the same time, the Overseers disallowed the by-law establishing a three-year term (ibid., pp. 11–12).

For the next half-century, over two-thirds of the Fellows elected to the Corporation were members of the Harvard faculty (Morison, 1936c, p. 157). The consequences of this development have been sketched by a student of university governance:

For more than fifty years from this time the residents usually had three of the five fellowships. This enabled them with the vote of the President to control the Board. In the election of the President they were in a position to prevent the choice of an undesirable candidate even if they could not name their own man. In all matters of business the residents would be in a position of advantage as compared to their non-resident colleagues. Their greater familiarity with the situation, their intimate relations with and personal interests in all the concerns of the College, would cause them to exert a much greater influence than the two or three men who lived at a distance from the College and who were usually active pastors of churches (Kirkpatrick, 1922a, p. 190).

The reversion to resident government favored by the Overseers who would have preserved Harvard as a center of orthodox Calvinism did not have this effect, since some of Leverett's faculty opponents were not supporters of Calvinist orthodoxy. Harvard moved steadily in the eighteenth century toward greater tolerance for religious belief and, consequently, increased *lern freiheit* for undergraduates. Seen as a center of heresy, it declined in student enrollment, but improved in faculty quality, recruiting some men who were active in scientific research. Brooks Adams was to note, in highly partisan terms, that "in looking back through the vista of the past, there are few pages of our history more strongly stamped with the native energy of the New England mind than this brilliant capture of Harvard, by which the ancient cradle of bigotry and superstition was made the home of American liberal thought" (Adams [1887], 1962, p. 451).

In 1736, Harvard was 100 years old. Yet, it was still the only college located in or near a major colonial city. Neither Philadelphia, the home of clergyless Quakers, nor New York, founded as a commercial Dutch colony, bothered to form a college until Harvard was well into the second decade of its second century. The basic elements for Harvard's future greatness, however, were already present. They lay in a unique combination of values that emphasized education and free thought. The first condition was evident in the fact that alone among the English colonists the Puritans began a college as soon as they were settled and continued to support its growth. The Puritans, like the Jews, were a people of the "book," who believed both in the need for "an educated ministry," and that all should seek "understanding of the Bible" (Foster, 1962, pp. 2–3; Moore, 1972, pp. 8–10). They exhibited a strong concern for general, as well as higher education. "The unique Massachusetts law of 1647 [which] laid the foundation of the American system of tax-supported schools, being distinctly different from the English idea of privately endowed schools . . . required every township with fifty or more householders to offer free elementary instruction, and towns with more than one hundred families were ordered to set up 'grammar' or college preparatory schools" (Wish, 1950, pp. 436–437). They insisted on support for these diverse institutions, so that, in the words contained in the 1648 edition of *The Laws and Liberties of Massachusetts,* "learning may not be buried in the graves of our forefathers" (Foster, 1962, p. 3; Ziff, 1973, p. 68; Shipton, 1934; Shipton, 1958; Smith, 1966).

The same factors that led the Puritans in Britain to play such a disproportionate role in scientific creativity in seventeenth-century England were also present in New England. As Merton has documented, there was a close correspondence between the values of the Puritans and "the attributes [and] goals of science" (Merton, 1968, pp. 628–638; Merton, 1938). English Puritans not only contributed far beyond their proportion to the membership of the Royal Society, but in the American colonies, as well, most of the 18 elected to the Royal Society came from similar religious backgrounds (Morison, 1956, pp. 241–242).

Yet, though the most orthodox of the New England Calvinist divines, such as the Mathers, were strong supporters of higher education and scientific research, there was an inherent tension between their concern to maintain the faith in an absolute and unquestioning form and the willingness to tolerate or encourage the openness to new ideas and the literature of the world necessary for independent scholarship. The breakdown of orthodox Calvinism and the triumph of a more liberal religious outlook were also necessary for Harvard's intellectual growth (Hofstadter, 1961, pp. 98–113).

The clue to the triumph of religious liberalism at Harvard does not lie solely or even predominantly in the intramural developments thus far discussed. Rather, these must be seen as a part of, or a reflection of, the process that produced liberal Congregationalism in Boston and surrounding towns. Boston was the most important trading center of the colonies in the seventeenth and early eighteenth centuries. It became increasingly linked to the English world of commerce, status, and ideas from which its founders had fled. As Bailyn has documented, by the end of the seventeenth century the Boston merchants had close connections with the Anglican commercial elite in Britain, some of whom had moved to Boston for economic reasons. As a result, "Not only had membership in a Puritan church ceased to be a criterion of social acceptability among the merchant families, but by the third generation the interrelated merchant group showed signs of moving toward the still officially anathemized Church of England." Anglicans were able to marry into the families of leading clerical figures of Boston (Bailyn, 1955, pp. 137–139).

The Boston elite had become relatively "cosmopolitan" and somewhat Anglicanized by the end of the seventeenth century, and the church of the Puritans had gradually divided into two camps, one reflecting the system of values that accompanied the growth of an affluent urban upper class, which sought to imitate the behavior of the London elite, the other drawing support from outlying rural areas and the less commercially involved populations, whose ministers "reiterated the theme that New England had forsaken its original purpose and ran idolatrous after new Gods" (ibid., p. 140). Much as the more orthodox gradually lost control of the urban churches, they also found themselves defeated at their college, Harvard. As a nineteenth century Harvard President, Josiah Quincy, noted: "By the constitution of the College, its religious influences were made to depend upon those, which, from time to time, might prevail in the town of Boston and its vicinity, and in certain specified Congregationalist churches there situated. In the course of time liberal religious views predominated in these churches and this vicinity, and . . . the Calvinistic clergy . . . found they had lost control of the College" (Quincy, 1845, p. v). And believing that "the Colledge at Cambridge was under the Tutorage of Latitudinarians," the Mathers and others among them supported the establishment of a rival, more orthodox institution in New Haven in 1701 (Morison, 1936*b*, p. 546).

The conflicts between religious liberals and conservatives on one hand and between more popular and more elite-oriented parties on the other were to continue to affect Harvard and Massachusetts until deep into the nineteenth century. Religious conservatism, adherence to the traditional Calvinist beliefs of the Puritans, found its main support among the less educated rural and poorer urban groups, while theological liberalism, which ultimately became Unitarianism, appealed to the more cosmopolitan, better educated, and more affluent Boston and eastern Massachusetts middle and upper classes (Heimert, 1966, pp. 50–51). Fundamentalism, therefore, was tied politically to the more "popular" based party, while religious liberalism and deism in Massachusetts were linked to the more elitist political tendencies (Greene, 1932, pp. 36–37). This underlying basis of political and religious diversity meant that Harvard, intimately related to the Boston elite, would continue to be in the vanguard of religious liberalism, and thus also much more open to free thought and inquiry in secular and scientific matters as compared to the much younger New England colleges and the College of New Jersey (Princeton), which remained under Calvinist control.

From 1700 on, therefore, the necessary conditions for Harvard's maturing into the great university of English-speaking America existed, inherent in its close link to the elite of a relatively cosmopolitan wealthy community that combined the Puritan-inspired commitment to education and scholarship with the tolerance for diversity and new ideas needed for intellectual creativity. No other college in the country would have both for a long time to come.

The growth of religious liberalism did not mean that Harvard had given up its commitment to uphold many aspects of Congregationalist theology and morality, which would be regarded as traditional by modern standards. Some indication of both the breadth and limits of the tolerance encouraged by early eighteenth-century liberal Congregationalism may be seen in the treatment of a Jewish scholar, Judah Monis, described as "truly read and learned in the Jewish Cabbals and Rabbins, a Master and Critic in the Hebrew." Monis, who in 1720 submitted an essay on the teaching of Hebrew to Harvard, was awarded an M.A. degree by the College, the first degree given to a Jew in any British university. Two years later, he converted to Christianity, and soon thereafter, the Corporation appointed him "an Instructor in the Hebrew Language." A contemporary report suggested that he converted to secure the position. "Before he could be admitted, it was rendered necessary by the Statutes that he should change his religion, which he professes to have done with perfect disinterestedness." Although he married the sister of a minister and belonged to the First Church of

Cambridge, some indication that his Judaism may have endured may be seen in the fact that "Monis continued to his death to observe the seventh day as the Sabbath." Hebrew was not very popular among the students, but Monis continued on the faculty for 40 years, retiring when 77 years old (Friedman, 1911, pp. 621–628).

DISCIPLINE AND ACADEMIC FREEDOM

The summits of Harvard's authority structure, though willing to admit non-Congregationalists into the student body, continued to emphasize the status and authority of the governors, the President, and the faculty. Parietal rules were extremely strict, students were expected to show deference to the college officers, and they were required to attend chapel. Not surprisingly, the teenage undergraduates took part in various forms of indiscipline. Leverett's successor, Benjamin Wadsworth (1725–1737), was bothered by "internal turbulence." Faculty records include considerable material dealing with charges brought against students for a variety of violations of the disciplinary rules of the college, including "shameful and scandalous Routs [riots]." The administration of the next President, Edward Holyoke, which lasted for 32 years after he was inaugurated in 1737, was also marked with repeated student violations of the rules. Much of the troubles stemmed from the effort of the College to hold the students under close supervision and control. The violations mentioned in the records include, according to Peirce:

"the breach of the Sabbath, more especially in time of public worship," the remedy for which was "the Tutors sitting in the meeting-house so as more conveniently to oversee the scholars"; "combinations among the undergraduates for the perpetuation of unlawful acts"; "the disorders of which they were guilty by being absent from their chambers, contrary to law, at unreasonable times of night"; the "disorders upon the day of the senior . . . meeting to choose the officers of the class," when "it was usual for each scholar to bring a bottle of wine with him, which practice the Committee (that reported on it) apprehend has a natural tendency to produce disorders"; "riotous disorders frequently committed on the quarter-days and evenings," on one of which in 1764, "the windows of all the Tutors and diverse other windows were broken,". . . Occasionally some striking occurrence called for the interposition of the lawgivers of the College; as in 1755, when "great disorders committed, and even indignities and personal insults offered to some of the Tutors by some of the pupils," produced the appointment of a Committee of the Overseers to make inquiry into them, . . . and as in 1766, when there were "great disorders among the Students tending to subvert all government" (Peirce, 1833, pp. 216–217).

Student indiscipline was not simply a consequence of youthful highjinks or spontaneous acts of discontent. Students organized protests against the quality of the food, as well as against the way the compulsory chapel requirements were enforced. Thus a report of the President and faculty in 1766 complained about "an unlawful combination of a great number of the Students to force an execution of the laws of the College in such manner as they think proper, particularly, with respect to excuses for absence from prayers, and that there has been an agreement that, unless such excuses shall be accepted, that the Students would leave the Hall in a body." The faculty report advocated severe punishment for those involved in "such combinations," even if it meant that many students would be expelled. Two years later, "it appears ... that a combination had been entered into by a great number of the Students against the [College] government; that in consequence, great excesses had been perpetrated; that on one Saturday night brick-bats were thrown into the windows of Mr. Willard the Tutor's room, endangering the lives of three of the Tutors there assembled, and that for this audacious act four Students ... were expelled" (ibid., pp. 221–225).

The authorities of the College could also be severe in their treatment of members of the instructional staff who violated the norms of the community. Isaac Greenwood, the first Hollis Professor of Mathematics and Natural Philosophy, who introduced experimental methods into teaching and involved students as assistants in his research, was condemned by the Corporation in 1737 as "guilty of Various Acts of gross Intemperance, by excessive drinking, to the dishonour of God" (Morison, 1936c, pp. 80–81). His misdeeds, which included being "domineering with students and quarrelsome with his colleagues," apparently had gone on for some years. Both the Corporation and the Overseers had pressed him to reform before the Overseers finally voted in 1738 to confirm his dismissal (Stoeckel, 1958, p. 56). Nathan Prince, who was both a Tutor and a member of the Corporation, was found guilty of "speaking of contempt of the President and Tutors as to learning" and discharged by the Overseers in 1742 after 19 years of service. Behind this action was the fact that he "was also fond of the bottle and ... appeared drunk at church and made faces and gestures at the minister. . . ." The Fellows of the Corporation noted in response that dismissals should originate with them, but that since "so many of the Corporation have ... complaints against the said Prince ... it would not be for the interest and peace of the college for Prince to remain in office" (Quincy, 1840, vol. 2, pp. 30–37; Stoeckel, 1958, p. 17).

During this period, Harvard followed a mixed policy with respect to enforcing religious orthodoxy among the faculty, which reflected the continuation of variations in the religious outlook dominant on its two governing boards. As Hoffmann noted, "the liberal inclinations of the inner circle of Harvard's government were checked by conservative interests represented on the larger board" (Hoffmann, 1972, p. 626). In 1738 the Corporation nominated John Winthrop to succeed Greenwood in the Hollis Chair of Mathematics and Natural and Experimental Philosophy. He was the first person proposed for a professorship who had not prepared for the ministry. The nomination disturbed the high Calvinists among the Overseers, and they entered a motion "to examine Mr. Winthrop about his principles of religion." This proposal was defeated in favor of one "to examine the Professor elect as to his knowledge in the Mathematics." The Committee reported favorably on his scholarly qualifications, and the Board approved his election (Quincy, 1840, vol. 2, pp. 25–27). Winthrop, who served in the position for 40 years and was also elected a Fellow of the Corporation, became the foremost science professor in the English colonies, the only one among them to be elected to the Royal Society. Yet the same Board of Overseers that declined to examine his religious beliefs voted in 1735 to dismiss a Mr. Longloissorie, a teacher of French, who had been hired by the Corporation without being confirmed by the second board, for spreading "erroneous religious opinions . . . among the students." They "declared their right to examine all candidates for teaching positions on their principles of religion, 'upon any just suspicion of their holding dangerous tenents although no express charges be layed against them'" (Peirce, 1833, pp. 188–190; Stoeckel, 1958, p. 18). Again, in 1739, they refused to confirm the election of Joseph Matthew as tutor until they were given evidence as to the satisfactory character of his religious principles (Quincy, 1840, vol. 2, p. 27).

The majority of the Overseers apparently tried to distinguish between the requirements that should be met by professors in nontheological subjects who were expected to lecture solely on their subjects, and those for tutors who "at that period were required, not only to perform religious services in the chapel, but to give religious instruction in their respective classes" (Peirce, 1833, p. 188; Quincy, 1840, vol. 2, pp. 27–28).

The combination of teaching an increasingly liberal theology, faculty "immorality," and the continuation of student indiscipline continued to open Harvard to severe criticism from conservative religious forces. The English Calvinist evangelist George Whitefield, who played a major role in the Great Awakening—the revival movement that swept New England—denounced Harvard in 1740 as a place in which "Tutors neglect to pray with and examine the hearts of their pupils. Discipline is at too low an ebb: Bad books are become fashionable amongst them" (Peirce, 1833, p. 204). Although Whitefield's moral influence on students was at first welcomed, his continued criticisms led President Holyoke and the entire faculty to issue a pamphlet in which they denounced Whitefield for his slanderous "reproachful reflections upon the Society, which is immediately under our care; where are observable his rashness and his arrogance," and described him as "an enthusiast, a censorious, uncharitable person, and a deluder of the people" (ibid., pp. 209–210).

Yet it must be acknowledged that the summits of Harvard also defended themselves against such attacks by arguing that they really were as intolerant as their critics demanded they be. Thus, in replying to Whitefield's answer to the faculty pamphlet, Edward Wigglesworth, the first Hollis Professor of Divinity, rebutted Whitefield in an open letter which stressed Harvard's conformism.

We had not long before dropped one of our Tutors out of his place, for very corrupt and dangerous principles as soon as they came to be known. . . . We had also expelled a Professor for immoral and scandelous practices. . . . We have since, for immorality, expelled another Tutor. . . . And these acts of Discipline, we believe, will convince others, whatever you may think of them, that Discipline neither was, nor is at so low an ebb, as to deserve that we should be reproached publicly with the want of it—But you say, "Bad books are become fashionable among them; Tillotson and Clarke are read, instead of Shepherd, Stoddard, and such like Evangelical writers."—We make no doubt but that bad books were, and are, and always will be, too often read in a society of such numbers, where many are supplied with money enough by their parents to buy a bad book, if their inclination lead them to it. But the question is, whether bad books were then read with the approbation or knowledge of the Governors of the House. . . . Now upon a particular enquiry into the Library records on this occasion, . . . it was found, with respect to the books which you call bad ones, that "from the 28th Nov. 1732, to that very day (for almost nine years) Tillotson had not been as much as once taken out of the Library by any Undergraduate; nor any of Dr. Clarke's works for above two years; whereas, . . . [many Evangelical writers] have . . . been borrowed by Undergraduates . . . [so that] they are scarcely ever in the Library . . . " (Peirce, 1833, App., pp. 147–148).

To evaluate the nature of this debate and Wigglesworth's denials it must be noted that he was "one of the first theologians in New England who dared publicly to challenge the 'five points of Calvinism.'" He and his son, who succeeded him in the Hollis chair, "trained the pioneers of liberal Christianity in New England . . . " (Morison, 1936c, p. 68).

REVOLUTIONARY POLITICS

More important for the future of Massachusetts and of Harvard is the fact that the same generations of students, whose behavior and views so disturbed Whitefield and a host of other evangelical preachers, were being trained to play major roles in the American Revolution (ibid., p. 86). John Hancock, in a speech in 1781, described Harvard as "the parent and nurse of the late happy Revolution in this Commonwealth" (Quincy, 1840, vol. 2, p. 244). Some indication of the issues that concerned the students long before the Revolution can be seen from reports of topics of "Commencement Theses and Quaestiones" over the years. Thus, in 1729 Joseph Greene argued the negative on the issue "Is unlimited obedience to rulers taught by Christ and His Apostles?" In 1733, Nathanael Whittaker supported the affirmative on "Is the Voice of the People the Voice of God?" Five years later, in 1738, Harvard students debated "Are we bound to observe the mandates of kings, unless they themselves keep their agreements?" In 1743, Samuel Adams backed the affirmative on the question "Is it Lawful to resist the Supreme Magistrate, if the Commonwealth cannot otherwise be preserved?" In 1759, Joseph Suman took the affirmative on "Is an Absolute and Arbitrary Monarchy contrary to Right Reason?" In 1769, John Hunt supported the affirmative of "Are the People the sole Judges of their Rights and Liberties?" Six years later, in 1775, Elbridge Gerry argued the affirmative on the issue "Can the new Prohibitary Duties which make it useless for the People to engage in Commerce, be evaded by them as Faithful Subjects?" (Young, 1880, p. 125; Potter, 1944, pp. 23–24; Morison, 1936c, p. 91).

It would be wrong to see the majority of the students as deeply involved in liberal or progressive political activities, or for that matter any kind of political activities, until the Revolutionary crisis broke out. Real unrest was seemingly directed mostly against bad food. The first recorded rebellion by Harvard students on a collective scale took place in protest against bad butter in 1766 (Morison, 1936c, pp. 117–118). The continued serving of bad food sparked a disruptive student demonstration that obliged President Edward Holyoke to seek support from the College Overseers. According to a colorful contemporary account, the long simmering affair began when Asa Dunbar, grandfather of Henry Thoreau, confronted a senior tutor and defiantly proclaimed: "Behold, our Butter stinketh and we cannot eat thereof. Now, give us we pray thee Butter that stinketh not" (Harris, 1970, pp. 22–23; Eliot, 1848, pp. 70–71; Bush, 1891, pp. 57–60; Batchelder, 1924, pp. 135–137). Following efforts by the administration and the Corporation and Overseers to force the offending undergraduates to sign a humble apology, "the students, led by the governor's son, and including a future senator of the United States (George Cabot), drew up a formal brief in the style of patriots protesting against unconstitutional oppression" (Morison, 1936c, p. 118).

Later demonstrations took place directed against faculty members for behaving in a pretentious or autocratic manner. Thus in April 1769 when "the tutors attempted to enforce a rule limiting excuses from classroom recitation, a destructive student revolt occurred . . . which necessitated the intervention of the Middlesex County Deputy Sheriff" (Cohen, 1971. p. 3). This episode resulted in an interesting example of the power of wealthy and influential families on the Corporation. Some students were expelled and a number "rusticated" (sent home for specific periods). As a result of pressure from their families, three of those penalized were pardoned by the Corporation. President Holyoke bitterly protested against this action, lamenting "the weakness and injustice of thus allowing ringleaders in a rebellion to escape, because they were the sons of men of influence or wealth, at the same time that others, in truth less guilty, who were destitute of such external connexions, were subjected to the penalties, and made to suffer the highest severities the laws of the College could inflict . . ." (Quincy, 1840, vol. 2, pp. 117–118).

Toward the end of the 1760s politics began to take over at Harvard, as at the other colleges up and down the coast. The key year seems to be 1768 when the records tell us of the "liberty tree" or "rebellion elm" in Harvard Yard, around which students had first met to protest internal issues of mistreatment by faculty, but which became the center for political protest as well. In that year Elizabeth Smith, the sister of Abigail Adams, wrote to a cousin at Harvard: "What fine times you have at Colledge. A *glorious spirit of Liberty* prevails among you—I believe you have not found your retreat so agreeable to study in as you hoped for" (Cohen, 1971, p. 1). Andrew Eliot, a Fellow of the Harvard Corporation, reported of the students: "The young gentlemen are already taken up with politics. They have caught the spirit of the times. Their declamations and forensic disputes breathe the spirit of liberty. This has always been encouraged, but they have sometimes been wrought up to such a pitch of enthusiasm, that it has been difficult for their Tutors to keep them within due bounds . . . " (Quincy, 1840, vol. 2, p. 163).

The undergraduates engaged in a variety of acts directed against the

British authorities. In 1768 they determined to abstain from tea, while the seniors insisted that their degrees be produced on paper manufactured in the New World. Tory Governor Hutchinson in his *History of Massachusetts Bay* suggests that Harvard was predominantly for the patriotic cause by the time of President Holyoke's death in 1769. From 1770 to 1773, the political interests of the students were stimulated by the fact that the Massachusetts Legislature, the General Court, met in Cambridge in order to escape the violent mood of Boston. The students attended the meetings of the House and were excited by the protest speeches. A Speaking Club was formed in 1770 as a center for discussion. Although many of its meetings dealt with nonpolitical topics up to 1775, 17 of them heard orations "relating to British oppression" such as "The Pernicious Practice of Drinking Tea," "Oppression and Tyranny," "The Boston Massacre," and other such topics (Goodhue, 1937, pp. 107–112, 114–115). A military company of college students was formed in 1769 or 1770 as a result of the students' awareness that they might have to use arms in defense of liberty (Morison, 1936c, pp. 139–141).

The students of those pre-Revolutionary days were, of course, no more unanimous in their opinions than those of more recent times. There were Tories among them, and some students would show their loyalty by bringing "India tea" into the commons. "This proceeding gave great offense to the sensitive patriotism of the whigs, and some disturbances were the consequence" (Quincy, 1840, vol. 2, p. 164). The Corporation, then composed in part of professors and tutors, asked them not to do so in the future both not to antagonize popular opinion and more importantly to keep the intramural peace.

Since the carrying of Indian teas into the Hall is found to be a Source of uneasiness and grief to many of the students, and as the use of it is disagreeable to the people of the country in general; that they be advised not to carry it in for the future, and in this way that they, as well as the other students in all ways, discover a disposition to promote harmony, mutual affection, and confidence, so well becoming Members of the same Society: that so peace and happiness may be preserved within the Walls of the College whatever convulsions may unhappily distract the State abroad (Kahn, 1968, pp. 123–124).

There is some reason to suspect that the system of ranking students according to the social status of their families, a far from easy task for the tutors, also occasioned considerable unrest among the students. A graduate of the class of 1759 noted, "excitement was generally called up whenever a class in College was *placed*. . . . [T]he scholars were often enraged beyond bounds for their disappointment in their place, and it was some time before a class could be settled down to an acquiescence in their allotment." The status-ranking system was not simply a matter of social position; certain privileges were associated with it. "The higher part of the class . . . commonly had the best chambers in College assigned to them. They had also a right to help themselves first at table in Commons . . . " (Peirce, 1833, pp. 308–309). As evidence of the depth of the resentment felt at being placed low, Colonel Isaac Williams of the class of 1727, who led a movement to start a college competitive to Harvard, "had been largely prompted by chagrin at the low rank accorded to his eldest son in the Harvard class of 1751 (fourteenth in a class of thirty-five, while his father had been tenth in a class of thirty-seven)" (Dexter, 1918, p. 220).

The system became increasingly difficult to administer, as students and their parents raised objections to placements, and it ran counter to the growing antimonarchical and antielitist sentiments then emerging. And on May 1, 1770, following a new dispute about placement, the Overseers approved a recommendation to stop ranking students "according to the supposed Dignity of the Families whereto they severally belong, . . . and that for the future the names of the Scholars in each class be placed in alphabetical order" (Dexter, 1918, p. 219; Peirce, 1833, p. 311). As the historian Franklin Dexter noted: "By the 1st of May 1770, . . . Committees of Correspondence between the different colonies had organized public opinion, and most recently of all the Boston Massacre had tended to knit the community together against arbitrary power. It was a good time for any step in the way of abandonment of superior privileges and dignities, the prerogatives of rank" (Dexter, 1918, p. 220).

The strains occasioned by the turmoil of the Revolution, which witnessed Harvard's retiring temporarily in 1775 to Concord to permit Washington and the Continental Army to use its buildings, undermined the continuity of autonomy and intramural authority. A tutor accused of directing the British troops on the road to Lexington was driven out of Cambridge (Cowley, n.d., pp. 11–25). In April 1776, the politically dominated Overseers appointed a committee to examine the political principles of the officers and instructors of the College. The members of the committee stated "that they should be required to attend at the next Overseers' meeting, to be examined as to their political principles, agreeably to a resolve of the General Court. . . . " The staff did so on April 23, furnishing "a written declaration of their political principles, which proved satisfactory" (Quincy, 1840, vol. 2, p. 168). In this atmosphere, the faculty refused to readmit a student who had been absent during the Concord period on the grounds that he "had been found guilty, and imprisoned by the General Court, for frequent clamoring, in the most impudent, insulting, and abusive language, against the American Congress, the General Court of the Colony, and others, who are and have been exerting themselves to save the country from misery and ruin" (ibid., p. 169). Yet, it may be noted that the predominantly faculty Fellows of the Corporation became involved in a dispute with the Overseers, when in 1778 they chose William Kneeland as Steward of the Corporation, "a man of great worth and respectability, in every respect well qualified for the office, . . . but as he had been deemed unfriendly to the cause of American Independence, his political principles rendered his appointment objectionable to the Overseers" (ibid., p. 172). The Corporation did as they were told, although they contested the right of the Overseers to veto such an appointment, a challenge that the Overseers ultimately agreed was legally correct.

Such events seemingly encouraged the students to show their disdain of authority. Before the war was over, they found themselves in sharp conflict with President Samuel Langdon who, though a strong supporter of the Revolution, insisted on giving 90-minute orations on the scriptures every Sunday evening. In 1780 they flaunted their resentment in a signed petition to him saying: "As a man of genius and knowledge we respect you, as a President we despise you." Langdon resigned soon afterwards (Morison, 1936c, p. 162). The historical record suggests that the student protest against Langdon bore some resemblance to that which undermined his predecessor Leonard Hoar a century earlier. Members of the faculty appear to have been involved in promoting the student discontent (Quincy, 1840, vol. 2, pp. 179–181).

Harvard students were to become quite conservative politically in the next century, but the example of the Revolutionary generation in resisting tyranny inside and outside the Yard was to inspire successive classes of undergraduates. The "liberty tree," around which students had gathered to organize demonstrations and pass resolutions from 1768 on, remained standing for many decades (Morison, 1936c, p. 133). Known as the "Rebellion Tree," its limbs were to bear many "Harvard presidents . . . hanged in effigy" (Kahn, 1968, p. 123). Thus student rebellion against arbitrary misuse of authority became a Harvard tradition linked physically to the events of the Revolution.

CHANGES IN GOVERNANCE

Although Harvard had been strongly committed to the Revolutionary cause, events stemming from changes in ideology and general turmoil

resulted in major changes in the governance of the College that undermined the influence both of the clerical Overseers and the faculty. The
concern stimulated by the Revolution for public control of Commonwealth institutions extended itself to Harvard, which to some extent had been viewed as the equivalent of a state university, as *the* university of Massachusetts. It received grants from the Commonwealth,
and the Legislature determined the composition of the Board of Overseers who had the final power to confirm the election of officers of the
College (Whitehead, 1973, pp. 12–13). In 1780, a new constitution was
drawn up by John Adams for the independent Commonwealth containing a separate section devoted to Harvard. The clause included a major
change in the composition of the Board of Overseers from a predominantly clerical one to a board in which the political figures had a large
majority. They included "the Governor, Lieutenant-Governor, Council
and Senate, . . . the President of Harvard College, . . . together with the
ministers of the Congregational churches, in the towns of Cambridge,
Watertown, Charlestown, Boston, Roxbury, and Dorchester" (Peirce,
1833, pp. 72–73). The legislature was also given the power to make
"such alterations in the government of the said University, as shall
be conducive to its advantage, and the interest of the republic of letters . . . " (Quincy, 1840, vol. 2, p. 508). The legislature was to continue to
try to dominate directly or to make use of its power to determine the
composition of the Overseers until the end of the Civil War (Kirkpatrick, 1931, pp. 42–43; Whitehead, 1973, *passim*).

Clear indication that John Adams and the delegates to the Constitutional Convention thought of Harvard as the state university is revealed
by the fact that the chapter dealing with "Incompatibility and Exclusion
from Offices," spells out a long list of public posts whose holders may
not serve at the same time in the legislature. These include judges, the
attorney-general, the treasurer, sheriffs, registers of probate, and the
like, plus the positions of "President, Professor, or Instructor of Harvard College" (Handlin & Handlin, 1966, p. 469). The officers of Harvard are the only ones listed in the section who were not directly on
the public payroll.

The constitution contained a clause which stated, "it shall be the duty
of legislatures and magistrates, in all future periods of the Commonwealth, to cherish the interests of literature and the sciences and all
seminaries of them; especially the University at Cambridge. . . . " When
it was submitted to town meetings across the Commonwealth for discussion and ratification, some passed resolutions voicing "objections to
the privileges given to the University at Cambridge, since the legisla-

ture might in time 'find it Necessary to Curtail that Rich and Growing Corporation Least it should Endanger the Liberties of the Commonwealth' " (ibid., p. 29).

The town meeting of Middleboro demanded a complete accounting of all funds of any kind "heretofore and now Belonging to Harvard College or to any or Either of the officers.... Belonging to said college shall for the present Time and forever hereafter be given annually to the Senate and House of Representatives in order that it may be fairly known what further privileges or grants are Really Necessary which may be granted accordingly or not as the said Senate and Court shall see Cause from Time to Time" (ibid., p. 699). The town of Bellingham voted against the clauses dealing with Harvard on the grounds "that the inhabitants of this State have a Right to Know ... all the Gifts and Grants of the Generall Courts of this State, and of all the Gifts, Grants and Devices of Particular Persons to and for Said University and to any and all the officers thereof. And Said Inhabitants have a Right to know the Annuall Income to and for said University, and how the Same is annualy expended, the want of which has been Gratly Complained of ... " (ibid., pp. 746–747).

Reflecting these sentiments, the politicians exhibited increasing reluctance to furnish Harvard with the necessary financial support. The school "was in desperate financial straits, owing to war, currency inflation," and the ineffectiveness of John Hancock who had served as treasurer, while busy on more important political matters (Morison, 1936c, p. 153). The legislature, however, simply refused to continue making regular appropriations for the salaries of the President and the professors (Whitehead, 1973, pp. 17–18). And when passing ad hoc support bills, it clearly intimated in the language of such legislation "that the patronage of the College by the legislature was soon to cease; ... that new views and new influences were beginning to prevail in relation to the institution.... The temper of the times was unfavorable to the patronage of institutions, destined for instruction in the higher and more abstruse branches of learning" (Quincy, 1840, vol. 2, pp. 247–249). "The riches of the institution" began to be mentioned as a reason for rejecting the memorials of the Corporation (ibid., p. 253). Seemingly, populist sentiments pressed the General Court to devote its resources elsewhere.

Faced with the need to find private sources of support if the College were to survive, the professors and tutors who composed the Corporation found themselves forced to involve men of property, substance, and political influence in the governance of the school. "The new political relations and popular influence introduced by the declaration of American Independence, and the financial embarrassments consequent on the revolutionary war, indicated to the [faculty-dominated] Corporation the wisdom of selecting men of experience in business, and practically acquainted with public affairs, as members of the board" (Quincy, 1840, vol. 2, p. 255; Morison, 1936c, p. 157). In 1779, they elected a leading merchant, James Bowdoin, as a Fellow. The choice of Bowdoin may have had some relationship to the fact that at the time he was serving as president of the State Constitution Convention, which was in the process of adopting the section dealing with the rights and governance of Harvard. In any case, the decision paid off well, since he both raised and left considerable sums for the University. The next vacancy in 1784 was filled by a distinguished lawyer, James Lowell. And with but one exception, the ranks of the Corporation were afterwards almost invariably chosen from the ranks of the Boston area elite (Whitehill, 1966, p. 144; Kirkpatrick, 1922a, p. 190). Financial necessity stemming from populist resentments furnished the catalyst that provided "the final stage in the evolution of the Harvard Corporation from a group of teaching fellows on an English collegiate model to a board of external trustees, connected with the living organism of the University only through the President" (Morison, 1936c, p. 160).

The shift from faculty government to one involving leading members of the economic and social elite in control of the board (which legally owned the institution and effectively governed it), accompanied by a change in the composition of the majority of the second board, the Overseers (who held the power of review and veto, from clerics to legislators), was defended much later by Samuel Eliot, the Treasurer of the University, as a triumph for popular control. He contended that faculty control could not last since "expediency could in no way have sanctioned a system so entirely at variance with a jealous republicanism of the people of the State. It would be sure to become obnoxious, even if it did not deserve to be so; while there was certainly danger that it would merit the odium it might incur" (Eliot, 1848, p. 49). The people who had established and supported the institution, rather than a self-cooptating oligarchy, the faculty, should have ultimate control. As Eliot put the case:

[I]t was said, that justice to the community would not permit a permanent institution to be so organized, as to allow individuals, in successive generations, to prescribe their own duties and salaries; that in the course of time and events, human selfishness and weakness would manifest themselves, as had been often the case in similar institutions for public purposes; and therefore that such an organization would have been obviously unsafe (ibid., p. 48).

Some further indication that the growth of antimonarchical sentiments in the larger body politic played a role in undermining faculty self-government may be adduced from the fact that a somewhat similar process occurred in Virginia where the second oldest college in English America, William and Mary, had operated with a system of governance comparable to Harvard's. The original royal charter had established as the major corporate body of the college, the "President and Masters or Professors." As a second board, corresponding to the Harvard Overseers, the Southern school had a Board of Visitors. "There does not appear to have been any contest between the two bodies until just before the Revolution when the clergy who made up the faculty, came into conflict with the political powers over questions of taxation and of general college policy" (Kirkpatrick, 1931, pp. xvi–xvii). From 1750 on, the Board of Visitors, dominated by the political leaders of the colony and the House of Burgesses, came into increasing conflict with the professors of the College who were largely Tory in their opinions—a fact that may have been related to the professors having a royal charter and to the London authorities retaining and using their right to overrule decisions of the Visitors and the House of Burgesses. The latter tried both to modify the financial position of the College and to change it into a more applied center of learning which taught subjects such as medicine, law, and various sciences (Stoeckel, 1958, pp. 76–97).

The William and Mary faculty appealed against the rulings of the Board of Visitors, backed by the provincial legislature, the House of Burgesses, to fire some of them for insubordination to their "feudal lord," the chancellor of the College, the Bishop of London, as was their right under the original charter of the College. The Bishop ruled in their favor and the faculty regained "their former independence for a short time." They also sought a decision or new charter from the king, making it clear that they possessed the same powers as the (faculty) Fellows of Oxford and Cambridge. But as Kirkpatrick notes:

The day for appeals to the king, however, and for new charters, was passed. Men who would not take orders in political affairs from the king, his ministers, or parliament, were not likely to submit to royal, much less, to episcopal authority when the claims of clergy and professors were considered. The Revolution and Independence were just at hand and the cause of the British college failed with the passing of the king's authority. Self-government for the college in

America ceased with the winning of that right for the colonies. In this crisis the American lay governor of the college was born (Kirkpatrick, 1931, p. 58).

Following the outbreak of the Revolution, Thomas Jefferson as Governor and member of the Visitors pressed major reforms on the school. Two divinity professorships were abolished, and chairs of law, physics, moral philosophy, and modern languages were established in 1779. The object of the political reformers was to make the College serve the interests of the community, rather than the will of the faculty (Stoeckel, 1958, pp. 98–101).

The opposition to faculty control over universities was rooted in the fact that the faculty corporation was an example of the autonomous "constituted bodies" that had originated in the Middle Ages (Kibre, 1962, pp. 325–330). Such bodies, which were largely self-cooptating oligarchies or aristocracies, were internally democratic. "All defended their liberties as they understood them; there was in many places a busy political life; discussion, protest, airing of grievances, and a refusal of taxes were very common.... In defending their rights and justifying their pretensions, the constituted bodies elaborated a good deal of political theory. It was a political theory of a strongly historical kind, making much of the agreements, compacts, statutes, and charters of former times" (Palmer, 1959, p. 51). It was the genius of the American Revolution to be the first to express the idea of the people, rather than various estates and institutions, as the constituent power; and the first such formal expression of this concept was in the Massachusetts constitution of 1780 authored largely by John Adams. "The formula, *We the people ordain and establish,* expressing the developed theory of the people as constituent power, was used for the first time in the Massachusetts constitution of 1780" (ibid., p. 224).

Thus ironically, the power of self-government of college faculty, which had emerged in Britain and parts of Europe as a feudal right corresponding to the rights that other "constituted bodies" had under feudalism, died in America with the triumph of the "bourgeois" democratic revolution. Colleges like Harvard and William and Mary, viewed as institutions of the community, dependent in part on public funds, and expected to be in harmony with the views of the controlling political elite, could not claim the right of self-government for the faculty. In the quarter of a century after independence, only one Harvard faculty member was elected to the Corporation. Since then, none have been (Kirkpatrick, 1922*a*, p. 190).

In noting the changes accompaning the rise of democratic sentiments and institutions, it should be stressed that Harvard and William and Mary never enjoyed an autonomy from external community control comparable to that experienced by the colleges of Oxford and Cambridge. The latter, established on the model of religious orders, had large endowments in the form of income from lands, much like the monasteries and convents. From the beginning the two American colleges were forced to turn to the state, local communities, and private sources for grants and donations. Further, the external governing boards of the institutions, the Overseers and the Visitors, while initially not very active, had much more power than comparable groups in England. The concept of community control over the colleges was, therefore, present in the charters of the American schools from the very start, a fact which presumably helped to legitimate the changes precipitated by the Revolution.

3. From the Post-Revolution Era to the Civil War

The considerable increase in student unrest in the post-Revolutionary period should not be seen as indicative of radical political tendencies among the undergraduates. Initially, the liberal, democratic, and antimonarchical outlook flowing from the identity of the new republic with its revolutionary origins encouraged enthusiasm for revolutionary movements in Europe. William Ellery Channing, later the great leader of New England Unitarianism, recalled of the Harvard of 1794: "College was never in a worse state than when I entered it. . . . The French Revolution had diseased the imagination. . . . The authority of the past was gone. . . . The tone of books and conversation was presumptuous and daring. The tendency of all classes was to skepticism" (Channing, 1851, p. 60). A contemporary of his, Daniel Appleton White of the class of 1797, also attributed to the "contagion" of the principles of the French Revolution, and the "books embodying them, much of the disorderly conduct, and most of the infidel and irreligious spirit, which prevailed at that period among the students at Cambridge. . ." (ibid., p. 61). As the foremost historian of Harvard, Samuel Eliot Morison, was to conclude, "the typical student of the early seventeen-nineties was an atheist in religion, an experimentalist in morals, a rebel to authority" (Morison, 1936c, p. 185).

Undergraduate sympathies with revolutionary movements abroad declined about as rapidly as did the much later radical wave of the 1960s. New England elites and their student children reacted against the Jeffersonians whom they regarded as supporters of the terroristic excesses of the French regime. With the emergence at the end of the nineties of a two-party system—Federalist-Republican, conservative-liberal—the dominant strata of the country, particularly in New England, became strongly identified with Federalism, a pattern which strongly affected all groups within the colleges, from the trustees and faculty to the students (Fischer, 1965, pp. 209–210; Hofstadter, 1961, pp.

241–242). One historian of university life, Ernst Earnest, comments that in "the early days of the Republic the teaching, except in a few southern colleges under the influence of Jefferson, was mainly Federalist" in politics (Earnest, 1953, p. 31). This was certainly true of Harvard. The students tended overwhelmingly to follow in the political footsteps of their parents and teachers (Story, 1851, pp. 51–53). When tensions grew between the United States and revolutionary France, "almost the entire student body of 170 signed an address in support of President John Adams" (Feuer, 1969, p. 328; Morison, 1936c, pp. 185-186). Joseph Story of the class of 1798, who was to be a Justice of the United States Supreme Court and was to play important roles in subsequent Harvard history, wrote of the College atmosphere at the end of the century: "Party spirit ran excessively high, and indeed with almost irresponsible fury. . . . The students became exceedingly interested in the grave questions then before the country" (Channing, 1851, pp. 67–68).

The tensions occasioned by these conflicts resulted in a struggle between the Federalist students and the government of the College over the rights of the undergraduates to express themselves in a partisan fashion at official functions. In 1798, Channing was chosen by the senior class to give the closing oration at commencement ceremonies. The College, however, told him "that all political discussion should be excluded. The reason for this restriction was that the students of the previous year had given great offense to the Democratic Party by the severity of their remarks. And as the college faculty were on the Federal side, candor seemed to demand that commencement day should not be embittered by political jealousies" (ibid., p. 70). The members of the senior class were incensed and insisted that Channing should refuse to speak under such conditions. When Channing did so, the president capitulated and removed the constraints. In the commencement address, Channing discussed the French Revolution. In conclusion, as the editor of his *Memoirs* notes, with "an impassioned burst of feeling, he said with great energy, and a look directed to the faculty which showed how earnestly he was inclined to protest against any restraint upon free speech,—'But that I am forbid, I could a tale unfold, which would harrow your souls.' As the circumstances thus referred to were generally known, this sally was received with unbounded applause; and when he left the stage, some time elapsed before the cheering ceased" (ibid., pp. 71–72).

Pro-Federalist student activism took on a more violent character the following year, when as a consequence of arguments between students and anti-Federalist townspeople at a Cambridge town meeting, "the students apparently incensed at the verbal attacks made on them in the town-meeting by Dr. Hill [an anti-Federalist leader], proceeded to break the windows of Dr. Hill's house" (Warren, 1916, p. 487).

The local organ of the Federalist Party, the *Columbian Centinel* of April 13, 1799, after noting the provocations against the students, said, nevertheless, that students engaging in such behavior "ought to be told that such atrocious nocturnal assaults injure the objects less than the agents of them."

It is the boast of Federalists to be the advocates of order and of the sacred right of property. Dark and secret attacks should be left to Jacobins who seldom work any other way. Were every man who receives an affront to attack the house of the adversary and thereby endanger his life, what would it lead to?

The reign of anarchy and Jacobinism would soon commence (ibid., p. 487).

STUDENT INDISCIPLINE

The triumph of conservative political principles clearly did not mean that the undermining of authority and traditional values which accompanied the Revolution had ended. The first decade of the new nation witnessed recurrent struggles up and down the coast with university authority over purely college issues—food, examinations, discipline regulations—and over the requirements that students take part in the religious services conducted in the college chapel. As in earlier (and later) days, the northern, particularly the New England, elite, while conservative politically, was quite liberal on religious matters, a point of view which affected the outlook of students toward the continued efforts of the colleges to enforce religious observances. A survey of the situation nationally points out that "Deism made rapid inroads among the college students of the day. Disrespect for authority, a sense of impermanence, and liberal theological ideas were heightened and spread by the Revolution. . . . Skepticism and infidelity became rife and were accompanied by greater rowdyism in the colleges" (Kennedy, 1961, p. 52; Rudolph, 1962, p. 40; Morais, 1934, p. 161; Koch, 1933, p. 242; Stauffer, 1918, pp. 86–87).

As Channing was to note, under such circumstances, "the difficulties of education were necessarily multiplied. The work required men of comprehensive and original minds, able to adapt themselves to the new state of the world. It is not to be wondered at, that the government and teachers of the college, most of them of mature years, and belonging to the old school, should understand little of the wants of the times. The system of government and instruction went on very much as it had done for years before, and the result was a state of great insubordination, and the almost total absence of the respect due to individuals of so much worth" (Channing, 1851, p. 60). Apolitical student indiscipline was widespread. In 1788–89, faculty reports at Harvard comment on "disorders" in chapel, on dishes and knives being thrown at tutors, on noise and even stones being thrown at lecturers, and on students insulting "the *President* by shouts and yells, challenges, curses, threats of laying siege to, undermining, and burning his house, by throwing clubs and stones" (Morison, 1936c, pp. 174–175).[1] In 1791 there was a "wave of disorder" in protest of the new requirement of examinations at the end of each year. Among the student arguments was the claim "that the procedure was unfair, for it penalized the underprivileged who had come to the college unprepared," a contention which would be revived in the 1960s (Handlin & Handlin, 1971, p. 127; Quincy, 1840, vol. 2, pp. 280–281). Repeated conflicts over college regulations meant that the "undergraduates at this time looked upon their tutors as their natural enemies. . . ." (Feuer, 1969, p. 328; Handlin & Handlin, 1971, pp. 127–128). Relations between the two strata were not conducive to reduce such tensions. Story reported that socially, "the regime of the old school in manners and habits then prevailed. The President and Professors were never approached except in the most formal way; and upon official occasions; and in the college yard (if I remember rightly) no student was permitted to keep his hat on if one of the Professors was there" (Story, 1851, p. 49).

One of the most perceptive analyses of the source of the difficulties between faculty and students in the emerging post-Revolutionary society was written in 1872 by Henry Adams, in the course of editing the college diary of his grandfather, John Quincy Adams.

The relations between instructors and scholars were far from satisfactory. Thoroughly cordial these relations never could be so long as college discipline remained in the hands of the instructors. The duty of giving instruction and the duty of judging offenses and inflicting punishment could never be intrusted to the same hands without injury to the usefulness of the instructor. This evil was conspicuous in the last century. . . . The system was wrong. . . . [T]he assumption of social superiority galled everyone subjected to it. The assumption created opposition. . . . Rebellion after rebellion broke out among the undergraduates (Adams, 1891, pp. 107–108).

[1]The quote is from Eliphalet Pearson, Hancock Professor of Hebrew. See his "Journal of Disorders" (1788) in William Bentinck-Smith (1953, pp. 111–113).

Interestingly, the one report on the social background of the unruly indicates that then, as much later, the scions of the well-to-do were more discontented, while those from less privileged backgrounds took delight in their opportunities to benefit themselves. "If the college atmosphere seemed oppressive to young scions of rich mercantile families, it was Elysium to boys . . . who come up to Cambridge from poor or provincial surroundings, after a hard struggle to qualify" (Morison, 1936c, pp. 179–180).

THE UNITARIAN TRIUMPH

The reform in the constitution of Harvard in 1780 replacing domination of the Overseers with clerical members by a large majority of ex officio political members was decisive in affecting Harvard's next major change, the capture of both the Hollis professorship of Divinity and the presidency by the newly evolving Unitarian denomination. Both positions had come vacant because of deaths in 1803–1804. The contests for succession occasioned a bitter struggle between the proponents of liberal Congregationalism, dominant among the Boston-area elite who had drifted into a Unitarian belief, and those who upheld Trinitarian Calvinist doctrine. After "as much intrigue. . . as was ever practiced in the Vatican" (in the words of the Reverend John Eliot, a Fellow of the Corporation) that board nominated Henry Ware, a strong Unitarian, for the divinity chair. The defenders of orthodoxy sought to block the nomination at the level of the Overseers. Here, however, they were stymied by the fact that 45 of the political members of the Board, both Federalists and Jeffersonian Republicans, showed up to vote down the minority of Calvinist-minister members. This action was not only decisive in the future theological affiliations of Harvard, but it also led to the final split in the still established Puritan state church into two denominations, Unitarian and Congregationalist.

The scenario was repeated for the election of the President. Again the Corporation nominated a religious liberal, Samuel Webber, and his nomination was sustained at the Overseers meeting by a vote of 35 to 14 (Morison, 1936c, pp. 187–191; Quincy, 1840, vol. 2, pp. 284–287; Hofstadter, 1961, pp. 184–185). Webber died in 1810 after but four years in office. His successor, John Kirkland, typified in his strong Unitarianism the beliefs of the community elite and was elected without opposition. As Richard Hofstadter has emphasized, the "victory of the Unitarians" had much to do "with the advance of a free intellectual climate at Harvard. . . . [T]olerant principles were far more central to the religious views of the Unitarians than they had been to those of even the moderate Calvinists, and the victory of the Unitarians was a genuine gain for the principle that different shades of belief could coexist under the roof of the same institution" (Hofstadter, 1961, p. 185). These changes led the Calvinists to reemphasize their view of the school as a center of heresy and to send their children elsewhere, while increasing numbers of students began to enter from less evangelically orthodox sections of the country and from diverse denominations; now even some Catholics and Jews attended. By 1820, more than a quarter of the students were from outside of New England, a jump from less than 10 percent before 1810 (McCaughey, 1970, p. 325).

Again, it should be stressed that the continued liberalization of Harvard's religious outlook, which helped foster its commitment to scholarly excellence, was interwoven with developments in the Boston and other seaboard urban areas, much as had occurred in earlier times. As Adolf Koch described the situation at the beginning of the nineteenth century:

Many of the Congregationalist clergy had ceased to believe the Calvinist principles. . . . Rather, without much outward change or overturning of established institutions, they preached a doctrine which assumed that man was less depraved and God less exalted. By 1800 many Congregational churches were in fact Unitarian. The change had been effected with the dignity and propriety becoming a cultured upper class. But it needs to be remembered that, while the Unitarian movement in America is properly thought of as a liberalizing of the older New England religious tradition, paradoxically, it was also a triumph of conservatism. It was an upper-class movement for the liberalizing or, perhaps more correctly, the civilizing of life. It had its roots in prosperity, urbanity, and worldliness. . . . As has been well said, "the Unitarians were liberal in theology but conservative in wellnigh everything else" (Koch, 1933, pp. 294–295).

As the Boston churches became liberal Congregationalist and Unitarian, Harvard inevitably followed. At the same time, contact with Harvard encouraged more cosmopolitan views among the community elite. The connection was fostered particularly by the growth after the Revolution of various learned and literary societies that had a Boston-Cambridge membership, including many ministers. The most noteworthy of these was the American Academy of Arts and Sciences, formed in 1780, which alternated its meetings between Boston and Harvard. It included many leading Harvard faculty, churchmen, and important lay figures, and regularly heard papers dealing with scientific and religious issues. Writing of the relationship between the two communities at the end of the eighteenth century, Harvard alumnus Sidney Willard noted that "the sympathies between the literary men and patrons of literature in Boston and the learned Faculty at the University were too binding to be severed without violence.... The ties between the academical and the political capital... became more and more strengthened by the intercommunity of the learned, and by union in scientific, literary and charitable associations..." (Simpson, 1950, pp. 491–503). Three to four decades later, the British visitor Charles Lyell noted that the interaction of the Harvard "professors, both literary and scientific, with the eminent lawyers, clergymen, physicians, and principal merchants of the place [Boston] forms a society of a superior kind..." (Lyell, 1845, vol. 1, pp. 108–109). Thus the Harvard faculty and the Boston elite formed an "intercommunity of the learned," mutually supportive in religious and social beliefs. And not the least of the consequences was the financial support that the University secured from the emerging Brahmin society.

PARTISAN CONFLICTS

These happy relations among the elite, however, did not extend to those between the college authorities (particularly the faculty, who were responsible for discipline) and the undergraduates. Harvard faculty spent considerable time at their weekly meetings with problems of student discipline, producing the consequences noted by Henry Adams. An alumnus reminisced:

The students certainly considered the Faculty as their natural enemies. There existed between the two parties very little of kindly intercourse, and that little, generally secret. ... The professors... performed police duty as occasion seemed to demand; and in case of a general disturbance, which was not infrequent, the entire Faculty were on the chase for the offenders... (Peabody, 1888, pp. 200–201).

In 1805 a major demonstration that had ultimate partisan political ramifications again developed over food. It repeated much of the scenario of the "Bread and Butter Rebellion" of 1766. The students struck, and the college, as four decades earlier, suspended half of the undergraduates. The Board of Overseers divided on party lines over both the substantive issue and the severity of the discipline. A committee led by the Jeffersonian Republican Lieutenant-Governor Levi Lincoln recommended both reforming the eating commons and pardoning the students. The Overseers voted on straight party lines, Federalists versus Republicans, and turned down the Lincoln Report by 29 to 26 votes (Morison, 1936c, pp. 211–212).

Similar events continued to occur with regularity. In 1807 the students again protested "the unsatisfactory state of the commons. The usual sequence of events followed. Students left the commons in a disorderly manner. Apparently the three classes held a meeting to discuss their common interests. Students insulted members of the faculty. . . " (Harris, 1970, p. 24). The College was disrupted for over a month by "The Rotten Cabbage Rebellion." The faculty closed the Commons and demanded written apologies under penalty of dismissal. When most students refused, the faculty tried to bring pressure by calling in "the families of the transgressors, with a view to conciliating their erring offspring. Mothers wept. Fathers swore. Finally seventeen abdurate spirits were dismissed, the rest apologized, and a semblance of discipline was restored. . . " (Batchelder, 1924, pp. 139–140). Among those expelled as ringleaders were Richard Henry Dana and Edward T. Channing. Neither ever received his A.B., although Channing was to become the Boylston Professor of Rhetoric at Harvard (ibid., p. 138).

Reactions to the behavior of the undergraduates occasioned a decade of partisan debate between the Jeffersonian Republicans and the Federalists for control over the Board of Overseers (Whitehead, 1973, pp. 18–20). Following the close partisan vote by the Overseers over the question of reversing the Corporation's expulsion of those involved in the 1805 rebellion, the Federalists, on regaining control of the legislature in 1810, changed the composition of the Overseers by reducing the number of ex officio public members to 11, with 15 holdover clerical members, and adding 15 new laymen to be "elected by the Board itself; and the new Board, thus constituted, would fill future vacancies by cooption" (Morison, 1936c, p. 212; Elliott & Chambers, 1934, p. 217). The change was designed, of course, to assure Federalist control in perpetuity. But when the Republicans regained power in the Commonwealth, they repealed this statute in 1812 and put the State Senators back on the Board. The game continued with the next reversal in party fortunes. In 1814 a Federalist legislature restored the 1810 composition while continuing the State Senate on it as well, thus creating a board of 77 members (Elliott & Chambers, 1934, p. 218; Morison, 1936c, p. 213; Goodman, 1964, pp. 164–165; Whitehead, 1973, p. 20).

These partisan conflicts for control of the University may have affected the tenure of "the only Republican" on the Harvard faculty, Benjamin Waterhouse, who had served as Professor of Theory and Practice of Physics, from the founding of the Harvard Medical School in 1782 until he was dismissed by the Corporation in 1812 (Morison, 1936c, pp. 169, 222–223). Although Waterhouse was a difficult character, often in conflict with professional colleagues, he was a major figure in medicine and had introduced vaccination to this country. He contended that he had been dismissed because of his political activities. As he described the situation:

> In 1806 this ancient University was taken possession by the notorious [Federalist] Essex Junto, who consider it their castle, or stronghold, and have accordingly manned it with picked men of their own cast. . . . I was gradually stripped of the fruits of all my labor, [and in 1812] set adrift with the loss of everything but my honour. . . .
>
> When Mr. Jefferson came into office, the late Judge Lowell, a leading man of the Junto. . . gave us, of the college, to understand, that the church and all our other sacred Institutuions were in danger, particularly the University, that therefore it behooved us Professors to rally with the clergy, and together form the front-rank in the Massachusetts army of federalism, in opposition to infidelity, Jacobinism and Jeffersonianism (Struik, 1948, pp. 156–157).

Perhaps more important than Waterhouse's well-known anti-Federalist views may have been the fact that in 1811 he had joined a group of Republican physicians to request the General Court to "give them a charter as the Massachusetts College of Physicians," an action perceived as the first step in establishing a competitor with the Harvard Medical School. Jeffersonian Governor Elbridge Gerry strongly supported the proposal stating "ominously that educational monopoly was a bad thing, excluding 'men of the most enlarged, liberal, and informed minds,' and providing 'an opiate to genius' " (Morison, 1936c, p. 222). The matter was heatedly debated in the press and in pamphlets and not surprisingly was strongly opposed by the Harvard Corporation. The then Federalist-controlled legislature turned down the petition by a close vote.

STUDENT POLITICS

Partisan controversy also extended within the student body as the nation approached its second war with England in 1812. The large majority of students continued to reflect the Federalist sentiments of the Massachusetts social and economic elite. When the Democratic-Republican Governor Gerry delivered the Thanksgiving Proclamation in the fall of 1811 at the compulsory Sunday service, he spoke of the country being blessed by "a national Government and Administration whose wisdom, virtue and firmness have not been circumvented, corrupted or appalled by the arts, seductions or threats of foreign or domestic foes," many students made scraping noises to indicate their displeasure.

The College authorities, although Federalist in sympathy themselves, required the students to submit a written apology to the minister of the service, Dr. Abiel Holmes (father of Oliver Wendell Holmes). The President, however, told them, according to a contemporary newspaper account, "that beside condemning their conduct as it required, . . . *he advised them to insert the reasons which betrayed them into this act of indecency.*" When a document to this effect was drawn up, the Republican supporters among the students, who numbered "a fifth part of the College," opposed the section that criticized the Governor, "notwithstanding it had passed the inspection of the President." Forty-five students then sent a separate address to the Governor objecting to the "pretended apology" by their Federalist compeers and informing him that in their judgment "this act of disrespect was neither general nor caused as has been asserted by the impulse of the moment; but was a preconcerted plan originating in rooted and inveterate prejudice." The Governor, in replying to this address, took the occasion to argue that encouragement of student involvement in political protest served to undermine all forms of authority, including that of the University itself.

In all systems of government, subordination is indispensible, and the University has had too much reason to deplore the want of it. . . . The students cannot be too deeply impressed with the necessity of supporting the Academical, State and National Government; for the habit of opposing any will inevitably extend to all of them, and Harvard will thus become the Alma Mater of miners to sap the foundation of our liberty and independence (Warren, 1916, pp. 488–490).

Further evidence that partisan issues continued to concern the undergraduates may be seen in the subjects debated during commencement exercises in these years. Thus in 1812, as the war began, the debate topic was "Whether extensiveness of territory be favorable to the preservation of Republican government" (Potter, 1944, p. 49).

President Kirkland and the Fellows of the Harvard Corporation, were, of course, strongly opposed to the War of 1812, which they saw as a misuse of federal power for an unjust cause. At the 1814 Commencement, Harvard conferred "honorary degrees on John Lowell, the secessionist; H. G. Otis, leader of the [antiwar prosecessionist] New England Convention movement; Judge Isaac Parker, who advised Federalist Governor Strong [of Massachusetts] to withhold [the state] militia; and Chief Justice Tilghman of Pennsylvania, who had defied the federal government in the Olmstead case" (Morison, 1970, pp. 5–6).

A few years later, in 1818, President Kirkland faced a new student protest against bad food which began with crockery being thrown in the commons. The students "rallied round the Rebellion Tree [its name still stemmed from the 1770s]. Each swore to stick to his comrades, and plucked a twig from the tree as a sign. 'Lord Bibo' (President Kirkland) summoned the leaders to his presence and forbade them to return to the tree." The undergraduates ignored this demand; and a number of them, including Ralph Waldo Emerson and Josiah Quincy, Jr., the son of Kirkland's successor as President of Harvard, were "rusticated" for some time. This was a mild punishment compared to what some demanded. The aged ex-President John Adams publicly proposed the revival of flogging as a penalty. Perhaps the supreme irony of this event was the fact that young Quincy, whose father was to have more severe trouble with students and suffer more opprobrium for his actions than any nineteenth-century Harvard president, had led a forbidden rally around the "Rebellion Tree," proclaiming that "Resistance to tyrants is obedience to God." These actions, of course, pointed up the continuing influence of the Revolutionary tradition in undermining authority among the scions of well-to-do conservative Federalists (Morison, 1936c, pp. 209–210; Harris, 1970, p. 24; Feuer, 1969, p. 328; Bowes, 1964, p. 96; Wagner, 1950, p. 87; Batchelder, 1924, pp. 144–145).

The year 1823 witnessed a "Great Rebellion," led largely by members of the senior class who had had a history of illegal class meetings, "battles in commons, bonfires and explosions in the Yard, cannonballs dropped from upper windows, choruses of 'scraping' that drowned tutors' voices in classroom and chapel, and plots that resulted in drenching their persons with buckets of ink-and-water." The rebellion broke out as a protest strike against a senior having been expelled. Before it ended, 43 seniors out of a class of 70 had been dismissed, including a son of John Quincy Adams, who vigorously protested the penalty to no avail (Morison, 1928b, pp. 65–96; Harris, 1970, p. 25).

A detailed description of the activities of the class of 1823 written by one of its members gives an excellent picture of the repeated turmoil of those days, as well as of the student side of the "Rebellion." He noted that after four students had been expelled, "the bugle was sounded under the Rebellion Tree, when forty-one out of seventy bound themselves by an oath that they would not return to order until the four expelled members were recalled. . . . Various resolutions were taken, among the rest that 'they would attend prayers the next morning for the last time. . . .'" (Morison, 1936c, pp. 84–85).

EFFORTS AT REFORM

The recurrent student unrest of this period may have reflected conflicts among the upper estates of the University over efforts to upgrade the institution. Kirkland's administration was marked by a considerable growth in the budget occasioned by a sizable increase in the number of professors, from 10 to 25, as well as in their quality, which required raising salaries and making major improvements in teaching, library, scientific, and residential facilities. Funds for these increases came about not only because of grants from various private sources, but also because of the decision of the Federalist-controlled legislature in 1814 to sizably increase state support by giving to Harvard the majority of the revenues from a new bank tax (Hoffmann, 1972, pp. 328–329; Whitehead, 1973, p. 20).

These efforts to improve quality were paralleled by changes in the governance of the University designed to reduce the power of the faculty by vesting the President with "unprecedented powers in the management of its affairs. Previously to the election of Dr. Kirkland . . . the general superintendence of the seminary, the distribution of its studies, the appointment of Tutors in case of any sudden vacancy, and in short all the executive powers relative to discipline and instruction, when not exercised by the Corporation itself, were carried into effect by the President, Professors, and Tutors, constituting a board denominated 'the Immediate Government.' In this respect the President always stood in the relation of *'primus inter pares,'* without other authority than that of a double vote, in case of equivote" (Quincy, 1840, vol. 2, pp. 335–336). The new regulations assigned to the President the right to make "alteration in the course of studies" and "from time to time to make such regulations respecting the instruction and the government of the students as he shall think reasonable and expedient" (ibid., p. 336).

The crisis of authority dramatized by the events of the Great Rebellion only served to emphasize a chronic state of affairs. There was widespread recognition that student indiscipline had taken on continuous as well as massive proportions. As one prominent faculty member, George Ticknor, described the situation, it clearly called for some action.

[I]n the course of the seventeen years ending in 1824, the whole number of students expelled, rusticated, dismissed, and suspended, was three hundred and fifty-four. Now, if we assume, that in the same time fourteen hundred persons were admitted to College, which is probably an over estimate, it will give an average of one of the higher and more disgraceful censures to every fourth student.... [This] proves plainly, that great and radical defects have existed at Cambridge, and satisfied the best friends of the College, that great and thorough remedies must be applied... (Ticknor, 1825, p. 10).

As in earlier and subsequent waves of student unrest, the President and various segments of the College, faculty, and Corporation used the opportunity to press for the adoption of their favorite reforms. In 1824, both the Corporation and the Overseers designated investigative committees (the latter, as in 1969, was convened under the chairmanship of an important judge, Joseph Story of the United States Supreme Court). Different faculty leaders also organized to gain their ends.

Both the Story Committee, representing in its composition the Boston Establishment, and the most numerous group of organized faculty, calling themselves the Eleven Resident Instructors, concentrated in their proposals for change on the governance of the institution. Not surprisingly, they came up with sharply variant suggestions. The Overseers Committee suggested the need for more administrative authority in the person of the President and of chairmen of proposed new departments. The 11 faculty demanded that the most powerful of the governing boards, the Corporation, consist of faculty as it had been for much of Harvard's earlier history.

As its first and presumably most important suggestion, the Story Committee proposed that "the President of the University... shall be the real, effective Head of the University, having a general superintendence of all its concerns, and have a complete visitatorial authority with respect to the several departments of the Professors and other Instructors. He shall have an independent and responsible negative [veto] upon the acts and proceedings of the other Boards and Departments...." Second, it recommended, for the first time in American academe, the creation of "separate departments... arranged as to embrace... studies of an analagous and connected nature...." The professor at the head of each department was to be given authority to nominate new appointees and in general to control the type and manner of instruction (Story, 1824, p. 5).

The Story Committee also suggested changes in teaching procedures, particularly smaller classes, and recommended that teaching be done "as much as possible in oral, familiar instruction, in preference to formal, written lectures" (ibid., p. 7). It sought as well to tighten up discipline, indicating that "a regular record shall be kept of the conduct of every student... and a copy of the same sent, every quarter... to his parents or guardians, so that they may be perfectly warned of his diligence or misconduct: ... [and] [t]hat the room of every student shall be visited every evening, at nine o'clock by some officer or Instructor of the College... and that the Instructors in the University should, so far as possible, act as guardians of the morals of the students" (ibid., pp. 8–9).

The Story Committee also saw a need to change the composition of the student body through having older and less affluent students. Noting that younger undergraduates were most likely to engage in "gross irregularities," they proposed that no person be admitted as a student into the University under the age of 16 years. "They also argued the importance of lessening the expenses of a collegiate education... [so] that parents of moderate property, and in the middle rank of life, may not be deterred from sending their children to Cambridge, nor obliged to seek a cheaper, or more defective education elsewhere" (ibid., p. 9). This latter suggestion may have had its inspiration in the fact that Justice Story (Harvard A.B. 1798) had come from an economically poor background and that, during the period in which he was an undergraduate, objections to college discipline had arisen largely among the sons of the privileged (Morison, 1936c, p. 180).

While the committee of Overseers advocated a more authoritarian regime for Harvard College, the Eleven Resident Instructors, almost half the total faculty, insisted that what Harvard needed was more faculty self-government, not less. A spokesman for the group blamed the "present evils in the state of the College" on the weak state of faculty authority. He denounced the proposals of the Story Committee as antithetical to a democratic society and so "degrading" to faculty esteem as to make it demeaning for anyone who did not need the job for economic reasons to continue to teach. "The system of government proposed is foreign from the whole spirit which breathes around us in our republican habits and institutions; and is such as no man of proper feelings would submit to, unless the necessities of a family compelled him to make a choice between different duties, his duty to himself and his duty to those dependent upon him" (One, Lately a Member... , 1824, pp. 4–5).

The faculty critics, reviving the controversy of a century earlier, declared that both because of the original intent of the founders of the College and because it was the best policy, the major governing board, the Corporation, should be composed of resident instructors rather than outside notables. They noted that they had been ignored in the past, writing, "It is well known to many, that for a considerable number of years past, great dissatisfaction with the condition of the college has existed in the minds of the resident officers," and claimed that the Corporation had paid no attention to various proposals for reform, particularly in the way students were handled, made by faculty members in 1821 (Norton, 1825, p. 3).

They maintained "the chartered right of the resident instructors to be elected to vacancies in the Board of the President and Fellows of the College" (Quincy, 1840, vol. 2, p. 340; Norton, 1825, pp. v–vi; Ticknor, 1825, pp. 12–15). As in 1722, the faculty protestors contended that they sought to return to ancient custom, "that, in the English universities, where many of the founders of Harvard College were educated, this was part of the meaning of the word Fellows, all of whom, by the laws of their foundation, are represented, as residing within the walls of their respective colleges; that the ancient usage under the charter of Harvard College, was the same; and that the words of the charter, fixing the college as a corporation *in* Cambridge, make it essential that the members of the corporation should be there resident" (Ticknor, 1825, p. 17). They argued that the faculty were better qualified than a governing board composed of outsiders to deal with the problems faced by a college.

The real object of the resident instructors, in all their proceedings, was to obtain such control over the discipline and instruction of the college, as might enable them to introduce those reforms and improvements which its condition required. From the circumstances of their intimate connexion with the college, their constant presence with it, and their consequent full acquaintance with its concerns, they were, and they are, the only body capable of introducing such reforms and improvements. The resident instructors are, at the same time, more deeply and personally interested in the institution, than any other individuals can be. But they have been wholly destitute of the ability to effect any of those changes which they might deem expedient or necessary to its prosperity (Norton, 1825, pp. 7–8).

It is difficult to reconstruct a century and a half later the principal concerns that motivated the renewed thrust for power on the part of the small Harvard faculty of the 1820s. Although occasioned, like the Story Committee, by the student revolt, the faculty documents dealt little with the problems of undergraduates. Rather, it would appear that many instructors were incensed over the disdain for their position implied in the absence of faculty representation on the Corporation, and the seeming rebuke to their effectiveness as teachers contained in the Story Committee's recommendations for changes in instructional procedure, and more significantly, for reduction of faculty authority to deal with discipline and curriculum matters. Their principal spokesman, Andrews Norton, Dexter Professor of Sacred Literature, contended that subjecting the faculty to the control of a board of outsiders served "to degrade their offices, and to lay all those who may hold them under a standing imputation of incapacity." He noted that "The resident instructors have been called their [the Corporation's] servants; and the name, perhaps, may express the relation which actually exists between these two bodies; but certainly does not correspond to the state of things which ought to exist. The station of master is one of more honor and dignity than that of servant; but in a literary [academic] institution there should be no offices of more honor or dignity, than those given to the literary men who are its instructors. They, indeed, should be the servants of the public, but not of any other body of men" (ibid., pp. xvii–xviii). And the document submitted by Norton on behalf of the eleven contended that increased faculty power "would render the stations of the resident instructors more respectable and desirable . . . ; and that every thing which may do this will tend to . . . promote the literature of the country, by rendering literary distinctions more an object of ambition" (ibid., pp. 13–14). They insisted, therefore, that in a college, the faculty "should receive the honor which may properly belong to the institution. Its reputation . . . belongs in the nature of things to individuals. . . . But the resident instructors are marked out by every circumstance as the proper representatives of the college; and with whose offices all the honor due the institution ought to be associated. No other body should intervene, as at present, to obscure them from public view; and to take from their offices, the rank and respectability which should be connected with them" (ibid., p. xvii).

In making their case, the memorialists also showed a concern with what today would be described as an issue of academic freedom, namely, the right of the faculty to choose colleagues solely on the basis of academic qualifications in open competition. They identified the then system of selection as giving too much power to the prejudices of the President and a lay board which had nonacademic concerns. They argued in criticism of the power of the President to initiate appointments: "the real effect of the present mode of election [of faculty] is to give to the President of the College, a weight of patronage, unfavorable to literature, because unfavorable to competition. . . . It is rendering the state of the college much too dependent on the personal characteristics of an individual" (ibid., p. 13).

They went on to challenge the competence of a board composed of busy, important people to handle these and other matters, and to act impartially in terms that have a modern ring:

The governors of the college have. . . , for some time, consisted, with the exception of the President, of gentlemen who either are, or have been, during the greater part of their lives, actively engaged in occupations or pursuits, foreign from the objects of the institution; men of high eminence in the profession of the law, whose minds, in consequence, were continually occupied with the cares and labors which this profession imposes upon its most distinguished members; men of business engaged in a great variety of private and public concerns; and clergymen, some of them of the very highest eminence, and already placed in situations, where their health was wasting under the necessary demands upon their time and thoughts and strength. . . .

They are its governors in the most extensive sense of the words. . . . The whole character of the institution is to be determined by them. By their regulations, especially those regarding the expenses of the students, and the charges upon them, they may lay open its advantages to a greater, or confine them to a smaller number. They may make it an institution merely for the rich, and for those who are supported by its charity; or they may extend its benefits to the whole community. But in selecting non-resident gentlemen as members of the Corporation, men of distinguished eminence will, of course, be taken. . . . When there is any warmth of political contention, the members of the Corporation will, in filling a vacancy in their body, select a candidate whose opinions correspond to their own. The Corporation will thus be perpetuated in one political party, and the college will be in the hands of one political party. . . . What has been described is only the natural and almost necessary course of things. But the effect of it is, to give a foreign, adventitious, political character to the college. . . (ibid., pp. 25, 31–32).

While the faculty memorialists identified possible political interests on the part of the nonresident upper-class members of the Corporation, they contended somewhat naively that faculty were free of such concerns. "The resident instructors are little likely to be distinguished as political partisans. They have kept aloof, and in all ordinary times, may be expected to keep aloof from political contests. As literary men, as instructors of the college, their objects in life must be very different from those of political ambition. As governors of the college, they will excite no political jealousy or enmity" (ibid., p. 32).

Basically, however, the faculty rested their case on the American individualistic doctrine of the day, namely, that self-interest produces the best results and that the faculty had a much higher interest in applying pure meritocratic standards in the appointment procedures than did a governing board of lay outsiders. As they put it:

The resident instructors have a personal and peculiar concern in the prosperity of the institution, which, from the nature of the case, cannot be felt by others. They are bound to it, not merely by public duty, but by private interest. The desire of its prosperity and reputation, which in them must be so active a feeling, would always induce them to be very careful in selecting not merely a proper candidate, but the most proper candidate for any office. Their personal interest in making the college as distinguished and useful as possible, would act in constant opposition to any improper motive or bias. Operating generally through the whole body, it would serve effectively to counteract any particular influence from individual prejudice, partiality, acquaintance, friendship, connexion, or from any less excusable motive. When the relation between a patron and a candidate for office is such, that the former will be affected neither in his interest nor reputation by the manner in which the latter may perform the duties assigned him; men are very liable to be influenced by other consideration than a mere regard to the superior fitness of the candidate. . . . But on the other hand, when those who have the power of nominating to an office, have themselves a stronger personal interest than any other individuals, that its duties should be properly discharged, there is then every security that the power will be properly exercised (ibid., pp. xvi–xvii).

The faculty were not unanimous in this demand. George Ticknor, perhaps the main advocate of curriculum reform and greater freedom for students, strongly opposed faculty participation on the governing boards. He felt that "the qualities necessary to constitute a valuable and useful member of the Corporation. . . are very different from the qualities necessary to constitute a valuable teacher." Specifically, he did not see faculty as having the ability to handle well "the funds of the institution." But more significant perhaps was his belief that a faculty in complete control of a university would be conservative with respect to academic issues, that they would create "a monopoly for their own benefit," resisting changes that might adversely affect the position or interests of those composing the teaching staff. Ticknor also argued against having a few faculty on the board on the grounds that a "professor or Tutor chosen into the Corporation, would be constantly acting in affairs, that concerned his own conduct and his own interests; voting over again upon his own votes; discussing the relations and duties of other instructors, who are necessarily in close connexion with himself. . ."(Ticknor, 1825, pp. 27–30).

The proposals to change the composition of the Corporation were rejected by the Overseers, then dominated by members of the Massachusetts Legislature. The faculty protest, however, succeeded in negating the proposals to enhance the power of the President to the point where he could veto their decisions. In a real sense, this open struggle over changing the power relations among the governing boards, the teaching staff, and the President, had the effect of stimulating the tendencies toward structural differentiation within higher education that Ticknor had argued were necessary for its administrative and intellectual vitality. The teaching staff were formally organized as the Faculty of the University "with the addition of the authority to act by committees. The President... was placed at the head of the Faculty, without any visitorial power or independent negative. He was... invested with those of general superintendence, and of carrying into effect the measures of the Faculty. The University was divided for purposes of instruction into departments, each to have a general superintendence of its own studies" (Quincy, 1840, vol. 2, p. 352).

Although the faculty lost the main battle, their struggle for increased power was not in vain. In the revised statutes of the University enacted by the Overseers in 1825, they gained a variety of powers that placed them in a much stronger position to determine educational policy than was enjoyed by the faculty of any other American institution, powers that many institutions would not obtain until the end of the century. As one student of Harvard organization notes:

Among the more important duties incumbent upon the faculty under the new regulations were the following: first, a general supervision of admissions, second, "authority to make all orders and regulations necessary for carrying into effect their powers and duties," third, control of student discipline, fourth, "power to administer the instruction and discipline of the University," which included the right "to propose at all times to the Government, any laws or measures, which they [the faculty] may find requisite or useful for the effectual exercise of their functions."

... In logic and in fact these statutes permitted the faculty to legislate on policy within their province. The governing boards were not composed of experts on curriculum and instruction—they had to depend upon those who were. ... In a practical sense the faculty had gained effective control over educational policy which has not been seriously challenged since (Wert, 1952, pp. 44–45).

The faculty of Harvard did not gain the most important power that may be delegated to the instructional staff, the right to play the principal role in selecting their colleagues. Yet, it may be noted that in 1830,

Jared Sparks, the first professor of secular history in any American university, who later served as President of Harvard (1849–1852), described the selection process at Harvard in terms that indicated considerable faculty influence at a time when professors at most other schools had little. After noting that new appointees were nominated by the Corporation and confirmed by the Overseers, Sparks asserted, "this is seldom done without consulting the members of the faculty into which a Professor is to be chosen. No good policy would introduce an efficient member into a small body, where such a step would be likely to endanger harmony of feeling and action" (Sparks, 1961, pp. 300–301). Sparks went on to urge "a new constitution . . . to provide for the nomination of a Professor by the members of the faculty, with whom he is to be associated," a reform which did not become the common practice at Harvard until late in the century. The Presidents retained the nominating power.

The faculty not only sharply improved their formal power as a result of the reforms of 1825, they also were able to demonstrate that governing boards and administrations were unable, even then, to force faculty to act in ways they oppose. Among the changes the majority of the instructors found objectionable were the provisions advocated by Ticknor that class sections be divided according to student ability and that able students be allowed to advance on their own rather than being held to a fixed schedule. As Morison notes, Ticknor and the Corporation, which had enacted these regulations, "soon discovered (what many academic reformers have since learned to their cost, and the regimenters and patrioteers have yet to learn) that a professor's power of passive resistance is immense and unpredictable" (Morison, 1936c, p. 233). The faculty simply ignored the provision or applied it "in a way that produced disorder among the students." As a result, President Kirkland recommended that the Corporation yield, and the law was made optional. It was dropped everywhere but in Ticknor's Modern Languages Department.

ACADEMIC LOSSES

The bitter internecine struggles of these years, as well as the frustrations involved in trying to discipline an unruly undergraduate body, severely harmed Harvard's academic standards. Enrollment declined as parents identified the school as a troubled place which was lax in enforcing order. Three of Harvard's most brilliant younger faculty, George Bancroft, Joseph Cogswell, and Edward Everett, who together with

Ticknor had been sent to study at the University of Göttingen in Germany in the late teens preliminary to taking up teaching positions at Harvard, resigned after a few years on the staff, fed up with the school. Everett, who entered politics after holding the Professorship of Greek Literature for five years and playing a leading role in the governance controversy, wrote in 1828, a few years after his resignation, words that might be seconded by many veterans of faculty wars:

The academic life presents fewer attractions to a man of letters than you probably think. . . . I assure you, that my share of the government of the college, as a professor, gave me more anxiety, than I have ever encountered as a member of Congress. In the latter capacity I have never lost ¼ of an hour's sleep. In the former, I had my digestion destroyed for a week together, by intense anxiety (McCaughey, 1970, p. 356).

The College also lost the considerable state funds that it had been receiving from 1814 on. In 1824, the Federalists, who had almost disappeared nationally, finally lost control of the Massachusetts legislature to their Democratic rivals. "The college petition that the state grant be extended for another five years fell on deaf ears in the Democratically controlled lower house. Not only was the grant not renewed, intimations were made the Commonwealth would never again underwrite the riotous goings-on in Cambridge" (McCaughey, 1970, p. 349; Whitehead, 1973, pp. 92–94). Ironically, although the Democrats chronically charged Harvard with failing to serve the less privileged strata because of its high tuition, the cancellation of support by the college's largest benefactor resulted in the elimination of almost all its scholarship funds for poor students, and a consequent severe drop in enrollment. The faculty was also cut in an effort to balance the budget (McCaughey, 1970, pp. 349–352). As a result of these troubles, Kirkland resigned in 1828 and was succeeded in 1829 by Josiah Quincy, former Federalist mayor of Boston and Unitarian layman, who had a reputation as a strong-minded able administrator. He was confirmed by the Overseers in a partisan vote.

RENEWED STUDENT REBELLION

From the student point of view, the troubles of Kirkland's adminstration had one important beneficial effect, the introduction of a mild version of the elective principle, student choice of courses; but this was probably far outweighed by the loss of some of their most brilliant young teachers, the decline in the numbers teaching them, the loss of scholarship funds, and not least, the introduction of a rigorous marking and ranking system that enhanced faculty-student tensions.

Marks had begun as a result of the reforms of 1825, and from these marks the first ten scholars were named in each class, beginning with that of 1826. . . . This system poisoned the already hostile relations between students and instructors, and made social intercourse between them impossible (Morison, 1936c, p. 260).

Richard Henry Dana, Jr., who was to write *Two Years Before the Mast*, left a detailed *Journal* which included a description of the next rebellion in 1832.

Toward the end of the second term a difficulty occurred between my class and the government which made a great change in my affairs. An offense had been committed in class, and the faculty wished to discover the offender. The *esprit du corps* was strongly against tale-bearing. . . . The story that came to us was that a charity-student . . . accidentally knew the actual offender and had been required by the faculty to disclose his name; that he had refused to do so, and by reason of the refusal, had been served with some process by a sheriff to bring the matter before a Grand Jury. . . . What motives regulated others I do not know but I can sincerely say that for myself, an aversion to tale-bearing, and a determination to sustain a young man who was willing to endure imprisonment rather than disclose what had been committed to him perhaps in confidence, were the causes that had led me to take part in the rebellion.

A meeting was called, at which all the class but two or three very timid and mean spirited lads attended. We passed resolutions that we would sustain our classmates, and proceeded to act accordingly. On Friday evening at prayers . . . my class set up a hissing, groaning and scraping. . . . The same thing was repeated on Saturday morning. Here was an open rebellion. I believe, too, that we refused to attend recitations. Suspension or expulsion was the certain consequence of discovery in any overt act, yet we persevered. . . . Some were sent off, others were taken away by their parents, and to those who remained, submission or suspension was the only alternative.

. . . I went in with the remnant of my class on the next morning, and, as was inevitable, had a summons to the faculty meeting and was suspended for six months (Dana, 1968, pp. 26–27).

In 1834 Harvard experienced even more severe student turmoil. The revolt began over a minor incident which led to some sophomores being penalized by the faculty. In reaction, their classmates protested; and during the subsequent uproar, windows were broken and furniture destroyed. The entire class was suspended for a year, and President

Josiah Quincy, unable to find the students responsible for the property damage, decided to call in the public authorities, thus breaking the "unwritten law that no police are ever called in. . ." (Harris, 1970, p. 29). This violation of university norms by the President brought a drastic reaction from the students comparable to the events of 1969 when police were summoned to Harvard Yard to break up the SDS occupation of University Hall.

Then, hell broke loose! Quincy had violated one of the oldest academic traditions: that the public authorities have no concern with what goes on inside a university, so long as the rights of outsiders are not infringed. The "black flag of rebellion" was hung from the roof of Holworthy. Furniture and glass in the recitations room of the University were smashed, and the fragments hurled out of the windows. The juniors, led by Ebenezer Rockwood Hoar, voted to wear crepe on their arms, issued a hand-bill with an acute dissection of the President's character, and hanged his effigy to the Rebellion Tree. A terrific explosion took place in chapel; and when the smoke had cleared, "A Bone for Old Quin to Pick" was seen written on the walls. A printed seniors' "Circular," signed by a committee who were promptly deprived of their degrees, gave their version of the Rebellion in language so cogent that the Overseers issued a forty-seven page pamphlet by Quincy to counteract it. . . . Quincy never recovered his popularity (Morison, 1936c, pp. 252–253).

The senior faculty were severely divided over Quincy's hard-line disciplinary policies. Although he generally won a majority among the nine voting members, the professors turned down his proposal to expel the entire senior class for issuing the "Circular" criticizing him. A minority faction led by Karl Follen (the professor of German Literature forced to flee Europe because of complaints by the Prussian government that "his Republican ideas were poisoning German youth"), and including John Farrar and Henry McKean, regularly opposed the President. Follen was subsequently let go by the Corporation for "encouraging student rebelliousness. . . and conspiring against the President during the 1834 disturbances" (McCaughey, 1970, p. 391). Since he was also deeply involved in the antislavery cause, his friends charged at the time that he had been dropped for his abolitionist activities, a claim that appears to have had little substance since Quincy himself was privately a strong opponent of slavery. Morison concluded that it "seems more likely that the real reason lay in the fact that Professor Follen opposed President Quincy's autocratic methods, and that Mrs. Follen, a rival queen to Mrs. Quincy, fomented the student Rebellion 'by her wit and talent'" (Morison, 1936c, p. 254).

Quincy was also in trouble with the Board of Overseers, even though it was controlled by elitist Whigs who dominated the politics of the state as the successors to the Federalists. Many Whigs were angry with the President because he had insisted in 1833 on giving an honorary degree to President Andrew Jackson, who was passing through Cambridge at the time. Quincy insisted, however, that Harvard had to do this for any incumbent President who came to Cambridge, as an earlier Federalist board had voted an honorary degree for James Monroe in 1817. Although many of the Whig Overseers remained unconvinced, the Board voted the degree at a hurriedly called meeting at which only 30 of the 80 members were present. Quincy was accused of rigging the meeting by setting it at a time when many could not be present (Davis, 1906, pp. 490–512).

The depths of feeling on the issue may be gauged from the comments of an Overseer at the time, John Quincy Adams, Jackson's predecessor in the Presidency:

[A]s myself an affectionate child of our Alma Mater, I would not be present to witness her disgrace in conferring her highest literary honors upon a barbarian who could not write a sentence of grammar and hardly could spell his own name. Mr. Quincy said he was sensible how utterly unworthy of literary honors Jackson was, but the Corporation thought it was necessary to follow the precedent and treat him precisely as Mr. Monroe. . . had been treated. . . . Mr. Quincy said it was thought also that the omission to show the same respect to President Jackson which had been shown to Mr. Monroe would be imputed to party spirit—which they were anxious to avoid. I was not satisfied with these reasons; but it is college ratiocination and college sentiment. Time-serving and sycophancy are qualities of all learned and scientific institutions (Davis, 1941, pp. 510–511).

The opponents of the award to Jackson seized on the 1834 student upheaval as an opportunity to get back at Quincy. They introduced a motion to condemn the appeal to the courts over an internal dispute, which resulted in a decision to appoint an investigative committee. John Quincy Adams was designated chairman of the committee, an act which boded ill for the President, not only because of Adams' bitter resentment about the degree for Jackson, but also because Adams, 11 years earlier, had petitioned in vain against the expulsion of his son John, who had been among 25 or so disciplined for involvement in the Great Rebellion of 1823 (Morison, 1936c, p. 231). Adams, however, followed his basic political instincts and strongly supported President Quincy in his calling in of the public authorities and endorsed the severe punishments handed out to the students, which made the class of 1836 one of the smallest since the turn of the century (Harris, 1970, pp. 26–27). Adams wrote, however, of Quincy that "he can never again regain his popularity with the students, and the public [will] treat him ... with cold neglect and insulting compassion" (McCaughey, 1970, p. 401).

Quincy was to continue to experience student troubles and violent rebellion. The "Gunpowder Plot" occurred in 1842. A college house and a recitation room were both blown up, and a "bombshell. . . exploded in University Hall doing much damage" (Harris, 1970, pp. 29–30).

The penchant of the undergraduates to take militant, sometimes violent, action against college authority should be seen in the context of the tactics used or recommended by President Quincy himself in the town-gown conflicts that pitted the well-to-do students against workers in Cambridge and Boston. A contemporary account of such a struggle in 1833, which may have involved many of the students expelled a year later, describes a "hot fight" with the workers then building the Unitarian church in Harvard Square:

[The fight may have begun when] the students crowded upon the workmen or in some way offended them, and as was natural hard words led to blows. . . . The workmen all had tools of some kind, and axes, saws, sledge-hammers, and crow-bars made very effective and deadly weapons. . . . All the elements of a bloody combat were at hand. . . .

Just then a commanding figure, in full black costume, appeared on the scene. . . . It was President Quincy! Passing on horseback, he sprang from and abandoned his horse and suddenly presented himself. Seizing the belligerent carpenter [in personal combat with a student] by the throat, with one hand he hurled him backwards, at least ten feet, over a pile of bricks, and controlling Pendleton with the other, in the most emphatic manner ordered all the students to go to their rooms (Cushing, 1899, pp. 17–18).

Almost a decade later, just a month before the "Gunpowder plot," a much more serious conflict erupted between Harvard students and workers in Cambridge and Boston which resulted in serious brawls. On one occasion when "a mob composed of Port-Rowdies and Boston truckmen, three hundred strong. . . " marched on Cambridge, the Harvard students armed themselves to defend the Yard. President Quincy "told the students if attacked to defend themselves in any way, pistols implied" (Porter, 1971, pp. 276–277). The mob broke up before bloodshed occurred.

The unfortunate similarities between President Quincy's experiences and those of another Harvard president over one hundred years later were not limited to the consequences of their calling in public authorities. Quincy, too, "was plagued with the problem of nonconformity of dress by the students" (Bowes, 1964, p. 108). In addition, he publicly criticized "the whiskers which (greatly to his disgust) began to sprout toward the end of his administration" (Morison, 1936c, p. 251).

RELIGIOUS LIBERALISM

If Quincy's administration may be faulted for recurrent tensions with students, it should be noted that he set a model for the schools of the country with respect to support for religious freedom. The University continued to be virulently attacked as a center of "infidelity," "atheism," and "Unitarian Sectarianism." At a time when Calvinism still dominated many other New England institutions, a pamphlet put out by the Corporation in 1831 reported that of the fourteen faculty, six were Unitarians, three Roman Catholics, and one each Calvinist, Lutheran, Episcopalian, Quaker, and Sandemanian. And in 1845 Quincy replied to repeated attacks by proclaiming Harvard's "purpose of avoiding as much as possible, the communication of any peculiarities of religious opinion to students ... " (Morison, 1936c, p. 259).

Tolerance for various forms of Christian religious belief, support for religious rationalism rather than revelation or Biblical doctrines, and enthusiasm for scientific discoveries led many followers of evangelical religion to reject higher education, to feel that "worldly learning might destroy the spirit. This attitude was to a large extent a reflection of the distrust the country folk felt toward the wealthy and easygoing residents of the town. Till deep in the nineteenth century there were families who objected for that reason to their children going to college" (Struik, 1948, p. 31).

Still there were clear limits to Harvard's religious liberalism. In 1838, Ralph Waldo Emerson, though no longer a Unitarian, was invited to give an address to the senior class of the Unitarian Harvard Divinity School. He used the occasion to make "a devastating criticism of all organized religion; the Church was contrasted with the Soul, at the end they heard the Messianic prophecy of a 'new Teacher' who would 'see the world to be the mirror of the soul, shall see the identity of the law of gravitation with the purity of the heart' " (ibid., p. 299). Emerson was severely attacked by members of the faculty, and the speech appears to have cost him his desired ambition to secure the Chair of Rhetoric (Morison, 1936c, p. 244; Struik, 1948, p. 299).

POLITICS AND MERITOCRACY

The dedication of Harvard to religious liberalism in the form of Unitarianism was paralleled by an equally fervent commitment on the part of the members of the Corporation and many faculty to political conservatism. As indicated earlier, this combination had characterized the views of the educated urban elite of Massachusetts and of Harvard from the eighteenth century on. As Samuel Eliot Morison, the preeminent historian of the University, noted: "Harvard in politics has always reflected the sentiments of the economic ruling class in Boston" (Morison, 1936c, p. 185). At the University's bicentennial celebration in 1836, the two graduates designated to make the major addresses were Edward Everett, now a leading Whig spokesman, and Harrison Gray Otis, who had been a leader of the Federalist party and a Fellow of the Corporation. In the lengthy speech prepared for the occasion, Otis attacked the Jacksonian views:

These persons do not admit, that the Revolution was completed by the establishment of independence. They would identify revolution with perpetual motion. They would put all ancient institutions, laws, customs, and schools upon wheels, and keep them whirling forever with the steam of their own eloquence. . . . Hence, mischievous errors respecting. . . the distribution of property, vested rights, the administration of justice, the natural and harmless distinctions of society (harmless because ephemeral and attainable by every class); and hence the subtleties by which the working classes, though fully employed and well paid, and inclined to be content, are stimulated to unjust pretensions, and assured that they are victims of oppressions and abuses, against the evidence of experience and their senses (Quincy, 1840, vol. 2, p. 666).

The Jacksonians, a minority within the effective governance of the University, challenged Harvard on composition of the student body, the relevance or practicality of the courses taught, and the role of the faculty. In many ways the issues raised appear quite similar to those debated in the 1960s and 1970s. The Jacksonian Democrats on the Board of Overseers and in the legislature increasingly attacked the University as an elitist institution during the 1840s. Having the "reputation of a Harvard baiter [was] a prerequisite for advancement within the Jacksonian ranks" (McCaughey, 1970, p. 480). A typical complaint registered by former faculty member and Jacksonian intellectual leader George Bancroft was "the disproportion between the magnificent endowments of Cambridge and the comparatively small number who derived benefit from them" (Bancroft & Child, 1845, p. 61).

The Democrats charged that the University was largely serving the children of the Boston Unitarian well-to-do. Bancroft and his supporters particularly emphasized the need for "Diminishing the Cost of Instruction," arguing that Harvard was one of the most expensive schools in the country, and that since it had a number of endowed professorships, it was in a better position than less well-endowed colleges to reduce tuition. In order to cut costs, Bancroft and other Jacksonians also urged that the size of the faculty be reduced and that the teaching load be increased. They pointed to how few hours a week professors taught compared to the work of other professions, noting that the academic "year is a succession of holidays; long periods of leisure, such as the merchant, the lawyer, the physician, the mechanic, the divine, cannot hope to enjoy," which gives the faculty the easiest jobs in the country (Bancroft & Child, 1845, p. 7).

In seeking to open Harvard to the able offspring of the less privileged, the Jacksonians explicitly advocated that Harvard become a meritocracy. "Bancroft was committed to academic excellence, and rather intolerant of anything short of it. . . . For he felt that educational institutions should be structured in a way that would reward only the intellectually gifted" (Gilmore, 1970, p. 44). His main complaint about Harvard was that it failed "to take students on the basis of merit alone," that less qualified students were able to enter because they could afford to attend. In so arguing, he was giving renewed expression to the meaning of egalitarianism in America as equality of opportunity, as enabling all to enter equally into the race for success.

Whig spokesmen such as Overseers John Gray and Leverett Saltonstall agreed that Harvard should emphasize excellence. As Daniel Appleton White put it, the best education as provided by a faculty "of well-known and eminent scholarship. . . [and a library]. . . beyond comparison more valuable than any other in America" was necessarily very expensive (Peabody, 1845, p. 38). And he suggested that the real need of the school was to raise more money through increasing tuition, arguing, as would others more than a century later, that "Raise its cost, and it will be more highly esteemed, and more ambitiously sought" (ibid., p. 41).

Samuel Eliot, the Treasurer of the University, also openly defended the elitist character of the school. "It results from the unavoidable constitution of human society, that a portion only of its members require the more extended education which is given in colleges. . . . It is for the interest of *all* then that *some* should be carefully and thoroughly prepared for the pursuits referred to [the professions], by the best education that can be given to them" (Whitehead, 1973, p. 98).

Similar values were stressed by Quincy, who, while admitting that the costs of a Harvard education were greater than elsewhere, suggested that this was necessary since a Harvard education was the best obtainable. Quincy also emphasized the fact that Harvard had a fund to aid poor students. Yet he admitted that Harvard had had a more heterogeneous student body in the past when it had received "large amounts of beneficiary money under the express authority of the legislature" (Gilmore, 1970, pp. 25–26).

In defending existing tuition and admission policies, however, Quincy exhibited his "elitist" biases. He opposed enlarging the size of the student body on the grounds that greater size was unmanageable and that crowding inevitably meant a reduction in the quality of education (Quincy, 1845, p. 19). More curious was his discussion of the problems created by the presence of larger numbers of students from the "West." He suggested that such undergraduates, while studious, presented a threat to order since they carried knives and were accustomed to using them. He anticipated that a professor might be knifed by a student and voiced the belief that "should. . . such an event ever occur here, I earnestly hope that. . . the offender shall not escape through the payment of money. . . [so that] the lives of professors and tutors enjoy the same protection as those of other members of the community" (ibid., p. 22). Quincy's concern on the subject of physical violence may have been occasioned by the shooting of a professor by a student at the University of Virginia in 1840 (Lipset, 1972*b*, p. 133).

Quincy also sought to refute Bancroft's attacks on the work of the faculty in terms closely resembling contemporary discussions. Thus he countered to Bancroft's totaling up the limited number of hours that professors spend in the classroom the long hours they must spend in preparing, the time they devote to faculty meetings, particularly the many concerned with student "disorders." Beyond these, however, given the rapid growth of knowledge, occurring then "with a zeal and activity never before witnessed," he noted that professors "must labor daily and diligently to preserve and enlarge the knowledge they have acquired" (Quincy, 1845, pp. 25–26). Quincy then went on to suggest that teaching was not the sole or even the primary responsibility of college faculty. Rather he stressed that the prestige of the institution rested on their research output, their publications.

New books, new views, new projects are daily put forth in relation to every art and every science. A professor in a University is, . . . if possible, to do justice to his position; to throw his contribution into the general stock everywhere forming by men of science. Every height, every distinction he attains, is an honor acquired for the University with which he is connected. Its glory is, in a greater or less degree, identified with his success (ibid., p. 26).

This statement was not simply an assertion of intent. As President, Quincy had sought to recruit eminent faculty by the inducement of a light teaching load. Thus in 1842, Asa Gray, already a nationally known botanist, was offered a chair at Harvard, under terms that, according to Quincy's letter of invitation, would allow him to limit his teaching in the subject "to the branch, in which you have already attained such eminence and celebrity," with a limited classroom schedule that would "leave you time, to prosecute the important work, in which you are engaged. . . . " Quincy went on to inform Gray that "an arrangement of this kind is not new, in our seminary" (Dupree, 1959, p. 110). Quincy may have been referring to arrangements made with Henry Wadsworth Longfellow, Ticknor's successor as Professor of Romance Languages, and Jared Sparks, the McLean Professor of Ancient and Modern History. Sparks had successfully "insisted on being allowed to instruct by lectures, assigned reading, and essays, rather than by set recitations, and in having eight months out of every twelve free for his researches in European and American archives" (Morison, 1936c, p. 264).

As a corollary to the emphasis on research, Quincy also gave strong support to those members of the faculty who sought to move toward a much more elective system of course requirements, in part to reduce the drudgery involved in teaching required subjects to uninterested students. Benjamin Peirce, the Hollis Professor of Mathematics, proposed in 1835 to drop the requirement that students must take three years of mathematics, making all courses beyond the freshman year elective. Peirce stated openly that he was uninterested in teaching large numbers of lazy students or those uninterested in mathematics. He preferred to concentrate on the very few who "have a taste and aptitude" for the subject (McCaughey, 1970, p. 430). Despite initial opposition from other faculty, the professors of Greek, Latin, and English came around to this position, and these four subjects became optional after the first year (Morison, 1936c, p. 262; McCaughey, 1970, pp. 442–445). The experiment, however, was short-lived, since it was not popular with Quincy's immediate successors. It remained for the post-Civil War administration of Charles Eliot to finally institutionalize the emphases on faculty research and student electives.

Other Whig spokesmen in the higher education debate of the 1840s were ready to move even further in the effort to make Harvard a more significant center of creative scholarship. Andrew Peabody and Daniel

Appleton White proposed as a reaction to the generally low state of undergraduate education in America compared to Europe that Harvard should become a graduate school, that it be the "University of America," requiring a degree from another college as a condition for entrance (Gilmore, 1970, p. 36). As White put it:

Why might there not be instituted at Cambridge a course of studies for students of much higher attainments than those now admitted—a course, on which the graduates of other colleges might be just qualified to enter?... If pupils were received at Harvard at nearly the point of literary acquisition, at which they are now sent forth, the institution would become at once, and long continue, without a rival, the University of America. Studious young men from all other colleges, and from every part of the United States, would be drawn together there. . . .

Could such a course as this be established, many of the features of the German university system might be advantageously adopted. The studies to be pursued, the books to be read, might with propriety be left, in a great degree, to the option of the student. Recitations might, for the most part, be superseded by lectures. . . .

An institution thus organized would be of incalculable benefit to the whole country. . . . It would raise up a generation of scholars worthy of the name, and. . . give them such facility in the acquisition of knowledge, that they could not fail of eminence as profound critics, original thinkers, and able writers (Peabody, 1845, pp. 45–47).

PARTISANSHIP AND GOVERNANCE

These public debates over Harvard's activities, stemming from its position as a quasi-state university, continued into the 1850s. Democratic party Overseers and public officials continued to challenge admission and curriculum policies as supporting Unitarianism and serving the children of the affluent. They called for greater emphasis on applied subjects, for giving students greater freedom to choose courses designed to prepare them for specific occupations (Hawkins, 1972, pp. 7–8).

A committee of the General Court, chaired by Democratic leader and soon to be Governor George Boutwell, stated in 1850 that the College "fails to answer the just expectations of the people of the State," and demanded that it be opened to those who "seek specific learning for a specific purpose." As a means of assuring that the students received the kind of courses they wanted, the committee proposed an elective system under which professors would be paid according to the size of their classes. "If a professor fails to draw students to his room, he should suffer pecuniarily. . . . The result would be, that those only would succeed who taught . . . in a manner acceptable to the public. That which was desired would be purchased, and that which was not, would be neglected" (Morison, 1936c, p. 287). To gain control of Harvard policies, the Boutwell Committee pressed for passage of a bill which would give the legislature the power to elect the Fellows of an enlarged Harvard Corporation for six-year terms (Whitehead, 1973, pp. 144–145). As a Democratic paper editorialized, "Harvard College belongs to the people of Massachusetts and by the grace of God, the people . . . will yet have it and hold it, if not in one way, then in another" (Morison, 1936c, p. 288).

The bill came close to being enacted. Boutwell had been elected Governor in 1850 and a coalition of Democrats, "who represented rural piety and orthodoxy," and Free Soilers controlled the legislature (Morison, 1936a, p. 508). The latter regarded the Corporation as a stronghold of opposition to the antislavery cause. One of the Fellows had actually voted for the Fugitive Slave law (Hoar, 1900, p. 62).

The Harvard Corporation addressed a memorial strongly opposing these suggestions. For the first time, in contradiction to past history and the position the Corporation took in earlier controversies with the faculty, they argued that the University was a private one, that the General Court "had permanently given away its rights of visitation in 1650 when it chartered the college without expressly reserving the right to change the charter" (Whitehead, 1973, p. 148). The legislature did not accept this limitation on their powers, but a compromise was reached. The General Court, which took office in 1851, left the Corporation alone, but changed the Board of Overseers to one of 30 members, to be elected by a joint ballot of both houses, plus seven ex officio ones (Elliott & Chambers, 1934, pp. 218–219). By dropping clerical and Senatorial representation, the Democratic–Free Soil majority of the legislature hoped to create a governing board of politically chosen community representatives, who, unlike officeholders, would have the time and inclination to effectively affect educational practices (Whitehead, 1973, pp. 149–150).

These changes in governance and sharp criticisms coming from both the left and the right led to much discussion but had little immediate effect on Harvard's admissions and instructional policies. Those who would open the College to poorer students were not able to secure the necessary additional "Beneficiary Funds," while the elitist exponents of higher admission standards could not deny that such changes would result in a further decline in the numbers enrolling. Harvard had become one of the most expensive schools in the country. Costs of attendance "were double those at Yale and Brown" (Hawkins, 1972, p. 8). The vast majority of undergraduates were, to cite an 1849 commentator, "the sons of wealthy parents. . . [whose] standard of expense, in regard to dress, pocket money, furniture, etc. . . . renders it almost a hopeless matter for a young man of slender means to obtain an education at Harvard" (Harris, 1970, p. 93).

The partisan conflicts also produced an academic freedom *cause célèbre* in 1850 when Francis Bowen, who had been nominated for the McLean Professorship of Ancient and Modern History, was turned down by the Board of Overseers by a vote of 39 to 33. Bowen, who was an avowed conservative, had been attacked for his public opposition to the cause of Hungarian freedom, then an issue because of Louis Kossuth's visit, and for his defense of Daniel Webster and the Compromise of 1850. "It had never been suggested in the course of the discussion that Mr. Bowen was unqualified, so far as knowledge was concerned to act as professor of history; and his junior and senior classes signed a petition to the overseers praising the quality of his lectures and begging that he be continued" (Morison, 1936a, p. 511). The record seems clear that Bowen was punished for his defense of Webster and his compromise on slavery. He was turned down by a vote that followed party lines (Whitehead, 1973, p. 153). Two years later, however, Bowen was appointed and confirmed to a chair in "Natural Religion, Moral Philosophy and Civil Policy" (Hawkins, 1972, pp. 8–9; Morison, 1936a, p. 511).

Removing the Senate and representatives of the clergy from the Board of Overseers also opened the University to further attention from the politicians, since there was considerable pressure from individuals who sought to serve on the Board. "The lobby became influential in the selection of the overseers and unemployed clergymen of various denominations were active in lobbying for themselves" (Boutwell, 1902, vol. 1, p. 95). In 1854, a Harvard graduate, George Washington Warren, serving as a Whig State Senator, introduced a bill to eliminate political control over the Overseers by shifting their election from the legislature to the alumni. To secure Democratic support, he proposed that the bill would take effect "when Harvard raised $200,000 from private sources to provide a hundred free scholarships for Massachusetts boys." A minority report from the committee dealing with the bill opposed it, in part, because separation from the state would leave "Harvard solely in the hands of the Unitarians," and argued that "far too many Massachusetts boys had been alienated from Harvard by this sectarian quality." The bill failed to pass (Whitehead, 1973, pp. 151–152).

The following year, 1855, the Corporation decided to directly attack the powers of the politically nominated Overseers. It accepted funds for a new Plummer Professorship of Divinity and filled the chair without submitting these actions for approval to the larger board. In defending these actions against Overseers' objection, the Corporation argued in contradiction to past history that the Overseers "had absolutely no right to demand confirmation on donations, salaries, or the appointment of officers of instruction; the overseers possessed the right of confirmation only in filling vacancies on the corporation [including the election of the President] and in 'the enactment of *orders* and *by-laws*, embracing statues and foundations of professorships and any new offices in the government or instruction of the institution' " (Whitehead, 1973, p. 154).

The Overseers not unnaturally attacked this limited conception of their function as reducing them to "a mere cypher." The Corporation continued to deny their rights. For the next ten years the two boards remained deadlocked (Whitehead, 1973, pp. 155–156).

The failure of the politicians to have much influence on Harvard educational policy was rooted in the fact that though they retained the right to ultimate control through their ability to choose the Overseers and modify the Charter, they refused to provide funds for the school. Thus Harvard President (1846–1849) Edward Everett, though a former Governor, was rebuffed when he twice appealed to the Legislature for public funds in 1848 and 1849. In his plea, he sought to combat the argument: "The schools are for the many; the Colleges for the few; the legislature must take care of the many, the few may take care of themselves; let those who want college education—the few—get it as they can" (Everett, 1961, p. 385). Even though many politicians attacked Harvard as a school for the "few," they effectively refused to try to control it by rejecting the requests that they support it financially, and make it a school for the many. It would appear, therefore, that given the tiny numbers actually interested in attending college at the time, many of Harvard's political critics only wanted to use the University as a symbolic elite target. Although the University was the subject of debates in the legislature, and was denounced on the hustings, "ordinarily very few of the Senate or Council took the trouble to attend the Overseers' meetings" during the period that they could outvote the nonofficial clerical and alumni members. The meeting at which Bowen was turned down was one of the very few in which there was "a full turnout" (Morison, 1936a, p. 509). The General Court curiously also remained aloof from the struggle between the Corporation and the Overseers whom they elected.

Those seeking to avoid political interference with the operation of the University did not, of course, see the power relationship in these terms. Thus Josiah Quincy noted feelingly:

It is the fate of Harvard College. . . to be cast, by the Constitution of its Board of Overseers, into the very trough of a politico-theologico sea, which has tossed that seminary in successive periods of its history, always to its injury, sometimes nearly to its destruction. In consequence of party spirit in politics and party spirit in religion, sometimes in hostility, sometimes in coalition, contesting for power, or endeavoring to oppress political rivals or religious opponents, the prosperity of the College has been mischievously affected, from the days of Dunster to the present, its literary advancement obstructed, and the peace and happiness of its governors and instructors, at different periods, disturbed or destroyed (Quincy, 1845, pp. vi–vii).

THE SLAVERY ISSUE AVOIDED

The troubles Quincy and Harvard had experienced as a result of partisan and religious controversies may have affected the determination of the heads of the school to keep it out of the growing conflict over slavery that was dividing the country. Quincy himself had been an early foe of slavery as a member of Congress and the State Senate before he became President of Harvard, had actively encouraged antislavery politicians in his private correspondence while President of the College, and again became an outspoken advocate of antislavery efforts after he left the post in 1845. Yet he discouraged "John Gorham Palfrey, then a professor in the divinity school, from using Harvard as a forum for his antislavery views. Although he shared Palfrey's views, Quincy told him he was anxious to avoid alienating any 'friends of the college'" (McCaughey, 1970, p. 478). As it entered the pre-Civil War decade, Harvard not only had to worry about attacks from the traditional populist and Calvinist critics of Unitarian intellectual elitism, it was under attack from another source. Many in the growing class of the newly rich, in industrializing New England, also pressed the school to serve practical ends, to fulfill the vocational and ideological needs of the business elite. Many of the affluent Boston Whigs traded with the South and therefore strongly favored the Compromise of 1850 and shunned antislavery agitators.

Harvard, by the 1850s, seemingly had come to view any involvement in extramural politics as posing a threat to its autonomy, to its role as the upholder of intellectual standards against those who would debase them on the hustings or in the marketplace. James Walker, Harvard President for most of this period (1853–1860), saw the colleges as "naturally allied to the great conservative interests of society," in an effort to stem the pressures for "intellectual anarchy." But at the same time, he denounced the "self-conceit" that characterized the wealthy (Smith, 1956, pp. 168–169). The scholarly community had the obligation to protect culture against both those whose power was based on the "mob" and those based on money. As passions grew in Boston and the nation, Walker in 1856 critically analyzed the growing divisions and hysteria, which reminded him of the witchcraft-trial days. He attacked "ultraism" and the "passionate assertions of zealots or demagogues." He saw the need for men who "operate as a check on violent and headlong counsels. . . [and help] to save both Church and State from those panics and violent and disasterous convulsions, which have done so much. . . to trouble and retard the progress of humanity and civilization" (Frothingham, 1891, pp. 466–467). As Wilson Smith sums up the predominant Harvard orientation as enunciated by Walker:

[His] reluctance to commit himself on public issues was due to a scholarly caution that asked for, if it did not get, full and free inquiry into all aspects of a given situation. His belief [was] that the unity of learning would be preserved through an impartial devotion to academic truth. . . . [He] and. . . other Harvard men. . . were intellectually wounded by the secular and utilitarian attacks upon their educational redoubt and. . . did not understand the secular chaos outside the university. They believed that man was indeed perfectible; the search for scholarly truth within the framework of a humane and tolerant theology would further the realization of this Unitarian credo in their society (Smith, 1956, pp. 182–183).

Given this lead from their President and most of the faculty, Harvard students also remained surprisingly uninvolved in the great moral debate. There is some suggestion that the presence of a large contingent of southern undergraduates may have imposed an unwritten truce with respect to debating the issue (Morse, 1933, pp. 154–156). In the early fifties, "almost one-third of the undergraduates were from the South" (Morison, 1936c, p. 281). Henry Adams, though an ardent Free Soiler and Republican, in giving the Senior Class Day Oration in 1858 told his classmates: "For four years we have associated together on the common ground of toleration; years during which the bitterest party spirit has excited the whole country, and stretched its influence over us at times" (Samuels, 1948, p. 42). But during that year, a sophomore from Mississippi, who was later to serve in the Confederate army as a brigadier general, "returned home saying frankly that he could not stand the political atmosphere around him" (Morse, 1933, p. 155).

The limited evidence available suggests divisions among the students reflecting the sentiments of their class and sectional backgrounds. Thus, the great majority from the North, particularly New England and Massachusetts, coming from Whig families tended to support the Whig-sponsored compromise of 1850. A number of leading abolitionists, such as James Birney, Gerit Smith, Harriet Beecher Stowe, and Theodore Weld, however, also sent their sons to Harvard (Smith, 1956, p. 151).

The professional school students appear to have been particularly unsympathetic to the antislavery cause. Those in medicine helped drive out the first three Negroes who had been accepted in the School in 1850. Following expressions of student opposition, the faculty voted that Negroes would not be accepted in the future. Not surprisingly, the three black students dropped out within three months of enrollment (West, 1972, p. 24). The Law School students were equally antagonistic. Edward Pierce, who received his law degree in 1852, reported that only six among 100 in the law school backed the anti-Compromise Free Soil movement (Morison, 1936c, p. 290). Two years later, when the Overseers chosen by a legislature controlled by foes of slavery removed Judge Edward O. Loring, who had upheld the Fugitive Slave Law, from his post as a part-time Lecturer, the Law School students voted to censure the Board for its action. On the other hand, a number of Free Soil undergraduates, including the then freshman Henry Adams, "backed the anti-slavery board" (Samuels, 1948, p. 40).

Not surprisingly, the strong feelings about slavery led to demonstrative actions. Charles Sumner, Harvard graduate and radical foe of slavery, "made a Free Soil speech in Cambridge Lyceum Hall (on the site of the Harvard Cooperative) which his friend Longfellow compared to a Beethoven symphony played in a saw-mill, so beautiful was Sumner's language, and so harsh the shouts, hisses, and 'vulgar interruptions.' " Horace Mann and Ralph Waldo Emerson were treated in a similar fashion by heavily student audiences, when they spoke against the Compromise and slavery in 1851 and 1852 (Morison, 1936c, p. 290). Emerson had strongly attacked Edward Everett for his support of the compromise. After the highly charged meeting, "some 200 students marched to the Everett residence," and cheered the former Harvard President. At the time, the total enrollment was 600, of whom half were undergraduates (White, 1913, p. 428). A contemporary description suggests that Law School students were the principal activists in opposing Emerson. On another occasion during this period, the tutors broke up "a noisy parade for Melon, the anti-slavery enthusiast," in Harvard Yard, the center of undergraduate life (Combs, 1950, p. 203). This event and the varying reactions to the Loring ouster may point to a difference in sentiments between the undergraduates and those studying in the professional schools.

The small band of Harvard instructors active in the Free Soil and other antislavery causes did little to mobilize student support. Yet it should be noted that Charles Eliot, then a tutor in Chemistry, and subsequently Harvard's most important President, took part in 1854 in an unsuccessful effort to free a captured fugitive slave by force (Schirmer, 1972, p. 25). The "aftermath of the Anthony Burns 'rescue' violently excited the student body" (Samuels, 1948, p. 40).

Whatever the expressions of support for antislavery activity among the different estates of Harvard, it is clear that the school was regarded as a center of conservative opposition by the abolitionist forces.

As Beriah Green cried out: "Harvard University! Was not Charles Follen there spurned? Were not Horace Mann and R. W. Emerson there hissed? Thence, did not Webster derive encouragement in supporting the Fu[gitive] S[lave] Bill?" (Thomas, 1950, pp. 232–233). The Democrats, though less concerned with slavery, continued to see the College "as the haven of smug aristocracy," while the Calvinists remained convinced that it was a center of infidelity (Morison, 1936c, pp. 286–287; Hofstadter, 1961, p. 252).

Harvard students had taken part in torchlight parades in support of different presidential candidates, and they continued to do so in the fateful election of 1860. There is some indication that controversy in the Yard was particularly heated that year. At the Commencement in June, the valedictorian, Charles Spaulding, provoked, for the first time in the history of such events, "plaudits mingled with hisses," when he praised Theodore Parker, Unitarian leader, who had arraigned Boston society for its guilt over slavery, as a "brave reformer." Again when he referred to the radical Republican foe of slavery, Charles Sumner, as " 'Massachusetts' favorite son.' ... after a moment of dubious silence a burst of spirited applause swept through the church only to be instantly followed by an opposing denunciatory storm of hisses.... As the class was leaving the church, one of them, a southerner, remarked to the classmate who walked beside him that what Spaulding had been saying presaged civil war—and so it did" (Morse, 1920, pp. 238–239).

A report by a member of the class of 1863 indicates that during "the autumn months of 1860 there was plenty of political talk and discussion" (Appleton, 1891, p. 4). The only available evidence as to actual student opinion at the time suggests that antislavery sentiment may have been stronger than the absence of student abolitionist activities implied. In mid-year 1860 the large majority of the class of 1860, 74, "declared themselves at graduation to be Republicans, nine to be Democrats, and twenty-three to be Constitutional Unionists" (Morison, 1936c, p. 320).

Curiously, with the exception of the leave-taking of most southern students, the Civil War itself did not much affect Harvard. With the departure for the war of the garrison at the Cambridge arsenal, Eliot formed a student cadet corps under his command to protect the arsenal against rumored plans by rebel supporters to seize it (Appleton, 1891, pp. 9–10). But relatively few students enlisted in the actual military forces, a pattern in northern colleges. In general, the well-to-do were allowed to stay out of the fighting; the conscription law of 1863 permitted draftees to hire substitutes to take their place, and students were not required to serve. Lincoln's own son graduated with his class from Harvard in 1864 (Morison, 1936c, pp. 302–303; Hawkins, 1972, pp. 21–22).

THE STATE OF EDUCATION

The students of this era were also much less disposed to engage in nonpolitical forms of collective indiscipline, in part perhaps because the College eased its responsibility to provide food, whether good or bad, by closing the commons in 1849, and also gave up required evening prayers in 1855. The Presidents of this period, for example, President Sparks (1849–1852), tended to "let the boys alone" (Morison, 1936c, p. 281; Harris, 1970, p. 30). But from the other side, Charles Francis Adams of the class of 1856, brother of Henry and Brooks and subsequently long-term Harvard Overseer, described in dismal terms the nature of his formal education and relations with faculty.

In one word: the educational trouble with Harvard in my time was the total absence of touch and direct personal influence as between student and instructor.... [O]utside of the recitation room, it was not good form—it was contrary to usage—for the instructors and the instructed to hold personal relations. Our professors in the "fifties" were a set of rather eminent scholars.... But as for giving direction to, in the sense of shaping, the individual minds of young men in their most plastic stage, ... it never entered into the professorial minds.... I was left absolutely without guidance (Adams, 1916, pp. 35–37; Duberman, 1961, p. 159).

But if Charles Francis Adams could complain, as myriad Harvard students before and after him have, that "I got as nearly as I can now see almost nothing at all" from his courses and teachers, he also reported in words comparable to many others that "from the college atmosphere and the close contact with a generation of generous young fellows containing then, as the result showed, infinite possibilities I got much of all that I have ever had of quickening and good" (Adams, 1916, p. 37).

Yet in spite of Adams' complaints about his teachers, it should be noted that the Harvard of the Civil War era contained many important scholars. The Lawrence Scientific School, which had been formed in 1849, possessed a distinguished group of scientists including Louis Agassiz in zoology, Asa Gray in botany, and Wolcott Gibbs in chemistry. Other distinguished faculty included Benjamin Peirce in mathematics, James Lowell in romance languages, and the Orientalist, George Rapall Noyes. With 70,000 volumes, its library was the second largest in the country (Morison, 1936c, p. 298). Yet, there was also a real sense that the school was in the doldrums, that it was not the exciting, stimulating place that a college which viewed itself as the best in America ought to be. Various faculty sought to reform it, to tighten up and to change the system of education. Charles Eliot, as an assistant professor, tried to change the curriculum of the Scientific School in the early sixties, proposing to stiffen the requirements for admission and to give science students a chance both for a broad general education and for real specialization (James, 1930, vol. 1, pp. 94–96). Eliot failed in his efforts, did not get promoted, complained bitterly about academic "conservatism," and subsequently took a professorship at the newly founded Massachusetts Institute of Technology.

The struggle between the two Harvard Governing Boards continued into the war period marked by, as the then Harvard Librarian noted, "the antagonistic feelings of the Overseers, the Overseers endeavoring to control the funds and consequently the college by insisting that all salaries shall be submitted to them for approval, and, if possible, annually" (Land, 1933, p. 125). The Corporation continued to refuse to acknowledge these powers, but in 1862 they were faced with the need to request that their nominee for President be confirmed by the other board. Seeking to satisfy a variety of objectives, John Lowell, the senior and dominant Fellow, determined that "the University needed as President a clergyman to quiet the religious element, a Republican (or at least a strong Union man) to placate the politicians, an administrator to build up the professional schools, and a scientist to give new subjects their due place in the collegiate sun" (Morison, 1936c, p. 304). To accomplish these, the Corporation nominated Thomas Hill, president of Antioch College and a Unitarian minister who was also "an excellent mathematician" and a "progressive educator." The proposal was particularly welcomed by the scientists on the faculty, who actively campaigned on his behalf. The Overseers, however, turned him down by 16 to 9, in large part, according to contemporary accounts, as a way of carrying on their power struggle with the Corporation. Other issues entered as well, including objections to Hill's religious beliefs, to the possibility that as a scientist he would seek to reduce the role of the classics, and even to his manners (Land, 1933, pp. 125, 133–134). The struggle was quite bitter and produced charges that "bribery and corruption" were being used to secure favorable votes from Overseers. "Mr. Bassett made a speech against Mr. Hill accusing him of eccentricity... [and] that the orthodox had put Mr. Hill in, contrary to the wishes of leading Unitarians. ... Mr. Sears made a speech setting forth his views upon the importance of the classics and the dangerous tendencies of the physical sciences." Six months after showing their muscle by rejecting the Hill nomination, the Overseers gave in and confirmed him as President in October 1862 (ibid., pp. 132–133).

Hill's election represented a considerable victory for those faculty, particularly scientists, who sought to press the idea that the University should not only teach, but "should also add to knowledge." They felt that Americans should not have to go to Germany to become scholars, that American universities should train them (ibid., pp. 137–138). The concern for graduate work and for original research, which had been growing in America in the decades before the Civil War, was intensified during the Civil War as it became clear that victory was related to industrial prowess and that scientific and technological research and education were both an economic and military asset. President Hill proposed that Harvard take the lead in this direction. In his first year in office, he proposed that Harvard become "the first American university," and in his report for 1863–64, he proclaimed: "If the genius of our colleges is such that they must be confined to the diffusion of knowledge, and not allowed to contribute to its increase, then it is time that we should found a new institution, whose purpose it shall be to further sound learning..." (ibid., p. 141). To accomplish these objectives, Hill proposed to enlarge the faculty, to provide graduate work leading to advanced degrees, and to introduce a largely elective system for undergraduates, which would encourage them to specialize.

These innovative proposals occasioned considerable controversy within the faculty, with some members of the governing boards, and with parents and alumni. Hill proved unequal to the task of political leadership. "He felt it the duty of his position to carry out the decisions of the Corporation rather than to initiate its measures" (ibid., p. 159).

He failed to carry the faculty with him on a number of measures and finally, faced with difficult family problems, resigned in 1868. In his final annual report, he outlined a program for the University, which his successor, Charles Eliot, was to fulfill.

The report was revolutionary in the importance it attributed to resident graduates, a category of students officially recognized since the Ticknor reforms, but tolerated rather than nurtured. According to Hill, future graduate students would be ambitious "to advance science, rather than to receive knowledge and diffuse it," and they should be encouraged by a program of fellowships and a new higher degree. It was more important . . . to provide teaching at the highest level of knowledge, than to add large numbers to the learners from textbooks (Hawkins, 1972, pp. 38–39).

THE END OF STATE CONTROL

The split between the two Governing Boards, exacerbated by the struggle over Hill's election, occasioned renewed efforts to finally eliminate any control over the institution by representatives of the state. "The controversy had leaked into the public press, and literally the ability of Harvard 'to keep its house in order' had been called into question." President Woolsey of Yale was to comment that he had "seldom been more disgusted than when the debates of this body on the qualifications of a gentleman elected as president of the University by the corporation were spread through the world by the newspapers, . . . " thus undermining Hill's position on taking office (Whitehead, 1973, p. 202). The 1854 proposal to turn election of the Overseers over to the alumni was revived and passed by the General Court at the very end of the war on April 28, 1865.

Although the act retained the format of two independent Governing Boards, and thus, did not eliminate the possibility of continued clashes between them, it was hoped that the "fact that the constituency which the overseers represented would change from the public at large to the alumni might lessen the struggle over finance and appointments. If both boards were composed of 'insiders,' the natural antagonism between an 'inside' and and 'outside' party might not be as tense" (ibid., p. 203). The act, moreover, was deliberately designed to avoid the possibility that the faculty or students might be able to have direct or indirect representation on the Overseers and thus be in a position to carry conflicts with the Corporation into the alumni elected board. It specified that no faculty member was eligible to serve as an Overseer or even vote in the election, and that alumni could not vote until five years after their graduation. The latter provision was intended to prevent "any possibility that the overseers might fall into the hands of very young graduates who might represent the 'student interest' " (Whitehead, 1973, p. 206).

The "Second American Revolution," the Civil War, like the first one, served to facilitate a series of political circumstances that changed the relation of Harvard to the state. As we have seen, the Revolution stimulated the politicians to try to take over control of the Governing Boards. The Civil War, however, reduced the tension between Harvard and the political community since the end of the conflict left the same forces in control of both. "The college and the state were predominantly Republican." The Republican leaders of the state were free, therefore, to agree to the request turned down in 1854, as "it was no longer opposed by the majority of the public" (Morison, 1936c, p. 278; Hofstadter, 1961, pp. 252–253; Shattuck, 1916, p. 426; Elliott & Chambers, 1916, pp. 219–221). Harvard became the first university to give alumni a major role in the governance of higher education, a practice which was to spread in ensuing years to many other schools (Wert, 1952, pp. 53–54). The school had seemingly learned the lesson "that to protect academic freedom she must at the earliest opportunity free her government from political elements; and that, as a price for freedom, she must look to her own alumni and to the public, not to the Commonwealth, for support" (Morison, 1936c, pp. 290–293; Hofstadter, 1961, pp. 252–253).

The new alumni-elected Board of Overseers expressed its agreement with the recommendations of outgoing President Hill that Harvard become a great university on the model of the German universities. In a report adopted in 1869, before Hill's successor was chosen, the Overseers explicitly distinguished between a college and a university, indicating that the former is concerned with "instruction," the latter with "the pursuit of science." The board called for expanding the faculty in the natural and social sciences, and proposed a wide extension of the elective system after the freshman year. And they went on to note:

The emancipation of Harvard from its confused relation to the State, and its new basis, resting on the love and help of its Alumni, opens to it a prospect of great progress and usefulness. The common aim of all its friends should be to second the movement now taking place, by which it is gradually changing from a gymnasium or college into a true university.... Professors are more interested in what they teach, and so are better able to inspire interest in others, when surrounded by an opinion favorable to the most thorough investigation. A university attracts students by the reputation of its professors, and by obtaining a number of great names it becomes conspicuous at a distance... (Morison, 1936c, pp. 326–327).

The choice of Charles Eliot as the head of the school was clearly related to these objectives. He had advocated many of the same innovations in two articles published in the *Atlantic Monthly* and was known intimately to the members of the Corporation and the Overseers as a former faculty member, as a professor at MIT, and from June 1868, as a member of the Overseers. Yet Eliot's candidacy occasioned considerable opposition from faculty members, both humanists and scientists alike. The former feared that in view of his "pronounced views in favor of new subjects, that all the subtle values of a liberal education, accumulated over two centuries, would be dissipated." The scientists "despised him" as a former colleague who had sought to change their curriculum and mode of operation, and who, they thought, would favor a more "practical" engineering approach to science (Morison, 1936c, pp. 327–328; James, 1930, vol. 1, pp. 186–187). Faced with faculty opposition, the alumni Overseers first returned his nomination to the Corporation, but following a renewed unanimous vote by the Fellows, the Overseers voted to confirm by 16 to 8, thus setting into operation what would become the most innovative administration in the history of American higher education.

4. The Golden Age of Eliot

Historians of American higher education have generally emphasized that the post-Civil War era was marked by a considerable decline in collective forms of student indiscipline (Brubacher & Rudy, 1968, p. 59). As David Allmendinger (1971, p. 17) noted: "the disorder and unrest of the antebellum period subsided, and the student population entered a long period of pacification." Congruent with this development, and possibly causally related to it, was a change in the role of the faculty away from that of disciplinarian in the recitation room and the dormitory to that of lecturer and scholar. The diffusion of the Germanic emphasis on original research among the major institutions, however, produced a new basis of conflict inherent in the consequent enunciation by leading professors of findings and opinions at odds with the interests and views of extramural religious, economic, and political elites (Metzger, 1961, pp. 63–64; Veysey, 1965, pp. 121–179). Tension grew between the "powers" and the academy, which resulted in efforts to restrict academic freedom and eventually culminated, in the late nineteenth century, in a number of bitter power struggles involving faculty (often in alliance with students) against autocratic administrators, governing boards, and politicians. In Harvard history, this period, identified as the Golden Age administration of Charles Eliot (1869–1909), took on somewhat different characteristics, responsible in many ways for its final emergence as the preeminent center of American scholarship. As elsewhere in the post-Civil War period, student unrest almost disappeared, but under Eliot the institution was able to provide faculty with an environment which avoided the destructive academic freedom and power struggles that occurred elsewhere.

Before turning to the Harvard developments, it is important to indicate some of the changes in the system of higher education which appear related to the decline in student indiscipline. First, the average age of both undergraduates and faculty increased. Some argue that the very young students of the early period of American higher education, many in their early and mid-teens, were inherently prone to be rambunctious and indisciplined away from home. By the second half of the century, the admission requirement of high school graduation had brought about a much older, and presumably more responsible student body (Kennedy, 1961, p. 78). More important, probably, was the even sharper increase in the average age of the faculty. Until mid-century the bulk of the teachers, and even College Presidents, were quite young. The vast majority of them were tutors, usually in their twenties, who had only a Bachelor's degree. By the 1860s, however, older professorial faculty began to dominate (ibid., pp. 100–114). As a group, they were more dedicated to teaching and scholarly careers, and less willing to closely supervise undergraduate life in police-like fashion (ibid., p. 114).

Paralleling this was the gradual breakdown in the controlled residential environment. The early nineteenth-century institutions had emphasized the role of the college as a "total institution" with the school providing room, board, and religious observance in addition to education. "The system made possible the supervision of and parental care for their charges. . . . [It] also brought students into close proximity usually under poor conditions. . . . The dormitory was a place where tempers were tried to the breaking point. It was a hatching ground for pranks and plots. . . . The fact that the system concentrated into groups active, healthy, high-spirited young men who were as capable of being whipped into a destructive, explosive riot as into a religious revival, should have been apparent early" (Bowes, 1964, pp. 84–86; Cowley, 1934, pp. 710–711).

By dropping the insistence that students live in College buildings, eat at the College Commons, and faithfully attend chapel, Harvard and many other schools eliminated some of the grounds for grievance; and by dispersing the students territorially, they reduced some of the potential for the easy organization of riots. Many university presidents, including Eliot, welcomed this reduction in the "collegiate way of living," although the support for such a policy remained stronger at Harvard than elsewhere and ultimately gave rise to the modern House System (Morison, 1936c, pp. 418–420).

At Harvard, in the latter half of the nineteenth century, freedom to live off campus resulted in the creation of privately run, luxurious "Gold Coast" residences and socially prestigious clubs that limited membership to those from high-status backgrounds. These developments segregated the student body according to family social class and income background, with the poorer undergraduates continuing to inhabit College buildings in the Yard (Veysey, 1965, p. 93). Since the more well-to-do had traditionally been more disposed to disdain faculty authority and to engage in various forms of indiscipline, this form of class segregation may have also worked to keep the peace. The less affluent, more studious, undergraduates were housed in the center, but were much less likely than the social elite scattered on the periphery of the community to foster collective protest.

These changes, of course, did not mean that the colleges had given up their efforts to control their students. As David Allmendinger points out, the increased use of frequent examinations and rigorous grading, introduced as we have seen at Harvard in 1825 as a reaction to a period of unrest, became an "alternate system of discipline," which spread out from New England.

[S]lowly, cumulatively, a transformation of great magnitude began to take place—the most significant consequence of all the unrest and disorder in the student population of antebellum America. Hereafter, order would be imposed through a student's daily academic performance. . . . Scholarship would become a competitive activity. . . . The intellectual life of the student was transformed; here was born the modern system of discipline (Allmendinger, 1971, p. 16).

Yet these changes did not eliminate the sources of class hostility between faculty and undergraduates. As Laurence Veysey reported, "a personal relationship had seldom existed in the past, and least of all in the mid-nineteenth century. . . . The coming of the elective system eased some of the tension, but it did not, as its advocates hoped, fundamentally alter the problem. The separation of aims and values remained, masked now by a veneer of mannerly politeness. . . . So out of touch was the Harvard faculty with the realities of the student world that it believed the undergraduates were devoting twice as much time to their studies as actually proved to be true" (Veysey, 1965, p. 295).

STUDENT REACTIONS

The Eliot regime started off with a bang, and considerable faculty suspicion of undergraduates. A group of Harvard students succeeded in blowing up an entire University building in 1870 (Mason, 1920, pp. 725–726; Grant, 1897, p. 558). Some sense of the mood and behavior of the students a century ago may be found in the memoirs of Robert Grant of the class of 1874, who was to subsequently become an eminent judge, novelist, president of the Board of Overseers, and member of the Governor's commission that reaffirmed the guilt of Sacco and Vanzetti.

Grant cites a letter from the Dean to his father reporting that he had been publicly admonished and put on special probation at the end of his freshman year (1870) "for participating in disorders in the recitation room of Mr. ———." His files revealed also that "a deduction of 32 was marked against Grant, Soph. , . . . for inattention and disorder at Italian exercise"; on June 13th of the same year (1871) he was "publicly admonished for twenty-two unexcused absences from prayers," etc. (Grant, 1897, pp. 557–558). Not surprisingly, Morison reports that at the time the relation between the two strata "was one of mutual hostility. It was perfectly good form to break up lectures with uproar and 'scraping' . . ." (Morison, 1928, p. 295). And in 1871 the Harvard Faculty forbade students to congregate in large groups, with the provision that any professor might "at his discretion forbid the collecting of students in groups within the precincts of the College" (Veysey, 1965, pp. 173–174). By 1877, however, the Harvard Faculty had dropped these and many other detailed regulations of undergraduate behavior, accepting the Eliot policy of giving the students as much freedom as possible, first with respect to behavior, and ultimately though reluctantly with the free choice of courses through a comprehensive elective system (Morison, 1936*c*, pp. 341–346, 357).

With few formal restrictions on student activity there was little in the way of collective outbursts. Early in the seventies, there were frequent conflicts between students and proctors when students would start bonfires from building materials in the Yard. "Finally the President [Eliot] had a bright idea. He ordered proctors to keep to their rooms in the event of a bonfire; and the students, deprived of the delicious spectacle of distracted proctors, took no more interest in that particular form of riot" (ibid., p. 401).

The elective system not only reduced direct control over student course choices, thus, as Barrett Wendell noted, eliminating a source of friction with the faculty, but it also lessened the potential for collective action through class activity (Wendell, 1887, p. 161). Many of the riots and other group protests of earlier years had usually begun as the action of classes, for example, seniors or sometimes the lower classmen. Under the old system of a required curriculum, students in the same year necessarily had to interact frequently in class, particularly in the first two years, and, therefore, had common interests outside. The "elective system. . . has tended to destroy that community of interest upon which the class depended for vitality. . . . Two students might enter Harvard from the same school and by the same examinations, and never meet again in any academic work during their entire course" (Sheldon, 1901, pp. 196–197; Morison, 1936*c*, p. 416). It should be noted that these consequences were not unanticipated by Eliot. In his inaugural address in 1869 he pointed to a number of changes which would necessarily make for a different relationship between students and teachers:

It has been alleged that the elective system must weaken the bind which unites members of the same class. This is true, but. . . . The increased size of the college classes inevitably works a great change in this respect [as well]. . . . This increase is progressive. Taken in connection with the rising average age of the students, it would compel the adoption of methods of instruction different from the old, if there were no better motive for such change. The elective system fosters scholarship, because it gives free play to natural preferences and inborn aptitudes, makes possible enthusiasm for a chosen work, relieves the professor and the ardent disciple of the presence of a body of students who are compelled to an unwelcome task. . . .

The petty discipline of colleges attracts altogether too much attention both from friends and foes. It is to be remembered that the rules governing decorum, however necessary to maintain the high standard of manners and conduct which characterizes this College, are nevertheless justly described as petty. What is technically called a quiet term cannot be accepted as the acme of University success. . . . Each year must be judged by the added opportunities of instruction, by the prevailing enthusiasm in learning, and by the gathered wealth of culture and character. . . . The manners of a community cannot be improved by main force any more than its morals (Eliot, 1969, pp. 10–11, 23–24).

The effort to widen the free choice of students led to an interesting proposal by Henry Adams, then an assistant professor of history. He wrote to Eliot in March 1877 proposing to establish a "rival course" to his own in American history, arguing that he knew "of no means so likely to stimulate both instructors and students. . . ." Specifically, he suggested that Henry Cabot Lodge "should have a course in U.S. history coterminous with mine. His views being federalist and conservative, have as good a right to expression in the college as mine which tend to democracy and radicalism. The clash of opinions can hardly fail to stimulate inquiry among the students" (Cater, 1947, pp. 80–81). Eliot accepted the proposal. Unfortunately for the future of this effort to enlarge the principle of *lern freiheit* to include planned political diversity in course offerings, Adams soon resigned from teaching to concentrate on his research, while Lodge followed him out two years later and entered politics.

Every relaxation of requirements seems to bring with it concern that students take advantage of their freedom, and consequent reversals of policy (Santayana, 1967, pp. 61–62). Thus in 1889 in response to parental protests about students not being in Cambridge during the academic year, the Overseers adopted a rule "that every undergraduate be requested to report in person early every morning, with a moderate and fixed allowance for occasional absences" ("College Discipline," 1889, p. 154). In a discussion that year in the *Atlantic Monthly*, Harvard Dean N. S. Shaler argued that "the public remark as to the evil behavior of Harvard students," which presumably underlay the pressure to tighten standards, was unwarranted. He contended that relatively few were "unfaithful or foolish." The criticism, in his judgment, was occasioned by the extreme actions of 2 to 3 percent which were well publicized, and "carry alarm into the households whence come some twelve hundred normally well-behaved young men" (Shaler, 1889, pp. 34–35).

The reforms of student life introduced by Eliot stemmed in some part from his desire to turn Harvard from a college primarily concerned with training youth to one dedicated to creative scholarship. This necessitated, as he noted in his inaugural address, that Harvard be both "rich" and "free" and that faculty be attracted to it because it supported them well financially and freed them both from petty concerns about handling students as well as from any anxiety about adverse repercussions from challenging conventional verities. He set a model for efforts to strengthen faculty "by increasing salaries, by setting scholars free from traditional dull routine, and by seeking unusual men from all over America and even in Europe. Almost his first act was to increase professorial salaries from $3,000 to $4,000 [at a time when other major schools were paying well below $3,000]. . . . By means of this one action Eliot had placed Harvard in a position to get almost any man it wanted in America" (Earnest, 1953, pp. 154–155; Harris, 1970, pp. 136–158). Among other inducements which Harvard pioneered under Eliot were the establishment of the sabbatical year's leave and a pension system, both in 1880. In the same year, Eliot wrote to "a prospective faculty member that Harvard professors had life tenure" (Hawkins, 1972, p. 67). Harvard's advanced policies enabled it to secure the most eminent faculty by far of any institution in the country, so that by the late nineteenth century it gained a sufficient modicum of prestige to be able to resist the competition from other universities, which in later years were to offer various Harvard "stars" more than they were receiving in Cambridge. Eliot, of course, did not rely on Harvard's nonmaterial assets to retain faculty. When a young scientist, Theodore Richards, came to him in 1901 with a higher salary offer, the president told him: "This is a very pleasant affair for everybody concerned. I have always thought that an occurrence of this kind is chiefly used as an opportunity to improve one's situation at home. Now, what do you want?" (James, 1930, vol. 2, p. 81). Richards received a promotion, and Eliot worked out a reduced load "which will leave him a teacher, and yet give him time and facilities for chemical research, and for creating a school of chemical investigators." Although Eliot preferred that all Harvard scholars teach, he anticipated "without complaint the development of research professorships" as a result of faculty desires and market pressures (Hawkins, 1972, p. 66).

George Santayana, Harvard philosopher, in 1894 summed up the "spirit and ideals" of Eliot's Harvard by distinguishing the college in which men were hired primarily to teach and infuse morality from the university in which they were employed to further scholarly truth. He compared Yale, which still sought "to be a mother of men rather than a school of doctors," which emphasized its links to national tradition and religion, which believed that the "work of education is to instill . . . revealed principles and to form habits congruous with them," with Harvard, which sought "after new gods," and which "therefore has no protective tariff on ideas" (Santayana, 1967, pp. 54–56).[1] This reflected a fundamental change in the character of the faculty. As he put it:

Some teachers of the old school naturally remain—teachers in whom the moral and personal relations to their pupils is still predominant, but the main concern of our typical young professor is not his pupils at all. It is his science. His vocation is to follow and promote the development of his branch of learning by reading the new books and magazine articles on his subject and contributing himself to its "literature." He gives lectures and reads his students' theses, and often, no doubt, finds this a welcome labor. There are times when light and inspiration come to him in the process of sifting and communicating his

---

[1] A decade earlier, *The Nation*, edited by E. L. Godkin, had stressed a similar distinction between the two ancient New England schools, viewed from the vantage point of teaching policies. As Godkin noted, Harvard is "representative of those who think that the true function of the university is simply to provide the means of learning for those who wish to learn, and that no part of the energy or ability of its instructors should be expended either in stimulating the stupid or inert, or in bringing to punitive justice those who neglect their opportunities.

"Yale on the other hand has . . . represented . . . those who consider a university a place for general training, moral as well as intellectual, in which the professor would stand literally *in loco parentis*, and not only provide the student with the means of instruction, but see that he gets it whether he likes it or not" ("Yale and Harvard," 1882, p. 52).

knowledge, times when he takes a natural delight in expressing his ideas—which he is here so free to do—and in planting the seeds of scholarship in the rising generation. But generally speaking, he wishes to be a scholar, and is a teacher only by accident, only because scholars are as yet supported only by institutions whose primary object is the education of youth. The pupils whom he really welcomes are those who have chosen his own profession and can encourage him in his labors by their sympathy and collaboration. His real colleagues also are not so much the other professors at the university as his *Fachgenossen* all the world over (Santayana, 1967, p. 59; Lipset, 1972*b*, pp. 225–232).

To recruit the best scholars in the world, to considerably reduce their teaching load, and to provide them with research and library facilities obviously required considerable additional funds. Eliot spent much of his time raising money, and although student enrollment quadrupled between 1870 and 1900, the endowment per student increased by 50 percent during the noninflationary period (Harris, 1970, p. 143). To a considerable degree his success in these efforts reflected Harvard's continued good fortune in being linked to the Boston-Cambridge elite. "Here Puritan respect for a learned clergy had survived the emergence of mercantile fortunes, a Unitarian and Transcendentalist liberation of the mind had stimulated social reformism, profits of the industrial revolution early found their way into philanthrophies of intellectual value, and Europe seemed at least as close as the American frontier" (Hawkins, 1972, pp. 62–63).

It is clearly not a coincidence that the "Golden Age" of Harvard coincided with "the time when New England's domination of American high culture reached its peak" (Green, 1966, p. 121). At the very start of the Eliot era, E. L. Godkin noted that Boston was "the one place in America where wealth and the knowledge of how to use it are apt to coincide" (ibid., p. 41). As early as 1807, members of the elite in founding the Boston Athenaeum had emphasized that in their city, "the class of persons enjoying easy circumstances, and possessing surplus wealth, is comparatively numerous. As we are not called upon for large contributions to national purposes, we shall do well to take advantage of the exception, by taxing ourselves for those institutions, which will be attended with lasting and extensive benefit, amidst all changes of our public fortunes and political affairs" (ibid., p. 42). Their descendants in the latter part of the century continued to feel this sense of responsibility as exhibited by their support for libraries, the symphony, hospitals, the Perkins Institute for the Blind, the Lowell Institute (for free, highly paid public lectures by the most distinguished intellectual figures of the day), and Harvard. As the historian of culture, Martin Green, notes:

[T]he whole world of learning was integrated into Boston society. The Lowells, the Eliots, the Adamses, the Quincys, the Cabots, between them ran Harvard—as trustees, as benefactors, and as scholars. . . . There was nothing like this in Germany, or in England either, and at its best such a system served to give all learning a social position and importance. These individuals served and indeed created Boston humanism, an assimilation of every kind of knowledge into a complex whole which is itself shaped into a significant relation to the individual's imagination and conscience. . . .

Boston merchants, and to some extent the bankers and industrialists who succeeded them, had the idea that commerce should go hand in hand with philanthrophy, and even culture; and should give way to them as soon as the individual had secured himself an adequate sum. . . . Family connection was one of the main ways in which the money made in Boston commerce passed into the hands of Boston scholarship. Samuel Eliot (who also founded the chair of Greek at Harvard) was the father-in-law of Andrews Norton and George Ticknor. [His son, also Samuel, the father of the President, was a member of the Corporation and Treasurer of the University.] Nathan Appleton was the father-in-law of Longfellow. . . . At the very least like Augustus Lowell, they urged their sons to pursue knowledge. In Boston, more than in the rest of America, business sincerely acknowledged intellectual as well as social obligations.

The great families represented Boston also in their relations with contemporary England. They had close ties with the Liberal intellectual families there; James Russell Lowell was a close friend of Leslie Stephen's, and in fact the god-father of Virginia Woolf; Charles Eliot Norton was brother-in-law to a Darwin. They were in fact very similar to the great chain of those families described by Noel Annan in his essay on "The Intellectual Aristocracy." . . . But within their own city, the Bostonians were much more completely a ruling class than the English; there was no-one above them; they were *more* responsible for their culture (ibid., pp. 52, 56–57).

ACADEMIC FREEDOM

Curiously, however, it must be noted that Eliot's career as President began with an effort in 1870 to inhibit the freedom of a faculty member, the same Francis Bowen whose appointment had occasioned so much difficulty in the early fifties. Bowen was instructed by Eliot and the other members of the Corporation "to remove from an economics textbook he was about to publish, either his support for repaying the national debt below par or all mention of his Harvard connection." They seemed to differentiate between textbooks and other activities, since Eliot wrote to E. L. Godkin, as a prospective faculty member: "The Corporation have no thought of interfering in the remotest manner with the writings or speeches of any person employed by them, unless indeed these writings are College textbooks. A professor here is free to think or say what he pleases" (Hawkins, 1972, pp. 70–71). As evidence of his dedication to academic freedom, it should be noted that in the same year (1870) in which the controversy occurred over Bowen's textbook Eliot succeeded in a struggle with the Overseers, now elected by the alumni, over the designation of a rationalist Comtean, John Fiske, as a history instructor. The appointment was denounced in religious media as evidence of "Harvard's drive on religion," and many Overseers opposed it. Following Eliot's strong defense, the Board voted 12 to 10 to confirm Fiske. The Overseers apparently were prepared to differentiate between outrageous statements voiced by one of unknown social origins and by a member of a Brahmin family, for the proposal made a few months later to appoint a "more advanced 'infidel' than John Fiske," Henry Adams, to an assistant professorship in history, was unanimously approved (Morison, 1936c, p. 348). The effort to modify Bowen's textbook proved to be the one occasion in which Eliot lent any support to restrictions on faculty activity. In 1880, in writing to an English scholar being offered a professorship he described Harvard's policies, designed to protect the freedom of faculty and students.

Within his sphere [a Harvard professor] is master. He may adopt a pure lecture method, or require his students to translate, "recite," or answer questions. He may be strict or lax as to discipline in the classroom. He may cultivate social relations with his pupils, or never speak to them except in the lecture room. Since there will generally be found among his students a considerable variety of opinions and conditions—religious, political, and social—he will naturally give to others the same freedom which he enjoys himself. He may present his own views with all the force he possesses, but he cannot authoritatively impose his personal opinions upon his students (James, 1930, vol. 2, p. 26).

On a subsequent occasion in 1893, he told another prospective appointee that Harvard conveyed "an absolute freedom from all restriction—governmental, academic or social—on freedom of thought or speech" (Hawkins, 1972, p. 71).

Eliot's liberal policies and successes with respect to student life and education, internal peace, and growing institutional prestige and affluence did not make him popular with any of the Estates of Harvard. His proposals for free electives were strongly opposed for many years and were the subject of heated debate at endless faculty meetings, often by teachers of required courses who argued that student freedom to choose their courses would enable them to avoid "hard intellectual work." The various reforms he proposed challenged the traditional ways followed by the faculty, and many opposed each one. Thus the establishment of a Graduate Department in 1872, with courses listed as "primarily for graduates" met with much opposition on the grounds that it would weaken undergraduate instruction. Morison judges that the opposition came largely from the "weaker brethren [who] knew they could never teach graduate students, and did not wish to be put to the test" (Morison, 1936c, p. 335). The record seemed to sustain Eliot's early judgment of his colleagues made as a young professor. "The head-quarters of Conservatism are in the Colleges and other Institutions for teaching. The conservative spirit in politics is not nearly as stiff and invincible as literary [academic] conservatism" (James, 1930, vol. 1, p. 72).

Eliot was to have more success with the faculty in later years, when he sought to reorganize the graduate program by combining the Graduate School, the Lawrence Scientific School, and the College into the Faculty of Arts and Sciences, with twelve Divisions, some of which would include a number of separate Departments. After four years of commit-tee work and faculty deliberations, the proposals were approved over-whelmingly by the Faculty and the Governing Boards (Wert, 1952, pp. 142–182; Hawkins, 1972, pp. 72–73). These changes enhanced the power of the faculty, since the Departments were given chairmen, rather than executive heads, whose role was to represent rather than direct their units. More importantly, departments gained the authority to initiate appointments and promotions, thus replacing the existing practice then still common in almost all other universities of presiden-tial nomination, after informal consultation with some of the profes-sors and the Dean. This decisive shift in power relations, which often occurred in other schools following bitter faculty-administration strug-gles, evolved at Harvard without a fight (Morison, 1936c, pp. 372–373).

The long years of the Eliot administration had witnessed a gradual but drastic change in the governance of the school. When he first took office, determined to change the character of the school, Eliot empha-sized the powers of the presidency in dealing with both the faculty and the Governing Boards. Seeking to upgrade the faculty, he consulted lit-tle with the existing staff; and as Barrett Wendell noted, there were oc-casions "where Mr. Eliot has appointed professors from outside without the advice or consent of the departments, much to the good of the department in question" (Hawkins, 1972, p. 62). Over the years, however, as the caliber of the faculty improved, Eliot increased the practice of consultation, until after the reorganization of the nineties the policy of nominations by departments was finally institutionalized.

All reports on the Eliot administration agree that he "had a strong concern for faculty participation in institutional government," and in spite of the fact that it required him to preside over endless controversial meetings, he sought to involve the faculty in the decision-making process through both committee and general meetings. But coincident with this objective, he also enlarged the administrative staff, those involved in handling what he described as the "mechanics of colleges," so that the faculty might lead an "undistracted life."

Not surprisingly, the same faculty that sought and welcomed increased powers also complained about the time they had to give to such activities. William James, finding himself on four committees, complained that committee work overwhelmed "the lives of men whose interest is more in learning than in administration." The Dean of the College, LeBaron Briggs, noted that committee assignments were feared as "a serious interruption . . . to original work, not only from the time taken by meetings, but also because of the break in the train of thought and the fatigue from this exacting and different work." In 1903, Eliot agreed to the recommendation of a special faculty committee to reduce professorial involvement by cutting down the number of committees.

REACTIONS TO ELIOT'S POLICIES

By the last decade of his administration, it was clear that the faculty had confidence in the admistration and sought limits on their own participation. As a recent biographer of Eliot notes: "At Harvard, the professors more than the president desired the creation of new administrative offices and increased powers for the administrative offices and increased powers for the administrative staff" (Hawkins, 1972, p. 73). This was borne out by a survey conducted in 1911 of faculty opinion at a number of universities concerning a plan to increase faculty control of universities, including election of presidents for limited terms by professors. More Harvard professors objected to such proposals than those at any other school except Wisconsin. Many argued in favor of what one described as "tempered autocracy" (Cattell, 1913, pp. 23–25, 65–84).

Eliot's educational reforms were bitterly disliked by important alumni who had favored his efforts to enhance the scholarly prestige of the school. Many felt that the elective system and the growing importance of graduate work would undermine the College to which they were dedicated. "Any outsider who heard the conversation of Boston clubs and drawing rooms in those days might well have concluded that President Eliot was 'Public Enemy No. 1' " (Morison, 1936c, p. 358; Wert, 1952, p. 167). Yet Eliot was generally able to carry the day with the alumni-controlled Overseers. The one major proposal that they refused to grant him was his plan for a three-year B. A., perhaps because the scheme was opposed by a large faculty minority (Wert, 1952, pp. 165–172).

In spite of the relaxation of disciplinary regulations and the enormous increase in *lern freiheit*, the students disliked him. "To the average undergraduate he seemed a pretty grim person. . . . All that he had done to make their studies more varied and pleasant and their life more free, they took for granted." He received few cheers at the annual Class Day (Morison, 1936c, pp. 358–361; James, 1930, vol. 2, p. 311). But as the years of the four-decade-long Eliot administration went on, as other universities followed the lead of Harvard with respect to electives, as honors came to the President and the University, both faculty and students were also to come to regard him as a "great man" (Morison, 1936c, pp. 396–398).

The period of the Eliot administration was clearly the most peaceful one in Harvard's long history. Yet the various writings about the university, not surprisingly, indicate continued sources of tension with both Governing Boards and faculty stemming from the commitment to emphasize research creativity as a basis for judging faculty, as well as the accompanying involvement in graduate teaching. In answering an objection to this policy, Eliot said that as long as the faculty regarded their job as one of simply teaching undergraduates "we can never get first-class teaching here. If they have to teach graduate students as well, they will regard their subject as infinite, and keep up that constant investigation which is necessary for the best teaching. Undergraduates will benefit as much as graduate students" (Morison, 1928b, p. 28).

Many disagreed and were to continue to argue all through the Eliot regime and beyond that emphasis on research and graduate education necessarily are at the expense of the education of the undergraduates. Late in the Eliot era, a comprehensive and highly praised survey of the *Great American Universities* discussed in some detail the supposedly deplorable situation of Harvard undergraduates and concluded that the weak point of Harvard and other leading schools was "the lack of personal contact between teacher and student . . . partly due to defective organization and partly to the development of a new school of teachers, who detest teaching, who look upon students as a nuisance, and class work as a waste of time" (Slossen, 1910, pp. 17–18).

Impersonality was also blamed on increased size, another change inherent in the commitment to become a great university. As Wendell noted in 1887, "it cannot be denied that the relations between students and officers are not as intimate as could be wished. . . . [T]he great size of the college . . . prevent[s] these relations from generally becoming more than professional. A few exceptionally good scholars find warm and sympathetic friends in their instructors, and students who are personally introduced to instructors are sure of a warm welcome. But here the matter ends" (Wendell, 1887, p. 161).

Twenty years later, at the very end of the Eliot administration, a young Harvard student radical, Van Wyck Brooks, reiterated the complaint that "the relations between the faculty and students of Harvard College . . . have been Germanized and depersonalized into a pure intellectualism. There is no rule laid down by the faculty except that students shall keep their university appointments, or, in other words, 'cut' only a limited number of lectures, and pass their examinations" (Brooks, 1908, p. 647).

Still it must be noted, as a tribute to the success of Harvard's relaxed policies under Eliot, that the school almost completely escaped the new wave of mass student protest concerning issues of discipline and student self-government that swept through many colleges and universities in the last two decades of the century. Student demonstrations focused on the doctrine of *in loco parentis*, curriculum content, administration power, discipline, due process, student self-government, and in a few state universities military training as well. "Disaffected young men rebelled through boycotts, strikes and demonstrations. . . . Frequently the most promising students led the agitation" (Solberg, 1968, p. 275; Feuer, 1969, p. 341; Lipset, 1972b, 137–140; Earnest, 1953, pp. 150–151). Presidents were toppled in state universities such as California, Illinois (twice), Minnesota, and Wisconsin, as well as in a number of New England colleges. Faculties were also frequently involved in the agitations in their effort to gain an increased share in university governance, sometimes stimulating student protest (Feuer, 1969, p. 332; Peterson, 1964, pp. 139–140; Lipset, 1972b, pp. 137–142). An answer to why the students (and faculty) behaved differently in Eliot's Harvard may be found in an editorial on "College Discipline" in *The Critic* which discussed why "American youths in college behave worse than German youths." Its explanation was "the German policy of non-interference by faculty with students," supposedly derivative from the fact that German professors were primarily dedicated to research. And both to improve "real learning in American colleges" and to reduce student unrest, the editorial writer of *The Critic* urged: "The time has evidently come for the return of ... the mere pedagogue ... to his proper sphere and the establishment in professorial chairs of zealous [research] specialists" ("College Discipline," 1881, p. 204).

SOCIAL-CLASS DIFFERENCES

Much more deep-rooted than the conflicts between students and college authorities was the emergence of division among the students themselves, occasioned by variations in social-class background across the country. The growth of fraternities in many schools and of a number of secret societies at Harvard, Yale, and Princeton served in large measure to formally divide the students in economic class, and to a lesser degree in ideological political terms. In some western states in the late nineteenth century, the Populists backed laws to outlaw or hamstring fraternities in state institutions (Brubacher & Rudy, 1968, pp. 127–128). The intramural division brought about "clear-cut internal cleavages of a political sort." In many schools, "a fairly permanent two-party system emerged in student politics on this basis; it was evenly balanced because the fraternity minority was so much better organized" (Veysey, 1965, p. 293). Wendell noted that "the most conspicuous social line at Harvard today is that between the 'society' men and the 'non-society.' So marked is this that the non-society men have been known formally to organize themselves on occasions when class politics grew warm, and that during the past few years several students of a radical turn of mind have declined invitation to any society on the grounds that societies establish invidious distinctions" (Wendell, 1887, p. 153). "As early as 1877 a revolt brought victory for the non-society men in class elections. ... Another peak of conflict was reached in 1909 – 1910, when again the Class elections were won by the 'democratic' element. Randolph S. Bourne, noting these events, perceived that politics in the Yard was run, not by the 'born' aristocrats, but by those with intense social ambitions" (Veysey, 1965, p. 151).

Many were concerned about the manifest social-class differences within Harvard. To those alumni who were upset at the presence of growing numbers of "unclubable" students, poor commuting "day scholars," and "New Americans" not of Anglo-Saxon Protestant stock, Eliot argued that the University must be open to all regardless of "class, caste, race, sect ... or political party." And he fought strenuously to eliminate those admission requirements, such as Greek, which served to keep graduates from public high schools out of Harvard, while at the same time raising those standards which tested intellectual aptitude. He believed firmly that higher education, including Harvard, should be meritocratic. "The essence of freedom is in equality of opportunity, and the opportunity of education should be counted the most precious of all" (Hawkins, 1972, pp. 181–182). At the end of Eliot's administration in 1908, less than half of the Harvard undergraduates, 47 percent, were from private schools. It was clearly far more open to talent than Yale and Princeton, where the corresponding figures were 68 and 78 percent, respectively (Thelin, 1973, p. 48).

Yet Eliot, in spite of his strong public commitment to the principle that Harvard should be open to Negroes and Jews (at a time when many other schools had overt restrictionist policies) and his efforts to support poor boys with "brains," strongly argued that the University should not interfere with socially exclusive clubs or luxurious Gold Coast residences, saying: "For some reasons one could wish that the University did not offer the same contrast between the rich man's mode of life and the poor man's that the outer world offers; but it does, and it is not certain that the presence of this contrast is unwholesome or injurious. In this respect, as in many others, the University is an epitome of the modern world" (Veysey, 1965, p. 93).

In an autobiographical work, W. E. B. DuBois of the class of 1890 noted that black students were not accepted socially by their white classmates. He indicated, however, that he had not been upset by this at the time, since he assumed that racial segregation was the norm, and he delighted in being treated more than fairly by his teachers (DuBois, 1940, pp. 34–35). When two Negro students, Clement Morgan and DuBois, placed first and second in the Boylston Oratorical Contest in 1890, both were given their just due by their fellow students and faculty. As DuBois reports: "Morgan became the center of a revolt within the college. By unwritten rule, all of the honorary officers of the class went to Bostonians of Back Bay. No westerner, southerner, Jew, nor Irishman, much less a Negro, had thought of aspiring to the honor of being class day official. But in 1890, after the oratorical contest, the students of the class staged an unexpected revolt and elected Morgan class orator" (ibid., pp. 30–37). DuBois, himself, was designated as a Commencement Orator, and received considerable applause for his satirical talk, "Jefferson Davis as a Representative of Civilization" (West, 1972, p. 28). Following this breakthrough at Harvard, which occasioned much comment nationally, other "northern colleges elected colored class orators" (DuBois, 1940, p. 37).

POLITICAL ACTIVITY

There is little mention in the reports of student life at Harvard in these years of much political activity. Writing of the undergraduates in the 1880s, George Santayana reported that about "high questions of politics and religion their minds were open but vague; they seemed not to think them of practical importance; they acquiesced in people having any views they liked on such subjects; the fluent and fervid enthusiasms so common among European students, prophesying about politics, philosophy, and art, were entirely unknown among them" (Santayana, 1956, pp. 30–31). Yet they were in an environment which presumably took ideas more seriously than the larger society, and the faculty were necessarily involved with politics. The available reports on faculty opinion suggest that they were predominantly Republican during and after the Civil War, but that the visible links between Republican administrations and aggressive industrial capital, plus concern over the need for civil service and other reforms, gradually shifted them. In effect, they became "mugwumps," that is, they "supported the Republicans through 1880, then voted for Grover Cleveland, then returned to the Republican fold in 1896 (though unenthusiastically, regarding McKinley as a lesser evil), and (commonly though not always) adopted some form of Progressivism after 1900." Veysey notes that at the time, "academic mugwumpery symbolized the professor's relationship to all institutions, including his own: uneasy discontent, yet an unwillingness to 'throw his vote away.' He far preferred to purify one of the major political parties . . . " (Veysey, 1962, pp. 160–161).

To a considerable extent, the reformist and clean government ideals of the Mugwumps stemmed from the colleges. Many Harvard faculty members and President Eliot were deeply involved. Eliot was the most prominent of the academic Mugwumps, and went further than most of them by advocating an independent "New Party" in 1884. He even drew up a platform for this stillborn third party, which "included integrity in office-holders, merit civil service, lower tariffs, . . . an end to unearned pensions and bounties,' immigration 'without distinction of race, nationality, or religion . . . ' " (Hawkins, 1972, pp. 140–141). As one historian notes: "Harvard was of course the great seminal source for the whole cluster of ideals that gave Mugwumpery its drive" (Blodgett,

1960, p. 31). The faculty Mugwumps included men like James Barr Ames, Francis Child, William James, Charles Eliot Norton, and Barrett Wendell. Eliot justified participation in politics on the grounds that "he thus set for Harvard students a proper example of an educated man's social involvement" (Hawkins, 1972, p. 141).

Harvard students occasionally played an active role in election campaigns that concerned their President and teachers, particularly in those of William Russell, who was leader of the Democrats in the class of 1877, was then elected to the Cambridge City Council in 1881 at the age of 24, and was mayor of the city three years later. He ran for Governor in 1888, when he was only 31 years old, and was elected in 1890. As in the case of Democratic reform campaigns eight decades later, some were concerned that visible student involvement in Russell's campaigns would lose him more votes than they gained. As one Harvard man put it: "Untidy chaps with [ballot] stickers would only deter people from using them" (Blodgett, 1960, pp. 122–130).

Russell and the state Democratic party built a coalition between a Harvard-based segment of the old elite and the workers to whom they appealed in class terms, arguing that the high tariff imposed by the Republicans and favored by business was impoverishing labor and turning over spoils directly to the trusts.

ALUMNI ATTACKS ON ACADEMIC FREEDOM

The involvement of Harvard faculty in economic controversies in opposition to the position taken by many in the business community did not go unnoticed and occasioned pressures from parents and wealthy alumni who particularly objected to the liberal free-trade ideas of members of the Economics Department. The teachings in this department were to prove a continuous source of controversy from the efforts to force Bowen to change his textbook in 1870 down to the 1970s. In 1883, Eliot replied to a Harvard parent who had complained about slanted teaching on the tariff issue, in a letter which defended the freedom of students as well as of professors: "We leave [our teachers] free, as we leave our students free to form their own opinions. . . . As to what Harvard can 'afford' to be or do, I believe that she can afford to be open-eyed, impartial and free, and that she could not afford to be anything else" (Hawkins, 1972, p. 218). The matter became an issue of public controversy six years later, when Republican businessmen alumni denounced the Economics Department, particularly in the person of Frank Taussig, as the source of subversive ideas and as responsible for their currency among the student Democratic activists. A Visiting Committee of the Overseers, headed by an active Republican, investigated the Department in 1889 and reported that it was a partisan body and should be reformed. The report stated:

These members of your committee regard the present organization of the department at Harvard as illiberal, one-sided, and therefore unjust to the student. It seems to them a somewhat singular thing that an institution which owes so much of the support and of the wealth which have made it prosperous to a community of protectionists and to the gifts of money earned in protected industries, should now so obstinately refuse to recognize protection except as a heresy.

The issue of whether the wealthy, through their ability to grant or withhold contributions, should influence appointments at Harvard was faced directly by the minority of the Visiting Committee, which denounced the idea that Harvard had a special intellectual obligation to its donors as "extraordinary and unworthy." The minority report declared:

If any wealthy donors and patrons of the College have expressly or impliedly made it a condition of their generous gifts that specific economic doctrines should be taught, and that the opinions of the College should be immutably fixed and mortgaged in perpetuity in the midst of a free community and in a world of change and progress, the College could better afford to return every dollar of its donations than to submit to such conditions. Its professors could better be starved than either pledged or subsidized in matters of scientific opinion.

The minority report was to carry the day. The controversy was heatedly debated in the Boston press and in national magazines. This was a time when social scientists were under comparable attack in many universities, and when a number were indeed fired. President Eliot spoke up vigorously on the side of academic freedom, and before the matter was dropped, the chairman of the committee, John T. Morse, commented that he had been "searchingly harrowed" by the affair (Blodgett, 1960, pp. 113–116; Church, 1965, p. 70).

The affair led Harvard to look for a competent protectionist economist, but William James Ashley, the man appointed in 1892 to fill that role, "combined his eminent scholarship with a belief in socialism of the Fabian variety." He strongly and publicly backed trade unions as the only available means for workers to remedy "social inequalities," and predicted "that the principal branches of production and exchange will ultimately be organized socially is as certain as the rising of tomorrow's sun." He was active in the Consumer's League of Boston which organized boycotts of "goods produced under unfair labor conditions." A historian of the department's activities believes that since "his historical method and his socialism were so interwoven, it is doubtful that Ashley could have kept his social viewpoint out of the classroom, especially in light of the fact that, for him, the economist's duty was to determine matters of welfare and to suggest means for the implementation of reform" (Church, 1965, pp. 61–68). There is no indication of any protest against Ashley from wealthy alumni, perhaps because they anticipated rebuff, or possibly because they realized Ashley's presence at Harvard in part stemmed from their last one.

STUDENT POLITICAL VIEWS AND ACTIVITIES

Most of the students probably entered the mugwump atmosphere of Harvard from conservative Republican backgrounds. In spite of the contention by Eliot in 1869 (reiterated by successive Harvard presidents) that "no good student need ever stay away from Cambridge, or leave college simply because he is poor," the statistical evidence clearly shows that "Harvard has been and still is a college for the children of business and professional families" (Harris, 1970, p. 11). During the latter part of the nineteenth century, between two-thirds and three-fourths of the students were graduates of private high schools (Veysey, 1965, p. 288; Harris, 1970, p. 15). Straw votes at such schools indicated predominant Republican views among the students in the latter part of the nineteenth century (Baltzell, 1958, p. 316).

A detailed examination of expressions by Harvard students of their political preferences from 1860 to 1892 suggests that their views reflected the extent to which the opinions of the faculty challenged or reiterated those of their parents. Thus from 1860 to 1868 graduating classes were between four or five to one Republican. No quantitative data exist between 1868 and 1880, but in three presidential elections—1868, 1872, and 1876—"that the Republican majorities were very great is shown by the fact that ... Harvard students always marched in the Boston torchlight parades of the Republicans—never in those of the Democrats" (Caffey, 1893, pp. 407–408). From 1880 to 1892 party choices may be differentiated by college class. During this period of faculty mugwumpery, they indicate that while Republicans always outnumbered Democrats, there was a steady increase over the four years a given class spent at Harvard from Republican to Democratic and "Independent" strength. As Caffey reported:

Many students who came to Harvard from Republican families during these years were drawn into the Democratic party, and we find nearly every Class of which there is any record becoming less Republican during its College career. For instance, the Freshman Class ('92) in the fall of 1888, in the mock presidential election, voted as follows: Cleveland, 82, Harrison, 171; total, 253. At graduation, four years later, according to the Class Secretary's Report, '92 voted as follows: Democratic, 93, Independent, 17; Mugwump, 4; Free Trade and Tariff Reform, 1; anti-Republican, 115; Republican, 126; total 241.

What is true of '92 is also true of '86, '87, '88, '89, and '91. . . . The total vote of the eight Classes—'85 to '92—in the presidential elections of 1884 and 1888 were 715 Democratic, 907 Republican; or in the proportion of 44 Democratic to 56 Republican. At graduation these same Classes voted 838 anti-Republican, 820 Republican; or in the proportion of 50.5 to 49.5.

. . . [A]t the presidential elections of 1884 and 1888 we find that the Freshmen of the College were largely responsible for the size of the Republican lead in both years. . . . If we subtract the votes of the Freshmen and Sophomores from the totals, it will be seen that Cleveland led Blaine by 21 votes and Harrison by 8; and by subtracting also the vote of the Special [probationary] Students, the majority of whom are apt to be young, that Cleveland led Blaine by 32 and Harrison by 18. These facts sustain the assertion that as men grow older at Harvard they are more likely to vote the Democratic ticket (ibid., pp. 408–409).

The election of 1892 is noteworthy in that large numbers of students were involved in political campaigns. Two large groups were organized—the Harvard Republican Club and the Democratic Campaign Club, each with about 600 student members. The Republicans sent speakers to campaign around New England and New York. The university did not welcome the outburst of political activity, at least within the College. In 1894 the Corporation banned partisan meetings from Harvard Yard (Veysey, 1965, p. 410). There is no indication in the historical record of Eliot's personal position on the matter, but one biographer notes that "Eliot sought to put the decision in the most permissive light, saying that only political rallies were banned and that there was no wish to lessen discussion of social and political problems" (Hawkins, 1972, p. 142).

These restrictions seemingly had little effect on undergraduate involvement in politics, for the bitterly fought election of 1896 between McKinley and Bryan produced an even higher level of activity. A contemporary description gives some of the flavor of that campaign year.

Campaign clubs, mass-meetings, brass bands, and torchlight parades kept the political pot boiling vigorously at Harvard from the time campaign buttons began to swarm in the Yard until the returns were in. . . . Activity began Oct. 6, when in response to a call for a mass-meeting to organize a non-partisan Sound Money Campaign Club, 500 men crowded into Upper Massachusetts, and after a due amount of speech-making and enthusiasm elected . . . officers. . . . The election, largely a cut and dried affair, was enlivened by points of order and disorder from the floor. Half the officers had been chosen when a parliamentarian pointed out that as no organization had been formed the election had been merely formal nonsense. The meeting, with true American respect for forms, extricated itself from the muddle by voting first to form the club and then to confirm the previous action. . . .

The same evening the Republican Club reorganized. . . . It had been a bad year for Democrats at Harvard, but Gold men and Silverites alike stood by the faith that was in them and organized. . . .

Two torchlight processions were the great events of the Campaign. The . . . Republican parade . . . was the first and largest. At 6:30 P. M., Oct. 30, the classes gathered around Harvard Square and in compact, orderly division, headed by the Harvard Band, marched into Boston. . . . The 1,500 or more Harvard men all uniformed in crimson gowns and white mortar boards made a fine show. . . . The procession abounded in transparencies with mottoes drawn from the Bible, Shakespeare, and Dante, or springing from native student wit (Dorr, 1896, pp. 256–258).

Like the rest of the eastern elite, and the bulk of the electorate as well, Harvard, both faculty and students, was frightened by William Jennings Bryan and overwhelmingly backed McKinley (Veysey, 1962, pp. 118, 160).

RELIGIOUS LIBERALISM EXTENDED

The greater liberalism among the Harvard population as compared with the rest of the socioeconomic elite was particularly reflected, as in earlier days, in their religious views and behavior. A report by a Harvard professor to Eliot in 1869 soon after he took office contended that "The non-church-going professors have exerted a very strong adverse influence" in the College. And Veysey concluded that as compared with other university faculty of the second half of the century, "Harvard was far more liberal at an early date and remained so" (ibid., p. 159). General opinion of the day also assumed that Harvard students were more likely to be irreligious.

Only one Harvard student in five was considered a professing Christian (in the evangelical sense) in 1878. At Dartmouth it was one in three; at Yale, two-fifths;

at Michigan and Western Reserve, half; at Princeton and Brown, three-fifths; at Amherst, Williams, Wesleyan, and other denominational colleges, four out of five; at Oberlin and a few other exceptional places, nine in ten . . . (ibid., p.122).

The religious liberalism prevalent at Harvard was at odds with the University's maintaining the practice still common at all American colleges of compulsory attendance at chapel. Eliot had proposed abolishing the rule in the early seventies, but the Overseers refused. Ironically, among the strong supporters of compulsory chapel was Overseer Ralph Waldo Emerson, who four decades earlier had lost his chance for a professorship because he denounced all forms of organized religion. The faculty repeatedly petitioned for the change, to no avail (Morison, 1936c, pp. 366–367). "From time to time a wave of protest had swept up from the students upon the Governing Boards, and in 1885 it became again formidable" (Peabody, 1926, p. 249). Eliot, backed by the Reverend Andrew Peabody, in charge of conducting chapel prayers, was finally able to have the change approved. Harvard thus became the first American college to abandon compulsory chapel.

Eliot, with his concern for the scholarly greatness of Harvard, insisted that Harvard must be an "undenominational university." He successfully pressed the Divinity School to modify its emphasis on propagating Unitarianism and to include distinguished scholars from all Christian denominations. Uniquely for the times, he urged the school to conceive of "theology as a science, correlated with law or medicine, with the same method of free research and the same spirit of single-minded devotion to truth . . . " (ibid., p. 249). Within the College, he lent support to Catholic and Jewish student organizations, and at a time when the Mormons were highly unpopular as polygamists, he praised the presence of a "Mormon colony" at Harvard. Early in his career as President he took a strong stand with the Overseers "that a man's religion should not be considered in judging his fitness to teach" (Hawkins, 1972, pp. 128, 130). Eliot was able to demonstrate that he meant what he said about the religious background of prospective faculty members when, in 1888, he personally appointed Charles Gross to teach medieval history. Gross, who was Jewish, had received his doctorate, *summa cum laude*, from the University of Göttingen, but had been turned down for a position at a number of colleges. He was about to go to work in his father's clothing business when Eliot called him to Harvard. Gross went on to become one of the stars of the University (Morison, 1936c, pp. 375–376).

Given the "long tradition of freethinking among Harvard faculty members and graduates," it is not surprising that the school was under frequent attack from diverse religious leaders and conservatives. One professor reported on his return from a trip to Europe in 1886 that the impression was widespread among the (presumably quite well-to-do) Americans whom he met on his travels "that Harvard College is a hotbed of atheism and of dissipation," a view that may have had a selective effect in determining the type of student who enrolled (Hawkins, 1972, p. 123). Eliot did little to dissipate this image when he informed faculty members under attack for their religious and moral views, as he did the German-born Jewish psychologist Hugo Münsterberg, who strongly supported drinking alcoholic beverages, that "You will, of course, feel perfectly free to express your views either in public or in private" (ibid., p. 131).

But if the University encouraged religious diversity and the rights of its members to reject the morality of the ascetic Protestant tradition of Harvard's past, it still insisted on adhering to conventional morality in the realm of sexual behavior. Thus in 1897, the chairman of the "Parietal Board" of the College sent a letter to all students notifying them that "No young lady or ladies, unattended by an older lady as chaperon, should be received in a student's room.... It is desirable that ladies should not enter or walk through the halls of the dormitories unattended; and a student, when entertaining ladies, should see that they are escorted to and from his room either by himself or by some other gentleman" ("University Notes," 1897, p. 613).

SETTLEMENT WORK

As the century came to an end, growing concern among the more liberally disposed segments of the affluent for the plight of the underprivileged emerged as a response to the problems of the rapidly growing cities with their teeming immigrant slums, corruption, and high crime rate. Among students the desire to apply the growing social idealism found its initial and most continuing fulfillment in settlement work, in seeking to better the condition of the poor in the urban slums. Across the country, many thousands of students and young graduates helped to staff the rapidly growing number of settlement houses. As one historian of *The New England College* notes: "The settlement movement . . . offered students the chance to put the collegiate ideals to work in these cities, just then beginning to dominate national life, and spread their problems across the country.... Students would go into cities ultimately because only there could they save themselves from atrophy. It was their defense against the kind of deterioration into irrelevance that had so frightened their elders in the elite" (Peterson, 1964, pp. 179–184).

Harvard students were part of this national tendency, taking part in settlement work in Boston and helping to man two Cambridge night schools, the Prospect Union and the Social Union (Morison, 1936c, pp. 367–368). In 1894 the Student Volunteer Committee was formed to coordinate activities such as these. "By 1902 almost four hundred students were engaged in volunteer social work" (Potts, 1965, p. 96). The University itself helped to foster the sense that the children of the well-to-do were obligated to help improve the circumstances of the underprivileged through first establishing Phillips Brooks House in 1900 as a center for those interested in such activities, and second, creating the Department of Social Ethics in 1906 (Morison, 1936c, pp. 367–368). William James suggested the name "Social Ethics." The new department was designed to meet the desires of many undergraduates for relevant courses which faced up to the problems of urban poverty. It was to include in the first decade of its existence courses in Immigration, the Housing Problem, the Alcohol Problem, Social Insurance, Criminology, and Radical Social Theories (Ford, 1930, pp. 223–236; Potts, 1965, pp. 94–95).

ANTIWAR ACTIVITY

Political controversy continued to intrude itself into the confines of Harvard Yard in debates over American foreign policy. In 1895 various "Harvard professors and students had opposed President Cleveland's ultimatum to England over the Venezuelan–British Guiana boundary dispute" (Freidel, 1970, p. 69). They wrote a letter to the *Crimson* on December 21, 1895, urging both undergraduates and faculty to write Congress protesting Cleveland's bellicose policy. Alumnus Theodore Roosevelt replied in the *Crimson* of January 7, denouncing the President's opponents as "traitors," and arguing that only a high level of military preparedness and boldness could prevent war. Many in the university community joined the argument in the *Crimson*. William James wrote defending the right to dissent against the President even in serious international situations and urging the students to take up the fight to bring "the threatened increase of armament to naught" (Schirmer, 1972, p. 40). The evidence of widespread pacifist feeling at Harvard outraged Roosevelt, who wrote bitterly about the cult of "non-virility" in Cambridge (Freidel, 1970, p. 69).

A few years later, Harvard was again divided over the prospect of war, this time with Spain, which "brought a flood of meetings, pro- and anti-administration . . . " (Morison, 1936c, p. 412). A number of prominent faculty members spoke up strongly against the war, both before and after it broke out. A week before President McKinley went to

Congress for a declaration of war, on April 11, 1898, "eighty-six members of the Harvard faculty led by President Eliot ... [declared] against war and for peace" (Schirmer, 1972, p. 53). William James, in opposing the war, expressed the hope "that in this University if nowhere else on the continent, we shall be patriotic enough *not* to remain passive whilst the destinies of our country are settled by surprise. ... Let us refuse to be bound over night by proclamation, or hypnotized by sacramental phrases through the day." He ended a class lecture saying: "Don't yelp with the pack!" Charles Eliot Norton told the students that "the war was needless, inglorious, and criminal, and advised them to consider carefully whether the best use they could make of themselves in their country's service was to enlist" (Morison, 1936c, pp. 412–413). He compared the new war to the Mexican War, both being equally evil. The students applauded him, and when he gave his final lecture of the year, on the verge of retiring, the hall was packed with those who came to do him honor. A Boston newspaper reported: "The entrance of the professor was the signal for a burst of applause such as has rarely been seen at Harvard" (Vanderbilt, 1959, p. 141). But in the press of the nation, Norton became "the object of considerable condemnation and abuse ... " (Schirmer, 1972, pp. 51–59; Brown, 1948, pp. 150–151). During the summer of the brief war, Oliver Wendell Holmes, Jr., reported to a friend: "I confess to pleasure in hearing some rattling jingo talk after the self-righteous and preaching discourse, which has prevailed to some extent at Harvard College ... " (Freidel, 1970, p. 17). Academic dissent continued at Harvard and elsewhere as the controversy over war turned into the even more divisive issue of "imperialism," whether the United States should retain any of the Spanish colonies and the continuing sore of the Philippine Insurrection. Bliss Perry—editor of the *Atlantic Monthly*, Cambridge resident, close friend of Charles Eliot, and subsequently a Harvard professor—wrote in his magazine in 1902:

Within a twelve-month college teachers have been openly denounced as "traitors" for advocating self-government for the Filipinos. In many a pulpit and newspaper office, last September, it was declared that the utterances of college professors were largely responsible for the assassination of President McKinley. ... One must admit that a good many college professors have taken the Irish members of Parliament as their exemplars. ... Miss Evelina Burney once wrote of Sir Philip Jennings Clerk, "He is a professed minority man." This type of man is familiar in academic circles (Perry, 1902, p. 286).

James and Norton continued an active role in opposition to the American effort to take over the Philippines. President Eliot also openly spoke up against the treaty with Spain (Schirmer, 1972, pp. 15, 132). As Schirmer notes: "Intellectuals gathered around the anti-imperialist movement as they had around slavery. . . . 'Harvard and the slums' was the taunt thrown at the Mugwumps; it also described the basic components of the local [Boston] anti-imperialist movement" (ibid., p. 15). James was particularly outspoken: "He saw the United States after the Spanish-American War 'perversely rushing to wallow in the mire of imperialism,' and for frequently saying so brought on his head only less wrath than that endured by Charles Eliot Norton. . . . Likewise James thought the British Colonial Office had blunderingly driven the Boers into war, and he took a stand in that situation, too" (Brown, 1948, p. 81).

There is little evidence of continued student opposition to the war after United States entry. Many, in fact, enlisted to help free Cuba from Spanish tyranny (as William Jennings Bryan also tried to do). Most interesting for its anticipation of the future of student anti-imperialist ventures was the establishment of a student committee to raise money for a "Boer Relief Fund," by Franklin Delano Roosevelt, then in charge of the *Crimson*, and other students (Freidel, 1952, p. 60).

SUPPORT FOR ACADEMIC FREEDOM

As American academe began to deal with political and social problems from a critical, sometimes even radical posture, academic freedom issues involving faculty critical of various establishments occurred around the country. Harvard, as was frequently noted by supporters of minority rights, stood out in rejecting pressures against such faculty. One of Charles Eliot's last major addresses as President, his Phi Beta Kappa speech in 1907, was devoted to a defense of "Academic Freedom." Under this heading he not only included the conventional appreciation of freedom of ideas, but also "the student's freedom to choose his studies, to refuse to attend chapel, to compete on equal terms for scholarships, and to choose his own friends, as well as the professor's freedom to teach in the manner most congenial to him, to be free from harassing routines, to enjoy a secure tenure, and to receive a fixed salary and a retirement allowance" (Metzger, 1961, p. 124). As a leading historian of academe notes, Eliot's "catholic approach was exceptional" (Veysey, 1965, pp. 96–97).

Eliot's commitment to academic freedom was, of course, of long duration. From the start, in his 1869 inaugural address, Eliot had a clear vision of the necessary relationship between academic freedom and intellectual achievement.

A University must be indigenous, it must be rich; but above all, it must be free. The winnowing breeze of freedom must blow through all its chambers.... An atmosphere of intellectual freedom is the native air of literature and science. This University aspires to serve the nation by training men to intellectual honesty and independence of mind. The Corporation demands of all its teachers that they be grave, reverent, and high-minded, but it leaves them, like their pupils, free. A University is built, not by a sect, but by a nation ... (Eliot, 1969, pp. 23–24, 14).

That these statements did not simply represent unfulfilled verbal commitments may be seen not only in Eliot's defense of the Economics Department in 1889, in his subsequent approval of the appointment to it of Ashley (the Socialist supporter of trade unions) in 1892, and the presence at Harvard of war-time critics of the Spanish-American conflict, but also in the total acceptance of two highly disparate but equally unconventional members of the Philosophy Department, Santayana and James. The former's close friend, William Lyon Phelps of Yale, pointed out that he "could hardly have lasted at any American college but Harvard beyond that point in 1891 when he defined his position, elegantly and without emotion, as that of an atheist and pessimist" (May, 1964, p. 62). Eliot worked hard to prevent one of Harvard's most distinguished, but also highly controversial scholars, William James, from retiring in 1904. James had not only opposed the Spanish-American War and the United States involvement in the Philippines; he was also identified with the newly born concept of the "intellectual" as radical critic and encouraged student activism, soon to take the form of Harvard's first Socialist Club. At the 1903 commencement, on the eve of reaching retirement age, James said of Harvard students: "Our undisciplinables are our proudest product. Let us agree together in hoping that the output of them will never cease" (James, 1903, p. 8). And a few months later, almost as if in response to this declaration, Eliot begged him to stay on (Veysey, 1965, p. 323). Such behavior and public utterance by the President and prominent faculty must have served "to reinforce the public view of Harvard as a place of independence and dissent" (Hawkins, 1972, pp. 142–143). James gloried in this reputation, boasting that the "true Harvard" was composed of students who had been attracted to the school because "they have heard of her persistently atomistic constitution, of her tolerance of exceptionality and eccentricity ... " (James, 1903, p. 7).

STUDENT SOCIALISM

A new test of Eliot's and Harvard's commitment to political freedom was to come with the emergence and growth to major proportions of a student socialist movement. The growth of radicalism, as reflected in a steady rise in Socialist electoral support and membership through the first decade and a half of the new century, was paralleled by the emergence of socialist sentiment among professors and students. The Intercollegiate Socialist Society (ISS)—the forerunner and direct ancestor of all subsequent student socialist groups, including the Students for a Democratic Society (SDS) of the 1960s—was founded in 1905 "for the purpose of promoting an intelligent interest in Socialism among college men and women" (Lewack, 1953, p. 4; Altbach, 1974, pp. 22–28). Its earliest chapters were formed at Wesleyan, Columbia, Yale, and Harvard. Among the charter members of the latter unit were Walter Lippmann, Arthur N. Holcombe, Nicholas Kelley, Osmond Fraenkel, Kenneth Macgowan, and Heywood Broun (Lewack, 1953, p. 4). The Society grew in the leading universities and colleges so that "just before World War I, the ISS had chapters in the major New England colleges, most of the state universities outside of the South, and the most prominent Protestant denominations." A historian of socialism, David Shannon, reports that it had about two thousand dues-paying members among a national college population of under four hundred thousand in 1912–1913 (Shannon, 1967, pp. 55–56; Kipnis, 1952, pp. 259–260; Altbach, 1974, pp. 24–25). "[T]he major strength of the ISS was in the prestige colleges of the eastern seaboard" (Altbach & Peterson, 1972, p. 14). According to a statement issued by the national office of the ISS in 1911, "the strongest of the group of chapters is the Harvard Socialist Club" ("University Notes," 1911, p. 396) with a membership of under one hundred. These figures may appear to be small, but there were undoubtedly many more students on the fringes of the movement. The ISS was in the situation comparable to that of the SDS in late 1968–69, which clearly had a much greater impact on the campus population than would be suggested by its reported national dues-paying membership of seven thousand out of a college student body of seven million. As Hal Draper, student leader of the 1930s and senior "adult" advisor to the Berkeley Free Speech Movement (FSM) in 1964–65, has suggested:

Around the 1 percent who actually joined a radical student group were concentric rings of influence, embracing different portions of the student body as different forms of commitment were demanded. For every one who joined there were perhaps two who agreed in the main with what the student movement was trying to do, but who did not join, either for lack of time to devote to such activity or for other reasons which did them less credit. There was another circle of students who were ready to support most of the campaigns or actions which the student organizations might launch on a given issue... (Draper, 1967, pp. 183–184).

Contemporary reports by observers of American higher education and student socialist activities indicate that socialism deeply penetrated the life of faculty and students in the leading universities of the pre-World War I era. In 1908, a conservative English visitor, Alexander Francis, noted that among those "who have had a college career, a considerable number... may be said to have professed socialism. Socialist societies have established themselves at the Universities... " (Francis, 1909, pp. 228–229). After commenting on the factors that led "undergraduate youth" in this direction, Francis indicated that faculty radicalism was most prevalent at leading universities, an impression that coincides with the results of quantitative studies completed from 1913 to the present (Lipset, 1972a, pp. 211–289). "I met not a few professors who hold and teach socialistic doctrines; and it is significant that most, certainly the most extreme, of these have positions in colleges and universities which have received large pecuniary gifts from millionaires" (Francis, 1909, pp. 228–229).

The young socialist intellectual Randolph Bourne, while still an undergraduate at Columbia in 1912, generalized in the same fashion concerning the spread of socialism among undergraduates and the role of the faculty at the leading American universities. "Settlement work and socialist propaganda... are now the commonplaces of the undergraduate." And he went on to argue that these tendencies were clearly a function of his experiences at college, for "his education, if it has been in one of the advanced universities, will have only tended to confirm his radicalism.... " He called on the dedicated undergraduate to "ally himself with his radical teachers in spirit and activity.... The college thus becomes for the first time in American history a reorganizing force. It... now finds arrayed against it, in spirit at least if not in open antagonism, the churches and the conservative molders of opinion" (Bourne, 1913, pp. 48, 295, 325–326). Some years later, in 1916, Bourne went on to argue in the *New Republic* that student radicalism had become too popular for its own good. "Let the college man or girl... join the Intercollegiate Socialist Society or some similar institution, and discover how discouragingly respectable they are." However, Bourne also noted that many of the young socialists of his day dropped away from the movement when they failed to make contact with the working class. "The young radical soon learns to be ashamed of his intellectual bias, and after an ineffectual effort to squeeze himself into the mind of the workingman drifts away disillusioned from his timid collegiate radicals" (Bourne, 1916, p. 161).

John Reed, who took part in the Harvard Socialist Club, although he did not join it as an undergraduate, left behind two autobiographical essays that were published long after his death in the Soviet Union in 1920. The first was written in 1912, two years after his graduation, while the second was drafted five years later. His description of events and student ideology bears strong resemblance to latter-day activities in Harvard Yard:

What's wrong with Harvard? Something is the matter. Numbers of letters from alarmed alumni pour into President Lowell's office every day, asking if Socialism and Anarchy are on the rampage among undergraduates. . . . Old graduates shake their heads mournfully and agree the place is going to the dogs. . . .

[The] group that founded the [Socialist] Club were Fabians, that is, they believed in "permeating" the University with the doctrine which they stood for. . . . The idea was to stir up criticism, revolt, discussion, opposition, not only on the present state of things in the outside world, but of the state of things at Harvard. They wanted to make undergraduates take sides on every issue that concerned them; to learn what they wanted to learn, and demand of the Faculty that the "dead wood" among the teachers be cleared away. . . .

So Lippmann and MacGowen, the inner circle of the Socialist Club, deliberately planned to get control of every organization that would help them, or at least to be represented therein. . . . They set themselves enthusiastically to become accomplished dialecticians, indomitable arguers, to be able to talk, and talk well, on any subject that might be brought up. . . . [T]he Harvard Socialists turned their theories upon themselves, determined to work them out at Harvard University. . . .

[W]ithin half a year, the active enrolled members of the Club amounted to fifty, with about twice as many interested [out of about 2,000 undergraduates]. . . .

Many of the professors and instructors had become interested in the various undergraduate movements. . . . the Socialist Club received the warm sympathy and support of the great William James, of Professor Adams, of Professor S. B. Johnson (Reed, 1939, pp. 8, 10, 22; Hicks, 1936, pp. 24–50).

In elaborating further on the activities of the Club, Reed pointed up its extensive influence throughout the College.

[They] criticized the faculty for not educating them. . . . Some men, notably Walter Lippmann, had been reading and thinking and talking about politics and economics, not as dry theoretical studies, but as live forces acting on the world, on the university even. . . . The Club drew up a platform for the Socialist Party in city elections. It had social legislation introduced into the Massachusetts Legislature. Its members wrote articles in the college papers challenging undergraduate ideals, and muckraked the University. . . . Prominent radicals were invited to Cambridge to lecture. . . . The result of this movement upon the undergraduate world was potent. All over the place radicals sprang up, in music, painting, poetry, the theatre, etc. The more serious papers took a socialistic. or at least progressive tinge . . . (Reed, 1936, pp. 332–333).

Lippmann himself has described the activities of the Club in terms which indicate its desire to influence everyone: "In a general way our object was to make reactionaries standpatters; standpatters, conservative liberals; conservative liberals and liberals, radicals; and radicals, Socialists. In other words, we tried to move everyone up a peg. . . . We preferred to have the whole mass move a little, to having a few move altogether out of sight" (Evans, 1961, p. 63; Schapsmeier & Schapsmeier, 1969, pp. 1–6; Binger, 1959, pp. 29–36).

The Socialist Club was able to affect the curriculum. In 1910 it secured 300 signatures (close to 15 percent of the student body) for a petition requesting a course on socialism, which was granted by the College (Feuer, 1969, p. 346). Like its campus successors on the left, the Student League for Industrial Democracy in the 1920s and early 1930s, the American Student Union in the latter part of the depression decade, and the SDS in the 1960s, the Socialist Club in its effort to build an alliance with workers took as one of its tasks improving the conditions of Harvard cafeteria and cleaning workers. It also set a precedent, followed by the other groups in subsequent decades, of campaigning on local off-campus issues, particularly with reference to housing conditions in Cambridge and Boston (Thwing, 1911, pp. 260–263; Henderson, 1912, pp. 463–465).

In this heady atmosphere of pre-World War I, Harvard students, as Reed also noted, "attacked the sacred institution of intercollegiate athletics, sneered at undergraduate clubs so holy no one dared to mention their name." They formed a variety of other socially oriented societies, e.g., the Harvard Men's League for Women's Suffrage, the Single Tax Club, and even an Anarchist group. "The Social Politics Club, founded in 1909 'to bring together men who believe the world is not finished,' was composed half of faculty (such as Edwin F. Gay, Lewis J. Johnson, and Comfort Avery Adams) and half of undergraduates. . . . [T]he International Polity Club [was formed] 'to promote the thoughtful discussion and study of modern international problems.' . . . [It] invited men like Norman Angell to discuss ways and means of consolidating peace . . . " (Morison, 1936c, pp. 435–437).

Unlike the situation in more recent times, when research on student activism has become almost a major academic subspeciality, no data exist as to the types of students involved before World War I. One published 1911 report by a then Harvard undergraduate, himself not a radical, has an authentic ring to it.

Among the Radicals are some of the most brilliant men in college; indeed the Socialist Club cultivates brilliancy. . . . [T]he Radicals have learned with good reason to consider themselves the intellectual backbone of the college.

. . . [But] they lack a sense of humor. . . . [T]he Radicals are intolerant; they fail absolutely to get the point-of-view of the undergraduate who wants to do his work, do his athletics. . . . [The] apathy—even hostility—of the Socialists to anything bearing the name of Christianity is especially noticeable,. . . by far the larger part of them are proud to say that they are not Christians . . . (Thwing, 1911, pp. 260–262).

Although the Harvard socialists called attention to the fact that the members of the Harvard Corporation were drawn from the ranks of the "leaders in business and finance, . . . whose families have been looked up to in the Back Bay for generations," a president of the Socialist Club, Gerard Henderson, noted in 1912 that there had been no effort to inhibit or restrain their activities (Henderson, 1912, pp. 463–465). Harvard not only did not repress its pre-World War I radicals, it showed some sign of accepting William James' pride in them. Thus, the lead article in the June 1914 issue of the *Harvard Graduates' Magazine*, written by its editor W. R. Thayer, was "The Mother of Radicals." Thayer defined radicals as "persons who brave ridicule or social ostracism, poverty or peril to life and limb, in defense of principles hateful to their community." He stretched Harvard's radical record as beginning long before its vaunted contribution to the ideologists and leaders of the American Revolution, noting,

The roll of Harvard's Radicals would be headed by the name of Harvard's first President, Henry Dunster. Rather than abandon his convictions against infant baptism, he gave up his office and retired to die in want. His successor, Charles Chauncy, fearlessly opposed the popular views on baptism and also suffered persecution. A generation later, President Leverett upheld the principle of toleration against the attacks of the Mathers and their bitter sectarian friends, and he, too, found life thorny in consequence.

Thayer went through the record of Harvard participation in nineteenth century liberal and radical religious, cultural and political movements—Unitarianism, literary radicalism, for example, Lowell, Thoreau, and Emerson, and political movements, the antislavery cause, "the Mugwumps in 1884, and . . . the Anti-Imperialists in 1898"—claiming that Harvard Radicals were their "backbone." "The above roll is obviously incomplete, and different compilers would add or subtract certain names: but it serves to show that at no period since its foundation has Harvard College failed to produce Radicals—or rebels, if you prefer that name,—who have led in every important movement." And as he proudly told his well-to-do alumni readers: "There is today no social, political, or economic cause, no matter how advanced or how unpopular, which has not its quota of Harvard names" (Thayer, 1914, pp. 561–563).

There is, however, no record of active concern by Harvard undergraduates for the plight of the Negroes, whether by the organized radicals or others. In this respect, they were not much different from those outside. Still it may be noted that on three occasions, in 1890, in 1903, and again in 1914, the Senior classes chose as their class-day orator, one of their black fellow-students ("Praise from Sir Hubert," 1914, p. 557).

THE SOURCES OF NONCONFORMISM

In his detailed history of the "emergence of the university" after the Civil War, Laurence Veysey also stresses that turn-of-the-century Harvard stood out among the major American schools with regard to both its encouragement of and toleration for "discordant elements." As he comments, the various important critical intellectuals who came out of Cambridge "all demonstrated that at Harvard, unlike most American universities, the serious student need not be stifled by his less imaginative fellows. A mild literary bohemianism became so well entrenched as almost to be part of the established order." Only Stanford rivaled it in these respects, but "the Stanford nonconformists lacked the talent of some of their Harvard counterparts, and the atmosphere at Palo Alto, as it lost its original pioneering quality, became increasingly less hospitable to these stray individualists" (Veysey, 1962, pp. 141–143).

As a consequence of this active undergraduate intellectual and political life, Harvard became the principal source of creative intellectual rebellion in the outside world, particularly in the growing New York radical bohemia. As the intellectual historian Henry May noted, a "Harvard contribution to the Rebellion was almost the whole original corps of Young Intellectuals, the new critics who mixed political and aesthetic revolt. These centered around Walter Lippman, Van Wyck Brooks, and John Reed, but there were many others: Lee Simonson, Edward Eyre Hunt, Robert Hallowell, Alfred Kuttner, Harold Stearns. At Mabel Dodge's salon, on the staff of the *New Republic* and later the *Seven Arts*, Harvard influence was obvious and pervasive" (May, 1964, pp. 56–62, 289–299; Ostrander, 1972, pp. 308).

Both Veysey and May addressed themselves to the question of why was Harvard so different from the rest of American academe? Why did Harvard lead in the "production of rebels"? Both credited it to the success of Charles Eliot's policies. Veysey stressed the emphases on the conditions affecting the environment and background of undergraduates; May emphasized the intellectual quality and variety of the faculty.

The introduction of a totally open elective system had attested to Harvard's unique willingness to encourage undergraduates to experiment to find their way. But perhaps more important than this were the admissions and recruitment policies which led it to become more socially heterogeneous than any other university. The rest of the Ivy League had a student body more limited to the socioeconomic elite; the undergraduates of the major midwestern and western state universities came from more local and provincial backgrounds.

"Harvard's ideal is diversity," declared a perceptive observer in 1910.

The Harvard students are gathered from all over the world, admitted under all sorts of conditions, and given the most diversified training. Harvard's policy of admitting Negroes and campaigning actively to receive Chinese students would have been unthinkable at Princeton. For these reasons, southerners generally avoided Harvard, but it drew heavily from the Middle Atlantic states and the Pacific Coast, as well as from upper New England.... New Englanders themselves began deserting Harvard for smaller colleges after 1903 (to some extent), in a reaction against this catholicity.... By 1893 Boston Catholics had become numerous enough to form their own club; Russian and Polish Jews organized a similar student society in 1906....

Although only an eighth of Harvard graduates were sons of Harvard men, a nucleus of fashionable families did send their offspring to Cambridge generation after generation. From these ranks came "gentlemen" whose values were aristocratic in a carefree sense unknown at Yale (Veysey, 1962, pp. 136–137, 139).

As Veysey also argued, to produce an environment that encouraged heterodoxy, diversity in background was not enough, "it was also essential that the nonconformist be inspired by a tradition of his own; one of detachment from the materially ambitious spirit of the society around him." And Harvard alone seemed to combine the latter, derived from the "gentlemanly aloofness" of its elite students, with the variety in outlook secured from trying to recruit the best from varying social environments (Veysey, 1962, p. 143; Earnest, 1953, p. 211).

But Harvard's "production of rebels" was also, in part, "explained by the revolution through which she had passed in the last generation. Earlier than any other old American institution, Harvard had been changed from a New England college into a great university," incorporating "a national center of strenuous educational reform . . . [and] a world center of research." And as Henry May went on to argue, this meant that Harvard students were more in touch with the rapidly emerging new ideas of the turn of the century than others.

[T]he real sources of insurrection lay not within Cambridge but in the whole Western World, and Harvard, more than some other colleges, was in touch with that world. The tolerance and diversity of the University's academic life . . . exposed some students to strange and foreign ideas. As Santayana put it, Harvard would have been willing to have any point of view whatever represented on the faculty. . . .

[R]ebellion came from Harvard *because* Harvard was so much a center of American nineteenth century culture. At Harvard the stresses and strains of that culture were intensified (May, 1964, p. 57; Earnest, 1953, pp. 154–156).

INTELLECTUAL ACHIEVEMENTS

A variety of statistical indicators confirmed the general impression that Eliot's Harvard had become "the foremost of American universities." A detailed study of the relative position of different American universities as reflected by the numbers listed in *American Men of Science* as significant figures in their fields placed Harvard far ahead of any other school when judged both by the absolute number of faculty so listed, and also by the criterion of department standing. Thus, its author J. McKeen Cattell, noted that in the 12 fields covered in his survey, Harvard was either first "or so nearly first that a small change would place it there. This is a remarkable record, and all honor should be given to the men responsible for it. The departments of Chicago and Columbia stand next to Harvard with about half its strength" (Cattell, 1910, p. 686). Although Cattell was only able to make quantitative comparisons in the natural sciences, he commented that "Harvard has the strongest schools of law and medicine . . . so that its primacy would not be affected if these were fully accounted for" (ibid., p. 684). And in discussing these results, another leading student of American universities, E. E. Slosson, indicated that "there is no doubt that in the humanistic branches the relative standing of Harvard would be quite as high" (Slossen, 1910, pp. 4, 8–10).

It is noteworthy that four graduates of late nineteenth-century Harvard who went on to become distinguished leaders of liberal and radical intellectual thought, Norman Hapgood, W. E. B. DuBois, Robert Morss Lovett, and Oswald Garrison Villard, were in later life to describe the "golden age" of Harvard around 1890 in almost idyllic terms. Hapgood commented in his autobiography: "If there could be a place intellectually more attractive than Harvard University toward the end of the Nineteenth Century, my imagination does not give it form" (Hapgood, 1930, p. 46). How this intellectual atmosphere looked to a bright black undergraduate who was to become a celebrated radical may be seen from the impressions of W. E. B. DuBois, who graduated in 1890.

Harvard in 1888 was a great institution of learning. . . . Among the active teachers were Francis Child, Charles Eliot Norton, Charles Dunbar, Justin Winsor and John Trowbridge; William Goodwin, Frank Taussig, Nathaniel Shaler, George Palmer, William James, Francis Peabody, Josiah Royce, Barrett Wendell, Edward Channing, and Albert Bushnell Hart. A young instructor who arrived in 1890 was George Santayana. Seldom, if ever, has any American university had such a galaxy of great men and fine teachers as Harvard in the decade between 1885 and 1895. . . .

I was repeatedly a guest in the home of William James; he was my friend and guide to clear thinking; I was a member of the Philosophical Club and talked with Josiah Royce and George Palmer. . . . I sat in an upper room and read Kant's *Critique* with Santayana; Shaler invited a southerner, who objected to sitting beside me, out of his class. . . . I became one of Hart's favorite pupils (DuBois, 1969, pp. 132, 143; West, 1972, pp. 24–28; Earnest, 1953, p. 235).

Villard, later the fighting editor of the *Nation* and the New York *Post*, echoed DuBois's listing of the "great teachers and unusually rare personalities" on the faculty and recalled that he enjoyed life at Harvard "to the brim" (Villard, 1939, pp. 80–87). Lovett detailed similar reactions:

This period [the late eighties and early nineties] was a golden age in the history of Harvard. . . . [T]he intellectual excitement arising from the new freedom in choice of studies was contagious. Although the elective system, unguided, was properly criticized as tending to a scattering of interest and energy, its immediate effect was stimulating and broadening.... Perhaps as a result of being treated as adults undergraduates developed a certain sense of superiority, which was called "Harvard indifference" (Lovett, 1948, pp. 33–34).

These enthusiastic reports of life at Eliot's Harvard by some of the most intellectually successful among its graduates are reinforced by quantitative evidence that the large majority of the students appreciated their courses and relaxed environment. A faculty committee established in 1902 to consider ways of improving instruction undertook to query a sample of undergraduates, selected by lot, as to their reactions to their courses. Of the 1,757 who filled out questionnaires, 83 percent indicated complete satisfaction with the courses they selected, 11 percent "were negative," and another 6 percent "declared that the choice of the course in question was but partly justified." There was a steady relationship between grade received and satisfaction, but even among "C" students, only 20 percent reported unhappiness with the instruction and course content (Briggs et al., 1904, pp. 612–613). The faculty committee had been concerned about the growth of large lecture courses; "in 1901–02 there were 25 with between 100 and 200 members, and 14 with more than 200." The major complaint of students was with the graduate-student assistants who handled the small discussion sections. The committee also worried that the bulk of the teaching at turn-of-the-century Harvard "must rest chiefly with the assistants, who come into more contact with the students. As the University is now organized, these assistants are necessarily young men, and therefore without experience in teaching. The Committee feels the extreme importance of selecting the very best available men.... Some of the men are not as good as could be desired, but even these have charge of too many students. The need of a larger number of competent assistants is felt by instructors and students alike." Still, it was noted that the "great majority of those [students] thought ... [large lecture courses] valuable, because they opened large subjects of thought, or because they introduced many students to 'big men' in the Faculty, or even because they brought a large body of students together" (ibid., pp. 616–617).

RENEWED DISSATISFACTION

If the large majority of the undergraduates surveyed by questionnaire indicated satisfaction with the instruction which they received in the greatly expanded Harvard of Eliot's fourth decade, there was evidence of renewed dissatisfaction with some of the educational consequences of growth and of relaxed control on the part of some alumni, members of the Governing Boards, and faculty. Although the focus of the criticisms varied, they centered in large part on the lack of direct influence over the education of undergraduates supposedly inherent in the structural and policy changes that had occurred. Thus, Charles Francis Adams, completing his 24th and final year in 1906 as a member of the Board of Overseers, who, as noted earlier, had complained about his own education in the 1850s, as "in essentials radically defective," stated that "I find myself led to believe that the condition of affairs . . . has since grown steadily worse." From his contact with "the run of undergraduates of the present time as I have met them in my own family or in the offspring of my classmates and friends," Adams concluded that "the gulf which divides the usual college instructor from the average undergraduate is even more impassable in 1906 than it was in 1854. . . . The lecture has taken the place of the recitation. . . . [T]he periodical examination paper is the nearest approach to personal contact. The average undergraduate is merely one unit in an impersonal mob" (Adams, 1907, pp. 105, 110–111). He objected as well to the system of free electives, arguing that students were not qualified to judge the preparation that they require.

Many of the misgivings of Adams and other Harvard graduates and governors with Eliot's "system of liberty" were shared by a growing number of faculty. Under the leadership of A. Lawrence Lowell, Professor of Government, opposition grew to the elective system and to Eliot's proposals to make it possible for most students to get their B.A. in three years. The report of the 1902–03 committee, largely written by Lowell, was concerned over the fact that students reported themselves putting in much less work for courses (three hours a week) than the faculty had estimated necessary (six hours) (Briggs et al., 1904, pp. 613–614). They were also bothered by the fact that a large proportion of the undergraduates took the bulk of their course work in elementary subjects, that relatively few sought to specialize or graduate with honors. A previous faculty report had documented "that the percentage of students who elected little or nothing but elementary courses was as high as 55 percent in the class of 1898," and that close to three-quarters scattered their courses without emphasizing work in any given field (Morison, 1930, p. xlv).

Many faculty believed that these concerns were shared by the more intellectually oriented among the undergraduates. One of the most creative among them, Van Wyck Brooks, writing in 1904, argued that the freedom to select all courses permitted many a student to go through college only taking easy courses or those which "harmonize with his own point of view," thus serving to "intensify his own narrowness and to encourage in him the line of least resistance." At the same time, Brooks pointed out, the Germanic emphasis on professional schools and graduate education, which also characterized Harvard, had produced a "general tendency . . . to look upon the degree of A.B. mainly as preparation for one of these graduate schools." This meant that studiously inclined freshmen are faced "immediately upon entrance into college" with "the increasingly intellectual modern idea of effective specialization." And this perceptive budding young radical intellectual anticipated a complaint that would become widespread in Harvard Yard more than a half century later that the "inevitable and inexorable" growth of the graduate university "will sweep away the gentle sentiments of Puritan tradition, and make of Harvard the factory of American imperialism," that with the decline of "the College the old fashioned humanist fades away, with the [growth of the] University the efficient practitioner of the future emerges" (Brooks, 1908, pp. 645, 647, 649).

The trend toward easing the work of students was reversed in the first years of the new century, the last decade of Eliot's regime. In 1902, faculty legislation required that students had to receive at least a C grade in two-thirds of their courses to graduate. The following year, the professors turned down Eliot's renewed proposals to make it possible for most students to get their A.B. in three years even though similar plans had won faculty approval in 1890, before the Overseers rejected them. And as a consequence of the report of the 1902–03 committee, a number of "notoriously easy courses were stiffened up" (Morison, 1930, pp. xlv–xlvi). The continuing opposition led to the establishment in 1908 of a new faculty committee to investigate the learning situation at Harvard directly under Lowell's chairmanship. Its report sharply criticized the effect of the elective system on undergraduate education. Emphasizing the responses to questionnaires by alumni, the Lowell Committee found evidence to sustain views which its chairman had frequently voiced at faculty meetings. The report contended that there was little respect for learning among Harvard students, in large part because it was easy to manipulate the elective system. A majority of the graduates reported that "they were dissatisfied with the amount of scholarly work they had done in College," and many recommended "some curtailment in the elective system."

Lowell's report stressed the need for all students to concentrate or major in a given field, and to be required to select from those courses that the chosen department designated as necessary for competence in that subject. Students also should be encouraged to compete for publicly acknowledged "honors" based on grades in courses which stressed ability to handle general principles, rather than facts, as well as on their work on a thesis. Fundamentally, it assumed the need to so change the atmosphere of undergraduate education as to make the student who received honors, "an object of general admiration," a result which could be obtained by imitating Oxford and Cambridge, where undergraduate scholarship was supposedly sustained by "an elaborate system of competition and prizes" (Lowell et al., 1910, pp. 478–484). The report stressed the need to recreate an emphasis on College education, to make the task of training the minds of undergraduates as important as that of graduate work. Lowell's views had support among a majority of the faculty, but more importantly, even before the report was published, the Governing Boards of the University chose him to succeed Charles Eliot as the President.

5. The Lowell Administration

With Lowell's appointment, the Harvard Corporation followed a pattern not uncommon to many institutions, choosing a successor who is sharply different from his predecessor. Leaders of organizations tend to be selected because they exhibit talents enabling them to effectively deal with the institutional problems at the time. As we have seen, Charles Eliot, a creative scientist who had shown much interest in fostering the conditions for a major science center, was chosen in 1869, at a point when his predecessor and the Governing Boards had advanced the objective of scholarly greatness for Harvard. And Eliot had more than fulfilled this aim. In so doing, however, he gave less attention to other functions of the institution, in particular to the total education of undergraduates. Eliot's Harvard acted almost as if undergraduates were a necessary nuisance who were to be given freedom so as to make them as little a burden as possible to the scholarly faculty (Jencks & Riesman, 1962, p. 734). By selecting Lowell, the Harvard Corporation chose as Eliot's successor a man who proposed to remedy some of the negative effects of the emphasis on creating a great graduate and scholarly university with a research-oriented faculty, a university that also emphasized freedom from interference with respect to curriculum, residence, and the like for the students. Eliot, who lived to be 90, continued, however, to defend the emphasis on scholarship long into the administration of his successor. In 1922 he complained that there are many who "do not see that the service Harvard University renders to the country through its graduate professional schools is greater than it renders through Harvard College proper. A Harvard tradition that is still an obstacle to progress!" (Land, 1933, p. 148).

A. Lawrence Lowell was a student of Britain, and his model was Oxbridge. He wanted Harvard to become the university that turned out a gentlemanly ruling elite. With this interest, he had been strongly critical of Eliot's laissez faire policies concerning student life. To Lowell, the absence of an Oxbridge residential-college system meant that Harvard undergraduates were separated outside of class along social class, ethnic, and religious lines (Earnest, 1953, p. 216). He "was more interested in creating a closely knit community than he was about 'democracy' in its more usual connotations." And his solution was to try once more to house Harvard students in college residences (Lowell, 1934, pp. 27–31; Veysey, 1965, pp. 250–251; Jencks & Riesman, 1962, pp. 737–738). In his inaugural address he proposed to bring the freshmen "together in a group of dormitories and dining halls, under the comradeship of older men, who appreciated the possibilities of a college life, and took a keen interest in their work and their pleasure" (Lowell, 1934, p. 43).

He also reiterated his criticisms of the elective system. By requiring concentrations (majors) together with a system of "honors," he hoped to motivate students to work harder on academic subjects (Lowell, 1934, pp. 32–45; Slossen, 1910, p. 597; Morison, 1936c, pp. 440–448, 507). When the plan for concentrations was introduced in 1910–11, the largest group of students chose to major in one of the social sciences, particularly economics, a tendency interpreted by one observer as, in part, a result of the "prominence of economic and governmental questions..." (Munro, 1912, pp. 76–77).

There is little hard evidence with which to evaluate the reaction of undergraduates to the changed emphasis on concentrations. Economics, the largest department, undertook an evaluation of its teaching in 1912–13. The most frequent complaint of the undergraduates was to the large required introductory course, and questionnaire responses indicated "their belief that more real instruction is obtained from the assigned reading than from lectures or discussions." They complained most about the teaching abilities of the graduate assistants who handled the weekly section meetings, a complaint voiced in a survey a decade earlier, and reheard for more than a half-century in the future (Munro, 1917, p. 254; Dewey, 1918, p. 606).

Thanks in no small degree to the freedom from faculty and administrative oversight that students enjoyed during Eliot's administration, Harvard, as noted earlier, had escaped the wave of student unrest that had swept most other New England colleges and schools in other areas during the 1890s (Lipset, 1972b, pp. 142–143). As a result the University also did not share in the various experiments in student senates and councils that emerged as a response to unrest. But Harvard students finally requested a Student Council in 1908. The faculty agreed and an elected body was established which had a modicum of success. There was apparently not much undergraduate interest in it. The political activists concerned with larger social problems ignored it. President Lowell, however, saw in the Council a potential ally in placing greater emphasis on undergraduate activities and devoted considerable energies to encouraging student self-government (Batchelder, 1913, pp. 621–622).

The politicization of the University that had occurred in the last decade of the Eliot administration resulted in some slight efforts to limit it under Lowell. In 1912, the University, which had not placed any restrictions on the activities of the Socialists, Anarchists, or other political groups, refused the "use of a hall to the League for Woman Suffrage, for a lecture by Mrs. Pankhurst," with the curious argument that since Harvard was not a coeducational institution, women could not lecture before a College group unless they "are officially invited by the authorities" (Henderson, 1912, p. 464). Two years later, in 1914, the Corporation ruled that student groups could invite anyone they wanted to meetings that were "open only to members of the University." University facilities, however, could not be used for public meetings at which only one side of a contentious question was presented, or to speakers carrying on "persistent propaganda." This action resulted in recurrent agitation every time an application for a meeting was denied by the University on these grounds. As Harvard Professor William Bennet Munro noted just before America's entry into the First World War, "nowadays every request raises the question as to what is propagandist and what is not. Every speaker on every topic is a propagandist to some degree" (Munro, 1917, p. 358).

WORLD WAR I

The period of radical activism and broad interest in social reform at Harvard and many other schools was ended by world war. The Harvard Socialist Club was still strong in 1914. It had over 60 members and 250 attended a meeting at which John Spargo spoke ("In the Colleges," 1913–14, p. 23). During the first year of the war in Europe, most Harvard groups and publications assumed that the United States should and would stay neutral. Socialists like John Reed and Jane Addams spoke to student meetings opposing American involvement. When General Wood proposed summer military training camps for students, the *Crimson* strongly opposed them. In March 1915 the Harvard chapter of the Collegiate Anti-Militarism League was formed to oppose proposals to arm the country. Gradually, however, the dominant sentiment at Harvard, led by President Lowell and retired President Eliot, became increasingly pro-Ally. The class orator at the 1915 Commencement spoke in favor of American support for freedom to a friendly audience. By the fall of 1915 the *Crimson* had shifted to support preparedness. Pacifists and antiwar radicals on campus felt isolated and even persecuted socially through 1916 (Stange, 1939, pp. 7–11). As the war went on, even the left and progressive supporters divided sharply over whether to support or oppose the Allies and America's entry into the war. Many alumni of the Harvard Socialist Club, such as Walter Lippmann and a host of progressively inclined faculty, identified with the cause of democracy against Prussian tyranny, particularly after the February 1917 Revolution in Russia.

Harvard as an institution began to prepare for war even before the government requested universities to do so. Lowell encouraged students to enroll in summer military training. A course in Military Science taught by General Leonard Wood and two other officers was given in 1915–16 before the passage of the National Defense Act of 1916 that provided for such courses. Early in 1917, while the United States was still at peace, Lowell invited the French government to send Harvard a few disabled officers to train students in the latest tactics developed in the conflict. After war was declared, the University faced the problem of restraining students from enlisting before they could complete their curtailed requirements for degrees and ROTC training. There is little evidence of any continued antiwar activity among the students (Morison, 1936c, pp. 450–451, 456–460). A report in the Socialist-party newspaper, the *New York Call,* of an antiwar march held in Boston on July 1, 1917, with 8,000 paraders detailed the composition of the demonstrators by various occupational, ethnic, and other group categories. It made no mention of students from Harvard or elsewhere (Peterson & Fite, 1957, pp. 45–46).

The war placed a considerable strain on academic freedom. The pressure to fire pro-German or antiwar faculty was intense in many schools. Many state universities discharged or suspended faculty whose loyalty was in question (Metzger, 1961, pp. 221–223; Peterson & Fite, 1957, pp. 102–109). At Columbia President Nicholas Murray Butler "formally withdrew the privilege of academic freedom for the entire duration of the war, stating in a commencement day address in June that 'what had been wrongheadedness was now sedition'" (Metzger, 1961, p. 255).

At Harvard President Lowell and the other members of the governing Corporation, though at least as pro-Ally and prowar as Butler and the Columbia trustees, maintained the tradition set by Eliot and resisted repressive pressures from alumni and others. They were subject to a greater temptation than any other institution to do so. In 1916 a Harvard alumnus, George Wiener, declared that he would give the University $10 million if Hugo Münsterberg, an eminent psychologist who had remained a German citizen and publicly defended Germany in debate, were let go. Münsterberg himself announced that he would resign as soon as Wiener deposited $5 million in Harvard's account. The Harvard administration and the Corporation put a quick stop to this activity, announcing that the "University cannot tolerate any suggestion that it would be willing to accept money to abridge free speech, to remove a professor or to accept his resignation" (Yeomans, 1948, pp. 314–316; Metzger, 1961, pp. 228–229; Morison, 1936c, p. 453; Harris, 1970, p. 277). Since the Münsterberg case reached public attention and occurred before the United States was actually at war, it may be argued that Harvard was not really subject to as strong pressures as those schools which were to yield on academic freedom during wartime. But in contradistinction to President Butler, Lowell also made a public statement in June 1917 in his annual report for the academic year which included a long eloquent defense of academic freedom. After arguing that research and teaching must be completely free and uninhibited by anyone, that a professor "must teach the truth as he has found it and sees it," Lowell went on to discuss the more difficult issue of public utterance on political subjects.

The gravest questions, and the strongest feelings, arise from action by a professor beyond his chosen field and outside of his classroom. . . . The argument in favor of a restraining power on the part of the governing boards of universities and colleges is based upon the fact that by extreme, or injudicious, remarks that shock public sentiment a professor can do great harm to the institution with which he is connected. That is true, and sometimes a professor thoughtlessly does an injury that is without justification. . . .

In spite, however, of the risk to the institution, the objections to restraint upon what professors may say as citizens seem to me far greater than the harm done by leaving them free. . . . It is not a question of academic freedom, but of personal liberty from constraint, yet it touches the dignity of the academic career. . . .

If a university or college censors what its professors may say, if it restrains them from uttering something that it does not approve, it thereby assumes responsibility for that which it permits them to say. This is logical and inevitable, but it is a responsibility which an institution of learning would be very unwise in assuming. It is sometimes suggested that the principles are different in time of war; that the governing boards are then justified in restraining unpatriotic expressions injurious to the country. But the same problem is presented in wartime as in time of peace. If a university is right in restraining its professors, it has a duty to do so and it is responsible for whatever it permits. There is no middle ground. Either the university assumes full responsibility for permitting its professors to express certain opinions in public, or it assumes no responsibility whatever, and leaves them to be dealt with like other citizens by the public authorities according to the laws of the land (Lowell, 1934, pp. 267–272; Morison, 1936c, pp. 454–456; Yeomans, 1948, pp. 308–312; Metzger, 1961, pp. 228–229).

In replying to his wartime critics, Lowell took over some of the ideas and even the language that had been voiced three years earlier by the editors of the *Crimson* in a reply to protests that had been made to the University and some of its publications about radical statements made by some professors. The *Crimson* at that time stated in words which would be repeated in wartime by the President: "No censorship should be imposed upon thoughts or their utterance. If the University were to decree what its professors and students should or should not say, then it would be making itself responsible for any statement made by its members" (*Harvard Crimson*, 1914, p. 365).

POSTWAR THREATS TO ACADEMIC FREEDOM

Lowell's commitment to the principles he enunciated at a time when few university presidents were supporting them was even more tried in the repressive hysteria of the postwar years when the fear of Bolshevism resulted in both governmental and vigilante efforts to suspend the civil liberties of radicals and other political dissidents. The colleges were seen as centers of disloyalty. Calvin Coolidge, former governor of Massachusetts and Vice President-elect, wrote articles dealing with the activities of the "Reds" in colleges, blaming faculties for the threat to the political order. The ISS reported severe repression of rights of free speech for radicals on campuses, and partly as a reaction to such pressures it changed its name to the League for Industrial Democracy (LID), or on campus, the Student League (SLID) (Lipset, 1972b, pp. 162–163; Altbach, 1974, p. 27). The Harvard affiliate continued to call itself the Socialist Club and ran a variety of educational meetings. In a "straw vote" held before the 1920 U. S. Presidential elections, the majority of the 2,030 Harvard students who balloted voted for Harding, the Republican (53 percent); 39 percent voted for Cox; 5 percent were for the Socialist, Eugene Victor Debs ("Harding Leads at Harvard," 1920, p. 17).

A variety of liberal groups organized to fight the repressive atmosphere. The most important, the Intercollegiate Liberal League, was formed at Harvard and merged in 1921 with others into the National Student Forum (Altbach, 1974, pp. 34–35). The Harvard Student Liberal Club published a magazine, *The Gadfly*, for some years, which indicated that it and the Club were "a protest against the existing academic order" ("Who Is Responsible...," 1922, p. 3). The journal praised the "cooperative movement," "the spread of the movement for workers' education," and the "Non-Partisan League in North Dakota," and called for "an examination of the fundamental premises on which society is based" (Edsall, 1922, p. 9). The magazine openly discussed discrimination against Jews at Harvard and backed pacifism. Its first Editorial Board included John T. Edsall, who became a professor of biochemistry, and down to the 1970s a staunch backer of liberal and strong antiwar views at Harvard, as Chairman, and J. Robert Oppenheimer, as one of the other three members. Right-wingers saw in the Club and its journal evidence of Harvard's subversive character. One argued:

It is safe to say that no institution of learning in the country has been so thoroughly saturated with the "liberal" activity as Harvard University. The institution has stimulated such a spirit of democracy among the students of the past generation that the radicals have had a more fertile field in which to work at Harvard than in a less liberal establishment. The professors themselves have not been inactive in the encouragement of the movement, and the names of several of them ... are known in the "illegal" circles of the Communist party of America (Whitney, 1924, pp. 58–59).

The student Liberals were supported in their efforts by a group of Harvard alumni who had organized themselves into the Harvard Liberal Clubs seeking "to elect Liberals as Overseers and Directors of the Alumni Association," so as to be able to influence University policies (Gardiner, 1920, p. 227). At a meeting during the 1918 commencement exercises, they indicated "that the chief purpose of a university should be to give its students a sense of social duty and prepare them for leadership in the reconstruction of modern society." A critical observer of their meeting argued that their real argument with Harvard was that its work in social science was "not sufficiently radical to meet their approval ... [and that] they are displeased with the failure of the university to give greater emphasis in these days to the work in social science than to that in military science. The social upheavers have shown less appreciation than any other class of citizen of the necessity, first, of America's getting into the war, and, second, of America's getting on with the war" ("From A Graduate's Window," 1918, p. 37–38). The Boston Liberal Club, which had a membership of 250 and met weekly, had various educational, labor, and liberal spokesmen talk to it. At one session, President Lowell replied to their criticisms stating "very frankly some of the difficulties in doing everything that one might wish for, not the least of which is the extreme difficulty of selecting the proper men to give courses of instruction in the newer social sciences because the whole thing is so recent that it has hardly produced its leaders" (Gardiner, 1920, p. 228). At another meeting in "the winter of 1920, following the raids conducted by the Department of Justice on the 'reds,' a 'free-speech' banquet was held, [which was] largely attended" (ibid., p. 230).

At Harvard a number of Law School professors, including Dean Roscoe Pound and Professors Felix Frankfurter and Zechariah Chafee, Jr., came under severe attack by conservative alumni for preparing together with law professors from other schools, a "Report upon the Illegal Practices of the United States Department of Justice," protesting the repression of radicals. Chafee's dismissal was demanded for an article he published in the *Harvard Law Review* in 1920. Lowell defended him and secured the backing of the Overseers. Harold Laski, then a young lecturer in Government and still relatively unknown as a scholar, occasioned even more aggressive demands for his dismissal when in 1919 he publicly defended the Boston policemen's strike, and in speaking to a meeting of wives of the strikers praised their husbands' contributions to pluralism and political science. Laski was denounced as a foreign "traitor and Bolshevik." Lowell, who had strongly supported then Governor Coolidge in his effort to suppress the strike, encouraging Harvard students to join the temporary strike-breaking police force (200 did so), would not budge on the academic-freedom issue. When it appeared that some Overseers might be sympathetic to the anti-Laski efforts, Lowell indicated that if they "ask for Laski's resignation, they will get mine" (Yeomans, 1948, pp. 316–317; Earnest, 1953, p. 263; Morison, 1936c, pp. 465–466; Kahn, 1968, pp. 97–98). Agitation against Laski continued in the Boston press, and more significantly among students, even after the decision to retain him was announced. The undergraduate humor magazine, *The Harvard Lampoon*," published a special anti-Soviet number which announced that Lenin owned 148 personal motor cars, Trotsky 52—and that Dr. Laski was one of the Bolsheviks' chosen emissaries. The journal also explained that the visiting lecturer was an ardent exponent of free love" (Wechsler, 1935, p. 348). Laski received an offer in his native land soon after and left. (The editors of the 1935-36 *Lampoon* would officially apologize to Laski for the earlier attacks made on him by their magazine.) (Cain, 1963, p. 227)

Lowell's record in defending academic freedom and scholarly integrity was demonstrated also by his actions in a much earlier case in 1914 in which a law professor was fired "when it was discovered that he was receiving a secret retainer from the New Haven Railroad to write articles and make speeches opposing the regulation of public utilities, which were supposed to be the results of purely academic research" (Morison, 1936c, p. 443; Felix, 1965, p. 194).

In a letter written to a student of faculty government, who had argued that Harvard would have had more academic freedom under a faculty-controlled Corporation, Lowell wrote persuasively that nonfaculty trustees were in a stronger position to ward off external threats to academic freedom than the faculty. As he put it:

May I point out that since the war the Corporation has stood absolutely steadfast in defending its professors under . . . very heavy pressure. It may be that a Corporation composed of professors would have stood the test as well; or it may be that—had they been urged by the alumni that the increase of supplies on which every University must depend was liable to be cut short if a certain professor was not muzzled—they would not have been so steadfast. . . . [The] faculties are not aware of the amount of pressure that has been brought upon the Corporation, because they are saved from feeling it by the presence of the Corporation, which absorbs the shock. The Corporation has stood the test . . . (Kirkpatrick, 1922b, pp. 67–68).

In his President's report in 1920, Lowell took the occasion to lay out his interpretation of the relationship of the role and power of the faculty to that of the Governing Boards in terms not unflattering to the professors. He laid stress on the conception of a university as "a society or guild of scholars." But "given the vast complexity of a modern university [which] has compelled specialization of functions, . . . one aspect thereof is the separation of the scholarly and business organs." And he described the consequent relationship.

Let it be observed, however, that although the governing board is the ultimate authority it is not in the position of an industrial employer. It is a trustee not to earn dividends for stockholders, but for the purposes of the guild. Its sole object is to help the society of scholars to accomplish the object for which they are brought together. They are the essential part of the society. . . .

In the words of a former member of the Harvard Corporation, their business is to "serve tables." The relation [between board and faculty] is not one of employer and employed, of superior and inferior, of master and servant, but one of mutual cooperation for the promotion of the scholars' work. . . . There is no natural antagonism between trustees and professors. To suggest it is to suggest failure in their proper relation to one another; to suppose it is to provoke failure; to assume it is to ensure failure.

He went on to note the differences between the way the worth of an employee is judged in private industry and the university, pointing out that the notion of "an unprofitable employee" cannot apply in the latter. "[I]n the university the usefulness of the scholar depends largely upon his sense of security, upon the fact that he can work for an object that may be remote and whose value may not be easily demonstrated. In a university, barring positive misconduct, permanence of tenure is essential for members who have passed the probationary period . . . [even] if they do not prove so valuable as they were expected to be . . . " (Lowell, 1921, pp. 397–401).

RACISM AT HARVARD

As suggested by his attitude and role with respect to the Boston police strike, Lowell's stands on academic freedom did not stem from liberal views on social issues. As against Eliot, he favored restriction on student freedom of choice, was more conservative politically, and somewhat bigoted, as reflected in his attitudes toward the composition of the Harvard student body. Veysey implies that some of Lowell's dissatisfaction with the Eliot administration was connected with policies which encouraged increases in the numbers of Catholic, Jewish, Negro, and Chinese students, and the consequent decline in attractiveness of Harvard to New Englanders (Veysey, 1965, p. 288). "Southerners avoided Harvard after the Civil War because it admitted Negroes on the same terms as whites, allowing them to eat at Memorial Hall, room in college dormitories, and participate in debating and athletic contests," but the school openly yielded to bigotry under Lowell (Morison, 1936c, pp. 416–417). In spite of his concern for breaking down the social barriers among Harvard's white students by requiring them all to live in college residences, he saw no contradiction in imposing a ban on Negroes living in the freshman dormitories established in 1914. He stated that it would be unwise "for a Negro to apply for a room in the dormitories. . . . It has nothing to do with the education he receives; that, of course, we furnish equally to all men without distinction as to race, color, or previous condition of servitude. It is a different matter from the social commingling in the Freshman dormitories . . . " (Harris,

1970, p. 17; Yeomans, 1948, p. 175). Black freshmen alone had to live in segregated quarters off campus.

Although Negro students did not protest publicly until 1922, various alumni and faculty had begun to question the practice even earlier. In 1922, a petition signed by 143 alumni protesting the policy was submitted to the Corporation calling on "the Alma Mater of Channing, of John Quincy Adams, of Sumner, of Robert Gould Shaw, of the 54th Massachusetts Infantry, and of the Lowells...," to change its policy. Among others, the letter was signed by Heywood Broun, Herbert Croly, Ernest Gruening, Walter Lippmann, Robert Morss Lovett, Samuel Eliot Morison, and Oswald Garrison Villard (Hixson, 1972, pp. 120–121). The affair became a matter of public notice when a statement appeared which President Lowell had made in reply to the Negro alumnus father of a freshman who had prepared for Harvard at the elite Exeter Academy, that since living in dormitories was compulsory for freshmen, "I am sure you will understand why ... we have not thought it possible to compel men of different races to reside together" (Painter, 1971, pp. 627–628; Hixson, 1972, p. 121).

Public protest now became intense. Among the many Harvard alumni who joined in was Franklin Roosevelt, who wrote that though there were "many colored students in Cambridge" when he was an undergraduate, the matter of where they lived never arose. Although Eliot had defended the right of undergraduates to discriminate socially with regard to privately owned residences and social clubs, he also strongly criticized limiting access to any University-controlled facility to black students in 1923 (Hawkins, 1972, p. 193).

Lowell and the Fellows of the Corporation nominally yielded in March 1923, unanimously approving a statement that dormitories "should not be restricted on account of race " (Fox, 1970, pp. 261–263), but that no one should be required to live with someone of another race. Segregation policies continued for Negroes until World War II. When housed in college buildings they were separated from white students (Painter, 1971, p. 634). Not surprisingly, the situation gave Lowell and Harvard an anti-Negro reputation among militant blacks. In May 1923, the *Messenger*, edited by A. Philip Randolph, stated in terms and arguments not unlike those to be made a half century later:

The Ku Klux Klan spirit has captured Harvard. Doubtless, if an examination of Harvard's investments is made, it would be found that millions of her enormous endowment are reaping large and "unfair" dividends from Southern cotton, lumber, city bonds, etc., that rest upon the backs of Negro labor (ibid., p. 633).

Lowell's efforts to restrict Jewish enrollment occasioned an even greater *cause célèbre*. Under Eliot, there was no effort to limit the number of Jews at Harvard. This policy was followed even though as Eliot noted in 1901: "It is doubtless true that Jews are better off at Harvard than at any other American college; and they are, therefore, likely to resort to it" (Veysey, 1965, p. 92; Harris, 1970, p. 16).

As the number of Jews applying to colleges increased sharply during the second and third decades of the twentieth century, various schools began imposing fixed quotas on Jewish students. At Harvard, the proportion had grown from 6 percent at the end of Eliot's term in 1908 to 21 percent in 1922. Suddenly in June 1922, Lowell's office issued a public statement indicating that the matter of "the proportion of Jews at the college . . . is in the stage of general discussion" (Steinberg, 1974, pp. 21–22). In a subsequent exchange of letters with a Jewish alumnus published in the New York *Times*, Lowell defended the proposal to limit Jewish enrollment on the grounds that it would prevent the growth of anti-Semitism.

The anti-Semitic feeling among the students is increasing, and it grows in proportion to the increase in the number of Jews. If their number should become 40 percent of the student body, the race feeling would become intense. When on the other hand, the number of Jews was small, the race antagonism was small also . . . (Steinberg, 1971, p. 32).

Although the discussion of the rights of black and Jewish students at Harvard was couched completely in terms of the way alternative policies might affect education (and all public statements deprecated anti-Negro and anti-Jewish sentiments), these debates took part in the context of a larger political atmosphere that witnessed the rise of the multimillion member Ku Klux Klan, the diffusion by Henry Ford of virulent anti-Semitic propaganda in his widely circulated Dearborn *Independent*, and the overt expression of explicit racist sentiments by leading national figures such as Presidents Harding and Coolidge and cabinet member Herbert Hoover. The strength of such feelings was attested to by the election of many Klan-supported candidates in northern as well as southern states, by the fact that resolutions condemning the Klan could not pass at either the Republican or Democratic national conventions in 1924, and by the passage of restrictive immigration legislation, biased against nonnorthern Protestant European immigrants (Lipset & Raab, 1970, pp. 110–149). These events did not pass unnoticed within Harvard Yard. In May 1922, a group of undergraduates formed a committee to combat the anti-Jewish propaganda of Henry Ford, which included the editor of the *Crimson*. In an editorial in 1924, the *Crimson* discussed the appeal of the Klan and argued that its "causes are not so much economic discontent as they are chauvinism, bigotry, and intolerance. . . . Klanism is simply a sad commentary on the condition of education and religion in the United States" ("Hooded Ignorance," 1924, p. 2). Yet though some white gentile students formed committees to oppose racial and religious restrictive policies at Harvard, there was little indication of widespread opposition to them. Harvard students, like the rest of middle-class America, were at best insensitive to the rise of bigotry in the nation, and at worst, were sympathetic to the efforts to turn back a threat to the traditional values of evangelical white Protestant America, perceived as coming from Jews, Catholics, blacks, and radicals.

ANTI-SEMITISM AND ADMISSIONS QUOTAS

Some evidence that Lowell was right in assuming the existence of considerable anti-Semitic feeling among the undergraduates was indicated by a survey taken among 83 students in a Social Ethics course, presumably among the most liberal of the undergraduates. Almost half of them, 41, supported quotas, while 34, including seven with obvious Jewish names, opposed them, and eight were undecided (Ham, 1922, p. 225). Those students in favor of restrictions assumed "that the number of Jews in Harvard College was increasing out of all proportion to the increase in the number of other races," and insisted that this was wrong, that the college should be "fairly representative of the country at large." The advocates of quotas complained that Jews were too bright or that they were too conscientious about their studies.

"In harmony with their policy of getting all they can for as little as possible, Jews incidentally take a majority of the scholarships. Thus they deprive many worthy men of other races of a chance." Here, however, we must discriminate. There is a diversity of opinion as to the intellectual powers of the Jew. A considerable number of our gentlemen deny that he is, on the average, more able mentally than his critics. "He does nothing but grind. Is it surprising that he should make better grades than those of us who have broader interests?" One aggrieved individual who drew a rock-bottom grade in the examination exclaims bitterly: "They memorize their books! Thus they keep the average of scholarship so high that others with a high degree of common sense, but less parrot-knowledge, are prevented from attaining a representative grade" (Ham, 1922, p. 225).

The opponents of restrictions argued as vehemently that an effort to make the College representative of the country undermined its essentially educational purpose, its obligation to those who are motivated to benefit from intensive education.

"An educational institution should not be representative of all people, but only of those with ambition and ability to do its work. This has nothing to do with race or religion." "To tell a Cohen, whose average on the college board examinations was 90, that he cannot enter because there are too many Jews already, while a grade of 68 will pass a Murphy, or one of 62 a Morgan, hardly seems in line with the real interests of the college" (ibid., pp. 225–226).

In supporting admission restrictions, many students, including the editors of the *Crimson*, voiced arguments that assumed negative Jewish traits. One group of undergraduates issued a statement supporting Lowell: "Were it only a matter of scholarship, there could be no objection to Jews at all. But they do not mix. They destroy the unity of the college" (Bloomgarden, 1960, p. 152). These arguments and concerns might have carried more weight in a situation in which the "nonmixing" Jews were not barred from membership in many of the prestigious eating clubs.

Lowell's protestations that he was primarily concerned with preventing anti-Semitic feeling were somewhat discredited by the published report of a private discussion he had had with an alumnus, in which he indicated his belief that Jews would have to give up their "peculiar practices" if they wanted to be treated equally (Hixson, 1972, p. 121). On another occasion, he told a distinguished alumnus who pressed him on the Jewish admissions issue that 50 percent of the students caught stealing books from the Library the previous year were Jewish. When the alumnus, who reported this discussion to Felix Frankfurter, subsequently, under Frankfurter's urging, asked Lowell, how many students had been caught, he was told, "Two." Another version of the story had Lowell saying that 100 percent of the book thieves were Jewish, and it turning out that the 100 percent was composed of one person (Broun & Britt, 1931, pp. 53–54).

The issue of Jewish quotas was even more widely debated in the national media than that of segregation of blacks. Harvard again was under severe attack for its illiberality. Given the position of the university as the oldest and preeminent college in the country, it is understandable that many not connected with it felt that they had a right to criticize Harvard's admissions policies. The liberal organ, *The New Republic,* which included a number of Harvard men among its editors from its founding on, contended that as a result of "the position Harvard occupies, or has occupied in American life," it is necessary to recognize that "Harvard is essentially a public institution." And like the patriots in Revolutionary times, and Jeffersonians and Jacksonians in the early nineteenth century, they insisted that Harvard must conform to the democratic will. As graduates of Eliot's school, they argued that it must return to the freedom that characterized "the hey-day of President Eliot's sway."

Harvard stood for freedom of thought, of expression, of personality. In the lesser institutions one was always being dragooned. . . . But at Harvard one could be free, and oneself. . . .

The Harvard of Eliot and the scholars and idealists exerted influence upon all American academic institutions, an influence making for liberation and a genuine respect for the individual. But times have changed. . . . The ideal of a republic of letters may be obsolete: possibly we ought to prepare for a world of cliques and castes. . . . [O]ur premier institution for the training of leaders is occupying itself with flavors and savors, nuances and shades. . . .

Let the seventh sons of the seventh sons of Harvard form a club, if they choose, and flavor it highly or subtly as they like. But the flavor for the whole of a great public institution like Harvard? It is a fair rule that flavors widespread become an abomination. The flavor of fish may be very delectable, in a tureen. In the public water supply it is discouraging ("The Flavor of Harvard," 1922, p. 323).

As protests mounted against the quota system both within and outside Harvard, the Overseers sought to defuse the issue by turning it over to a faculty committee of 13, including three Jews, which was assigned the general task of reevaluating all admissions policies. Lowell was seemingly defeated when the committee brought in a report in 1923 that was accepted by the Governing Boards, repudiating quotas, and reaffirming Harvard's tradition of "equal opportunity for all, regardless of race and religion." The committee also argued that the College must be aware that "even so rational a method as a personal conference or intelligence test, if now adopted here as a means of selection, would inevitably be regarded as a covert device to eliminate those deemed racially or socially undesirable." It went on, however, to then recommend in the interests of making Harvard a much more national university than it was that in regions outside of the East and North, where high schools were not as good as in the Northeast, the entrance examination be waived "for students in the highest seventh of their graduating class, if they had completed an approved course of study, and had the recommendation of their school."

This new policy of reducing Harvard's rigorous standards of admission for those outside the eastern seaboard in order "to raise the proportion of country boys and students from the interior," to gain a "regional balance," would mean, according to a contemporary article in the *Harvard Graduates' Magazine,* that "the proportion of Jewish students will be reduced," since it will "bring to Harvard more students from the high schools of towns and smaller cities, especially of the West and South" (Holmes, 1923, p. 533). The committee also proposed to make it more difficult for students to transfer to Harvard, and to bar from admission "students who cannot write acceptable English." As the alumni were informed: "These two provisions will keep out a group of students in which many are certainly unfit. Of these, at present, a considerable proportion are Jews, but they will not be excluded, either in name or in fact, on racial grounds" (ibid., p. 533). Thus the report rebuffed President Lowell publicly, but the admissions policy was effectively changed to accomplish the purposes he desired. Jewish enrollment was to drop from well over 20 percent to about 10 percent of the undergraduate body (Steinberg, 1974, pp. 28–30).

Debates over the "composition" of the student body continued to concern faculty and students. A faculty committee report in 1925, while reiterating the principle of nondiscrimination with respect to race or religion, discussed the need to consider "personality" factors. But as an article in the *Gadfly,* the organ of the Liberal Club, commented: "Boys with 'personalities' bearing a marked racial stamp will not be excluded on grounds of race"; but "racial traits" associated with Jews are often regarded as personality ones ("The New Admissions Plan," 1926, p. 5). More strikingly, a Student Council Committee on Education submitted a report in the spring of 1926 which emphasized that "no college can admit unassimilables with impunity." It urged that Harvard "avoid all extremes and preserve a certain proportion between more or less 'unassimilable' groups. There should not be more than 10 percent of all the latter groups at the very most." Those who cannot "be prepared in all qualities of mind, character and personality to assume positions of active, helpful leadership in the world," and "who show no desire, and perhaps have no capacity for entering in the larger life of the college are to be rejected" (ibid., 1926, p. 5).

This report is illustrative of the close rapport which Lowell had established with the campus politicians who controlled student government. Almost from the day he took office, the President spent considerable time supporting extracurricular undergraduate life, both athletic and nonathletic, and his concerns paid off, particularly in the 1926 report of the Committee on Education. The report strongly reflected Lowell's values not only with respect to admissions policies, but even more importantly for the future of the school, it recommended as its own independent plan his life-long ambition to create the equivalent of Oxbridge residential colleges, which would house almost all undergraduates in units to which faculty tutors would be affiliated. Support from the Student Council proved to be Lowell's trump card with which to defeat the critics of the plan, who were quite numerous among both students and faculty.

Soon thereafter, in his annual report for 1927–1928, Lowell announced that a benefactor, who turned out to be Edward Harkness, a Yale graduate, had agreed to finance the costs of building the residential units. The $10 million which were donated were used to build seven Houses, with masters' residences and rooms for tutors. Lowell had his way against considerable opposition through his ability to raise the funds and secure Student Council endorsement. The Houses were well in operation by the time of his retirement in 1933 (Lowell, 1934, pp. 318–322; Yeomans, 1948, pp. 180–195; Morison, 1936c, pp. 476–479; Harris, 1970, pp. 36–37; Jencks & Riesman, 1962, pp. 731–773).

There seems little doubt that Lowell also had his way with respect to limiting the number of Jews among the student body and on the faculty during the 1920s and 1930s. Reports from faculty indicate that the percentage among undergraduates in the early thirties at the end of the Lowell administration was about ten and that there were only a handful of Jews who attained senior faculty status. In at least two cases, Jews were kept on with the understanding that they would be paid from outside funds contributed by a wealthy Jewish family. No Jews were appointed to the Law School faculty after Felix Frankfurter until 1939, although Frankfurter had proposed some distinguished ones on earlier occasions. In these respects, of course, Harvard was no worse, and with respect to student enrollment, perhaps somewhat better than other elite universities. An effort to evaluate the extent of restrictions against Jews in 1930 by Heywood Broun and George Britt placed Harvard in the "moderate" category, below those judged "none," or "slight," but better than those placed in the "pronounced" class, which included Columbia, Cornell, Johns Hopkins, Northwestern, Virginia, and Yale (Broun & Britt, 1931, pp. 89–90). Harvard, which had a few Jewish senior professors in the early thirties, may have been far from the most discriminatory in this respect as well. A comprehensive report prepared for the American Jewish Committee in 1937 concluded that "It is very difficult these days for Jews to become full professors in the leading universities. In order to attain such rank, they must have achieved distinction in their respective fields of national and international character" (Karpf, 1937, pp. 61–62). The limitations in the job market for Jews were used by various graduate schools as reasons for curtailing admissions on the assumption that they would be unable to place their Jewish students. Albert Sprague Coolidge of the Harvard chemistry department told a Massachusetts legislative committee shortly after World War II that his department had followed such a policy (McWilliams, 1948, pp. 138–139). James Conant, Lowell's successor as Harvard President, had been unable as a Professor of Chemistry to place Jewish students, some of whom he had regarded as among the best he ever had.

POLITICAL ACTIVITY IN THE YARD

The Harvard Liberal Club, although quite weak in the apolitical atmosphere of the mid-twenties, also took on the President with respect to a less significant internal issue, the proposal to build a Memorial Church in the Yard in honor of the World War I dead. The Liberal Club strongly opposed the suggestion, and the *Gadfly* reported a poll in which only 251 voted for the new chapel while 656 were against it. The majority of those surveyed favored using the money for a new gymnasium or swimming pool. When the club set up tables in the Yard to collect petitions against the Memorial, the University ordered them to stop ("Student Poll Resurrected," 1927, p. 1). The church was, of course, built.

Small socialist and other left groups existed at Harvard in the twenties in addition to the relatively vigorous Liberal Club, which was able to get out its magazine, the *Gadfly*, for most of the decade. A report on student activities in 1924 stated that "the one topic which came close to rivaling football in interest this fall was politics. Early in the year, the liberal minded of the University gathered together into a highly inflammable LaFollette-Wheeler [Progressive-Socialist candidates] Club, and did their best to prove that the Harvard banner and the red flag of liberalism were as one. At this the Harvard Democratic and Republican Clubs, long dormant, awoke with a start, and began to defend themselves against the liberal menace" (Nichols, 1924, p. 301).

Although LaFollette secured a respectable vote in the 1924 straw vote, the majority were clearly Republican and conservative. An indication of the distribution of sentiment in the Yard in the mid-twenties may be seen in the fact that in 1924, a majority, 56 percent, backed the conservative Republican incumbent, Coolidge; 26 percent supported the conservative Democrat, Davis; while 17 percent voted for the Progressive and Socialist parties' candidate, LaFollette. The Harvard left vote was slightly higher than the 14.5 percent reported as a total for 120 colleges polled and almost identical to what LaFollette received among the electorate in the November elections ("The Vote . . . ," 1924, p. 2).

The most important single issue arousing leftist sentiment among intellectuals and students in the mid to late 1920s was the case of the two anarchists, Sacco and Vanzetti. Their conviction in 1921 for murder had resulted in a crescendo of protest among liberals and leftists around the world. Gradually, many caught up in the protest became convinced that the American juridical and political system had been deliberately mobilized to execute two innocent men. The conflict between the protesters in the American intellectual world and the lay powers enlarged the cleavages between the two to the point where each was ready to believe the worst about one another (Earnest, 1953, p. 279; Felix, 1965).

Since the trial took place in Boston, Harvard was much involved in the protest on both faculty and student level. Law School Professor Felix Frankfurter was probably the most persuasive legal mind writing on their behalf (Felix, 1965, pp. 146–160; Frankfurter, 1927). President Lowell chaired a three-man Advisory Committee appointed by Governor Fuller, which concluded that the two anarchists were guilty (Felix, 1965, pp. 191–202). As one historian of higher education reported on its impact on academe:

The case . . . emphasized the dichotomy between the professors and the powers which ruled the academic community. . . . The socially and politically aware members of the academic community were imbued with a deep distrust and hostility to the conservative elements in the church, business and government. A. Lawrence Lowell will go down in history not as the man who tried to introduce greater democracy among Harvard freshman or as the defender of academic freedom, but as the man who sent Sacco and Vanzetti to death.

For hundreds of professors and students this long agony had brought an awareness of the world outside the colleges. Increasingly academic life shifted from books and football to a concern with the social, political and economic order. Many a student who knew nothing about the trial of Socrates became deeply stirred over that of Sacco and Vanzetti (Earnest, 1953, pp. 280–281).

At Harvard, the Socialist Club published a denunciation of President Lowell for his part in the execution as the lead article in their periodical ("Students in Revolt . . . ," 1933, p. 7). Yet in the Presidential straw vote in 1928, a majority (52 percent) supported Herbert Hoover—much less, however, than the two-thirds among collegians nationally. The Democratic candidate Al Smith was the choice of 44 percent of the 4,005 Harvard students who voted, while 4 percent opted for Norman Thomas on the Socialist ticket ("Harvard Poll for Hoover," 1928, p. 27).

Any effort to evaluate Lowell's actions inside or outside of Harvard Yard must be premised on his basic commitment to his conception of the *noblesse oblige* values of a ruling class of gentlemen, an aristocratic elite, which included both those born to the status and those assimilated to its values and manners at establishment schools. Harvard's main contribution to American society must be new highly trained members of the elite, who had been disciplined and socialized in the classroom, on the athletic field, and in the Houses. As he once put it:

The elite should be, if possible, both intellectually and physically superior. That among them some should be in mind and others in physique above the ordinary level is not enough. We should strive to develop mind and body to the intent that men may be fit for the calls that will be made upon their force and endurance. The Japanese samurai were both warriors and scholars, bearing two swords and a tablet for writing poetry (Yeomans, 1948, p. 336).

Yet a survey of the backgrounds of those who participated in varying ways in the Harvard of the 1920s suggested that, in spite of Lowell's efforts, the separation between undergraduates of different social-class backgrounds that clearly characterized Eliot's regime, continued. In 1924, Corliss Lamont, then a Harvard student, found that students who had prepared for college at private high schools dominated all the formal extracurricular activities "with hardly a single exception." Men from public schools, on the other hand seemed "to spend a larger proportion of their time in study. . . . They win far more than their due share of honors and distinctions." Thus, Lamont's data appeared to show that the control of undergraduate life by the "Preppies" was not a result of the activities of "cliques of men from the private schools," but rather "arises from a fundamental difference in the major interests of the two groups" (Munro, 1924, pp. 439–440). The Harvard "elite" remained sharply divided between those who took seriously Lowell's emphasis on the extracurricular and those who focused on their studies, and the difference was class-related.

Lowell's conservative political views were expressed not only in the role he played in endorsing the execution of Sacco and Vanzetti (a trial whose validity still remains a matter of controversy today), but also in his strong opposition to labor unions, in his efforts to prevent liberal Louis Brandeis from being confirmed as a Justice of the U. S. Supreme Court, in his fight against the Child Labor Amendment, in his antagonism to various welfare measures of Harvard alumnus Franklin

Roosevelt in the 1930s, and in his support of proposals to create a third conservative party to beat back the reform wave stimulated by the Depression (Yeomans, 1948, pp. 326, 410–424, 483–496; Felix, 1965, pp. 193–194).

THE DECLINE OF SCHOLARSHIP

If Lowell is to be praised for his creation of elements of a collegiate system of living and learning, a condition for accomplishing this was to concentrate much of his energy and Harvard's resources into construction. As Morison notes: "Mr. Lowell was the greatest builder of any Harvard president; and during the last twenty years of his presidency, more new construction was completed than in all Harvard history previous to his day" (Morison, 1936c, p. 449). The building was, of course, motivated by Lowell's desire to surround the students with a total intellectual and social environment with college tutors in the Houses who would produce an educated elite fit to govern, regardless of social origins, on the model of the English governing classes. Such an emphasis necessarily led him to be less concerned with maintaining the scholarly character of the Harvard faculty, evidenced in part by the frequent departure of young Jewish scholars who had made their mark in graduate school or in low-level appointments. A survey conducted in 1925 which asked departments in liberal arts disciplines around the country to judge the top departments in their fields indicated that Harvard had slipped from the top position it had in 1910 to second behind the University of Chicago (Keniston, 1959, p. 119).

The findings of the 1925 survey were reiterated in a more informal canvass of "the preferences of the winners of fellowships, both foreign and domestic," reported in 1933, the year of Lowell's retirement from the Harvard Presidency, by Frederick Keppel, the head of the Carnegie Corporation. He credited Harvard's decline in "men of outstanding scholarly distinction" to the fact that Lowell "is quite frankly more interested in the urbane scholar of the British type, who will charm and stimulate the undergraduate, than in the authority of the multiple-footnote variety, who might prove more useful to the candidate for the doctorate." More devastating, however, was his belief that Harvard under Lowell had fallen out of touch with the rest of academe, that it could be said that "Harvard College has had practically no influence upon American education during the past twenty-five years" (Keppel, 1933, pp. 759, 762).

Similar complaints about the Lowell regime had been growing within Harvard Yard among both students and faculty. Bernard DeVoto, writing in the *Harvard Graduates' Magazine* at the end of the period, noted, as did others, concern that the physical quality of Lowell's Houses was not matched by the academic quality of the low-paid, low-status tutors. He reported the common "belief that the faculty of Harvard is not, on the whole, as good as it used to be. . . . One hears that the distinction of this department has lapsed, or that there is much dead wood in another one, or that the best students of a given field now go to Chicago or Columbia or Wisconsin, whereas once they came to Harvard. . . . One hears . . . that Harvard has lost her leadership, . . . is letting universities once less important surpass her in the only thing for which a university exists, its faculty." And he concluded by making a plea which in effect reversed that which Lowell and others had voiced against Eliot a quarter of a century earlier.

We have the College now, splendidly overbuilt, tricked out with new methods of instruction whose defect is that not enough of the men who manipulate them are good men, remodeled, redesigned, re-Housed. . . . So—let the College rest awhile. It is time to give us back the University. That cannot be done with bricks and mortar, or with systems and teaching plans and graded classifications of degrees. It can only be done with men.

A good many of us believe that the greatness of Harvard has been its great men, not its buildings, not even its innovations. . . . It is possible, remember, for Harvard to lose its honored place at the head of American universities. . . . If it does, it will happen because we have chosen other objectives than a faculty of first-rate men. Some of us have been genuinely afraid. We don't care where the faculty is recruited or how it is housed, but we do care who belongs to it (DeVoto, 1933, pp. 95–97).

The conclusion that Harvard had declined severely in scholarly quality was also attested to by none other than Lowell's successor as President in 1933, James B. Conant. Conant impressed some members of the Corporation, before he even was on their list of 40 candidates for the succession, by the clear quality of his judgment that Lowell's concentration on building the collegiate system harmed the intellectual standards of the institution.

I was disturbed by its effects on appointments. Looking over the fence at other departments and listening to the usual faculty gossip, I was convinced we were filling up the younger ranks with mediocre men whose merit consisted largely in their willingness to be tutors. . . . The standards for promotion were not high enough to suit me. . . .

A university . . . was a collection of eminent scholars. If the permanent professors were the most distinguished in the world, then the university would be the best university. The quality of those appointed to life positions was therefore fundamental. If a man was made a professor for personal reasons, as I believed was happening, or even for being a helpful member of a department or for devotion to Harvard, then Harvard was to that extent betraying its trust.... To fill one of these positions with a second-rate person was to betray a trust—to be guilty of almost criminal negligence.

I don't doubt I showed considerable emotion (for a New Englander) in describing what I thought was going on at Harvard in this matter of choosing professors. Of course, I was not speaking or, indeed, thinking solely in terms of natural scientists. I knew from my friends in the humanities and social sciences what was happening in these areas, and I thought the present policy was leading Harvard downhill (Conant, 1970, pp. 82–83).

In selecting James Conant to replace Lowell, the Governing Boards of the University once again followed the model established when choosing his two immediate predecessors, Eliot and Lowell, scholars who had been "reformers," critics of administration policies. The boards used the election of a new President as an opportunity to reverse direction, to modify the deficiencies caused by apparent overconcentration on one aspect of the University's function. Eliot, the dedicated chemist and advocate of the great University, was chosen to convert a college into a university. He was replaced by the humanistic Anglophile political scientist Lowell, who had sharply criticized Eliot for neglecting the College, undergraduate education. And he, in turn, was now succeeded by one of his sharpest faculty critics, another chemist, who sought a return to Eliot's emphasis on building a great research faculty.

6. The Protest of the Thirties

The various waves of protest that had characterized the American campus in the twenties—first the revulsion over the results of the war and the postwar repression; then the severe changes in "manners and morals" with respect to law obedience (bootleg whiskey), dress, and sex; and finally the demonstrations against the conviction of Sacco-Vanzetti—seemed to have vanished by the last year of the prosperous decade (Lipset, 1972b, pp. 159–174). The magazine, *The New Student*, which had been the chief expression of campus protest all through the 1920s, ceased publishing in the spring of 1929 convinced there was no longer an audience for it. Walter Lippmann, ex-Harvard Socialist, commented: "What most distinguished the generation who have approached maturity since the debacle of idealism at the end of the war is not their rebellion . . . but their disillusionment with their own rebellion" (Lippmann, 1929, p. 17). Another veteran of political wars along the Charles River, Harold Laski, after a trip to the United States in the first years of the depression, was surprised to find relatively little interest in politics of any kind among undergraduates. He wrote a plaintive article in 1931, "Why Don't Your Young Men Care?" (Laski, 1931, pp. 129–136).

Yet some of the students of the nation and at Harvard did begin to care in the sense that Laski desired. As compared to the late twenties, left-wing support grew rapidly. A national straw vote in 1932 revealed that 18 percent of the 58,686 students canvassed were for Norman Thomas, the Socialist candidate, while 1 percent favored the Communist, William Z. Foster. Half of them were for the reelection of Herbert Hoover, a sharp decline from the two-thirds he secured in 1928, and 31 percent backed Franklin Roosevelt. At Harvard, the Socialist vote was almost as high, 17 percent, but Hoover had also increased his strength to 61 percent of the 2,842 ballots, while Harvard alumnus Franklin Roosevelt secured but 22 percent (Cowan, 1960, pp. 5–7, 8, 17, 18).

Organizationally, the student section of the LID, which had been relatively moribund (2,000 members nationally in 1927), began to grow rapidly (Altbach, 1974, pp. 73–74). Its Harvard affiliate, the Socialist Club, which had declined after the Sacco-Vanzetti case, now revived; its most significant activity in 1929–30 according to an official history of the League was exposing "the shabby treatment of the scrubwomen by the university, which was paying them under the minimum prescribed by the state law!" (*Students in Revolt . . .* , 1933, p. 8). At the end of 1931 the national SLID held its largest conference in many years with 200 delegates present, and it continued to increase steadily in the next few years (Rawick, 1957, p. 275). The Communists formed their own group, the National Student League (NSL), to compete with the SLID. From 1932 to 1935, the two groups frequently cooperated on individual campuses until their national organizations merged into the American Student Union (ASU) in 1935.

One of the key experiences which affected the concerns of the emerging campus radical movement involved Harvard students, a jointly sponsored SLID-NSL tour in 1932 to the mining regions of Kentucky then undergoing violent strife between coal miners and owners. The 80 students from various eastern colleges were threatened with being lynched, and were then forced by the District Attorney of Harlan County and sheriff's deputies to leave the state. Two of the students, including Herbert Robbins of Harvard (now a Professor of Mathematical Statistics at Columbia), presented a petition for a federal investigation to "the secretary of the secretary of the secretary of" President Hoover, but nothing followed (Wechsler, 1935, pp. 97–105). The official reaction to this trip was to become a major part of the folklore of the student movement of the thirties, informing those involved of the biases of authority, much as stories of dealings with southern sheriffs and governments were to affect their successors in the movements of the 1960s.

Robbins, upon his return to Harvard, helped to form a chapter of the NSL, of which Harry Marks (now Professor of History at the University of Connecticut) became president. A small SLID also existed, which included George Edwards (later a judge in Michigan) and Lewis Feuer (currently Professor of Sociology at the University of Toronto, and chronicler of worldwide student activism). Cooperating with them was the Harvard Liberal Club, which had become particularly active in calling campus attention to conditions in Fascist Italy and Nazi Germany.

By the spring of 1934, the Harvard radicals were sufficiently numerous and aggressive to gain considerable publicity through their efforts to protest against Nazism and war. A visit to Boston in the spring by the German cruiser, the *Karlsruhe*, was met by a large demonstration which included many Harvard and MIT students. A Harvard student was arrested for gaining access to the deck of the cruiser, and the crowd was forcibly dispersed by the Boston police. The event was later described in a detailed report by a group of Harvard students whose conclusions were supported in an "Introduction" by three leading faculty members, Arthur N. Holcombe, Ralph Barton Perry, and William Ernest Hocking. They protested the "unenlightened, uncalled for, and brutal [police] tactics," in which "arrests were made without due cause and with completely unjustified violence," with some of the arrestees being "slugged" in the station house (Dennet et al., 1934). Concern over the arrests and mistreatment of Harvard students enabled the radicals to form a broad protest committee, including representatives from a variety of nonpolitical campus groups. This effort was notable publicly for the aforementioned report, and privately for a demand from the representative of the *Crimson* that as a condition for its support no Jew serve as a member of the protest committee.

The bigoted behavior of the *Crimson*, which generally took an antiradical position through the thirties, pointed up the predominantly conservative character of the student body. On April 13, 1934, when about 200 Harvard students took part in a mass meeting for peace held at Widener Library as part of a national antiwar "strike" called by the SLID and the NSL, the *Crimson* announced that the Michael Mullins Marching and Chowder Club also intended to demonstrate:

At exactly eleven o'clock the meeting began. Within three minutes could be heard the oncoming tread of the men of Michael Mullins who strode on to the grounds with large, flamboyant placards. As they marched in goose-step fashion, they raised their arms in Hitler salutes while the men in front lifted a placard: DOWN WITH PEACE.

One of the leaders was draped in towels; another wore a full-fledged Nazi uniform; still a third, dressed in Boy Scout attire, tooted a bugle. When a speaker sought to address the crowd, the men of Mullins rushed forward to present him with an engraved medal. When another arose, he was immediately pelted by missiles and shouted down.... Tiring of this exhibit, the marchers adjourned to another section of the quad to conduct their own mock-meeting; speakers, somewhat self-consciously but gradually won over by the force of their own personalities, heiled Hitler, war and the extermination of heretics. And hundreds of residents of Harvard University joined enthusiastically in the show, halting only momentarily to shout final defiance at the outnumbered, hapless sponsors of the antiwar meeting (Wechsler, 1935, pp. 348–349; Cain, 1963, pp. 231–232; Cowan, 1960, p. 5–17).

Conflict between Harvard opponents and supporters of Nazism (there was a campus chapter of the Friends of New Germany) reached a new crescendo later that spring. The chief marshall of the alumni events at commencement, Dr. Eliot Cutler, named Ernst F. S. Hanfstaengl, a German member of the twenty-fifth reunion class, to the honorary post of aide to the marshall. Hanfstaengl was a leading Nazi and close personal friend of Adolf Hitler. The announcement aroused considerable protest from students, faculty, and alumni. Although President Conant was deeply offended by the designation of Hanfstaengl, there was nothing he could do, since the alumni celebration was completely in the hands of the reunion class marshall. The *Crimson*, on the other hand, expressed its displeasure at the protests, which it regarded as exhibiting "bad manners." To make amends, it proposed that the Nazi be granted an honorary degree in view of his role as a distinguished German alumnus.

The *Crimson's* reaction did not typify the dominant sentiment at Harvard, or at least the most impassioned feelings, which were anti-Nazi. Hanfstaengl did not have an easy visit to his alma mater. He was "guarded to the hilt by police in and out of uniform." Anti-Nazi slogans were on many buildings. "His hat was stolen and readdressed to him 'Care of Adolf Hitler.' On its crown, in Hebrew letters, were inscribed the words: 'Thou shalt not kill' " (Wagner, 1950, p. 277).

At the meeting of the alumni, a demonstration broke out while Conant was delivering the customary address by the President. Protesters interrupted the speech to scream denunciations of the Nazis, Hitler, and Hanfstaengl. Four were arrested in the Yard, and seven others taking part in a demonstration in Harvard Square were also taken in custody. The University was able to get the charges against those held for the interruptions at the meeting squashed (Conant, 1970, pp. 140–142; Wechsler, 1935, pp. 350–351; Kahn, 1969, p. 100).

Although Conant could not have been happy about the interruption of his talk, his deep-rooted hatred of Nazism led him, in effect, to welcome the publicity that it gave to Hanfstaengl's ties to Hitler. Before coming to the alumni reunion, the German alumnus had written to Conant offering to donate $1,000 to establish "the Dr. Hanfstaengl scholarship," to "enable an outstanding Harvard student, preferably the son of one of my old classmates, to study in Germany in any field of art or science." Conant recommended to the Corporation that they refuse the money, and he credited the demonstration with helping to convince the Fellows to agree with him. "The protesters on commencement afternoon had achieved one end. They had given vast publicity to Hanfstaengl's relation to Hitler—a relation, it is important to note, that Hanfstaengl never denied. . . . [T]he demonstration commencement afternoon now meant that the Corporation's action was bound to be regarded by the public as a judgment on the Nazis" (Conant, 1970, p. 350). The *Crimson*, however, disagreed and attacked the President for "his outspokenness and his lack of 'good taste.'" His style was not a "gentleman's way" (Wechsler, 1935, p. 350).

The issue was renewed in the fall of 1934 when Matthew T. Mellon, who had been a student at the University of Freiburg and was now enrolled at the Harvard Graduate School, offered the Corporation $1,500 to enable a Harvard graduate to study in Germany. The Corporation was about to accept the offer when the *Crimson*, reversing its role of the previous academic year, exposed the fact that a German newspaper had published a cable from Mellon indicating that his offer was intended as a protest against Harvard's rejection of Hanfstaengl's gift. The Corporation, thereupon, voted to decline Mellon's gift as well ("Hanfstaengl's Name . . . ," 1934, p. 287).

One year later, in 1935, the two radical groups were able to attract a much larger audience of 600 to their April peace-day strike, at which they asked the audience to take a version of the Oxford Oath: "We pledge not to support the government of the United States in any war it may conduct." The Michael Mullins brigade once again tried to break up the meeting, but they were stopped by Harvard police, under orders to protect the meeting, and general student attitudes, which, while clearly not sympathetic to the radicals, opposed vigilante tactics. The Mullins men again used Nazi symbols and chanted "We want Hitler." More frightening was the action of some of them in riding around the University with a machine gun mounted on a car (Wechsler, 1935, pp. 79, 351).

The voiced opposition to Nazism, the protection of the rights of free speech of radicals within Harvard Yard, the unwillingness to prosecute anti-Nazi demonstrators, did not stem from liberal attitudes among the members of the Governing Boards, who were largely conservative, wealthy Republicans. Their distaste for conventional liberal and New Deal policies was clear. Thus, in 1934, when faced with the need to provide financial assistance to students whose families had become impoverished, Harvard set up a student work program using its own funds. It refused to take part in a federal program to provide jobs for students through the Emergency Relief Administration. Although this was done ostensibly because Harvard did not need the money, there is some indication of principled opposition from within the Corporation. (In 1941, Harvard finally did accept $80,000 from the National Youth Administration for these purposes.) In 1935, when Henry Wallace, as Secretary of Commerce, was nominated to receive an honorary degree, some members of the Board of Overseers opposed the proposal—the only time this happened during Conant's presidency—which finally carried with Conant's strong support. In 1936, at the tercentenary celebration of Harvard's founding, former President Lowell, who was to preside at the meeting that closed the celebration, indicated that he would not do so if Franklin Roosevelt, President of the United States and Harvard alumnus, was to address it. Judge Learned Hand, the president of the Alumni Association, had to convince Lowell that not to have the President of the United States speak would be a public scandal. And as Conant noted, President Roosevelt, "who knew he was facing a predominantly hostile audience, began with a subtle yet bold defiance."

A hundred years ago when Harvard was celebrating its two hundredth anniversary, Andrew Jackson was President and Harvard men were sore afraid. Fifty years ago, when Harvard was celebrating its two hundredth and fiftieth anniversary, Grover Cleveland was its President and Harvard men were sore afraid. Today, I am President (Conant, 1970, pp. 113–118, 147, 153, 155–156).

The President faced a friendlier audience among the students, since in the 1936 *Crimson* straw vote he secured 45 percent of the 2,700 ballots, much more than four years earlier, but still less than the 51 percent for Republican Alfred Landon. Norman Thomas received but 3 percent, less than his vote in the Yard in 1928 ("University Favors . . . ," 1936, p. 1). The bulk of organized liberalism and radicalism as represented by the American Student Union was strongly behind Roosevelt this time.

Conant and the Harvard faculty had a target closer at home when they resisted the passage of a teachers' oath bill through the Massachusetts legislature in 1934–35. Conant rallied the presidents of other Massachusetts colleges in opposition. Samuel Eliot Morison wrote learned historical articles designed to "show the utter futility af attempting to control a person's attitude by demanding oaths." When the bill passed, a number of Harvard faculty announced that they could not sign the oath in good conscience ("The Teachers' Oath," 1935, pp. 86–87; Mather, 1935, pp. 181–182). A compromise was finally worked out with the attorney general which permitted the objecting professors to sign with addenda explaining their reservations (Conant, 1970, pp. 451–453). Faculty agitation against the law continued for some years. Students also took part in these protests.

FACULTY ACTIVISM

In commenting on the mood at Harvard in the mid-thirties, James Wechsler, then a national leader of the newly born American Student Union, noted that "One of the most curious paradoxes is that liberal sentiment and concern for social issues is probably more pronounced among faculty members than among students" (Wechsler, 1935, p. 353). The record, as recalled by participants, would seem to bear him out, particularly with respect to younger and nontenured faculty who were probably the most liberal or radical segment of the community. These faculty also formed an activist organization, the Cambridge Union of University Teachers (a chapter of the American Federation of Teachers), as their response to the strains and ideological developments of the Depression era. The group, which functioned for the rest of the thirties, had a membership of between 80 and 100, largely nontenured appointees.

The Cambridge teachers union was organized in the fall of 1935 by Lewis Feuer, an assistant in the Philosophy Department, and Alan and Paul Sweezy, who held junior positions in the Economics Department. J. Raymond Walsh, an Instructor in Economics, became its first president. Among the tenured faculty who joined the group were F. O. Matthiessen in History and Literature, Henry Hart in the Law School, Kirtley F. Mather in Geology, David Prall in Philosophy, Rupert Emerson in Government, and Crane Brinton in History ("A Teachers' Union," 1935, pp. 193–194). Among the junior faculty, it included at times men like Abram Bergson and J. Kenneth Galbraith, later professors of Economics at Harvard, Robert G. Davis and Ernest J. Simmons of the English Department, both later of Columbia, Robert K. Merton of Sociology, also later of Columbia, Max Lerner in Government, Granville Hicks in English, Frank Manuel of History, later of New York University, and Robert A. Gordon, later of Berkeley, in Economics.

The group, many of whose leading members considered themselves socialists, communists, or unattached radicals, operated more as a semipolitical group than a trade union organized for collective bargaining purposes. Alan Sweezy, in fact, announced "The Union is not being formed for the purpose of raising the standards of living or of improving the working conditions of its members. On the contrary most of its members are convinced that their position is a very favorable one, as compared with the great mass of the community" ("A Teachers' Union," 1935, p. 232). The union sought to influence units of the Boston-area trade-union movement to support a Labor party, and conducted meetings to discuss this issue (Sweezy, 1935, pp. 240–241). It also sponsored, together with the American Student Union chapter, well-known outside speakers, such as André Malraux on the Spanish Civil War and Louis Fischer on the Soviet Union. Curiously, the executive committee of the Union proved unresponsive to a request that they take up the issue of discrimination against Jews in appointments, presumably because they thought that the matter was hopeless.

The most controversial issue in the Union's history, which also concerned the ASU chapter, revolved around the failure of the University to reappoint two leading Union members, J. Raymond Walsh, its president, and Alan R. Sweezy, a member of its executive committee. Since stories about this *cause célèbre* still circulate and have appeared in subsequent discussions of the role of faculty radicals, a report on the event seems warranted. The failure to retain Walsh and Sweezy, both of whom were known as "leftist" economists, stemmed from President Conant's efforts to tighten Harvard's procedures for appointing and promoting faculty and in part from financial constraints imposed by the Depression. For various reasons the number of nonpermanent faculty on annual or three-year term appointments had grown considerably relative to the tenured staff. Since the number to be given tenure could not increase much, Conant determined in 1936 on a policy which would limit severely those who could be kept on by any given department beyond their initial three-year appointments. This meant that departments having more junior faculty than they could retain would have to decide whom among them to recommend for reappointment. The others would be given two-year terminal appointments ("Personnel and Promotions at Harvard," 1939, pp. 180–185). This new policy forced departments to make hard, competitive decisions. In many departments where there was a surfeit of first-rate junior faculty, extremely competent men were asked to resign. Given the scarcity of permanent positions, Conant felt that it was better policy to make such hard decisions while those involved were still young, rather than push them on the labor market when they were older and higher priced.

In 1937, the Economics Department had seven instructors completing their initial terms, and the Dean's Office had determined that it could only recommend two for reappointment. When the Department proposed two candidates for these openings, Dean George Birkhoff sent the other five, including Walsh and Sweezy, letters notifying them that they were being recommended for a two-year term, after which they would not be eligible for reappointment at Harvard (Conant, 1970, pp. 158–162; The Special Committee . . . , 1938, pp. 3–6). Considerable discussion ensued both by members of the Economics Department and by the Union of University Teachers. Department members indicated that when voting to promote two to fill positions assigned to the Department by the Dean, they had not understood this policy to mean that the unrecommended other five could not stay on unless the Department was assigned more vacancies. Many members of the Union and some accounts in the newspapers suggested that the decision in the case of the two Union activists was connected with Dr. Walsh's criticism of former President Lowell on February 13, 1937, at the public hearing on the Child Labor Amendment held before a committee of the Massachusetts legislature, with the activities of the two men in the Cambridge Union of University Teachers, and with their radical opinions (The Special Committee . . . , 1938, p. 12).

Two student committees were established, one of students of Walsh and Sweezy, and the other at a mass student meeting, supposedly to represent the student body, the Temporary Student Committee on Instruction in the Social Sciences. In fact, the latter group largely represented the more activist and radical elements among the students. It was chaired by Rolf Kaltenborn, who was also President of the Harvard chapter of the American Student Union ("Walsh-Sweezy Case . . . ," 1938, p. 1). The Committee circulated petitions among the students asking for further investigation and reconsideration of the two cases. The *Crimson*, on the other hand, in an editorial "Tempest in a Teapot," as well as in subsequent statements, defended the action of the administration and attacked student protests as "ill timed and impolitic." The Temporary Committee, which became popularly known as the "Committee of 14," countered with statements arguing that the University should be aware of the need to provide students with "various shades of opinion" among the faculty, and urged that the "knowledge of the actualities of social change" required "practical participation and observation of its present workings," presumably presented in the courses of the two dismissed instructors. The Student Council, however, supported and justified the position of the administration, although it also decided to appoint a committee to look into the general issues of research versus teaching, procedures of "hiring and firing," and related matters raised by University policy.

The Cambridge Union of University Teachers also protested the action vigorously, arguing that the University was opposed to "liberal or radical" thought in the social sciences. Its principal statement was titled, "Is Harvard's Liberalism Myth or Reality?" A number of Union members decided to circulate a petition among faculty other than full professors addressed to a group of nine distinguished senior professors, summarizing the case as they saw it and requesting the nine to investigate the situation and inform the community as to the facts. The statement was signed by 131 faculty, most of whom were not members of the Union. The professors so petitioned agreed but first wrote to President Conant telling him of their intention to launch such an investigation unless he chose to appoint a committee of his own to do so. The President responded by designating the professors chosen by the Union as an official University committee appointed by him to review the "Walsh-Sweezy" case. The Committee of Eight included some of the University's most distinguished men: Ralph Barton Perry of Philosophy as Chairman; E. M. Dodd, Felix Frankfurter, and Edmund Morgan of the Law School; Kenneth Murdock of English; Arthur M. Schlesinger of History; Harlow Shapley of Astronomy; and W. S. Ferguson, the new Dean of the Faculty of Arts and Sciences.[1] This was clearly a very liberal committee, one that could not be accused of doing the administration's business. Its appointment had the effect of defusing much of the organized agitation.

The Report of the Committee, published as an 85-page printed document with an introduction by President Conant in June 1938, concluded without equivocation that there was no reason to suppose that any prejudice had affected the decision of the Economics Department to recommend two others ahead of Walsh and Sweezy ("The Walsh-Sweezy Case . . . ," 1938, pp. 1045–1056). Walsh himself recognized that under the standards employed for promotion he could not be considered until he "furnished evidence of scholarly capacity in the form of a manuscript of merit." Similarly, Sweezy "realized that, because of the paucity of his production, the application of currently accepted standards [for promotion] prevented the Department from making any such recommen-

---

[1]Two of the original nine to whom the petition was addressed did not serve on the committee: Samuel Eliot Morison of History was going on leave and he was replaced by Ferguson; Elmer Kohler of Chemistry died.

dation." Since no one in the administration had been involved in these initial Department decisions to recommend more productive scholars ahead of Walsh and Sweezy, it was clear also that neither the President nor the Dean had interfered with academic freedom (The Special Committee . . . , 1938, pp. 23–26).

The Committee did not stop at these conclusions, however, but also argued that the sudden imposition of new and apparently confusing policies with respect to retention and advancement had been unfair to those who assumed they would have more time to demonstrate their competence. It recommended that the implementation of the new rules be put off and that Walsh and Sweezy be given new terms, without limitations on the possibility of their being retained subsequently. The President and the Corporation refused this request on the grounds that events had shown that the restrictive promotion policy was justified and that applying it to Walsh and Sweezy was not a special case, since it was already operative generally. Given the fact that this obviously unbiased committee had decided that all the evidence demonstrated that there had been "no departure from Harvard's tradition of tolerance and of untrammelled scientific inquiry," the rebuff suffered by the student and faculty supporters of Walsh and Sweezy did not occasion any further public protest. Both men chose to resign from Harvard and take other positions rather than serve out their terminal appointments, thus ending Harvard's best-publicized modern case involving charges of denial of academic freedom. The Committee remained in existence for another year to consider general personnel policy and brought in a recommendation that junior faculty be dropped within a definite period of time unless they were given tenure (A Special Committee . . . , 1939).

CONCERN FOR FACULTY QUALITY

In evaluating the deeply argued controversy over Harvard's personnel policies in the 1930s, it is important to recognize that at the heart of the changes, as viewed by Conant and many faculty, was a desire to find means to improve the scholarly quality of the faculty. By limiting the number of tenured positions to a fixed relationship to the endowment and forcing "up or out" decisions on all nontenured faculty within an eight-year period, Conant's policies made it impossible to carry men who were not first-rate scholars indefinitely because they were "useful" teachers or House tutors, as had occurred under Lowell. Although many criticize academic tenure as a system that permits incompetents to stay on, it is much more accurate to view it as a procedure which forces universities to make hard judgments about their faculty within a limited time-span. It is easy to continue faculty from year to year, and suddenly realize that the institution is no longer in a position to decide adversely, particularly if the faculty member has been a reasonably conscientious teacher and a loyal citizen. The new Harvard personnel policy went even further in making it difficult to retain junior staff for any reason other than creative scholarship, by insisting that when a department had a tenure vacancy it must be filled competitively, that is, by considering all scholars in the given field anywhere as possible candidates on the same basis as nontenured staff at Harvard. And when a department made a recommendation, it was to be reviewed by an ad hoc committee, composed half of people in the field outside of Harvard and half of Harvard professors not in the department making the recommendation. By such means, it was hoped that Harvard could reduce the impact of academic "nepotism," of senior men choosing their disciples to succeed them, or of departments promoting "useful" colleagues from the junior ranks.

Such a system of selecting tenured faculty members necessarily comes close to eliminating teaching ability as an important criterion. Open competition implies almost total concern for scholarly creativity, for published work that is well regarded. Not surprisingly, many students opposed the Conant emphasis. The Student Council argued that "the quality of teaching will be seriously affected by the lack of flexibility in the administration's tenure policy." Various undergraduate organizations formed the "Student Committee to Save Harvard Education," and argued: "[T]eaching is the most important function of the University as far as the students are concerned, and we venture to say that it is the most important function the College performs." They contended that the new policy "has had, and will continue to have, disastrous effects upon the quality of Harvard instruction." As a compromise solution, they suggested that junior faculty who did not qualify for tenure but who were excellent teachers "be offered associate professorships without any guarantee of eventually receiving full professorships," and tenure (Goddard, 1939, pp. 216–218). The student protest fell on deaf ears. Harvard made its commitment to giving indefinite appointments solely to those who could meet the judgment of their discipline peers that they were among the most creative scholars in their field, a system which remains in force today.

As if to demonstrate that the adoption of the new system was not a product of any fear of hiring young radicals, Harvard in February 1938 offered an appointment to Granville Hicks as "Counsellor in the extracurricular reading of American history." This was a low-level tutorial post attached to a House "to encourage undergraduate interest in the national past." Hicks was probably the leading open Communist party literary intellectual in the United States at the time. He had been an editor of the *New Masses* and had written a Marxist analysis of American literature, *The Great Tradition*, as well as a biography of John Reed, the hero of Communist intellectuals in the thirties. Hicks had been dismissed from his job at Rensselaer Polytechnic Institute (RPI) after teaching for six years. His dismissal had received wide publicity as politically motivated, a charge made explicitly by an investigating committee for the AAUP.

As must have been anticipated, his Harvard appointment occasioned serious and continuing criticism from the press and politicians. Conversely, the *Crimson* described it as "the most positive academic step that the university had taken forward this year." The job, however, only lasted for one year. The following February, the University announced that none of the seven Counsellors in American Civilization would be reappointed, that their appointments had been "for one year only and not subject to renewal." Hicks suspected that this policy, which had not been told to him or the other counsellors earlier, had been formulated to get rid of him, but there is no evidence on the issue. While at Harvard, he was active in the Communist party branch there. It was composed of younger faculty, "some fifteen instructors and tutors" who met weekly in an apartment near the Yard. As he described their activities:

We sought to control the Teachers' Union, which was not difficult since our policies in this period of Communist moderation were acceptable to most liberals. We supported all Democratic Front activities in the area. We prepared two or three leaflets, including a fairly ambitious pamphlet on anti-Semitism. We talked about Marxism, the European situation, the New Deal (Hicks, 1965, pp. 154–156, 161–164, 170–171; Aaron, 1961, pp. 354–364; *Hearing Before Committee . . .* , 1953).

THE END OF THE FACULTY COUNCIL

The controversies over the Walsh-Sweezy case and the new personnel policies had aroused intense faculty concern that, ironically, resulted in the end of an experiment in representative government within the Faculty of Arts and Sciences that had begun soon after Conant took office. A largely elected Faculty Council of 60 members had been organized to handle the work usually dealt with at faculty meetings because for "years attendance at regular Faculty meetings had been very poor, and it was felt that a representative council would provide more steady attendance and insure a more thorough conduct of business." Full faculty meetings were still held on occasion, and could be called on demand. The heated personnel dispute led to "several very fully attended and lively meetings of the whole Faculty," and ultimately to the "demand that the Faculty Council be abolished, that the whole Faculty resume what some proudly call its independence, and even its sovereignty."

The Faculty Council was dropped. But as the editor of the *Harvard Alumni Bulletin* noted, this only meant that what some called the oligarchy of "Politicians" on the Council, would be replaced by a "kind of oligarchy of volunteers, habitually attendant, [who] would almost certainly come to stand for the Faculty of Arts and Sciences" and who might be even less representative of faculty opinion than the Council. Once the controversy was over, there was no reason to anticipate "that any great number of the Faculty will continue to attend regular Faculty meetings. There is, indeed, in the experience of the last thirty years, ample evidence that they will *not* attend such meetings" ("The Faculty Council," 1939, p. 179).

EXTERNAL PRESSURES

In reporting on the controversies of the 1930s, it should be noted that the University was under pressure from wealthy conservative alumni who regarded it as a bastion of radicalism and refused to contribute on that account. The biggest fund-raising effort of the decade, the Tercentenary Drive, was the only one in Harvard history to fail of its objectives, undoubtedly because of the effects of the Depression. Yet Seymour Harris in his history of *The Economics of Harvard* concludes that "it was particularly the 1936 fund which seemed to suffer from the charge of radicalism."

President Conant's program had to contend with alumni criticism of those who had created the New Deal. Harvard was not without responsibility, and particularly Felix Frankfurter, who had trained many of the bright young lawyers later to become Roosevelt's aides, was under attack. . . .

In the spring of 1936 the university was getting fifteen or twenty Frankfurter letters a day (Harris, 1970, pp. 277–278).

Ironically, while the Economics Department was being denounced for procapitalist bias by the student radicals, the record indicates that it was also under heavy and recurrent criticism from conservative businessmen for having predominantly leftist faculty. During the Tercentenary Fund campaign, Conant was often told of fears "expressed that unsound doctrine was being taught in the department of economics" (Conant, 1970, pp. 434–435). Walter Lippmann—who chaired the Overseers' Visiting Committee for the Department from 1933–1936 and who, as a leader of the Harvard Socialist Club, had been involved in sharp attacks on the Department three decades earlier for its conservative biases—repeatedly answered such criticisms in the Committee's Annual Reports, arguing that the issue must never be a man's opinions but "whether or not he arrived at his views by thorough scholarship and by intellectual processes which command the respect of his peers."

DEVELOPMENTS IN THE STUDENT UNION

The student activists continued as a visible force on campus for the rest of the decade. The Harvard Student Union had been formed at the end of 1935, following on the creation of the national ASU. At Harvard, it incorporated the Liberal Club, the Peace Society, as well as the local chapters of the SLID and the NSL. A number of subsequently prominent figures were among its officers and leading members. They included Pete Seeger, the folk singer; Jerome Himmelhoch, sociologist now at the University of Missouri; Robert Lane, Yale Professor of Political Science; Irwin Ross, well-known author; Joseph Levinson, Professor of Chinese History at Berkeley, who died in 1969; Adam Yarmolinsky, University Professor at the University of Massachusetts; and many others.

The group continued the practice of April peace meetings, but these changed from "strikes" against all wars to advocacy of collective-security policies by the Western countries and the Soviet Union to stop the fascist powers. Under Communist pressure, but with the support of many liberal members, the national ASU had dropped the Oxford Pledge and increasingly agitated for an end to American isolation and neutralist policies. This switch was facilitated by the dedicated support that radicals and liberals gave to the Loyalist side in the Spanish Civil War, a concern which led them to advocate repeal of the American Neutrality law barring military aid to foreign nations at war. In effect, from an antiwar movement at birth in 1935, the ASU became a supporter of an activist American foreign policy designed by some to make the United States an ally of the Soviet Union, and by others to press it to take the lead in an international antifascist alliance. By the elections of 1936, the Communists had become strong supporters of Franklin Roosevelt, seeing in him an advocate of collective security, and the leader of an American "Popular Front," uniting labor, minority groups, liberals, and the Communists. Although the Communists clearly gained organizational control of the national group, many non-Communist liberals were active in it until the Communists once again shifted their line and that of the ASU to oppose the western "imperialistic bloc," and to favor neutrality after the Hitler-Stalin pact and the outbreak of World War II in the latter half of 1939 (Draper, 1967, pp. 174–182; Rawick, 1959, pp. 314–322). At the national convention during the Christmas break in 1939, the delegates from Harvard were a major group in the small, liberal anti-Communist bloc which was defeated by large majorities on resolutions involving the larger European war and the condemnation of the Soviet invasion of Finland (Ross, 1940, pp. 48–49).

Many in the Harvard group were clearly much concerned with having a liberal image. A leader of the Union, Sherman Maisel (who later became a Governor of the Federal Reserve Board and Professor in the Business School of Berkeley), wrote at the end of 1937 that "the Student Union is first and foremost a liberal organization . . . in accord with the major policy objectives of the Roosevelt administration." He complained, however, that "throughout the nation, whether on campus or in the press, it is labeled radical, red, or communist." He proposed that, as a condition for the Harvard's unit staying in, the ASU "be reorganized on a more Federalistic basis; that the power to issue statements and take stands be removed from the National Executive Committee and put into the hands of the member chapters" (Maisel, 1937, p. 4).

The Harvard Student Union, in line with the Popular Front approach, sought to cooperate with other groups. It rarely attacked its rivals, although in February 1938 an analysis of the role of the *Crimson* complained that the paper was not neutral as it ought to be, "that during the last few years the conservative majority on the Editorial Board has . . . editorialize[d] their own opinions." The 1938 April Peace Demonstration, however, was sponsored in cooperation with the *Crimson*, the Neutrality Council, Phillips Brooks House, Avukah (a national student Zionist organization), and many other groups. The *Progressive* boasted that the Student Union was finally "participating in a united front with all elements of the college" ("Harvard Rallies for Tomorrow," 1938, p. 1).

The membership of the group seemed to vary between 100 and 250 during its short history. Almost half of them were lowerclassmen. Freshmen were far more active than the upperclassmen in the group.

The Union's leadership repeatedly complained about the small numbers who turned out for general membership meetings. But the meetings, in turn, were criticized by members as poorly organized and badly conducted, and getting little accomplished because of the vehemence of debate. It seems clear that the Harvard radicals and their liberal allies in the 1930s, while more numerous in absolute terms (though not proportionately) than the Socialist Club before World War I, were not as effective and had less influence on the campus generally. The issues posed by the Depression, the rise of fascism, and the approach of war in Europe left them divided among themselves. They failed to build an effective student movement, in part because they could not agree as to what kind of movement they should build and what objectives or even specific policies the Union should work for. With the exception of the Walsh-Sweezy case, which was quickly defused by the designation of the Committee of Eight as an official Harvard body, the University did not present them with any issue of repression, the kind around which student radicals are best able to mobilize broad support. Unlike many other schools, Harvard never raised any objections to their activities, or to those of other radical groups. Perhaps the broadest coalition in which the radicals were involved in the whole prewar decade occurred during the protests against police brutality and the arrests of students in the *Karlsruhe* episode in 1934. Without a local target, and with a continuing depression which pressed students to relate their studies to future career goals, Harvard students remained largely inactive politically, and the radicals turned in on themselves.

It is interesting to note that an article in the *Crimson* in the fall of 1936, which sought to account for the lack of militancy of Harvard students as compared to those in other universities, came to similar conclusions about the role of the university:

[I]n a college where each member, student and faculty alike, is left free to pursue his given task and no official thought is paid to caste, creed, color or previous condition of servitude, the average Harvard man finds it hard to see just what he can really agitate about. Student publications, for instance, are not victimized by political censorship, such as [occurs elsewhere] ... ("Indifference," 1936, p. 2).

THE POLITICS OF INTERVENTION

The outbreak of war in Europe in September 1939 occasioned what was probably the most intense period of politicization in Harvard's history between the Revolution and the Vietnam War. When the school reopened for the fall semester, it was bitterly divided between isolationist and antiwar elements (who appeared to dominate among the student body) and those favoring support to the Allies (who had growing support among the faculty). Many groups opposed the war: the Harvard Student Union; the Youth Committee Against the War; the American Independence League (formed in October, with 750 members at Harvard); and the Harvard Anti-War Committee, which ran large united rallies (Albright, 1962, pp. 11–13). The *Crimson* strongly backed an antiwar position in its editorials and news stories.

A civil liberties issue emerged in November when the University refused to allow use of its facilities for a meeting at which Earl Browder, then the national secretary of the Communist party, was scheduled to speak. After this action brought protests from various groups including the Harvard chapter of Phi Beta Kappa and the *Crimson*, President Conant announced that the decision did not imply a rule against Communists speaking, but that Browder had been banned because he was under indictment at the time for passport fraud (Frye, 1939, pp. 257–259).

The antiwar groupings did not keep their hands clean with respect to civil liberties for their opponents. When the University announced the appointment of a former director of the BBC as a lecturer, the action was widely denounced by student groups as designed to bring a pro-British propagandist on campus. John K. Fairbank, then a new, young member of the History Department, told the students that their welcome to a new faculty member was "malicious in tone, entirely unsupportable, and naive." The following fall, when a meeting was called to form a student branch of the American Defense Committee, a propreparedness organization, an effort was made to break it up by antiwar radicals (Albright, 1962, pp. 19, 43).

The antiwar strength began to be eroded by events. The Soviet invasion of Finland in December 1939 resulted in a condemnation by the Student Union after a stormy meeting, and the chapter, as noted above, quit the national organization after the annual convention. Although it began the academic year with 250 dues-paying members, it declined to less than 50 in the spring. The remnants of the Union, while opposed to the Finnish invasion, were to continue their opposition to the Roosevelt interventionist policy. But after the invasion of the Low countries in May 1940, they divided again, with the antiwar group retaining a majority (ibid., pp. 18, 31). The leftist antiwar forces were split in addition between a socialist-oriented one in the form of the Keep America Out of

War Committee, and the American Peace Mobilization, in which the Communists were a major force. When the two groups called separate peace rallies on the day of the traditional April peace demonstrations in 1940, the *Crimson* reported that the University and the police feared a riot between the supporters of the rival meetings. Fortunately for the peace of Harvard Yard, it rained (ibid., p. 28).

Although the invasion of Norway and the Low Countries and the fall of France in the spring of 1940 brought about increasing public commitment to the Allied cause among the faculty, many of whom spoke up about intervention, a survey of student opinion in April "showed the majority remained firmly opposed to the sale of material to the Allies," while favoring a proposal for a national referendum before a draft could take effect. An antiwar committee with representatives from Phillips Brooks House, the Harvard Student Union, the Harvard *Guardian*, the Pacifist League, the Law Students Association, and Phi Beta Kappa collected petitions promising that the signers would "not fight in war" (ibid., pp. 28, 33; Conant, 1970, p. 217). At commencement in June, the graduating seniors carried antiwar and anti-Roosevelt signs and cheered the class orator when he denounced interventionist, pro-Allied policies (Albright, 1962, pp. 34–35). When an "old grad, David Sigourney, '15, who fought in the last war, undertook to lecture the graduating class on their attitudes toward this one, the seniors responded with boos. The booing arose in such volume from the black-gowned mass of 1000 seniors, that they drowned him out" (Harper, 1940, p. 17).

President Conant and many members of the faculty took up the cudgels for a pro-Allied position. Conant had been arguing with students as the war progressed, and recalls thinking after one session: "That is what comes of extreme left-wing criticism of our capitalistic society: a student decided the government is not worth defending" (Conant, 1970, p. 216). In June, he joined the Committee to Defend America By Aiding the Allies, the foremost interventionist group, chaired by William Allen White. During the summer of 1940, a large group of faculty led by Ralph Barton Perry formed a chapter of the American Defense League to back preparedness and support of the Allies. This group secured 600 members. Many professors began speaking up and writing articles that deplored the pacifist position of the student groups as playing into the hands of the fascists.

The widespread character of faculty criticism led the editors of the *Harvard Crimson*, Spencer Klaw, and of the *Yale Daily News*, Kingman Brewster, Jr. (who played a major role in the founding of America First, the major isolationist organization) to publish a joint article defending the student antiwar position. They argued that Germany could not be defeated militarily, that even if the United States entered, the war would be prolonged indefinitely, and that such a long-term state of war would destroy democracy at home (Brewster & Klaw, 1940, pp. 277–279).

A poll reported in the *Crimson* in September 1940 pointed up the split between the students and the faculty. A majority of the former opposed Roosevelt's policies, while most of the latter gave the President considerable backing. Conant, who had spoken in a chapel talk at Harvard and on national radio in favor of "all possible aid to the allies without reservation," bore the brunt of the counterattack from the antiwar militants. As he recalled the events:

The *Crimson* attacked in force. My office was picketed (an operation which received little national publicity since commercial television did not yet exist). The *Harvard Lampoon* published a cartoon of the president of Harvard beating war drums. Between the halves in the Yale Bowl at New Haven, I was burlesqued in a skit staged by the *Crimson* and the *Lampoon*. A student with a big "1941" on his back lay down on the field reading a book when a figure appeared attired in cap, gown and mortarboard and wearing the sign "Conant." He began to annoy the student by parading around him with a wooden-bayoneted rifle. After a short interval, the student reluctantly took the gun but then turned to prodding "Conant" with the bayonet and chasing him around the field. Finally "Conant" was presented with a large retort and removed from the scene on a cart, presumably back to the laboratory (Conant, 1970, p. 222).

It may be noted that Conant, though under repeated attack from the campus antiwar movement, chose the occasion of an address to the ardently interventionist Jewish War Veterans to defend the moral integrity of "those of the younger generation who are strict isolationists or ardent pacifists. . . . I believe they are wrong. But let us be chary of passing harsh judgment upon them. Let us above all not accuse them of lack of idealism. Nothing could be further from the truth. Many are, rather, suffering from overexposure to one particular ideal, a noble one, but not always sufficient: the ideal of peace. In short, the errors of the youth of today, if they be errors, are symptoms of their idealism" (ibid., pp. 216–217).

In the *Crimson* straw vote for 1940, Roosevelt dropped 6 percent as compared to 1936, securing but 39 percent of the undergraduate ballots. Wendell Wilkie captured 55 percent of them, while Norman Thomas received 4 percent, slightly more than in 1936, and Earl Browder, the Communist, 1 percent. Roosevelt did better among the Arts and Sciences faculty, with 48 percent as compared to 46 percent for his Republican opponent ("How They Voted," 1940, p. 4).

Student sentiment and the weight of campus political organization around the country began to shift rapidly by the end of the year. Former leaders of the ASU—such as Joseph Lash, its Executive Secretary from its beginning, and Robert Lane, past president of both the Harvard Student Union and the national Student Union, and Irwin Ross, former editor of the *Harvard Progressive*—helped to organize a variety of interventionist student groups to which the Harvard Liberal Union affiliated (Solomon, 1941, pp. 15–17). Student-opinion surveys conducted at Harvard in February and March 1941 revealed a large majority for "more aid to Britain at the risk of war." The March poll showed both an expectation and willingness to fight to protect democracy. The Harvard Liberal Union, which from the start was much larger than the Student Union, was organized by former members of the latter to foster an aid to Britain policy. The editors of the *Crimson*, it may be noted, remained faithful to their old position; as late as May 28, 1941, they attacked Roosevelt's war policy and called for support for both the American Peace Mobilization and the Keep America Out of War Congress. Commencement, early in June, revealed the drastic character of the change. The two main recipients of honorary degrees were Lord Halifax, the foreign secretary of Great Britain, and President Roosevelt. Both men were greeted with cheers by the graduating seniors (Albright, 1962, pp. 44–50).

On June 22, 1941, Hitler's Germany invaded Stalin's Russia, and the bottom fell out of what was left of the antiwar movement. In the fall as classes began, the *Crimson*, with the same board of editors as in the spring, declared in its first issue: "There can be no isolationism for America." Most student activity now involved support for intervention. The League for a Declared War for National Self-Respect was formed in October, and one-third of the student body signed a petition condemning neutrality. Before December when the Japanese bombed Pearl Harbor, the students of Harvard, by an overwhelming majority, had shown they had learned that their President and professors had been right (ibid., pp. 54–56).

RESISTANCE TO RACISM

The war was not the only issue to trouble Harvard at this time. Early in April 1941, Harvard was scheduled to play the U. S. Naval Academy in lacrosse. When the Navy refused to play the game because one member of the Harvard team, Lucien V. Alexis, Jr., was a Negro, the Harvard Athletic Association agreed to leave Alexis off the team ("Students Protest Alexis Episode," 1941). In so capitulating to the racism of the Naval Academy, Harvard backtracked on its earlier behavior in comparable episodes. "In 1903, William C. Matthews, '05, star third baseman, was the center of controversy when Harvard refused to play a southern team, because they wanted him benched. In 1911, Theodore Cable, '13, weight thrower, was prepared to go to the Oxford-Cambridge Track meet when dissension arose from some source. This was immediately checked by graduate pressure" (Davis, 1941, p. 31). This time, the students united in widespread protest cutting across all political divisions to demand that Harvard refuse to play against any team which discriminated on racial grounds ("Undergraduates Protest Action of H. A. A. . . . ," 1941). Two weeks after the issue arose, the Corporation issued a statement in which it called on the Athletic Association to "make it plain to other institutions with whom we are competing that it is Harvard's principle that there should be no racial discrimination among our students" (Davis, 1941, p. 28; " 'No Racial Discrimination' . . . ," 1941). Thus, unlike the United States Navy, Harvard could take part in a war against racism with the self-confidence that it was willing to strike a blow against domestic racism as well. There were, of course, still racially and religiously motivated restrictions at Harvard; their removal would form part of the postwar story.

7. The Postwar Era

Perhaps the most impressive changes that followed the war may be grouped under the heading of increased democratization. Statistically, the greatest shift occurred in the position of the Jews. There is some evidence that whatever assumptions supported the restrictions against Jews on the faculty level, they were beginning to erode even before the war began. Harvard took in many European refugees on a temporary or permanent basis, and some of these were Jewish. Jews began to appear on academic rosters of various departments as assistant professors, and some received tenured appointments. And with the end of the conflict, the dike broke, and Harvard hired Jews in significant numbers. Similarly, the informal quotas that existed on Jewish student enrollment ended. A survey conducted in 1952 by a group of Cornell sociologists based on samples of students at 11 universities across the country (Cornell, Dartmouth, Fisk, Michigan, North Carolina, Texas, UCLA, Wayne, Wesleyan, Yale, and Harvard) indicated that Harvard had a larger Jewish undergraduate enrollment, 25 percent, than any other school sampled. Among the other private colleges surveyed, Dartmouth had 15 percent, Yale 13, and Wesleyan 12. Even Cornell, drawing heavily on New York City, had fewer than Harvard, 23 percent.[1]

The 12-university survey also demonstrated that the Harvard student body was more heterogeneous in socioeconomic terms than the other private schools. A larger proportion of Harvard undergraduates, 27 percent, reported a family income of under $5,000 than at any of the other four. Dartmouth had the fewest in this category with but 15 percent, while Yale had 17. Not surprisingly, the ratio of Harvard students from public school backgrounds which had risen from less than half at the

[1]The statistics are drawn from my secondary analysis of the data which have not previously been published elsewhere. Other discussions of the changing admissions policy are contained in Harris (1970, p. 17) and Kahn (1968, pp. 53–54).

end of Eliot's regime once again passed the 50 percent figure after the war, while by the early fifties over 10 percent were of manual working-class origins. Given the preference in admission to the children of alumni and faculty and the concern for evidence of scholarly aptitude and proficiency, the admissions system was still producing entering classes four-fifths of whom had fathers in professional or managerial occupations, that is, largely second-generation college students. Only 2 percent were black as late as 1964 (Harris, 1970, pp. 12–15; Kahn, 1968, p. 110).

Faculty members give President Conant and Provost Paul Buck, who was in charge of the institution during Conant's wartime leave, considerable credit for the changes in mood and policy. As Seymour Harris noted: "[A]nyone who examines the Harvard developments, especially since the days of President Conant and Professor Buck, cannot help but be impressed by the great strides made since 1930. The gains are evidenced in the number of students and faculty from minority groups and also the advances of minority groups in important student activities. . . . For these great advances, no one deserves more credit than Conant and Provost Buck" (Harris, 1970, p. 17; Kahn, 1970, pp. 53–54). Although Harvard may have been in the lead with respect to such changes, it is obvious that academe generally modified its restrictions across the country during the postwar era, as part of a general change in the mood of America. National opinion polls revealed a drastic drop-off in anti-Semitic attitudes soon after the war (Stember, 1966, pp. 60–61, 65, 79, 83, 94, 104). But whatever the factors involved, under Conant and Buck, Harvard was implementing the policy enunciated by Eliot that its "officers are selected for their fitness only, without the least regard to their religious affiliation" (Harris, 1970, p. 16).

Conant's emphasis on rebuilding the scholarly quality of the faculty paid off. An evaluation of the prestige of various departments by their peers in 1957 reported that Harvard was once again the leading university (Keniston, 1959, p. 119).

THE RIGHTS OF COMMUNISTS UNDER ATTACK

As the postwar era began, Harvard students revived politically and revealed themselves as believers in cooperation with the Communists. In a referendum in 1946, the undergraduates voted three to one to send an official delegate, who turned out to be the chairman of the *Crimson*, to the Prague International Students Congress. The Liberal Union, backed by the *Crimson*, set up a booth to protest the scuttling of price controls and organized a boycott of Harvard Square merchants who raised prices. "A march of protest was also organized which brandished signs all the way from the Cambridge Common to Central Square" (Potter, 1953, p. 581).

The last year of the forties, 1949, witnessed a "Mass uprising of the student body," on a scale and over an issue such as would not be repeated again until the mid-1960s. It was directed against the Naval ROTC oath, particularly "the clause which required cadets to inform the authorities of anything 'subversive' they might have overheard, regardless of the status of whomever they overheard."

The Young Progressives (former Wallace-for-President-men) protested first, and they were soon joined by the *Crimson*, the Liberal Union, the Harvard chapter of the Advancement of Colored People [sic], the League for Industrial Democracy, the John Reed Club, and even the Young Republicans. The Navy demurred a couple of times, but when the persistence and ferocity of undergraduate objections finally convinced the Faculty of Arts and Sciences to consider the matter and to protest formally the so-called "stool-pigeon clause," the Navy gave way (ibid., p. 582).

The Communists secured some student strength at Harvard in the first few postwar years. The Harvard Liberal Union, beginning as an interventionist, anti-Communist split-off from the Harvard Student Union in 1941, had revived as the strongest left of center group (ibid., p. 581). In 1947, it refused to join the Students for Democratic Action (SDA), the campus unit of Americans for Democratic Action, because SDA barred Communists. The executive committee of the Liberal Union, which was dominated by Communists, was, however, removed by the members (Swirski, 1971, pp. 162–163; Potter, 1953, p. 581). In addition to Communist involvement in the Liberal Union, they were present in the form of the American Youth for Democracy (AYD), a clear front group; the John Reed Club, which largely involved graduate students and junior staff; and the campus unit of the Young Progressives of America (YPA). A survey by *Newsweek* of "communism on campus" reported that Harvard was one of six schools in the entire country in which reporters found organized Communist units. (The others were California, Chicago, North Carolina, Ohio State, Oregon, and Washington.) ("Reds vs. Academic Freedom," 1949, pp. 68–69; "Newsweek Surveys Communism in the Colleges," 1949, pp. 68–69.)

The Wallace campaign was to be the last major left student electoral effort in the country, and at Harvard, for some years.

An ugly problem now began to emerge for various units of the University, how to deal with the Comunists. Even before the cold war began, the American Youth for Democracy (AYD), the Communist youth group created during the war, was temporarily barred from Harvard in 1947 for violating university regulations (Altbach, 1974, p. 146). In 1949, the John Reed Club sponsored a talk by a well-known Communist, Gerhard Eisler, who was on his way to a job in East Germany after having been convicted for contempt of Congress. When the University was attacked for allowing students to be corrupted, William Bender, the Dean of Harvard College, defended the students' right to hear, stating: "If Harvard students can be corrupted by an Eisler, Harvard College had better shut down as an educational institution ... " (Kahn, 1968, pp. 100–101; Potter, 1953, p. 582). Harvard did not adopt policies, common at other institutions, barring Communist groups and speakers from using its facilities, but some nominally universalistic regulations formulated in 1951 had almost the same effect. The University required that all organizations file membership lists with the Dean of Students' Office. As a result, "the John Reed Club decided to go underground instead of publishing their names, and the Young Progressives had to lose their charter because they could not find twenty persons (minimum required) willing to have their names associated with the organization" (Swirski, 1971, p. 172). A student of Harvard affairs of this period also reports that the administration "did everything possible to make life difficult for the Labor Youth League [the Communist group in the early fifties]" (Swirski, 1971, p. 169).

These restrictions on the rights of pro-Communist groups did not simply represent impositions by conservative administrators. The bulk of the student body apparently agreed with them. Thus when the Radcliffe AYD would not submit a list of its members, the Radcliffe Student Council voted to expel them, and the *Crimson* praised the Council for this action. There is little record of any student opposition to administration policies. Arthur Schlesinger, Jr., was moved to write to the *Crimson* in May 1953 wondering why Harvard students showed such fear at hearing Communists. Protesting against the cancellation of an appearance by author Howard Fast and of a movie starring Paul Robeson, Schlesinger wrote: "I gather that in these cases the students acted on their own, without orders or even hints from the Faculty. It is a stirring commentary on the courage of this new generation that the faculties and governing boards of a university should be more in favor of free speech than the students" (Halberstam, 1953, p. 623).

THREATS TO THE ECONOMICS DEPARTMENT

The saga of the Economics Department continued: it was criticized in 1950 in the Report of the Visiting Committee appointed by the Overseers and chaired by the steel magnate Clarence Randall. The committee complained that the Department had "one or more Socialists, some zealous followers of British economist John Maynard Keynes, and some who advocate the extension of economic controls by Government." But it argued that the Department lacked "men of equal ability and zeal who hold opposing views" (Conant, 1970, p. 437). The issue was actually a continuation of a conflict over the tenure appointment of John Kenneth Galbraith in the late 1940s, one which some members of the Overseers had tried to block (Bundy, 1970, pp. 532–533). Although President Conant had strongly backed the Galbraith nomination and defended the Department to the Overseers, he did acknowledge the need for balance, and urged in his reply to the Visiting Committee that something be done to reduce the "atmosphere of hostility [that] exists to some degree throughout the country between the management of industry and academic economists" (Conant, 1970, p. 445). The Department, though not conceding the point in principle, did propose that their instruction would benefit from the appointment of an economist "whose major interest was what we might call the economics of enterprise," and two members of the much more conservative Business School faculty began giving courses in the Department.

The controversy over the issue of "balance" in the Department continued according to McGeorge Bundy "through most of my time as dean [1954–1960]. It was an intellectually dreary affair...." Bundy explains the failure of those who pressed for the appointment of different types of economists as stemming from the fact that Harvard emphasized intellectual excellence.

Certainly most members of the Harvard Economics Department were liberals, and certainly varieties of political and social belief are healthy in social science faculties. But a much more critical point than either of those was that appointment to the Harvard faculty was traditionally and deeply grounded in the affirmation of the personal intellectual excellence of the individual proposed. The proponents of "balance" did not understand the importance of this standard, and so all their share of the dialogue came to nothing. There was no appeal beyond the test of excellence. . . . So it was easy for the faculty to fend off the crude but zestful efforts of the Overseers' Committee to impose a conservative or even extract the nomination of one by the department (Bundy, 1970, p. 533).

In his discussion of these matters, Bundy does note the self-evident fact that professors in voting on nominations are affected by personal considerations, that, in fact, a good administrator must constantly check that these have not affected recommendations that come to him. It is not surprising, therefore, that one former chairman of the Economics Department, Seymour Harris, has "balanced" the story of the resistance to business pressure to change the appointment policies of the Department saying, "I can with intimate experience vouch that possibly at least one able teacher and scholar failed of promotion because he was a Marxist. Indeed later he also became a Stalinist propagandist, and experienced a deterioration of scholarly standards. But there is little doubt had he not embraced Marxism, he would have attained tenure" (Harris, 1970, p. 189).

COLD WAR PRESSURES ON SCHOLARSHIP

Outside private pressure on the University with respect to the political views of its appointees was not limited to that stemming from wealthy individuals. In 1948, Harvard experienced a demand from the officers of a major foundation, the Carnegie Corporation, that it get rid of the associate director of a research unit established under a foundation grant. Stuart Hughes, a Harvard Ph. D. in History, had resigned from the State Department in 1947 because of disagreements with the direction of American foreign policy and had been appointed as the associate director of the newly created Russian Research Center. Soon after his arrival in February he became actively involved in the Henry Wallace presidential campaign. Within a couple of months, Hughes was called in by the director of the Center, Clyde Kluckhohn, and notified that the Carnegie Corporation found his presence as an officer of the Center embarrassing, that the chances for a renewal of the Center's grant were endangered. Hughes, who was gradually dropping out of the Wallace campaign because of disagreements with its direction, indicated that he would cease the political activities that bothered the Carnegie officers. This action of his proved insufficient; he was subsequently informed by a Carnegie Corporation officer, later a very distinguished leader of liberal political action, that it was not simply his actions, but also his "opinions" that were objectionable. Rather than endanger the existence of the Center, Hughes resigned to take up an appointment as an assistant professor in the Harvard Department of History. Although Hughes reports that no one in authority at Harvard put any pressure on him to do so, he also indicates that he never received any suggestion that the University was prepared to fight out the issue with the foundation as a matter of principle. In all fairness it should be added that the Russian Research Center in the next few years supported the work of identified radicals and Marxists, such as Herbert Marcuse and Barrington Moore, Jr., both of whom published important books under its auspices.

As the cold war turned hotter, the issue of the rights of Communists in educational institutions led to severe conflicts among intellectuals, within universities, and with government units. The large majority of the liberal-to-left intellectual community had turned decisively on the Communists following events such as the emergence of overt anti-Semitism in Russia and other parts of eastern Europe, the purge of "Titoist" nationalist elements in eastern Europe, the Czech coup, and the Berlin Blockade in 1948. There was general agreement among liberal and socialist intellectuals in the United States and Europe that the Soviet Union was a totalitarian aggressive enemy, that it must be resisted, and that since local Communist parties represented the interests of the Soviet Union they should not be treated as domestic political parties. Given the view of the Communist party as a totalitarian one which requires obedience on all issues from its members, many came to the opinion that party members could not be regarded as free men, since they adhered to party positions on intellectual matters as on other issues. It necessarily followed to many that Communists should not be allowed to teach in free universities. About the same time, particularly after the outbreak of the Korean war in 1950, government agencies and Congressional committees escalated their investigations of the activities of persons believed to be present or former Communists. A tactic fostered by the Communist party of "taking the Fifth Amendment," refusing to answer questions about past or present membership in the party, was followed by many persons called as witnesses by House or Senate Committees. Universities were then faced with the problem of how to deal with persons who told such agencies that they could not answer their questions on the grounds of possible "self-incrimination" in a criminal prosecution.

At Harvard, President Conant, who in a number of statements and speeches made since he took office in 1933 had reaffirmed Eliot's and Lowell's position with respect to academic freedom and controversial ideas, decided that this position did not justify Communists' teaching. As a member of an Educational Policies Commission set up by the National Educational Association and the American Association of University Administrators, he put his name to a statement in 1949 proclaiming that "Members of the Communist Party of the United States Should Not be Employed as Teachers," that party "membership, and the accompanying surrender of intellectual integrity, render an individual unfit to discharge the duties of a teacher in this country." In subsequent statements, Conant argued both inside and outside of the University community that the issue was "not a question of heresy; this is a question of a conspiracy which can only be likened to that of a group of spies and saboteurs in an enemy country at a time of war. I am convinced that card-holding members of the Communist party today are not free agents. . . . [T]hey must be considered as essentially a group of persons who have declared war against American society and whose ethics are therefore exactly comparable to those of spies and saboteurs" (Conant, 1970, pp. 456–459; Swirski, 1971, p. 163). When asked publicly, however, what he would do "if a distinguished member of the Harvard Faculty walked into his office and announced himself as a Communist. Answered the President, 'I would send for a psychiatrist' " ("The University," 1949, p. 720).

Authority at Harvard was now clearly on record as opposed in principle to Communist party members' being allowed to teach, but it also strenuously and at length notified conservative alumni and others that it would refuse to investigate the beliefs and affiliations of professors involved in leftist activities, even those of alleged Communist fronts. The *Alumni Bulletin* in June 1949 carried an eight-page section, "Freedom at Harvard," which reprinted an exchange of letters between a protesting alumnus, Frank P. Ober; President Conant; and Grenville Clark, a member of the Corporation. Mr. Ober, who was chairman of a Maryland Commission on Subversive Activities, had written to Conant protesting Harvard's attitude toward "extracurricular activities of professors," specifically naming two who, in his judgment, had spoken under the auspices of Communist fronts, and stating that he would not contribute to the University because of this. Clark, who answered in the main for the Corporation, affirmed that "Harvard conviction and tradition [are] utterly opposed to your program." He asserted that the right of the faculty to express themselves "should not be restricted by the University by trying to keep a 'watch' on professors or otherwise." In his long published answer he summarized the Münsterberg, Chafee, and Laski cases, and quoted from Eliot's and Lowell's defenses of academic freedom in peacetime and during war. He concluded:

> I just don't know, and no one can know, whether, *on balance*, Harvard gains or loses money by its policy in this regard. . . .
>
> In any case, while that is an intriguing question, it is not the real one. For whether the policy gains money or loses it, Harvard, in order to *be* Harvard, has to hew to the line. That is what Mr. Eliot meant, I am sure, when he said, in 1869, that while a university "must be rich" it must "above all" be free. That choice is as clear today as eighty years ago ("Freedom at Harvard," 1949, pp. 729–736).

During this period, Harvard showed its ability to withstand pressures to which even the most eminent state university in the country was forced to succumb. In the spring of 1949, when the Cambridge School Board refused to allow Harold Laski to speak in the high school auditorium, he delivered his talk to the Law School Forum at Harvard's Sanders Theatre. The Regents of the University of California, however, turned down a proposal from the UCLA Chancellor that he speak on that campus (Gardner, 1967, pp. 20–21, 24, 31; Cain, 1963, p. 237). Harvard provided a haven to four of the 24 Berkeley faculty who had been dismissed by the California Board of Regents in the summer of 1950 as a culmination of the "loyalty oath" crisis there. More Berkeley "refugees" spent the next two years in Cambridge than at any other school in the country, a not unimportant fact given the considerable sense of rivalry for academic prestige which California administrators and regents held with respect to Harvard.

The opposition to Communists being allowed to teach extended beyond the ranks of the administration and governing boards. In the spring of 1949, a poll of the faculty and student body found that they took opposing stances. The professors voted by two to one against Communists on the faculty, while the students cast a similar large majority in favor of the academic rights of Communist party members ("The University," 1949, p. 720). Men present at Harvard at the time recall that the faculty support for the rights of Communists to serve as teachers appeared to come largely from the ranks of the younger non-tenured staff. It must, however, also be noted that a historical survey of student activism concluded that during this period, "the students at Harvard did not actively fight for civil liberties" for Communists. Rather, the "most active elements among them were torn by the issue of exclusion of Communists from their own organizations . . . " (Swirski,

1971, p. 163). To place the issue in its contemporary perspective, it should be noted that many socialists were concerned with keeping Communists out of left groups because of their long history of having had to fight party members who had often used subterfuge about their beliefs and objectives in order to capture non-Communist organizations. As diligent a supporter of civil liberties and opponent of American wars as Norman Thomas argued that "The right of the Communist to teach should be denied because he has given away his freedom in the quest for truth" (Goodman, 1968, p. 327).

STUDENT OPINIONS

Although the late forties tend to be viewed in accounts of campus behavior as the beginning of the political quietism of the fifties, at Harvard a sizable minority appears to have been receptive to radical ideas as late as the 1948 elections. Almost 20 percent of the straw vote was cast for "third party" candidates: Norman Thomas, 8; Henry Wallace, 8; and the Dixiecrat Strom Thurmond, 4. Thomas Dewey received the usual Harvard Yard Republican majority (56 percent), while Harry Truman, victorious in the nation, was backed by only 25 percent of the Harvard students ("Presidential Straw Vote . . . ," 1948, p. 1). Whether the large Socialist and Progressive party votes represented resistance to the emerging "cold war" foreign policy or an embryonic student radicalism are unanswerable questions. There is little evidence of comparable backing for Wallace and Thomas among students nationally.

Four years later in 1952, during the Korean war, few students supported the Socialist and Progressive party candidacies. For the first time since 1912, when Wilson ran ahead of a split Republican party in the Harvard vote, a Democrat, Adlai Stevenson, won a slight majority of the undergraduate votes, though he ran behind Dwight Eisenhower in the total University-wide balloting ("Eisenhower Carries . . . ," 1952, p. 1). Stevenson's Harvard strength was much greater than that received by him across the country in campus polls.

More detailed evidence that Harvard students were relatively liberal during the ebbtime of student activism may be seen in the findings of the aforementioned survey of students at 11 universities in 1952 (Goldsen, et al., 1960). The survey inquired into a variety of opinions concerning career, importance of fraternity (or high-status exclusive clubs) and social and political opinions. In general, Harvard students stood out as the most liberal of all on social and political matters, as less concerned with "careerism" as compared to opportunities for interesting and useful work, and as less committed to the value of prestige clubs or fraternities (among students belonging to them). The only school which was more liberal on some of the socioeconomic issues than Harvard was the black university, Fisk.

Harvard students were much less likely (46 percent) than students in the entire sample (62 percent) or at any other school sampled to think that democracy depends fundamentally on the existence of free business enterprise. Those at Yale, UCLA, and Wayne were much higher. Similarly, fewer Harvard undergraduates (23 percent) than in the sample (35) or than at any other school thought that "If people are certain of a minimum wage they might lose their initiative." Harvard had the lowest proportion of Republicans (28 percent) of any of the schools sampled outside of the South, with the exception of the "working-class" Detroit school, Wayne. This low Republican figure is particularly significant, since it represents a considerable drop-off from the percentage of Harvard fathers reported as Republican, 42 percent. No other college reported as much of a shift away from parental Republican loyalties. Further analyses of other unpublished data in this survey show that Harvard students of the early 1950s were less inclined to deny Communists or "radicals" various political, civil, or economic rights than were the students at *any* of the other ten universities.

The same pattern of greater liberalism at Harvard held up with respect to foreign policy issues of the day and social values and behavior. Thus, the Cambridge undergraduates turned out to be less religious in their beliefs and practices than those at the other 10 colleges. When asked about qualities they would look for in a job, the Harvard students were more likely to mention "self-expression" values than those at the other places, and less disposed to list opportunity to "earn a good deal of money," or some assurance of "a stable, secure future." In responding to a question, asked only of those belonging to fraternities, or at Yale and Harvard, the exclusive "clubs," on the "sense of identification and solidarity with the organization," the Harvard club men were much less likely to have such feelings than those at any other school.

In spite of the continued greater commitment to liberal policies, and the considerable opposition to, or lack of support for, the Korean war, the Harvard record indicates as little active expression of antagonism to the war as to the Congressional investigations of Communism. A contemporary student account suggests that this absence did not reflect the success of the intimidators, as some latter-day commentators have argued, but rather the gradual collapse of the groups to the left of the Liberal Union, almost all of whom had dissolved by 1952 because of the behavior of the Soviet Union. The "realization of what the Soviet really wanted [led] Harvard's leftist groups [to] either wither or like the *Crimson* and the H. L. U. [to] move . . . right." Samuel Potter argued that McCarthyism did not meet with much organized protest because the interest in radicalism had vanished. It may be noted in support of Potter's thesis that much the same pattern of a sharp decline in leftist activity and support occurred on the campuses and among the intellectuals generally in western Europe and Canada, i.e., places where the Wisconsin Senator and his allies had no power or influence (Potter, 1953, p. 582; Lipset, 1972*b*, pp. 186–189).

Many were to interpret the passivity of college students and the decline of radical criticism among faculty and other intellectuals as a reflection of basic changes in American or western society which undercut a critical stance by the intelligentsia. Yet the signs were there that the underlying adversary culture of intellectualdom had not died. A study of the opinions of social scientists in the mid-fifties indicated that the large majority supported the rights of Communists even at the height of McCarthyism and that such views were more prevalent at the more distinguished schools and among the more prestigious and productive scholars. The authors, Lazarsfeld and Thielens, concluded that campus supporters of McCarthy stood in more risk of being sanctioned (ostracized) by their colleagues than did radicals (Lazarsfeld & Thielens, 1958, p. 104). Earnest noted in 1953 that "a professor pilloried by the Velde or McCarthy committees became a hero in the eyes of students." And as a historian of American academic life, looking over that history from Harvard's founding in 1636 to 1953, he concluded that "unless history fails to repeat itself, there will be another revolt of youth" (Earnest, 1953, p. 337).

THE ACADEMIC CULTURE

The limited political involvement of Harvard students in the early fifties, in spite of the heavy 1948 backing for left-wing candidates and the abundant evidence of considerable liberal and antiwar views in 1952, was also reflected, as Samuel Huntington has suggested, in the dominance after the war of a strong "academic culture," which deprecated political involvement even among the discontented. The dominance of the academic culture over the "clubby culture" (linked to family social status, social life, and athletics) was probably related to the new emphasis on pure achievement, meritocracy, which was involved in the Conant-Buck personnel and admissions policies discussed earlier. More than ever before in Harvard's long history, Huntington argued, what now counted on both a faculty and student level was academic achievement. "After World War II, with the permanent 'nationalization' of the Harvard student body and the temporary influx of veterans, the academic culture came into its own." As Huntington, who arrived at Harvard in 1948, as a highly politicized graduate student, comments:

The widespread participation in the academic culture at Harvard struck me, coming as I did to Cambridge after an undergraduate career at Yale and year of graduate work at Chicago. . . . It very quickly became clear to me that Harvard was different: those graduate students active in politics were on the periphery of a community whose central concerns were focused on intellectual matters. . . . Not only was intellectual achievement valued much more than political involvement, but it was also clear that unlike Chicago it would have been quite impossible to have any degree of success at the latter without sacrificing completely any reasonable chance of success at the former. So I abandoned caucuses, resolutions, manifestoes, and vote drives, for the stacks of Widener and the basement of Littauer. That was where almost every one else was. . . .

The respect if not the awe that . . . [a *summa*] status commanded among undergraduates equalled that which on most college campuses went to the star halfback or the escort of the spring festival queen, and which at Yale was reserved for Bonesmen [elite clubsmen] and at Chicago for the top student politicos. The important thing, of course, was not that an academic culture managed to exist among undergraduates but that it was widespread among them. . . . At Yale, at least when I was there in the mid-1940's, the proportion was only a small fraction of them (Huntington, 1969, p. 52).

A NEW PRESIDENT

The same election in November 1952, which by giving the Republicans a majority in both Houses of Congress put right-wing Republicans, McCarthy, Jenner, and Velde, in charge of committees to investigate subversive or un-American activities, also resulted in Harvard's getting a new head (Goodman, 1968, pp. 326–331). Even before he took office, Dwight Eisenhower asked James Conant to take the position of the United States High Commissioner in Germany. Conant accepted, went on leave in February, and retired as Harvard President in June 1953. He was succeeded by Nathan Pusey, president of Lawrence College in McCarthy's home town of Appleton, Wisconsin. Pusey, who held a Ph.D. in classics from Harvard, had at least three marks of distinction which were presumably relevant to his appointment. First, he had publicly and actively opposed Senator Joseph McCarthy in his home state, after

the latter had begun his crusade against hidden Communists in government and had denounced universities for harboring and producing
Communists. Second, like Lowell, he had shown considerable concern
with the education and treatment of undergraduates. Eliot the chemist,
dedicated to building a scholarly faculty, had been succeeded by the
humanist social scientist, Lowell, interested in the Harvard undergraduate as a whole man. Conant, the chemist concerned with faculty quality and graduate education, was now to be followed by a President
whose teaching and administrative careers had been almost entirely in
four year colleges and whose main pronouncements had been on
problems of education. Third, however, the new President differed
from his three predecessors and represented a throwback to an even
earlier era, in that he was a deeply religious man, who showed concern
during his presidency with religious activities and education.

Outside of government itself the most important target of Senator
McCarthy and his allies was Harvard. The University symbolized two
groups which he defined as un-American and corrupting of basic values, the cosmopolitan high status internationalist eastern WASP elite
and the intellectuals. These challenged the verities of nationalist, tradi-
tionalist, conservative America, both the lower-middle class old-stock
and the rising ethnics. In his first speech that opened his campaign
against internal Communism, in Wheeling, West Virginia, on February
9, 1950, Joseph McCarthy specified the target:

It is not the less fortunate, or members of minority groups who have been
selling this nation out, but rather those who have had all the benefits the
wealthiest nation on earth has to offer—the finest homes, the finest college educations, and the finest jobs in the government that we can give. This is glaringly
true in the State Department. There the bright young men who are born with
silver spoons in their mouth are the ones who have been worse (Lipset, 1964a,
p. 361).

McCarthy and his supporters frequently honed in on Harvard as the
center of this complex. Thus the *Freeman* magazine, the most important
right-wing journal in the early fifties stated: "Asian coolies and Harvard professors are the people . . . most susceptible to Red propaganda."
(This is reminiscent of the description of the Mugwumps of the 1880s,
and the "anti-imperialists" of the turn of the century as "Harvard and
the slums.") In discussing McCarthy's enemies, the *Freeman* stated: "He
possesses, it seems, a sort of animal, negative-pole magnetism which

repels alumni of Harvard, Princeton, and Yale. And we think we know what it is: This young man is constitutionally incapable of deference to social status" (Lipset, 1964*a*, p. 362).

Harvard's senior sociologist, Talcott Parsons, explained the charges that Harvard was "an alleged 'hot-bed' of Communism and fellow-traveling" as flowing from the fact that the University "has been particularly identified as educating a social elite, the members of which are thought of as 'just the type,' in their striped trousers and morning coats, to sell out the country to the social snobs of European capitals. It is the combination of aristocratic associations—through the Boston Brahmins—and a kind of urban-bohemian sophistication along with its devotion to intellectual and cultural values, including precisely its high intellectual standards, which makes Harvard a vulnerable symbol in this context" (Parsons, 1964, p. 222).

It must be said, in justice to Senator McCarthy and the others who were so concerned, that the record as assembled by a Harvard unit itself, bore them out, at least with respect to the undergraduate backgrounds of the diplomatic elite. Not only did McCarthy's *bête noir*, Dean Acheson, Truman's Secretary of State, hold Yale and Harvard degrees, but as the Harvard *Alumni Bulletin* pointed out at the time: "There seem to be enough Harvard ambassadors for a baseball team in Europe."

The new United States Ambassador to the Federal Republic of Germany (James B. Conant, Harvard '14, and former president of the University) will find, if he looks about him, fellow alumni in comparable positions. Across the border to the south and west, the Belgian ambassador is Frederick M. Alger, Jr. '30, and the French ambassador is C. Douglas Dillon, '31. Down the Iberian Peninsula the ambassadors to Spain and Portugal are John D. Lodge, '25, and James C. H. Bonbright, '25. A bit to the north, Ambassador Conant will find Ambassador Robert D. Coe, '23, in Denmark and John M. Cabot, '23, in Sweden. In the forbidden land to the east of him is Charles E. Bohlen, '27, Ambassador to the U. S. S. R. Near at hand, across the Channel, is the senior member of Harvard's ambassadorial galaxy, Winthrop W. Aldrich, '07, LL.D. '53, Ambassador to Great Britain ("Ambassadors," 1955, p. 617).

The public position of the University continued the Conant non-Communist hiring policy, as approved by a two to one faculty vote. On one hand President Pusey strongly and eloquently defended the purest form of academic freedom with respect to the investigation and presentation of ideas.

The idea that a scholar must be free to follow his own hunches in pursuing his special studies is not the whim of some modern educator. . . . Certainly it is not, nor was it ever intended to be, a question of academic "privilege." A scholar or scientist has an *obligation* to investigate and report new ideas in his field, even when his conclusions may be unpopular among the general public or among his colleagues. . . .

The way of a scholar is often a challenging, lonely journey. He usually works alone without much attention or encouragement from others. But it is of the greatest importance that he know—have unequivocal assurance—that whatever he finds or reports, within the limits of his own knowledge and skill, will not penalize him as a man. If he sees men around him dismissed from their positions for less than the most serious reasons—because of popular clamor, or on anything less than the most solid proof—it would not be surprising if he were then to shirk his own basic responsibility in the field of learning (Pusey, 1964, pp. 20, 22).

But in the same speech in which he urged such care to protect the rights and sense of security of the individual scholar, President Pusey went on to support the non-Communist hiring policy adopted by the Corporation before his appointment:

We need feel no uncertainty about Harvard's, nor any other university's attitude toward Communism. Harvard wants no part of it. Nor do the others. Inasmuch as Communism seeks to control and dictate to men's minds, Communism is any true university's inevitable enemy. The Harvard Corporation has stated that Harvard wants no one who has given up his conscience to Communist discipline. Such a man lacks the necessary independence of thought and action. Nothing could be more opposed to everything that Communism stands for than a free university . . . (ibid., pp. 28–29).

It is difficult to evaluate or even to report the manifold impacts of the phenomenon known as McCarthyism on American university life generally, or Harvard in particular. A leading conservative intellectual, the sociologist Robert Nisbet, has even credited Joseph McCarthy with primary responsibility for the radicalization and politicization of the university, which ultimately took the form of the New Left. As he identified the process, by "his challenging of the loyalty of intellectuals, his threats to 'get' Harvard and other universities, it would be extraordinary if the mind of the American faculty had *not* become visibly radicalized . . . " (Nisbet, 1971, p. 143; Ulam, 1972, pp. 57–58).

At Harvard in the early fifties, some unknown number of people who felt themselves vulnerable to attack from investigative agencies were deeply affected by the investigative atmosphere, if not by actual proceedings involving them. A number of persons associated with the University left the country, presumably to get out of the range of a subpoena. Others simply trembled, aware of their hidden stigmata, and hoped that no one would notice them. Some, I have heard with good evidence of three such, who never faced public charges, were told by various university authorities, including two Deans, that in one case he could not have a job promised to him, in a second be reappointed to one he had, or in third be recommended to one outside, if they insisted on refusing to cooperate with government investigators seeking information on past Communist activities in which these people were no longer involved. A very high-ranking Dean told one presumptive junior faculty member that Harvard had a limited amount of public credit, and that he had to see to it that the number of publicized cases in which Harvard people were involved was kept to an absolute minimum. Hence, the University preferred not to hire anyone whose position with respect to public testimony might make him a *cause célèbre.* Two law students who refused to testify about Communist associations on "Fifth Amendment" grounds before the Jenner Internal Security Committee "were deprived of honors they had achieved as outstanding students, including election to the *Harvard Law Review,*" by the student editorial board (Swirski, 1971, p. 170; "The University," 1953, pp. 537–539). On the other hand, Dean Griswold and the Faculty of the Law School refused to take any administrative action against these students after the President of the Massachusetts Bar Association demanded their expulsion on the grounds that they had proved themselves "unfit for admission to the bar in any of our states" (Cain, 1963, pp. 240–241).

In describing Harvard's record in resisting McCarthyism in positive terms, some point to the fact that Harvard did not fire three staff members who "took the fifth Amendment" with respect to questions concerning Communist party membership; that the one tenured faculty member, then an associate professor who did so, "eventually became a full professor and the chairman of an important academic department" (Kahn, 1968, p. 102). The three were the subject of an investigation by the Fellows of the Harvard Corporation in the spring of 1953, during the interregnum between Conant's leaving and Pusey's taking office. In the case of then Associate Professor Wendell Furry who had not only used the Fifth Amendment protection, but admitted to a Faculty Advisory Committee and the Corporation that he had given "incomplete or false information" on several occasions, and that he had been a member of the Communist party from 1938 to 1947, the Fellows concluded that his behavior had "fallen so far below the standard of moral conduct to be expected of a member of our faculty as to constitute grave misconduct." They indicated that they regarded use of the Fifth Amendment with respect to past Communist activities alone as a much lesser offense, "misconduct." What made the difference was not telling the truth, and they placed Furry on probation for three years, so that if "at any time during that period either because of Dr. Furry's future conduct or because of contrary evidence as to his past conduct, we should deem it to be for the best interests of the University to remove him, we will do so." In the other two cases, involving a teaching fellow and an assistant professor, which only concerned their reliance on the Fifth Amendment, the Fellows, finding that one had left the Communist party in 1950, and the other though involved in party activities had never actually belonged, regretted that they had not seen fit to testify, but decided each was not "guilty of grave misconduct and on the information we now have we will take no action against him [or her]."

The Fellows made it clear that they were opposed to the use of the Fifth Amendment and that they would not countenance membership in the Communist party.

We think membership in the Communist Party by a faculty member today, with its usual concomitant of secret domination by the Party, goes beyond the realm of his political beliefs and association. . . . In the absence of extraordinary circumstances, we would regard present membership in the Communist Party by a member of our faculty as grave misconduct, justifying removal.

We deplore the use of the Fifth Amendment by a member of our faculty. . . . [It is] entirely inconsistent with the candor to be expected of one devoted to the pursuit of truth. It is no excuse that the primary purpose of its use is to protect one's friends, or to express one's feelings that Congressional Committees are by-passing the Constitutional safeguards of due process of law, or to avert a danger of prosecution for perjury in case one's testimony should later be contradicted by the false testimony of others ("Statement by the Harvard Corporation . . . ," 1953, pp. 1–7).

Senator McCarthy, of course, did not accept this position. He denounced the Corporation, proclaiming that Harvard now had an admitted policy of allowing "Fifth-Amendment Communists" to teach undergraduates. Newly inaugurated President Pusey took umbrage to the assumption that use of the Amendment implied party membership, while reiterating that Harvard did not approve of faculty relying on it (Kahn, 1968, p. 102).

The issue revived in January 1954 when Massachusetts Republican Governor Christian A. Herter, who was a member of the Board of Overseers, asked the new President of the University to dismiss faculty members who used the Fifth Amendment. Pusey publicly refused, declaring that the behavior did not warrant such extreme action. The matter was hotly debated within both governing boards, the Corporation and the Overseers, and Pusey's position was upheld. McGeorge Bundy, who was Dean of Faculty for most of the fifties, while paying tribute to the President, has reported of that period, "what was decisive . . . in the general resistance of Harvard to McCarthyism, was the feeling of the faculty" (Bundy, 1970, p. 532). The Faculty, in turn, was impressed by the steadfastness of the President in speaking up for academic freedom, and in May 1954 issued him a special citation, a unique honor.

Nathan Pusey met this situation with a serene and quiet courage. . . . Stubborn in the right, strong in his convictions as an administrator and as a man, bold where the freedom of the human mind and spirit is concerned, Nathan Pusey has made himself, in the space of a few short months, the President of Harvard both in name and deed (Eichel et al., 1970, p. 8).

STUDENT REACTIONS

There is little evidence of organized student protest against the activities of the investigating committees other than an effort in March 1953 by a Boston-area "Combined University Students' Committee on Academic Freedom" to organize rallies at various colleges and on the Boston Common in opposition to a visit by the Jenner Senate Committee on Internal Security to Boston. The Harvard Student Council opposed these plans as "rash"; the student Committee dropped its plan for mass action in favor of petitions and small delegations. "Thus, the student organizations of the fifties did almost nothing about the biggest issue of the time" (Swirski, 1971, pp. 170–171; Ulam, 1972, pp. 60–62).

During the fifties, Harvard experienced a curious religious conflict between the President and many faculty and students. From his inauguration in 1953 on, Pusey had shown concern about "the present low estate of religion at Harvard" and devoted considerable energies to raising funds for reviving the Divinity School, a relatively unpopular objective among many professors in other parts of the University. In the spring of 1957, he became involved in a major controversy by declaring that the University's Memorial Church located in the Yard (the one the Liberals had opposed in 1927), "had always been a Christian institution and that accordingly the Memorial Church could not be used for non-Christian weddings, confirmations, or funerals" (Kahn, 1968, p. 272).

This meant, of course, that Jews could not use it. Many faculty protested privately and by formal written petition; there was a suggestion that unless the policy were changed it would be brought to the floor of the Faculty meeting for a debate and vote (Eichel et al., 1970, pp. 8–9). By late April, President Pusey yielded, and acknowledged that "Harvard had become a secular university . . . with a tradition of worship" (Kahn, 1968, p. 272).

Little other militant political activity was reported in the *Crimson* until the very end of the 1950s. In 1946, a number of student groups launched a campaign against a local bar which refused to serve black students. The effort, which involved a boycott of the bar and picketing by the students, resulted in a change in the policy. The only sustained activity involved the efforts of the Young Democrats and Republicans during presidential election campaigns. Students seemed "apathetic towards any type of political activity," a reaction which they shared to a considerable degree with their peers not only in the United States, but in much of the rest of the Western world (Swirski, 1971, p. 172). Although national surveys of students indicated considerable opposition to the Korean war, there was little action taken against it. The organized groups were very weak. At no time during the 1950s did the SLID, the direct lineal parent of SDS, have a membership of over 500 nationally, and it was usually much less (Lipset, 1972b, pp. 185–189; Altbach, 1974, p. 154). Negro student groups, of which the most important one was the campus section of the NAACP, did begin to grow and increasingly identified with the small emerging wave of militancy connected with the struggle for integration of southern schools.

At Harvard in the mid-fifties political clubs continued to exist. The Liberal Union, offshoot of the Student Union of the thirties, held regular meetings, while two conservative clubs, the Conservative League and the New Conservative Club, competed for right-of-center support, the latter rejecting Senator McCarthy, the former approving. The League had been engaged for some time in "compiling information on members of the faculty whom it considers subversive, . . . trying to root out any faculty members whose classroom lectures showed indications of radicalism." Its leader complained that liberals outnumbered conservatives at Harvard by at least four to one, and that given the general atmosphere it took courage to be an admitted conservative. The Liberal Union was headed in 1955 by Chris Niebuhr, the son of Reinhold Niebuhr. Young Niebuhr told a visiting reporter that its members were less ideological, "more practical, more pragmatic than the old timers." As evidence of the fact that Harvard liberals "don't go off half cocked," he pointed to their "realistic" position on academic freedom. The Liberal Union "backed the university administration when it said that it would discharge faculty members who are proved to belong now to the Communist Party." And Niebuhr went on to admit that in one sense the charge that his group had become "conservative" was true: "In a way, liberalism today is conservative. You talk about conservation of cultural values. I'm for that. But what are the values you want to conserve? *Liberal* values. The thing is that liberalism has won, and that has a tendency to make us conservative" (Reichley, 1955, pp. 12–16; Cain, 1963, p. 243).

A major complaint of direct interference with the activities of a student political group in the mid-fifties came not from the left, but the right. In 1957, when Harvard appointed J. Robert Oppenheimer, once an editor of *The Gadfly*, and then under attack for actions during the thirties and World War II, as the "William James Lecturer," the conservatives sponsored a debate on the question: "Should Oppenheimer Be James Philosophy Lecturer at Harvard?" between two conservatives and two lawyers affiliated with the ACLU. The leaders of the club reported that they had been harassed by the Dean of Student Activities, found it difficult to get University facilities, and finally held their debate in a private building, while their officers were closely questioned about each other and about the sources of funds for the club. The club's two faculty advisers resigned before the debate. William C. Brady II reported:

The spokesman and past officer of the club, who had appeared on the John Daly national television news program with some other students and criticized the appointment of Oppenheimer (although in measured language), was singled out for the longest session of all. He didn't mind; I know, for the student who stood longest on the carpet was myself. Being called to account for conservative agitation was only to be expected. . . .

I was told by the Dean of Students Activities that appearing on Daly's TV program was "extremely dangerous." In fact, he said, I was "playing with 'conduct unbecoming a Harvard student'" (Evans, 1961, pp. 225–227).

In seeking to get an impression of the political concerns of the student body, a correspondent for the *Reporter* magazine interviewed the *Crimson* editor who covered political activities. He described the situation:

The Liberal Union, the Conservatives, the New Conservatives, none of them amount to much with the mass of the guys. The majority are suspicious of all political organizations. Most of them are what you would call liberal Republicans, although Stevenson did a lot to make the Democrats respectable at Harvard. But they're not enthusiastic about either Stevenson or the Eisenhower administration.

The thing is *not* to be enthusiastic. It looks bad at cocktail parties. Even somebody like Schlesinger seems not quite polite. Nobody wants to be identified with anything that's at all out of the way (Reichley, 1955, p. 16).

The relatively passive apolitical mood on the campuses was but a part of a larger atmosphere characterizing the Eisenhower years, accentuated by the reluctance of intellectuals to criticize democratic systems during the cold war, and by prolonged economic prosperity. Harvard's most radical social scientist, Barrington Moore, Jr., gave voice to an analysis not too different from that of Chris Niebuhr:

In the United States today, with the exception of the Negro, it is difficult to perceive any section of the population that has a vested material interest on behalf of freedom. . . . There is, I think, more than a dialectical flourish in the assertion that liberty requires the existence of an oppressed group in order to grow vigorously. Once the ideal has been achieved, or is even close to realization, the driving force of discontent disappears, and a society settles down for a time to a stolid acceptance of things as they are. Something of this sort seems to have happened to the United States (Moore, 1958, p. 183).

Intellectuals find it hard to be apolitical, or to simply accept things as they are. Although less radical compared to previous decades, the faculty were probably still more active, more liberal, and even to some extent more radical than other strata, including the students (Lipset, 1960, pp. 310–343; Lipset & Dobson, 1972, pp. 137–198).

Faculty activism during this period revolved particularly around the two campaigns of Adlai Stevenson, in 1952 and 1956. Surveys of faculty opinion show that, although badly defeated by Eisenhower among the electorate, he had a majority among college faculty, particularly in his second campaign, with greatest support among social scientists, and professors in the major universities. Hence it is likely that even during the "silent fifties" the students in the major universities were in an environment in which prestige was associated with opposition to conservative views (Lipset, 1972b, pp. 188–189; Lipset, 1972a, pp. 211–289). In 1956, the *Crimson* poll of faculty and students found that Stevenson had a slight majority (51 percent) among the undergraduates, but that he secured almost two-thirds (65 percent) of the faculty ballots. Eisenhower had held his own among the students, but lost considerable faculty support as compared with the 1952 Korean war election ("Harvard Faculty Shifts," 1956, p. 40).

Paralleling the increased faculty participation in electoral politics during the fifties was an enormous increase in membership and activity in the Young Democrats and Young Republicans, nationally and at Harvard. The two national organizations claimed over a million members, with the Democrats reporting more chapters and members in 1956 than the Republicans. A contemporary analyst of student politics in this decade suggested that the "absorption of extra-liberal and extra-conservative elements into the youth organizations of the two major political parties probably had something to do with the disappearance of strident political activity from college campuses." It is possible to argue the opposite thesis, that the demise of the radical and militant-cause campus groups left the more ideologically politically disposed students without organizational homes, and that many of those who would have been militant activists joined the campus wings of the major parties.

This assumption is reinforced by the fact that both groups stood close to the ideological extremes of their respective parties. National conventions of the Young Republicans, headed in 1956–57 by John Ashbrook, Harvard graduate and conservative rival to Richard Nixon for the G. O. P. nomination in 1972, passed resolutions on relations with Communist states and domestic policy which put them considerably to the right of the Eisenhower administration. Conversely, the Young Democrats were to the left of their party leadership on foreign policy and social welfare issues, with delegates from college chapters more likely to favor recognition of Communist China than those from community units (McIntyre, 1957, pp. 927–928).

At Harvard in 1956 there was considerable enthusiasm and activity for Adlai Stevenson who was endowed by many of his supporters with heroic ideological, intellectual, and leadership qualities. For many, the Stevenson campaign took on the aura and intensity usually identified with more chiliastic radical movements. With the wisdom of hindsight, it is possible to see in the emotional enthusiasm for Stevenson the beginnings of the "New Politics," of the concerns for peace and race, and even of the "New Left" which emerged a few years hence.

Yet in the fall of 1957, following the launching of Sputnik by the Soviet Union, the *Crimson* could request the repeal of a liberal position taken by the Faculty ten years earlier. In that earlier era the Harvard Faculty had been relatively unique among American universities in adopting a formal rule which barred the University from accepting any funds for classified research. On November 27, 1957, the *Crimson* requested that it get rid of this limitation that prevented the government from making use of Harvard faculty members on research needed to catch up with the Russians. Fortunately for the faculty's relations with the *Crimson* another decade in the future, no visible attention was paid to the request, and the rule has never been revoked (Kelman, 1970, p. 205).

In an article in the first issue of the *Crimson* in the fall of 1960, which sought to review the Harvard political scene of the preceding decade from a generally sardonic left point of view, the author, who noted the lassitude of the student body politically, commented on the more active and positive record of the faculty.

At the beginning of the decade, as at its end, [non-Communist] disclaimer affidavits were being protested. The National Science Foundation loyalty checks were frequently protested.... If Harvard was soft on former Communists, it was not with ex-Nazis, and the presence in the Air Force medical corps of a former administrator of concentration camp "research" elicited a vigorous outcry at Harvard. The Faculty largely supported Dr. Oppenheimer in his battle with the AEC; his invitation as the William James Lecturer of Philosophy for 1957 caused another stir, and moved some alumni to protest vehemently (Buttenwieser, 1960, pp. 5–23).

LIBERAL STUDENT ATTITUDES

Perhaps the most telling report concerning the undergraduate opinion structure on the American campus during the 1950s was written by a then young conservative, M. Stanton Evans, in dealing with the conservative revival during the decade. In general, he reported the evidence from straw votes, formation of conservative clubs, and student reactions to various issues to point up the magnitude of right-wing strength. It clearly indicated greater political conservatism among the campus population during the early and mid-fifties as compared with the previous two decades. Eisenhower had widespread student support. Yet all during the period, sizable minorities expressed attitudes on various issues which can be best described as left-liberal, and even socialist. Evans concluded that the dominant student view toward the end of the decade was "permissive, antireligious, and relativist in the realm of ethics; statist in the realm of politics; anti-anti-Communist in the *sui generis* crisis which grips our age. In a word it is liberal" (Evans, 1961, p. 217).

A poll of Harvard undergraduates conducted by the *Crimson* in the spring of 1959 pointed up the liberal sentiment that was emerging at the end of the silent decade. On many items, opinion was almost as liberal or radical as would be reported by comparable surveys in the sixties. The existence of such feelings in the late fifties may help to explain the rapid growth of civil rights, antiwar, and leftist activities in the following decade. As the author of the *Crimson* article on the survey noted, while the mood was "liberal," the "program, in many cases, is decidedly radical."

Thus, whereas only a twelfth of Harvard's undergraduates describe their political temperament as "radical" . . . over a seventh support "full socialization of all industries," more than a fifth favor socialization of the medical profession, and nearly a third believe that the Federal government should own and operate all basic industries, such as steel and railroads. . . .

Much the same third that favor basic socialization also support "immediate unilateral suspension of atomic tests" by the United States . . . and "reduction of current unemployment by government action, even at the price of aggravating inflation." . . .

In the field of foreign affairs, a clear-cut majority of the undergraduates support "recognition of Communist China by the United States and its admission to the United Nations." . . .

Though the openly radical proposals of socialization won approval from up to a third, Harvard students reserve their overwhelming support for the "liberal" *status quo.* Two-thirds support such "Welfare State" projects as Social Security and Federal regional power development. Not surprisingly, current "liberal" proposals receive similar impressive backing: four-fifths approve of Federal aid to public secondary schools; two-thirds, of American economic and nonmilitary technical aid to other countries at its present level, of national health insurance, of Federal aid to private colleges and universities, of government wage and price control to check inflation; and half, of Federal financial assistance to American cultural activities (Comstock, 1959, pp. 7–8).

A majority (55 percent) identified themselves as "moderate liberal," 22 percent said "conservative," 8 percent were "radical," and 16 percent reported they were "politically indifferent." About "two-thirds believe that America's two-party system is 'satisfactory on the whole and should be essentially retained.' In contrast, only one-fifth . . . favor an alteration of the present party structure 'so that sharper lines could be drawn' between the two parties. . . . In addition, a tenth would like to see a Third Party successfully founded to crusade forcibly for their political beliefs. Though a few students ask for an American Conservative Party, most of the tenth are [left-wing] radicals. . . . "

As compared with the two-thirds who favored Communists' being allowed to teach in colleges and universities in 1953, three-quarters of those polled in 1959 supported the academic rights of Communist Party members. That neither these views nor the support given to recognition for Communist China represented pro-Communist or "neutralist" views may be seen from the fact that 72 percent stated that they would prefer "a world war with the Soviet Union" to "surrender" to it to keep the peace. A minority were willing to express religious prejudices. Thus, a year before John Kennedy ran for President, 22 percent of the non-Catholics said that they had objections to a Catholic's "election as president of the United States," more than the 19 percent who had similar negative feelings about a Jew among non-Jews, or the 16 percent who held such views toward an atheist or agnostic (ibid., pp. 7–8, 9–10).

More interesting perhaps than the answers to the specific attitude items was the response to the question as to whether "your political views changed" since entering Harvard. Over half, 54 percent, admitted to shifting. Of the groups which so indicated, "seven-tenths have changed" either "from conservative to more liberal," or "from liberal to more liberal." In absolute terms, 38 percent of the undergraduates thought they had become more liberal at Harvard, while 16 percent indicated they had moved in a conservative direction. When those who reported changing were asked to specify "what factors have influenced you?" slightly over half said "lectures and/or assigned reading in courses"; the second most frequent reason (21 percent) was "influence of friends," while 15 percent indicated "increased thinking about political questions," and 13 percent gave "increased independent reading." In interpreting these results, the *Crimson's* analyst concluded that they confirm the impression that undergraduates were "surrounded by a climate of liberalism," that the way in which liberal faculty deal with economic and political questions in courses "allows an unhealthy argument by omission to replace a complete presentation of all 'sides' of a question."

In evaluating these findings, in light also of the weak state of political activity, he concluded that "the College remains largely a hotbed of unconcern," that even the politically interested students "are at a loss to understand how they can act, if at all." And given this background, most efforts to form political clubs "end in quick failure. After one or two enthusiastic meetings, most members realize that they lack both the time and the special competence to gain an adequate understanding of" the various political issues (ibid., pp. 9–10).

8. The Sixties and Beyond

Almost as if political waves and moods respond to the calendar, the beginning of a new decade, the 1960s, witnessed the revival, first in a slow and tentative way, and then like a flood, of student activism. As the decade began, it was unclear as to whether the newly politicizing students were moving predominantly to the right or the left.

Discontent with the moderation of the Eisenhower administration had led to a new national right-wing conservative movement, gathered around Senator Barry Goldwater and William Buckley, the young editor of the newly founded magazine, the *National Review*. The youth and campus wing took the form in 1960 of the Young Americans for Freedom (YAF), formed from those active in Youth for Goldwater (Evans, 1961, pp. 109–112). Among the members of its first Board of Directors was Howard Phillips, Chairman of Massachusetts Youth for Nixon and President of the Harvard Student Council. (His identifying himself as Council President on political literature, however, brought forth a vote of "strong disapproval" of his actions by the Council— Cain, 1963, p. 257.)

In the first years of the decade, a number of journalistic commentators, including one in *Time* magazine, in discussing the revival of student "involvementism" were most impressed by the apparent "sharp turn to the political right" (Peterson, 1961, p. 6). A national survey which queried Deans across the country as to the formation of new political groups on their campuses during 1960–61 found agreement that there had been considerable increase in political involvement, and that more "conservative" (65) or Republican (104) groups than liberal-radical-peace (52) or Democratic (94) clubs had been established (ibid., p. 8). The reports by student government leaders and the returns in straw votes "seem to agree that the Republican Party is currently preferred over the Democratic Party on a majority of the nation's campuses. Student-leaders were approximately two to one in favoring

Republican-oriented ideologies and/or candidates" (ibid., p. 9). At Harvard, however, John F. Kennedy secured 64 percent of the undergraduate choices, far more than fellow alumnus Franklin Roosevelt or any other Democrat in Harvard's history (Woodroe, 1960, p. 1).

Although there was clearly considerable Republican support at Harvard, political activity was predominantly on the left. The YAF supporters organized the Conservative Club, but maintained a low profile, eschewing picketing and demonstrations. A study of its members reported that it "seems to serve mainly as an enclave for conservatives in the midst of an incompatible atmosphere." The club rejected right-wing zealots. Its members "clearly sought out the club as a place where their pre-college (family) values would be comfortably reinforced while yet maintaining themselves as Harvardmen in good standing" (Schiff, 1964, pp. 116–119). A national survey of members of campus conservative clubs in 1961 indicated that 77 percent of those at Eastern colleges felt that their campuses, students and professors, were dominated by liberalism, that as at Harvard they had to band together to create a protective environment (Opinion Research Corporation, 1962, p. A-1).

At Harvard the main issues of the early sixties were related to peace and civil rights. Two peace groups, the Committee for a Sane Nuclear Policy and the Committee to Study Disarmament, were very active in 1959. Most of the peace activists, concerned with the atom bomb, testing, and disarmament, merged in 1960 into Tocsin ("Ring the Alarm"). Tocsin was soon able to organize a large "all-day, university-wide demonstration, hailed as the first demonstration on such a scale in more than fifteen years" (Swirski, 1971, p. 150). Over 1,000 students and 50 faculty took part. The group had as its faculty advisers two professors who were deeply involved in national peace organizations, H. Stuart Hughes (SANE) and David Riesman (Committees of Correspondence). It affiliated to a national group, the Student Peace Union (SPU), a new national antiwar movement (Altbach, 1974, pp. 185–194). The group, which published a regular magazine, *Tocsin Forum*, was the most active political organization at Harvard for some years, sometimes attracting 300 people to its regular meetings. Serious research and study groups were formed which produced detailed memoranda addressed to government agencies dealing with foreign policy matters, generally in opposition to different forms of armament and the continuation of a "cold war" policy. In February 1962, Tocsin "masterminded" a large national demonstration in Washington under the sponsorship of SPU. The Washington Action Project was the largest and most successful student demonstration since the 1930s, attracting 10,000 participants (ibid., pp.

191–192). The Harvard leaders of the movement sought to talk to the new Kennedy administration, which included a number of their former teachers such as McGeorge Bundy (the President's Adviser on National Security matters), Carl Kaysen, and Arthur Schlesinger, Jr. It is interesting to note that the SPU leadership and chapters at other schools were initially opposed to Tocsin's desire to talk to government officials. This difference of opinion may have illustrated one of the major factors—the personal relations of Harvard men with the governing elite —that was to keep the subsequent Harvard protest movements from using confrontation sit-in tactics until some time after they had been employed at other major schools. As David Riesman once noted, all students at Harvard, even the newest freshman, were "at most, but one person and a telephone away from being able to speak to the White House." When one had such ties to the political establishment, transmittal of opinions and research memoranda could appear more effective than public pressure.

Tocsin's most ambitious project, one which may have led to its demise, was its involvement in the "independent" candidacy for the U.S. Senate of one of its faculty sponsors, H. Stuart Hughes, in the fall of 1962. Hughes, who campaigned actively, securing much support, credited Tocsin with being responsible for his running. The campaign aroused much undergraduate enthusiasm and appeared to be going well until the Cuban missile crisis broke out on October 22. Much of Hughes' support appeared to drop during the Cuban events. He wound up with less than 2 percent of the vote, considerably less than he and the members of Tocsin had anticipated. Following the election, participation in Tocsin dropped precipitously, never to be revived. Many of those once active in it either withdrew from politics or turned to the emerging domestic activism centered around the civil rights movement (Crawford, 1963).

ACTIVISM REVIVES

Civil rights protests had gradually mounted from the end of the fifties on, involving pressure on local institutions to change their discriminatory practices. The campus affiliate of the NAACP, the Society of Minority Rights, SNCC, and others organized picketing of stores charged with discrimination, mass rallies in support of southern campaigns, tutorial help for black children, and together with law students and faculty, legal efforts to eliminate discrimination in housing and employment. In general, the leaders of the predominantly black groups were uninterested in cooperation with organizations such as Tocsin which did not have civil rights as their main priority. Archie Epps, then one of the leaders of the civil rights movement at Harvard, now Dean of Students, "apparently spoke for his group when he stated that 'until Negroes have full civil rights, other movements will not be alive to us'" (Crawford, 1963, p. 12).

Organized political activity at Harvard in 1962–63 included many groups in addition to Tocsin, the Conservative Club and the civil rights organizations such as: "The Harvard Society of Individualists; . . . The Committee on Space Nuclear Weapons Development; The Young Republicans; The International Relations Club; The Young Democrats; The Liberal Union; The World Federalists; The Socialist Club; and several other organizations" (ibid., p. 4). Yet, as close and sympathetic an analyst of student behavior as Kenneth Keniston, who in the early sixties was deeply involved in social-psychological studies of Harvard undergraduates, was unable to believe that these stirrings represented a drastic change in the pattern of overall student political passivity. In an article on "American Students and the 'Political Revival'" in 1963, he dismissed the prospects for a "revival" and sought to explain why "our young men and women remain overwhelmingly uninterested in the state of the nation and the world." Among other things, he concluded: "It almost appears that affluence and education have a negative effect on political involvement, at least in America" (Keniston, 1963, pp. 40–41). Similarly, in a book based on case studies of Harvard students, which was completed in 1964, he continued to analyze in depth the reasons why students lack any faith that they can accomplish anything decent through political action (Keniston, 1965).

The new movement, which surprised many sympathetic to it, did not alarm Harvard's President who was eventually to become its target. In a speech at the beginning of the decade, "What Makes a College Good?", Nathan Pusey noted the tendency of past generations of students "to be much more intensely concerned with questions of politics and economics, and active participants in causes. Interests of this kind ebb and flow in college communities, but *these particular concerns appear—happily it seems to me—to be reviving in our time*" (Pusey, 1964, p. 153).

Almost as comic relief, it should be noted that the President had to continue to fight off the now almost century-old attack on the slanted antibusiness views of the Economics Department. A group of alumni published a book in 1960 (to appear in revised form in 1962 after 95,000 copies were distributed), *Keynes at Harvard: Economic Deception as a Political Credo* (Dobbs et al., 1962). They charged that Harvard was the center of a radical intellectual attack on American society.

A check of the pattern of the growth of leftist forces at Harvard soon revealed that the Economics department was the fountainhead of leftist ideology at the University. True other departments—Sociology, History and Anthropology—also reflected considerable leftist thought. But a comparison of reading material of all of them shows that the same references recur, and generally the economics courses took the lead (ibid., p. 10).

The book identified the "leftist" control of Harvard economics as the result of a long-term effort with links to the pre-World War I Socialist Club. It paricularly noted, therefore, that Walter Lippmann, once a leader of the Club, had served as Chairman of the Visiting Committee on the Economics Department while an Overseer from 1933–1939. "During this period the Keynesians and other leftists assumed control of the Harvard Economics Department" (Dobbs et al., 1962, p. 106).

In 1961, in replying once again to charges such as these in a speech to the Alumni Association, President Pusey read from the report of the Visiting Committee on the Economics Department in 1889, which as noted earlier (see p. 109), had attacked the Department for supplying "partial and one-sided instruction." He noted that those then under attack are now considered "very moderate, if not conservative." And he reminded the alumni present of William James' comment at the 1903 Commencement: "The day when Harvard shall stamp a single and hard type of character upon her children will be that of her downfall" (Pusey, 1964, p. 168).

SDS APPEARS ON THE SCENE

The decline of Tocsin and the reduced interest in foreign-policy-related activism following the Cuban missile crisis were paralleled on a national scale by the weakening of the Student Peace Union. The shift of white student activists to greater involvement in domestic issues took its most significant form in the creation in 1962 of the Students for a Democratic Society. SDS was founded as the latest affiliate of the League for Industrial Democracy, thus in a direct line from the Intercollegiate Socialist Society. It began as a mildly radical group, concerned much more with domestic problems than foreign affairs. Some members of Tocsin attended its founding Port Huron convention. On the Harvard campus SDS gradually replaced Tocsin. The latter formally dissolved in the fall of 1964 because its "members are turning away from a passive study of peace and foreign policy and instead, embracing direct participation in the domestic problems which they see facing the country" (Lake, 1964, p. 1; Swirski, 1971, p. 182; Eichel et al., 1970, pp. 27–28).

The Harvard SDS chapter emphasized direct participation in dealing with ghetto problems in Boston. It also opposed an effort to tear down the homes of working-class whites for a redevelopment project. Not yet fully radicalized, SDS supported Lyndon Johnson as the "lesser evil" against Barry Goldwater, and gave out buttons which read "Part of the way with LBJ." Whether part of the way, or all the way, the Harvard student body joined the rest of academe in giving overwhelming endorsement to the Democratic opponent of the right-wing Republican who favored bombing in Vietnam and opposed federal civil rights legislation. Johnson received close to 90 percent of the vote ("How Undergraduates Would Vote. . . ," 1964, p. 3).

Harvard spawned another student movement, the May Second Movement (named for the date of a demonstration), which, though short-lived, paved the way to a transformation in the local SDS. The May Second Movement (MSM) was basically the student section of the then pro-Maoist Communist party, the Progressive Labor Party (PLP). Concerned with the Vietnam war from its beginning, it pressed SDS to cooperate in antiwar protests in the fall and spring of the 1964–65 school year. SDS and other Harvard students also joined in support of various southern civil rights actions. Harvard students and faculty marched in Selma and Montgomery with Martin Luther King and took part in a Washington mobilization called by SNCC (Swirski, 1971, p. 183).

As American troops began to enter Vietnam on a massive scale, SDS shifted much of its focus to the war. The Maoist May Second Movement dissolved, telling its members to join SDS. By 1966, the Harvard chapter had 200 members and was the largest unit in the United States (Eichel et al., 1970, p. 30). Opinion against war was solidifying at Harvard. In May 1966, 1,500 signed an SDS petition protesting Harvard's furnishing draft boards with information about the class ranking of students. And from its success in this campaign, the Harvard SDS learned an organizational lesson: "campaigns against intangible enemies like racism and war might have their place, but supporters could be won only by attacking nearby visible enemies on specific issues. . . . [A] target in Cambridge was priceless" (ibid., p. 30). SDS was to apply this lesson many times.

SPRING RIOTS

All the demonstrations and riots at Harvard in the early and mid-sixties did not simply deal with political issues, Harvard had an old custom, the "Annual Spring Riot." It generally occurred on the first warm night each spring, which in chilly New England means late April or more usually early May. The Riot "provided an opportunity for harried undergraduates to vent their frustrations—academic, sexual, and emotional" (ibid., p. 30; Kahn, 1968, p. 125). Three major nonpolitical spring "riots" occurred in the sixties. In May 1960, when the university announced that it would no longer award handprinted diplomas in Latin, but henceforth would issue printed ones in English, the school erupted in loud protest. "Four thousand students participated in demonstrations, sit-ins and disruptions of traffic," which lasted for days. Thousands marched chanting "Latin si, Pusey, no." The administration, faced with the retirement of the man who had prepared the Latin diplomas, refused to give in (Swirski, 1971, p. 181). Three years later, hundreds of students organized to prevent the cutting down of the sycamore trees to widen the road along the Charles River. Some chained themselves to the trees. This protest was more effective; the trees are still there. In 1966, when the city of Cambridge passed an anti-jaywalking law, in part designed to speed traffic through the Harvard Square bottleneck, the students would have none of it. Again in May, a demonstration occurred. "Thousands of students poured into Harvard Square and proceeded to obey the electric pedestrian lights. When the lights said 'Walk' the students would walk, back and forth across the street. When the lights said 'Don't Walk' the crowd would stop, in the middle of the street. Traffic was backed up for miles" (Eichel et al., 1970, p. 20).

Although the more political demonstrations of subsequent years clearly cannot be explained, in the words of the reporters for Harvard's radio station, as a response to the "frustrations—academic, sexual, and emotional," that boil over on the first warm day of spring, it is perhaps noteworthy that old grad (and veteran of the ASU of the 1930s), E. J. Kahn, Jr., refers in his book dealing with the late sixties at Harvard to "the Spring '69 riots," i.e., the SDS sit-in at University Hall, and that on the first warm day in 1972, Harvard's Center for International Affairs was "trashed" (physically ripped apart) by a crowd of young people, estimated at 1,500. All this may attest to the wisdom of the Story Committee in 1825, which suggested a causal link between the weather and riots at Harvard.

From 1966 on, Harvard increasingly became a politicized institution, with students, faculty, and administrators involved in acting and reacting to political events and demonstrations. To report these developments in detail would have extended this work to far beyond its present length. Fortunately, a number of persons involved, or in close contact, with the University have written substantial analyses. These include: an excellent book of reportage by four undergraduates, then reporters for WHRB, the Harvard radio station; a comprehensive journal and descriptive-analytic book by Steven Kelman, then the head of the Harvard Young People's Socialist League (YPSL), written from a social democratic, strongly anti-SDS stance; a report sympathetic to SDS, and particularly to the confrontation and massive strike in 1969; by a young Englishman, then an undergraduate at Harvard, Richard Zorza; an analysis of the general Harvard scene at this time by an alumnus, E. J. Kahn, Jr., who happens also to have been active in the Harvard Student Union in the late thirties; a highly personal account by a faculty member, Adam Ulam; and a detailed report by a private research group, the Urban Research Corporation. In discussing events for the rest of the sixties I have drawn on these descriptions plus other more specific sources. The reader who wants to get a more thorough picture may read these accounts (Eichel et al., 1970; Kahn, 1968; Kelman, 1970; Zorza, 1970; Ulam, 1972; Urban Research Corporation, 1970; "The Committee of Fifteen. . . ," 1969, pp. 1–60; "April Crisis at Harvard," 1969, pp. 1–24; "The University: April 1969," 1969, pp. 1–16).

ANTIWAR PROTEST

A variety of evidence drawn from events at various campuses and a host of opinion polls from 1965 on suggest that the rapid growth in student protest around the country was basically a reaction to the Vietnam war (Lipset, 1972b, pp. 40–72). As American participation in the war escalated without producing apparent military success, the judgment that something was basically wrong with a war in which the powerful United States could not defeat a small impoverished nation in Asia grew. The very values of self-determination, of American anti-imperialist concern, which have always been used to justify American foreign policy, were now turned against it, particularly among that segment of the population which had been reared to perceive liberal egalitarian ideology as the content of Americanism, the college student children of the liberal part of the middle and upper classes. This group is concentrated in the most selective, more intellectually oriented colleges of America, and the student revolt of the late 1960s took hold in these schools.

At Harvard, which might be considered a prototype of the category, student political activity rose greatly during the 1966–67 school year. SDS organized successful, often confrontationist, civil disobedience protests against visits to Cambridge by Vice-President Hubert

Humphrey, and to Harvard by Secretary of Defense Robert McNamara. Humphrey's off-campus visit to Cambridge in October was greeted with pickets, outcries, and egg throwing. When McNamara came a few weeks later under the auspices of the (Kennedy) Institute of Politics and would not debate an antiwar spokesman (50 faculty and 1,000 students had signed a petition requesting him to do so), 800 students assembled at a SDS-initiated demonstration and blocked his car from moving. He escaped through tunnels under the school (Eichel et al., 1970, pp. 31–35; Kelman, 1970, pp. 51–62; Kahn, 1968, p. 106; Ulam, 1972, pp. 129–132). In spite of this treatment of a member of the President's Cabinet, the Dean of Harvard College, John Monro, announced that he would not levy any charges against those involved: "I hate to make any kind of political activity or demonstration a matter of disciplinary action." Instead, he invited the leaders of SDS to supper, a tactic which, together with much faculty consultation with SDS members, prevented another confrontation when Arthur Goldberg, U.S. Ambassador to the U.N., visited in the spring (Kahn, 1968, pp. 106–107). There was, however, general agreement among the officials of the Institute of Politics that the Goldberg visit would probably have to be the last one by a high-level government official until the war ended.

By the end of the 1966–67 school year, antiwar sentiment was dominant. Almost a quarter of the students had signed "We won't go" statements or had applied for C.O. status (Swirski, 1971, p. 183). Following a spring of demonstrations by both moderate and radical students, a group of undergraduates financed by faculty members formed a summer project, "Vietnam Summer." Kenneth Keniston attempted to put their backgrounds and social supports in a larger context of knowledge about student activism which had emerged out of the many studies by himself and others. After noting, among other things, the strong relationship between family background (the activists tended to be children of liberal-left parents) and type of school (the intellectually more selective), he emphasized also that in contrast to the fifties, "student protestors are . . . actively defended, encouraged, lionized, praised, publicized, photographed, interviewed, and studied by a portion of the academic community. Since the primary reference group of most activists is not the general public, but rather that liberal segment of the academic world most sympathetic to protest, academic [faculty] support has a disproportionate impact on protest-prone students' perception of their own activites. In addition, the active participation of admired faculty members in protests, teach-ins, and peace marches, acts as a further incentive to students" (Keniston, 1968, p. 315).

In the fall of 1967, soon after school began, over 1,000 Harvard students went to Washington to take part in a march on the Pentagon. In late October, a group of students prevented a job recruiter for Dow Chemical, which manufactured napalm, from leaving the office he was using in a Harvard building. They finally let him leave in the evening. University officials secured the names of students involved in the demonstration, and at the biggest faculty meeting in the history of the Faculty of Arts and Sciences (478) voted to approve the recommendations of the Administrative Board to place 74 students on probation and "admonish" another 171 (Eichel et al., 1970, pp. 36–39).

The growth of student protest led to the beginnings of organized counterreaction from a segment of the faculty. A group of senior professors under the leadership of the late Robert McCloskey, Professor of Government, began meeting privately to plan for collective faculty action in case classroom or other university activity was disrupted. They were particularly concerned to secure a united faculty front, to avoid the appearance of a divided professoriate at faculty meetings. This was the beginning of what was to be known as the "moderate" or "conservative" caucus, as distinct from the "liberal" or "left" group, which was formed some time later.

President Pusey, while rarely speaking out directly, indicated his feelings about the situation in his "Report to the Overseers" of January 1968. He clearly placed himself in opposition to radical activism.

Perhaps the most objectionable feature of such disturbances is the sheer wastage of time they occasion with no ascertainable educational or any other kind of benefit. But beyond this, I find it painful to accept in Harvard men either such behavior or the reasons now being given by some of their contemporaries in justification of it. . . .

Safe within the sanctuary of an ordered society, dreaming of glory—Walter Mittys of the left (or are they left?)—they play at being revolutionaries and fancy themselves rising to positions of command atop the debris as the structures of society come crashing down. Bringing students of this persuasion back to reality presents a new kind of challenge to college education (ibid., p. 43).

A second demonstration precipitated by a visit by a Dow recruiter occurred in late February. The Student-Faculty Advisory Council (SFAC), created just three months earlier to establish formal channels of communication between students and faculty representatives (16 faculty and 21 elected student members), had asked the University to postpone the visit from Dow. On February 22nd, the Faculty voted not to interfere, arguing, in the resolution that passed, that the University must be open to all outsiders. An SDS meeting decided that this action justified an attack directly against the University for its conscious complicity in the war effort. On the next day, 200 students engaged in a "nonobstructive" sit-in in University Hall, administrative center of the Arts and Sciences Faculty. They allowed those in the building to continue their work and ended the demonstration by early afternoon. This action, however, marked the targeting of the University, as such, as a surrogate for the government and its war policy.

Later in the spring many of the more moderate students at Harvard joined their peers at other schools in the McCarthy and Kennedy antiwar presidential campaigns. Hundreds went regularly to New Hampshire before the primary; many traveled to distant states later on. Some were at the Chicago convention and lived through the disturbances there.

Yet though the University obviously had been intensely politicized, Harvard administrators and faculty could congratulate themselves that unlike many other institutions, Harvard remained relatively peaceful. Columbia, which had experienced a disastrous spring with massive sit-ins, police actions, a general strike, and the repudiation of the administration by a large section of the faculty, was in everyone's mind (Ulam, 1972, pp. 147–149). In an interview, President Pusey indicated that he did not think what occurred at Columbia could happen at Harvard, since the sort of issues that had existed at Columbia were not present at Harvard. He and others also argued that the lack of communication among students, faculty, and administration, which had been noted by many as characteristic of Columbia, was not true of Harvard. Pusey "told reporters that lines of communication between students, faculty, and administrators remained open at the University" (Eichel et al., 1970, p. 44). Others suggested that various qualities of the House system, as compared to dormitories and off-campus housing of other schools, helped make Harvard a happier and more peaceful place. Through the Houses, students were supposedly in close and intimate contact with a variety of faculty, especially the masters and tutors, as well as the associate members.

Yet, at the same time, the editor of the *Crimson*, Joel Kramer, in an article in the *Alumni Bulletin*, also discussed the Columbia situation "and why it didn't happen here." He had a different and simpler explanation, which he exemplified by comparing the results of the demonstration against the Dow recruiter at Harvard with the Columbia events.

Regardless of the issues involved [at Columbia] or the conduct of students or administrators before the police raid, the bloody battle turned almost everyone against the Columbia administration. . . .

The Harvard demonstration, by contrast, was resolved without police intervention ... [although] the Harvard administration alerted Cambridge police,
and there were some University policemen ready in the basement of Mallinckrodt. ...

If Harvard had called on University police to break up the demonstration,
there probably would not have been blood—but they might not have been able
to clear Mallinckrodt, either. If the Cambridge police had been called in, it
would very likely have been a different story. ... Most policemen do not like
student radicals, whom they usually call "filth," and student radicals do not like
policemen, whom they usually call "fascists." ...

Kramer assumed that the Harvard administrators had read the
Columbia story the same way that he had, that the fact it had happened
at Columbia would now assure that it would not happen at Harvard.

College administrators will probably learn a lesson from the Columbia fiasco.
Before they were reluctant to use police but ... [thought it might be] necessary;
now, to avoid another Columbia, they will not find it necessary. The administrator has little choice, because even if a majority of students stands with him
before the violence, it will turn against him afterwards. This happened at
Columbia. Moderate students who had opposed the sit-in reacted to the police action by joining the radicals in a coalition calling for President Kirk's resignation
(Kramer, 1968, p. 10).

Kramer was, of course, not alone in his evaluation of the consequences of calling police to a campus. After the Columbia events, the
Harvard administration and governing boards consulted various experts as to how to handle student unrest. Harvard's own Chief of Police,
Robert Tonis, in such a discussion "outlined the 'bust' scenario,
explaining the need for outside police assistance, the probable violent
student reaction, and the prospect that many police might lose control
of themselves if confronted by a crowd of taunting students" (Eichel et
al., 1970, p. 109).

SDS PLANS FOR ACTION

Harvard's year of the "bust," 1968–69, has been described in such intimate detail in the various publications discussed above that little
more would seem necessary than to present the outline of the events of
the most momentous year in the University's history in the century
since Eliot took office. It was clear as the year opened that Harvard was
the primary target for a major confrontation by SDS. To escalate beyond
their success at Columbia required a similar accomplishment in

Cambridge. And optimally, it would be deliberately designed to provoke authority to be repressive, a strategy campus radical leaders had consciously followed at Berkeley and other institutions since 1964 (Lipset, 1972*b*, pp. xx–xxi). Mark Rudd, the leader of the Columbia sit-in and strike and a national spokesman for one of the main SDS factions, visited Harvard in October to urge students to launch their own sit-in. Rudd was very disappointed at his reception, since his audience "seemed listless; their response to his call for commitment was muted and restrained," and he commented later that "There's nothing happening there at Harvard" ("April Crisis at Harvard," 1969, p. 2). When a Harvard SDSer, in effect, reiterated President Pusey's point that the type of potentially inflammatory issues that had existed at Columbia were not present at Harvard, Rudd said not to worry about issues, since the major Columbia ones had basically been nonissues to him before the demonstrations:

Let me tell you. We manufactured the issues. The Institute of Defense Analysis is nothing at Columbia. Just three professors. And the gym issue is bull. It doesn't mean anything to anybody. I had never been to the gym site before the demonstration began. I didn't know how to get there (Levine and Naisbitt, 1970, p. 70).

The Harvard SDS was sharply divided into two major factions (as was the organization nationally), one linked to the Maoist Progressive-Labor Party, called the Worker-Student Alliance (WSA), while its opponents at Harvard, in reaction, formed themselves into the New Left caucus. The Maoist wing stressed the need to build a revolutionary movement based on the workers and looked for issues that might appeal to people outside the campus. The New Left was relatively pessimistic about the possibilities of changing the consciousness of well-paid white American workers and emphasized support for anti-American Third World movements, for "liberation movements," and at home, particularly those for blacks and women. It saw the changes in the outlook and style of students as reflected in the "counterculture," with its unique antibourgeois norms of dress, drugs, and sex, as pointing to the emergence of a mass revolutionary student-based movement.

Before the year began, SDS achieved a major success in gaining approval for a "radical" course, Social Relations 148–149. This course, headed in the fall by Tom Cottle and in the spring by Jack Stauder, two young junior faculty, was titled in its first semester as "Social Change in America," and in the second as "The Radical Perspective." As one of the teaching fellows in the course described it: "Harvard SDS organized

Social Relations 148–9. . . . Graduate students, older undergraduates and a few off-campus radicals teach the course in sections which are tied together through a common (and broad) reading list and weekly section leader meetings." Given for regular course credit, and enrolling 900 students in the spring, the course was explicitly designed by its organizers "as a bridge between interest in a politically radical interpretation of the world and a commitment to action in the Movement" (Finkelhor, 1969, p. 49). As noted also by the WHRB reporters:

The subject matter of the many seminars included in the courses was explicitly radical in viewpoint, the instructors made a conscious effort to break with the traditional academic ideology of detached liberalism. Titles of Soc Rel 149 seminars included "Imperialism and the University," "Women and Sex-Role Oppression," "Leninism," and other subjects which seemed "relevant" to student interests. . . . Most of the instructors were undergraduates, many were members of SDS who saw the teaching as a chance to radicalize students. . . . Course requirements like papers and examinations were deemphasized, the stress was put on the experience of students relating to one another (Eichel et al., 1970, p. 48).[1]

Although most of the students enrolled in the course were clearly not members of SDS, its existence gave the activists access to a large portion of the undergraduate student body. The instructors were somewhat heterogeneous in political viewpoint, but the range mainly covered differences of opinion within SDS. Members of the YPSL reported that when some of them tried to get authorization to lead a section from the group of graduate teaching fellows who seemed to determine the selection of seminar leaders, they were told that they could not have one because of their reformist politics.

Steven Kelman, the leader of the Harvard YPSL who spent a great deal of his time arguing with SDSers and seeking to recruit students for the more moderate young Socialist organization, contends that "Soc Rel 148/149 played a crucial role in preparing for the confrontation by indoctrinating a large number of wavering liberal-radical types and especially presenting them with a sense of the strength and invincibility of the New Left steamroller. . . . The simple fact is that, contrary to the legend promoted by SDS, most Harvard courses hardly present any political line at all in the sense that they give insights or attitudes in approaching current political problems. The simple fact is that *one* SDS

---

[1]Some indication of the nature of the course may be seen in a collection of materials used in it: See Christoffel et al. (1970).

course succeeded in reversing for many students the effect of *all* the other Harvard courses they had taken. This was because other courses do not deal with the questions in the headlines. . ." (Kelman, 1970, p. 248).

The major political issue of the year was the status of ROTC, Harvard's most direct involvement in the war (Ulam, 1972, pp. 157–160). A number of official student government groups demanded that ROTC lose its academic standing. In December, Hillary Putnam, a philosophy professor, who was a strong SDS backer, introduced a motion at a Faculty meeting advancing the SDS position that ROTC be totally removed from Harvard. SDS demanded the right of students to attend the faculty meeting called to discuss ROTC. When this was denied, they rallied a few hundred students to sit in Paine Hall, the site of the meeting, some hours before it began. The University postponed the session. Over 100 of the students in the Hall were brought up on charges. When the hearing committee, the Administrative Board, recommended that of 57 who could be proven present, 52 be put on probation and 5 who had participated in the earlier Dow Chemical incident be suspended, the Faculty divided sharply. Rumors abounded that if any students were suspended SDS would precipitate a Columbia-type sit-in.

Under considerable pressure from undergraduates, even many who were not sympathetic to SDS, to modify the severe recommendations on the grounds of the depth of the protestors' antiwar feeling, the Faculty at its next meeting overrode the Administrative Board, which included a number of administrators, and dropped the suspensions. A week later, the Faculty again defeated an administrative recommendation and voted that selected representative students concerned with issues under discussion could attend Faculty meetings and participate in the debate. It then went on in early February after heated debate to vote to withdraw academic credit and professorial status from the ROTC program and its instructors. Under the motion passed, however, ROTC might still continue as an "extracurricular activity," although without rent-free use of Harvard buildings and without scholarships to those taking military training.

The Corporation, two weeks later, voted to accept the faculty's proposals with respect to ROTC's academic standing as within faculty jurisdiction, but explicitly rejected the recommendations with regard to use of buildings and scholarships as matters within their authority, not the faculty's. This decision, not unnaturally, revived the ROTC discussion. For some faculty the controversy now became one involving questions of constitutional authority. Many of the moderate student government leaders were also incensed by an action which they interpreted as a rebuff to them from the President and the Corporation.

The WSA faction of the SDS now thought that they had the issue they needed to secure mass student backing for a confrontation with the University. Returning from the spring vaction in early April, they proposed a seizure and sit-in at University Hall. The New Left caucus, however, opposed the plan, arguing that the student body had not been sufficiently educated about the issue and would refuse to back them. At a series of SDS meetings, the Maoists were repeatedly turned down by the majority of the 350 members who attended:

Three times that night SDS had voted against the immediate seizure of a building, but the leaders of the Worker-Student Alliance Caucus had no intention of abiding by that decision. After the march around campus [by the entire organization] ended, they hurried to an apartment just across Massachusetts Avenue from the Yard to discuss secretly their own plans. . . . Before dawn they had reached their decision: they would seize University Hall at noon that day, April 9, when the first of the New Left's daily rallies was scheduled to begin (Eichel et al., 1970, p. 83).

THE "BUST"

From here on the action at Harvard followed the scenarios as acted out in Berkeley in 1964 and Columbia in 1968, much as had been predicted by Joel Kramer and Chief Tonis. The WSA students occupied the building, forcibly evicting several Deans. Many of the New Left caucus supporters reluctantly joined in the sit-in. The administration followed up plans made during the year, which reflected their understanding of the "lessons of Columbia" (call the police in early, don't convene the faculty, on the assumption that delay and faculty discussion will only result in confusion and inability to act). At five A.M. the next day, police, brought from various parts of the Boston area, entered the building, evacuated those in it, sometimes with use of physical force, and took the 196 arrested away in buses. All this took place under the eyes of a large part of the student body and some faculty.

As at Berkeley and Columbia, the "bust" was followed by a strike called at a mass meeting under the auspices of the heads of various student government committees. The moderates were now engaged in the struggle and adopted as their own many of the slogans and demands of the radicals. Before the faculty meeting on April 11, a second faculty caucus, the so-called "liberal" or "left" one, was fully operative.

The very hectic faculty meeting attended by over 500 professors voted predominantly for the proposals of the "liberals" to drop all criminal charges against those arrested, and to elect a faculty committee "to investigate the causes of the crisis, handle punishment, and recommend changes in governance." A sentence in the preamble to the motion, which had been part of an original proposal from the moderate caucus reading "The overriding moral issue is the initial violent seizure of the building," was deleted by 248 to 149 votes. In effect, the administration of Harvard University had been repudiated by its faculty, much as had occurred at other major universities following a similar set of prior events.

The single act of calling the police engaged and outraged the liberal feelings of the large majority of the student body and the faculty. In effect also, the sentiments of "class" or "peer group" solidarity which exist among students, as Dana pointed to in his *Journal of 1832* in accounting for the resistance of his classmates and their willingness to risk suspension, were equally operative in the more dramatic conflict of 1969. And President Pusey was to experience the same opprobrium for calling in public authority to enforce order within the Yard that Morison reported as the fate of his predecessor, Josiah Quincy, for a comparable action in 1834. Pusey, like many other university administrators, had been unable to appreciate the strength of the half-a-millenium-old norm that police should not be called to the precincts of a university. As one group of outside observers described the process at Harvard:

At 3:00 in the morning on April 10th, the University Hall occupiers had been a disruptive minority group that had tried to force its views on the majority through physical blackmail; at 6:15A.M. they were a martyred band that had destroyed the credibility of a university and its decision-making procedures....

[T]he administration inadvertently accomplished precisely what the SDS set out to do by its decision to conduct a swift police raid.... It is ironic that the SDS was able to generate the substantive debate it wanted largely because of student "liberal sympathies" about the police bust and concern for procedural guarantees—concepts that the SDS itself has often denounced (Urban Research Corporation, 1970, p. 20).

The "radicalization" of the students and faculty, the general loss of confidence in authority, were quickly to sweep away the ROTC issue. The Faculty voted overwhelmingly to deny ROTC any special rights or privileges. More significantly, however, under pressure from a more radicalized black student body, the Faculty changed policies it had adopted earlier in the year with respect to Afro-American Studies.

THE AFRO-AMERICAN DEMANDS

In January 1969, a Faculty committee on African and Afro-American Studies which had worked for 18 months brought in a report concurred in by the two black students who sat in on all its deliberations, recommending a Program of Afro-American Studies (not a department), which could be taken in conjunction with a concentration in some specific discipline. The leaders of the main black student organization and the *Crimson* had praised the report. In April, during the strike the leadership of the Afro-American students' organization, which had agreed to the report, was suddenly replaced by a more militant group. The shift within the Afro organization, in part, was a consequence of changes in Harvard's admission policies which sharply increased the percentage of black students entering from 2 percent in the early sixties, to 4 in 1968, and 7 in 1969. The composition of the black admittees also shifted from predominantly middle-class to a large segment from inner-city ghetto backgrounds. In effect, the change of leadership within Afro involved a shift from socially middle-class seniors to lowerclassmen from relatively underprivileged backgrounds, who were basically repudiating the conciliatory policies of traditional Harvard blacks.

The new leaders now publicly announced that the faculty had not lived up to its original commitments because the one-page outline presenting the content of the new field prepared by a junior faculty member of the Committee had only been shown to the three black student representatives on the Committee, not to the whole of Afro. They argued also that the outline changed some parts of the original understanding. As a result, they claimed to be free from their agreement, and now demanded a more elaborate program, including a separate department, that would be controlled by a joint faculty-student committee, the students to be chosen half from the Afro-American organization and half from black-studies concentrators. This joint committee would nominate faculty members for the new department, "generate its own courses," and be "responsible for establishing its own curriculum standards and course requirements," allowing for "courses that are radical both in subject matter and approach" (Urban Research Corporation, 1970, pp. 35–36; Eichel et al., 1970, pp. 261–276; Rosovsky, 1969, pp. 562–568). Some black students openly warned of another sit-in by their group unless their demands were met.

Henry Rosovsky, who had chaired the original Committee for the 18 months of its deliberations, took the floor at a faculty meeting held while the massive University-wide strike was still on and explicitly denied that there had been any breach of confidence, that the report had been modified in any way. At a subsequent meeting, two House masters, Alan Heimert and Zeph Stewart, introduced and seconded the motion as drawn up by the Afro-American student group. They presented as their own the black students' version of, in Stewart's words, the "functioning of a mechanism which had betrayed them so soon and might betray them again" (Eichel et al., 1970, p. 284). Representatives of Afro took part in the ensuing debate. With consent of the black students present, the motion was amended slightly to change the words "radical and relevant" courses to "innovative." After long argument, in which the leaders of *both* faculty caucuses opposed the Heimert-Stewart motion, it passed by a vote of 251 for and 158 against, much to the surprise of most people present. The Harvard faculty had voted to allow students to take part in running a department, designing courses, and choosing faculty.

How did this happen in spite of the agreement by most of the leaders of both caucuses that this was a bad thing? There was general agreement among those who watched the hand voting that the pro-Afro votes had come largely from younger faculty and natural scientists. The student reporters for WHRB, generally sympathetic to the strike and student demands, suggest the following explanation:

Why had the Faculty taken this radical step? Certainly, fear was an element in the vote. Just one day before, professors had seen in the *New York Times* the frightening picture of armed black students leaving a seized building at Cornell. They could easily visualize the same thing happening in Cambridge. Skip Griffin's [an Afro leader] speech to the Faculty and the intimidating presence of 70 Afro members in the lobby must have made that threat even more real. [In a note, they mention: On the day after the vote, the *Crimson* showed one black student leaving the theatre with a meat cleaver in hand.] But Afro also appealed to the Faculty's sense of reason and fairness; for the most part Afro's presentation was clear, calm, and rational even in the Faculty's own terms. Clearly, some faculty members were convinced that the Standing Committee had broken its brittle covenant of faith with the blacks. Others wanted to restore a sense of community to Harvard by dramatically reasserting their faith in a group of students. Finally, the actual vote showed a preponderance of natural scientists voting in favor of the Afro resolution. Natural scientists, always suspicious of social scientists, were prepared to endorse such academic experimentation precisely because they considered Black Studies to be less than a legitimate field of intellectual endeavor (Eichel et al., 1970, p. 288).

Henry Rosovsky had a similar but also different set of explanations. First, he pointed to a variety of threatening acts and speeches made by Afro leaders, before and during the faculty meeting:

The acting dean ... told us that the A.A.A.S. resolution should not be amended; the black students wanted us to treat it on a take-it-or-leave-it basis. . . . Faculty members were standing twenty-four hour guard at Widener Library, people were worried about the safety of paintings in the Fogg Museum, and the shadow of Cornell was spreading. . . . I do not see how the Faculty vote of April 22 can be interpreted as anything else but action in the face of threats. . . .

I believe that many nontenure members voted for the radical proposal because they were generally more sympathetic and identified with white and black student demands. They also were not averse to backing any step opposed by the administration and some of the more conservative senior faculty. After all, "if the old bastards oppose the black demands, we might as well back them."

Then there was also the peculiar attitude of some physical scientists. I will never forget a conversation with a famous Harvard scientist who told me that the Afro proposal was just fine for their area of study, and he would vote for it with enthusiasm. He added, that, of course, "this sort of thing would never work" in his own department. When I was bold enough to ask for an explanation, he pointed out to me that science possessed a "pyramid of knowledge". . . .

Undoubtedly some faculty members were entirely sincere and believed that they were simply riding the wave of the future. . . . Many were bearing the heavy burden of liberal guilt (Rosovsky, 1969, pp. 571–572).

Whatever the reasons explaining the behavior of the Harvard faculty on this and other issues during the strike, the passage of the Afro motion led to an end of the student strike, and the protest of 1969 was over.

THE RESTORATION OF AUTHORITY

There were still a number of matters that had to be settled. The Faculty elected a committee to suggest administrative changes, and to handle the problem of disciplining the students who had sat in University Hall. The demand of the strike for amnesty never generated much faculty support. In presenting the liberal caucus motion which, in effect, totally repudiated the actions of the administration, their then spokesman, Wassily Leontief, had stated also that "the action of the student group, particularly of its leaders, who perpetrated that physical attack on the university should be punished. . . . They should be expelled from the university" (Eichel et al., 1970, p. 209). Thus, though the candidates of the liberal caucus running in the election for the new faculty "executive" committee, to be known as "The Committee of Fifteen," won the majority of the seats against a moderate slate, there was to be no question of amnesty. Ultimately, 16 participants were dismissed, separated, or required to withdraw from the University for various periods of time. Another 20 were given suspended "required to withdraw" sentences, while 102 were given warnings. Jack Stauder, the instructor in charge of the "radical" course, Social Relations 149, was one of those arrested. His three-year appointment was cancelled by the Corporation, with the proviso that he might be reappointed to a one-year contract, without being allowed to teach in the following fall semester. The Faculty Committee on Educational Policy, which had been evaluating the radical Social Relations course, decided that the permission they had granted for a one-year experiment should not be renewed, that the course would have to live up to the same rules as all other Harvard courses, a ruling that would drastically reduce the number of sections and students it could have. Those handling the course decided to drop it under these conditions. A number of changes occurred in the administration. Franklin Ford, the Dean of Faculty, had a mild stroke during the strike, and eventually resigned, as did Dean of the College, Fred Glimp. President Pusey replaced these men with two leaders of the moderate caucus, Economics Professor and labor expert, John Dunlop, and diplomatic historian, Ernest May.

The restoration of authority at Harvard following the bust was essentially the accomplishment of the faculty. As Samuel Huntington, a leader of the moderate caucus, pointed out: "After the bust, there was basically no legitimate authority in the university" (Oberle, 1969, p. 49). Essentially, the leaders of the two caucuses took over and made policy through prolonged discussions with each other before all faculty meetings. As one observer noted: "The caucuses' basic willingness to cooperate has produced a negotiated agreement between the two groups on almost every major issue." Recognizing that the institution was in danger, that other schools had come close to destruction, each group seemingly placed compromise ahead of power. The liberal leaders took as one of their responsibilities holding the more radical faculty and students in line; conversely, the moderate spokesmen worked to prevent the more hard-line faculty from pressing their dissatisfactions.

Behind the comity was what some professors describe as an overwhelming desire to cooperate in "saving the institution"—a slogan that reformers and conservatives alike have wielded to counter student extremists' attempts to shut down the University. Harvard's professors seem very much aware of the experience of Berkeley and Columbia, where, they say, factionalism poisoned the academic atmosphere and prevented the faculties from taking effective action (Oberle, 1969, p. 50; Urban Research Corporation, 1970, pp. 53–54).

Once the immediate crisis was over, the main topic of discussion, writing, and to a limited extent, research, was an analysis of the causes of the disaster. There was widespread agreement among students, faculty, and outside observers that the administration had erred in calling the police. And given the fact, noted earlier, that many in the Harvard community had cautioned various administrators against such action, anticipating that it would lead to a mass repudiation of their authority, the obvious question was why did they do it. The issue was particularly pertinent since in February the University of Chicago had demonstrated an alternative course of action. When Chicago students occupied their administration building, President Levi refused to negotiate with them, but at the same time did not call the police. The faculty supported him almost unanimously, and following the evacuation of the building after two weeks, the University expelled or suspended close to one hundred students involved.

The team of investigators from the Urban Research Corporation who descended on Cambridge after the immediate crisis was over took as one of their tasks finding an answer to this question. From my observation of the events, their analysis warrants repeating:

The administration has offered several reasons for the immediate police bust. Noted earlier were several practical problems: the paralysis of the administrative center of Harvard; the need to protect confidential files on faculty, students, and university finances; the dangers of a massive influx of outsiders over a prolonged period of time; and the pressure of the Cambridge community for action against the occupiers.

More important in determining the administration's decision, however, seemed to be less tangible factors. First, Harvard was profoundly impressed by Professor Cox's analysis of the Columbia University seizure, in which he particularly blamed excessive administrative delays in taking action, too many independent professorial mediators, and the success of the disrupters in using this time to capture more buildings and broaden campus support. Because Harvard was determined not to repeat this mistake, it rejected the University of Chicago experience as a model. The administration also foresaw long-term disadvantages in delaying action. Dean Ford stated at the April 11 faculty meeting that judging from the University of Chicago and elsewhere:

"there is evidence that the prolonged occupation of a building does produce some effects in the (University) community, the hardening of positions, the formulation of factional demands, so that by the time you take any action, whatever it is, including no action, you have a built-in residue of bitterness on the part of a lot of people."

A rationale for the quick police bust was offered by Dean Glimp in an interview. He commented first on the symbolic position of Harvard: "Given the style of the takeover here—the forcible occupation rather than a peaceful sit-in coupled with the high visibility of Harvard, if we hadn't moved in a great hurry, the demonstrators would have stayed a month." He went on to argue that the prolonged University of Chicago sit-in was harmful to students in "causing the 'unthinkable' to become 'thinkable'—increasing a gradual deterioration of standards about what types of behavior, what degrees of harassment, are permissible...."

It is known that once the police are called in, they run their own show, and, as the Committee of Fifteen noted in their report, the administration should have considered more carefully "the well-known principle that if something can go wrong in an operation of that sort, it will" (Urban Research Corporation, 1970, pp. 37–38).

As occurred following the Great Rebellion of 1834, the Overseers appointed a committee to investigate the sources of the 1969 crisis, under a leading federal judge, Henry Friendly. In seeking to explain the basic causes, the Friendly Committee, though crediting the war and the draft as major precipitating factors, emphasized, as had various efforts to evaluate comparable crises at Berkeley and Columbia, educational and structural factors. Thus, they explained a large part of the Harvard difficulties on blockages in channels of communication among the various Estates of the university, and called attention to legitimate sources of student malaise—a decline in the quality of their education as reflected by the impersonality inherent in large courses, the inadequate attention paid to undergraduates by faculty, often overly involved in outside commitments and research, and the growing inadequacies of the Houses as educational and living centers, as compared to earlier periods. Their only immediate recommendation was the creation of a University-wide committee to study and report on structural changes.

Some of the causal analysis of the Friendly Committee may be evaluated by reference to a detailed survey of the Harvard students by a young faculty member, Marshall Meyer, now at the University of California at Riverside. Meyer sampled the opinions of 937 students three weeks after the seizure of University Hall (Meyer, 1971, pp. 245–268). The results indicated clearly that by 1969 most Harvard students saw their politics as left of center. When asked to locate themselves on a nine-point scale, one in the center, and four to the left or right of it, over three-quarters (76 percent) chose a left of center position; only 14 percent, one on the right. This did not mean, however, that the far left was dominant. Only 1 percent, in fact, located themselves in the most extreme left category though another 19 percent said they were in the next position.[2] In effect, the answers to this and other questions suggest that the large bulk of Harvard undergraduates, at the time of the bust, were strong antiwar liberals, though unsympathetic to confrontation tactics. The vast majority, 80 percent, "strongly disapproved" of the Vietnam war, another 14 percent disapproved in less strong terms; but 6 percent indicated they were for the war. Three-quarters disapproved of Richard Nixon as President.

Some indication of the nonradical character of their views may be seen in the fact that 82 percent said they thought the sit-in was *unjustified* at the time it took place. Only 15 percent said that they had "wanted Harvard to end all connection with ROTC" before the sit-in. The students, however, were opposed to calling the police to end the occupation of University Hall by 78 percent to 20. Bringing them in clearly shifted the attitudes of many on various issues. Thus, the proportion who thought the sit-in had been justified rose from 17 percent before the bust to 30 percent afterwards. Those who favored ending any Harvard connection with ROTC more than doubled to 32 percent (Meyer, 1969).

In an analysis of these data, Meyer pointed out that his findings, like those of earlier surveys at Berkeley and other crisis-torn schools, did not agree with the commentaries that credited much of the student protest to dissatisfaction with major elements of their education. Educational malaise was *not* related to support for the sit-in or strike. He concluded that to "dismiss the political elements of student dissent as a verbal cover for frustrations arising from lack of supportive contact with faculty members is shortsighted, as is the conclusion of a committee of Harvard overseers that loss of intimacy between students and faculty is a major source of tension" (Meyer, 1971, p. 257). As he noted, if the Committee were right the data should show a relationship between lack of contact with faculty and political protest involvement, but they do not. Eighty-two percent of his respondents were positive about a Harvard education; 78 percent said they were friendly with one or more faculty members; "three-quarters talked with a faculty member outside of class once a week or more"; a quarter did so more than three times a week; about half thought the senior faculty were concerned about "the personal problems of students"; and 80 percent thought the junior faculty

[2]The survey, as Meyer himself noted, undoubtedly underrepresented extreme radical opinion, as SDS called on students to refuse to answer the questionnaire on the grounds that its results would be of use to the administration.

were so concerned. Even more significant, however, is the fact, as noted above, that none of these items were correlated with political views. That is, those students who were discontented with their education, or who reported little or no contact with faculty, were no more likely to be leftist or protest prone than those who reported very positive educational experiences (ibid., p. 257).

Meyer noted that the main source of support for the demonstrations and antagonism to Harvard's political role was the strength of commitment to a leftist ideology. Student respondents were classified on a nine-point scale from left to right. When surveyed, almost two-thirds (65 percent) of those who were grouped in the two most leftist categories thought that "the takeover of the building was justified," a proportion which declined to one-third (33 percent) for the next category (moderate left), and to *two* percent for those whose views placed them in the three most conservative categories (ibid., p. 260). Meyer's findings are of especial interest with respect to the impact of police action on the students. The leftist students backed the strike demands on substantive political issues, but were relatively unconcerned about the police action; the moderate students were less interested in or even disapproving of the strike demands, but were offended by the use of force.

A student's support of the strike that followed the police bust was closely related to his political beliefs. Ninety-one percent at the far left of the political spectrum, in contrast with only six percent at the right, supported the strike. But . . . *most of the students at the extreme left of the political spectrum struck primarily in support of the eight demands* [of the strike]. Fifty-four percent were most concerned with the demands, and 28 percent were most upset by the use of police. Concern for the demands declines, in fact vanishes, as one goes from left to right on the spectrum. At the same time, reaction to the police intervention increases. . . .

[I]t appears that the decision to call the police had a variety of effects. Students at the right of the political spectrum welcomed the university's firm policy, while radicals who were not particularly happy about this policy were not particularly upset by it either. In all likelihood, some of the militants had hoped for police intervention as a means of dramatizing their position, and they were not disappointed. It appears that the moderate or liberal students, those slightly to the left of the political center, were most disconcerted by the appearance of outside forces. . . . [The moderates] overwhelmingly disapproved of the seizure of University Hall . . . and had little more enthusiasm for calling the police. . . . After the bust . . . nearly sixty percent of the moderates went on strike, two-thirds of them because outside forces had been brought into the university. . . .

The moderates, I sense, were confounded by events, but most went on strike feeling that the university's impropriety in calling in the police was greater than the militants' in taking a building. . . . To most moderates, I imagine, what is at stake is not a set of non-negotiable demands but rather a conception of the university that precludes the use of forces to solve its problems (ibid., pp. 265–266).

Who were the SDSers in that year? The many surveys taken around the country during the late sixties all indicate that left-wing students tended to come from relatively well-to-do families, that the core activists were even more affluent, that activist children of manual workers were relatively more likely to be involved in the Young Americans for Freedom than in SDS (Lipset, 1972b, pp. 80–113). The limited Harvard data available are generally similar with respect to family wealth. As Steven Kelman reports: "Family income: average for the U.S., $8000 a year; average for Harvard, $17,000 a year; average for SDS, $23,000 a year. . ." (Kelman, 1970, p. 140).

POSTCRISIS CHANGES

The following year, 1969–70, was relatively peaceful at Harvard until the massive strike which occurred on most campuses of the country following the Cambodian incursion in May 1970. SDS had split in two at its summer 1969 convention. The Maoist WSA faction had both the majority and the organization name, nationally and at Harvard. Much of the local New Left caucus functioned separately under the name the November Action Committee for much of the year. The Center for International Affairs was targeted by the radical groups, much as was done to similar international centers on other campuses, as a supposed local collaborator with the government's war and foreign policy. (Henry Kissinger had been Associate Director of the Center before he went to Washington.) The underground Weatherman organization, which had split from SDS, "trashed" the Center in the fall of 1969.

The years immediately after the bust witnessed a number of other efforts by different activist groups, more often than not centered around the SDS or black groups, to find issues around which to mobilize student sentiment. Black students, usually backed by SDS, protested the University's hiring policies with respect to construction and other labor, and its investment program in southern African countries. SDS organized a protest at the 1969 commencement, which resulted in one of their spokesmen being allowed to give an unscheduled speech. They also helped to stimulate a disruption of the 1970 ceremonies by a largely black community group, demanding assistance from Harvard for low-cost housing in their neighborhood. A scheduled talk by Edwin Land of the Polaroid Corporation was cancelled because of threats that it would be disrupted by protests against Polaroid's operations in South Africa. On one occasion the Center for International Affairs was bombed, and on another a meeting of its Visiting Committee was broken up by a group of students who invaded the building. A "teach-in" on Vietnam called by Young Americans for Freedom and other conservative groups, at which the South Vietnamese ambassador and other supporters of the war were to speak, was so disrupted that it had to be stopped. Individual faculty members who were identified with advising the administration on confrontations (Archibald Cox), consulting with the government on Vietnam (Samuel Huntington), criticizing welfare policy in the ghettoes (Edward Banfield), or publishing an article which concluded that genetic factors were more determinative of intelligence than environment (Richard Herrnstein) were harassed in class, and in a number of cases were followed around the campus, bothered in their office, and annoyed on the telephone.

None of the disruptive events, however, with the one exception of the Vietnam "teach-in," involved many students. Yet in the postbust climate, having been repudiated by both faculty and students, the administration was clearly chary of invoking discipline. Occasionally, the ringleaders of some of the protests, particularly when some physical force had been used, were suspended. Yet for the overwhelming majority of students and faculty, peace seemed to have returned to the Yard. Protest meetings, apart from those linked to escalations of the Vietnam War in May 1970 and 1972, tended to be very small. Attendance at faculty meetings also declined greatly. In the fall of 1971, two of the regular monthly sessions were called off for lack of business, and it was difficult to obtain the small quorum necessary for the other two. The faculty seemingly was tired of debate and discussion. This pattern was to continue into the mid-seventies.

During the debates about the establishment of the Department of Afro-American Studies, some argued that permitting students to take part in the decision-making apparatus in that Department would lead to pressure on other departments to do the same. The prediction was borne out, although with mixed results. Students have played significant roles in three of the smaller professional schools—Design, Divinity, and Education. Graduate students secured voting membership in the full Department meetings in Social Relations and Sociology. In the former, which encompassed social anthropology, social psychology, and personality psychology, they also were given considerable weight in the initial processes of recommending and evaluating faculty. The Department of Economics and the Social Studies Committee rejected similar demands. In 1972, when Social Relations and Psychology merged, the rights of graduate students to elect representatives with voting rights in department meetings were dropped. Such "co-government" policies disturb many faculty. There have been suggestions that the Faculty Council, or the Faculty as a whole, adopt policies to rule out such participation. Thus far they have not been pressed formally because of the strong norm of noninterference with the internal business of departments.

Within Harvard College, however, students have rejected various proposals passed by the Faculty to reestablish a more powerful student government, or to include student representatives on a joint faculty-student discipline committee, the Committee on Rights and Responsibilities (CRR). It proved difficult to get enough candidates to run for the various posts available under the rules establishing a Harvard Undergraduate Council. Only 10 percent bothered to cast ballots, and the Council never functioned because of lack of student interest. There has been even greater opposition to student participation in discipline, and almost all Houses have refused to conduct elections for membership on the Committee. As a result, the CRR has operated for years without any student members.

The faculty caucuses gradually stopped meeting, although until 1974 their "former" leaders continued to run opposing "slates" for the Faculty Council, established in 1970, to advise the Dean of the Faculty of Arts and Sciences between Faculty meetings. Again, as at a number of other schools, once the great bust and strike crisis faded into memory, while the radicals continued to be burdensome by engaging in various minor confrontation and trashing actions, the mood of the faculty shifted in a more conservative direction. The moderate candidates have been able to win ensuing elections by substantial majorities in all elections since the first one.[3]

The establishment of the Faculty Council within the Faculty of Arts and Sciences was a direct response to criticisms levied by the "liberal" caucus after the "bust." They sought to limit the power of the administration to determine who among the faculty could formally give them advice. The "liberals" objected that committees appointed by the Dean

---

[3]Similar patterns occurred at a number of other schools of faculty supporting the more left caucus immediately after police were called in to handle a confrontation, but subsequently shifting to back the more conservative faction. See Lipset (1972b, pp. 220–223, 261–264) and Kinsley (1970, pp. 15–17).

and other administrators were not representative of faculty opinion. Within a few years, however, some of the more liberal faculty began complaining, much in the same terms as had been voiced against a prior Faculty Council in 1939, that the existence of the Council gave undue influence to more conservative faculty politicians, and that its existence is responsible for the fact that attendance and controversy at faculty meetings has declined greatly. Like their critical predecessors of the 1930s, they identify a Council elected in quiet times, when it is difficult to get people to run and voting participation declines, as a mechanism for administrative control rather than as a vehicle for faculty expression.

During the crisis, some faculty reviewed the old complaint against the Corporation that it did not include faculty members. Although the issue never reached the level of a formal demand and was never considered at a faculty meeting, the Corporation, apparently feeling a genuine threat to their legitimacy, responded by electing two graduates of Harvard, holding professorial appointments at other universities, as Fellows of the Corporation. Ironically, many faculty were unhappy with this development, since it involved placing on the principal Governing Board scholars who had not been offered professorial posts at Harvard, but who would now have the power to review all appointments in their own field.[4]

CHANGE IN ADMINISTRATION

As at Berkeley, Columbia, Cornell, and many other universities, the student revolt led to a change in the administration. Nathan Pusey, who had taken office in 1953 to lead Harvard in the fight against McCarthyism, notified the Governing Boards that he would resign as of July 30, 1971. All the accomplishments of his administration were largely forgotten by most students, and many faculty, as he joined the ranks of "deposed" college presidents. In all fairness, it should be noted that he not only maintained the tradition of academic freedom with respect to the Economics Department and the rest of Harvard, but that in a period in which most leading private universities declined sharply in

[4]A University Committee on Governance chaired by John Dunlop to evaluate the governance procedures, the majority of whose members were faculty, suggested in its report that "it is possible to argue that academic persons should not be members of the Corporation. The grounds are that their qualifying experience might lead them to meddle in the matters of their discipline, while charged with being, on the basis of generalist qualifications, Fellows of the whole University" (The University Committee on Governance, Harvard University, 1971, p. 34).

academic stature because of an inability to expand their faculty and roster of departments to keep up with the increasing resources of leading
state universities, Harvard held its own. In the two efforts conducted by
the American Council on Education in 1964 and 1969 to evaluate the
scholarly status of graduate departments in various fields, the University of California at Berkeley turned out to have more of the first-ranking
departments than Harvard, suggesting that Harvard had slipped again
as it had done in Lowell's day (Roose & Andersen, 1970). But E. J. Kahn
noted: "On close inspection, Berkeley's preeminence seemed a mite
tainted. In four of the five fields [humanities, social sciences, biological
sciences and physical sciences], Harvard had outranked Berkeley. In
the fifth field, engineering, Harvard hadn't been given any rating at all
[since Harvard does not have engineering, which it leaves to MIT] . . . "
(Kahn, 1968, pp. 47–48). A comparable study of the ranking of 17 professional schools in 1972 reported that Harvard had more first-ranking
schools (four) than any other university. Harvard, however, only covered eight of these areas; for example it does not have schools of veteri-
nary medicine, forestry, optometry, or social work. Among the eight
Harvard schools covered in the 1972 survey, seven were judged by their
peers to be among the top three in their field (Margulies & Blau, 1973,
pp. 22–23).

In describing the faculty personnel policies as he knew them as Dean
of Faculty during part of the Pusey era, McGeorge Bundy pointed to the
continued stress on conceiving of a Harvard professorship as "one
which was held to have been earned by election in a highly competitive
contest." In this respect, he acknowledged their "debt to the work of
James B. Conant."

Building on the best of a tradition he knew from the inside, he created a process
of deliberation and discrimination in the making of senior appointments which
literally forced the asking of an arrogant question, every time a vacancy was
filled: is the candidate who is proposed the best man *in the world* for this job?
Even its true believers found the process a shade pretentious, but its stimulating effect cannot be overstated; it was a strong, if not infallible, protection
against mediocrity and a persistent stimulus to "think big" (Bundy, 1970, p.
539).

In choosing a new President in the fall of 1970, the Fellows of the Harvard Corporation refused to follow the lead of many other universities,
which "democratized" the process by including spokesmen of faculty
and students on selection committees, or inviting formal recommen-

dations from representatives of these two strata. Rather they kept the selection procedure entirely in their own hands. In practice, however, they moved to give all segments of the University a sense of being consulted. All students, faculty, and alumni received letters asking for their suggestions, both as to the qualities necessary for the next president and as to specific names for consideration. Lists of names were drawn up and investigated at length; the process involving personal interviews with 200 faculty, and many student leaders, by individual members of the Corporation. Many also received phone calls from Fellows of the Corporation inquiring as to their knowledge or opinion of a given candidate.

The two faculty factions in the form of their steering committees were active during the presidential nomination period. Although the moderates were in a clear majority among the faculty, the liberal committee was more active. During the presidential selection period, the 12 members met weekly to consider information and strategy. They early recognized that the most likely candidates from within the Faculty of Arts and Sciences were identified with the rival caucus, particularly the Dean of the Faculty, John Dunlop. The liberals' strategy, therefore, was to urge their supporters to point out to the Corporation that any appointment from within the Faculty would be "divisive," that it would have to be someone who was objectionable to a portion of the faculty because of his behavior during the crisis. Alternatively, they urged selecting a President from one of the professional schools, whose faculty and administrators had not formally been involved in the Arts and Sciences' debates. At least three of the Deans of these schools had opposed the calling of the police in the Council of Deans which had met with the President before the bust. In practice, however, this meant that the effective liberal candidate was Derek Bok, the Dean of the Law School, who had been appointed to that post a few years earlier, while still in his thirties. The liberals, however, did not advance Bok as their nominee. To have done so would have eliminated him. Rather, they suggested a number of others who were ideologically close to them, while concentrating their energies on undercutting any possible moderate.

Their rivals, in turn, clearly preferred John Dunlop. Given the fact that his age, 55, was regarded as a liability, they also suggested a variety of other possibilities. And like their caucus opponents, they emphasized to the Fellows the impossibility of certain persons, particularly House masters, whose names had been mentioned as possibilities. Recognizing that Bok was a serious candidate, a number of them tried to undercut his candidacy with arguments indicating their opinion that he had tried to handle student-activist-induced crises in his School by an overly conciliatory policy, and stressing his apparent close personal friendship with some of the more liberal members of the faculty. Not as well organized for this struggle as the liberals, the moderate leadership met irregularly. They were more disposed to accept the authority of the Corporation, to assume that the Fellows of the Corporation were basically in agreement with them. The moderate case and feelings were, therefore, less strongly put. In addition, their concerns about Bok were countered by the fact that he and Dunlop were close friends; they had co-authored a book on labor problems, which had appeared shortly before the crisis. Dunlop himself was positive in his evaluation of Bok as a possible President.

No one is as yet privy to the deliberations of the Corporation, or the considerations of any of them. But journalists who spoke to a number of the Fellows during the selection process were early impressed with the extent to which a number of them had Kingman Brewster, Jr., president of Yale, in mind as a model. Brewster had seemingly kept the peace of New Haven, had prevented any campus confrontation with the police by frequent discussions with student groups, including the radical leaders, by various gestures indicating his sympathy with their general objectives and by rolling with the punch with regard to specific demands and issues. And as one reporter told me early in the selection process, only one man at Harvard looked like Brewster. Derek Bok's record and actions at the Law School were similar to Brewster's. It is a debatable question, therefore, whether the strategy of the liberal steering committee worked, or whether members of the Corporation used the liberals to knock down various candidates whom they did not want in any case. Whatever the factors that determined the outcome, the Fellows chose Derek Bok, and he was confirmed by the Overseers in January (Jacobs, 1971, pp. 19–21). In electing Bok, the governing boards once again followed the pattern of choosing as a "successor" a man who symbolized a repudiation of important policies identified with his predecessor. In this case, the concern was not with educational or scholarly programs, in the traditional sense, but rather with tactics to be employed in dealing with student activism, which ironically was over.

The presidential election "was the last skirmish in a two year feud" between the two caucuses. There is little evidence of any continued activity by either since that time, although somehow as noted above, until 1974, there were almost invariably two candidates for each vacancy on the Faculty Council, who turned out to be related to the "deceased" caucuses.

THE NEW PRESIDENT

Bok, who took office in July 1971 at the age of 40, is the first Harvard President since the early days of the school not to be a Harvard College graduate; he went to Stanford. (At the 1971 Commencement, he was awarded an honorary B.A. to continue the tradition.) Bok, however, like many of the earlier presidents of Harvard, though not Pusey, comes from an old high-status background, the Boks of Philadelphia. His views on matters politic as well as academic have been liberal. Since taking office, he has seemingly fulfilled the expectations of his faculty endorsers. Chosen as a "crisis manager," he has followed a conciliatory policy, avoiding reliance on force, whether outside or internal. When a group of black students occupied Massachusetts Hall, the President's office, during May 1972, demanding that Harvard sell its stock in Gulf because that corporation had investments in Angola, thereby helping the repressive Portuguese regime in its civil war with native rebels, Bok permitted them to stay until they finally left a week later. Bok and/or the Corporation refused, however, to sell the stock (Yale and Columbia had done so).

Thirty-four of the students involved were brought up on charges for illegally occupying the building, but the Committee on Rights and Responsibilities voted to give them a "suspended" sentence, in effect, no punishment. In explaining its action, the CRR reported that it took "into account the long, peculiar history of racial frustrations present at Harvard." Although this action by the CRR was one by a faculty committee, it was congruent with the trouble-avoiding policy of the new administration. Many feared, at the time, that it would sanction similar tactics by white activists in the future.

The administration also tried to avoid for a long time getting involved in a conflict between SDS students and a psychology professor, Richard Herrnstein, who had been harassed inside and outside his classroom on charges of being a "racist" because he had published an article in the August 1971 *Atlantic* concluding that intelligence was largely determined by genetic factors, and that in an open society this relationship could lead to a meritocratic caste-like social system. (The article, however, never mentioned blacks or race, although leaflets and speeches denouncing Herrnstein said that it did.) The President did, however, denounce the year-long harassment in April after the Faculty Council became actively involved, and demanded that action be taken. The administration also allowed SDS to hold its annual convention, billed as an antiracist one designed to organize a campaign against racists like Herrnstein, Jensen, and Shockley, at Harvard in early April, in spite of protests against the decision by various leading faculty, and the majority of the Faculty Council, acting informally. Following the convention, Bok vigorously defended his action at the Faculty meeting, arguing that Harvard opens its doors to all kinds of organizations, that it could not deny the same rights to SDS, that to do so "would have seemed to imply. . . that this University was not prepared to accept free discussion and debate when it was uncomfortable to do so" ("Mr. Bok on Free Speech," 1972, p. 14).[5]

These temporizing policies of the new administration naturally pleased those who had been identified with the former liberal caucus, and disturbed the moderates. One of the leading spokesmen for the defunct moderate caucus, James Q. Wilson, then chairman of the Government Department and member of the Faculty Council, was moved to publish a depressing view of the situation at Harvard in an article in *Commentary* in June 1972. Writing of events that had occurred during the weakened authority of the last two postbust years of the Pusey regime, and of the failure of the first year of the Bok administration to reverse the trend, Wilson argued that Harvard no longer ranked high on the list of institutions in "which free and uninhibited discussion was possible." He noted a series of happenings that had taken place:

In the last two or three years, the list of subjects that cannot be publicly discussed there in a free and open forum has grown steadily, and now includes the war in Vietnam, public policy toward urban ghettoes, the relationship between intelligence and heredity, and the role of American corporations in certain overseas regimes. To be sure *certain* points of view about each of these matters can be, and are, discussed, but a serious discussion of *all* sides of these issues is risky, if not impossible. To be specific: a spokesman for South Vietnam, a critic of liberal policies toward the ghettoes, a scientist who claimed that intelligence is largely inherited, and a corporation representative who denied that his firm was morally responsible for the regime of South Africa have all been harassed and in some cases denied forcibly an opportunity to speak (Wilson, 1972, p. 51).

Still, this was only one view of the situation at Harvard in 1972. The retiring editor of the *Crimson*, Garrett Epps, in his farewell article in

[5]He also defended Herrnstein against SDS harassment in the same talk.

February dealing with the way Harvard looked to a radical member of the class who had been freshmen in the year of the bust, the last physical undergraduate link to that event, evaluated the scene quite differently. To him, the slickness of Harvard, as exemplified by Bok's "cool" and "with it" style had undercut the radicals, had regained for Harvard, at a minimal cost, its authority and power within and outside the Yard. He concluded that "the real victor in April 1969 was Derek C. Bok, student hero and A student extraordinary."

[T]o Bok, the form is all. His only discernible goal as President is to avoid risk to his institution and to minimize conflict which might threaten it by making cosmetic concessions which divide and pacify the constituencies he must manipulate. . . . But neither will he make a profitless stand on principle. Instead he adjusts Harvard just enough to take the initiative away from those demanding changes, makes the minimum effort necessary to blur the issue. . . .

[C]ontrast Pusey with Bok. Nathan Pusey was a nasty old man obsessed with reactionary beliefs and values. Yet for all that he was more human than Bok. He [was] . . . willing to fight to the death with any weapon he had to preserve his principles. . . .

Our day, [those] . . . who briefly shut Harvard down in 1969, like Pusey's had passed and the future belonged to them, the smartest, most dynamic, most skillful group of technocrats the world has ever seen. Thus far, they are winning (Epps, 1972, p. 2).

By the end of the spring term, however, a younger postbust *Crimson* reporter evaluated Bok's first year in a more balanced fashion, one which reflected not only the President's actions, but the increasing moderation or deradicalization of the undergraduate paper itself.

There is no doubt that Bok's style varies drastically from that of his predecessor, Nathan M. Pusey '28. His reputation is that of a crisis solver; in this respect, he has demonstrated an irritating, but apparently effective, knack of avoiding direct confrontation through postponement. Rather than meet an issue head-on, he defers to "a need for further discussion. . . ."

He avoids discussion of SDS and its efforts to get rooms for a national convention at Harvard, saying that it is a matter for the College to decide. Then he quietly arranges for rooms at the Law School to avoid a potential disturbance.

Similarly, he puts off a statement on the Herrnstein issue until harassment has reached the point that the University community is almost united in its revulsion. Then, a statement is a safe and expedient move. . . .

Bok's tendency to let controversy run its course, with only limited involvement on his part, makes it hard for him to convey sincerity when he does act. . . .

Student protests are the product of institutions as much as the men who run them: no President however clever or sincere can avoid serious disagreements over policy in a community as diverse as this one ("Bok Receives Mixed Reviews. . . ," 1972, pp. 1, 3, 8).

THE ISSUES OF THE "CALM"

Yet such discussions of Bok's tactics as a "crisis manager" who could deal with student protest turned out to be largely irrelevant. For by the following academic year, 1972–73, it had become clear that a great "calm" had descended over the American campus from the Berkeley Hills to the banks of the Charles. In fact, in retrospect, it appeared clear that the wave of student activism, which had escalated from the Berkeley Revolt in the fall of 1964, had begun a steady decline from 1969 on, following the decline of American involvement in Vietnam. The massive protest occasioned by U.S. intervention in Cambodia in 1970 proved to be a short-lived interruption. Whatever the tactics or educational policies pursued by institutions across the country, they could be given little credit or blame for the change. A political revolt on campus had ended as its main issues, conscription and the Vietnam war, disappeared.

The new scene brought with it a variety of old and new issues.[6] The faculty legislation creating an independent Afro-American Studies Department in 1969 had called for a review after three years. Controversy over the merits and policies of the department occasioned considerable writing, committee, and faculty meeting activity in 1972–73. Some black scholars, particularly Martin Kilson in Government and Orlando Patterson in Sociology, bitterly criticized the department for a lack of scholarly seriousness, which they blamed in part on its political character, and on the fact that students were involved as voting members in the selection of and evaluation for retention of faculty members. After much heated debate, the faculty voted to require that all new members of the department must have a joint appointment with one of the established discipline fields, and to eliminate the provisions for student participation in faculty selection.

The department's position within the University remains insecure as it ends its fifth year of existence (1974–75). Other academic discipline departments have been reluctant to approve joint appointments. Student interest has declined sharply. During the school year, 1973–74, only 13 students among the three upper years were concentrating in Afro-American Studies. Although critics contend that grades assigned

[6]I have not attempted to cover in detail the various continuing efforts to revive activism at Harvard, since these have been treated by Marshall Meyer (1973, pp. 127–153).

by department faculty are considerably above the Harvard average, enrollment in its courses has also dropped considerably.

Black students showed more interest in the plight of Africans under colonial rule than they did in the changes proposed for the Afro-American department. In the spring of 1972, two dozen of them occupied Massachusetts Hall, the site of the President's office, demanding that Harvard divest itself of 680,000 shares of Gulf Oil, because the company was exploring for oil in Angola. As noted, the university took no action and allowed the sit-in to go on, until the blacks left after one week, "perhaps because they sensed diminished support from other students, perhaps out of boredom, perhaps out of concern about possible penalties" (Meyer, 1973, p. 139). The Committee on Rights and Responsibilities, sensing the pacific mood of the campus, voted in favor of a *suspended* sentence of withdrawal, thus avoiding any confrontation over the punishment issue.

With declining external support for graduate students, the latter organized in various groups, including an abortive union, which called short-lived strikes, seeking more funds from the University. This battle for self-interest resulted in administration commitments to increase support for graduate students from institutional funds, as well as in a decision to sharply curtail the number of graduate students admitted to Harvard to save money (Meyer, 1973, pp. 136–138). In spite of considerable opposition by many faculty to this curtailment of Harvard's role as a center of graduate education, little opposition has been voiced at faculty meetings, a response which appears to reflect reluctance to engage in serious controversy on any issue.

ECONOMICS AND POLITICS AGAIN

That perennial source of debate, the Economics Department, maintained its century-long record of being subject to attack for ideological biases. This time, the attack came from the student left, much as it had done in the early years of the century when the Harvard Socialist Club had complained, or during the thirties, when the ASU had requested that student desire for more relevant and radical courses, and the favorable undergraduate evaluations of radical teachers, be considered when choosing economics faculty. In May 1972, the president was visited by a group of students who presented him with a petition signed by 700 graduate and undergraduate students in support of the reappointment or retention of four nontenured "radical" economists. The petition noted the relative absence of radicals among the senior faculty (only one was recognized as falling in that category among over 30 professors), and stated that the courses taught by the younger radicals are "popular, not only because of the teaching ability and interests shown by these men in their students, but also because of the radical perspective they present in their courses."

The Economics Department has continued to devote much energy to dealing with such criticisms. A 14-member graduate student–faculty committee was established to consider the demands for more "Marxist" work and recommended that "Marxist and neo-Marxist analysis and socio-economic structure" be established as regular fields within the Department, a proposal which would legitimate the search for "Marxist" professors. While the Department turned down this suggestion as such in May 1972, it recommended to its nontenured faculty search committee that it "give special attention" to candidates in this field. It also approved "socio-economic analysis," interpreted to mean Marxist and neo-Marxist analysis, as one of the special fields in which students could be examined (Bluhm, 1972, p. 5; "Economics Department Weighs Marxism," 1972, pp. 1, 6; "Economics Department Bars Marxism . . .," 1972, pp. 1, 6).

In the following two years, however, the Department refused to retain or grant tenure to four self-described "radical" junior faculty. The ever-weakening group of radical student activists sought to raise support around the issue of political discrimination, but found few willing to protest vigorously. But the issue did not die. In the spring of 1974, the Economics Department was once again debating a recommendation by a joint graduate student-faculty committee which recommended that the Department hire at least two faculty to teach courses on "Marxism economics." The chairman of the committee, Kenneth Arrow, indicated that "student criticism of the Economics Department had influenced the move for change and that student pressure would affect the implementation of the Committee recommendation" (LeMoyne, 1974, pp. 1, 6). Although the department turned down major aspects of the recommendations, particularly that Marxian analysis of socioeconomic problems be a required part of its graduate program, it made some important concessions to the demands of the radicals. A departmental vote "endorsed a statement placing first priority on the hiring next year of an assistant professor with a Marxist background in the socio-economic field" and endorsed the inclusion of "a section on Marxian readings in its syllabus for the general theory examination and to permit students to use a course on Marxian historical theory to meet part of their history requirement" (Rabinowitz, 1974, p. 1). By so doing, the Harvard Economics Department seemingly has agreed to the use of explicit political criteria in filling a teaching position.

Criticism of the Economics Department from conservatives has not disappeared. Four undergraduates wrote to the *Crimson* in the spring of 1974 indicating their agreement with the Marxist critics that it is "fruitless to argue that economics should be an apolitical, value-free science of analysis, that setting social objectives is outside its proper realm." They, too, argued that the department is unbalanced, that it "is conspicuously overloaded with Keynesians and monetarists." They complained, however, that in addition to Marxism, "another significant and perhaps more important body of economic thought has been unjustly slighted by Harvard. . . laissez-faire, free-market economics." And like their fellow students on the left, these young conservatives called on the department to at least provide for "token representation" on the faculty of different points of view (White et al., 1974, p. 2).

FREE SPEECH AND OTHER ISSUES

Free speech for faculty members and outside lecturers has remained an issue. Radical groups continue to attack Richard Herrnstein for his views on genetics and intelligence, but find little interest among the student body (Meyer, 1973, pp. 134–136). A scheduled debate between William Shockley, the Stanford Professor of Electrical Engineering who contends that blacks as a group are genetically inferior to whites with respect to intellectual aptitude, and black leader Roy Innis, scheduled before the Law School Forum, was cancelled in 1973 as a result of protests by some students, and fear that the meeting would be broken up. Various faculty and students criticized the Law School for capitulating to pressure, but again the issue had little continuous backing.

John Dunlop, appointed by President Pusey as Dean of the Faculty of Arts and Sciences during the aftermath of the 1969 crisis, resigned in the spring of 1973 to take over direction of the federal government's price-control program. After a search by a faculty committee, the decision narrowed down to two candidates, James Q. Wilson of the Government Department, who had been a prominent member of the now defunct "conservative" caucus, and Henry Rosovsky of the Economics Department, who had played a prominent role in the events leading up to the creation of an Afro-American Studies Department. Some faculty, once active in the "liberal" caucus, reentered the political arena and submitted a petition to the President, signed by over 60 professors, indicating their opposition to Wilson, the rumored leading candidate. Whether the intervention of the "liberals" was important is not known, but President Bok appointed Rosovsky as the new Dean. Since Rosovsky was viewed in sympathetic terms by the "conservatives," his appointment also could pass into the annals as a noncontroversial action. Almost unnoticed was the fact that Rosovsky happens to be a Jew, and as such, is the first one appointed to his post, the second-highest administrative position in the University.

In 1886, Harvard ended the practice of having a Unitarian minister as the Preacher to the University, and the leader of the weekday and Sunday service, by establishing a Board of College Preachers which included men from a variety of Protestant denominations. In 1974, President Bok received a recommendation from a faculty committee, strongly endorsed by the Dean of the Divinity School, to have three Preachers to the University, one Protestant, one Catholic, and one Jewish. The school had come a long way from 1636, although the proposal was not accepted by the Corporation.

Perhaps the most controversial set of issues affecting the University in the mid-seventies revolves around its response to the pressures from the federal government, minority groups, and women to establish and implement a program of affirmative action, which would result in a significant increase in the number from such groups on the faculty. Graduate student and junior faculty women have been particularly active in pressing this cause. Like most other schools, Harvard slowly responded to such pressures but faces difficulties inherent in having relatively few new tenure positions in any given year and in its selection policies and procedures, which prescribe filling tenure vacancies with the presumably best scholar in the field, regardless of background. As of the academic year 1974–75, only ten women and four blacks held tenure professorships in the Faculty of Arts and Sciences.

Intramural political controversy in the second half of the seventies is also likely to reflect the discontents of the faculty over the way in which universities respond to an era of declining revenues, and little, if any, expansion of positions. Students, competing hard with each other to achieve the high grades which will give them an edge on admission to professional schools or in securing jobs, have little time available for politics. In less affluent and more authoritarian schools than Harvard, professors have increasingly turned to collective bargaining as a method of restraining the salary-saving propensities of governing boards (Ladd & Lipset, 1975). While Harvard faculty are not likely to adopt this approach with its antimeritocratic emphasis, there are signs, as the second half of the seventies begins, that even in this institution with its billion-dollar endowment, controversies over budget allocations in an age of austerity will again produce heated controversy at well-attended faculty meetings.

9. Conclusion

The oldest university in the United States has had a long history of student indiscipline, political unrest, and internal controversy. Although political and religious issues affected it from the seventeenth century on, student movements are largely a twentieth-century phenomenon. It is particularly striking how repeatedly in the modern era Harvard has thrown up the largest segment of student radicalism. The Harvard Socialist Club was the biggest unit of the Intercollegiate Socialist Society before World War I. The Harvard Liberal Club generated the most important postwar student movement, the Intercollegiate Liberal League. The Harvard Student Union was reported to have been the largest chapter of the American Student Union in the late 1930s. The most important student Zionist organization of the depression decade, Avukah, which strongly cooperated with the ASU and socialist groups, also had its largest unit at Harvard. Tocsin was clearly the most influential, and close to the biggest, segment of the Student Peace Union of the early sixties. The Maoist May Second Movement had its main center in Cambridge. And for a time, the Harvard SDS chapter outnumbered all others in the national organization. The one important exception to the pattern occurred in the early thirties, when in spite of the large vote for Norman Thomas in the 1932 Harvard straw vote, the local chapters of the socialist SLID and the Communist NSL were relatively weak.

This record, of course, does not mean that radical groups dominated the student body even during waves of student radicalism. When Adlai Stevenson barely defeated Dwight Eisenhower among undergraduates in the 1952 and 1956 straw votes, these were the first occasions that a Democrat did so since Woodrow Wilson in 1912. Wilson, who was the first Democrat to lead in Harvard Yard balloting, was only able to do so because the Republican vote that year was divided between Taft and Roosevelt. Harvard's record of predominant support for Democratic presidential candidates only began in 1960 with the victory of John F.

Kennedy. His triumph, of course, was followed by overwhelming votes for Democrats in succeeding contests, and by equally strong majorities for the liberal peace candidates, Eugene McCarthy, Robert Kennedy, and George McGovern, in prenomination canvasses. During the period of Republican dominance in the Yard, Socialist and other third party support peaked with LaFollette's 17 percent in 1924, Thomas' 18 percent in 1932, and the 16 percent which Henry Wallace and Thomas together secured in 1948.

The available materials from surveys of student opinion in 1952, 1959, and various times in the 1960s suggest that liberalism has been the dominant ideology in Harvard Yard since early in the post-World War II era. The kind of behavior represented by support among undergraduates for religious and racial quotas or segregation, the efforts to break up peace rallies, or the majority opposition to Franklin Roosevelt which occurred in the 1920s and 1930s, was impossible by the end of the 1940s. The domination of Harvard extracurricular life including the editorial board of the *Crimson* by upper-class, conservative, and antipolitical students had also declined sharply, and was soon to vanish totally. By the late sixties, the *Crimson* was regarded by many, including the socialists, as an SDS organ. During the quiet seventies, it has continued to promulgate a cynical "antiestablishment" stance. Since the bust, it has faced opposition from a "moderate" student weekly, the Harvard *Independent*. The latter seeks to give the community a nonradical though quite liberal version of the news.

Any effort to explain the presence of a greater radical minority at Harvard, as compared with all other "elite" schools, must tie back to some of the generalizations about the institution made by Veysey and May, who examined the history of the American university and intellectual life up to World War I. As noted earlier, they stressed the presence at Harvard of a larger group of "unorthodox" elements among the student body, some of whom became important critical intellectuals after graduation, than at any other school. Veysey suggested that the backgrounds of Harvard students were socially more diversified than elsewhere in academe. Further, as May noted, its faculty included a much larger proportion of the genuinely creative. This meant that in spite of the fact that most Harvard students had private school backgrounds, and that the socially elite "clubbies" tended to dominate the scene until World War II, Harvard has included a considerable emphasis on intellectualism, on rewarding individuals for scholarly attainments, for close to a century.

Intellectuality, as many surveys of both faculty and students completed since the pre-World War I era suggest, is related to heterodox behavior in other areas, including particularly political and religious outlooks (Lipset, 1972a; Lipset, 1972b; Ladd & Lipset, 1975). Basically, both theory and empirical evidence indicate that the cast of mind necessary for intellectual creativity, originality, and the rejection of the traditional and accepted within given arts or disciplines, is associated with a socially critical outlook. In the United States, a number of studies of academic and other intellectuals indicate that the higher they rank on indicators of intellectual achievement, the more likely they are to have left social and political views. The better a university, as reflected by measures of academic scholarly achievement, the larger the percentage of its faculty who have been sympathetic to and involved in critical politics, whether these be opposition to Joe McCarthyism, or the Vietnam war, or support for left views. Roughly speaking, the same indicators of institutional eminence correlated with a propensity to sustain student activism during the era of the sixties.

It would follow from this line of argument, as Henry May and Laurence Veysey noted, that the transformation of Harvard under Eliot into the preeminent center of academic intellectuality on the faculty side, and the encouragement, through both admissions policies and faculty orientations, of intellectuality among the student body, should have produced a continuing minority of students oriented toward creativity and social criticism, thus providing the bases from which the various Harvard radical political clubs could recruit.

Lowell's policies may have inhibited this tendency in the 1920s and early 1930s, but the changes toward increased meritocracy fostered by the Conant regime in the 1930s and brought to fruition after World War II heightened the domination of the academic culture over the club and athletic ones which were in ascendency among the student body in the 1920s and early 1930s. As Samuel Huntington pointed out, by the latter decade "the clubby culture. . . . had apparently come under serious challenge by the spread of the academic culture among some portions of the College students. After World War II, with the permanent 'nationalization' of the Harvard student body and the temporary influx of veterans, the academic culture came into its own" (Huntington, 1969, pp. 51–52).

As noted earlier, Huntington suggested that the prevalence of the academic culture was responsible for the weakening of political involvement in the fifties, that politically disposed liberal and left students were pressed to spend their time in the stacks rather than at meetings because of the prestige of academic accomplishments. I would question this conclusion, given all the evidence of the high interrelationship of the academic or intellectual culture with the political at other times. In my judgment, the fifties at Harvard and other scholarly prestigious institutions set the stage for the protest waves of the sixties in these schools because they became much more committed to intellectual creativity as a value than they had ever been. The propensity of intellectuality to foster an "adversary" political culture was repressed in the fifties by the larger political events, subsumed under the heading of anti-Stalinism, which turned intellectuals in the Western world generally away from political criticism. As I noted at the end of the fifties, these events inhibited the "obligation" normally felt by "intellectuals to attack and criticize. Their solution to this dilemma is to continue to feel allied with the left, but to vote Democratic; to think of themselves as liberals—and often even as socialists—but to withdraw from active involvement or interest in politics and to concentrate on their work, whether it be writing poetry or scholarly articles" (Lipset, 1960, p. 342).

The academic culture of the 1950s was peculiarly nonpolitical not because of the strains between scholarship and political activism, and there are many such, but because the fifties were a special and unique period in the history of intellectualdom, one in which events sharply contradicted the intellectuals' propensity to oppose established institutions, resulting then "in a feeling of malaise which takes the form of complaining that everyone, including the intellectuals, is too conformist" (Lipset, 1960, p. 342).

If this analysis has validity, it would follow that once the political "inhibitors" broke down, as they began to do with Khruschev's Twentieth Party Congress Speech (1956) exposing the crimes of Stalinism and the consequent breakdown of the appearance of a monolithic, totalitarian, expanding Communist empire, political criticism and activism would revive in the major centers of intellectual creativity. The reawakening of student and faculty activism at Harvard was but a special case of an almost worldwide phenomenon.

And given this logic, the question becomes not why Harvard repeatedly has been a major center of student activism, but rather why so many other schools from Berkeley through to Columbia, Chicago, Cornell, Michigan, and Wisconsin, experienced a major internal upheaval earlier than it did? One answer to this question may lie in noting another aspect of the various activist clubs and movements which have existed in Cambridge since 1906. While all of them were relatively large, they also tended, with but few exceptions, to be on the "right" of the national left tendency of which they were part. Thus, there is no indication that the members of the Harvard Socialist Club had any sympathy for the rather large revolutionary left-wing of the pre-World War I Socialist party, or the assorted anarcho-syndicalist tendencies of the time. Rather they deliberately followed "Fabian" gradualist policies. The Liberal Club of the 1920s was clearly not radical in ideology or tactics. The Harvard Student Union of the 1930s, though containing a large pro-Communist faction, was one of the very few major units of the American Student Union which adhered to a distinctly non-Communist ideology after 1937. Its delegates to national conventions were usually among the small minority who opposed the pro-Soviet line. Tocsin was the most policy-oriented segment of the Student Peace Union of the early 1960s. As T. J. Crawford noted in a contemporary study of the group:

From the beginning the difference between Tocsin and most other peace groups was apparent. The emphasis on positive alternatives is an example of Tocsin's most outstanding approach. Other groups have typically adopted a moralistic and emotional stance. . . . They have been long on demonstrations and attention getting civil disobedience activities, but short on specific and workable suggestions for alternatives to the arms race. . . . By contrast, Tocsin seems to. . . have adopted a "structuralist" approach in attempting to develop specific and feasible proposals for altering the social structure. . . .

The student peace demonstration [in 1962] in Washington, D.C., involving over 5,000 students, was initiated and organized by the Tocsin leadership. . . . But the controlled intellectual tone of the demonstration clearly showed the effects of Tocsin's leadership. The eight page Tocsin-authored policy statement around which the demonstration was centered took cognizance of the problems of the cold war, and recommended several specific unilateral initiatives. The contrast with the "Ban the Bomb" approach of many previous student peace demonstrations is obvious. While in Washington, students discussed the policy statement with members of the State Department, the Atomic Energy Commission, the Congress and presidential advisors (Crawford, 1963, pp. 5, 8).

The Harvard SDS, incorporating former members of Tocsin, also was relatively moderate in its first years. It moved drastically to the left in 1967, in part reflecting the entrance of a number of Maoists formerly active in the May Second Movement. But as indicated earlier, it then remained divided between a "right-wing" faction known as the New Left and the Maoist Worker-Student Alliance. The former, who found reasons for objecting to a major confrontation, had a majority in the Harvard group until after the bust; this destroyed their credibility. In effect, the Harvard SDS included many who, unlike their colleagues at

Columbia, were for foregoing confrontation until they had more assurance of victory, assurance which could only be secured by further educational efforts.

The presence of a large Maoist movement at Harvard in the May Second Movement and then in SDS does, of course, confound the thesis that Harvard radicals tend to be on the more reformist end of their particular brand of radicalism. But it does so because of some other peculiarities. The Harvard Maoists, both in the May Second Movement and SDS, differed considerably in social background from the dominant strand of student activism as reported in various surveys. Studies from both the 1930s and the 1960s agree that left students have tended to come from liberal to left backgrounds (though usually somewhat to the left of their parents), from families which loosely qualify as belonging to the "intelligentsia," highly educated liberal to radical professionals, disproportionately Jewish and liberal Protestant (Keniston, 1968, pp. 306–310; Lipset, 1972*b*, pp. 80–113).

At Harvard, however, these background variables characterized the YPSL and the New Left members, but *not* the Maoists, either in the May Second Movement or the WSA. The latter tendency drew support from the scions of well-to-do WASP elite, often conservative, family backgrounds. They represented a true "generation conflict" in ways that those in other left groupings did not. The founders of the May Second Movement were sons of a Texas oil magnate. Of the students arrested in University Hall, almost all of whom were WSA (few of the New Left were arrested), "approximately 50 percent attended prep school, with the largest representation from the most exclusive ones like St. Paul's. Just over 40 percent of the Harvard student body as a whole comes from prep school" (Kelman, 1970, p. 140). A similar emphasis on WASP elite private school background was reported for the Maoist students tried by the Committee of Fifteen for their role in the sit-in.

Steven Kelman, the then leader of the YPSL, particularly emphasized the differences between the "hereditary radicals" of the New Left caucus, whom he, as a Social Democrat, described as "good people" with whom one could argue, and the WSA Maoist group whom he characterized as "WASP rebels." Without explaining why the particular group of Harvard "aristocrats want to rebel," he argued that they were the source of bitter extremism:

It is in the guilty aristocrat that we see clearly politics not for politics' sake, but for self-expression, the possibility of recapturing a lost vitality that one feels too weak to create for oneself. . . .

The declining aristocrats in SDS are all, *to a man,* pro-PL. Not only is there not a single one who's attracted by the weak reformism of the Young People's Socialist League, but there is not a single one of them in the New Left caucus. PL's rantings are about on the intellectual level that such students, whom I always considered products of favoritism at the admissions office, can comprehend (Kelman, 1970, p. 146).

It is difficult to offer a satisfactory explanation for the conversion to a form of radical extremism of a segment of the scions of privileged WASP America at Harvard in the late sixties. Possibly, the very generality of the strong antiwar, anti-Establishment stance which took over within the intellectual academic culture left those of the social elite who were affected with a need to go all the way once they were intellectualized and radicalized. An upper-class radical is vulnerable to attack from others as reflecting his privileged social background unless he totally radicalizes himself so that no one can accuse him of being moderate. Perhaps, the "aristocrats" lacked the sense, which children of radicals or active liberals had, that the left cause could not be expected to triumph overnight. Possibly, unlike the "hereditary radicals," they had the fervor of the converted true believer. But whatever the source of their commitment, the fact remains that in the Great Rebellion of 1969, it was the children of the true blue, of the WASP elite, linked by social origins to the classes which had manned the clubs, not the scions of the "unassimilables," who brought a Harvard administration down, who forced capitulation on the Corporation and faculty.

The politics of confrontation, as fostered by the more extreme activists, are clearly, however, not the style of Harvard undergraduates. Their position at a university with strong links to politics and government, the presence among them of many children of governing elites, the realistic aspirations of many to enter the elite, and thus seemingly to have an opportunity to reform the country, moderated Harvard radicalism in the past, and continues to do so today. During the Cambodian events in May 1970, and the revived bombing and mining of North Vietnam in December 1972, the predominant response of Harvard protestors was to go en masse to Washington to lobby for antiwar proposals with Congressmen from marginal constituencies, that is, with men whose vote could be affected. Many more students were involved in the practical politics seminars of the (Kennedy) Institute of Politics, which meet regularly but do not give credit, than participated in the Maoist remnant of SDS in the seventies or the New Left New American Movement. Support for McGovern was almost the only cause on campus with any widespread support in the spring of 1972.[1] In the ensuing years, the political atmosphere at Harvard remains one of a generalized liberalism, although it must be noted that in 1973–74 and 1974–75, the largest undergraduate political group was the Young Republicans, a fact which attests more to the passivity of the more liberally oriented students than to any dominance by the Republicans.

Evidence that the underlying structure of attitudes developed in the 1960s has not changed fundamentally in the subsequent less politicized era has been presented by Marshall Meyer (1974), who in the spring of 1974 repeated his 1969 survey of Harvard students. As indicated in Table 1, there is very little difference in the response pattern in spite of the considerable variation in the political climate. Thus five years after the occupation of University Hall, only 24 percent of the students identify their politics as center or right of center, as contrasted to 23 percent in the earlier period. About one-fifth in both eras placed themselves in the two furthest left positions on a nine-point scale. A similar majority (56 and 58 percent) located their politics on the moderate left. Not surprisingly, when asked to describe where they thought most junior and senior faculty were politically, they projected the faculty's opinions as much more conservative than their own, with the junior faculty more liberal than the senior. The students also identified their parents' politics as significantly more conservative than their own, while they perceived the population of the United States as preponderantly conservative.

The pattern of a similar distribution of responses by both samples held up with astonishing similarity with respect to a number of questions about specific issues. Thus 80 percent "strongly disapproved" of United States involvement in Vietnam on both occasions. The identical percentage, 77, "strongly approved" of the civil rights movement in 1969 and 1974. Thirty-three percent in 1969 and 37 percent in 1974 "disapproved" of black power. In 1969, 37 percent of the respondents indicated that they had taken part in the "McCarthy campaign"; five years later, 38 percent reported having participated in McGovern's Presidential effort. The only political question which produced any difference between the two eras pertained to "labor." Forty-nine percent in 1969 and 64 percent five years later agreed that "Labor does not get its fair share of what it produces," a variation which may reflect the impact of different economic circumstances, prosperity and recession.

[1]For a report on the attitudes of Harvard students based on a survey taken in the summer of 1972 by a mail questionnaire to which 42 percent of the 150 sent questionnaires replied, see Meyer (1973, p. 142).

TABLE 1 *Perceived political position of different strata by Harvard students, 1969 and 1974 (in percentages)*

		Yourself		Most Harvard students	
		1969	1974	1969	1974
Furthest left	− 4	1	3	1	0
	− 3	19	16	7	4
	− 2	32	40	33	32
	− 1	24	18	41	39
Center	0	9	8	11	12
	+ 1	8	7	5	9
	+ 2	4	6	2	4
	+ 3	2	2	0	0
Furthest right	+ 4	0	1	0	0
		(893)	(516)	(900)	(504)

		Junior faculty		Senior faculty	
		1969	1974	1969	1974
Furthest left	− 4	0	0	0	0
	− 3	10	6	0	1
	− 2	33	22	4	6
	− 1	37	45	28	21
Center	0	12	17	27	28
	+ 1	5	7	23	21
	+ 2	1	3	14	17
	+ 3	0	1	4	4
Furthest right	+ 4	0	0	0	0
		(872)	(489)	(881)	(488)

		Your father		The average person in the U.S.	
		1969	1974	1969	1974
Furthest left	− 4	1	1	0	0
	− 3	2	3	0	0
	− 2	8	14	0	3
	− 1	16	24	1	1
Center	0	18	17	15	25
	+ 1	18	16	32	38
	+ 2	20	15	35	28
	+ 3	14	8	13	5
Furthest right	+ 4	3	3	2	1
		(888)	(520)	(890)	(516)

SOURCE: Meyer (1974, pp. 3–6).

But if the students of the Watergate era strongly resembled their compeers of the Vietnam protest period in their general political views, a change between these generations was indicated with respect to attitudes toward political tactics. Here the 1974 group revealed less enthusiasm for militant or violent tactics, a shift back to support for gradualist or moderate methods. Thus 66 percent of those queried in 1974 expressed "strong disapproval" of urban violence, as contrasted to 53 percent earlier. Forty percent disapproved of "student unrest" in the mid-seventies, compared to 28 percent with similar views in 1969. Immediately after the "bust," 68 percent agreed that "There are times when it almost seems better for the people to take the law into their own hands rather than wait for the machinery of government to do it." Ten percent fewer felt this way in 1974. A fifth of the late sixties respondents agreed that "in order to make the world better a lot of innocent people will have to suffer," a view which only 14 percent supported five years later. During the interval, of course, 18-year-old youth had gained the right to vote, a fact which may have affected student attitudes toward the electoral process. Fully 80 percent of the Harvard students reported that they were registered. As might be expected, given their predominant liberal to left views, only 9 percent were registered as Republicans, a third, 34 percent, were Independents, while the majority, 56.5 percent, were identified Democrats.

The five-year interval since the "troubles" had not made Harvard students friendlier to the University. Over half, 54 percent, the same percentage as in 1969, believed that "more radical courses are needed." Thirty-five percent in 1974, almost identical to the 33 percent in 1969, believed that "morale among students is very low." The proportion reporting being "friendly with one or more faculty members" had declined slightly from 78 to 72 percent, while those who indicated that they talked two or more times a week with faculty members outside of class also had fallen from 55 percent to 49 percent. Those who would rate senior faculty as good teachers declined slightly over the period from 75 to 73 percent, although junior (nontenured) faculty improved their positive ratings a mite from 77 to 81 percent. Yet it must be noted that on questions dealing with the extent of concern exhibited by faculty "with *personal* problems of students," a sizable change in attitudes was recorded by Marshall Meyer. In 1969, half the respondents felt that most senior faculty were "hardly" or "not at all concerned," a figure which had jumped to 70 percent by 1974. While junior faculty were rated as more concerned than their seniors, fully 40 percent complained of their lack of interest in students' personal problems, as contrasted to 19 percent five years earlier.

Marshall Meyer suggests that this heightened student malaise about faculty concern for their "personal problems" reflects the increased career consciousness produced by the depressed labor market of the mid-seventies. Students are seemingly more personally insecure about their futures than they were during the more prosperous 1960s. Whether this interpretation is valid or not, the fact remains that the decline in overt activism in the mid-seventies at Harvard, as in academe generally, does not reflect a significant shift to the right among students or greater satisfaction with their educational experience.[2] Many of the students at Harvard and other highly selective institutions come from highly educated family backgrounds in which the adversary culture of the intelligentsia is dominant. And the cynicism about established institutions diffused during the 1960s and reinforced by the experiences of the Watergate era has weakened the legitimacy of the university as well.

In his discussion of the decline of the meritocratic academic culture, written after the bust in 1969, Samuel Huntington deplored the strength of the anti-intellectual "counterculture" at Harvard. He suggested that many students were again worshiping at different altars from the intellectually oriented faculty. And he concluded that as in earlier times when a scholarly faculty had faced undergraduates who predominantly reflected the anti-intellectual culture of the socially elite "clubbies," the faculty now must deal with a student body many of whose members accept the new anti-intellectual orientations of the "counterculture" and the New Left. Thus, as in the past, many students complain about professors, and professors resent students. The results of Meyer's 1974 survey would appear to support Huntington's concerns.

Given the continued strength of the intellectual or academic culture among the Harvard faculty, however, it is possible to still hope that the academic culture may regain much of the ground it has lost. The strength of that culture has been fostered by many faculty who have strongly supported the emergence of student activism, and who have personally been deeply involved in the antiwar movement and other political activities. Many of them, even during the heyday of the protest era, turned strongly to arguing with the politicized students that their easy solutions for university problems were wrong, that politicization of the university at the expense of scholarship was bad. Thus radical sociologist Barrington Moore emphasized to Harvard students during the sixties that in his experience they always have had a major influence on the faculty with respect to educational policy, that formal

---

[2]Meyer's findings that the "calm" of the mid-seventies is not reflected in more conservative collegiate attitudes are paralleled in national surveys which also indicate the persistence of left-oriented antiestablishment views (Yankelovich, 1974).

student power would reduce rather than enhance that influence. David Riesman, active in Tocsin and other peace movements of the early sixties, strongly urged the need to keep explicit politics out of the university, and also argued after the "bust" against student participation in the governance of departments or other parts of the university. H. Stuart Hughes, Third Party candidate and national peace leader, deplored the demands of activists for special student privileges with respect to meeting classes or taking exams during periods of war-induced crisis, and noted that he has always met his academic obligations, even when running for office (Lipset, 1972*b*, pp. 210–215).

Such arguments do not win over those for whom politics is a way of life and for whom the university is primarily a fortress from which to recruit troops to attack the larger society, or its surrogate, the administration building. But since Harvard still tries to draw both faculty and students from those who have shown very high achievement or aptitude in intellectual pursuits, since it still has the arrogance, as Bundy pointed out, to think of itself as the "best," by so doing it fosters the commitment of all the Estates of the University to scholarship. Whether it succeeds in this, however, depends more on the state of America and the world than on what happens inside Harvard Yard. In a sane and only reasonably troubled world, Harvard will continue its history of political activism and concern, while doing its primary job of scholarship and education as well. Those conservatives who fear challenges, and radicals who fail to understand that a commitment to intellectual creativity is the most continuing source of change in the modern world, will be unhappy. But as McGeorge Bundy once explained of Harvard "the extraordinary freedom . . . was sustained . . . more by the universal commitment to the ideal of excellence," than by anything else (Bundy, 1970, p. 539). The price of freedom and innovation is often disturbing; the rewards are very high. In February–March 1971, the International Gallup Poll asked leaders in 70 nations: "What university do you regard as the best in the world—all things taken in consideration?" The poll reported that Harvard topped the list ("Harvard Named Best University," 1972, p. 23).[3]

[3]This survey is only the most recent of a large number of quantitative measures of the contributions of the faculty and students of different universities which have placed Harvard in the lead. Yale historian of education, George W. Pierson, in his *Education of American Leaders* (1969), has published over one hundred tables listing the contributions of American colleges and universities from American Independence down to the mid-1960s to various leadership roles in political, economic, religious, cultural, and academic life. Harvard stands out as the leading contributor in the very large majority of them. Although high on various business and other nonacademic lists, its greatest lead over other schools has been in cultural and intellectual fields.

References to Part One

Aaron, Daniel: *Writers on the Left,* Harcourt, Brace & World, Inc., New York, 1961.

Adams, Brooks: *The Emancipation of Massachusetts,* (1887) Houghton Mifflin Company, Boston, 1962.

Adams, Charles Francis (ed.): *The Works of John Adams,* vol. 7, Little, Brown and Company, Boston, 1853.

Adams, Charles Francis (ed.): *Memoirs of John Quincy Adams,* vol. 1, J. B. Lippincott Company, Philadelphia, 1874.

Adams, Charles Francis: *Three Phi Beta Kappa Addresses,* Houghton Mifflin Company, Boston, 1907.

Adams, Charles Francis: *Charles Francis Adams, 1835–1915: An Autobiography,* Houghton Mifflin Company, Boston, 1916.

Adams, Henry: *Historical Essays,* Charles Scribner's Sons, New York, 1891.

Albright, A. P.: "Arms and the Student: A History of Isolationism at Harvard University, 1939–1941," honors thesis, Department of History, Harvard University, 1962.

Allmendinger, D. F., Jr.: "Student Unrest in the Decades Before the Civil War," unpublished paper, Department of History, Smith College, 1971.

Altbach, Edith H.: "Vanguard of Revolt: Students and Politics in Central Europe, 1815–1848," in S. M. Lipset and Philip G. Altbach (eds.), *Students in Revolt,* Houghton Mifflin Company, Boston, 1969, pp. 451–474.

Altbach, Philip G.: *Student Politics in America: A Historical Analysis,* McGraw-Hill Book Company, New York, 1974.

Altbach, Philip G., and P. M. Peterson: "Before Berkeley: Historical Perspectives on American Student Activism," in P. G. Altbach and R. S. Laufer (eds.), *The New Pilgrims: Youth Protest in Transition,* David McKay Company, Inc., New York, 1972.

"Ambassadors," *Harvard Alumni Bulletin,* vol. 57, p. 617, May 21, 1955.

Appleton, Nathan: "Harvard College During the War of the Rebellion," *The New England Magazine,* vol. 4, pp. 3–23, March 1891.

"April Crisis at Harvard," *Boston Sunday Globe,* pp. 1–24, October 12, 1969.

Bailyn, Bernard: *The New England Merchants in the Seventeenth Century,* Harvard University Press, Cambridge, Mass., 1955.

Baltzell, E. D.: *Philadelphia Gentlemen,* The Free Press, Glencoe, Ill., 1958.

Bancroft, George, and Linus Child: *Report on Diminishing the Cost of Instruction in Harvard College Together with a Minority Report on the Same Subject* (by John C. Gray), The University Press, Cambridge, Mass., 1845.

Batchelder, Roland B.: "The Student Council," *Harvard Graduates' Magazine,* vol. 21, pp. 621–622, June 1913.

Batchelder, S. F.: *Bits of Harvard History,* Harvard University Press, Cambridge, Mass., 1924.

Bell, Daniel: *The Coming of Post-Industrial Society,* Basic Books, Inc., Publishers, New York, 1973.

Binger, Carl: "A Child of Enlightenment," in M. Childs and J. Reston (eds.), *Walter Lippmann and His Times,* Harcourt, Brace and Company, Inc., New York, 1959.

Blodgett, G. T.: "Massachusetts Democrats in the Cleveland Era," unpublished Ph.D. dissertation, Department of History, Harvard University, 1960.

Bloomgarden, L.: "Our Changing Elite Colleges," *Commentary,* vol. 29, pp. 150–154, February 1960.

Bluhm, J. S.: "Students Give Petition to Bok: Demand Radicals Be Rehired," *Harvard Crimson,* vol. 155, pp. 1, 5, May 11, 1972.

"Bok Receives Mixed Reviews in His First Year as President," *Harvard Crimson,* vol. 155, pp. 1, 3, May 31, 1972.

Bourne, Randolph: *Youth and Life,* Houghton Mifflin Company, Boston, 1913.

Bourne, Randolph: "The Price of Radicalism," *The New Republic,* vol. 6, p. 161, March 11, 1916.

Boutwell, George S.: *Reminiscences of Sixty Years in Public Affairs,* McClure, Philips & Co., New York, 1902.

Bowes, H. P.: "University and College Student Rebellion in Retrospect and Some Sociological Implications," unpublished Ed.D. dissertation, School of Education, University of Colorado, 1964.

Brewster, Kingman, Jr., and Spencer Klaw: "We Stand Here," *The Atlantic,* vol. 166, pp. 277–279, September 1940.

Briggs, L. B. R., et al.: "Report of the Committee on Improving Instruction in Harvard College," *Harvard Graduates' Magazine,* vol. 12, pp. 611–670, June 1904.

Bristed, C. A.: *Five Years in an English University,* G. P. R. Putnam, New York, 1874.

Brooks, Van Wyck: "Harvard and American Life," *Living Age,* vol. 259, pp. 643–649, December 12, 1908.

Broun, Heywood, and George Britt: *Christians Only,* The Vanguard Press, New York, 1931.

Brown, Rollo W.: *Dean Briggs,* Harper and Brothers, New York, 1926.

Brown, Rollo W.: *Harvard Yard in the Golden Age,* Current Books, New York, 1948.

Brown, W. G., and John L. Dodge: "Student Life: The Political Clubs," *Harvard Graduates' Magazine,* vol. 1, pp. 303–306, 1893.

Brubacher, J. S., and W. Rudy: *Higher Education in Transition,* Harper & Row, Publishers, Incorporated, New York, 1968.

Bundy, McGeorge: "Were Those the Days?" *Daedalus,* vol. 99, pp. 531–567, Summer 1970.

Bush, G.: *History of Higher Education in Massachusetts,* Government Printing Office, Washington, D. C., 1891.

Buttenwieser, P. A.: "In Fifties, Anti-Communist Hysteria Challenged Harvard's Independence as Student Politics Ignored Issues," *Harvard Crimson,* Registration Issue, vol. 138, pp. S–1, 23, September 1960.

Caffey, C. G.: "Harvard's Political Preferences Since 1860," *Harvard Graduates' Magazine,* vol. 1, pp. 407–415, April 1893.

Cain, E.: *They'd Rather Be Right,* The Macmillan Company, New York, 1963.

Cater, Harold Dean (ed.): *Henry Adams and His Friends,* Houghton Mifflin Company, Boston, 1947.

Cattell, J. McKeen: "A Further Statistical Study of American Men of Science," *Science,* vol. 32, pp. 672–688, November 11, 1910.

Cattell, J. McKeen: *University Control,* Science Press, New York, 1913.

Channing, William Ellery: *Memoirs of William Ellery Channing,* William Crosby and H. P. Nichols, Boston, 1851.

Christoffel, T., D. Finkelhor, and D. Gilbert (eds.): *Up Against the American Myth: A Radical Critique of Corporate Capitalism Based Upon the Controversial Harvard College Course, Social Relations 148–149,* Holt, Rinehart and Winston, Inc., New York, 1970.

Church, R. L.: "The Economists Study Society," in P. Buck (ed.), *Social Sciences at Harvard, 1860–1920,* Harvard University Press, Cambridge, Mass., 1965, pp. 18–90.

Cohen, Michael D., and James G. March: *Leadership and Ambiguity: The American College President,* McGraw-Hill Book Company, New York, 1974.

Cohen, S. S.: "Student Unrest in the Pre-Revolutionary Decade, 1765–1775," unpublished paper, Department of History, Loyola University, Chicago, 1971.

"College Discipline," *The Critic*, vol. 1, pp. 204–205, July 30, 1881.

"College Discipline," *The Nation*, vol. 48, pp. 145–155, February 21, 1889.

Combs, P. C.: "Harvard College 1846–1869: The Age of Transition," honors thesis, Department of History, Harvard University, 1950.

"The Committee of Fifteen: Interim Report on the Causes of the Recent Crisis," *Reports*, pp. 1–60, Harvard Printing Office, Cambridge, Mass., June 9,1969.

Comstock, D. K.: " 'Moderate Liberals' Predominate Politically," *Harvard Crimson*, vol. 137, pp. S–9–10, June 11, 1959.

Conant, James B.: "Academical Patronage and Superintendence," *Harvard Educational Review*, vol. 8, pp. 312–334, May 1938.

Conant, James B.: *My Several Lives*, Harper & Row, Publishers, Incorporated, New York, 1970.

Cowan, P. S.: "Thirties: Decade of Postponed Consciousness," *Harvard Crimson*, Registration Issue, vol. 138, pp. S–7–8, 17–18, September 1960.

Cowley, W. H.: "Student Participation," unpublished paper, School of Education, Stanford University, n. d.

Cowley, W. H.: "History of Student Residential Housing," *School and Society*, vol. 40, pp. 710–711, 1934.

Crawford, T. J.: "Tocsin and the Harvard-Radcliffe Conservative Club: A Study of Student Political Groups," unpublished paper, Department of Social Relations, Harvard University, May 1963.

Cushing, Thomas: "Town and Gown in Old Times," *Harvard Graduates' Magazine*, vol. 8, pp. 15–18, September 1899.

Dana, Richard Henry, Jr.: "Here Was an Open Rebellion," *Harvard Alumni Bulletin*, vol. 70, pp. 26–27, May 25, 1968.

Davis, A. M.: "Jackson's LL.D.," *Proceedings of the Massachusetts Historical Society*, vol. 20, pp. 490–512, December 1906.

Davis, Paul: "Fair Harvard," *Harvard Guardian*, vol. 6, pp. 28–31, June 1941.

Dennet, R., et al.: *Official Report of the Committee on the Investigation of Police Tactics in Charlestown on May 17, 1934*, privately printed, Cambridge, Mass., 1934.

DeVoto, Bernard: "The Faculty First," *Harvard Graduates' Magazine*, vol. 62, pp. 90–97, December 1933.

Dewey, David R.: "The Teaching of Economics at Harvard," *Harvard Graduates' Magazine*, vol. 26, pp. 605–607, June 1918.

Dexter, Franklin B.: "On Some Social Distinctions at Harvard and Yale, Before the Revolution," *Proceedings of the American Antiquarian Society*, New Series, vol. 9, pp. 34–59, October 1893.

Dexter, Franklin B.: *Miscellaneous Historical Papers of Fifty Years*, Tuttle, Morehouse, and Taylor, New Haven, Conn., 1918.

Dobbs, Z., et al.: *Keynes at Harvard: Economic Deception as a Political Credo*, Veritas Foundation, New York, 1962.

Dorr, G. H.: "Student Life," *Harvard Graduates' Magazine*, vol. 5, pp. 255–260, 1896.

Draper, H.: "The Student Movement of the Thirties: A Political History," in Rita Simon (ed.), *As We Saw the Thirties*, University of Illinois Press, Urbana, 1967, pp. 151–189.

Duberman, Martin: *Charles Francis Adams, 1807–1886*, Houghton Mifflin Company, Boston, 1961.

DuBois, W. E. B.: *Dusk of Dawn*, Harcourt, Brace and Company, Inc., New York, 1940.

DuBois, W. E. B.: *The Autobiography of W. E. B. DuBois*, International Publishers Company, Inc., New York, 1969.

Dupree, A. Hunter: *Asa Gray*, Belknap Press of the Harvard University Press, Cambridge, Mass., 1959.

Earnest, Ernst: *Academic Procession*, Bobbs-Merrill, Indianapolis, 1953.

"Economics Department Weighs Marxism," *Harvard Crimson*, vol. 155, pp. 1, 6, May 19, 1972.

"Economics Department Bars Marx Option from Graduate Theory Examination," *Harvard Crimson*, vol. 155, pp. 1, 6, May 24, 1972.

Edsall, John T.: "The Experimental Attitude in Economics," *The Gadfly*, p. 3, December 1922.

Eichel, Lawrence E., Kenneth W. Host, Robert D. Luskin, and Richard M. Neustadt: *The Harvard Strike*, Houghton Mifflin Company, Boston, 1970.

"Eisenhower Carries Crimson Poll," *Harvard Crimson*, vol. 29, p. 1, October 31, 1952.

Eliot, Charles W.: *University Administration*, Houghton Mifflin Company, Boston, 1908.

Eliot, Charles W.: *A Turning Point in Higher Education: The Inaugural Address of Charles William Eliot as President of Harvard College, October 19, 1869*, Harvard University Press, Cambridge, Mass., 1969.

Eliot, Samuel: *A Sketch of the History of Harvard College and of Its Present State*, Little, Brown and Company, Boston, 1848.

Elliott, Edward C., and M. M. Chambers (eds.): *Charters and Basic Laws of*

Selected American Universities and Colleges, Carnegie Foundation for the Advancement of Teaching, New York, 1934.

Epps, G.: "A Parting Shot," *Harvard Crimson,* vol. 155, p. 2, February 7, 1972.

Erikson, Erik H.: *Identity: Youth and Crisis,* W. W. Norton & Company, Inc., New York, 1968.

Evans, M. Stanton: *Revolt on Campus,* Henry Regnery Company, Chicago, 1961.

Everett, Edward: "Edward Everett on Harvard's Need for State Funds, 1848–1949," in Richard Hofstadter and Wilson Smith (eds.), *American Higher Education,* The University of Chicago Press, Chicago, 1961, pp. 379–387.

"The Faculty Council," *Harvard Alumni Bulletin,* vol. 42, pp. 178–179, November 3, 1939.

Felix, David: *Protest: Sacco-Vanzetti and the Intellectuals,* Indiana University Press, Bloomington, 1965.

Feuer, Lewis S.: *The Conflict of Generations,* Basic Books, Inc., Publishers, New York, 1969.

Finkelhor, D.: "Radical Education at Harvard," *Leviathan,* vol. 1, pp. 49–50, March 1969.

Fischer, D. H.: *The Revolution of American Conservatism: The Federalist Party in the Era of Jeffersonian Democracy,* Harper & Row, Publishers, Incorporated, New York, 1965.

"The Flavor of Harvard," *The New Republic,* vol. 26, pp. 322–323, August 16, 1922.

Ford, J.: "Social Ethics," in Samuel Eliot Morison (ed.), *The Development of Harvard University Since the Inauguration of President Eliot, 1869–1929,* Harvard University Press, Cambridge, Mass., 1930, pp. 223–230.

Foster, M. S.: *Out of Smalle Beginnings; An Economic History of Harvard College in the Puritan Period, 1636 to 1712,* Harvard University Press, Cambridge, Mass., 1962.

Fox, S. R.: *The Guardian of Boston: William Monroe Trotter,* Atheneum Publishers, New York, 1970.

Francis, A.: *Americans: An Impression,* Andrew Melrose, London, 1909.

Frankfurter, Felix: *The Case of Sacco and Vanzetti,* Little, Brown and Company, Boston, 1927.

"Freedom at Harvard: An Exchange of Letters by Frank P. Ober of Baltimore, President Conant, and Grenville Clark, Fellow of Harvard College," *Harvard Alumni Bulletin,* vol. 51, pp. 729–737, June 25, 1949.

"Freedom of Speech," *Harvard Graduates' Magazine,* vol. 23, pp. 364–365, December 1914.

Freidel, Frank: *Franklin D. Roosevelt, The Apprenticeship,* Little, Brown and Company, Boston, 1952.

Freidel, Frank: "Dissent in the Spanish-American War and the Philippine Insurrection," in Samuel Eliot Morison, et al., *Dissent in Three American Wars,* Harvard University Press, Cambridge, Mass., 1970, pp. 65–95.

Friedman, Lee M.: "Judah Monis, Harvard's First Instructor in Hebrew," *Harvard Graduates' Magazine,* vol. 19, pp. 621–629, June 1911.

"From a Graduate's Window," *Harvard Graduates' Magazine,* vol. 27, pp. 37–40, September 1918.

Frothingham, Octavius Brooks: "Memoirs of Rev. James Walker, D.D., L.L.D.", *Proceedings of the Massachusetts Historical Society,* Second Series, vol. 6, pp. 443–468, May 1891.

Frye, William R.: "The Undergraduate Week," *Harvard Alumni Bulletin,* vol. 42, pp. 257–259, November 17, 1939.

Gardiner, Robert H.: "The Harvard Liberal Club at Boston," *Harvard Graduates' Magazine,* vol. 29, pp. 226–231, December 1920.

Gardner, D. P.: *The California Oath Controversy,* University of California Press, Berkeley, 1967.

Gilmore, John A. D.: "Jacksonians and Whigs at Harvard: The Politics of Higher Education," honors thesis, History and Literature, Harvard University, 1970.

Goddard, John W.: "The Students Ask for Teachers," *Harvard Alumni Bulletin,* vol. 42, pp. 216–218, November 10, 1939.

Goldsen, Rose, et al.: *What College Students Think,* D. Van Nostrand Company, Inc., Princeton, N. J., 1960.

Goodhue, Albert: "The Reading of Harvard Students, 1770–1781, as Shown by the Records of the Speaking Club," *Essex Institute Historical Collections,* vol. 73, pp. 107–129, April 1937.

Goodman, Paul: *The Democratic Republicans of Massachusetts,* Harvard University Press, Cambridge, Mass., 1964.

Goodman, Walter: *The Committee,* Farrar, Straus & Giroux, Inc., New York, 1968.

Grant, Robert: "Harvard College in the Seventies," *Scribner's Magazine,* vol. 21, pp. 554–566, May 1897.

Grant, Robert: *Four Square, An Autobiography,* Houghton Mifflin Company, Boston, 1934.

Green, Martin: *The Problem of Boston,* W. W. Norton & Company, New York, 1966.

Greene, E. B.: "A Puritan Counter-Reformation," *Proceedings of the American Antiquarian Society,* vol. 42, pp. 17–46, April 1932.

Halberstam, Michael J.: "The Undergraduate," *Harvard Alumni Bulletin,* vol. 55, p. 623, May 9, 1953.

Ham, William T.: "Harvard Student Opinion on the Jewish Question," *The Nation,* vol. 115, pp. 225–227, September 6, 1922.

Handlin, Oscar, and Mary Handlin: *Commonwealth,* New York University Press, New York, 1947.

Handlin, Oscar, and Mary Handlin (eds.): *The Popular Sources of Political Authority. Documents on the Massachusetts Convention of 1780,* The Belknap Press of Harvard University Press, Cambridge, Mass., 1966.

Handlin, Oscar, and Mary Handlin: *The American College and American Culture,* McGraw-Hill Book Company, New York, 1970.

Handlin, Oscar, and Mary Handlin: *Facing Life: Youth and Family in American History,* Little, Brown and Company, Boston, 1971.

"Hanfstaengl's Name Comes Up Again," *Harvard Alumni Bulletin,* vol. 37, pp. 287–289, November 3, 1934.

Hapgood, Norman: *The Changing Years,* Farrar & Rinehart, Inc., New York, 1930.

"Harding Leads at Harvard," *New York Times,* vol. 70, p. 17, October 21, 1920.

Harper, Yandell: "Harvard Holds Out For Peace," *Harvard Progressive,* vol. 4, pp. 17–19, September 1940.

Harris, P. M. G.: "Setting the Social Dynamics of American Higher Education, 1636–1745," paper read at the meeting of the Organization of American Historians, New Orleans, April 15, 1971.

Harris, Seymour E.: *The Economics of Harvard,* McGraw-Hill Book Company, New York, 1970.

Harvard Crimson: "Freedom of Speech," *Harvard Graduates' Magazine,* vol. 23, pp. 364–365, December 1914.

"Harvard Faculty Shifts," *New York Times,* vol. 106, November 5, 1956.

"Harvard Named Best University," *Gallup Poll Index,* no. 72, June 1972.

"Harvard Poll for Hoover," *New York Times,* vol. 78, p. 27, October 26, 1928.

"Harvard Rallies for Tomorrow," *The Harvard Progressive,* vol. 1, p. 1, April 26, 1938.

Hawkins, Hugh: *Between Harvard and America. The Educational Leadership of Charles W. Eliot,* Oxford University Press, New York, 1972.

Hearing Before Committee on Un-American Activities, House of Representatives, Eighty-Third Congress, First Session, February 25, 1953, and February 26, 1953, Hart and Hartkins, Washington, Shorthand and Stenotype Reporting, Multilith, 1953.

Heimert, Alan: *Religion and the American Mind: From the Great Awakening to the Revolution,* Harvard University Press, Cambridge, Mass., 1966.

Henderson, G. C.: "The College and the Radicals," *Harvard Graduates' Magazine,* vol. 20, pp. 463–465, March 1912.

Herbst, Jurgen: "The First Three American Colleges: Schools of the Reformation," unpublished paper, Department of History, University of Wisconsin, Madison, 1973.

Herbst, Jurgen: "The Challenge to Government by Church and State: Harvard College, 1636–1707," unpublished paper, Department of History, University of Wisconsin, Madison, February 1974.

Hicks, Granville: *John Reed,* The Macmillan Company, New York, 1936.

Hicks, Granville: *Part of the Truth,* Harcourt, Brace & World, Inc., New York, 1965.

Hill, G. B.: *Harvard College By an Oxonian,* The Macmillan Company, New York, 1894.

Hixson, W. B.: *Moorfield Storey and the Abolitionist Tradition,* Oxford University Press, New York, 1972.

Hoar, George F.: "Harvard College Fifty-Eight Years Ago," *Scribner's Magazine,* vol. 28, pp. 57–72, July 1900.

Hobbes, Thomas: *Behemoth: The History of the Causes of the Civil Wars, and of the Counsels and Artifices by which They were Carried on from the Year 1640 to the Year 1660,* Walter Crooke, London, 1682.

Hoffmann, John Maynard: "Commonwealth College: The Governance of Harvard in the Puritan Period," Ph.D. thesis, History of American Civilization, Harvard University, 1972.

Hofstadter, Richard: *Academic Freedom in the Age of the College,* Columbia University Press, New York, 1961.

Holmes, Henry W.: "The University," *Harvard Graduates' Magazine,* vol. 124, pp. 531–534, June 1923.

"Hooded Ignorance," *Harvard Crimson,* vol. 86, p. 2, October 25, 1924.

"How They Voted," *Harvard Crimson,* vol. 110, p. 4, November 6, 1940.

"How Undergraduates Would Vote: Results by House, Class, and Party," *Harvard Crimson,* vol. 142, p. 3, October 22, 1964.

Huntington, Samuel P.: "The Changing Cultures of Harvard," *Harvard Alumni Bulletin,* vol. 72, pp. 51–54, September 15, 1969.

"In the Colleges," *Intercollegiate Socialist,* vol. 2, p. 25, December–January 1913–1914.

"Indifference," *Harvard Crimson,* vol. 107, p. 2, November 28, 1936.

Jacobs, Scott: "How Harvard Chose Bok," *Change,* vol. 3, pp. 19–21, March–April 1971.

James, Henry: *Charles W. Eliot, President of Harvard University, 1869–1909*, vols. 1 and 2, Houghton Mifflin Company, Boston, 1930.

James, William: "The True Harvard," *Harvard Graduates' Magazine*, vol. 12, pp. 5–8, September 1903.

Jencks, Christopher S., and David Riesman: "Patterns of Residential Education: The Case of Harvard," in Nevitt Sanford (ed.), *The American College*, John Wiley, New York, 1962, pp. 731–773.

Kahn, E. J., Jr.: *Harvard Through Change and Through Storm*, W. W. Norton & Company, Inc., New York, 1969.

Karpf, M. J.: "Jewish Community Organization in the United States," *American Jewish Yearbook*, vol. 39, pp. 47–48, American Jewish Committee, New York, 1937.

Kelman, Steven: *Push Comes to Shove: The Escalation of Student Protest*, Houghton Mifflin Company, Boston, 1970.

Keniston, Hayward: *Graduate Study and Research in the Arts and Sciences at the University of Pennsylvania*, University of Pennsylvania Press, Philadelphia, 1959.

Keniston, Kenneth: "American Students and the 'Political Revival,'" *The American Scholar*, vol. 32, pp. 40–64, Winter 1962–63.

Keniston, Kenneth: *The Uncommitted*, Harcourt, Brace & World, Inc., New York, 1965.

Keniston, Kenneth: *The Young Radicals*, Harcourt, Brace & World, Inc., New York, 1968.

Kennedy, M.: "The Changing Academic Characteristics of the Nineteenth Century American College Teacher," unpublished Ph.D. dissertation, Department of Education, St. Louis University, 1961.

Keppel, F. P.: "President Lowell and His Influence," *The Atlantic*, vol. 151, pp. 753–763, June 1933.

Kerr, Clark: *The Uses of the University*, Harvard University Press, Cambridge, Mass., 1963.

Kibre, Pearl: *Scholarly Privileges of the Middle Ages*, Medieval Academy of America, Cambridge, Mass., 1962.

Kinsley, M.: "Student Government at Harvard," *Change*, vol. 2, pp. 15–17, July–August 1970.

Kipnis, Ira: *The American Socialist Movement: 1897–1912*, Columbia University Press, New York, 1952.

Kirkpatrick, John E.: "The Rise of Non-Resident Government in Harvard University," *Harvard Graduates' Magazine*, vol. 31, pp. 186–194, December 31, 1922a.

Kirkpatrick, John E.: "The Rise of Nonresident Government in Harvard University," unpublished paper, Department of Political Science, University of Michigan (in Harvard Archives), 1922*b*.

Kirkpatrick, John E.: *Academic Organization and Control,* The Antioch Press, Yellow Springs, Ohio, 1931.

Koch, G. A.: *Republican Religion,* Henry Holt and Company, Inc., New York, 1933.

Kramer, J. R.: "The Undergraduate: The Lessons of Columbia's Police Raid and Why it Didn't Happen Here," *Harvard Alumni Bulletin,* vol. 70, pp. 10, 12, May 25, 1968.

Ladd, Everett C., Jr., and Seymour Martin Lipset: *Academics, Politics and the 1972 Election,* American Enterprise Institute for Public Policy Research, Washington, D. C., 1973.

Ladd, Everett C., Jr., and Seymour Martin Lipset: *The Divided Academy,* McGraw-Hill Book Company, New York, 1975.

Lake, Ellen: "SDS Mark Change in Campus Left," *Harvard Crimson,* vol. 142, p. 1, October 3, 1964.

Land, William G.: *Thomas Hill, Twentieth President of Harvard,* Harvard University Press, Cambridge, Mass., 1933.

Lane, William C.: "Report on 'The Telltale, 1721' and 'A Harvard College Society, 1722–1723,' " *Publications of the Colonial Society of Massachusetts,* vol. 12, pp. 220–231, January 1909.

Lane, William C.: "Early Harvard Records," *Harvard Graduates' Magazine,* vol. 36, pp. 350–362, March 1928.

Laski, H. J.: "Why Don't Your Young Men Care?" *Harper's,* vol. 163, pp. 129–136, July 1931.

Lazarsfeld, P., and W. Thielens, Jr.: *The Academic Mind,* The Free Press, Glencoe, Ill., 1958.

LeMoyne, James: "Ec Reviewers Want 'Radical Program,' " *Harvard Crimson,* vol. 159, pp. 1, 6, March 14, 1974.

Levine, M., and J. Naisbitt: *Right On,* Bantam Books, Inc., New York, 1970.

Lewack, H.: *Campus Rebels,* Student League for Industrial Democracy, New York, 1953.

Lippmann, Walter: *A Preface to Morals,* The Macmillan Company, New York, 1929.

Lipset, Seymour Martin: *Political Man,* Doubleday & Company, Inc., New York, 1960.

Lipset, Seymour Martin: "The Sources of the 'Radical Right,' " in Daniel Bell (ed.), *The Radical Right,* Doubleday-Anchor Books, Garden City, N.Y., 1964*a*, pp. 259–312.

Lipset, Seymour Martin: "University Students and Politics in Underdeveloped Countries," *Minerva*, vol. 3, pp. 15–56, Autumn 1964*b*.

Lipset, Seymour Martin: "Youth and Politics," in R. K. Merton and R. A. Nisbet (eds.), *Contemporary Social Problems*, Harcourt Brace Jovanovich, New York, 1971, pp. 743–791.

Lipset, Seymour Martin: "Academia and Politics in America," in T. J. Nossiter et al. (eds.), *Imagination and Precision in the Social Sciences*, Faber & Faber Ltd., London, 1972*a*, pp. 211–289.

Lipset, Seymour Martin: *Rebellion in the University*, Little, Brown, Boston, 1972*b*.

Lipset, Seymour Martin, and Richard Dobson: "The Intellectual as Critic and Rebel: With Special Reference to the United States and the Soviet Union," *Daedalus*, vol. 101, pp. 137–198, Summer 1972.

Lipset, Seymour Martin, and Earl Raab: *The Politics of Unreason: Right-Wing Extremism in the United States, 1790–1970*, Harper & Row, Publishers, Incorporated, New York, 1970.

Lovett, Robert: *All Our Years*, The Viking Press, New York, 1948.

Lowell, A. Lawrence, et al.: "Report of the Committee to Consider How Tests for Rank in College May Be Made a More Generally Recognized Measure of Intellectual Power," *Harvard Graduates' Magazine*, vol. 18, pp. 478–484, March 1910.

Lowell, A. Lawrence: "The President's Report," *Harvard Graduates' Magazine*, vol. 29, pp. 393–401, March 1921.

Lowell, A. Lawrence: *At War with Academic Traditions in America*, Harvard University Press, Cambridge, Mass., 1934.

(Lowell, John): *An Alumnus Remarks on a Pamphlet Printed by the Professors and Tutors of Harvard University Touching Their Right to the Exclusive Government of that Seminary*, Wells and Lilly, Boston, 1824.

Lyell, Charles: *Travels in North America, with Geological Observations on the United States, Canada, and Nova Scotia*, J. Murray, London, 1845.

McCaughey, Robert A. P.: "Josiah Quincy, 1722–1864: The Last of the Boston Federalists," Ph.D. thesis, Department of History, Harvard University, 1970.

McIntyre, W. R.: "Student Movements," *Editorial Research Reports*, vol. 2, pp. 913–929, December 1957.

McWilliams, Carey: *A Mask for Privilege*, Little, Brown, Boston, 1948.

Maisel, Sherman J.: "Maisel Asks Broad Program," *The Harvard Progressive*, vol. 1, p. 1, December 8, 1937.

Malia, Martin: "What Is the Intelligentsia?" in Richard Pipes (ed.), *The Russian Intelligentsia*, Columbia University Press, New York, 1961, pp. 1–18.

Margulies, Rebecca Z., and Peter M. Blau: "The Pecking Order of the Elite: America's Leading Professional Schools," *Change,* vol. 5, pp. 21–31, 34–37, November 1973.

Martin, Edward S.: "Undergraduate Life at Harvard," *Scribner's Magazine,* vol. 21, pp. 531–553, May 1897.

Mason, Daniel Gregory: "At Harvard in the Nineties," *The New England Quarterly,* vol. 9, pp. 43–70, March 1936.

Mason, William C.: "The Explosion in Stoughton Hall," *Harvard Graduates' Magazine,* vol. 28, pp. 725–726, June 1920.

Mather, M. F.: "On Saying It with Oaths," *Harvard Alumni Bulletin,* vol. 38, pp. 181–182, November 1, 1935.

Matthews, Albert: "Introduction, Harvard College Records, Part I," *Publications of the Colonial Society of Massachusetts,* vol. 15, pp. xiii–clxxvi, 1925.

May, Henry: *The End of American Innocence,* Quadrangle Books, Inc., Chicago, 1964.

Merton, Robert K.: *Technology and Science in Seventeenth Century England,* Saint Catherine Press, Bruges, Belgium, 1938.

Merton, Robert K.: *Social Theory and Social Structure,* The Free Press, New York, 1968.

Metzger, Walter P.: *Academic Freedom in the Age of the University,* Columbia University Press, New York, 1961.

Meyer, Marshall W.: "Attitudes of Harvard Students, May 1969," unpublished report, School of Labor and Industrial Relations, Cornell University, September 1969.

Meyer, Marshall W.: "Harvard Students in the Midst of Crisis," *Sociology of Education,* vol. 44, pp. 245–269, Summer 1971.

Meyer, Marshall W.: "After the Bust: Student Politics at Harvard, 1969–1972," in David Riesman and Verne Stadtman (eds.), *Academic Transformation,* McGraw-Hill Book Company, New York, 1973, pp. 127–153.

Meyer, Marshall W.: "Attitudes of Harvard Students, May 1974," unpublished report, Department of Sociology, University of California, Riverside, October 1974.

Moller, Herbert: "Youth as a Force in the Modern World," *Comparative Studies in Society and History,* vol. 10, pp. 237–260, April 1968.

Moore, Barrington, Jr.: *Political Power and Social Theory,* Harvard University Press, Cambridge, Mass., 1958.

Moore, Kathryn McDaniel: "Old Saints and Young Sinners: A Study of

Student Discipline at Harvard College 1636–1734," Ph.D. dissertation, Educational Policy Studies, University of Wisconsin, Madison, 1972.

Morais, H. M.: *Deism in Eighteenth Century America,* Columbia University Press, New York, 1934.

Morison, Samuel Eliot: "The Great Rebellion in Harvard College and the Resignation of President Kirkland," *Publications of the Colonial Society of Massachusetts,* vol. 27, pp. 54–112, April 1928*a*.

Morison, Samuel Eliot: "The History of Harvard," in S. E. Morison et al., *The History and Traditions of Harvard College,* Harvard University Press, Cambridge, Mass., 1928*b*.

Morison, Samuel Eliot: *The Development of Harvard University since the Inauguration of President Eliot, 1869–1929,* Harvard University Press, Cambridge, Mass., 1930.

Morison, Samuel Eliot: "Precedence at Harvard College in the Seventeenth Century," *Proceedings of the American Antiquarian Society,* New Series, vol. 42, pp. 371–431, October 1932.

Morison, Samuel Eliot: *The Founding of Harvard College,* Harvard University Press, Cambridge, Mass., 1935.

Morison, Samuel Eliot: "Francis Bowen, An Early Test of Academic Freedom in Massachusetts," *Proceedings of the Massachusetts Historical Society,* vol. 65, pp. 507–511, January 1936*a*.

Morison, Samuel Eliot: *Harvard in the Seventeenth Century,* Harvard University Press, Cambridge, Mass., 1936*b*.

Morison, Samuel Eliot: *Three Centuries of Harvard,* Belknap Press of Harvard University Press, Cambridge, Mass., 1936*c*.

Morison, Samuel Eliot: "Student Ranking," *Harvard Alumni Bulletin,* vol. 57, p. 417, March 12, 1955.

Morison, Samuel Eliot: *The Intellectual Life of Colonial New England,* Cornell University Press, Ithaca, N.Y., 1956.

Morison, Samuel Eliot: "Dissent in the War of 1812," in S. E. Morison et al., *Dissent in Three American Wars,* Harvard University Press, Cambridge, Mass., 1970, pp. 1–31.

Morse, John T.: "Henry George Spaulding, 1837–1920," *Harvard Graduates' Magazine,* vol. 29, pp. 236–240, December 1920.

Morse, John T.: "Recollections of Boston and Harvard Before the Civil War," *Proceedings of the Massachusetts Historical Society,* vol. 65, pp. 150–163, October 1933.

"Mr. Bok on Free Speech," *Harvard Today,* p. 14, May 1972.

Munro, William Bennett: "The End of the Year," *Harvard Graduates' Magazine,* vol. 21, pp. 75–84, September 1912.

Munro, William Bennett: "The Winter Term," *Harvard Graduates' Magazine,* vol. 25, pp. 350–361, March 1917.

Munro, William Bennett: "The Autumn Term," *Harvard Graduates' Magazine,* vol. 26, pp. 248–258, December 1917.

Munro, William Bennett: "The Winter Term," *Harvard Graduates' Magazine,* vol. 32, pp. 434–444, March 1924.

Nagai, Michio: "The Development of Intellectuals in the Meiji and Taisho Periods," *Journal of Social and Political Ideas in Japan,* vol. 2, pp. 28–32, April 1964.

Namier, Lewis: *1848: The Revolution of the Intellectuals,* Doubleday-Anchor Books, Garden City, N.Y., 1964.

"The New Admissions Plan," *The Gadfly,* vol. 2, pp. 3–6, May 1926.

"Newsweek Surveys Communism in the Colleges," *Newsweek,* vol. 34, pp. 68–69, July 18, 1949.

Nichols, William: "Student Life," *Harvard Graduates' Magazine,* vol. 33, pp. 297–302, December 1924.

Nisbet, Robert A.: *The Degradation of the Academic Dogma,* Basic Books, Inc., Publishers, New York, 1971.

" 'No Racial Discrimination' at Harvard, Orders Corporation," *Harvard Crimson,* vol. 111, p. 1, April 21, 1941.

Norton, Andrews: *Speech Delivered Before the Overseers of Harvard College in Behalf of the Resident Instructors of the College,* Cummings, Hilliard, and Co., Boston, 1825.

Oberle, M. W.: "Harvard: Faculty Organizes in Response to Crisis," *Science,* vol. 165, pp. 49–51, July 4, 1969.

One, Lately a Member of the Immediate Government of the College: *Remarks on a Report of A Committee of the Overseers of Harvard College, Proposing Certain Changes, Relating to the Instruction and Discipline Of The College,* The University Press, Cambridge, Mass., 1824.

Opinion Research Corporation: *Conservatism on the College Campus,* Opinion Research Corporation, Princeton, N. J., 1962.

Ostrander, G. M.: *American Civilization in the First Machine Age: 1890–1940,* Harper Torchbooks, New York, 1972.

Painter, N.: "Jim Crow at Harvard: 1923," *The New England Quarterly,* vol. 44, pp. 627–634, December 1971.

Palmer, R. R.: *The Age of the Democratic Revolution: A Political History of Europe and America, 1760–1800—The Challenge,* Princeton University Press, Princeton, N. J., 1959.

Parsons, Talcott: "Social Strains in America," in Daniel Bell (ed.), *The Radical Right,* Doubleday-Anchor Books, Garden City, N.Y., 1964, pp. 193–200.

Peabody, Andrew: "The Condition and Wants of Harvard College," *North American Review*, vol. 60, pp. 38–63, January 1845.

Peabody, Andrew: *Harvard Reminiscences*, Ticknor and Co., Boston, 1888.

Peabody, Francis Greenwood: "Charles William Eliot," *Harvard Graduates' Magazine*, vol. 35, pp. 239–251, December 1926.

Pearson, E.: "Journal of Disorders," (1788), in William Bentinck-Smith (ed.), *The Harvard Book*, Harvard University Press, Cambridge, Mass., 1953, pp. 111–113.

Peirce, Benjamin: *A History of Harvard University*, Brown, Shattuck & Co., Cambridge, Mass., 1833.

Perry, Bliss (B.P.): "College Professors and the Public," *Atlantic Monthly*, vol. 89, pp. 282–288, March 1902.

"Personnel and Promotions at Harvard," *Harvard Alumni Bulletin*, vol. 42, pp. 180–183, November 3, 1939.

Peterson, A. L.: "Current Political Trends on American College Campuses," *Ohio Wesleyan University Research Bulletin*, 1961.

Peterson, G. E.: *The New England College in the Age of the University*, Amherst College Press, Amherst, Mass., 1964.

Peterson, H. C., and G. C. Fite: *Opponents of War, 1917–1918*, University of Washington Press, Seattle, 1957.

Pierson, George W.: *The Education of American Leaders: Comparative Contributions of U. S. Colleges and Universities*, Frederick A. Praeger, Inc., New York, 1969.

Porter, K. W.: "The Oxford-Cap War at Harvard," in A. DeConde (ed.), *Student Activism*, Charles Scribner's Sons, New York, 1971, pp. 273–279.

Potter, David: *Debating in the Colonial Chartered Colleges*, Bureau of Publications, Teachers College, Columbia University, New York, 1944.

Potter, S. B.: "The Undergraduate," *Harvard Alumni Bulletin*, vol. 55, pp. 581–582, April 18, 1953.

Potts, D. B.: "Social Ethics at Harvard, 1881–1931: A Study in Academic Activism," in Paul Buck (ed.), *Social Sciences At Harvard, 1860–1920*, Harvard University Press, Cambridge, Mass., 1965, pp. 91–128.

"Praise from Sir Hubert," *Harvard Graduates' Magazine*, vol. 22, p. 557, March 1914.

"Presidential Straw Vote Puts Dewey Well Ahead in University, Radcliffe," *Harvard Crimson*, vol. 121, p. 1, November 1, 1948.

Pusey, Nathan: "Freedom, Loyalty, and the American University," (an address delivered before the National Press Club, Washington, D. C., May 25, 1954), in Nathan Pusey, *The Age of the Scholar*, Harper Torchbooks, New York, 1964.

Quincy, Josiah: *The History of Harvard University,* vols. 1 and 2, John Owen, Cambridge, Mass., 1840.

Quincy, Josiah: *Speech of Josiah Quincy, President of Harvard University Before the Board of Overseers of that Institution,* Charles C. Little and James Brown, Boston, 1845.

Rabinowitz, Daniel: "Economics Faculty Votes Against Marxian Program," *Harvard Crimson,* vol. 159, pp. 1, 6, May 1, 1974.

Rawick, George P.: "The New Deal and Youth," unpublished Ph.D. dissertation, Department of History, University of Wisconsin, 1957.

"Reds vs. Academic Freedom," *Newsweek,* vol. 34, pp. 68–69, July 18, 1949.

Reed, John: "Almost Thirty," *The New Republic,* vol. 86, pp. 332–336, April 29, 1936.

Reed, John: "The Harvard Renaissance," *The Harvard Progressive,* vol. 3, pp. 8–10, 22, March 1939.

Reichley, A. James: "Young Conservatives at Old Harvard," *The Reporter,* vol. 12, pp. 12–16, June 16, 1955.

Reid, Whitelaw: "The Scholar in Politics," *Scribner's Monthly,* vol. 6, pp. 605–616, September 1873.

Reisner, Edward Hartman: "The Origin of Lay University Boards of Control in the United States," *Columbia University Quarterly,* vol. 23, pp. 63–69, March 1931.

Riesman, David, and Verne A. Stadtman (eds.): *Academic Transformation: Seventeen Institutions Under Pressure,* McGraw-Hill Book Company, New York, 1973.

Roose, Kenneth D., and Charles J. Andersen: *A Rating of Graduate Programs,* American Council on Education, Washington, D.C., 1970.

Rosovsky, Henry: "Black Studies at Harvard: Personal Reflections Concerning Recent Events," *The American Scholar,* vol. 38, pp. 562–572, Autumn 1969.

Ross, Irwin: "The Student Union and the Future," *The New Republic,* vol. 102, pp. 48–49, January 8, 1940.

Rudolph, Frederick: *The American College and University: A History,* Vintage Books, Random House, Inc., New York, 1962.

Saltonstall, Leverett: *Report of a Committee of the Overseers of Harvard University Concerning the Requirements for Admission to the University,* The Gazette Office, Salem, Mass., 1845.

Samuels, Ernest: *The Young Henry Adams,* Harvard University Press, Cambridge, Mass., 1948.

Santayana, George: *Character and Opinion in the United States,* Doubleday-Anchor Books, Garden City, N.Y., 1956.

Santayana, George: *George Santayana's America,* University of Illinois Press, Urbana, 1967.

Schapsmeier, E. L., and E. H. Schapsmeier: *Walter Lippman: Philosopher Journalist,* Public Affairs Press, Washington, D.C., 1969.

Schiff, L. F.: "The Conservative Movement on American College Campuses: A Social Psychological Investigation," Ph.D. thesis, Department of Social Relations, Harvard University, 1964.

Schirmer, D. B.: *Republic or Empire,* Schenkman Publishing Co., Inc., Cambridge, Mass., 1972.

Shaler, N. S.: "The Problem of Discipline in Higher Education," *Atlantic Monthly,* vol. 64, pp. 24–37, July 1889.

Shannon, David A.: *The Socialist Party of America,* Quadrangle Books, Inc., Chicago, 1967.

Shattuck, G. B.: "The Final Extension of the Franchise to Vote for Overseers," *Harvard Graduates' Magazine,* vol. 24, pp. 425–431, March 1916.

Sheldon, Henry D.: *Student Life and Customs,* D. Appleton, New York, 1901.

Shipton, Clifford K.: "The Puritan Influence in Education," *Pennsylvania History,* vol. 25, pp. 223–233, July 1958.

Shipton, Clifford K.: "Ye Mystery of Ye Ages Solved, or, How Placing Worked at Colonial Harvard and Yale," *Harvard Alumni Bulletin,* vol. 57, pp. 258–259, 262–263, December 11, 1954.

Shipton, Clifford K.: "The Puritan Influence in Education," *Pennsylvania History,* vol. 25, pp. 223–233, July 1958.

Simpson, Lewis P.: " 'The Intercommunity of the Learned': Boston and Cambridge in 1800," *New England Quarterly,* vol. 23, pp. 491–503, December 1950.

Slossen, E. E.: *Great American Universities,* The Macmillan Company, New York, 1910.

Smallwood, M. L.: *An Historical Study of Examinations and Grading Systems in Early American Universities,* Harvard University Press, Cambridge, Mass., 1935.

Smith, Wilson: *Professors and Public Ethics,* Cornell University Press, Ithaca, N. Y., 1956.

Smith, Wilson: "The Teacher in Puritan Culture," *The Harvard Educational Review,* vol. 36, pp. 394–411, Fall 1966.

Solberg, W. U.: *The University of Illinois, 1867–1894,* University of Illinois Press, Urbana, 1968.

Solomon, Harold: "Organizing Youth for War," *The Harvard Progressive,* vol. 4, pp. 15–17, April 1941.

Sparks, Jared: "Jared Sparks on Professorial Appointments at Harvard, 1830," in Richard Hofstadter and Wilson Smith (eds.), *American Higher Education,* vol. 1, The University of Chicago Press, Chicago, 1961, pp. 300–301.

A Special Committee Appointed by the President of Harvard University: *Report on the Terminating Appointments of Dr. J. R. Walsh and Dr. A. R. Sweezy,* Harvard University Printing Office, Cambridge, Mass., 1938.

A Special Committee Appointed by the President of Harvard University: *Report on Some Problems of Personnel in the Faculty of Arts and Sciences,* Harvard University Printing Office, Cambridge, Mass., 1939.

Sperry, Willard L.: *Religion in America,* Beacon Press, Boston, 1963.

Stange, G. Robert: "Harvard 1914: Betrayal of Innocence," *The Harvard Progressive,* vol. 4, pp. 7–11, November 1939.

Starr, H.: "The Affair at Harvard," *The Menorah Journal,* vol. 8, pp. 263–276, October 1922.

Statement by the Harvard Corporation in Regard to Associate Professor Wendell H. Furry, Teaching Fellow Leon J. Kamin, and Assistant Professor Helen Deane Markham, Harvard Printing Office, Cambridge, Mass., May 20, 1953.

Stauffer, V.: *New England and the Bavarian Illuminati,* Columbia University Press, New York, 1918.

Steinberg, Stephen: "The Religious Factor in American Higher Education," unpublished Ph.D. dissertation, Department of Sociology, University of California, Berkeley, 1971.

Steinberg, Stephen: *The Academic Melting Pot: Catholics and Jews in American Higher Education,* McGraw-Hill Book Company, New York, 1974.

Stember, Charles H.: "The Recent History of Public Attitudes," in C. H. Stember et al., *Jews in the Mind of America,* Basic Books, Inc., Publishers, New York, 1966, pp. 31–234.

Stoeckel, A.: "Politics and Administration in the American Colonial Colleges," unpublished Ph.D. dissertation, Department of History, University of Illinois, 1958.

Story, Joseph: *Report of the Committee of the Overseers to Inquire into the State of the University,* Phelps and Farnham, Boston, 1824.

Story, William W. (ed.): *Life and Letters of Joseph Story,* Little, Brown, Boston, 1851.

Struik, Dirk J.: *Yankee Science in the Making,* Little, Brown, Boston, 1948.

"Student Poll Resurrected," *The Gadfly,* vol. 3, p. 1, March 9, 1927.

Students in Revolt: The Story of the Intercollegiate League for Industrial Democracy, League for Industrial Democracy, New York, 1933.

Sweezy, Alan R.: "Union of University Teachers," *Harvard Alumni Bulletin*, vol. 38, pp. 240–241, November 15, 1935.

Swirski, S.: "Changes in the Structure of Relations Between Groups and the Emergence of Political Movements: The Student Movement at Harvard and Wisconsin, 1930–1969," unpublished Ph.D. dissertation, Department of Political Science, Michigan State University, 1971.

"The Teachers' Oath," *Harvard Alumni Bulletin*, vol. 38, pp. 86–87, October 11, 1935.

"A Teachers' Union," *Harvard Alumni Bulletin*, vol. 38, pp. 193–194, November 1, 1935.

"Teachers' Unions," *Harvard Alumni Bulletin*, vol. 38, pp. 232–233, November 15, 1935.

Thayer, William Roscoe: "The Mother of Radicals," *Harvard Graduates' Magazine*, vol. 22, pp. 559–563, June 1914.

Thelin, John R.: "Images of the Ivy League, 1890–1960: The Collegiate Ideal and the Education of Elites in American Colleges," Ph.D. thesis, History of Education, University of California, Berkeley, 1973.

Thomas, B. P.: *Theodore Weld, Crusader for Freedom*, Rutgers University Press, New Brunswick, N. J., 1950.

Thwing, F. B.: "Radicalism at Harvard," *Harvard Graduates' Magazine*, vol. 20, pp. 260–263, December 1911.

Ticknor, George: *Remarks on Changes Lately Proposed or Adopted in Harvard University*, Cummings, Hilliard and Co., Boston, 1825.

Ticknor, George: *Life, Letters and Journals*, vol. 1, Houghton Mifflin Company, Boston, 1909.

Ulam, Adam: *The Fall of the American University*, The Library Press, New York, 1972.

"Undergraduates Protest Action of H. A. A. in Barring Negro from Lacrosse Contest," *Harvard Crimson*, vol. 111, pp. 1, 3, April 9, 1941.

"The University," *Harvard Alumni Bulletin*, vol. 51, pp. 719–725, June 25, 1949.

"The University," *Harvard Alumni Bulletin*, vol. 55, pp. 537–539, April 4, 1953.

"The University: April 1969," Special Edition of *Harvard Today*, Spring 1969.

The University Committee on Governance, Harvard University: *The Organization of the Governing Boards and the President's Office: A Discussion Memorandum*, Cambridge, Mass., 1971.

"University Favors Landon by 165 Votes," *Harvard Crimson*, vol. 107, p. 1, October 15, 1936.

"University Notes," *Harvard Graduates' Magazine*, vol. 5, pp. 609–613, 1897.

"University Notes," *Harvard Graduates' Magazine,* vol. 20, pp. 395–398, December 1911.

Urban Research Corporation: *Harvard's Student Strike: The Politics of Mass Mobilization,* Urban Research Corporation, Chicago, 1970.

Vanderbilt, Kermit: *Charles Eliot Norton: Apostle of Culture in a Democracy,* The Belknap Press of Harvard University Press, Cambridge, Mass., 1959.

Veysey, Laurence R.: "The Emergence of the University," unpublished Ph.D. dissertation, Department of History, University of California, Berkeley, 1962.

Veysey, Laurence R.: *The Emergence of the University,* The University of Chicago Press, Chicago, 1965.

Villard, Oswald Garrison: *Fighting Years,* Harcourt, Brace and Company, New York, 1939.

"The Vote by State and Schools," *The New Student,* vol. 4, p. 2, November 1924.

Wagner, C. A.: *Harvard: Four Centuries of Freedom,* E. P. Dutton & Co., Inc., New York, 1950.

"The Walsh-Sweezy Case," *Harvard Alumni Bulletin,* vol. 40, pp. 1045–1050, June 10, 1938.

"Walsh-Sweezy Case Successfully Concluded," *The Harvard Progressive,* vol. 1, pp. 1–2, September 28, 1937.

Warren, Charles: "Student Politics in Anti-Federalist Days," *Harvard Graduates' Magazine,* vol. 24, pp. 485–490, March 1916.

Wechsler, James: *Revolt on Campus,* Covici, Friede, New York, 1935.

Wendell, Barrett: "Social Life at Harvard," *Lippincott's Magazine,* vol. 39, pp. 152–162, January 1887.

Wert, Robert Joseph: "The Impact of Three Nineteenth Century Reorganizations upon Harvard University," Ph.D. thesis, Stanford University School of Education, 1952.

West, E. J.: "Harvard's First Black Graduates, 1865–1890," *Harvard Bulletin,* vol. 74, pp. 24–28, May 1972.

White, James C.: "An Undergraduate's Diary," *Harvard Graduates' Magazine,* vol. 21, pp. 423–430, March 1913.

White, Lawrence H., et al.: "Economics Department," *Harvard Crimson,* vol. 159, p. 2, March 29, 1974.

Whitehead, John S.: *The Separation of College and State: Columbia, Dartmouth, Harvard and Yale, 1776–1876,* Yale University Press, New Haven, Conn., 1973.

Whitehill, Walter Muir: *Boston in the Age of John Fitzgerald Kennedy,* University of Oklahoma Press, Norman, 1966.

Whitney, R. M.: *Reds in America,* Beckwith Press, New York, 1924.

"Who Is Responsible for 'Classroom Constraint?'" *The Gadfly*, vol. 2, p. 3, December 1922.

Wilson, James Q.: "Liberalism versus Liberal Education," *Commentary*, vol. 53, pp. 50–54, June 1972.

Wish, Harvey: *Society and Thought in Early America*, Longmans, Green & Co., New York, 1950.

Woodroe, Clark: "Kennedy Wins 56% of Vote in University-Wide Survey," *Harvard Crimson*, vol. 138, p. 1, October 27, 1960.

"Yale and Harvard," *The Nation*, vol. 34, pp. 52–53, January 19, 1882.

Yankelovich, Daniel: *The New Morality: A Profile of American Youth in the 70's*, McGraw-Hill Book Company, New York, 1974.

Yeomans, H. A.: *Abbot Lawrence Lowell, 1856–1943*, Harvard University Press, Cambridge, Mass., 1948.

Young, Edward J.: "Subjects for Master's Degree in Harvard College from 1655 to 1791," *Publications of Massachusetts Historical Society*, vol. 18, pp. 119–151, June 1880.

Ziff, Larzer: *Puritanism in America*, Viking Press, New York, 1973.

Zorza, R.: *The Right to Say "We,"* Frederick A. Praeger, Inc., New York, 1970.

Part Two

Educational Reform at Harvard College: Meritocracy and Its Adversaries

by David Riesman

Prologue

In the fall of 1973, a year after I had completed the ensuing manuscript, I was asked by Robert Kiely, Associate Dean for Undergraduate Instruction, to attend a meeting of the student-faculty Committee on Undergraduate Education (CUE). The meeting had been called to consider whether the erection of a new dormitory in the Harvard Yard, the first in many decades, could conceivably provide a chance for an educational departure, perhaps some kind of coherent program of General Education; as a possible model we had all been sent the outline of a subcollege inaugurated at Stanford by Mark Mancall—a program which, occupying about three-quarters of the students' time, bore resemblances to the short-lived "Tussman College" at Berkeley or the Columbia College Western Civilization sequence.[1]

I had supposed that student and other members of the CUE would object to the constraint or the supposed Western provincialism of a

ACKNOWLEDGMENTS: My research and reflection on American higher education have been supported by the Carnegie Corporation and the Ford Foundation. I am indebted to Gerald Grant, my colleague in this work. In addition, I have had helpful comments on the manuscript and help in the compilation of data from Daniel Bell, Leon Bramson, Reuben Brower, McGeorge Bundy, Barbara Norfleet Cohn, Humphrey Doermann, Peter Elder, John Finley, Nina Fosburg, Martha Fuller, Zelda Gamson, Nathan Glazer, Stephen Graubard, David A. Harnett, Edwin Harwood, Gerald Holton, George Homans, Richard M. Hunt, Christopher S. Jencks, Carl Kaysen, Kenneth Keniston, Dorothy Lee, Christopher Leman, Martin Lipset, Michael Maccoby, Ernest May, Marshall W. Meyer, Barry Munitz, Barry O'Connell, Gary Orren, Martin Peretz, Chase Peterson, Gerald M. Platt, Nathan Pusey, Paul Sigmund, Verne Stadtman, Byron Stookey, Jr., Richard M. Sullivan, Rebecca S. Vreeland, Robert S. Weiss, Dean K. Whitla, James W. Wickenden, Jr., Edward T. Wilcox, and Dorothy Zinberg. It should be understood that none of these critics bears any responsibility for what is said in the article; some quite strongly disagree. The article was principally written during a visiting year at the Institute for Advanced Study in Princeton, the helpfulness of which is here acknowledged.

[1]On the Tussman College, see Tussman (1969); on the Columbia as well as the Harvard and Chicago Programs, see Bell (1966); and for a recent commentary, see Bell (1973, pp. 1, 4–6).

"Great Books" proposal, and there was some of this. But virtually all the discussion was occupied instead with the question as to the alleged elitism of any program which did more for some freshmen than for others—an objection already strenuously raised against the overapplied Freshman Seminar Program, and of course in many other colleges, such as Swarthmore and many state universities, against honors programs of any sort.

I sought to counter this now quite predictable current of feeling by asking whether there would be similar objection if a new program were made extraordinarily demanding, so that, for example, students had to learn an esoteric language (not a language like French, which the children of the favored might have been thought to learn at home or school), and if the program were intrinsically of great difficulty—I made an analogy to the physically strenuous Outward Bound program and spoke of it as an intellectual Outward Bound program; suppose, then, all who were willing to surmount these barriers would then be chosen by lot if there were more than there was room for, would there still be objection on the ground of unfairness? Indeed, in the minds of many students, there would. One student commented that a program such as the one proposed would almost necessarily exclude premeds, who would have to get on with their work in the sciences, as if this alone were enough to make the program unfair. Yet the "unfairness" of being a premed at Harvard or being at Harvard at all never entered the discussion, which in fact, like a good many other such discussions in which I have participated in my capacity as an educational reformer, never really grappled with the issues of content or such practical issues as to how faculty could be found capable of teaching in such a program.

In one aspect, this necessarily abbreviated account illustrates the way in which many privileged enclaves within our society are influenced by an egalitarian ethos partially at odds with the world outside, not socialism in one country, as some Russians had hoped to build, but a quasi-socialism in what is largely still a capitalist society.

I have some sympathy with this attitude. I like the fact that Harvard has a ceiling on faculty salaries, and unlike the more aggressively upwardly mobile universities, does not need to operate by the star system, making extraordinary concessions to a few luminaries who will advertise the institution while neglecting those who merely serve it. And I have long contended that places in the Freshman Seminars should be allocated by a lottery where special talents are not required, and that this should also be done with overenrolled undergraduate courses; I have followed this policy in my own seminar and course work. I would like to go further, and provide a kind of ration system for the scarcities within Harvard College which defeat many of the less aggressive or well-connected students on arrival, who are turned down by a series of Freshman Seminars, fail to achieve admission to such overenrolled fields of concentration (majors) as History and Literature or Social Studies, and fail as sophomores to be admitted to one or another of the more popular residential Houses.[2] I have argued in favor of some kind of rationing through which students who, for example, secure entrance into their first-choice Freshman Seminar have slightly less chance of admission to an oversubscribed field of concentration or popular House, although I have no ready answer to the problem as to how students would decide the necessary tradeoffs between goodies now and goodies later, in the absence of full knowledge of how good the goodies are for them. But the general Harvard spirit, among students and faculty alike, is too anarchic to make such a scheme seem feasible or desirable, though the complaints are strong enough to make some students who win a prize feel uncomfortable and guilty, while many who do not win one feel either that they have failed or that "the system" has failed them.

To be sure, those who would be willing to serve as student representatives on the Committee on Undergraduate Education would almost certainly be more sensitive to the charge of elitism or unfairness than would the general run of students, particularly in the present climate of severe competition for grades that will assure entry to the scarce resource of medical schools and to the accordion-like but unevenly desirable resource of law schools. Still, I found it interesting to compare the attitudes of this small group of students with the reflections of the members of the Student Council Committee on Education of 1939, whose report of June 12 of that year recommended a sharp turn away from the prevailing elective system, with its minimal distribution requirements, toward a program astonishingly similar to the one the faculty was later to recommend when it introduced General Education after World War II. This Committee, of which James Tobin '39, now the distinguished Yale economist, was cochairman, was seeking another kind of equality, namely, a common content which students from a variety of backgrounds could share, as against the more specialized trajectories their surveys showed students were taking. Their principal worry was not equity but the seriousness and breadth of student undergrad-

---

[2]That the differences among the Houses are in fact small, though magnified in legend, does not reduce the feeling of defeat and even humiliation students suffer who are not admitted to one or another of the Houses which are overchosen. See Jencks and Riesman (1962).

uate careers. The carefully reasoned and studied work of this Committee (unfortunately never published) is testimony to the cyclical nature of reform, which is one of the themes implicit in Lipset's companion essay in this volume. Its impact also illustrates the way in which Harvard students, like students elsewhere, can influence the curriculum; indeed, Harvard's House Plan itself is in part the outcome of a Student Council report of 1926, which strengthened the hand of President A. Lawrence Lowell both vis-à-vis the prospective donor of the Houses and vis-à-vis objecting faculty and students.

At the present moment (fall 1973) however, the prospect of economic recession and budgetary constraints on families and on institutions seems to limit opportunities for educational reform at Harvard as elsewhere—surprisingly, recent efforts at Harvard to renew the perennial discussion of a three-year baccalaureate degree elicited little interest in spite of the rising cost, especially of private, though subsidized, higher education.[3]

In the tradition of some eminent predecessors, Harvard's President Derek Bok is deeply interested in undergraduate educational reform and has done his best to stimulate it among students and faculty. In general, in my observation, such impetus for reform generally comes from administrators, although they may be aroused by faculty, supported by students (as in the case of the Student Council Reports already referred to), and provided with leverage by outside sources of intellectual and financial support. But I am speaking here of College-wide reforms, not of the very great changes that occur within the bulkheads of departments which at least in a large research-oriented institution are the major arenas for the concerns of faculty, graduate students, and often undergraduate concentrators as well.[4] Harvard's Chemistry Department, for example, makes a serious effort at student evaluation of

[3]About a quarter of the Harvard students who on entry are offered advanced standing on the basis of their high school work graduate in three years, while others use the year of grace to take leaves of absence or stay on for a fourth post-baccalaureate year. (See the pamphlet, *An Informal Discussion of Advanced Standing at Harvard and Radcliffe Colleges,* Office of Advanced Standing, Harvard University, no date.) On Charles W. Eliot's pressure for a three-year degree, see Hawkins (1972, pp. 272ff). The renewed discussion of the three-year degree at Harvard was partly stimulated by the Carnegie Commission report *Less Time, More Options: Education Beyond the High School* (1971).

[4]In a characteristically evocative essay, Martin Trow contends that the major sorts of innovation in American higher education occur incrementally within departments or within individual courses, without ever being given the (frequently pretentious) label of "innovation"; see "The Public and Private Lives of Higher Education," paper read at the Second National Forum on New Planning and Management Practices in Post-Secondary Education, Education Commission of the States, Chicago, November 16, 1973.

courses, far beyond the uneven bite of the *Crimson's Confidential Guide to Courses* or the new survey of courses primarily open to freshmen undertaken in 1973 by newly appointed Dean Robert Kiely. Indeed, I think one could argue that the publicized overall reforms in Harvard College are less important for the fate of students than the subtle changes in the microclimates of departments which are themselves sometimes mini-universities with many subclimates.

Yet it is the publicized College-wide changes which tend to have an impact—whether of acceptance or rejection of the model—on other selective colleges and sometimes on educational institutions more generally. Both Eliot and Lowell, in considering their reforms, were concerned with the consequences for education in the secondary schools, just as the Program of Advanced Standing was adopted as an aspect of the effort to encourage and upgrade the high schools by rewarding via their students those that offered college-level work. Furthermore, even in a period when major reforms are in abeyance at Harvard (in part reflecting the fact that budgetary issues predominate as demands far outrun resources) there are still expanding state colleges and universities where there is leeway for and interest in experiment. Although they may appear alike to tourists, no two educational institutions, like human beings, lack idiosyncrasy; Harvard's are evident from Martin Lipset's essay and from my own; nevertheless, there are enough similarities, actual or assumed, so that issues discussed at Harvard may have relevance as well as resonance elsewhere.

That is all the justification I need for asking readers to follow me on a very personal journey through the Harvard College I myself experienced as an undergraduate in the late twenties and as a faculty member since 1958. The chair I hold was specifically mandated to a concern for undergraduate education, and I have participated from the beginning in the General Education program and have served for many years on its supervising Committee on General Education. (I serve on the Administrative Board of the Graduate School, which, among its other preoccupations, is concerned with the role of Teaching Fellows; I am also a member of the Faculty Committee on the Social Studies Program, an interdisciplinary undergraduate concentration more fully described hereafter. At an earlier point I was one of the several elected faculty members of the Harvard-Radcliffe Policy Committee, a student group concerned with educational reform, now superseded by the Committee on Undergraduate Education. And I have been a Fellow and Associate of both a Harvard and a Radcliffe House, although last year the concern for fairness and the fear of oligopoly required me to limit my affiliation to a single House; I chose the Radcliffe one and have in general been active in specifically Radcliffe affairs. I was a member of the so-called Kagan Committee which ended the formal separation of Harvard and Radcliffe living arragements and which introduced coresidential living both at Harvard and Radcliffe, helping along with many other pressures to compel a move away from the long-standing 4-to-1 ratio of men to women students, to the present 2.5-to-1, itself an unstable compromise.) In addition, of course, I became on arrival a member of the interdisciplinary Social Relations Department out of which I moved along with other sociologists when a separate Sociology Department was reinstituted in 1970. These are some of the limited vantage points from which I write about contemporary Harvard. I have had in addition very great benefit, not only of the institutional researches of Dean Whitla and others, but also of the many colleagues who have been connected with Harvard who gave me abundant criticism of earlier drafts of my chapter. Some senior colleagues, notably former Provost Paul Buck and Professor John Finley, were particularly generous in discussing Harvard history with me from their own long-time experience of it.

In my own history, I owe an interest in education to my parents. My father, a student of the history of medicine, was preoccupied with medical education, while my mother was not only deeply involved in Bryn Mawr affairs, but alert to the works of John Dewey, Arthur Morgan, the refounder of Antioch College, Bertrand Russell, and many others.[5] Thus when I became an editor of the *Crimson*, I made education my beat, rather than seeking, like many of my colleagues who later distinguished themselves, such as Paul Sweezy, to become adept at sports stories; I covered the House Plan from its inception and was one of its few undergraduate defenders. While I did not, as legend would have it, inaugurate the *Crimson*'s *Confidential Guide to Courses*, I did occasionally contribute to a column called "The Student Vagabond," the result of my auditing of courses in fields far outside my own concentration in biochemistry. I have drawn on these memories, recognizing their certain fallibility, in the brief sketch I give hereafter of President Lowell's effort to right the balance in favor of Harvard College, which he thought his great predecessor, Eliot, had tipped too much in favor of the University.[6]

The major theme I have chosen around which to weave my digres-

---

[5] I have sketched a portrait of my mother's concerns in "Two Generations" (Riesman, 1964, pp. 711–735).

[6] Hugh Hawkins' *Between Harvard and America* (1972) is an engrossing account of Eliot's innovations, and in his chapter, "The Resurgence of Collegiate Concerns," of what he refers to as Lowell's counterreformation.

sions concerning Harvard College involves the way in which Harvard College became increasingly national and oriented toward achievement, for its faculty and to a lesser degree for its student body, thus defining and serving some aspects of American professional and academic life which are meritocratic. The now-common term, "meritocracy," gained currency from a social science-fiction fantasy by Michael Young, which traced the rise of a bureaucratic society stratified in terms of measured intellectual qualities, and envisaging a contest for preferment in which most of the winners would have high morale while most of the losers would feel their lot justified. However, a few surly, old-fashioned populists and some romantic, high-status women would side with the losers and lead an eventual revolt.[7] I employ the term "meritocracy" as Michael Young does, to distinguish educational or occupational selection by some more or less formal process, based on judgments as to qualifications, as separate from historically earlier modes of selection based on lineage, on patronage, on immediate political pressure, or on personal impressions by the person or group doing the selecting. Thus the Civil Service System aims to be meritocratic, as did the traditional Chinese written examinations for bureaucratic positions.

There is no call for meritocracy when there is no surplus of candidates for opportunities in the educational world. Harvard screened students in an earlier period by expecting them to know Greek; when the orbit of recruitment widened in the late nineteenth century by relaxing this and other prerequisites, Charles W. Eliot helped institute the College Entrance Examination Board as an alternative route of entry.[8] In the earliest years there was also no great surplus of tutors who wanted to teach at Harvard. Professionalism—hence, in our sense, meritocracy—on the Harvard College faculty can be traced back to the impetus of Continental, especially German, scholarship on an increasing number of can-

---

[7]See Young (1959); see also Riesman (1967, pp. 897–903).

[8]In his old age, Charles Francis Adams wanted Harvard College kept as a preserve for the rich and well-born, and in a series of letters in 1904, Eliot argued forcefully against this, noting that Groton and St. Paul's had suffered from such recruitment, that public school graduates did better at Harvard than those from preparatory schools, and that democracy demanded a wider draw. Some of this exchange is reported by Hawkins (1972, pp. 170–171); I owe thanks for copies of the letters to Jennings Wagoner, Jr., who has been doing research on the papers of Eliot; Wagoner also quotes a letter to President Eliot from his cousin, Amory Eliot, about the "excessive strictness" of the Board of Examiners, which is "depriving Harvard of a class of men who are often her best representatives, both as graduates and undergraduates; and trying to turn the college into a hot-house for finished scholars only" (Amory Eliot to CWE, August 13, 1906; Box 284, Eliot Papers).

didates for American college faculties as early as the mid-nineteenth century.[9]

Eliot's preoccupation with visible scholarship meant a focus on the University rather than the College, and a deprecation of what he came to regard as merely local, nonprofessional, or parietal concerns; he sternly applied impersonal criteria to judge the loyal locals. Even before he left office in 1909 a counterattack had begun. But A. Lawrence Lowell, who became President in 1909, after increasingly vehement attacks on Eliot for neglect of the College, did not want to return to an era where a place at Harvard depended on local connections, a rich wife, and simple serviceability as a college teacher. What Lowell sought both in recruiting students and in recruiting faculty might be defined as an aristocratic variant of Eliot's democratic and more impersonal meritocracy. It is this latter with which we are largely familiar in American life. It is egalitarian in the sense that placement depends on a contest judged in terms applicable to expanded candidate pools, with "merit" being assayed in publicly defensible forms. Grades became virtually all-important, not because there is complete confidence in them, but because judgments based on them, if not always easy to defend vis-à-vis either individuals or groups, provide an available mechanism for distributing scarce resources both in college and in graduate and professional education.[10]

[9]See the biographies and discussion in *The Lazzaroni: Science and Scientists in Mid-Nineteenth Century America* by Miller, Voss, and Husse (1972). I am indebted to an unpublished manuscript by Robert A. McCaughey which traces the cycles of recruitment of faculty to Harvard College for most of the nineteenth century, suggesting that the development of a professionalized, research-oriented faculty at Harvard College was by no means a straight-line development culminating in the Presidency of Charles W. Eliot (1869–1909). There were periods even before the Civil War when the College was moving away from being a refuge for ministers awaiting a call or for a failed businessman, and becoming a locale for independent scholarly work, although for much of this period it was more like an academy where the faculty were drill masters who often had to make bedchecks and deal, as Lipset's essay indicates, with restless and unruly students. As the supply of European-trained potential faculty increased, Harvard College moved unevenly to recruit them, even outside its own provincial orbit; indeed, as both Hawkins and McCaughey explain, Eliot himself had been denied a professorship at Harvard because, in competition with Wolcott Gibbs, he was not deemed a sufficiently accomplished chemist. Hawkins' book as well as Wagoner's and McCaughey's unpublished researches show that President Eliot's commitment to scholarship came slowly, was very greatly prodded by the Johns Hopkins model and the competition it offered, and as is implicit in the correspondence referred to in the preceding footnote, was greeted by some of his Bostonian constituency with hostility, since it meant denying tenure to socially agreeable but academically unpromising faculty members; Eliot came to the point of quite directly warning such men that they had better produce or get out. See Robert McCaughey, "The Transformation of American Academic Life: Harvard University (1821–1892)," (1974).

[10]The distinction is similar to that of Turner (1969, pp. 855–867).

In an unequivocally democratic meritocracy, any number can play —or rather, work. What I have here termed the aristocratic variant would only appeal to those who felt confident in their fair-minded but sprightly ability to bet on able young people and to advance them, but who did not believe themselves required to consult widely and to justify their selections to a large and distant audience. (Eliot had himself proceeded in just this way at the outset, before building up a faculty on whose professional judgments he could place reliance and which, once recruited, sustained the pressure toward academic professionalism.) The aristocratic style of selection tends to disparage tests, and to put its faith instead in the unarticulated judgment of men who are satisfying each other and their own consciences.[11] Such a process has operated in the selection of Rhodes Scholars. It is epitomized in Harvard's Society of Fellows, which was set up by President Lowell in 1933 in an effort to break what William James called the Ph.D. octopus and to create an opportunity for a small number of gifted young men to pursue their studies without the need for credentials or departmental supervision.[12]

Aristocratic meritocracy comes increasingly under attack because the obscurity of the processes of selection encourages the criticism that prejudice or caprice enters into the enterpise. Thus for most of this article we shall be talking about meritocracy in its common-man or democratic forms. But even these forms have in recent years come under attack on the ground that prejudice of another, nonpersonal sort may be built into the definitions of merit or into the procedures for discovering it.[13] There is the now familiar charge that seemingly meritocratic procedures are biased in favor of the usually white, educated middle

[11]Cf. the discussion of the role of an influential in science in bringing forward the capable and purging the shoddy in Donald Fleming (1954, Ch. 10).

[12]The Society of Fellows offers such attractive terms to its Junior Fellows, given three-year renewable stipends for postbaccalaureate study, that it has had great success in attracting able candidates, especially now that it has lost one of its original rationales and allows Junior Fellows to pursue the doctorate during their fellowships. It has also been successful for Harvard in helping turn up potential faculty; about a third of former Junior Fellows are now on the Harvard Faculty. McGeorge Bundy, Arthur Schlesinger, Jr., and Harry Levin are among a number of notables who did not get the doctorate, but presently virtually all Junior Fellows earn the doctorate.

The University of Michigan has just now begun a program modeled on the Society of Fellows but which will presumably lack some of the ceremonial aspects—the elegant dinners of Junior and Senior Fellows in Eliot House—that have brought Harvard's program both some of its luster and a certain contemporary unease.

[13]Since my chapter was written, Daniel Bell (1972, pp. 29–68) has dealt with this whole range of issues. Bell discusses the resentment that arises where, because of the degree of meritocracy which prevails, there is equality of opportunity within a given system, with corresponding inequality of result or outcome.

classes, and this is often linked to the contention that "merit" has been defined in a self-serving way by already dominant elites. Sometimes the alternative criterion for distributing scarce positions and opportunities appears then to be a political or cultural one, such as a quota system for blacks, other nonwhite minorities, women, or whatever group can make common cause in its deprivation. But there is also a more thorough-going attack on meritocracy based on the idea that ranking and distinctions with respect to merit engender coldness, rivalry, and even viciousness, violating the principle that all people are fundamentally equal—an axiom I myself can accept as a religious mandate, but not as an educational one. "Meritocracy" comes to be linked in the minds of many with another word, namely "bureaucracy," which I would like also to see used neutrally rather than pejoratively; both terms become symbols for all that is disliked in a complex industrial society.

Michael Young was prophetic 16 years ago in seeing that what had been regarded as a progressive principle, namely, that people should be promoted on the basis of achievement rather than on the basis of ascribed qualities, would fall into disrepute with many, so that even some of the winners in the contest would be joyless and guilt-laden, and in fact more often antagonistic concerning the processes of selection than the losers. In other words, there is doubt about the merit and the very meaning of merit. Paradoxically, the triumph of the democratic version of meritocracy had hardly occurred before a counterattack began not only on behalf of the large numbers still excluded at the points of intake, but also on account of the damage competition produces to the human qualities of those included.

Many of the attacks on meritocracy seem to me to be criticisms of the prestige and dramatically large compensation given to the winners; however, one can conceive of a society in which meritocracy is employed as a device for selecting those who will do the more specialized work of society, work which may or may not have intrinsic rewards, while compensation might be distributed in quite other ways, for example in inverse proportion to the intrinsic enjoyment of the work, or even of prestige. Thus, some of the attacks on meritocracy seem to be attacks on hierarchies of prestige and perquisites that do not seem to be inevitable concomitants.[14]

---

[14]For an argument in favor of achieving greater equality in income and status in the United States while playing down the attempt to upset educational meritocracy, see Jencks et al. (1972).

The issues swirling around meritocracy involve the tenuous link between the educational and the occupational orders; the conflict (to which much of Talcott Parsons' work is devoted) between the need for performance and the need for nurturance; the costs and benefits of social mobility as these operate in society and in American higher education. My own position on many of these matters is ambivalent and tentative.

1. *Edging Toward Meritocracy in the 1920s*

When I came to Harvard in 1927, President Lowell had been battling the young barons of ascription with only modest success. He had wanted an honors College even before he became President. While the elective system had been for his predecessor a way to encourage the faculty, in current parlance, to do their (ever more scholarly) thing,[1] Lowell saw that it allowed many students to glide indolently through Harvard. Lowell sought a more strenuous, more engaged undergraduate body. In helping to establish the tutorial system, he hoped that the tutors would be able to draw their students into a more intense academic involvement. Like Woodrow Wilson at Princeton, he saw the social exclusiveness of student housing and dining as an interference with his aims; the so-called Gold Coast on Mount Auburn Street where the well-to-do and socially acceptable students lived in privately built (though later Harvard-owned) residences in splendid isolation from the unwashed (a term then in use; how quaint it sounds now!) seemed to Lowell to deny opportunities for fruitful mingling between the already arrived and the upwardly mobile. His first response was to build dormitories for freshmen along the Charles River, and in the 1920s to begin establishing the Harvard Houses in which students would be compelled to reside and pay for (if not necessarily eat) their meals—a move bitterly opposed by many undergraduate clubmen and alumni.

What Lowell wanted was a greater equality and seriousness within the Harvard gates; his modified version of meritocracy is the one I have called aristocratic. While he had little patience with dilettantes and idle snobs, he would not, were he alive today, want to fill Harvard College with students at the 800 ceiling on the College Boards. He hoped to recruit to the College forceful, intelligent young men, who

---

[1]This phrase will have to suffice as shorthand for the far more interesting and intricate enterprise in which Eliot was engaged, as recounted by Hugh Hawkins (1972—especially Ch. III and IX). Robert McCaughey's research referred to above makes clear that the elective system as a way of encouraging specialized scholarship had been unevenly explored in the years preceding Eliot.

would take part in the major institutions of American life: in law and government, in the management of the economy, in international affairs; would-be scholars were all right too, so long as they did not give the place an anemic cast.

One way of putting all this in contemporary terms is to say that the Harvard of President Lowell's day muted the ascriptive by means of the meritocratic, but only in part. Harvard's Final Clubs, now nonresidential eating clubs which had earlier broken away from national fraternities to avoid having to mix with their assorted brothers from elsewhere, suffered marginally at first from the building of the Houses. (Members had to pay board to Harvard, although not until Conant's Presidency were some 50 holdout clubbies forced into the Houses to sleep.) Election to such clubs as Porcellian or AD (so named after breaking away from the Alpha Delts) in the Lowell era was much more a matter of descent than of popularity or other personal qualities; save for a few marginal cases, there was nothing the individual could do to get in.[2] What the House did do was enhance the possibility that a student could participate in a social and intellectual life without having to join either a Final Club or one of Harvard's rather low-status fraternities. House facilities for intramural athletics, for artistic and theatrical performance, and other non-College-wide pursuits eventually attenuated the attractiveness of the Final Clubs even for their members.

Martin Lipset's essay details the way in which Eliot's Harvard had become ethnically and socially more heterogeneous than its Ivy League competitors.[3] Harvard suffered the loss of some actual or would-be aristocrats who preferred the geographic and social isolation then offered by Williams or Dartmouth. But Harvard was never completely deserted by the social elite who regarded it as "their" college, and to this day it has retained its attraction for Brahmins, provided they are capable enough to get in. As social exclusiveness may have allowed many well-to-do Americans to accept and even encourage waves of immigration to the United States, so the Final Clubs may have allowed Harvard to

---

[2]It is interesting that Yale's senior (and secret) societies in contrast depended to a much greater degree on good works and not on grace. In that sense, Yale was more characteristically American, somewhat more attracted to go-getters, perhaps somewhat more homogeneous socially. For evidence that this remained the case right down through the 1950s, see Allan Blackmer (1960). Blackmer compares Andover students who chose Harvard with those who chose Yale, noting the subtle differences as well as the great overlap in outlooks.

[3]On Eliot's antagonism to nativist restrictionism, see Hawkins (1972, Ch. 6). However, in an unpublished essay Jennings Wagoner, Jr., discusses the conflict Eliot faced between his desire to bring Southerners back to Harvard who had, of course, left at the time of the Civil War, and the treatment of Negroes in the life of the College.

remain (despite temporary interruptions in the Lowell era) relatively open to a diverse flow of applicants; for it should be remembered that during the twenties, Harvard College was not overapplied and that graduates of private and good public schools could readily do sufficiently well on the College Boards to get in.[4]

In the twenties and thirties, Columbia and the University of Pennsylvania lost their local elites to more suburban ivied institutions; Harvard did only in part. Moreover, Harvard was attractive to the sons of German Jewish families of established wealth, to Lehmans, to Warburgs, Strauses, Loebs, and others who sometimes have buildings named after them or are responsible, like the late Paul Sachs, for great art collections.[5] I think one can infer that Harvard's present academic and intellectual distinction depends in some measure on the fact that the College has managed to retain a mixture of distinctions, including lineage.[6] All Presidents since Eliot have struggled with the tension endemic between an undergraduate college and a research-oriented university; yet in the American grain these tensions seem to me essential if scholarship is to be fertile and free.

The Harvard College I entered in 1927 had the atmosphere of a New England college, despite its considerable Mid-Atlantic appeal. For many students who came as commuters with their lunches in a bag, it was one of the Boston area's city colleges.[7] A good many of these commuters were premeds who were unavoidably serious. Only in a later day, however, were professors in the science departments markedly successful in recruiting disciples among premeds, whom they hoped to "save" from becoming what the scientists regarded as mere careerists in applied technology. (One of the similarities of the seventies to the earlier collegiate era is that the science departments are now again being faced

---

[4]Harvard's heterogeneity led to social cruelties, whether in the exclusion of Negroes from the new freshman dormitories built by President Lowell (see Lipset's essay in Part One, pp. 142–145) or in the more subtle but cutting social snobberies which are captured in George Anthony Weller's novel, *Not to Eat, Not for Love* (1933); Weller had been an observant *Crimson* editor. For discussion of Weller's book and of the era described, see Thelin (1972—especially Ch. 11).

[5]Paul Buck, in conversation, has emphasized the importance of these resources for Harvard's present distinction in terms of the quality of the student body as well as the munificence of the legacies.

[6]It seems possible to me that this is a waning asset. In the future, Harvard may depend more on attracting to its faculty researchers who can get government and foundation grants as against continuing to turn out alumni, divided into Classes, e.g., Class of '76, whose alumni loyalty and training in generosity of a patrician sort are strong.

[7]There are almost no commuters of this sort now, thanks to affluence, plus scholarship aid. Those who do commute are married students and others who choose—and get permission—to live off-campus in apartments. In my day there was no public higher education in the liberal arts to be found in the Boston area.

with an "unredeemable" flow—indeed a kind of "brain drain"—of premeds.)

The deprecated Radcliffe students were another serious if not always scholarly cadre, helping provide an audience (taught in separate classes until World War II) for otherwise indifferently regarded faculty. Before World War II, Harvard students looked down on Radcliffe girls as drips and pretended never to notice them; indeed, in that now vanished era, many of the more elegant as well as some of the more intelligent local young women preferred to "come out" rather than attend college at all. In the new era after World War II, even well into the 1960s, a good many Harvard undergraduates regarded Radcliffe students as intellectually, and at times also socially, too formidable for them and claimed to prefer the supposedly but often not actually less brilliant, more beautiful and demure girls from Wellesley or, less threatening still, from the nonelite colleges in the Boston area.

There were many students at Harvard who were bright enough to do well academically, especially in fields like English, history, Romance languages, economics, or government, without obedience to the democratic version of meritocracy, that is, of hard work, but only to the more aristocratic version of insouciant talent. It was common then to pretend that one did no work. Seventy to a hundred or so men went on each year from the College to Harvard Law School, for whose abrasively competitive atmosphere they were often quite unprepared; the Law School had gone national long before the College did. In addition, the College included a small minority of potential scholars and another minority who looked forward perhaps after a certain amount of graduate work to teaching in such secondary schools as Exeter, Milton, Western Reserve Academy, St. Louis Country Day School, and an occasional suburban public school.

In my own of course extremely limited observation, the Harvard College faculty of the late 1920s was only occasionally capable of the intensity that President Lowell valued. It included many frustrated pedants, angry at having to teach the sons of the well-to-do and often embittered when kept for indefinite periods in the status of instructor or assistant professor.[8] There were many exceptions. I found excitement in the physiology course I had with Lawrence J. Henderson. He stimulated many to an interest in Pareto, and introduced me to Elton Mayo in the Business School (a school even then looked down upon by College faculty and by an increasing number of students who, though of bourgeois

---

[8]The Harvard Teachers Union, discussed in the Lipset article, mobilized in the 1930s some of the resentment that this pattern promoted and helped nudge Harvard to adopt the present up-or-out AAUP-style policy.

origin themselves, were already learning to despise the "bourgeois arts"). Charles McIlwain was a presence. I was not the only student to respond to my young, magnetic mentor, Carl J. Friedrich, who had recently come from Germany and gathered a coterie of disciples in Government and related fields. A number of my classmates wanted to write, and some found support of a Chips-like kind from "Copey," Charles Townsend Copeland, who holed up in digs in the Yard and paraded his eccentricities for his young admirers. The College was then, and long remained, quite barren in the arts.[9] A group of us were interested in the theater and grieved that George Pierce Baker had gone off to teach drama at Yale; we rather innocently cultivated a few rich men in the hope that they would give Harvard a theater.[10]

It was not difficult in the Harvard College of that day, nor in any later Harvard College, to remain in good academic standing if one were reasonably well prepared, chose one's courses guilefully, and did a modicum of work after the first term of freshman year. To do outstanding academic work was difficult, then as now. Then as now, there were very great differences among fields, both in terms of grades and in terms of the amount and intensity of work required.[11] About a third of

[9]I speak here of the creative and performing arts, not of art history or the work of the Fogg Museum of Art. Compare with my own account in the text the detailed record of Harvard luminaries in the late Lowell era in Morison (1936, pp. 473–476). Like many others, I am greatly indebted to Morison's work on Harvard.

[10]The hope which many had had was not fulfilled until 1959, when, under President Pusey's auspices, the Loeb Theater was opened, with its superb facilities for drama. President Pusey was the first President in my lifetime to care about the arts, including architecture. To this day, however, the endemic conflict in the humanities between the performing arts and the critical or historical fields is strong, and was illustrated again when Daniel Selzer left Harvard for Princeton a few years ago because the latter institution offered more scope for curricular work in the theater.

[11]Dean Whitla, Director of the Office of Tests at Harvard College, has compiled data showing how much wider is the spread of grades in science courses than in "softer" fields; more people are likely to fail a science course, and honor grades (A's and B's) are not as automatic as they have become in a great many courses. Whitla also has a profile showing how individual courses grade students vis-à-vis each student's grades in his other courses; allowing for exceptional involvement of some students in some courses, this profile could be regarded as a table of "guts," many of which show rising enrollments. But the same profile also shows that there are courses known to grade severely vis-à-vis a student's average which also show rising enrollments, notably Bernard Bailyn's taxing and challenging courses in Colonial and early nineteenth-century American history. Thus Gresham's Law does not entirely operate vis-à-vis grade inflation. There is also enormous disparity in the recommending of summa cum laude degrees among the various departments; for example, in 1972, History was notably chary and History and Science (a limited honor's concentration) was notably generous in this respect. Of course, Whitla's survey is external evidence which can only lead to inferences about the level of work required in individual courses or departments; however, its publication was intended to lead faculty members and departments to consider their procedures for awarding grades and honors with some awareness of Collegewide norms.

the entering students graduated with honors.[12] For the great majority of my classmates, though they may have cared desperately to establish their adequacy vis-à-vis each other and the world, the arena for this was not the classroom. But the new Houses made a difference for those of us who needed adults who would support our intellectual and academic concerns, since we could not always find enough support for these among our peers. And many of the faculty who became involved with the Houses as Tutors or Associates welcomed the chance to meet with undergraduates in casual fashion, over sherry or tea in the tutor's quarters or in the Common Rooms, rather than in a formal classroom setting or in one of the Final Clubs. (The Signet Society, then and later, provided a locale in which students of artistic or literary bent could meet with faculty over a meal.) The Houses helped provide a "critical mass" of people potentially alert to conversation about books and ideas, and to redeem for adult faculty an undergraduate body previously regarded as largely indifferent to ideas.

My roommate, Alexander Langmuir (later a public health physician), and I moved into Dunster House as seniors and benefited greatly from the kind of conversation the House facilitated. Carl J. Friedrich, already referred to, was a tutor in the House; so was the late Crane Brinton, who was engaging as well as stimulating, and Seymour Harris, the young economist. With a friend from childhood, Benjamin West Frazier III, I attended Boston Symphony Orchestra concerts and shared an amateur interest in architecture which had led us earlier to be critical of the neo-Georgian design of the Houses and to argue with President Lowell that Gropius should be given the commission rather than the old Boston firm of Coolidge, Shepley, Bulfinch and Abbott. I talked with the intense James Agee, a junior, about the South and about literature, and I read some of the work of the Southern agrarians. But I do not recall from those years much discussion of national or international politics. This was so even though I was studying Berlitz Russian and preparing, more out of a desire for adventure than from a political or cultural interest, to visit the Soviet Union in the summer after graduation. A plurality of my classmates, as Lipset's essay notes, were for Herbert Hoover in the election of 1928, as were the great majority in the election of 1932. But this was more a matter of reflex, of family and class. Also there was very little social consciousness of the contemporary sort.

I was one of those who mocked Roger Baldwin and Corliss Lamont, civil libertarians and Harvard alumni, when they protested the wages of Harvard scrubwomen. Indeed, it is astonishing to me in retrospect how

[12]For data on the classes of 1934 and 1935, see Morison (1936, p. 448–449).

little class guilt my friends and I felt and how little aware we were of the agony of many Americans even after the onset of the Great Depression in 1929. This is so even though some of us, myself included, worked in settlement houses under the auspices of Phillips Brooks House or, as I also did, spent a summer with the Grenfell Mission in Labrador. Some of my friends, and my younger brother also, went around quoting T. S. Eliot to each other, and managed to remain fairly insulated from the political currents of which Lipset's essay treats.[13] (Several years later when I was a law student, I got irritated with the many people I knew who even in 1933–34 were saying that anybody who wanted a job could get one and that the unemployed were simply lazy. Never having had a real job in my life other than a half job working for a summer at the Mt. Desert Island Biological Laboratory near my family's summer place, I took off for Detroit and later Chicago with the minimal equipment I thought a hobo would have to see if I could get a job. I stood in lines at the River Rouge Ford plant and at Armour and Company at Chicago so obviously unfit that I could not possibly have gotten a job; lacking a car I could only go to a single place in a day; in a federal transient shelter I found many men who had been craftsmen, electricians and others who were roaming the country without jobs, pictures of their children in their wallets. I got no job but only the flu and ended up recuperating at a friend's house in Detroit—then spent the rest of the summer with a roommate canoeing in the North Woods of Canada. But I did conclude that there really was unemployment, not simply indolence!)

Lipset's essay delineates exceptions to what I have said here about the nonpolitical attitude of Harvard undergraduates with whom I had intellectual or social commerce; but he also suggests that at Harvard, as in perhaps the majority of academic institutions in this period, there was more radicalism among faculty members than among the vast majority of undergraduates.[14] I do not have data on the academic and social origins of Harvard College faculty in the 1930s. Undoubtedly, many on the faculty were not to the manor born. Yet, when I was an undergraduate, there were a number of eccentrics on the faculty who had the style of gentlemanly amateurs on the British model, whatever their actual

[13]When several years earlier I had been Chairman of the Speakers Committee of the Liberal Club, I brought to Harvard some academic innovators, including Alexander Meiklejohn, Clarence Cook Little (then of Michigan), and Hamilton Holt of Rollins. [There is a fascinating picture of an autocratic Hamilton Holt in his controversy with John Andrew Rice in Duberman (1972, Ch. 1).] I cannot say, however, that my college mates had much interest in issues of educational reform.

[14]Students in the liberal arts at CCNY would be an exception. See Nathan Glazer's vignette of City College (1973, Ch. 4).

family backgrounds. I have arbitrarily selected the Chemistry and History departments to assess the degree of inbreeding among tenured faculty at Harvard at various recent historical points, and our estimate is that in the Department of History about 50 percent of the Harvard faculty in 1936 had their undergraduate degrees from Harvard, and 60 percent their doctorates from Harvard. In Chemistry, about 30 percent of the faculty had their undergraduate degrees from Harvard, and 46 percent their doctorates.[15] The stream of distinguished, displaced Europeans was just beginning to come when I was a student. Thus Harvard offered a place to the Russian sociologist, Pitirim Sorokin, and the Russian chemist, George Kistiakowsky, in 1930; Gaetano Salvemini came as a refugee from Italian fascism; after 1933, distinguished German refugees began to appear on the faculty, sometimes on a temporary basis.

The European and especially the German sense of the university as a place for research and scholarship, not for the general education of undergraduates, had been brought back to the United States for decades by Americans who had studied abroad and by occasional immigrants and visitors from Europe. This flow of influence was, however, intensified

[15]I consulted former President James Bryant Conant concerning the correctness of my assumption that he developed the Ad Hoc Committee system for faculty tenure appointments (see below) to widen the orbit of recruitment and impose quality control on departmental comfort with mediocrity. He responded (in conversation and then in a note) that as a chemist he was a member of a national professional world and could judge the degree of provinciality in Harvard's local setting; he inaugurated the Ad Hoc Committee system to nationalize (indeed, internationalize) recruitment for faculty, just as he also moved to nationalize recruitment of undergraduates. He had been, unlike Charles W. Eliot, a distinguished chemist (I had been one of his undergraduate students). Paul Buck (in conversation) fully agreed with Conant that the Ad Hoc Committee system served to widen orbits of recruitment and, at its installation, to frustrate local clusters of expectation among friendly faculty. In addition, he emphasized the use of the system, not only to defend Harvard's efforts to raise standards vis-à-vis its own faculty, but also to defend departmental choices from political interference by alumni and, on at least one occasion, some of the Overseers. In effect, the Ad Hoc Committee disfranchised the Governing Boards, for as Conant and Buck explained, once this sort of peer review had occurred and had been approved at the highest internal levels, it would not be feasible to maintain the system and to recruit outside reviewers if their judgments were not to be final. Most Harvard faculty are insulated from awareness as to how the system of Ad Hoc Committees has served to protect academic freedom, especially now that the undulating clamor over the Department of Economics comes largely from the political Left rather than the Right.

Professor Buck feels that the system has been least successful where, in a particular field, there is no good candidate, and where, correspondingly, Harvard should give up the field, but where pressures to fill the vacant chairs and the vacant slot in the roster of disciplines can be pretty overwhelming. (Harvard did, however, at one point drop Geography—I recall a comment by Clark Kerr that to terminate a field at Berkeley, even when it involved only a single incumbent, was the most courageous action of his administative career.)

by the new cadre of European emigres who, whatever institutional loyalty toward Harvard they may have developed, rarely acquired loyalty to traditional collegiate Harvard. Indeed, these men provided for homeguard Harvard faculty a personal witness to the outlook of Continental faculties with their relative lack of any mystique about the "Harvard community" and their generally whole hearted pursuit of scholarly distinction.[16] Similarly, the many men who came to teach at Harvard after study at one of the great state universities may have become converts, for example, to Lowell's ideal of the Houses as counterweights to the University, but this too was rare.[17]

With great variation among departments and, to some extent, among generations, the Harvard of my undergraduate days was still somewhat provincial, despite the efforts of some departments to maintain distinction on a world rather than a local scale. Many thought it somehow unbecoming for a Jew to teach English literature or American history, much as the University of Georgia would have been uncomfortable with a New Englander teaching Southern history. The Boston Brahmin—and widely American—prejudice against Catholics, and especially Irish Catholics, which is still not completely attenuated, was part of the landscape. In the humanities and social sciences, the tone I remember was Anglophile or Francophile; an interest in Weimar Germany or in the Soviet Union (other than an immediately political one), not to speak of the rest of the planet, was uncommon. Yet these preferences and prejudices were not ironclad. As already mentioned, Harvard, like Oxford and Cambridge, made room for elegant eccentrics, as it had done earlier for Santayana, and that magnetic and troubled son of an Albany Irishman of the Swedenborgian persuasion, William James. Birth and breeding had long since not sufficed to secure a permanent place on the Harvard faculty, and an increasing number of students of good family were taking their studies more seriously than they often let on. Intellectual pres-

---

[17]The quizzical detachment of George Santayana, on which his contemporaries commented, was a detachment from professionalized scholarship as well as from Harvard itself. The flamboyant Austrian economist, Joseph Schumpeter, in a later generation, enjoyed teasing some of the locals, but in his own grand way did identify himself with scholarship and made himself available to lively and talented students, much as did my own teacher, Friedrich.

[18]An examination of the Harvard degrees of the senior tutors of the Houses since the inception of the House system turns up only four without some Harvard degree, out of 96 altogether, although there is only one House (Kirkland) where the majority of senior tutors have also been Harvard College graduates. The senior tutor is the second in command in the House under the master, and in effect a dean of students in the House, with the responsibilities a dean of students would generally have. (The analyses of where Harvard faculty received their degrees was the work of Martha Fuller.)

tige could heighten social prestige for individuals, as it did for Harvard itself. Those institutions such as Johns Hopkins, Clark, and Chicago, which began with a search for intellectual and academic prestige, were never quite able to accomplish Harvard's amalgam of the social and the academic.[18]

Yet the cases are too few and the institutional circumstances so idiosyncratic that it would be unsafe to generalize from these instances and to declare that scholarship and research thrive best in America where they are not the only reigning passions. Harvard survived its first several centuries as a public-private amalgam. That it surpassed in eminence such early rivals as Union College or William and Mary seems to me to reflect in part the "great men," notably, of course, Charles W. Eliot, whose long tenure enabled them to develop a complex institution with such built-in mechanisms of self-correction as the Ad Hoc Committee system instituted by Conant. But just as in a medical school the tension between the scientists teaching preclinical subjects and the practitioners on the clinical side is often difficult and sometimes intractable, so the Harvard symbiosis between an undergraduate college and a research-oriented faculty with their comet's tail of graduate students and, in many fields, a fair supply of postdoctoral researchers, has led to conflict and distraction in the lives of individual faculty members and to struggles over limited resources—struggles moderated by the relative bounty of financial support from private donors and the federal government in the two decades following World War II. As McGeorge Bundy once put it in a joking way, he could allow Widener Library to flourish because the chemists were not starving.

In the kind of cyclical pattern that Lipset describes, the emphasis on research has periodically come under attack on the ground that it leads to neglect of undergraduate teaching or responsibility to civic virtues and causes. In some of my own writings, using a dairyman's metaphor, I have been critical of the use of "Holstein" rather than "Jersey" measures of faculty productivity and of the narrowness with which research sometimes comes to be defined.[19] The necessity to teach undergraduates if they are reasonably talented and if the teaching comes in small, not too exhausting installments, can, in some fields or at some points in the researcher's life cycle, be refreshing even for esoteric pursuits. But what must not be forgotten is that research is hard and often frustrating, and that, as is well-known, the vast majority of those who win the doctorate do no further research, even though some may main-

---

[18]For a succinct description of this process, see Ben-David (1972, pp 37–47).
[19]Cf., however, Riesman (1972, pp. 17–32).

tain cultivated, scholarly interests. To practice most professions makes no special claims other than the achievement of a certain minimal level of competence—a level which in such fields as neurosurgery or patent law can be quite high. To define oneself as a schoolteacher or college teacher in regular subjects and for the ordinary run of students also makes few special claims. To declare that one is a research scientist does not necessarily make larger claims (Price, 1961). But at the highest levels research is like the practice of the arts: it does make a claim to potential uniqueness: a new discovery, a new angle of vision, some synthesis of old and new. The worlds of scholarship and high culture act at the same time as a brake (sometimes too tight, now often too loose) on delusions of originality, and provide the support and peer legitimation that researchers need because otherwise few would take the risks of failure and frustration. This says nothing about the inherent value of these respective activities; for example, that college teaching may sometimes be a fall-back position by failed or frustrated researchers does not mean it is less socially useful or less personally satisfying. Indeed, serious and innovative teaching is at least as difficult as innovative research, as likely to fail, as much in need of peer support and legitimation, and very likely as rare as innovative research.

2. Meritocracy Triumphant

For many on the Harvard faculty, and not only the German newcomers, the concessions that had been made traditionally to the social and the collegiate seemed excessive.[1] Even before American entry into the Second World War, Lowell's successor, President Conant, had turned attention to the graduate and professional schools and had begun to create for the College a wider network of national recruiting and those financial aid measures which allowed the College to offer financial support to any accepted student who needed it, thus diminishing social and economic barriers to entry. Less visibly, his administration reflected a move toward the democratic kind of meritocracy represented by the Harvard National Scholarships which were offered to students whose College Board scores reached a certain level, while placing less emphasis on the aristocratic kind, which favored a few specially chosen, glamorously talented and well-sponsored young men, as exemplified in the Society of Fellows.[2]

[1] Cf. Riesman (1953, Ch. 4, pp. 99–113), "Scientists versus Captains of Erudition." Abraham Flexner, in his book of 1930, took a purist view of university functions, one which is endemic in discussions then and now. However, he exempted Harvard and several other Ivy League colleges, and the major women's colleges, from his severest strictures (Flexner, 1967, pp. 64ff).

[2] When I was teaching at the University of Chicago just after the Second World War, an exceptionally able and erudite but somewhat unpolished graduate student in sociology journeyed to Cambridge for his interview with the Senior Fellows in the hope of being accepted by the Society of Fellows. As he reported the occasion to me, he found people making social conversation with him, at which he was ill at ease; and at dinner in the Eliot House Society of Fellows Dining Room, he sprang to life when his dinner companion, the late Arthur Darby Nock, asked him, so he thought, about Hobbes. The Chicago student started to hold forth on Hobbes, only to be cut short: "Hobbies, not Hobbes!" Alas for his election, his main hobby had been writers like Hobbes. My guess is that today, holding other things relatively equal, he would not have been turned down.

A series of consequences flowing from World War II greatly increased the role of meritocracy in its democratic version in Harvard College. For one thing, the constraints of the war led to having Radcliffe students taught jointly with the men. Since women students are generally DARs (Damned Average Raisers), throwing them in with the men added to the scholarly pressure. And then all over the country at the war's end, the GI Bill of Rights brought to the universities a new surge of seriousness and began the demolition of the now-fading fraternity systems.[3] Delayed and often matured by the war, frequently married, with a pretty good idea of the careers they were headed for, veterans did not want to fool around with collegiate fun and games. They were impatient with what seemed trivial distinctions of status, such as the lowly position of college freshmen; they insisted on being regarded as adults. Furthermore, as the boom in higher education began, private colleges and major state universities could become more selective, allowing the more visible private institutions and such public eminences as Virginia to recruit in wider catchbasins. This brought the news of the availability of colleges like Harvard to a much larger group of high schools than before the war.

Of course the image of Harvard College has been such that many prospective students have regarded it as out of their social, cultural, and intellectual league, even if they could afford to attend. Furthermore, many young men of 17 or 18 who will end up as scholars and researchers do not know this of themselves in high school, and are put off by a college that seems monolithically scholarly, since they cannot then make such a commitment.[4] Admissions Dean Wilbur Bender did not believe that Harvard could only benefit the top 2 percent among the test score winners, but he argued that by presenting Harvard to high

[3]This chapter was first drafted in the fall of 1971. Since then, there have been reports of fraternity resurgence, including an interest in fraternities among some Vietnam veterans. Quite possibly, just as the Masons and other lodges and orders have been, so to speak, downwardly mobile in the social-class hierarchy of America, fraternities may now be attracting some working-class and lower-middle-class students who are the first in their families to attend college.

[4]The psychologist David Ricks has described the way in which winning a national scholarship made it legitimate for students like him to leave their local orbit (in his case, Utah) and to attend a national university college without being rejected by his peers as snobbish and high-hat (Cf. Ricks, 1961). Such considerations are overlooked by Michael S. Schudson in his critique, "Organizing the 'Meritocracy': A History of the College Entrance Examination Board" (Schudson, 1972, pp. 54–69).

school seniors as suitable not only to would-be scholars, he widened the pool of scholars who would in fact come.

At the same time, as rising ethnic groups became more affluent and as their young shied away from provincial ties, Harvard became—in part because of active work on the part of admissions officers and alumni—a legitimate goal, for instance, for Irish Catholic boys who would once have aspired to Holy Cross, Georgetown, or Notre Dame, if they were capable, or who, in the absence of scholarship aid, might have gone to the local state school. The College Boards, now so casually deprecated by political and pedagogic radicals, sometimes protected students in Catholic high and prep schools from the resistance they encountered from school authorities when they applied to places like Harvard. (Of course, some first-rate Catholic prep schools like Portsmouth Priory have encouraged their graduates to attend secular colleges.)

Decisive for the changed temper and tempo of Harvard both on the faculty and student sides was the great increase of Jewish recruitment and acceptance.[5] The faculty shift was that of the leading academic institutions generally, although it was and remains uneven in terms of field, with more Jews in theoretical physics and microbiology than in organic chemistry and engineering, more in sociology than in archaeology, more in intellectual history than in diplomatic or military history. Furthermore, not only was a larger number of Jews recruited but a representation of Jews from a wider range in terms of social origin. The earlier Jews on the Harvard faculty and to a lesser degree in the student body had been, or seemed to be, German Jews with several American generations behind them; the postwar influx brought many more Eastern European Jews who were less "Americanized" and less prepared to be. (In the 1960s, on many predominantly white campuses, a similar development occurred among black students, who in an earlier time had been middle class in origin and destination; both among blacks and Jews the more "proletarian" styles came to prevail, with the same moral hegemony that these had among elite youth generally.)

It would be a very rough guess that Jews now number a quarter of the student body and a third of the faculty. As individualistic as the Brahmins, they compete with each other and with everybody else. In an earlier more leisurely Harvard, such behavior would have been stigmatized as unmannerly, but in the Harvard that was being shaped under the successive auspices of Conant and Pusey, such achievement-

[5]Cf. Martin Lipset's essay in this volume on the question of a Jewish quota.

oriented behavior was admired and, where possible, imitated or sur-passed.[6]

The contemporary impact of Harvard admissions policy is succinctly described by Cass and Birnbaum: "Pressures for academic achievement are rigorous. College environment likely to be extraordinarily gratifying to the scholar, the intellectual, the grind, the highly motivated plod-der—to all but the traditional candidate seeking a leisurely gentleman's C. Today's Harvard student body is probably the most truly national of any in the country, and one in which a majority of the freshman class is expected to graduate with honors."[7]

The faculty counterpart to nationwide recruiting for undergraduates was another innovation of Conant's which has already been discussed, namely, the Ad Hoc Committee system. That system required any department or school which wanted to promote an incumbent or recruit an outsider to a permanent chair to submit the candidate's qualifica-tions to a committee appointed for this task only, one that included some faculty members from within Harvard in neighboring fields as well as faculty members from outside Harvard in the same field. Department members and perhaps others at Harvard were to be called to testify before the Committee as to why the person in question should be appointed, what other persons had been considered, and what the

---

[6]See Ricks and McCarley (1965, pp. 39–53), and McCarley (1959) on which the Ricks and McCarley article draws. McCarley, working with Ricks, compared the responses to Har-vard College of freshmen from elite prep schools and the responses of freshmen from good public high schools and brought the two cadres together for mutual interchange; while the prep school products seemed adapted to Harvard in superficial terms, such as clothes and manner of speaking, they realized that, in competition with the public school graduates, they were ill-adapted to the new, more meritocratic Harvard, and that if they were to feel adequate they would have to change in profound ways. The study was not a comparison of Jews and non-Jews, but of students from different social and school backgrounds; many Jewish entrants, for example, those from the South, felt as little prepared for the prevailing subcultures of Harvard College as any scion of five Harvard generations drifting in with his classmates from St. George's School.

[7]See Cass and Birnbaum (1971, p. 278). In various surveys, Harvard undergraduates do in fact declare that the environment is gratifying—as on Carnegie Commission national sur-veys, students generally did even during the highly rhetorical debates of the late 1960s. In the present atmosphere of intense competition for places in medical and law schools, the students who seek to enter these professions often work under the most intense pres-sures—but a large proportion, perhaps as many as a quarter, who have no idea what they will do on graduation, are by no means seeking a leisurely gentleman's C. For one thing, that grade has been replaced by the antiacademic, antigentleman's B. The fifth edition (1972) of Cass and Birnbaum has eliminated the reference to the gentleman's C and notes that the College environment can be gratifying to "the highly motivated student of more modest academic aptitude who has serious interests in a wide range of extracur-ricular activities, from Athletics to Zen" (p. 252).

state of the art has been and may perhaps become in the particular discipline that has made the requested choice seem desirable for the department, for Harvard, and for the field.[8]

It is difficult to estimate how the Ad Hoc Committee system has worked over the years; however, it would be my guess that it has advanced meritocracy in its democratic version, on the one hand providing some modest insurance against those nonkin nepotisms of preference and provincialism by which distinguished faculties can slowly become mediocre,[9] or mediocre faculties remain so, while on the other hand perhaps intensifying the temptation of departments to select candidates who have visible national reputations and thus can easily survive Committee scrutiny, even though they may not be optimal for Harvard in other respects. The quality of the process of course reflects the sagacity of the President and Dean in helping to select and then in questioning the members of an Ad Hoc Committee and the Harvard witnesses. Unconventional, "aristocratic" choices have been approved by such committees. However, it seems possible that outside the Natural Sciences and Mathematics, the system has been disadvantageous to junior Harvard faculty who are unlikely to have had the record of publication of older men (sometimes ex-Harvard junior faculty) elsewhere.

[8]The existence of the Ad Hoc Committee system depends not only on Harvard's belief in its own importance, but on the wide sharing of that belief, for the faculty members elsewhere who are asked to come to Harvard for a half-day meeting after having read materials by and about the candidates must believe that it matters whom Harvard appoints. Other universities rather commonly ask outsiders for their judgments on particular candidates in a letter or in a phone conversation: they may have permanent tenure committees which review all promotions. Occasionally a department that for example wishes to embark on graduate work may solicit a site visit from an ad hoc committee of (generally sympathetic) outsiders, in part to impress its own administration or a state coordinating council; still more occasionally, a department will be subjected to a review by an outside committee in the hope of updating it, or to resolve conflicts.

The working of the Ad Hoc Committee system can be clumsy and self-defeating. Some of the persons whom Harvard has sought have been unwilling to wait until an Ad Hoc Committee meeting could be scheduled (a matter of weeks or months) or even to take their chances at being turned down.

[9]In general, however, the more distinguished a faculty becomes, the more scrupulous it is likely to be in recruiting its own successors. At times, such a department can become so choosy that no candidate satisfies its exalted criteria—particularly if these are mixed, as they generally are, with canons as to appropriate method and style of work—eventually forcing a depleted department to recruit only moderately capable individuals on pain of losing its share both of students and appointments. And of course intellectual distinction is no guarantee against personal pettiness and misjudgment of people and projects in or out of one's own field.

However, since promotions do at times occur from within Harvard's junior ranks (where assistant professors are appointed for five-year terms), the competitiveness of those wanting to stay at Harvard seems more relentless than comparable competitiveness elsewhere, reflecting in part Harvard's actual superiority in terms of students, opportunities for research and colleagueship, prestige, and, in part, a complacency that transcends its realistic supports. Accordingly, senior faculty tend to assume that all junior faculty want to stay at Harvard, intensifying the strain between those Harvard refers to as "permanent members" and those outside. And as happens elsewhere too, junior faculty are torn between their often dedicated commitment to teaching and the pressure they feel to compile a scholarly record that will facilitate their going to a good position elsewhere if Harvard does not keep them; the dilemma may be intensified for those who want to teach outside their departmental fold with the (at times exaggerated) fear of risking the loss of departmental sponsorship.[10]

At Oxford or Cambridge, a College can appoint a don on the basis of personal acquaintance and perhaps because one or two articles have shown that he is bright. This is meritocracy in its aristocratic version, only somewhat mitigated by the British system of advertising open positions throughout the English-speaking world. The Ad Hoc Committee system is no doubt only one, perhaps mainly symbolic reason, why it is difficult for the Harvard Faculty of Arts and Sciences to behave in the same way except in rare instances. It has become almost un-American to make this kind of clubby judgment. Moreover, the competitive individualism of the Harvard faculty has the consequence that those few faculty members given permanent tenure as lecturers for principally nonscholarly activities, such as serving as Master of a House[11] or gaining reputations as superior undergraduate teachers, have often been unhappy in the absence of prestige among colleagues. But there are also faculty members at Harvard with national reputations who publish widely and who would be regarded as illustrious in most institutions who nevertheless, within the small world of a subdepart-

[10]For an account of how the vicissitudes struck a sensitive, self-observant junior faculty member, see Cottle (1973, Ch. 2). The present tight faculty market, combined with pressure from within and outside Harvard to appoint women and members of minorities to open positions, has increased the malaise of (mainly white male) junior faculty, although with quite uneven impact among the departments.

[11]A Master or other administrative officer does not have academic tenure as such, but only so long as he holds his administrative post.

ment, are looked down upon as insufficiently original and distinguished.[12] And just as undergraduates often feel that they got into Harvard or Radcliffe by mistake, some sensitive faculty may occasionally wonder why they were chosen when talented young men and women are regularly sent elsewhere.[13]

The majority of senior Harvard faculty do not appear to others to harbor such self-doubts, but instead, especially in the post-Sputnik and Kennedy-Johnson era, have given an impression of supreme self-confidence. This is true not only of the scientists who have served on federal commissions, but of many of the social scientists and even of people in the humanities. A number of undergraduates have been attracted to this aura of power and influence and, like other seaboard provincials, have exaggerated its importance. Even now in Harvard College a minority of students develop a quite extraordinary self-possession, rarely matched by students of comparable ability at otherwise comparable universities. More graduating seniors at Harvard are likely to have published books than is true elsewhere. Recently, in terms proportioned to numbers of students, more are likely to have become leaders of radical movements or influential among organizers for Eugene McCarthy, George McGovern, and other peace candidates—a topic developed at length in Lipset's companion essay. The shy, the less sophisticated, the self-doubting, both among students and faculty, seem to me more likely to be damaged by the Harvard milieu than they would be at a university with a less exclusive emphasis on overt evidence of bright-

[12]To be sure, in some cases these individuals misjudge the extent of the collegial respect they do have at Harvard, being wounded by the combination of their own self-doubts and the lack of supportive response.

It is possible to have the respect of one's colleagues at Harvard—and I speak here of colleagues within one's own guild—without publishing much, if one is known to be brilliant, to keep up with one's field, and to take scholarship with due seriousness. And being at Harvard may itself in some marginal cases give individual faculty members the benefit of the doubt. But once that benefit is removed, Harvard faculty can be cruel and cutting in side-of-the-mouth deprecation of disesteemed colleagues, and this narrowly meritocratic judgment will pass down the transmission belt of graduate student teaching fellows to the undergraduates. Lipset has observed that eminent Berkeley faculty members are apt to be even more cruel, since (outside the natural sciences) Berkeley still thinks of itself as Avis to Harvard's Hertz, and no mantle of marginal acceptance is thrown over the only moderately talented.

[13]It should be added that, once one is at Harvard, one's salary reflects market value or how well an individual advertises the University only in part; Harvard does not match the star salaries paid by both upwardly mobile and many established institutions.

ness and a somewhat less competitive forum for establishing adequa-cy.[14]

In a way, this is a survival of the aristocratic version of meritocracy, which looks down on merely solid worth and the achievements that can be won by diligence, uncoupled with flights of brilliant fancy. In formal terms, Harvard does not have a two-class faculty, one for undergrad-uates and lower-division teaching, and the other mainly for graduate students; just as undergraduates can take graduate courses, so all faculty have access to both cadres of students.[15] But Harvard may subtly have a two-class faculty (and student body), in astronomer's language, of red giants and dwarfs. A number of Harvard's most noted scholars enjoy teaching undergraduates, sometimes giving the introductory courses in their fields. Furthermore, since permanent appointments at Harvard depend on the preexistence of "hard money" to support the chair and not on student numbers, there are some departments which are rela-tively overstaffed and where senior faculty must teach undergraduates if they are to do any teaching at all. Moreover, departments differ in the ethos they establish concerning senior men teaching underclassmen either in the department or in Freshman Seminars or General Education courses. Nevertheless, there are many fields where the regular load of undergraduate teaching, particularly tutorial and the leading of sec-tions, falls on junior faculty and graduate students, leaving senior facul-ty free to concentrate primarily on their apprentice entourage of post-doctoral fellows and graduate students. President Lowell's hope that sen-

---

[14]Cf. Davis (1966, pp. 17–31). Davis demonstrates that the big high school frog in the small campus pond is more likely to continue on to graduate school than the valedicto-rian who finds himself dismayingly thrown in with 500 other valedictorians.

Problems comparable to those that Davis discusses can be observed in those few un-dergraduate colleges where academic values have triumphed even more unmistakably than at Harvard College. Reed College, for example, has in recent years offered its students no alternative careers other than imitating the faculty, and it has had a very high rate of attrition. Cf. Clark (1970, pp. 129–144). Similarly, in The College of the Uni-versity of Chicago after World War II, the student subcultures tended to reflect the cog-nitive preoccupations and verbal combativeness of many of the faculty, leading, as at Reed, to a tendency for students of different orientation to feel inadequate and to drop out. On Chicago, see Spady (1971, pp. 38–62); Spady found that the lack of social integra-tion was especially problematic for women students. For discussion of attrition due to severe grading at Chicago, see Spady, "Peer Integration and Academic Success: The Dropout Process among Chicago Freshmen," unpublished PH.D. dissertation, Univer-sity of Chicago, 1967; recently, there has been a deliberate effort to raise grades at Chicago, both for equity vis-à-vis less stringent competitors and in the hope of diminishing attrition.

[15]For clarifying discussion of the two-class faculty problem at Chicago and Columbia, and of the general issues dealt with in this article, see Bell (1966).

ior faculty would assume a major part of the tutorial enterprise has never been fulfilled.[16]

The initiative in making appointments at Harvard as in most universities lies with the departments. The assumption has been that by appointing the "best man" in a particular field, a good atmosphere for scholarship and learning would evolve, for students as well as for faculty. But there is also the belief, often justified, that the incremental growth of disciplinary preoccupation expands the ties among the disciplines. Yet given the many narrow definitions of what an academic discipline is in topic or method, these judgments may be regarded as an academic equivalent of the belief in the Invisible Hand.[17] What has been lacking in the Harvard procedure, for all its carefulness, has been any large sense that the search for the best available person in a particu-

---

[16]There has been since World War II, and especially since 1960, an enormous increase in the number of teaching fellows, that is, graduate students, and in the extent of the teaching burden carried by them. For one thing, a larger proportion of students has entered honors programs with their characteristic requirement of a senior thesis; supervision of such thesis work is extremely time-consuming. Tutorials themselves have tended to grow more specialized and demanding. Furthermore, as straight lecture courses have come under critical attack, there has been a tendency to supplement them with section meetings supervised by teaching fellows—meetings which are not intended as mere drill sessions. The hope has been that the teaching fellows would themselves be supervised, thus learning to become better teachers and better masters of their subjects. See *Teaching Fellowships in Harvard College*, a survey by the Committee on Teaching as a Career (October 1960), and to similar effect, the still unpublished report of the Committee on Graduate Education, chaired by Professor Michael L. Walzer, of June 8, 1973. As fellowship aid from the government and foundations has fallen off, graduate students have needed teaching fellowships to earn their keep, which has meant that an assignment as a Teaching Fellow may be seen not as an honor or opportunity but as a necessary expedient. Correspondingly, with considerable variation among departments, teaching fellows (and junior faculty as well) have increasingly made vocal their resentment that they are the front-line troops vis-à-vis undergraduates, protecting the senior faculty from bearing their full share of tutorial or sectioning, even though the senior faculty have the greater job security. With the spread of egalitarian attitudes, such disparities within the teaching ranks are no longer accepted as part of the natural order of things. Similarly, the fact that senior faculty frequently carry a greater load of University-wide committee responsibilities which they feel as onerous tends to be viewed by the young outsiders not as a compensatory burden on the former, but as another aspect of professorial privilege.

[17]Both in new and old institutions there is now such frequent talk about the interdisciplinary that many people may forget that men with a departmental base have often felt secure enough to move away from it. Many of the departments we now see are the result of such migration. See Ben-David and Collins (1966, pp. 451–465). Those institutions which have rejected departmentalism have sometimes discovered that the men and women they recruit are antidisciplinary out of incompetence or allergy rather than out of transcendence and originality, or out of an interest in problems whose understanding requires multidisciplinary paradigms and skills.

lar subfield would often be less fruitful than the effort to recruit a cadre who could work well together and with other faculty and students.[18]

Yet some cadres were in fact built up. Starting with the Russian Research Center after the Second World War, Harvard developed, as other institutions did, a group of area-focused centers where researchers could come together, along with their graduate or postdoctoral apprentices, to pursue enterprises which assisted their own self-education. West European Studies has recently been added to East Asian Studies, the Center for Middle Eastern Studies, and the (repeatedly bombed or invaded) Center for International Affairs. The Joint Center for Urban Studies of MIT and Harvard has brought together, mostly for individual projects, faculty members from all the social sciences. The Cambridge Electron Accelerator was also a joint venture of MIT and Harvard; it was closed down in 1973 for want of federal support.

The Social Relations Department also began after the war, joining what had been a very small Sociology Department with Social and Clinical Psychology and Social Anthropology in a research and teaching enterprise that for 25 years attracted able students and served as a model of attempted, though of course incomplete, integration of these disciplines. At the undergraduate level, Social Relations took its place along with Government, History, and Economics as a major field of un-

---

[18]When, in the academic year 1970–71, a Committee on the Status of Women at Harvard held a hearing on faculty appointments, I testified that, both at Chicago and Harvard, recruitment had invariably been of "the best man": "the best man" in Balkan history, or "the best man" in urban sociology. I said that such individualistic recruiting did generally produce a man, not a woman. I proposed that if the policy were modified to seek a person who might be catalytic for the cadre already on hand, assuming that the department was not sunk in cozy mediocrity, it seemed likely that one would in fact discover more women and would create more productive and less self-destructive departmental microclimates. I made plain my judgment that women were not necessarily less egocentric or more nurturant or catalytic than men, but that this might be so on average. This was regarded as a sexist bias by many women on the Committee and at the hearing, whose reaction was, in effect: "Don't give us that nurturant bit! We can be as vicious as any man, and should be recruited on the same basis of individual superiority as men." Whatever may be the case as to the balance between the sexes, which varies undoubtedly among fields and over time, I would still maintain that recruiting should not be only for "the best man" in those institutions where mediocrity is less of a problem than the damage done by sadism and exploitativeness. Naturally, one would need to be vigilant lest such a procedure as I propose be used to screen out lone-wolf innovators or political dissidents.

In 1954, a faculty committee published a 500-page report, "The Behavioral Sciences at Harvard," which illuminates the tradition of Harvard individualism not only in making appointments but also in an inclination to disparage team research—an inclination now somewhat attenuated, but still evident. See, on the Ad Hoc Committee system, "The Behavioral Sciences at Harvard" (pp. 197ff); on individualism and research (pp. 44–59, 246–268).

dergraduate social science interest; at the graduate level, it was far more successful than the short-lived postwar attempt to promote a Doctor of Social Science degree: Ph.D.'s in Social Relations have continued to be in demand as researchers, teachers, and often as administrators. However, when some of the initial enthusiasm for building ties, for example, between psychoanalytic psychology and cultural anthropology waned, and when major founding fathers (including Gordon Allport, Clyde Kluckhohn, Henry A. Murray, and Talcott Parsons) died or retired, departmental fission began. The sociologists formed an independent department in 1970, and in the following months the Psychology Department was rejoined in a larger structure with Social Psychology and other Social Relations subunits.

The proliferation of centers and institutes at Harvard, however, has been limited in comparison with Berkeley, where it sometimes seems as if every senior faculty member has his own institute; indeed, by state university standards, the departments at Harvard are small enough so that centrifugal tendencies are minimized. And while, as already suggested, Harvard senior faculty work less intensively with undergraduates than their counterparts at Princeton or Yale, the bright and somewhat assertive Harvard College students have considerable seductive power in securing access to the Harvard notables.[19]

Indeed, the appointment as President of Nathan Pusey—himself a Harvard College graduate, with later experiences at Scripps, Wesleyan, and Lawrence—reflected a decision by the Governing Boards to focus once again upon Harvard College (as Lowell had done) and to achieve a balance between its claims and those of the graduate and professional schools. This search for balance did not reflect the demands of undergraduates—they then seldom voiced demands—but rather the concern with the College among the alumni themselves, including many devoted and influential ones who raised money for Harvard, served on

---

[19]See Martin Trow, "Notes on Undergraduate Teaching at Large State Universities" (1966). Trow emphasizes the fact that the freshman class at Berkeley includes students who in terms of aptitude are the equal of freshman classes at Harvard or MIT, but that same freshman class at Berkeley will also include students who are the equal of the freshman class of an undistinguished teachers college. They reflect in this way the disparities among the high schools, whose top 12 percent can be admitted to the University of California. That is, the exceptionally adept students at Berkeley, for example, are mixed in with many less adept ones, so that a faculty member there faces a constituency which appears less inviting to all but missionaries than the numerically smaller constituency of able students at a selective private university college such as Harvard. (To be sure, not only missionary types enjoy teaching a diverse lot of state college or university undergraduates; bright faculty do not invariably want to teach only those students who resemble themselves.)

its Visiting Committeees, recruited students locally, and otherwise concerned themselves with College affairs. The main assignment in holding this balance was given to McGeorge Bundy, then a young member of the Government Department, who became Dean of the Faculty of Arts and Sciences in 1953.[20]

In his essay "Were Those the Days?" delineating Harvard in the 1950s, Bundy reflects that he did not succeed in holding the balance fairly.[21] He observes also that the faculty in those postwar years were animated by a passion for excellence, but that on the whole they defined excellence narrowly. I have already touched on this in describing the strategy of securing "the best man," seen in the nonaristocratic version of meritocracy as the person with the best track record on a single racecourse. However, since energy and self-confidence are significant elements of attainment in a single field, it must in fairness be added that many senior Harvard faculty possess wide-ranging professional and cultivated personal interests, are generous to colleagues and to students, and find time for loyalty to their institution as well as to their discipline.[22] Correspondingly, there were and remain enormous

[20]President Pusey deserves credit for his willingness to appoint as Dean a man of such dazzling assertiveness and virtuosity as an administrator, a person in sharp contrast to his own more muted (and, outside the company of close friends, more formal) manner. In the appointment of Deans, Nathan Pusey consulted the relevant senior faculties, but followed the aristocratic line of trusting his own judgment rather than relying on consensus; often his choices turned out well. While President Pusey had many supporters in the professional schools, a large number of Arts and Sciences faculty members seemed to me from the very beginning not to forgive him for sharing some but not all of their values, for taking organized religion seriously (but not all of the faculty's secular or civic religions), and for possessing a very different, often slower, tempo and style. Meyer (1973, pp. 134ff) summarizes the very different style with which incoming President Derek Bok approached students and faculty. Almost inevitably, any successor for the 1970s, in the dialectic such matters take, would have had to be a person of more informal manner, more habituated to participative (as distinguished from consultative) procedures, and more comfortable with the give-and-take of bargaining.

[21]See "Were Those the Days?" (Bundy, 1970, pp. 531–567); I have found this essay extremely helpful for my own analysis.

[22]Carl Kaysen believes that the Junior Fellows recruited to Harvard helped play a part in broadening faculty interests, since during the time of their Fellowships these individuals were not bound to a departmental racecourse, but had the run of the University in curricular terms, and, through their contacts with each other and with Senior Fellows, to some degree in personal terms as well. Yet less friendly beneficiaries have seen the Society of Fellows as a cruelly self-confident group of undeniably talented men who paraded their knowledge of wines and other esoteric things after the stag manner of a British common room; the range of topics at the Fellows' dinners may have been broad, but the tone had a game-like monotony, the effect of which could be narrowing.

differences among departments in the prevailing styles of judgment of colleagues and students. During the fifties and much of the sixties, the minority of virtuosos in the undergraduate student body tended to model themselves on the more dazzling and self-confident faculty members, who, of course, as in any other college, were more available to them as potential models than were other professionals, government officials, or businessmen. Not all the student virtuosos were summa cum laude prospects; some were *Crimson* editors who, as we shall see, generally managed to do well if not always outstandingly in academic terms, while others were writers or playwrights or in a few cases, musicians and, in the late sixties, political activists.[23]

The virtuosos I am talking about overlap with another much larger group, ranging from a fifth to a quarter of the entering student body, who came to the College with advanced standing on the basis of superior high school preparation. This program gained momentum after Sputnik, and was intended not only to accelerate college graduation for some students, but also to encourage excellence in teaching and learning in the high schools. Thus, at many universities, a student who had had college physics at the Bronx High School of Science, or college French at Andover, would be given credit for these. However, Harvard faculty members were very unevenly prepared to concede that someone could learn French or physics outside their own orbits, or that any examination not framed by them could test this. Nevertheless, Bundy's elegant and incisive wit managed to persuade the faculty that if one had three such advanced placement subjects, one could enter college as a sopho-

---

[23]For a penetrating account of this impetuous and scholarly Harvard after World War II, in contrast to the Harvard of the late 1960s, see Huntington (1969, pp. 51–54). Huntington's judgment coincides with my own, that the Harvard neighborhood was tipped in the direction of scholarly competition, among undergraduates as well as among graduate students, in the late 1940s. At several points of detail, however, my judgment both of Chicago and of Harvard differs from that of Huntington. Thus, I do not believe that prewar Harvard was quite as clubby as in Huntington's portrait. Moreover, Huntington's picture of turbulent political activism dominating the University of Chicago as against Harvard's greater emphasis on academic virtuosity in the years immediately after the Second World War, though it captures a facet of Chicago, does not jibe with my own picture of the hegemony academic matters held at Chicago. In fact, I have known quite a few highly intelligent students who have chosen to come to Harvard because the Cambridge-Boston ambience offered a greater variety of alternatives if academic intensity proved unsatisfying, in comparison with the enclave of the University of Chicago; similarly, I have recently observed quite academically adept students deciding on Harvard as against Yale or Princeton, Williams or Swarthmore, precisely on the ground that Harvard faculty would pay less attention to them, allow them to be more anonymous and hence, according to their preference, less involved and serious academically.

more even if this violated life's inherent phasing.[24] A third of the entering students who were offered the possibility of advanced placement
declined it, while many others chose to go through in three years and
then to exercise the admirable option of staying on for a fourth year, a
year in which they could either be free entirely of requirements or
could use to begin graduate work while still having undergraduate
benefits such as life in the residential Houses. Currently, only a tenth
of the students eligible for sophomore standing leave the College after
three years.

The Harvard College term "wonks," referring to the excessively studious, was a way of putting down those students, admitted to Harvard
under a democratized meritocracy, who were not cavalierly brilliant;
the dazzling students could escape the designation of "wonk" even
when admitting to occasional long bouts of work. I am told by students
that the use of the term "wonk" has declined, perhaps as one of those
aristocratic snobberies that can no longer be justified, even though, as
we shall see, the term "jock" is used derisively toward athletes, whose
competitive striving and mere diligence as players is rarely admired. In
these years, Harvard College has been a milieu in which many who
rejected an academic career came to do so *faute de mieux*, for example,
because they had gotten their first B+ in biology and had decided that
they had best go to medical school, since they would never become a
James D. Watson.[25]

During these years, two-thirds or more of the men and four-fifths of
the women have graduated with honors; in some ways even more striking is the fact that most freshmen do eventually graduate.[26] While achiev-

---

[24]The very few students admitted to Harvard after the 10th or 11th grades of high school as
early entrants seem to have fared less well, perhaps because the Cambridge environment
is difficult even for high school graduates and differs in degree from the environment
that early entrants encounter at Shimer College, or even at The College of the University of
Chicago, where their experiences appear to have been more benign.

[25]In those years of the hegemony of Arts and Sciences, some of these students redis-
covered their scientific calling in a medical school and then went on for the Ph.D. with
their M.D. kept as insurance. Today of course the situation is almost completely reversed,
with many Ph.D.'s in the sciences hoping to go to medical school to have a secure as well
as legitimate vocation.

[26]Quoting Cass and Birnbaum again: "About 85 percent of students entering as freshmen
graduate four years later (94 percent in six years); about one percent do not return for
sophomore year; student transfers 'nil' in the course of four years to other colleges ...
about 77 percent of [Radcliffe] students entering as freshmen graduate four years later;
one percent do not return for sophomore year; two percent transfer in the course of four
years to other colleges" (Cass and Birnbaum, 1971, pp. 252–253). Actually, I do know a
handful of Harvard College students who have transferred, but overall the statement
seems accurate.

ing top academic honors is difficult in a setting where National Merit Scholars number 700 (matched only by Michigan State University), it is extremely rare for a student to fail academically; and perhaps the majority of the failures which appear to be academic result from efforts to defeat a pressureful parent or to avoid (for example, by oversleeping examinations) a test of one's shaky belief in one's own outstanding brilliance. Once within the Harvard gates, the meritocratic pressures that exist are principally those that are internalized, and only a relatively small number of so-called high-risk students find staying on at Harvard really arduous; many can use the *Crimson's Confidential Guide to Courses*, or the grapevine, to discover easy routes through the curriculum. (Others, more ambitious, use some easy routes, including pass/no-credit courses, because they are pursuing taxing programs in other areas.) Even for the tiny minority of students who are failed out or put on probation for academic deficiency, and are often encouraged to take leaves of absence, reentry into Harvard is generously open—a policy that implicitly discriminates against applicants to enter Harvard as transfer students who have done outstanding work elsewhere and would have a great deal to offer Harvard.

In some measure, it seems to me, these policies reflect a residue of antimeritocratic, aristocratic snobbery at Harvard which both favors those already admitted, almost no matter how badly they perform, and also makes possible recruitment of the high-risk students without fear for the institution's reputation; as admissions officers like to point out, many of these "risks" finish with commendable academic records and go on to socially useful careers.[27] But as I have already indicated, it is easier to escape the Harvard meritocracy academically than psychologically, and the self-regard of many students, high-risk or low, is often grievously wounded, just as being an "ordinary" student at Harvard does not satisfy many high school valedictorians. The low attrition is itself a symptom of trouble in some respects because many students who should never have come to Harvard or who lose their footing there continue for fear of admitting defeat; moreover, Harvard tends to loom larger than life for those who are alienated and antagonistic to it, quite

---

[27]Having established early the policy of a nationwide search for outstanding academic and intellectual talents and also for high-risk students, Harvard also began recruiting nonaffluent, nonwhite students several years before many other selective colleges did; Harvard has a very large number out of the total pool of National Achievement Scholar Program students. Harvard's black undergraduates average somewhat lower SAT scores than their peers and end up on average with somewhat less distinguished academic records: they have done somewhat less well in terms of graduation rates.

as much as for those who uncritically regard it as the center of the intellectual universe.[28]

In this situation of intense intramural pressure, the Admissions Committee has sought to discover students, who, if they found themselves in the bottom quarter of the class, would have alternative reasons for some self-respect or happiness.[29] However, about three-quarters of the graduating class has until recently gone on immediately to graduate or professional schools; indeed, doing well academically became both a measure of one's personal adequacy and a passport to postbaccalaureate opportunities. Most graduates of Harvard College, even without an honors record, have been able to gain admittance to a good if not luminous graduate or professional program (except recently in the fantastically competitive medical arena, although even there, really determined Harvard premeds generally manage to get in somewhere, often as the result of further premedical work after graduation); but in my observation, many Harvard students who have done well academically as far as the outward eye can judge have suffered damaging blows to self-esteem, and an unknown but I would guess substantial number of those who go through Harvard without honors have found it difficult to maintain self-confidence. (Today, as we shall see hereafter, there have been changes both in postbaccalaureate plans and in undergraduate attitudes toward academic success.)

Even when I was an undergraduate, lineage was not a sufficient solace to students with no other claims to distinction. Groton particularly, but also some of the other prep schools, turned out men who believed they had to earn their way. Nevertheless, as already noted, lineage did matter when it came to admission to the various Final Clubs, and this had to be lineage recognized beyond the local coterie, so that a young man who came from a respected provincial family and had all the correct graces might still not feel wholly accepted socially, al-

[28]In my observation, Harvard College benefits greatly by students who transfer in—a number held extremely low in the past because of the absence of attrition and because of a prejudice in favor of a regulation four-year stint; for the year 1971–72, a more generous transfer policy was adopted, partly on revenue grounds, only to be abandoned for the subsequent year because of the decision to admit more women at the freshman level. In some small measure, Harvard students may be held captive by the impression that they cannot easily transfer to another topflight institution, though since they would be welcome at most excellent state and private colleges, this may again be a rationalization for their reluctance to give up a Harvard degree.

[29]Contrary to legend, the Admissions Committee has not gone out actively to recruit students who will fill up the so-called happy bottom quarter of the entering class, in order to help make those on top content.

though many exceptions were made on the basis of personal friend-ships and unusual talents. In contrast, social status in the Society sense has become increasingly something of an embarrassment in the present era. It seems possible that Radcliffe students suffer more from this than Harvard students do: they have in fact come from a smaller pool and are more well-to-do; as women, the socialite image is more apt to haunt them; as women, they may be more vulnerable to the aggression typified in the British play, *Look Back in Anger.* Perhaps this is one reason why, as Lipset's essay shows, there was a high proportion of "preppy" men arrested in University Hall in April 1969. In my generation, upper-class men might cultivate the mucker pose, but their reactions were more in-nocent and less ideological than those of many children of America's First Families today. Nevertheless, a fifth-generation Harvard scion who had hopes of becoming an art collector or an Arctic explorer might be reasonably content to have gotten into Harvard, and to move through his education without distinction, ready in his turn as an alumnus to pick up the burdens of the Harvard Class Fund and of the philanthropic traditions of his family.[30] Students of this kind of assured standing are but a tiny fraction of an entering Harvard class.[31]

What about the athletes, last survivors of the nineteenth-century Anglo-Saxon world where American football began?[32] In the General Education Course I direct on American character and society, the only formal requirement is a long paper, and a number of Harvard athletes over the years have written about their experiences in trying to live in the double world of the training table and its powerful antagonists. The failed athlete tends to be a sad person at Harvard, without even the col-leagueship of teammates and frequently unable to find a second career in time to readjust. In the residential Houses, occasionally they form a defensive union of the rejected, and I have in mind here chiefly white

[30]It would be interesting to know whether my impression is correct that there are now more children from families of intellectual or artistic or academic distinction at Harvard than from those of wealth and social standing. Harvard offers such students a certain degree of anonymity, but even so, they are apt to feel shadowed by their fathers' or, rarely, their mothers' or grandparents' attainments.

[31]The roster of colleges attended by graduates of leading New England prep schools is one indication of this, a roster now expanded well beyond the Ivy League and the Northeastern quadrant plus Stanford; most of these prep schools have themselves followed the lead of the selective colleges in widening their own orbits or recruitment, often to the dismay of their alumni. They have also followed the collegiate trend toward coeducation.

[32]Cf. Riesman and Denney (1951, pp. 309–325), reprinted in Riesman (1954), for discus-sions of the origins of the game at Harvard, Yale, and elsewhere.

athletes, who lack any ideological banner under which to maintain their self-assurance, however ambivalently. But even the successful varsity athlete is sometimes hardly less torn. Even the time taken out for travel in a team's schedule is a handicap to a student who is also running in the academic race. And the athlete often feels that he must prove that he is not merely an athlete; in short, prove himself in the enemy camps. I am speaking here principally of football, for the tennis or squash star, like the fencing champion or the track star or skier, operates within the conventions of the culture and is the better off for combining a good academic record with distinction in a non-big-time sport. I am inclined to think that the antijock hostility at Harvard (and in other universities where it may meet more opposition among both faculty and students) reflects the fact that many faculty members and quite a few bright students suffered in their school if not in their college days from envy of the star athlete and his prowess with women, perhaps from a sense of their own inferiority by old-fashioned definitions of competitive masculinity. At Harvard, they can have their revenge.[33]

The enormous power of the meritocratic academic culture over undergraduates can be illustrated not only by the experience of athletes, but in some ways more dramatically by the changing attitudes of *Har-*

---

[33]Readers may be curious as to how athletes who are less than brilliant get to Harvard in the light of the current intense pressure for admissions. Perhaps because Harvard's academic reputation is so exalted, the College has been willing and able to take risks with many types of students, including athletes, who can do the work and who may make unusual contributions, but who are not outstanding academically. Competing Ivy League colleges, less secure about their academic reputations or less sure that they can control their own more fervent alumni, have had to be more cautious (although when their coaches discover that they have no athletes signed up for major sports, there may be a desperate last-minute scramble). Whereas in the early 1950s Princeton and then Yale attracted a large proportion of the athletes who were also adequate as scholars, Harvard now has done so well in that race as to alter the forms of acrimony in meetings among Ivy League presidents. Harvard College itself, as I have attempted to show, is in no way demoralized by what may be the very slight margin of favoritism shown to athletes on admission—perhaps only the fact that alumni have eagerly cultivated them for Harvard's sake. At most, only the athlete himself suffers from the shock of disesteem at Harvard while he might have been a less diminished hero at many other schools. But some real damage can periodically occur at a secondary school where teachers have used the possibility of admission to Harvard on meritocratic grounds as bait to tempt the potential scholars in the face of a Philistine or anti-intellectual milieu, only to find the diligent student who is not seen as "exciting" turned down, and the sometimes high-living athlete of good intelligence but poor work habits (or the outstanding musician or writer) accepted. Today, in a few of these same schools, I could imagine some teachers being happy to see Harvard regarded as a reward for any kind of strenuousness in the face of the much greater demoralization brought about by drugs, racial conflict, and countercultural antagonism to all energetic pursuits.

vard Crimson editors toward grades.[34] To responsible editors, the *Crimson* is nearly a full-time job, six days a week during the school year. Over generations of editors, great care has gone into writing if not always into the reporting; and the Comment Book in which editors criticize the day-to-day work can bear down as savagely as any don on sloppy writing, on inept composition of the page, or on poor editorial judgment. I have already indicated that in my own day, many *Crimson* editors took it for granted that they would not get top grades but would get by manageably well; the paper was their life, their club, in some measure their paycheck, and for some their prospective vocation. But in the post-World War II era, increasingly editors seem to have felt that the *Crimson* was not an alibi for a merely passable academic record.[35] Some editors felt this way in spite of the fact that their work and renown brought them many contacts with faculty and often admiration from them. Distinction on the *Crimson* became insufficient if one did not win out in the major meritocratic contest of the curriculum.[36] And, indeed, by the same facility that brought them onto the *Crimson*, many have managed to get good grades and even to graduate magna cum laude.

The Loeb Theater, handsome and ultramodern, was opened in 1959 and provided another extracurricular career with visibility greater than the earlier House productions had allowed. Here one might launch a successful career as a playwright (as Arthur Kopit did at Radcliffe's small Agassiz Theater); perhaps as a director or actor or actress. But here also, as with the *Crimson* and even the most outstanding musical activities, it was difficult for students to feel justified by extracurricular renown if they did not do well academically. Of course, this is especially true of students working in the plastic arts, who unlike the glamorous editors of the *Crimson* or winners of piano or violin competitions in performance have no public forum. Indeed, they get little appreciation for

[34]I speak in the text of the editorial and news boards of the *Crimson* and not of the business and photographic staffs.

[35]I have the impression, not based on any solid evidence, that somewhat comparable pressures were simultaneously being felt among the editors of outstanding college dailies such as the *Michigan Daily*, the *Daily Texan*, the *Cornell Sun*, the *Cardinal* (University of Wisconsin-Madison), the *Daily Bruin* (UCLA), and others. Everywhere, editors could believe themselves *intellectuals*, at odds with the pedantic or meretriciously *academic*, but yet this distinction, also to be found among *Crimson* editors,was not a wholly adequate defense against a poor academic record. Cf. Willie Morris's description of his experience on the *Daily Texan* in the middle 1950s (Morris, 1967, pp. 180ff).

[36]Cf. the bitter valedictory column of *Crimson* editor Garrett Epps, speaking for the "C" students against the "A" ones, February 2, 1972, p. 2.

their work and are apt to say apologetically that they are just messing around with paint or sculpture. Neither has student politics provided an alternative avenue of esteem. I am speaking here of student government in the old-fashioned sense, not of the radical student politics of the late 1960s; the former was often regarded as evidence that one was vulgarly gregarious and harbored juvenile ambitions.

In their ideology, Harvard undergraduates talk like academicians in good universities, who at least profess to disdain and deprecate administrative work. However, in producing plays and concerts, or in initiating House or College-wide periodicals, or later in civil rights or antiwar activities, many Harvard undergraduates proved themselves to be superlatively good organizers. Often their work could be both energized and given luster by the supreme self-confidence that, as I have already indicated, some Harvard students muster as if to parody the outlook of their faculty models. I think of the organization called Tocsin, which a dozen years ago lobbied for a nuclear test ban, quickly accumulating the necessary technical knowledge and manifesting considerable political finesse. Three students from this group journeyed to Geneva to discuss seismic detection with delegates to the disarmament conference there. Of course students with this sort of self-possession are not the creation of the Harvard mystique, for they generally arrive from cosmopolitan backgrounds with considerable sang-froid; but Harvard helps propel them on arrival. I sometimes think that Harvard's self-confidence is a zero-sum game, in which a few students gather a great deal more than the lot they had when they arrived, while others lose a great deal on discovering, often overapprehensively, the competition they face.

Yet it would be a mistake to give the impression that, even at the height of meritocratic pressures in the decade just past, Harvard students (or Harvard faculty) spent all their time and concern in proving how bright and competent they were. That large number of students who came to Harvard from provincial backgrounds often found it a joy to be allowed to indulge their more esoteric intellectual interests and to find these responded to rather than regarded as inappropriate for would-be manly boys, or would-be feminine girls. Harvard and its metropolitan environment provided a "critical mass" for many interests which had been cultivated in isolation and misgiving in high school. To compete unequivocally for scholastic honors was attractive to those who came from schools where only athletic honors could be competed for without accusations of grade-grubbing or apple-polishing. Moreover, Harvard, like most other American colleges, is loose enough for students (and faculty too) to change their interests as these develop. While fields of concentration (majors) are supposed to be chosen at the beginning of the sophomore year, a great many students switch majors in the course of that year, or even in some cases in the junior year, and still manage to encompass enough courses (usually six or eight) for a degree. However, Harvard's looseness as an institution says nothing about the particularities of individual departments, which differ enormously in their openness to such switches as well as in other respects. (Indeed, while the *Crimson Confidential Guide* describes individual courses, it has only tentatively begun to say anything about the all-important climates of individual departments. Moreover, a large department, such as History, consists of a series of microclimates, with the Americanists, for example, having a very different style vis-à-vis undergraduates from those in East Asian History.) As in any large university, much depends on the luck of the draw in which students are matched with section men, House tutors, departmental advisers; and for honors work, their thesis supervisors and readers.[37]

The senior thesis is in my observation often the most valuable, as well as the most taxing, academic experience a Harvard student has. But since students can progress to the senior year with little experience in writing, culling a satisfactory thesis out of a series of attempts is a high-wire act over an invisible net.[38] Furthermore, those more accomplished students who have grown up in milieux in which academic and ancillary extracurricular achievements have been supported and rewarded are often also those who, because of their own intelligence and because of what their parents had accomplished, tend to take their own achievements for granted. If their senior theses and other work are highly

[37]There are many kinds of disparities. For example, some departments will allow or even encourage a determined student to write a senior honors thesis even if he has not fulfilled departmental requirements and even if his grades have not been of honors caliber. Or again, the Faculty Committee Report on the Behavioral Sciences at Harvard in 1954 noted that student-faculty ratios were far higher in the new fields of Social Relations than in long-established ones like History, Government, and Economics. (See "The Behavioral Sciences...," pp. 27–34.) Similar disparities still prevail. Also see the discussion of the impact of particular departments on Harvard undergraduates in Vreeland and Bidwell (1966, pp. 237–254).

[38]One reflective alumnus termed it "the most exhilarating and humbling act of an undergraduate"; see Gordon (1965, p. 56). At Princeton which (like Reed) requires a senior essay of every graduating student, this fact appears to cast its shadow before it, so that the floor under literacy is somewhat higher than at Harvard; in part it is raised by the preceptorials, sections of courses traditionally but now decreasingly taken over by senior faculty for close supervision of undergraduates. For discussion of Princeton preceptorials in an earlier day, see Heath (1964).

acclaimed, they are inclined to believe themselves frauds; if they achieve merely ordinary distinction, they are convinced that they have failed. Most such students in my observation have come from families whose own achievements had been won in meritocratic terms; and for these students to enter Harvard College involved no great liberation, no great change of pace. A number of the undergraduate educational reformers in the College who, after 1968, attacked the selective devices and what they regarded as the affective dehydration of meritocracy came from such backgrounds.[39] It is also true that students for whom some measure of high meritocratic achievement is no problem—though living up to their own and their parents' exalted expectations for them remains a problem—could most easily attack both the aristocratic and the democratic versions of meritocracy at Harvard without being accused of a sour-grapes attitude.

Such considerations may help explain why particularly vehement attacks on elitism and on Harvard College in general have come in the last few years from students in one of the two most eagerly sought-after fields of concentration at Harvard, namely, the Committee on Social Studies (the other equally selective and much more established field is History and Literature). This program was set up in 1960 under the supervision of a committee drawn from the social science departments to provide for a small number of undergraduates who wanted to pursue an interdisciplinary concentration on such themes as political development in the new nations or psychoanalysis and history. The formal program would necessarily be minimal, with students farmed out to take courses in areas relevant to their particular concerns. At the outset, the number admitted was kept small in part because the Government and Economics departments feared that they would lose many able students to Social Studies (History now also fears such loss); presently, the problem of finding competent tutors (mainly graduate students in history, government, philosophy, sociology, and economics) also limits the program to an intake of some 50 students each year. (Moreover, relative smallness is itself often an asset, both in selective and more esoteric nonselective fields of concentration, making possible although by no means guaranteeing closer personal and intellectual ties among faculty and students.) The program reflects the rigorous intellectual standards

---

[39]I am indebted to Barry O'Connell for correspondence and conversation on this theme. He has also noted that a number of the leaders of the New College, which briefly served as an experiment station for educational reform at Harvard, 1969–71, were from California where, one might surmise, a more casual attitude toward the fixity of the four-year college syndrome prevails, reflecting in part easy transfer within the state system, and in part a somewhat greater feeling of transiency in general.

of its most influential faculty members, and the level of performance expected of students is high (thus avoiding implications of sloppiness in a nondisciplinary concentration); the tutors who do the bulk of the teaching and the students themselves seek to live up to expectations for both scope and erudition. As graduating seniors, these students have garnered some of the prizes: Rhodes and Marshall Scholarships, Harvard Traveling Fellowships, and admission to the most selective post-baccalaureate programs; several years ago, three of the seniors had already published books by the time of Commencement. Yet their angry reaction to the selectivity of the program itself and of Harvard, like a good many contemporary reactions to Phi Beta Kappa, does seem to reflect the turning against meritocracy by some of its most favored beneficiaries. As Michael Walzer declared in a talk at the Senior Dinner of the Committee on Social Studies in May 1971, these students were facing the dilemma Yeats posed between the work and the life, and they were opting for life rhetorically without being prepared to surrender the work and its rewards.[40] Student critics complained that the Social Studies program, like Harvard College in general, was simply grooming students for slots in the all-powerful "Establishment,"[41] again raising

---

[40]
"The Choice"

The intellect of man is forced to choose
Perfection of the life, or of the work,
And if it take the second must refuse
A heavenly mansion, raging in the dark.
When all that story's finished, what's the news?
In luck or out the toil has left its mark:
That old perplexity an empty purse,
Or the day's vanity, the night's remorse.

From *Collected Poems of W. B. Yeats* (Macmillan: New York, 1962, p. 242).

A woman colleague, reflecting on the issues raised here, declares that in spite of the softening of sex-role boundaries at the present time, it remains more difficult for women to make the choice, incremental though it be, between perfection of work and of life; whereas for men, the traditional pressures of masculine ambition still remain powerful, so that resisting them demands a more radical alienation. Paradoxically, women who choose "work" over "life" in such liberationist enclaves as Radcliffe have the support of sisterhood, which as a network of affective ties is a reminder of women's traditional affective role; there would appear to be less peer support for men at Harvard, whichever road they take.

[41]In an editorial spoof in its first issue for 1972, the *Crimson* prophesied: "Declaring that History and Lit. has become too large, Professor John Clive [elegant Chairman of the Program] announces its division into two new elite concentrations, 'History' and 'Literature.' 'This way,' Clive explains, 'you can study what you are really interested in but still feel superior to your friends in English.' Not to be outdone, Michael Walzer [Chairman of the Committee on Social Studies] leads a surprise dawn takeover of the Fly Building [a Final Club] and announces that Social Studies has become a Final Club." See "The *Crimson* Predicts: 1972" (January 3, 1972, p. 2).

the note of sponsorship rather than blindly bureaucratic recruitment, though the latter would hardly be admired or accepted either.

Similar charges have recently been raised against the Freshman Seminar Program (instituted in 1959 to provide an opportunity for freshmen to work in small groups on manageable topics with a great diversity of seminar leaders) on the ground that because nearly twice as many freshmen regularly apply for Seminars as can be admitted, the program is necessarily elitist.[42] These reactions to the Freshman Seminar Program have a paradoxical quality in light of the fact that the Program was instituted in part to moderate the impersonal rigors of the Harvard College curriculum. The Seminars provide a more relaxed setting for meeting faculty, and other students as well, and the report which compared Seminar students with those not in Seminars but equivalent in aptitude (though probably not in venturesomeness, assertiveness, or luck) indicated that the students who had been in Seminars found faculty more accessible to them throughout their College career.[43] In most universities, Harvard included, freshmen and sophomores pay the same tuition as juniors and seniors, but cost a lot less to teach (much of their instruction is in the hands of graduate students); thus, in effect, they subsidize senior faculty to teach small upper-division courses or seminars in their specialties. In some degree, the Harvard Freshman Seminar Program sought to reverse this pattern on the theory that freshmen may require even more individualized instruction than students further along in college. Some freshmen may apply to half a dozen Seminars, be interviewed for them, and admitted to none—hardly an auspicious beginning to their Harvard careers, especially if they are inclined, as so many are, to doubt their adequacy. Yet in discussion with students I have not found support for any system of rationing of scarce Harvard resources, which for example might notify students that if they are admitted to a Freshman Seminar, they will go to the end of the line in applying for the oversubscribed Social Studies or History and Literature concentrations. Nor is there support for a lottery, which

---

[42]Such objections of course are not peculiar to Harvard College. The Swarthmore Honors Program is under similar attack (Mangelsdorf, 1973, pp. 327–329), as is the Echols Scholar Program for outstanding undergraduates at the University of Virginia. During 1971, a committee chaired by Bentley Glass discussed the future of Phi Beta Kappa in the light of objections coming from many Chapters against selectivity based on grades or academic performance, however modified by other considerations; there was the additional belief that the Chapters should directly serve some socially relevant purpose, whether educational reform on their own campuses or some extramural involvement, rather than merely honoring the membership and, through the elected members, superior scholarly performance. See *Report of the Committee on the Role of Phi Beta Kappa* (1973).

[43]See Stookey (1963).

students regard as too impersonal and denying them the opportunity to plead their own particular cause. There is a widespread belief today that there are no real scarcities, and if one is denied an opportunity it means only that one is discriminated against or that monopolists are holding out on one.[44]

The Social Studies Program, the Freshman Seminar Program, and a number of other changes in the curriculum, which will be discussed in the next section, had a variety of aims, among them the hope that, given greater freedom and leeway, the pressures under which undergraduates work might become less confining. Yet as already indicated, their effect has been ambivalent in this respect. They have offered closer contact and generally earlier contact with faculty—but this very connection may also make for more effective demands on students. Indeed, although Freshman Seminars are ungraded, this fact has not diminished the need to establish one's adequacy in a situation where there is no place to hide, unlike the anonymity of a lecture course.[45]

The greater leeway for choice offered by these new programs inevitably intensified pressures for still greater freedom from academic constraint. The spread especially in the elite colleges of antielitist and egalitarian sentiments meant that Harvard, despite its residual ascriptive legacies such as the (now rapidly democratizing) Final Clubs could not create an enclave for guilt-free assurance among students from privileged families. For one thing, upper-class and upper-middle-class families rarely surrendered on behalf of their ideology the chance to give their children the superior educations in private and suburban public schools that might help them enter "the college of their choice." In the post-Sputnik era, some children of the upper strata felt themselves pressured at home and at school to ever more precocious performance in competition with diligent strivers who, lacking birth or breeding or even brass, had to depend on meritocratic selection for their chance to

---

[44]See Shils (1969, pp. 37–43). Since Shils' article and my own comments were written, of course, students everywhere, like everyone else, have become extremely conscious of ecological scarcities, without necessarily altering their attitudes toward scarcities arising within their own academic communities.

[45]Conversely, when faculty know students personally, they tend to evaluate them more generously; see the discussion of "personalism" in Riesman, Gusfield, and Gamson (1970, pp. 267–268). However, not all small settings at Harvard have this quality of intense mutuality, for the section meetings of a good many large lecture courses, directed by teaching fellows, are sometimes poorly attended quiz sessions, sometimes lecturettes; there is great variation in the quality of these smaller settings at Harvard and the degree to which undergraduates feel any responsibility to prepare themselves and to take part in discussion.

get ahead. In 1959, a Harvard freshman from a leading prep school declared in an interview, "I am frittering away my time, not applying myself, and so on, but I am a natural, friendly, genuine person... not one of those lonely, inhibited, overly conscious grinds. By the time I graduate, I will be more independent and serious, more interested in study... but not yet" (Ricks & McCarley, 1959, p. 47). By the late 1960s, some young people torn in this way between competing values, between striving for meritocratic success and fearing both success and failure, became leaders of the contrameritocracy, sometimes wholly inappropriately projecting on the first-generation students the dilemmas arising from their own elite backgrounds, even in some cases calling for open admission to Harvard College.

The fear of worldly success as a kind of moral stigma or as isolating one from harmonious relations with other people is not a new theme in American life; there was not only a single Protestant ethic which could be interpreted as equating success and probable grace, but various religious ethics less compatible with competitive accomplishment. The sects of socialism often secularized these more cooperative doctrines, and although these have been relatively weak in America, their influence has, as Lipset's essay points out, been intermittently felt at Harvard College. That influence could easily combine, in the educated upper-middle class, with the attraction of aristocratic disdain toward the "merely" bourgeois values of striving and place hunting. Among my own friends when I was an undergraduate, such attitudes were widely prevalent. Even the (partial) pretense that one did virtually no academic work was not simply a game of displaying one's fearless valor and cavalier indifference, but also an effort to show that one was not rivalrous, not a "rate-buster" or teacher's pet. For many of us to go on then to the Harvard Law School, with its ferocious competitiveness, was a tremendous culture shock. Competition for grades which determined Law Review, which in turn determined placement, was unabashed; and since papers were read and graded by numbers, anonymously, faculty members, although they could torment students in the often bombastic, supposedly Socratic give-and-take of the large lecture classes, could not play favorites.[46]

In the 1960s, Harvard College came in some respects to resemble the

---

[46]James Angell McLaughlin (a fervent Orangeman who later changed his name to MacLachlan) told me years later that on the basis of my class performance in Property I, he was sure I would fail and was astonished to learn that I had written the best paper. However, it was said that Thomas Reed Powell did play favorites; a whimsical man, he did not share his friend Felix Frankfurter's admiration for undiluted meritocracy.

Harvard Law School of earlier decades, even while the Law School somewhat moderated its monolithic atmosphere. In part, the sheer size of the competing cohort of the 1960s helped give ambitious young people the feeling that they were being crowded by each other as well as pushed by adults, whether parental or professorial.[47] The heavier the pressures of meritocracy were felt to be, the stronger grew the ambivalence of those subject to the pressures.

Furthermore, members of the parental generation themselves were not immune to this attack, particularly when they came in their own lives to doubt the value of what began to be thought of as "merely" meritocratic success, which left them unfulfilled and vulnerable. Many senior academicians are of course also parents, and not immune from their children's sometimes harsh judgments.[48] The delegitimation of academic authority and hence of selectivity had of course many other sources. The student movement at Berkeley grew directly out of the civil rights movement, from which many of its tactics were drawn; only later did the antiwar movement assume hegemony.[49] Meritocratic selectivity, earlier of course seen as the path of equity, became in the eyes of many another form of racial discrimination, once it was evident that equality of opportunity produced anything but equality of results.[50] It was at this point that the enemies of meritocracy, based on those excluded, joined the enemies based on the consequences for those included, the winners; in other words, there was a loss of humane solidarity consequent upon competitiveness in a society where equality of opportunity results in the losers condemning themselves for nonachievement, the winners for manipulativeness.[51]

Thus we are back at the very outcome that Michael Young had prophesied in his social-science fiction. A full analysis of these developments is beyond the scope of this essay. Social Darwinism is of course discredited; the more Calvinist versions of the Protestant Ethic have lost support among the affluent and educated; the "poor but honest" classes

---

[47]On the importance of the demographic bulge reflecting the post-World War II baby boom, on events and outlook in the 1960s, see Daniel P. Moynihan (1973, pp. 3–12).

[48]In the last few years I have for the first time had colleagues who would glowingly if perhaps ambivalently report that their droput son was a carpenter in Vermont, or that a daughter had decided not to attend college or had chosen the local state school.

[49]For a general discussion, see Martin Lipset (1971) and his essay in this volume for the particular Harvard story.

[50]Let me mention again the cogent discussion by Bell (1972—especially pp. 42ff).

[51]For discussion of this theme, see Sennett and Cobb (1972). Cf., however, Deutsch and Edsal (1972, pp. 71–79).

often believe in the work ethic for other people, although the desire of most Americans to go on working even without the spur of economic compulsion seems relatively unimpaired.[52] Perhaps more important, meritocracy is like bureaucracy in lacking glamor or heroism in its focus on measured accomplishment, diligence, and specialized work—where the outcome is a society torn between the dominion of experts in a particular specialty and experts in the mobilization of charismatic and often demagogic appeals.[53]

A few segments of American higher education had striven toward meritocracy for only a short period of years, not much more than two decades. The impact of meritocracy in the educational order on occupational careers was modest at best.[54] Weighing the very modest effectiveness of meritocracy, in terms of equity and in terms of getting the world's work done, against its onerousness as a process for channeling human energies and organizing human invidiousness, many from the ranks of both potential winners and losers were prepared to mount an attack on it.

[52]See for fuller discussion Weiss, Harwood, and Riesman, "Work and Automation: Problems and Prospects" (1971, pp. 545–600).

[53]Compare Joseph Schumpeter's discussion a good many years ago as to the way in which capitalism would be undone as the result of its very bounteousness, the lack of charisma of its no longer entreprenurial leaders, and the discontents of its no longer driven beneficiaries. See Schumpeter (1942).

[54]This conclusion, arising from the cumulative work of James Coleman, Alexander Astin, Christopher Jencks, and others, results from averaging educational attainment and averaging occupational attainment and/or income. If one should examine more specialized sectors, e.g., the impact of making the law review on later legal careers, one might come to marginally different conclusions for a limited portion of the occupational spectrum.

3. Moderating Meritocracy

When the counterattack on meritocracy gathered strength in the late 1960s, its impact at Harvard was softened by the diversity and looseness I have already referred to. When a college of such uniformly high standards as Oberlin decided in 1971 that its long-standing commitment to sexual and racial equality and to the civil rights movement involved greatly increasing its already considerable recruitment of nonwhite students, it had to be prepared for change in modes of teaching and perhaps of grading if it was to adjust to the heterogeneous newcomers. Similarly, an institution like California Institute of Technology, with its SAT scores all over 700, would have to make a drastic adjustment if it were to admit students of merely average verbal and quantitative abilities. Harvard, however, even in the McGeorge Bundy era, continued to admit a small number of (mainly white) athletes and alumni and faculty children, without fear of breaching the general intellectual intensity of the College, and certainly without compelling faculty to take special measures, either in teaching or evaluation. Harvard had in effect, though not in name, continued a "pass" degree, as at Toronto or at Oxford or Cambridge, inherited from the old gentleman's C.[1]

[1] I have not been aware of pressure at Harvard to give a passing grade either to the son of an alumnus or to an athlete. I suspect that this is because, as already indicated, Harvard is pretty loose at the floor if tight at the ceiling. (However, I have sometimes heard scions complain that they feel discriminated against in the contemporary atmosphere of Harvard; as with some extremely beautiful young women, a few faculty may tend to regard them with suspicion, assuming that they cannot really be bright and motivated.) Like faculty elsewhere, however, I have experienced intense pressure not to fail a senior when that would prevent his graduating; in such cases I have sometimes concluded that the student in question had gotten by until the second term of his senior year on flimsy performance and on alibis, in rare cases mobilizing the senior tutor in the student's House or other faculty as advocates. It should be clear that I am talking here about students—in my experience, perhaps adventitiously, invariably male—who in the large General Education course I direct attended virtually no lectures, few section meetings, failed to discuss their paper topics, as required, with their section leaders, and turned up 10 days after the deadline with 40 semiorganized, semiliterate pages. Students would not imagine they could get by with this in a course in physics or classics. It was not Harvard but Boston University which made an effort to cripple the active term-paper companies in the Boston area.

However, this reasonably comfortable compromise began to change in the 1960s when the growing number of black students presented the faculty with a visible cadre of students whose average preparation was below traditional norms.[2] As mentioned earlier, Harvard welcomes "risk" students who are white as well as black, but the whites generally tend to be invisible, uncomplaining, and unrelated to each other, while the black students came together in the late sixties at Harvard as elsewhere to organize and develop feelings of responsibility vis-à-vis each other and vis-à-vis other blacks in such low-income areas as Roxbury. Far from being "invisible," black students began to appear to white students and faculty both vocal and visible.[3] There is no transitional year or special remedial network for these students, other than the network provided by the general advising system and the admirable facilities of the Bureau of Study Counsel, which is equipped to deal with the emotional problems generally wrapped up with cognitive difficulties.[4] There is a Board of Freshman Advisers, some of whom are also Proctors who live in the freshman dormitories in the Yard; the majority of them are graduate students in Arts and Sciences or in the Law or Business (or rarely, Medical) Schools; they are generally compassionate

[2]The pool of black high school seniors with SAT scores over 500 remains small. See Doermann (1971, pp. 131, 134). The pool of Spanish-speaking high school seniors with such scores and good high school backgrounds is proportionately even smaller.

[3]For a reflective account by a black student of divisions—sexual, political, cultural—among black students at Cornell in 1968–69, see Donald (1970, pp. 153–204). See also the critical comment on Harvard College by Monroe (1973, pp. 45–48).

[4]See Perry (1970), who details the way in which Harvard College examinations have changed in recent decades, from single frames of reference demanding largely factual answers to shifting and ambiguous frames demanding subtleties of interpretation quite different from the styles of many secondary schools which, in a system of national recruiting, send students to Harvard College. Mr. Perry is the founder of the Bureau of Study Counsel.

The Bureau of Study Counsel conducts a regular series of meetings with groups of Teaching Fellows and other faculty members to discuss teaching. Anonymous tape recordings of sections and tutorials serve as a basis for exploring the ways in which teacher-learner interaction helps or hinders the learning which was the purpose of the hour. As members of these groups develop confidence in each other, individuals present recordings of their own work. The intent is less to define "good teaching" than to extend the teacher's awareness of those classroom contingencies and those assumptions of his own from which he generates his response in action. Cf. Kiyo Morimoto, "On Trying to Understand the Frustrations of Students" (1972); Mr. Morimoto is presently Associate Director of the Bureau of Study Counsel.

and concerned, but their knowledge of Harvard College may be limited (even if they are graduates of the College), and their time is severely limited.[5] Even the most skillful—quite irrespective of color—may not know how to approach a proudly defensive black student who not only insists he needs no remedial work but plunges into an advanced course in applied mathematics or physics which would give pause to the most well-prepared entrant.[6]

Black students may plunge into such courses for many different reasons. They may be, as it were, fleeing forward in the face of their fright that they cannot cope at Harvard. To be sure, black students know very well how difficult it is for a white liberal faculty member to grade them severely, though a few may seek in a course in a "hard" area an honest grade they suspect would be denied them out of fear or sympathy in other fields.[7] Some black students may regard the applied sciences as the best prospect Harvard offers for undergraduate vocational preparation, and it is such preparation most first-generation students seek. A handful may be boasting to their friends about the advanced courses they are taking.

Such attitudes of some black students differ in degree but not in kind

[5]I had once thought, on coming to the Harvard faculty, that freshmen should not be segregated in the Yard but should be assigned to the residential Houses, much as Yale freshmen are assigned to the Yale residential Colleges. But many Harvard sophomores have reported in informal conversation that the Proctor in their entry in the Yard was more available as someone with whom to talk over one's problems, whether academic or otherwise, than the tutor in one's residential House or in one's half-heartedly chosen field of concentration, whose main preoccupation might be with juniors and seniors fully committed to the field and already pressing for advice on postbaccalaureate careers. Such considerations gave me pause in pressing for inclusion of the freshmen in the Houses. Until the academic year 1972–73, Radcliffe freshmen were not segregated from upperclassmen, but lived in the Radcliffe Houses; now some have been placed in the Harvard Yard and a few students who are not freshmen also placed in the Yard, to act as informal advisers.

[6]The feeling of some black students that they are demeaned by having to be tutored seems to me analogous to the reaction of some atom-bombed Japanese who feared and resented the help offered by American physicians and regarded it as counterfeit nurturance. Cf. Riesman (1968).

[7]Sometimes, instructors will privately declare that, because they are giving passing grades to black students who would have failed if they were white, they are giving honor grades to white students who do work which is in comparison superior—perhaps one source of what seems to be a general inflation of grades in the last few years.

from attitudes endemic among white students.[8] Harvard and Radcliffe students, thrown into a situation where they are told that they must regard themselves as adults, find it difficult to admit that they need help. Often, as at many other institutions, students seek out relatively unstructured programs such as the Committee on Social Studies, or select as many morsels as they can of Independent Study, with little opportunity for adult help in realistic self-appraisal. A curriculum may be considered as a partial substitute for advising systems that even in small colleges are generally inadequate, since advising is seldom considered a regular part of a faculty member's teaching obligations, and since many know too little about their own institutions or about particular undergraduates to become more than perfunctory advisers.

A similar ideology that one must be wholly independent tends to prevail when it comes to questions of adjusting to the coresidential life of the now "liberated" Houses. There was a time, up until a few years ago, when a Radcliffe freshman was required to get permission from her housemother before signing out for the night; the generally routine contact could lead to a conversation in which the student's difficulties, first with a French course and then with something more personal and underlying, could casually surface and perhaps receive some informal, seemingly unsought, advice. However, when all signout restrictions were abolished, and housemothers with them, this casual opportunity

[8]Of course there are many black students at Harvard College, from all sorts of backgrounds, who are admirably equipped for the institution's academic demands. Many have attended prep schools, have taken part in ABC or similar programs, and/or come from upper-middle-class and professional backgrounds. These well-equipped black students often are subjected to pressures for black solidarity and can sometimes (like affluent or otherwise privileged white students, but perhaps even more so) be made to feel that the fact that they are doing well academically exhibits not only disreputable desires for acculturation to bourgeois white middle-class norms, but also lack of sympathy for fellow blacks who are in academic difficulty. Such pressures appear to have moderated in the last several years, and blacks have responded to their situation of at least potential privilege in an increasing diversity of ways. For some, tutoring in Roxbury or perhaps in a prison may be a preferred response; a few make an effort to discover roots by travel and work in Africa; still others become active on behalf of black construction workers, Harvard employees, or anti-Portuguese revolutionaries. David Evans, a black Admissions Dean at Harvard College, has proposed an exchange program between Harvard and some Southern Negro colleges in order to give Harvard black students an opportunity to see the sorts of collegiate life and middle-class aspirations of black students who come from truly deprived settings: Evans hopes such exposure will moderate the romantic fantasies about the oppressed hence rebellious poor prevalent among middle-class Harvard students, white or black. He believes that such a term or year of intranational exchange would give students going on to Law or Medical School a more realistic grasp of what it would mean as fully qualified professionals to devote themselves to "the community." He hopes some would conclude that they want to do exactly that.

for adult encounter was lost. Now, with the abdication of adults from such occasions of benign nonneglect, what one master of a Radcliffe House terms "the tyranny of the enlightened" prevails and students tend to be subjected to the unalleviated hegemony of the peer group.

Although originally designed to introduce students to the heritage of Western civilization, rather than to adults or to each other, Harvard's General Education program, even though it did not possess the coherence that had been urged on Harvard by the report of the Student Council in 1939 or the famous "Red Book," did serve in an ancillary and uneven way to reduce the anonymity of the freshman year and to provide locales for serious discussion through the sections into which many of the large courses were divided. For example, Samuel Beer, Professor of Government, in his famous course Social Sciences 2: "Western Thought and Institutions," recruited a corps of talented graduate students from the Departments of Government, History, and Sociology, and other fields, who met undergraduates in a weekly section to discuss the lectures and the readings in the classics; some of these teaching fellows were also House tutors and thus had additional opportunity for informal conversation with neophyte students.[9] Similarly, Reuben A. Brower's Humanities 6: "Introduction to Literature" built an esprit de corps among the section leaders for a demanding course of close reading of significant texts; and there were similar ventures in the natural sciences, in several cases with faculty brought to Harvard especially because of what they could contribute in General Education. Often, these year-long General Education courses were oversubscribed, and it depended on assertiveness or good fortune whether one knew of their quality and whether one managed to gain access to them. At best, these courses provided for their students the kind of close attention from concerned adults that is taken for granted at such superb liberal arts colleges as Amherst, Swarthmore, Carleton, Mount Holyoke, Oberlin, and many others.

When I came to Harvard in 1958, I was especially attracted to Samuel Beer's example, and in fact recruited several teaching fellows who had worked with him. But when I proposed to offer my own General Education course with only the single requirement of a term paper (and attendance at section meetings) but without a final exam (or the then-conventional mid-term hour exam), the Faculty Committee on Educational Policy was fearful that students might goof off; they were also worried

---

[9]One of the intellectual harvests of this course is a volume of essays by former staff members, edited by Melvin Richter (1970); see Richter's introduction, pp. 1–37.

about possible plagiarism of papers.[10] The Committee on Educational Policy did, however, consent to allow me to proceed, although in subsequent years I was again required to appear before the Committee to defend the procedure—one which has now, at Harvard as almost everywhere, become widespread. The procedure had, for those teaching in the course, its unavoidable costs: thus, the absence of the sanction of an examination made it difficult for teaching fellows to depend on compulsion to get students to read the assigned books; they were instead faced with the task of creating a climate where students would want to read the books in order to be able to take part in discussion and not to let down the rest of the group. Given the pressure of other courses which did have examinations, the results for our own course were inevitably uneven. Undoubtedly, some students took advantage of the course, throwing together a paper in the last few weeks or days of the term; however, in general students used the opportunity, for instance, to explore as juniors what might become a thesis topic for their senior year, and in many cases to extend their range of skills by embarking on a small-scale empirical study. Changes in modes of examination and in grading do not necessarily imply changes in standards of performance. For example, though in the Freshman Seminars grading was from the outset on a credit/no-credit basis, a provision greeted with some anxiety by many faculty, it turned out that the freshmen put at least as great energies into their seminars as into their graded courses. Some freshmen, in fact, have preferred not to volunteer for the Seminar program because a mere "credit" would mean one less chance to pull down an A grade.[11] Nevertheless, as I have already indicated, there has been a general inflation of the currency of grades at Harvard, which has been the more marked because of the increase of more personalistic settings such as tutorial or independent study and the relative diminution of courses where the final grade is based entirely on examinations. As elsewhere,

[10]Since students in the course are required to discuss their term papers with their section leaders well in advance and since the section leaders are generally aware of the capacities of individual students, attempts at plagiarism would seem to have been rare, although there have been more instances where students sought to use for my course a paper already written for another, without letting either instructor know about a practice that in some cases would be quite legitimate. The rise in the Boston area as elsewhere of companies engaged in selling term papers reflects among other things the spread of the once novel idea of substituting such papers for written examinations, though of course many seminars and lecture courses require both.

[11]When the faculty granted academic amnesty to students after the Cambodian invasion, the term "credit" was then employed for students who did not take final examinations but still wanted to pass a particular course. One result was to lower the value of the mark of "credit" also on freshman transcripts, an unfair consequence of an emergency action.

there has been an attack on grading per se as inevitably repressive or at least an interference with truly motivated learning and spontaneous relations between students and faculty.[12] In the controversial radical course, Social Relations 148–149, given for some 900 undergraduates in 1968–69, the instructors attacked the grading system by giving honor grades almost uniformly—an action which did not so much show the irrelevance of grades (the alleged and often actual intention, of course) as the usefulness of grading by other people on which one could be parasitical.[13] Contrary to what is often thought, it is not only junior faculty who raise the grading curve or refuse to use any traditional curve, but many senior faculty also give generous grades, not only on political or pedagogic grounds, or to attract student traffic, but also simply to escape the aggravation of student complaints about grades.

I can testify from personal experience how relentless such complaints can be, especially in fields where there is no clear right or wrong answer, or where the evaluation of a term paper can always be argued about. Students are quite prepared to telephone at all hours, to come to one's home—and in cases where it is a failing grade, to appeal to the senior tutors of their Houses as advocates.[14] In the area of grading as in so many others, the tacit if uneasy consensus on standards of judgment among faculty can no longer be taken for granted.

In cases of plagiarism, whether via one of the term paper companies

[12]There is a temptation in such attacks to treat examinations stereotypically and to overlook the possibility that certain kinds of examinations could be experiences from which a good many students could learn. Yet I regard an apprentice relation between student and teacher as preferable, or the view of the teacher as a coach, as in the Swarthmore Honors Plan, where the examining is done by outsiders. And of course evaluation and grading, though they often overlap, are not the same thing. See for further discussion of these concerns Riesman (1963).

[13]The course was organized in part by SDS and mobilized graduate students, undergraduates, and nonstudents as teaching fellows. In my own view, this was a course which students should have taken on a pass/fail basis since it was concededly experimental. But as one of the instructors reported to me, students were unwilling to surrender an almost guaranteed A for a mere pass, preferring to hold their pass/fail option in reserve against more intractable obstacles. For a study at a state university demonstrating that students perform less well in courses they take pass/fail than in graded courses, see von Wittich (1972, pp. 499–508).

For a detailed report illustrative of the forms which a conflict over grading can take, see "Report of the Department of Sociology, 1971–72" by Richard F. Tomasson (1973), then Chairman at the University of New Mexico. Tomasson dismissed several teaching assistants who gave honor grades to all students, contrary to instructions; the teaching assistants appealed to the AAUP and to a chain of legalistic hearings at the University on the ground that their academic freedom had been violated.

[14]On the emotional hazards of the job of senior tutor, see the perceptive article of Kevin Starr (1972, pp. 21–26).

or another student, some faculty avoid argument by what seems to me a surprising leniency, such as giving the student a low or possibly a failing grade, but not reporting him (such offenses are almost invariably committed by male students) for possible disciplinary action. As already mentioned, student preoccupation with grades in the last several years has risen markedly, as it has become widely believed that Harvard students find it harder to get into medical schools or top-flight law schools and as the job prospects have looked generally more somber.

One area in which many faculty have felt traditional standards inappropriate has been that of creating a Department of Afro-American Studies—a department that would, contrary to general Harvard practice at the time, have students in equal number to faculty as members of the search committee for a chairman and for other faculty, and playing a formal role in departmental affairs. Well before that, Harvard black students had originated the *Journal of Negro Affairs* (later changed to the *Journal of Afro-American Affairs*). As at other institutions, articulate black student leaders sought to create a milieu at Harvard responsive to their particular concerns, both with respect to the situation of blacks in the wider University and with respect to their own relation to blacks in the metropolitan area and elsewhere. Even before the student turmoil of April 1969 (described in Martin Lipset's essay), some of the black student leaders had begun to believe that the "bureaucratic" faculty and student authorities were not being responsive to their interests as to the shape of the proposed Department of Afro-American Studies. These smoldering objections and resentments surfaced in the wake of the SDS seizure of University Hall and the police evacuation that followed. At that point, organized black students demanded of the entire faculty that they receive formal leverage in the selection of faculty and, with strong faculty support, they demanded that a concentration in Afro-American Studies (rather than a combination of such studies with the already established disciplines) get under way that fall, modifying the procedures and timetables earlier proposed and agreed to by the so-called Rosovsky Committee.[15] A divided faculty agreed. In the light of the role given to black students, and of the tensions among various factions of black students, separatists and otherwise, as well as various

[15]See Rosovsky (1969, p. 568) and a history of the Afro-American Studies Department in *Report of the Committee to Review the Department of Afro-American Studies* (1972, pp. 20–34). See also *The First Three Years of the Afro-American Studies Department, 1969–72*, a report to Harvard's Faculty of Arts and Sciences on October 16, 1972.

cadres of white faculty beset by guilt, idealism, sentimentality, and fear, it is understandable that the Department came to be viewed by many as lacking the meritocratic standards believed to prevail in the College. Several years later, some black students privately declared that the Department has lacked academic distinction. They complain, also privately, that white faculty and administrators were condescending and humiliated them by acceding to the appointment of staff who would not have been accepted in the regular departments—even though they recognize that the departmental staff was in part chosen by their activist predecessors.

It is not inevitable that a department where undergraduates have a large managerial share will be less meritocratic than others. A department of physics or of classics might be hardly at all different with students on search committees, as of course students are in many places. However, in fields such as sociology, urban studies, or black studies, in which the role of field or community service and activism as legitimate academic exercises may exacerbate the tension in a department as to its aims and methods, a formal student voice in appointments may make the field unattractive to potential scholarly candidates, thus diminishing the pool of potential faculty of high quality, as this would be defined at Harvard, and hence of faculty authority.[16] In the first year of operation, 1969–70, there were charges that white students were edged out of concentration in Afro-American Studies. As has happened elsewhere, only a small proportion (less than one-fifth) of Harvard's black undergraduates are themselves concentrators in the Department, although many take courses under its auspices and use its facilities as a kind of student center. (Harvard has never had a regular student center—perhaps in part because the center idea is snobbishly associated in the Harvard milieu with Midwestern gregarious Philis-

---

[16]On comparable problems in black studies programs at other institutions, see Slaughter (1972). The unattractiveness of a department riven by student and faculty partisanship is of course no monopoly of Black Studies programs! Many departments are bitterly split between "hards" and "softs," politically, pedagogically, and along many other dimensions. And in many, activist students have a hand, tacit or formalized, in all departmental affairs. The situation is exacerbated in Black Studies because of the novelty of the field and the competitive premium placed on black candidates, many of whom understandably prefer appointments in regular departments where they may be subjected to fewer cross-pressures of a political, budgetary, and "community" sort.

On a much smaller scale, problems of an analogous sort have arisen vis-à-vis efforts to establish educational programs which will satisfy students and faculty from Spanish-speaking backgrounds, whether Mexican-American, island-born or mainland-born Puerto Ricans, and other more fragmentary groups.

tinism—with reliance being put instead in the residential Houses and the rather barren ambience of the Freshman Union.)[17]

The major new department created at Harvard in recent years, the Department of Visual and Environmental Studies, begun in 1967, reflects newly emphatic student preoccupations quite as much as does the Department of Afro-American Studies. It is not entirely new because it could build on an undergraduate predecessor, Architectural Sciences, which gave students an opportunity to deploy talents of manual and artistic dexterity as well as the verbal and conceptual facility more generally recognized at Harvard. While the English Department has been reluctant to provide course credit for work in the theater, and the Music Department gives only grudging and marginal credit to undergraduates for musical composition or performance, "Vis. Stud." allows students to work in film, photography, and design for credit. Correspondingly, it grants faculty status without demanding the Ph.D. or its equivalent. Thus, it is in some respects a departure from the traditional plateau of democratic meritocracy, which rests on formal credentials. While it may be true that celluloid is the narcotic of a certain kind of chic student (indeed many people will do almost anything to acquire film), in fact Vis. Stud. students for the most part work with very great intensity and dedication. Only a small number of the besieging applicants can be admitted to the workshop and studio courses which have an enviable shop atmosphere of seriousness.[18]

Other modifications in the requirements for an undergraduate pro-

[17]I have heard it said that since some Harvard administrators, as undergraduates, were members of Final Clubs (or of the literary-intellectual Signet Society whose membership includes a number of faculty), they have been less sensitive to the need for a student center than might have been the case had they been less well provided for as students. Presently there is an effort loosely to affiliate the freshmen with the Houses (as is automatically done with freshmen in the Radcliffe Houses) even though this affiliation (unlike the arangement in the Yale Colleges) is not binding either way.

[18]Two Vis. Stud. concentrators, Rob Cohen and Michael Williams, produced for their joint senior thesis (1971) a film, "Experience," subsidized by the Committee on Admissions, which indicates the virtuosity some of these students attain. The film is also illuminating for its dramatically antiphotogenic, antielitist view of Harvard College students. It makes amply clear that in a post-meritocratic era not all Harvard students are winners nor want to be. The Committee on Admissions could use the film for antirecruiting in Middle America!

For reasons adumbrated in the text, the Department of Visual and Environmental Studies has not gathered a stable and permanent faculty—which in the Harvard system would require the present availability of larger resources to fund the Chairs—but has made do often with part-time staff; the tensions within the Department over its directions, refracting those we have stereotyped as conflicts between "creators" (including craftsmen) and "critics" in a situation of scarce resources, are periodically aired in the *Crimson*.

gram have been occurring at Harvard as elsewhere, many of them having begun before the days of vocal student discontent in 1968 and later.
For example, one course a year, on the average, can be taken pass/fail
(which in practice means that hardly any fail). In 1965–66, the Harvard
Radcliffe Policy Committee, a largely undergraduate body, sent out a
questionnaire to see what courses would be taken on a pass/fail basis if
opportunity arose. Some of us had hoped that students would be encouraged to take serious courses in the natural sciences when the threat
of a poor grade had been greatly reduced. But the survey indicated that
the preferred courses students would hope to venture into under
pass/fail were those in Fine Arts and Music. This represented another
"two cultures" gap at Harvard: many students feared that in a course in
history of art or music they would be at a disadvantage vis-à-vis the
preppies whose mothers had taken them to the Louvre at the age of ten.
Harvard College attracts a number of students who have immersed
themselves in mathematics or the natural sciences in high school and
who choose Harvard in preference to MIT or Cal Tech because they now
feel that they should "broaden out"; many have told me that science
was the only well-taught subject in their schools, the only demanding
one. In my observation, most science concentrators at Harvard move
easily into all other fields without any handicap and do as well in those
fields as those who have made them their métier. Still, some of the science students do feel shy about courses in the arts (much less so in
music), and the pass/fail proviso is an encouragement for some of them.
A recent survey showed that over 80 percent of the undergraduates do
make use of the pass/fail option.

Even when I was a Harvard undergraduate, it was possible to get
course reduction (from the standard load of four courses) if one were
pursuing honors, in order to have more time available for the senior
thesis. A few years ago, independent study was also available to students
with honors standing, who might want course credit for activities not
traditionally regarded as academic. But honors students usually have
enough ability to undertake both a regular course load and extracurricular activities, while less adept students sometimes have felt they
could not afford to undertake activities for which they did not get credit, at least if these were not simply recreational. Presently independent
study is available to all students; but the faculty, reacting to the belief
that there have been abuses in this area, has now separated independent study, which requires supervision and a report, from independent
work, which is less formal and cannot be given a grade.

Taken one by one, these curricular changes have left unimpaired the

hegemony of the traditional departments, although the relative attractiveness of these has fluctuated, with a great rise in the social sciences
(including, until its recent fissure, the interdisciplinary Department of
Social Relations), and presently something of a vogue for studies which
promise that they are *not* "relevant," such as medieval history (although
here lies mysticism), classics, art history, etc. At the same time, the
cumulative result of the changes of recent years has been to diminish
the relative monopoly of departments as the principal routes to the
bachelor's degree. The attractiveness of the two principal interdisciplinary honors programs, Social Studies and History and Literature,
testifies not only to their oversubscribed "elite" character, but also to
the attraction of fields which exist only at the undergraduate level and
which are explicitly nondepartmental. A proposed new honors major in
Religion will similarly be taught by an interdepartmental committee.
However, enterprising students can link fields of concentration, for example philosophy and science, creating what would in other institutions be a double major. In 1970–71, after approval by a student-faculty
committee, it became possible for a student to design his own field of
concentration, provided the student could show that his or her plans
could not be fitted into one of the existing departments or interdepartmental committees and the program seemed to make sense in its own
terms. To secure approval, a student applies to a newly created Committee on Special Studies after securing approval from the Senior Tutor in
his or her residential House; the option is open to nonhonors as well as
honors candidates. Up until June 1972, some 30 students had taken advantage of the opportunity.

But the existence of these opportunities not only represents the now
formalized role of students in educational reform, so that the Committee on Undergraduate Education—taking the place of the appointive
Committee on Educational Policy—has both student and faculty elected
representatives, but also signals to students still within a field of concentration that they are not necessarily prisoners there, but can, if they
want, write their own tickets. With the partial loss of their monopoly,
the departments therefore must compete not only with each other but
with nondepartmental offerings, competition which many faculty
members, fully identified with their departments, regard as "unfair,"
lowering standards and cheapening the degree. Correspondingly, many
departments have loosened their own requirements as well as broadening their offerings, so that for example the Department of Government
offers courses which easily fall within the orbit of philosophy,
history, sociology, psychology, and at times psychiatry.

The departments have been particularly, though unevenly, resistant to the very modest decentralization of the curriculum to the Houses that has occurred in recent years—even though the limited offerings in the Houses are far fewer than those now laid on in the Yale Colleges.[19] It had originally been hoped that sections of large courses, including the General Education courses, would be taught in the Houses, and that students in large departments would be able to have a tutor who was a resident of their own House. Some of this does occur, but the undergraduates themselves do not always respond to opportunities that a Housemaster or tutor has made available, leading to a loss of morale and momentum which in turn puts a damper on further experiments. Department chairmen have tended to see House tutorships as prerogatives handed out in terms of some balance of financial need and departmentally defined merit, rather than with reference to what a House Master might seek in terms of contribution to the House—and it is the department which has the budget, while the House Master has at best a limited veto and no monetary power.[20] Overcrowded in recent years especially by the increase in the number of women students without drastic decrease in the number of male students, the Houses generally lack facilities for accommodating courses or seminars. The result is that students in a House are only rarely aware of taking courses with fellow residents.

It is difficult to estimate the proportion of faculty who have more than perfunctory identification with the Houses. Many faculty members who are listed as House Associates might go to their House once or twice a year. Probably the majority of faculty is indifferent to the Houses. Perhaps a quarter to a third of faculty has more than nominal involvement; a number of these are men and women who received some of

[19]Sophomores and juniors, unless they are married or have special permission, are required to live in a House; seniors can more readily get permission to move off campus. But all students, including commuters and those living in several cooperative houses, are attached to a House and are entitled to its facilities, including special advisers for premedicine and prelaw.

[20]What House Masters can offer to the minority of tutors who are residents is a more or less attractive suite of rooms, not always suitable for married couples especially if there are children, and subject to all the older alcoholic- and newer Harman Kardon-style noise pollution of contemporary dormitory life. All tutors are given a certain number of free meals in the House in order to encourage them to eat with students who often resent the sight of tutors eating mainly with each other. At the University of California at Santa Cruz, the Provosts of the Colleges have a much larger budgetary stake, paying half the salaries of faculty, so that the Boards of Studies (departments) must haggle with them to agree on a mutually acceptable recruit. The fear is widely prevalent at Santa Cruz, in my judgment not altogether justified, that the Colleges have lost their power to shape the curricular climate of the University, especially in appointments to tenure, because the Boards of Studies have unevenly become more discipline-oriented and because many students themselves have become avidly and understandably preprofessional.

their education at Harvard and perhaps as graduate students held a House tutorship.

How one assesses the degree of faculty involvement in the Houses, or indeed the vitality of the House system, depends on one's perspective. If one compares Harvard with most public or private universities, one might conclude that undergraduates are served in the Houses by arrangements which go far beyond the ordinary dormitory complex: the students have access to tutors fairly readily and to senior Faculty Associates by making only a slight effort. If one examines Harvard from within, one sees that some Houses have active Senior Common Rooms and that the Master and his colleagues go to considerable pains to lay on courses that build on the interests and energies of Faculty Associates and tutors as well as to develop other activities, with artists in residence or lecture series, responsive to student interests. Other Houses in contrast are dormitories plus: all do provide the academic and personal help of the Senior Tutor and his staff, who along with the Master write recommendations to graduate schools as well as help solve conflicts among roommates or other problems such as noise and vandalism. (Most Houses, like other Harvard buildings, have instituted heavy security precautions in the last several years.) If one compares Harvard, however, with Yale or with superb undergraduate colleges such as Haverford, Pomona, Smith, or Dartmouth, in that comparison Harvard's senior faculty are much less involved with undergraduate teaching and culture than, from the point of view of undergraduates, might be optimal. Thus one can say that to have a quarter of the faculty with some involvement in the Houses is either a large or an all-too-small quotient, depending on one's point of view.

Indeed, there is a considerable group of Harvard faculty which sees the Houses critically as undercutting the democratic meritocracy of College-wide competition. They see the Houses as too comfortable and cozy, almost as if they were coed fraternities. To them, the notion that a student's ability to get into a course, or even a section of a course, might depend on where he lives, seems an ascriptive invasion into an achievement-oriented system.[21] They also fear that faculty members

[21]Although it is widely believed among faculty that House courses attract mainly people from the sponsoring House, a survey done by Edward T. Wilcox, Director of the Committee on General Education, showed that in the three terms beginning with the spring term of 1971, less than 30 percent of the students in the House courses had come from within the particular sponsoring House. Indeed, freshmen are eligible for House courses but through ignorance or lack of initiative rarely apply to them. Professor Robert Kiely, appointed by Derek Bok as Associate Dean for Undergraduate Education, has been encour-

who have House affiliations will be "soft on students," given to a personalistic rather than a didactic mode of teaching.[22] The size of a Harvard House ranges from 300 to 450 and in a sense the Houses are in competition with the College-wide activities for student energy and interest. Intramural sports, managed through the Houses, are more cheerful and less competitive, of course, than varsity sports, and marginally, the same thing is true in the academic realm.

While there is no prohibition against a department's offering a House course, virtually all House courses thus far have been offered in General Education and hence must receive approval by its supervising Committee. While General Education has been the sponsor of some of the more experimental modes of teaching and of courses which could not be mounted in a regular department, it nevertheless continues to serve some of its more traditional functions. It has not been especially hospitable to the House courses, forcing them to pass a scrutiny more severe than would be exercised by departments over courses given with almost automatic academic freedom—a kind of senatorial comity—by department members. And paradoxically, while the heritage aspect of the General Education program has nearly evaporated, and while no consensus exists on what form a program of General Education should take as requirements are relaxed, the courses offered by the Committee are more popular than ever. At present, the General Education requirements are minimal, not much more than a mild expectation that a student will take several courses outside his own area of specialization. However, General Education courses, beyond the minimum required, figure increasingly in the choices students make for time which is not under the aegis of one's department.

The program itself dates only from the Second World War and was created in a response to the belief that new kinds of students were coming to the College who needed immersion in the Western heritage, an immersion they could not be expected to get at home or even in a good secondary school.[23] Just as House masterships with notable exceptions

---

aging the Houses which have in the past not offered House courses to do so, in an effort to spread the benefits of this sort of valued small group instruction more widely among some of the less entrepreneurial undergraduates.

[22]For a discussion of these styles of teaching, see "Teaching Styles and the Polarities of Work and Play," in Riesman, Gusfield, and Gamson (1970, Ch. 7).

[23]See *Harvard Committee* (1946). The original idea of the "Red Book," as this volume came to be called, had been to encourage the creation of a single full-year course in each of the three major areas—the Social Sciences, the Humanities, and the Natural Sciences—with the aim of bringing the students onto a common level of discourse, whatever their points

were in the early years filled by Ivy League-type men in English or History or Classics, so the General Education courses appeared in their inception to be something of a refuge for an older, less scientific, and less academically entrepreneurial Harvard. At their glamorous best, as in the Humanities course led by John Finley (also the long-time, devoted Master of Eliot House), intellectual virtuosity might compensate for the absence of the hard-driving, specialist preoccupations of a more departmentalized postwar faculty. But in general, a proper choice among required General Education courses was regarded by some students and many faculty as a way of escaping departmental rigor, with its steplike prerequisites and insistence on cumulative competence.[24]

As a member of the Committee on General Education, I know what struggles my colleagues and I undergo to decide what in the way of content or mode of approach justifies a course's being included in the program. The older "Red Book" theories of General Education have dissipated. Yet there remains a certain spirit which is more characteristic of courses in General Education than in the departments, that is, a more exploratory and less competitive atmosphere. Even when courses cover identical material, their climate is subtly altered by the auspices under which they are given. A General Education course in fact is not primarily for the instructor's departmental disciples. While perhaps the majority of the faculty members have preferred to teach potential disciples in their own specialty,[25] a substantial minority has enjoyed the prospect of teaching a more diverse student body in a broader way.[26]

---

of origin. Such a coherent program, like the ones at Columbia and Chicago, never came into existence. For if the departments at Harvard are relatively autonomous vis-à-vis the Dean of the Faculty, each individual faculty member is also quite autonomous even vis-à-vis his department, let alone the College as a whole. Given these traditions of faculty independence, which date back to the Eliot reforms, and even earlier, it proved impossible to secure agreement on single courses in each of the three major areas. Instead, half a dozen or more alternative options were created in each area.

[24]When in 1958–59 as a member of the Committee on Advanced Standing I interviewed students who were electing to enter Harvard as sophomores, they often declared that they wanted to get out of all that "Gen. Ed. dilettantism" and get on with serious things. In this stereotypical judgment there was as usual some truth and some falsity. Many General Education courses were at least as demanding as departmental courses, but as windows on Harvard for entering students, the General Education courses were more visible, and it could be a point of pride to be able to avoid them.

[25]A report to the Faculty by Acting Associate Dean Earnest R. May, February 15, 1972, presents data on the dramatic rise in the last decade of specialized courses with tiny enrollments, as well as illustrating the immense diversity among departments in the degree to which they seek at all to meet the needs of undergraduates and in particular of those who are not their own concentrators.

[26]There are, however, some General Education courses which meet both departmental requirements and also the now inchoate expectations of the Committee on General Edu-

These very qualities of the General Education Program have led a small number of reflective faculty to believe that its existence permits the departments to extrude their more innovative faculty and to shirk departmental responsibility for a broad range of offerings for concentrators and nonconcentrators alike. The problems raised here are analogous to those presented by the creation of an experimental college within a traditional university—or the problem created at Harvard by inventing the Social Relations Department and drawing into it some of the less behavioristically minded psychologists and anthropologists who were not what one of my colleagues calls the "stone and bone" men. By providing a shelter in Social Relations for psychologists who had been beleaguered in their original home, that home became more monolithic, while the Department of Social Relations was seen by some faculty as amorphous and lacking in proper standards. It is easy for outsiders who have not experienced the periodic savageries of intradepartmental warfare, particularly as it involves vulnerable graduate students, to lay down the mandate that individuals should stay and fight within their own bailiwick rather than escape to a more comfortable academic purlieu. (There is a not entirely far-fetched analogy with those who condemn anyone who becomes an exile from an oppressive regime.) On such matters I would not want to lay down a general rule, either as to the proper conduct of individuals or as to institutional organization. I am, for example, convinced that the Social Relations Department was a creative enterprise and that the psychologists who helped make it so would not have done much to alleviate the more monolithic aspects of the Psychology Department had they remained in it. Similarly, to return to the question of General Education at Harvard, I am not persuaded that the departments would actually pick up their responsibilities for the General Education potential of their fields if the General Education Program itself were to be abolished. On the contrary, it often occurs that someone will venture a General Education course outside his department (or, as mentioned earlier, a Freshman Seminar) about which the department will then develop enough confidence to recapture the course as its very own. Undoubtedly, some departments are under less pressure from students because General Education exists as a safety valve, but one can also observe instances where the departments have been influenced by the success of the General Education courses to modify their own courses in incremental ways even while some of

cation: Humanities 6, developed by Professor Reuben Brower, and Natural Sciences 5, inaugurated by Professor George Wald, are illustrations.

their members may publicly denounce the General Education Program for its lack of standards.

Students are themselves frequently ambivalent about the diversity they encounter in General Education courses. In those where discussion is encouraged, they can be snobbish about having to listen to each other and complain that they came to Harvard to hear the big shots and not naïve students. But at other times, they can enjoy the diversity they meet in the classroom, the more so since in their Houses they are often confined to a colony of the like-minded. Surveys conducted by Dean K. Whitla, Director of the Office of Instructional Research and Evaluation, demonstrate that Harvard College students recognize that the institution draws a diverse student body. But some of the more articulate nevertheless declare (as students in selective colleges characteristically do) that their peers are all too homogeneous: alas, they say, they are mostly affluent, white suburban, upper-middle-class, from professional and educated families, etc., etc. These students do not recognize a far greater source of homogeneity in residential colleges, namely, the chronological one, ranging from the age of about 16 to the early 20s. Harvard's Extension Program for adults is rarely mixed in with undergraduates, although there is a small category of Special Students, many of them belated premeds, who are given permission to do postbaccalaureate work in undergraduate courses. However, the College does have the advantage for students and faculty of including a minority of adults who, as Nieman Fellows (journalism) or Kennedy Fellows (mostly government), Trade Union Fellows, Center for International Affairs Fellows, Advanced Management Business School Students, etc., have the free run of the curriculum and may have House affiliations.

One of Harvard's attractions for entering students is its recognized diversity, the lack of any single defining type of "Harvard man," yet freshmen sometimes find their friendships limited to the luck of their roommate or entry draw. Coresidential living and the preference for cross-sex dyads is one element in this confinement; the discovery that Harvard frowns on gregariousness and Big-Man-on-Campus types is another; a certain guardedness that prevails among competitive yet unsure students is still another handicap. In the large lecture courses for freshmen and even in their smaller sections, students seldom take the opportunity to get to know each other. Very different in this respect are the Freshmen Seminars that began in 1959. The program encouraged faculty members to offer Seminars on any subject they chose to as many or as few students as they chose; the Seminar program would buy a faculty member's time from his or her department and the Freshman Seminar would count as a full course in terms of teaching load. Every year since the program began, nearly twice as many freshmen have sought to enter Seminars as could be accommodated. Because of the shortage of volunteers from the Arts and Sciences Faculty, some Seminar leaders have been recruited from other Schools at Harvard or from the many talented potential teachers around the area, such as, for example, researchers at the Cambridge Electron Accelerator; the departments have been uneven in their welcome to such temporary colleagues. Many departments, indeed, had not been enthusiastic about the Freshman Seminar program when it was proposed, but the administration was able to go ahead because it had a grant of outside money from a generously anonymous donor. But some departments have exercised an effective veto power over the appointment of Seminar leaders who did not meet their own tests of acceptance. Such approval, while not formally required, is invited as a kind of senatorial courtesy; the science departments have seemed relatively free of anxiety vis-à-vis the teaching prerogative, perhaps because they are pretty sure of a consensus on who is capable or possibly because they care less about freshmen, while the humanities departments have been a good deal more reluctant.

In atmosphere, the typical Freshman Seminar is less competitive than the large lecture-and-section courses regularly open to freshmen. The Seminar is small, ranging in size from half a dozen to 10 or 15, which allows the seminarians to get to know each other well; the instructor often has them to his or her home to meet over beer and pretzels or wine and cheese in the evening.[27] The lack of grades also reduces the pressure for some and encourages students to apply to Seminars that otherwise might have seemed too forbidding. (However, premeds and others desperate to get top grades may turn down Seminars because they are ungraded.) Yet as indicated earlier, the Seminars may have lessened certain competitive pressures without diminishing—perhaps even intensifying—the quest for meritocratic excellence at Harvard. In many

---

[27]In the Seminar of 40 Harvard and 20 Radcliffe students that with three colleagues I directed in the first year of the program, the relations within the group became extremely close. We had been told that students at Harvard College more than 100 points apart in their College Board scores had a hard time talking with each other. But in this situation that barrier fell easily. However, we failed in the serious effort we made to cross the "two-cultures" gap between the sciences and other fields; the students headed for the sciences ranged easily, for the most part, into the other fields, but this was not reciprocated, in spite of our efforts. On the way in which students of that period often rigidly and fearfully defined themselves on arriving at Harvard, see Riesman (1961, pp. 117–125).

cases, the Seminars moved freshmen into a specialized area of the instructor's own research, providing him or her with eager, if untrained, apprentices.[28]

It has been difficult to persuade senior faculty of top departmental reputation to offer General Education courses or Freshmen Seminars; they are of course under pressure from their own departments to offer courses to meet the expectations of undergraduate majors; and particularly in the sciences, they are often surrounded by a swarm of postdoctoral fellows who can fully occupy their pedagogic energies. It has proved even more difficult in recent years to recruit Masters of the residential Houses who command widespread faculty respect. In the early years of the House plan, President Lowell was able to persuade eminent men to accept masterships; I have already mentioned John Finley's long tenure at Eliot House, in which he set something of a model for other Masters to try to live up to. Harvard faculty today suffer more distraction and competition from constituencies than in an earlier, more tranquil era.

Correspondingly, the demands on a House Master are considerably greater now, since student expectations are much higher, and since students are less shy about voicing complaints and, despite the widespread belief that one should stand on one's own feet, in expressing feelings of unhappiness and anxious uncertainty. When a few years ago the Radcliffe dormitories were divided into Houses which, except for the new and dramatically handsome Currier House, do not have facilities comparable with a Harvard House or provisions for a Master's residence, the Masters who were chosen sometimes threw up their duties after a single year. If a Master is going to be able to recruit for his Senior Common Room academically distinguished faculty who will take a serious interest in the House, the President must choose a Master who has earned professional respect, but this may mean settling on someone who lacks the time, energy, or talent for making the House academically and culturally innovative. This is a way of saying that if the Masters are to moderate successfully the pressures of meritocracy, they must first

[28]Some faculty members objected to calling a class or program for freshmen a "seminar," a term reserved for graduate work, but those faculty who took part in the Seminars were astonished to discover how fast and how far freshmen could proceed. The discovery was being simultaneously made by some Harvard as well as MIT and other faculty members, especially in the natural sciences and mathematics, that secondary school students were also capable of what would heretofore have seemed extraordinary feats of intellectual mobility. Gerald Holton, Professor of Physics at Harvard, has been one of the leaders of both the General Education Program and of Project Physics, which has sought to introduce intellectually and conceptually demanding physics to students in the high schools.

have won its guerdons.[29] Of course, this is not a situation unique to Harvard.

What is not unique to Harvard, either, is the effort on the part of the administration to encourage some senior faculty to set a model of multi-disciplinary or at least nondepartmental teaching. At Harvard this took the form of another effort by President Lowell to find a place for the aristocratic version of meritocracy—a faculty counterpart to his plan for Junior Fellows, who were to be encouraged to create their own pro-grams free of the expectation that they would earn the doctorate and hence' be subjected to departmental control. Thus in 1935 President Lowell began to make a very small number of appointments to Univer-sity Professorships. As already mentioned, these appointments have tended to be given to senior men already at Harvard who possessed un-doubted intellectual distinction and who deserved well of the Univer-sity because of their institutional dedication. For example, the late Merle Fainsod, a political scientist who had directed the Russian Research Center and later the University Library, held such an appoint-ment; so does Paul Freund of the Law School, an unobtrusively capable University citizen, who offers a large General Education course, The Legal Process. Edwin Reischauer, who also involves himself in the Gen-eral Education Program, became a University Professor on returning from the Ambassadorship to Japan. Oscar Handlin, who has concerned himself with the Harvard University Press, with the library, and with the creation of the Charles Warren Center for Studies in American His-tory, was recently made a University Professor; so on his retirement from the arduous Deanship of the Faculty of Arts and Sciences was John Dunlop (who simultaneously took a leave of absence to head the Cost of Living Council in Washington). The Nobel Prize winning physicist, Edward Mills Purcell, also an institutional loyalist and, like Paul Freund, a Senior Fellow of the Society of Fellows, is a University Professor. Ernst Kitzinger, the eminent historian of art, served the University through the directorship of Dumbarton Oaks in Washington, D.C., and does have interests that cross departmental lines. The catalog declares that

---

[29]That minority of Masters who have not held the academic esteem of their departmental colleagues have had an unhappy time. (Somewhat comparable instances exist of peer disesteem for faculty members brought to or kept at Harvard principally for their con-tribution to the General Education Program, whose often large undergraduate following does not compensate for the judgment of their departmental colleagues that they are pun-dits rather than real scholars.)

For evidence that the Masters can have an impact on the outlook of students, provided that the Faculty Associates have values congruent with those of the Master, see Vreeland and Bidwell (1965, pp. 233–250).

the University Professorships exist "for men working on the frontiers of knowledge, and in such a way as to cross the conventional boundaries of the specialties." The chairs—unlike the many named professorships within departments—were designed to free men from affiliation with a department or even a school and hence to discover the constituencies for teaching they might prefer. One man of great distinction, Paul Tillich, was recruited to Harvard as a University Professor, beginning in 1954–55, and he taught courses in the General Education Program until his retirement in 1962. Since that time, so far as I know, Lowell's successors have not used the University Professorship to recruit new or controversial talent to Harvard—an action that might be seen by the departments as interference in their own supposedly unending search for talent.

Nevertheless, Nathan Pusey and McGeorge Bundy decided to use the pattern, but not the name of University Professor, in order to bring to Harvard men whom the departments might not consider as their first priority in making appointments. Laurence Wylie, Professor of French at Haverford, had secured training in anthropology and written his ethnographic *Village in the Vaucluse*, but this did not necessarily attract the attention of Harvard's Department of Romance Languages and Literatures. Bundy made use of a newly created chair in French Civilization, money for which was provided by Douglas Dillon, to make the Wylie appointment possible and then offered the Department of Social Relations the chance to give Wylie a departmental home, which was done. (Now, Romance Languages and Literatures and Anthropology both give him a home.)[30] With funds saved from a Ford Foundation grant for faculty salaries, Bundy brought me to Harvard with a special mandate for undergraduate education in the social sciences, but with freedom to choose my own agenda; again the Social Relations Department became the legatee of a free gift. Erik Erikson was another such acquisition, again in Social Relations. In none of these cases was a departmental appointment a prerequisite, only an opportunity or an administrative base. All three of us taught General Education courses.

It seems unlikely that new appointments of this same sort will be made in the future. The egalitarian has overtaken the aristocratic meritocracy, and in a faculty of those who consider themselves stars (and the best judges of other stars) what administrator these days would have the

---

[30]Professor Wylie has kindly provided me with a memorandum detailing all the intricate steps by which he came to Harvard, which would seem to me to make clear that his was a case of what Ralph Turner would call sponsored rather than contest mobility.

courage to take it upon himself to assume the aristocratic over the democratic style? Moreover, with the new pressure on teaching contributing to the current academic climate, it is difficult to justify giving a professor complete control over his own time.

Bundy's appointment as Dean of Faculty in 1953 was itself a case of sponsorship—by President Pusey. Indeed, when Bundy was appointed to tenure, under President Conant's regime, the Ad Hoc Committee is said to have marveled at the fact that he had not taken a single course in Government; he had been a Junior Fellow and he was obviously bright. That won the day. And he had been far down on the list of those recommended to Pusey as possible choices for the Dean of the Faculty of Arts and Sciences; selecting him took a certain courage. Bundy had confidence in his own judgment, and although he consulted professors he respected, he was not necessarily impressed by the consensus of any particular department. Nevertheless, looking back some years later on his stewardship (1953–1961), Bundy concluded that, in effect, he had let meritocracy get out of hand: narrow definitions of excellence came to prevail over all other considerations. He had not managed to hold the balance vis-à-vis the departments, or to moderate the claims of competition vis-à-vis those of wide-ranging competence and such personal qualities as compassion.[31]

Yet some of Bundy's unfulfilled agenda have come to pass since his departure. Student representatives now attend faculty meetings and sit on many departmental committees, including in some cases those on admissions (at the graduate level) and on junior faculty recruitment. Senior faculty used to get jobs for their favorite graduate students or those of their departmental friends through an old boy network, whereas now most departments have regular procedures by which letters of inquiry to a department are available to all graduate students, who can follow up such leads themselves—although there is great unevenness in the degree to which departments regularize and energize their search for employment for their graduates. And by the usual Tocquevillean rule, as students have been given more power, they have sought still more. For example, while financial issues predominated in the formation in the spring of 1972 of the Harvard Graduate Student and Teaching Fellow Union, this somewhat disparate group formalized and partially solidified what previously had often been the private resentments of graduate students, unhappy with their particular departments or with Harvard in general. While the strikes called by the Union in the spring

---

[31]See Bundy (1970, pp. 545ff).

of 1972 and again in 1973 proved abortive, with many undergraduates and most senior faculty crossing the picket lines, the demands of the graduate students nevertheless had an impact on policy. Financial aid was shifted, though with some qualifications, from "merit" to "need," over the objection of many departments which felt that they could no longer compete for the brightest cohort, as a coach would for top athletes, but could only offer a financial package based on family income, student assets, loans, etc. While the Graduate Student and Teaching Fellow Union was much stronger in some departments (not surprisingly, Anthropology and Sociology, but also Biology and Biochemistry) than in others, its outlook crossed departmental lines. And as elsewhere, there are now self-conscious cadres of women faculty and of black faculty whose identifications and concerns are nondepartmental.[32]

Moreover, the hegemony of the curriculum today is less than it was a few years earlier, also reducing the leverage of the departments. Many fewer students now plan to go on to the Ph.D.; many more are uncertain about the postbaccalaureate future; there is a widespread uneasiness about the whole concept of a career. Furthermore, with the disappearance of the draft, students once again feel free to take leaves of absence from Harvard; the notion of an uninterrupted four-year stint comes increasingly into question. There are many available ideologies which justify for both black and white students not doing well at academic games, and these ideologies have made a dent on a good many faculty, and not just the junior ones. In consequence, just as there is a greater variety of postbaccalaureate careers or moratoria regarded as legitimate for Harvard College graduates, so there are also many more routes through and around the curriculum and way stations in between.

Yet many of the more sensitive educational reformers at Harvard believe that these changes have been—again that favorite expression—mere tokenism. Some suggest that the loosenings and relaxations of pressure have only made it possible for "the system" to go on much as before, like the permitted license of a fiesta which allows a corrupt monarchy to continue. Furthermore, the educational reformers discovered that there was no latent pool of undergraduate dissatisfaction with

---

[32]As implied in the text, none of these things, of course, is distinctive of Harvard. On the generational split among faculty, see the Martin Trow study (forthcoming) to be published by the Carnegie Commission; see also the Carnegie Commission on Higher Education (1972) for survey data on faculty and student dissatisfaction and satisfaction with curricula. The survey was conducted with the cooperation of the American Council on Education.

the curriculum that they could mobilize; the students' persisting political and cultural radicalism could only spasmodically be connected to curricular and pedagogic themes.[33] With a new administration at Harvard that responds with tactical flexibility to confrontations, and with a marked return to studiousness in the last several years, the fulcrum of educational reform has again returned to the hands of the administration, where in my observation it generally lies in American universities.

But the despairing pessimism of student educational reformers is not shared by a substantial group of faculty, who believe that traditional standards have been debased at Harvard, perhaps beyond redemption. They declare that the changes which have been introduced allow students to slip by without ever having to learn to read or write intelligently, or to learn a foreign language, or to struggle with a demanding science, or indeed to do anything particularly onerous. But this is no novelty. Such faculty are basing their judgments on the post-World War II years and particularly on a dozen post-Sputnik years. Even in those years Harvard had students who just slipped by. There has probably been a change in the number of such students today, but more important, in the moral legitimacy now given such behavior.[34]

[33]See Meyer (1973). Meyer's survey of undergraduate attitudes shows that in 1972, as in 1969, three-quarters of the undergraduate respondents declare that they are friendly with one or more faculty members and that they talk with faculty outside of class at least once a week; half conclude that senior faculty are concerned with students' personal problems and over three-quarters that junior faculty have such concerns. In this context, the responses of 10 Harvard faculty members in 1969 to the question, "Is it getting more difficult to teach?" indicate the efforts of these respondents to understand student preoccupations with "relevance," and to respond to the altered student temper without abdicating to demands for instant activism. See "Ten Harvard Professors Answer a Question for the Faculty: Is It Becoming More Difficult to Teach. . ." in the *Harvard Alumni Bulletin* (pp. 43–50, 1969).

I cannot explore in this monograph the subtle interplay between the feelings of students of being under pressure for performance in the larger pool of competitors and the attraction of extramural radicalism for many of them. That in Meyer's and other surveys activist students voice minimal objections to the curriculum does not foreclose the possibility that some of their antiwar sentiment may have increased in intensity as a result of the malaise engendered by competitive pressures. See, for further discussion, Grant and Riesman (forthcoming).

[34]Here again, Huntington (1969, pp. 51–54) is a useful text on the contrast; it appears in the same issue of the *Harvard Bulletin* in which some of his and my colleagues laud the moral intensity of student activism and claim that their own teaching has profited from the need to justify what they are up to in the face of the new student mood.

4. *Altered Student Climates*

For the first time in a generation it has become possible for the children of the affluent professional and educated classes to choose not to go to college without bringing on a crisis in their families or in their secondary schools. So understanding have many parents and faculty members become of dropping out and of countermeritocratic attitudes generally that such conduct may not bring the satisfactions of defiance that were sought—leading possibly to ever more ferocious attempts to cut the ties of dependency.[1] However, dropping out of educational streaming makes it possible to declare that one has rejected elite society and thus to identify with the down-and-outers, culturally or politically or both. One is at least not part of what now is so widely seen as the great gray, bland, plastic, bourgeois middle. The difficulty is that such a dramatic all-or-none position can seldom be achieved by a single unequivocal act: one must be constantly vigilant, and one's friends will surely be vigilant, against conduct or fantasy suggesting that one still harbors material or career ambition or the taste for any sort of conventional comfort or status. Herbert Marcuse's concept of repressive tolerance speaks to this fear of being embraced by the poisonously tolerant, uncombative middle. What dissenters describe as cooptation is in my observation a two-way process of mutual influence and infiltration; the fact that radicals regard it as exclusively defanging and deviant suggests how desperate is their need to believe in and maintain the heroism of an outcast position. In the late 1950s, Kenneth Keniston studied a number of alienated Harvard undergraduates who did not find enticing the adult world of jobs, careers, marriages, commitments; these isolated forerunners would today find themselves at least vicariously sharing a

---

[1]Barry Munitz, who helped clarify this phenomenon for me, notes the analogy to student protests against liberal and uncertain administrators, forcing the protesters to go to ever wilder lengths to provoke a reaction.

substantial subculture with wide appeal outside its immediate membership.[2]

But most of the classmates of Keniston's subjects despised what they regarded as commercial callings and regarded the professions as both more pure and less constraining. In the class of 1967, over a third of Harvard College students intended to pursue careers in the academic professions, that is, in higher education. Three-quarters were going on to some form of postbaccalaureate education. This reflected only moderately the graduate school sanctuary from the draft but much more strongly a rising assumption that careers in the professions were worthwhile, reasonably well-paying, and reasonably interesting.[3]

In the humanities and the less quantitative social sciences, there began to be widespread doubts that an academic career was desirable long before the market situation changed and the question arose as to whether there would be any jobs. Some students returned through the paradoxical route of the counterculture to an old American folk tradition that professors are somehow ridiculous, incompetent to handle the situations of ordinary human life. But other students took a very different tack and sought from their instructors in fields like literature, philosophy, religion, and sociology, keys to the meaning of existence and ways to express the moral imperatives of dissent. These students insisted upon a personal, reciprocally egalitarian relation with faculty members, not confined to the classroom or the instructor's formal expertise.[4] This outlook among many students, widely shared among faculty, has led as elsewhere to the judgment that lectures are by definition hierarchical,

---

[2]See Keniston (1965). For a different typology, see Heath (1964).

[3]When I brought an eminent and reflective businessman, who had headed the Volunteers for Adlai Stevenson, to talk to the Freshman Seminar I led, the students were rather contemptuous of him as an "organization man"; they were more responsive to Dr. Edwin Land, the inventor-president of Polaroid, though even here, in an adumbration of later attitudes, some wondered why he was so aggressive against nature as to try to understand what crystals were like, analyzing and breaking them up: why could he not let nature alone?

[4]"The task of the teacher, unlike that of the professor, is not only to teach how to learn science, but how to live." This is a quotation from Michio Nagai (1972, pp. 225–226).

A number of men and women who entered graduate school during this period in the hope that this was a way, if not to change the world, at least to change American sensibility, have been disappointed by the limits on activism and on personal and pedagogic change they find themselves up against as young faculty members, at times even in the more experimental colleges. Cf. for an autobiographical account, Cantarow (1972, pp. 50–61); see also the critique of Cantarow by Bensman (1972, pp. 653–654). See also, for reflective discussion of the limits that candidly self-conscious academics might set on their effort to abdicate as authorities, Elbow (1973, pp. 247–258).

authoritarian, and constraining toward feeling and spontaneity. The implication that only small discussion groups are legitimate comes up against the logistical limits not only on the availability of faculty but even of small seminar rooms and other facilities for handicraft education. The Harvard Graduate School of Business Administration does have lecture and seminar rooms arranged to facilitate group interchange. While at Harvard College the number of discussion sections in lecture courses has increased tremendously, most classrooms still look like nineteenth-century high schools with their desks and podiums, and some of the few available seminar rooms tend to be guarded in almost the style of a German Herr Professor by individual departments or research centers. Even in the newer buildings, there has seldom been close cooperation between architects and educators which would have reflected changes in preferred modes of teaching. And of course there is a general shortage of space for classrooms and offices, at least as defined in terms of contemporary amenities. (These amenities include limits upon the hours when students and faculty in the more affluent institutions are prepared to conduct their mutual exercises.) In any event, despite the strong ideological opposition to large lecture courses, students continue to be attracted to them, and in spite of the belief in sincerity and dislike of playing games, some of the esteemed lecturers are among the more theatrical. Furthermore, although students believe that authenticity requires not doing anything which at the moment one does not want to do, most faculty members continue to feel constrained by their obligations and by students' expectations of them (in spite of declamations of mutual freedom), while the student remains free to come and go.

In large lecture courses such as my own at Harvard (which lacks the monitoring agency of a final examination), students now come and go at any time during the hour; they munch sandwiches and drink cokes; their pets wander up and down the aisles (it does not generally endear one to students to ask that pets be taken out because they are distracting, as I have occasionally done); hardly anyone enforces the posted regulations against smoking in the classroom. I am not, by implication, contending that students paid undiluted attention in an earlier day (when I was taking Irving Babbitt's course on Romanticism, students had a pool which was reported in the *Crimson* as to how many names he would drop in the course of the hour), rather, I am talking about the open expression of lack of interest which reflects the emphasis on spontaneity and candor. To be sure, spontaneity and candor are difficult to achieve, and students and others may parade rudeness as a ready substitute. These observations should not be exaggerated: there are great differences in the tone of student behavior precisely because of its fluid character. For example, when Lionel Trilling, in the spring of 1971, gave the Charles Eliot Norton Lectures, a large audience of students and faculty responded with intense and not merely polite attention, his topic being the historical ramifications of the cult and culture of sincerity and authenticity.[5]

At Harvard, as at other university colleges, the academic career is the most visible one for students, and often the one vis-à-vis which they define themselves as for or against. A decade ago, in speaking at a career conference at Harvard, I urged students to try to discover, perhaps by Antioch-style experiences, what different kinds of work tasted like, remarking that some students spend more energy learning to discriminate among wines than measuring their aptitude and temperament against various sorts of work. Some students replied impatiently that they had had extremely expensive educations and that these dictated what they ought to do apart from what they liked; one declared that he would really prefer to become a mechanic, but he could not waste a Harvard education that way, and was going to law school. Today, some of the most dedicated political activists might say that a Harvard education should not be wasted in self-scrutiny but used for the benefit of "the revolution" or some similar mission. But it is unlikely that students would consider it illegitimate to become a mechanic because of all the benefits they had received; to become a mechanic or an electrican (though perhaps not a plumber) would be regarded as a just verdict on those benefits.[6] As with gastronomic tastes, so enjoyment or distaste for various sorts of work and career involves some combination of personal disposition and social definitions and status. And while Harvard College students today are considerably freer than they were from pressures to live up to adult expectations, they are perhaps the more

[5]See Trilling (1972).
    In my own lecture course and other experience, first-year students are less blasé and more responsive—characteristics that also made them vulnerable in the late 1960s to become shock troops for older activist cadres or those agemates who had already been political leaders in their high schools.

[6]There is not yet enough experience about these attitudes toward careers to know how long they will last; for example, will the apprentice who has enjoyed working with his hands for a couple of years in the construction industry stick with it for a term of years? Of course some fairly permanent and fairly lucrative careers can now be found in the counterculture itself. Running head shops, putting out the underground press, indeed dealing in drugs are illustrations. For a study of the relation between the (sometimes guilty) successes and the many purposeful failures in this area, see an unpublished study by Jeff Goldsmith, a graduate student in Sociology at the University of Chicago.

vulnerable to the ideology of their peers. For example, many students who could actually appreciate structured situations have persuaded themselves that, like many of their fellows, they cannot endure any constraint. They intend to find their lifestyle first, perhaps their identity (which in reality often means defining what they are *not*, as the easiest way to begin defining what they are), and then to look for a way of supporting that lifestyle. Some have had the fantasy of being able to live with only a slightly reduced standard of living on an endless plateau of affluence, or at least that they will be able to return to this plateau at any time they wish. Others are prepared to sacrifice comfort if they cannot combine it with conviction.

Some professions, by redefinition of possible aims, have escaped the obloquy now visited upon many conventional careers. Many of the Harvard undergraduates (over 20 percent) who intend to go to medical school (and the rising number of Radcliffe students—16 percent—entering with the same aim) believe that they can live a life of community service and at the same time have the freedom of the independent professional person.[7] Law school has also been redeemed for a certain number of students by the prospect of practicing poverty law or consumer or environmental-protection law.[8] Law school, of course, is also regarded as a way station to something else—for example, some form of political work.

The preoccupation with discovering vocations of service within the older professions suggests a softening of traditional masculine definitions of ambition. The 1960s saw the development at Harvard and some other leading institutions of Masters of Arts in Teaching programs which attracted young men who would once have regarded school

[7]There has been a dramatic shift away from the ideal of the research medical scientist toward the ideal of the community-oriented physician serving a deprived population. However, studies by Daniel Funkenstein, M.D., Professor of Psychiatry at Harvard Medical School, suggest that many medical students will not be able to practice their ideal profession and will have to settle for something else within medicine, in part because community medicine turns out in practice to be frustrating even where it is not underfinanced. See Funkenstein (1968).

A survey of the intended careers of Harvard students entering as freshmen in the fall of 1972 reports that two-fifths aim at medical school, although when it comes to fields of concentration, presently over half are registered in the social sciences. Of course some of these are also headed to medical schools, especially since many of the latter prefer candidates with a broad liberal education, provided they have shown capability in the minimum of scientific premed courses.

The percentage of Radcliffe students who plan a medical career continues to rise, including many who turn toward it after starting out in something else—and including also a number of graduates returning as Special Students for a premedical preparation.

[8]See, for example, Wickenden, Jr. (1972); also Schendel (1973).

teaching, if not as women's work, then as work for men not capable of becoming college or university professors. Some of these students, like Jonathan Kozol, a former *Crimson* editor, became leaders in the movements for alternative or free schools. Similarly, talented Radcliffe students sought out constituencies of the deprived with whom to work: black children when that seemed feasible; retarded or handicapped children; and less commonly, the exceptionally gifted children who would once have been regarded as the most desirable clients. However, as Nathan Glazer has pointed out in a recent essay (Glazer, 1974), school teaching, along with many other traditional middle-level service careers, has been discredited for many students at colleges like Harvard by the radical critiques of the bureaucratic service professions on the ground that they support the status quo. School teaching, social work, juvenile court work, etc. are regarded as at best ineffectual, at worst constraining both for clients and professionals. Social science research has indicated the limited ability of schools to reduce inequality, as earlier it had indicated the limited ability of prisons to reduced recidivism. In a characteristic all-or-none syndrome, many students have concluded that if, let us say, school teaching does not produce instant benefits for the deprived, but only modest benefits for a few of them, and if it imposes bureaucratic constraints on its practitioners, then it loses its legitimacy as a career.

Thus the overwhelming drive into law and medicine reflects, in part, a rejection of other competing careers which were once seen as ways to help those in need. To be sure, many students point out that law and medicine are lucrative careers (this is true of law only at the top of the profession), and they insist there is a deep cynicism among many extremely career-minded students who may pay lip service to fashions in idealism, but who have concluded that, since all careers are corrupt, they might as well be fiercely competitive about grades and strike it rich. Indeed, in the last two or three years, the turn toward such careers has been greatly intensified by the recession, by the near-disappearance of jobs in teaching and the belief (often, in fact, overgeneralized vis-à-vis particular fields or the particular placement power of Harvard) that there are only a few careers, of which medicine and law are the chief ones, which offer above all a nonbureaucratic work setting, a competency or better in terms of livelihood, and a chance to exercise a skill.

At the same time, it is the very opening of meritocratic competition to so many more contestants that has helped spoil the contest for some young people of upper-middle-class origins. To compete to retain their inherited advantage would seem somehow unfair and would require a change in personal style. It is precisely that change which many Harvard freshmen coming from prep schools said they were prepared to make a dozen years earlier.[9] Success, viewed ambivalently by the sensitive for decades, has now become for many an even more questionable aim. It may be safer as well as more authentic not to try for it. Antielitist rhetoric disguises the extent to which the belief in the failure of success can be traced to an earlier ideal of aristocratic insouciance. But in the American democracy, aristocratic values can become readily democratized.

When in the spring term of 1970 Dean Ernest May of Harvard College invited the Houses to submit ideas for curricular reform, eager groups of student educational reformers talked about their hopes for more affectively oriented education, for encounter groups for credit, for social action groups for credit—for what sounded to me like a combination of the Antioch network[10] and perhaps Goddard and New College in Sarasota. One College-wide committee met all through the summer of 1970. Among both students and faculty, the idea of any hierarchy between students and faculty or within faculty came under attack; so did the idea of a degree, or of any credential.[11] However, as indicated in the preceding section, there has been considerably less talk of educational reform among students since that time. A good many students concluded that the endless participatory process got nowhere. President Bok, however, would like to revive the argument, and as already mentioned has appointed an Associate Dean of the Faculty of Arts and Sciences for Undergraduate Education (Professor Robert Kiely of the English Department) with a mandate to encourage educational reform.

Attrition at Harvard seems not to have risen appreciably despite the fact that dissatisfaction has become more vocal and intense. If one suggests either to applicants or to already matriculated students that, given their values and interests, they might be happier at Antioch or at Evergreen State College or any number of other alternatives, one hardly ever finds that they are dissuaded either from seeking to enter or from staying at Harvard. In a way, this is understandable, for they can make not entirely unsatisfactory careers out of being miserable at Harvard. In the course of that career, they may meet a number of stimulating and engaging faculty and assorted artists, journalists, and celebrities—for the Harvard trade routes are more widely traveled than those of any

[9] I refer here to the study by Robert McCarley briefly reported in Ricks and McCarley (1965) as well as longitudinal studies of Harvard undergraduates by Ricks at the Psychological Clinic directed by Henry A. Murray.

[10] See Grant (1973).

[11] See Riesman (1971).

other comparable university. The Kennedy Institute, the Center for International Affairs, the West European Studies Center—all of these bring both visiting luminaries and year-long visitors, a number of whom give noncredit courses open to undergraduates. Depending on a Master's energies and contacts, the Houses may also play host to visitors, and the student papers and official Harvard *Gazette* illustrate a musical, artistic, and intellectual bill of fare of remarkable range.[12] In some ways, the sense of glamour that surrounds the visitors to Harvard is a prop for the panache with which many students leave Harvard.[13] I might add that one reason New Haven is not Cambridge is that unhappy students at Harvard can take refuge in a considerable number of more or less communal groups of students and nonstudents in the Boston area whose support may somewhat compensate for abandoned academic hopes. Likewise, the minority of political radicals also have support in the area, and have been able to claim that they wanted the leverage and visibility of Harvard in order to make America over.

As I have argued, the political and cultural radicals, though they have not made Harvard over, have had a considerable impact on student attitudes. But there are still old-fashioned go-getters to be found, now perhaps drawn to Harvard by the wide net of recruiting and the continuing insistence of the Admissions Committee that Harvard should not become exclusively the prerogative of the (often disenchanted) suburbanite. The introduction of Radcliffe students into the Houses has altered their climate, moderating what were once stag-hearty and stag-precious enclaves.[14] Reflecting the egalitarian trend, there is a strong movement among undergraduates for sex-blind admission to Harvard;

[12]Commenting on this smorgasbord, Gerald Grant has written me: "At what other college in America would a student have as much entrée as a Harvard undergraduate? Yale would be second, I suppose, but New Haven is certainly not Cambridge. This extracurriculum may be the most important confidence-booster of all." Gerald Grant seems to me right in stressing the multitudinous cultural, academic, and intellectual flow through Harvard University. But it should be added that colleges and universities in more isolated areas often make extraordinary efforts to bring distinguished visitors to the campus in some kind of coherent sequence and to keep them there for more than a hit-and-run affair. Students at such colleges, because not surfeited with competing opportunities, may often make better use of intensive contact with visitors than many Harvard students do, who may be like the people in Queens or Brooklyn who never visit Manhattan!

[13]This panache, however, as I have noted earlier, is the property of a relatively small number of students who have easy access to faculty with similar panache or to celebrities invited by faculty. The self-confidence of the undergraduates and of the adults is mutually reinforcing. But there is another, quite converse process that also occurs: less self-assured students are frightened away from distinguished faculty and visitors and feel more comfortable in the company of some junior faculty and teaching fellows who are equally put off by the worldly assurance and preoccupied air of the elect. These less fluent and articulate groups then mutually reinforce attitudes of resentment and malaise.

[14]For a report of a somewhat earlier day, see Vreeland (1972, pp. 65–68).

in the light of this, faculty and alumni have accepted President Bok's decision to move quickly to a slightly reduced number of men and a larger number of women so that the ratio will become two and a half to one rather than four to one.[15]

To the outside observer, student life in Harvard College today seems in and out of the curriculum more relaxed and less outwardly competitive than hitherto. (Premeds are again, as they were in the Harvard of my own undergraduate days, a notable exception; however, unlike the earlier era, today's premeds along with others seeking to enter the handful of top-flight law schools spread competitive anxiety throughout the student body which, at least for some first-year students, can approach the level of panic.)[16] But as the obvious outward pressures have

[15]Omnipresent among egalitarian-minded students is the assumption that sex-blind admission would lead to a 50-50 sex ratio. If the applicant pools to Harvard and Radcliffe were equally inclusive and if one admitted students on the basis of verbal SAT scores, it is possible that women would greatly outnumber men. However, many middle-income families are much more ready to make sacrifices to send a son than a daughter to an expensive private college; Radcliffe students have come from a far more affluent population than do Harvard ones. Compensatory scholarships as well as greatly stepped up recruiting would be necessary to overcome this disparity, and even then would have to face the reluctance of women to go quite as far away to college as their male siblings do, once one gets outside the still relatively small circle of the liberated. Cf. for further discussion, Jencks and Riesman (1968, Table V, pp. 103, 293–295). College women seem not to have quite the lucrative summer and part-time job opportunities available to their male counterparts. Dean Whitla, Director of the Office of Instructional Research and Evaluation at Harvard, has reported that male applicants to Harvard come with more impressive extracurricular credentials than do women applicants: the men are more likely to have published though less likely to have written poetry, to have been class president, to have done a scientific experiment, etc.

[16]Since the foregoing was written, it has become evident that premed competitive pressure has intensified. Stories circulate about sabotage of fellow students' chemistry experiments, not to speak of the continuing problems of plagarism, the buying of term papers, and other desperate measures taken to improve grades. A vicious circle would seem to be operating here that says something about Harvard in particular as well as about the premed competition in general. The fact is that most Harvard premeds would be successful if they continued to want to attend medical school and that, apart from the steadily decreasing minimum of tough science courses they must take, they are quite free to pursue a variety of interests in and out of the curriculum. But to act with such sanguinity, even if one has a justified confidence, would itself seem elitist vis-à-vis one's more anxious fellow students. Thus, one pretends to greater panic than one actually is at first inclined to share, almost as a sign of fellowship. And if the most brilliant students seem panicky, then the less obviously talented become still more frightened, while if the former act sufficiently frightened for a long enough time, they will eventually persuade themselves that they really *are* frightened, especially if under family pressure and personal ambition they regard only half a dozen medical schools as worth consideration rather than the larger range of excellent schools the premed advisers are familiar with. Even today, the Harvard platform is a good boost for the medical or any other post-baccalaureate profession, but to treat it as such would itself be thought of by many students as elitism, so this too leads them to act as if they were unsponsored young people at an unknown state college.

been moderated, the inner anxieties have not stilled. Students ask themselves whether they are fully human. Are they experiencing life as they believe they should? Are they capable of love? Can they cope well enough with peers, and have they sufficiently cut their ties with parents and other supervising adults?[17] Students in my own undergraduate days were often—and in my opinion tiresomely—scornful of religion; today many search for a personal religion, and for those who do not, there is a growing tolerance and sometimes enough curiosity to attend a folk mass or other post-Conciliar ceremony with a Catholic friend. However, the muscular Christian of an earlier day has almost disappeared, and the religious quest is in avowed intention generally anticompetitive, anti-institutional, and antimeritocratic.[18]

[17]Antagonism toward parents, passionately felt by many students in the late 1960s and accepted as proper form by others, seems to me to have moderated a good deal in the last few years, and I have some support for this impression from unscientific surveys done for undergraduate social science courses. Among many parents there is an effort to accept, even to anticipate, the values of prevailing youth cultures, while among students there is often considerable compassion vis-à-vis adults, including parents, that at times spills over into condescension. The confusions among liberal faculty in the late 1960s are considered reflectively in Nathan Glazer's 1969 essay, "Remembering the Answers" (Chapter 13).

[18]The groups of Latter Day Saints (Mormons) in and around Harvard and other Boston-area universities constitute a dramatic exception, combining great warmth and solidarity within the group with apparently unimpaired belief in the traditional virtues of strenuous individualism.

5. *Altered Faculty Climates*

A reader of Lipset's companion essay could, I believe, reasonably infer that riots and disturbances have been cyclical events at Harvard College over the centuries; correspondingly, though the pressures and protests faced by Nathan Pusey differed in rhetoric and scale from those faced by President Josiah Quincy, both were episodes in a long historical continuity. This may be so: we cannot interview the dead, and no doubt they appear more invulnerable to us than they did to themselves. But what I think is easily forgotten or even suppressed is the climate of genuine physical fear and moral anxiety experienced by many faculty members at Harvard and at other troubled campuses in the late 1960s, the legacy of which is still with us. Very few Americans, perhaps especially male Americans, like to admit being sissies or physical cowards. (I am one myself, and when I was younger I used to take a number of counterphobic risks to "prove" otherwise.) If we were less afraid of seeming to be afraid, I believe our judgments would be more acute, for we would not have to rationalize our actions on ideological grounds when these actions have been based on grounds of, at one pole, fear of physical damage and, at another pole, fear of ostracism and rejection by faculty and student constituencies. This constellation is all the more powerful when the position which has powers of physical intimidation and personal ostracism also garbs itself in highly moralistic dress.

An illustration can be drawn from the debate, reported by Lipset, over the Rosovsky Report on Afro-American Studies, where the report's recommendations were overturned at a faculty meeting (see pp. 222–224). Martin Kilson later contended that white faculty surrendered to militant black demands out of fear, and some liberal whites responded that this was not the case: they changed their minds because of high principle, believing that black students had a special claim to inclusion on a committee to choose faculty for the new department because whites would not be competent in this area. I was away from Harvard that academic year, 1968–69, so cannot assess from personal observation the justice of Kilson's charge or the accuracy of those who responded to it. But my sense of similar events at Harvard and elsewhere leads me to believe that, in general, Kilson's assessment is probably correct.[1]

At Berkeley, Stanford, Harvard, Princeton, Columbia, and other leading universities, some of those who were most apprehensive concerning New Left–oriented student and faculty militancy were European refugees who had fled from social upheavals in which student activists had often taken a leading part. At evangelical mass meetings, where speeches were made against the Vietnam War, against racism, against what could be defined as university complicity, these sometimes twice-burned refugees listened to the music rather than to the frequently idealistic words—and the music was indeed often ominous.[2] Refugees had a certain advantage in one respect: they were outside the network of guilt and self-accusation vis-à-vis American racial struggles; thus they neither felt the need to prove themselves not to be racists nor were most of them vulnerable to the demand that they provide compensatory justice for their own or their ancestors' previous crimes and neglect.

What I have referred to as the smell of fear or at any rate of anxiety seems to have left the Harvard milieu now, but its legacies remain in the cautious and often self-censoring way in which faculty members and students discuss such topics as Women's Liberation, genetics, race relations, etc., where it is sometimes hard in the prevailing discourse to distinguish between one's own guilt, fear of offending, and civilized tact. These taboos have been much moderated in the last several years, and one could even say—a point I shall return to—that a certain faculty backlash has occurred from conservatives, either silent earlier or whose voices were drowned out. Nevertheless, Harvard is one of the few major selective universities where vestiges of radical activism

---

[1]Not so much the climate of fear as the climate of confusion on a troubled campus is described by Searle in his sardonic book *The Campus War: A Sympathetic Look at a University of Agony* (1971), delineating a typology of faculty reactions toward and contributions supporting the activist student movements at Berkeley. Compare, however, the very different, more sanguine picture of Berkeley that may be gleaned from Neil Smelser's article (1973).

[2]For an unsentimental retrospective account by a distinguished emigré, see Ulam (1972). What is said in the text about the emigrés has of course to be qualified by many exceptions who, like Herbert Marcuse for a time, became heroes of the New Left, or like Arno Mayer at Princeton, who was one of the leading spirits in the attacks on the Institute for Defense Analysis.

remain, even though some of the former activists have gone off campus into the arduous work of organizing and propagandizing in factories.

The attempted strikes conducted in 1972 and 1973 by the Graduate Student and Teaching Fellows Union made visible an often deep-seated bitterness among graduate students, some of whom had of course been among the activists as undergraduates in the late 1960s. The Cambridge-Boston area, with its many colleges and universities, high-technology corporations, and access to sea and ski resorts, has been a magnet somewhat comparable to the Bay Area in California. Harvard itself offers to some of its graduate students the unusual advantage of a resident tutorship in a House, and considerably more chance to be on their own in teaching than would be the case at Princeton, Yale, Stanford, and Chicago. But such attractions are a mixed blessing when they are unevenly distributed among a cadre which would like to create peer solidarity and when they are also felt to be generally but not invariably transitory. As already made clear, the chance for Teaching Fellows and Assistant Professors at Harvard to remain and be promoted to tenure is limited, at least outside the sciences and mathematics, where one can make one's mark while still under 35.[3] The Teaching Fellows and junior

[3]In my own Department, a brilliant computer expert was promoted from within to tenure within the last few years; in 1967, Professor Ezra Vogel, Director of the East Asian Research Center, gained tenure from within Harvard. In American History, Bernard Bailyn was the last such appointment, in 1958. However, the Government Department, with a very large enrollment of undergraduates and a notable magnet for able graduate students and junior faculty, enjoys a far larger number of tenure positions than Sociology and has perhaps a larger measure of self-confidence in bringing forward its own. Overall, more members of Harvard's tenured faculty have been promoted from within than brought from without, and as will be seen from the following table; many of the latter had been junior faculty at Harvard and/or have had some Harvard connection earlier:

Faculty of Arts and Sciences (tenured faculty as of March 13, 1974)

Natural progression to full professor with no break in service	201 (nontenure = 5)
Held prior teaching appointment but resigned and returned (break in service)	64
Came to University for first time (held no Harvard degree)	85 (nontenure = 2)
Came to University for the first time (holds Harvard degree but no previous appointment)	17

As already indicated, there are large variations among departments when it comes to promotion from within, and, of course, in terms of the proportion who do get such promotion as against those who are denied it. Furthermore, the tight job market in many academic fields, especially for white males, means not only many fewer vacancies at Harvard itself but far less attractive opportunities for those who must leave Harvard.

faculty are sometimes in the position of double agents, asked to support the academic position of senior faculty while they may identify more with talented and troubled undergraduates.

There are of course divisions among senior faculty too. For example, the Masters of the Houses, and sometimes senior faculty deeply involved in the Houses as well, have at times seen themselves at least as much as spokesmen *for* undergraduates as spokesmen *to* them. Thus, Winthrop House was for a time a major center of concern with experimental education and harbored a short-lived experimental college; its Master (whose retirement has just been announced) supported efforts at educational reform and was one of the main sponsors of House-based General Education courses. Tocsin had a major base in Quincy House, my own House at the time and that of Stuart Hughes (and Henry Kissinger also); currently, with women the leaders in some of the remaining activist efforts, several of the Radcliffe Houses have been the locales of dissenting activity. Black separatism centered for a time in Leverett House. These divergences remain despite the effort to include in each House a microcosm of the College.[4]

A minority of faculty including even several Masters finds the prevailing cultural styles in the Houses off-putting. They see themselves as too square and hence unwelcome; and since many House Senior Common Rooms are no longer sanctuaries for faculty, with such special privileges of place or position everywhere under attack, they take refuge at the Faculty Club (or the Boston dining clubs to which a few belong) or withdraw to the company of their graduate students or postdoctoral fellows.

Needless to say, genuine problems do exist for older faculty like

---

[4]Lowell House still manages to maintain its High Table every month or so, although dinner jackets are no longer *de rigueur*, whereas the dais in Quincy House, the stage in the past for similar gatherings, was preempted several years ago by the then separatist black students in that House. Dudley House, which offers nonresidential affiliation and some amenities for students living off-campus and in several student-run co-op dwellings, contributed the largest relative number of students to those arrested in the occupation of University Hall in April 1969. I have already mentioned research by Rebecca Vreeland and Charles Bidwell indicating the crucial role of the Master in setting the style of the House, provided that his own style is not too incongruent with that acceptable to other faculty and to undergraduates. See Vreeland and Bidwell (1965). In the article on the Houses by Jencks and myself already referred to, we attempt to explain why differences persist among the Houses despite quotas which prevent the establishment of Houses homogenously composed of academic stars, athletic stars, socialites, etc. See Jencks and Riesman (1962, pp. 731–773).

myself who continue to value and to seek associations with students in the Houses. A kind of physiological democracy prevails which favors those who are young and need little sleep, have loud (usually male) voices which can be heard over the hi-fi, and who have few other demands on them to complicate their agenda. The insistence on spontaneity means that students may invite a faculty member for an occasion and then forget to show up, or the noninvited will show up; sometimes a special dinner will be laid on for a visiting fireman with a sign-up sheet, and a group of students will turn up who have not signed up, eat the dinner, and run before the visitor's remarks begin. Students themselves, of course, suffer from various sorts of rip-offs in the Houses, but their principle, if not always practice, of tolerance forbids complaint. (The unobtrusive measure of doors and gates being locked may be an indication of a slight comeback for Hobbes vis-à-vis Rousseau.) In my own observation, faculty reactions to undergraduate political and cultural styles and values frequently reflect, as I have mentioned, the age and condition of a faculty member's own children.

On such issues as the Richard Herrnstein controversy, University investment policy, or the women's movements, some senior faculty have sought to be in the vanguard of activism. Some of these men and women are in the biomedical and other sciences and were early critics of the Vietnam War as well as of evils and disasters within American society; between them and the activist students may run currents of mutual reinforcement which can at times be interrupted when some radical students or nonstudents seek to test the limits of faculty willingness to take risks.[5] Other faculty, unevenly scattered through various departments and schools, have concluded that their previous work had been sterile or even complicitous, and have assured activist

---

[5]"It matters immensely—in the *feeling-life of leaders* . . .—that the energies of protest, the conviction that the men at the top are but flunkies for the system, if not self-serving liars, are fierce at this moment. The widely held belief is that the tide of affairs cannot and should not be ridden any longer by the uncommitted man, by the person who calls out ceaselessly for regard for the rights of others without establishing himself as an authentic person capable of radical individualism. . . . Those [leaders] who are not shot down outright . . . are edged, badgered, provoked, parodied, abused into exposure; 10,000 academics and undergraduates and media heroes . . . shape a public world in which authority, leadership, an office capable of arguing for restraint, comes to know that it has somehow to establish *its* own credibility through risks and through wager, through a legend of 'guts in crisis'"(DeMott, 1972, pp. 24–29, at p. 28).

students that they, the students, were the conscience of the University and of the society.[6]

In the social sciences particularly, a number of senior faculty members were both leaders in the antiwar movement and passionate critics of the tactics of students and faculty activists insofar as these involved efforts to disrupt University activities. For example, Barrington Moore, Jr., one of the most trenchant critics of contemporary society on the Harvard faculty, was also outspoken in opposition to efforts to "restructure" the universities in general or Harvard in particular. Thus when after Cambodia, Kent State, and Jackson State in 1970, there was a successful demand that the faculty grant a kind of amnesty vis-à-vis examinations and grades, Barrington Moore was one of the group of social scientists, myself included, who resisted the claim that students were so deeply disturbed emotionally or so involved in political work that they could not possibly respond to the usual academic requirements.[7] Because by May 1970, formal classes were virtually over and the Reading Period had already begun, there was less "restructuring" at Harvard than elsewhere at this time.

Yet there were also consequences of the amnesty, which permitted students to secure a "credit" without examination, which have lingered on both in the lives of particular students and in faculty memory. Thus some students who wanted to take their examinations were under social pressure not to, and a few of these are now seeking entrance to medical or other postbaccalaureate schools with transcripts in which the spring term, 1970, is a blank, which has also been a problem for some at Harvard College vis-à-vis election to Phi Beta Kappa. Some

[6]After the occupation of University Hall in April 1969, and the subsequent police bust, faculty meetings were broadcast on the student radio station, WHRB; understandably, some faculty addressed themselves to the unseen student audience rather than to their colleagues. In 1971–72, faculty meetings returned to their earlier pattern in the smaller Faculty Room at University Hall, and there have even been epidemic problems of securing a sufficient quorum to enable the faculty—which meets as an entire body and not as a representative senate—to legislate. (The agenda for legislation and discussion proceeds through the medium of the Faculty Council, which in 1969 was created in the wake of student disruption and took the place, *inter alia*, of the appointive Committee on Educational Policy; presently it is becoming difficult to get candidates to run for the overworked Council, whose vetting of proposals can be completely disregarded in response to eloquence, whim, or prior organization at faculty meetings: it would seem that Harvard faculty members quite often behave more like members of the United States Senate than of the House of Representatives, though in numbers the Faculty of Arts and Sciences approximates the latter.)

[7]See my criticism of this position in "The Business of 'Business as Usual'" (Riesman, 1972a, pp. 6–8).

students who refused to join the half-hearted strike called by the militants felt great conflicts of guilt—paralleled by the conflicts among teaching fellows over whether to hold classes or not during the unionizing strike efforts of the last several years.

The extraordinary outpouring of campus protest after Cambodia was a kind of spasm which was not succeeded, as many activists had hoped, by a large turnout of students to work in the Congressional campaigns of Father Robert Drinan, former Vermont Governor Philip Hoff, or other antiwar candidates. A good many more moderate students, at Harvard and elsewhere, felt that they had been exploited by what had already become the fragmented factions of SDS; the euphoric "high" of some of the post-Cambodia convocations was succeeded for many by despair and mutual mistrust, and the residual feeling that academic careers had been jeopardized by fellow students —and sometimes by faculty—with hidden agendas. In part perhaps because a good many students had already left the campus, the Harvard faculty at one of its last meetings of the 1969–70 academic year turned down the "Princeton Plan" for an election recess in the fall which would have allowed students to campaign and to vote at their homes. One argument in favor of the plan had been that this would encourage the more moderate students to work within the electoral process rather than be attracted by violence and terror outside it—a genre of argument used on other occasions also—as a justification for granting student demands.[8] I argued against the Princeton Plan on educational grounds, saying that we would be misleading our students

---

[8]I was exposed to an illustration of this tactic several years later as a member of the Administrative Board of the Graduate School of Arts and Sciences, when a small number of Jewish students contended that Saturday final examinations should be abolished, rejecting the so-called "Hillel exemption" which permitted devout Jewish students to wait at Hillel House until sundown and then take the examination scheduled for a Saturday; they argued that the Sabbath was meant to be a day of rejoicing, not of anxious waiting for an examination. However, there was also the contention that it was offensive to the devout Jewish students to compel them to stay at Hillel House an entire day so that they would not have leaked to them the questions that they would have to answer after sundown. One of the main arguments made on behalf of the claim of the Jewish students was that they should win their cause because, unlike the black students, they were not seizing buildings! I should add that this issue, with its overtones of the new ethnicity, mimicry of and backlash against blacks, and some genuine devoutness, was of interest to only a tiny fraction of the student body and faculty, although it occasionally intruded on the agendas of the Administrative Boards of the College and the Graduate Schools off and on over a two-year period, and was finally resolved by the Faculty Council to permit these students, on their own honor—and Harvard does not have an honor system—to take their examinations on the subsequent Sunday.

to respond as if we believed that short bursts of electoral activity in October would be decisive in most campaigns, when what was requisite was the drudgery of work in the precinct long before the primaries, and that in fact we should try to explain to students that they needed to learn how to listen to voters before they were in a position to persuade or mobilize them. The atmosphere of that period is well captured, I think, in the comment of a colleague who chatted with me after the faculty meeting, a politically and pedagogically conservative natural scientist, who said that if students were off-campus during the electoral period in October, they would not be at Harvard to trash or burn down buildings; hence, to save Harvard from damage, I should have supported rather than resisted the plan! I do not use this episode to show that I was brave and he was cowardly, for I have already mentioned that I was frightened also on many occasions, but rather to indicate the way in which educational considerations often gave way to expediential as well as righteous concerns.

What has in fact characterized the Harvard College faculty since those more agitated days has been the recognition of the fragility of the convictions and inertias by which traditional academic requirements had been maintained. I have already mentioned the dilution of the General Education requirements which now amount to a minimal distribution requirement (although many students take more than the minimum because of the attraction of individual courses in the General Education Program). It has been possible for quite some time to graduate with honors in General Studies which means that one does not write a thesis and gets a *cum laude* degree on the basis of course grades. Some departments will allow high departmental honors to be granted on the basis of some additional course work and high grades in courses, also without a thesis. Articulate and persuasive undergraduates have for many years been able pretty much to shape their own programs by finding the right sponsorship; such opportunities have now been, as it were, democratized and are also available to the less entrepreneurial, including many with extremely spotty course grades.

Furthermore, some relaxation at the undergraduate level occurs in a kind of two-step process as a result of changes at the graduate level. The Sociology Department has no specific course requirements, although before qualifying to write a dissertation, students must write a theoretical paper on a topic such as the logic of inquiry in social science or sociological theory or history; they must also pass an oral examination in any one of a number of substantive fields.[9] The Department has a small intake; as in other areas, much depends on the quality and intensity of advising which students receive, seek out, and are willing to accept.

The belief is widely prevalent among undergraduates that senior faculty prefer to spend time with their graduate students, but if one talks with many of the latter one finds them insisting that many of Harvard's most luminous faculty prefer, if they spend any time with students, to spend it with undergraduates, who frequently have more money and style, more energy and dash, and who in a time of tight budgets need to be courted if one's department is to maintain itself and even grow. There is here, as in every area, enormous variation among departments, but many have no regular program of courses specifically designed for graduate students, let alone any program (such as the Department of Germanic Languages and Literatures possesses) for helping graduate students become less awkward undergraduate teachers, either in terms of subject matter or of pedagogy.

In all this one must distinguish not only among departments (or, more accurately, the subfields among these so that, for example, East Asian history and European history have very different microclimates), but also between those graduate students who attended Harvard College and those who did not. Many of the latter, although they generally are at Harvard for a longer time than undergraduates, are often quite isolated from the institution, unless they have a House affiliation or some experience as teaching fellows which brings them into contact with undergraduates and with other graduate students. One teaching fellow illustrated the graduate student ignorance of Harvard College by the example of a fifth-year graduate student in mathematics who had never heard of the Social Studies Program or the Committee on History and Literature, although these are the two most overapplied undergraduate concentrations.

[9]Since the foregoing was written, the Sociology Department has reinstituted a "methods" requirement so that, beginning with students entering in the fall of the academic year 1973–74, candidates "must demonstrate two out of the following: (1) knowledge of mathematics through elementary calculus, (2) knowledge of elementary statistics, (3) ability to program any one computer language." Students are strongly urged to acquire command of a foreign language such as French or German and to acquire experience in field work. The Graduate School itself requires students to take the equivalent of 16 half-courses.

Of course, many graduate students conclude that they should put all "collegiate" things behind them and get on with what they have learned to call "their own work." They would see any effort to become knowledgeable about undergraduate life, perhaps even in their own departments, as a frivolity and a distraction. A number of faculty and some influential administrators are of the same opinion, believing that Harvard University's main task is to produce outstanding research scholars in the shortest possible time. For example, a reflective administrator, Edward L. Pattullo, Director of the Behavioral Sciences Center, argued in a recent article, not that Harvard should entirely abandon undergraduate education, but that it should more effectively come to terms with its inability, in a time of declining resources, to maintain both an outstanding liberal arts college and a graduate school geared to scholarship and the training of graduate students. He proposed that Harvard College should be geared to upper-division work, especially for transfer students who can take advantage of its opportunities for scholarly advancement, while encouraging freshmen and sophomore Harvard students who have concluded that they have no such prospects to transfer elsewhere.[10] I myself would like to see a much more liberal transfer policy, and I agree with Pattullo that those who have found their footing elsewhere may do better at Harvard than those who started at Harvard as Freshmen and continue through inertia or the reluctance to surrender the Harvard guerdon. (This would mean, given Harvard's low attrition, recruiting fewer freshmen.) And it should be evident that I share Pattullo's worry, and that of many other students of American higher education, that the major research universities try to satisfy too many constituencies, thus sacrificing what they can uniquely do in the way of research and training for research, inviting bankruptcy by overcommitment.

Where I differ from Pattullo and those who share his outlook is in my conclusion that research and training for research benefit more than they suffer from association with undergraduate education. Surely, the combination creates often nearly unmanageable tensions and stringencies. And we do not understand very well the kinds of support, other than financial, that graduate students need to sustain their moral and intellectual poise when they are working on their dissertations. Yet I believe that, for some, contact with Harvard undergraduates outside as

[10]See Pattullo (1972, pp. 20–25).

well as inside their own specialties is more refreshing and sustaining than distracting. Alternate bouts of thesis and course work with experience of teaching and life in the Houses has increased the intellectual range of many graduate students and helped them in the first stages of their post-Harvard careers. A graduate student whose principal contact is with a faculty mentor to whom he serves as an apprentice may have a marvelous opportunity which may only be diluted by teaching, for example, outside his mentor's orbit. But one has also to think in terms of the life cycle of those of us who try to engage in creative intellectual or artistic work, and of periods when we run dry, stare at our typewriters or the walls of our room—or of the time when, later in life, we may decide on a second career in some related field. Senior faculty need to bear in mind how diverse are the problems of the graduate students in their departments, some of whom are already at home in the Harvard milieu while others feel perpetual strangers to it. Some graduate students undoubtedly do delay too long, allowing their teaching to legitimate postponement of the real test of their adequacy in a thesis. But if one examines an institution as unique as California Institute of Technology, which is more monolithic than Harvard, one sees the dryness and loneliness of graduate work even there. Thus I would be cautious about following a formula like Pattullo's and would prefer to see what can be done within the characteristic American amalgam of graduate and undergraduate functions—an unstable relation analogous to that between preclinical and clinical echelons in a medical school.

Since it appeared, Pattullo's article has received little discussion. But it does symbolize a growing recognition among a minority of faculty members, senior as well as junior, that the undergraduate curriculum can no longer be justified simply because it exists: the faculty ought to decide what an educated person ought to know (or perhaps, ought to be like as a fully human being); this should then become the basis of a revised and coherent curriculum. There is talk at Harvard as elsewhere of a three-year A.B. as the regular pattern, and such talk in turn gives rise to the feeling that the whole process is arbitrary: why three years? Why not five years, or two years? Why not a wholly nonresidential degree, prepared for in any way that the students choose?

In the course of such reconsiderations, the linkage between a college degree and postbaccalaureate preferment, whether in jobs or in graduate school, also comes into question. Many students and faculty members do not see why colleges should serve the credentialing function either for graduate schools or for employers; colleges should serve only their internal audience—or the society at large in their role as critic (or, in a few cases, as preparing for the revolution).[11] Studies on the subject which show the tenuous or nonexistent connection between college attendance and grades and success in later life are used to support this effort to cut higher education loose from its service as a (more or less) meritocratic screen.

Undoubtedly, there would be advantages to freeing colleges from the captive audiences that they now have, because most jobs regarded as worth having require a college degree at the very least.[12] However, the costs of such a development are less often discussed. Precisely because higher education is in some measure meritocratic rather than ascriptive both in admissions policies and in grading, it seems to me a less unjust apparatus than the occupational order itself which is more subject to ascriptive pressures of power, wealth, and patronage.[13] Those colleges which have abandoned grading and which also have minimal requirements may make life easier for the well-connected, the charming, the obviously bright graduate; but correspondingly, they may make life more difficult for the "first generation" student who is unable to offer his potential employer or graduate school anything except his A.B. as

[11]For a general review, see Carnegie Commission on Higher Education (1972), including a report on a survey of student and faculty opinions on concerns and dissatisfactions throughout academia.

[12]See Faltermayer (1970, pp. 98–103); see also Berg (1970) and Berger (1971, pp. 89–98), who observes that young people are encouraged to stay in educational institutions searching for their identities until society, having defined them as mature, may be ready to absorb them.

[13]Personal nonintellectual qualities of charm and beauty appear to be partly ascriptive, partly achieved. I recall attending an admissions conference several years ago at which admissions deans of major selective universities were declaring their antielitist rejection of SAT's and other tests in favor of more "human" measures and obviously in part in order to appeal to nonwhite applicants. A black guidance counselor in a high school rose from the floor to declare that the result of such a shift would be to make life easy for the vivacious who made a good first impression on counselors and admissions officers while penalizing those able and diligent young people who lacked such instant appeal. The guidance counselor certainly had a point, but there are also admissions officers—and employers—who are skeptical of the vivacious and charming and who are more likely to bet on the person who seems conscientious, the upwardly mobile striver whom one can feel good about helping along over the obvious barriers of deprivation. While as I have indicated in this essay, the vivacious and self-confident often make their way at Harvard in competition with the shy and self-mistrustful. I have also seen a kind of reverse discrimination against the former, comparable to the prejudice I have sometimes found against quiet, well-mannered aristocrats on the ground that they cannot possibly be truly interesting.

testimony to his competence and seriousness.[14] Furthermore, it is in the interest of the survival of higher education to fulfill more than a single function, for universities are not supported in the United States because they represent the true, the good, and the beautiful when they do not also provide particular benefits to significant constituents. Education is both a producer's and a consumer's good, and the credentialing function in some measure serves the former and acts as insurance against abuses of the latter. The only relative freedom of an institution like Harvard College depends on a judicious balancing of constituencies rather than seeking an illusory divorce from all of them.[15] Meritocracy is both a procedure for distributing scarce educational and occupational resources and one for determining how the work of society shall get accomplished in an intricate, still largely industrial world. As such, it is like democracy: as the saying goes, "the worst possible system except for all the others."

Yet not all societies which rely more or less heavily on meritocracy are alike in the resulting costs for individuals or in the time of life at which these costs are heaviest. In Japan, the nightmare comes at the point of entrance to the university; some students, the so-called Ronin, take their entrance examinations over and over again, and we are all aware of the occasional suicides of those who fail.[16] There is sometimes another bout of examinations on entering employment with one of the large companies or government bureaus. But after these ordeals the selected cohort, with whatever internal jealousies, works with considerable cooperative spirit and, though with waning unanimity, is guaranteed a lifetime position with a single employer. In contrast, the United States is a country of many more second chances. One may move from a first degree at an undistinguished college to a doctorate at a more dis-

[14]To be sure, where grades have been subordinated, evaluations and student portfolios are supposed to take their place. Where small numbers are involved, the portfolios probably can provide better evidence than grades (although grades might help just a bit in interpreting the portfolios and vice versa). Use of a portfolio implies an aristocratic version of meritocracy where people are sufficiently sponsored so that others will take the trouble to peruse the portfolios. But portfolios can sometimes be even less informative than grades; I have been told by graduate admissions officers, who may only be exaggerating slightly, about evaluations sometimes coming in from grade-free colleges which report, e.g., "Jim has learned to relate well to people," or "Jane has been working toward a new identity."

[15]Cf. the discussion of Harvard's relative freedom during the McCarthy era and later in Bundy (1970); see also Ford in the same issue of *Daedalus* (1970, pp. 661–675).

[16]Cf. Vogel (1973, Ch. 3).

tinguished university and then in some cases to a postdoctoral fellowship under a Nobel Laureate. There are opportunities to change careers in postgraduate years and later. There is an altogether looser fit than in Japan (or in most European countries) between one's first degree and one's chances in life. But the converse of this recurring opportunity to "make it" is the recurring opportunity for one's career to go sour.[17] Harvard can do little to protect its classicists against a new vogue for African or East Asian studies; it cannot protect scholars in the latter areas against what I see as the growing "domestication" of American academic and intellectual life; it can go only a little way to protect old-fashioned natural history zoologists against the new vogue for molecular biology and its fissioning components. Similarly, those social and behavioral sciences that deal with the self are now experiencing a boom

[17]I am indebted to Everett Hughes for a better understanding of careers gone sour and of careers in general. In *The Hidden Injuries of Class*, Richard Sennett and Jonathan Cobb discuss the special wounds American society inflicts on individuals precisely because of the opportunities it opens to them: they must repeatedly face conflicts between competitiveness and collegiality and self-reproach both for failure and for success. While the book deals principally with the white working class, the themes it raises have wider application (Sennett & Cobb, 1972, Parts I & II).

What is said in the text about America as a second-chance country was true in many fields for the period of expansion after World War II. But the plateau of the 1970s in college and secondary school enrollment, not to speak of the prospects for serious recession (even with continuing inflation), are likely to limit opportunities for mobility or make these appear too risky. The growing tendency of faculty to unionize, which has concerned both Lipset and me, is evidence of a belief that one must depend on one's collective cadre rather than on individual talent and energy for graded advancement. See in this connection the argument made for instant tenure as a support for internal faculty cohesiveness and morale in Livingston's "Tenure Everyone?" (1972). The author of the article makes a good case, but I think takes insufficient account of another kind of demoralization that can ensue when, because all tenure slots are filled, stimulating potential colleagues must be turned away while one lives out one's life with the luck of an earlier draw; unless all institutions should adopt in Japanese style instant tenure and lifelong employment, able faculty in search of some stimulation may leave such settings and seek out more stressful but also more challenging ones. But a more important question concerns students rather than colleagues: whether an institution does not owe students the very best that it can muster even at a certain cost in intramural tension based on a testing and selecting process. No doubt the balance of costs and benefits will vary among institutions, bearing in mind that most institutions, educational and otherwise, provide de facto tenure because it is agonizing to fire people with whom one is working and easier all around to keep them on, the more so when one does not have to meet the test of the market, at least as long as the costs of instruction remain as heavily subsidized by public and private funding as they presently are—or were until the current great depression.

that may make later deflation all the more jarring. We have noted earlier that senior Harvard faculty do not necessarily feel secure because of where they are if they cannot perennially justify being there.

A number of young faculty members and graduate students at Harvard as elsewhere have turned against what they consider the game playing and craze for success of research-oriented academic departments. Often they declare that they want to spend themselves in working with undergraduates in a close and nonhierarchical relationship. Frequently they have assumed that, by rejecting the research-oriented model of scholarship, one automatically becomes capable of joining students in a living-learning community. When this turns out to be more complicated, some of these teachers become quickly disillusioned. They may have taken too much at face value what articulate students say about the kind of teaching they want, and not appreciated fully the diversity of motives and tastes, even within these students, let alone within a larger student body. For example, not all students want intimate student-teacher relations, even though they may say so; they may feel crowded by such a relation, and be unaware of their preference for diluting it through greater impersonality. Furthermore, those who reject what they call the rat race of academic gamesmanship may not appreciate how competitive a group of teachers can be when there are no boundaries or requirements to protect the potential student constituencies of any one of them. Indeed, if one of the problems of assessing research competitively is that there is pressure for speedy and sometimes for voluminous publication, as against a longer lead time and a greater succinctness, the lead time for assessing teaching may be even faster, as fashions change among student audiences and as these are manipulated by faculty and student politicians. It may be even riskier for a faculty member to venture on an innovative course that students may not find entertaining than for him or her to stake out a line of research that may come to nothing, for in the former case one cannot even publish one's negative results.

One sees at Harvard as at other institutions some faculty members who seem to have exhausted their intellectual inheritance at the behest of students who are concerned with the "income" they will receive now, and not with the faculty member's long-term interest in his or her own development. There is a certain measure of exhaustion among that minority of faculty who concern themselves intensively with undergraduates and with College affairs. Many, perhaps most, of the curricular reforms discussed in this article are expensive in terms of faculty time and energy.[18]

So-called Independent Study, if taken seriously by both faculty and students, requires a great deal of faculty guidance. In an earlier era when a freshman arrived at Harvard, the proctor in the Yard who might serve also as his adviser could see to it that he got started on his General Education requirements, took his place in English A, perhaps added a math or language course, and possibly also had room for an elective as a way to begin exploring possible fields of concentration. Once embarked on such a field, as a sophomore, the field was again fairly well marked out, perhaps dividing between honors and nonhonors programs along sequential steps. With many individual exceptions, students headed for Law School would major in Government or Economics; premeds might head for Biochemical Sciences; future museum curators to the Department of Fine Arts. Even then, venturesome students discovered that Harvard was sufficiently aristocratic to bend its rules in the service of talented students who were not to be bound by the ordinary routines. But on the whole, one could count on fairly predictable course enrollments and the assignments of graders, teaching fellows, and classroom space accordingly. Today in the natural sciences and in fields like economics which follow the natural science model, this kind of channeling remains, although there are many more variations. In other fields there can be enormous fluctuations; and because there are so many choices, the demand for advice is far more intense, and the advice if it is to be helpful must be informed far beyond the earlier simple norms. Just as the Senior Tutors of the Houses encounter an almost intolerable burden of personal, academic, and career advising, so the Head Tutors of the various departments who must approve undergraduate programs of concentration face comparable demands on their time, ingenuity, and responsiveness. Moreover, Harvard undergraduates, like others of their class and generation, are often fantastically

[18]Contrary to prevailing legends, most faculty members even in distinguished, research-oriented universities like to teach and do not necessarily want to teach only advanced students. This does not mean that such faculty members are eager for heavy undergraduate teaching loads, but only that they are prepared to do a certain amount of teaching both of undergraduates and of graduate students. See Parsons, Platt, and Smelser (1973) and Parsons and Platt (1972). Critics of this survey may state that faculty members believe that they should teach and therefore say they want to, but there are also settings where research has greater prestige than teaching, and even in these, teaching would seem to be valued, though only in modest amounts; what is not valued at all, at least in what people report, is administrative and committee service.

skilled as "Philadelphia lawyers," having learned how to play parents off against each other; they deploy sharp energies in testing the limits of bureaucratic constraint. Since in the current ethos everything must be done consensually, and generally in the open, department and faculty meetings occur even in politically relatively quiet times with a frequency more characteristic of a commune than of the impersonal mechanism that Harvard is sometimes supposed to be.[19]

I am not suggesting that all these added involvements are simply waste motion and emotion from the point of view of the faculty. In apportioning faculty time as between classroom teaching and advising, I would myself think advising even more important if it can be properly individuated and if it can serve to help students explore areas of which they have been frightened, as well as to pursue areas in which they already feel competent. And plainly, advising is a two-way affair, in which faculty learn what the impact of the curriculum is in a way that even the more alert cannot learn in most regular classroom settings. At the same time, the abandonment of lectures by many faculty on the ground that these are undemocratic has in practice often meant that people who are good at lectures run seminars or tutorials which either turn into unprepared minilectures, or allow a few assertive students to dominate what passes for discussion. I believe that students ought to learn to learn in settings which, for ideological or other reasons, they regard as less than optimal. And while it seems unlikely that most of us can give 90 good lectures a year, some of us can perhaps give 10 to 15, in which we are presenting material newly thought about. It is even possible with as many as 300 persons to combine lectures with discussion if one can find the proper shape and quality of hall and create the right atmosphere. (The Graduate School of Business Administration does have just such a lecture-discussion room in Aldrich Hall.)

As the Second World War drew to a close, it was possible at Harvard to bring together faculty members concerned about the Western heritage, about democracy and freedom, about the place of science, and to develop a philosophy of General Education grounded in these concerns. The war and its aftermath, including the flood of students, had helped

---

[19]Let me again stress the very great differences among departments in the degree and quality of student involvements. Students in the Department of Chemistry, for example, have conducted meticulous course evaluations which have influenced curricula. Graduate students in the Departments of Sociology, Anthropology, and Biochemistry and Molecular Biology have been among the most active in organizing the Graduate Student and Teaching Fellows' Union, while in other departments the Union has little if any support.

make these perennial issues more salient. In retrospect, the focus on these issues seems at once nostalgically admirable and at the same time cognitively restricted, territorially provincial, and naïvely sanguine. We still are faced with these same concerns, but they look quite different now, enormously more intricate and also more partial. The departments and the interdepartmental committees have preempted some of them for their own terrain, and the student is nearly as likely to find a course dealing with large questions of personal concern to him in one of the departments as in General Education. There is no longer a clear division of labor for General Education.

Correspondingly, the task of teaching has grown more difficult when the aim is not confined to the imparting of information or techniques. It seems to me important to strive for dispassionateness even while recognizing that it is an unattainable ideal—and of course for many the very opposite of an ideal.[20] In my own teaching I do very much hope students will become more curious about society and about the various methods scholars have employed toward understanding society. In some cases I find their curiosity inhibited by a sense of personal inadequacy: the student in effect is saying, "Who am I to make a judgment apart from what authorities, including my peers, say either about what American society has been and is becoming, or about how to investigate this?" In other instances, narcissism interferes with curiosity: sometimes even the entering student, politically and culturally doctrinaire, believes he already knows the answers to these questions, and that further exploration is boring, irrelevant, or even counterrevolutionary. Like Thorstein Veblen, I value "idle" curiosity, apart from prevailing pieties. But unlike the situation in Veblen's day, there is no need at Harvard College presently to be iconoclastic in his mode, but rather, if anything, to combat the prevailing iconoclasm with its unhappy but nevertheless anxiety-reducing simplifications. Furthermore, I would hope students might stretch themselves beyond the range of skills with which they come to college, whether this means immersing themselves in history or in understanding demography, or in learning how to express themselves on paper as well as orally or on film. Within sociology proper, I am a pluralist, and would like to see colleagues and students literate in, and if possible equipped for, a wide va-

---

[20]See Hughes (1969, pp. 35–38); see also Ulam (1969, pp. 29–34). For a penetrating discussion which takes a wholly relativistic position, in which the claim of truth is itself a lie, see Davis (1972, pp. 6–15).

riety of methods , none of which in our present state of knowledge deserves a monopoly.[21]

There are endless traps in the kind of teaching I seek to do. Demonstrations of candor and openness may be all too seductive for some students, who will take a professor's pronouncements too literally and solemnly, which for an influential teacher can become quite frightening as he realizes his own, one would hope, temporary power. Other students may fear that a professor has a hidden agenda, even though he claims to be genuinely interested in their development, quite apart from political or professional outcomes. Such suspicions may not be entirely misplaced. One of the reasons why I insist on discussion following a lecture is that I regularly uncover misconceptions of what I have said, or realize that what I have said is only half or less of what I have meant, and I discover also that I have misjudged the context of student concerns as these change from year to year. In fact, I am struggling with these pedagogic issues while simultaneously wrestling with intricate substantive problems, for my concern is never only with process or only substance; and there is always the danger in a General Education course for nonconcentrators that students in Harvard will become adept at subsumesmanship, so that at times I almost wish to find some student pedants, products of a catechismal training.[22]

As these dilemmas of the undergraduate teaching enterprise have become more manifest, and as there has been increased emphasis on teaching, there has not been any comparable effort to help either graduate students or faculty to become more capable and more responsible teachers. As I have mentioned earlier, graduate students are often

[21]These are themes to which I have kept returning in what I have written. See, e.g., "Values in Context" (1952, vol. 22, pp. 29–39); cf. also the discussion of "countercyclical policy" in *Constraint and Variety in American Education* (1958, pp. 83–131); see also Riesman and Watson (1964). See also Mills' admirable appendix "On Intellectual Craftsmanship" (1959).

[22]I have generally found a sex difference along this axis, with men much more willing to generalize on scant information than women—and a general Harvard bias that judges the women as merely docile as a result.

The more aware faculty members become of the multiple constituencies they face, of which sex differences are minor in comparison with many others, and the more aware they also are of the multiple aims they have to consider in their teaching, the more demanding their teaching becomes. Correspondingly, it seems to me important to oppose the current efforts, by legislation in some states and by other sorts of mandates elsewhere, to specify the number of hours professors should spend in the classroom, and to increase those hours in a merely quantitative way—with the end result often of diluting the quality of teaching and evoking resentfully routine performances.

chosen as teaching fellows, not because they are likely to be good at it, but because they need the money (some of the best prospective teachers who have research fellowships may be actively discouraged from teaching) or for other reasons that have little to do with their pedagogic promise. At the point when junior faculty are first recruited, some inquiry as to teaching ability is generally made, but it is seldom more than hearsay—although some departments wisely invite prospective faculty to come and give a lecture or hold a seminar in order to have some, not always ideal, setting in which to evaluate ability as a teacher. However, once someone is on the faculty, there is no determined effort either to assess or to improve the quality of pedagogic performance.[23]

As most faculty members recognize, excellence in teaching is more difficult to submit to a metrical meritocratic scale than excellence in research. Harvard College has not yet called together an ad hoc committee of insiders and outsiders to assess the teaching of a faculty member. The privacy of the classroom, regarded as a component of academic freedom, has protected neophytes from inspection by their colleagues, making teaching—quite unlike scholarly publication—a subject for only private anxieties, self-deceptions, and accomplishments. At the Harvard Law School and at the Harvard Graduate School of Business Administration, in both of which enormous attention is given to teaching, the classes of junior faculty are visited by senior faculty; syllabi and reading lists are scrutinized; attention to a teacher's ability to hold the student audience is coupled with recognition that some teachers may be useful whose appeal is more esoteric. Contrary to what

[23]One of the by-products of the Freshman Seminar Program has been to allow faculty to experiment with new course materials and new modes of presenting these in a less threatening setting than would be possible in a typical departmental course which is required to bear a certain amount of the load or preparing students for further work in the field; in addition, while the faculty member who offers a new departmental course may be under pressure from his colleagues to continue to give it in subsequent years, a volunteer offering a Freshman Seminar (or a junior tutorial to a group of students, such as has sprung up in the Social Relations and Sociology Departments and in other fields at the upper division level) is under no such constraint. Thus the Freshman Seminar Program may have encouraged the improvement of undergraduate teaching, although that was not one of its stated aims.

In the summer of 1973, the School of Education at the University of Massachusetts at Amherst ran a summer Clinic to Improve University Teaching, open to all faculty members of the University and outsiders also, in which faculty participants had the chance to videotape their lectures and to get criticism of their performance from members of the clinic staff and others (including visitors like myself). Some of the methods used resemble those employed by the Bureau of Study Counsel at Harvard, the services of which are known to and made use of by only a tiny fraction of Teaching Fellows, let alone faculty.

is generally believed, promotion to tenure at Harvard in Arts and Sciences does not ignore teaching; Harvard may be prepared to subsidize an absolutely outstanding person whether or not he or she is even audible, but in most cases within my own observation, teaching is weighed along with other factors in deciding among candidates who are not clearly geniuses. Unfortunately, this is generally done on hearsay evidence of a pretty fragmentary sort.[24]

Even though faculty members at Harvard now live in a moral climate which deprives many of them of older certainties of position, it seems to me unlikely that the current efforts to weigh teaching far more heavily in the assessment of faculty will make a great deal of difference in the quality of undergraduate life. The danger will still remain that the all too devoted undergraduate teacher will burn himself out unless by an enforced and liberal leave policy he can maintain his standing in his discipline as passport and insurance as well as for its bearing on the long-run quality of his teaching. Harvard should be aristocratic and snobbish enough to make occasional room for the gifted scholar-teacher

---

[24]The hearsay is, in my limited observation, reasonably reliable for the extraordinary teacher, for the obvious charlatan, and for the hopelessly unintelligible and intellectually incompetent; it is in the very large middle range that hearsay seems most unsatisfactory.

If throughout American academia, assessments of teaching became public, then faculty members who devoted themselves particularly to teaching might not thereby become captives of their own institutions through loss of visibility and lack of recognition. (There is an exception for the pedagogic experimenter who writes up his experiences as a teacher for an educational journal, thus creating a new professional peer group.) I have in mind here not only the characteristic recognition by scholarly colleagues in one's academic field but also recognition gained through artistic performances or consulting, or political activity or any other form of engagement with an adult extramural constituency. Colleges seeking "good teachers" would have a slightly more assured way of looking for them. But as already indicated, a meritocracy based on effectiveness as a teacher will be no less and perhaps more stressful than one based on effectiveness as a researcher. So far as I can judge, studies which attempt to assess the correlation, if any, between effectiveness as a teacher and as a researcher have been inconclusive; several have shown, however, that those who are judged good teachers by their students are also those who are "productive" as researchers. But other studies have shown no correlation; none, to my knowledge, has shown a negative correlation, i.e., that good researchers are bad teachers. I do not know of any studies which discriminate among different disciplines or even among levels of institutions.

Of course, in the country as a whole, the vast majority of faculty never do any research and have no intention of ever doing any. Indeed, in most American liberal arts colleges, even very good ones, most faculty in most fields publish nothing (biologists are an interesting exception), even when the institution claims to encourage scholarship and even when there are a few exceptional models around who combine the intense teaching and collegial life of a small college with a significant career in research. See Oliver Fulton and Martin Trow, "Research Activities in American Higher Education" (1972).

who publishes little or nothing but who keeps alive by scholarly work; there have always been a few such individuals around and, in the Oxford or Cambridge pattern, they have maintained collegial respect.

I have referred earlier to the advantage Harvard possesses because it has combined a liberal arts college with a major research university. In that context, I believe that Harvard can make its greatest contribution to undergraduate teaching, less by revision of the undergraduate curriculum than by more serious efforts to introduce graduate students to problems of teaching as a regular part of their training—a theme to which I have kept returning in these last pages. President Derek Bok has encouraged efforts of this sort, although they are still incipient. He has set up a fund for innovation on which Teaching Fellows can draw, for instance to develop experiments in programmed instruction; regular faculty can also draw on the fund. However, at Harvard as elsewhere, snobbery toward educationists leads to snobbery about pedagogy per se, hence the indefensible belief that it is sufficient to throw someone into a classroom because he has presumably been in a classroom as a student, and let him fend for himself. Some of the miseries of graduate students already referred to reflect their lack of an opportunity to teach; but there are also miseries among those who believe that they fail as teachers (sometimes this is a misperception), while at the same time they find themselves spending "too much" time teaching in comparison with what their mentors refer to as "their own work."

A thoughtful graduate student, Christopher Leman, has pointed out in correspondence that many Harvard senior faculty cultivate an apparent ease in both teaching and writing which makes it appear to many graduate students as if the latter can never attain a similar intellectual fluency. This image of effortlessness discourages the would-be apprentice. I know from long experience how hard it is for me to convince the graduate students who listen to my lectures (particularly when I am trying to hold a discussion where, of course, I am in large measure dependent on cooperation from the audience) that I am quite anxious and perspire profusely, because I appear to be at ease and in command; hence, what I say is put down as spurious modesty. And undoubtedly there are faculty who write and teach easily; sometimes these may be "reducers" in the typology of reactions to pain and stress worked out by Dr. Asenath Petrie (1967). Such exceptional individuals aside, graduate students tend to see themselves surrounded by more omnicompetence than exists—but, as this whole essay has indicated, students overimpress each other much in the same way that they are, in these respects, sometimes overimpressed by superorganized and supercompetent Harvard faculty. Some react with an excessive cynicism toward faculty.

In some fields, these obstacles can be partially surmounted by creating shop or apprentice settings, in which senior and junior faculty, graduate students and undergraduates, can all be working on a common task, and some of the departments with high morale such as Geology manage to accomplish this.[25]

Harvard faculty members have nominally light teaching loads in comparison with those at many good liberal arts colleges or lesser state institutions. However, because of Harvard's location, its visibility, and often the eminence of its faculty, there is a constant stream of visitors from within and outside the United States who are at once a stimulus and a distraction. And as a self-governing group, many also do a great deal of committee work and rotate the administrative burdens of departments and programs. Furthermore, as I have argued, the general faculty ethos supports attention to undergraduates, and the latter in surveys profess that the faculty are responsive and available to them—although less than they would like. (Martin Lipset's essay makes use of a survey of Harvard undergraduate attitudes in the spring of 1974 which suggests that there has been a change in this respect in the last several years, and that fewer students now believe that the faculty are available, responsive, and concerned with them. See pp. 254–255 of this volume.) Thus the Harvard faculty, like other faculties, believe themselves overworked and are not entirely mistaken. Hence it seems unlikely that they will accept new mandates such as the one proposed here of helping their graduate students become better teachers (which would also help them get better teaching jobs), since they will find it hard to cut down on their extant and exigent obligations. In a time of shrinking budgetary resources, the leverage

---

[25]Ingenuity is needed to find analogues for the apprentice or shop setting in the humanities (work in oral history might be one illustrative possibility) or in some of the more cumulative natural sciences, where the subject matter is mainly analytic and abstract; in an advanced social science such as economics, a shop setting might come about only through the sort of applied work that is deprecated among "pure" economists. In my own field, a survey research center can serve as a shop in which the neophyte has a chance along with the senior scholar to interpret data as well as to produce or code it. Anthropologists may create a shop atmosphere by their tradition of fieldwork.

In thinking about these matters we are handicapped by the fact that, although there has been an enormous amount of writing on higher education in recent years, there have been hardly any studies of the daily life of the department; and we know only in a general and anecdotal way how career lines differ among fields, with mathematicians often more like beauty queens, and historians more like sages.

the President has to reorient the faculty's span of attention in a community that prides itself on self-government would seem extremely limited.

The faith of many faculty in what we are doing has been shaken by the events of recent years and has been only relatively restored by the apparent calm of the 1970s. While there is a minority at Harvard who possess deep institutional loyalty, and whose caring and sense of responsibility are moderately contagious, there is also a good deal of cynicism, as in the country at large, and this too is contagious. The older convictions about what Harvard should be doing have unevenly lost their assurance; we live within the secular cathedrals of the higher learning in the absence of the convictions which built the cathedrals. Under these conditions, the future of Harvard, as of most major institutions of higher education today, seems to me opaque. While most of the changes discussed in this essay have been individually small scale, the change in attitude toward the legitimacy of curricular and faculty authority is not small scale. Thus it is hard to imagine Harvard going on as before. I might add that my imagination likewise stumbles when it comes to the country as a whole. Lipset's essay would lead one to suppose that everything will go on as before, with cyclical fluctuations. My own sense of things is more apocalyptic, although I recognize that an institution, like an individual, can continue to live with a lot of ruin within the system.

References to Part Two

"The Behavioral Sciences at Harvard," Faculty Committee Report, Harvard University, Cambridge, Mass., 1954.

Bell, Daniel: *The Reforming of General Education: The Columbia College Experience and Its National Setting,* Columbia University Press, New York, 1966.

Bell, Daniel: "Meritocracy and Equality," *The Public Interest,* no. 29, pp. 29–68, Fall 1972.

Bell, Daniel: "A Second Look at General Education," *Seminar Reports,* Columbia University, vol. 1, pp. 1, 4–6, Dec. 7, 1973.

Ben-David, Joseph: *American Higher Education: Directions Old and New,* McGraw-Hill Book Company, New York, 1972.

Ben-David, Joseph, and Randall Collins: "Social Factors in the Origins of a New Science: The Case of Psychology," *American Sociological Review,* vol. 31, no. 4, pp. 451–465, August 1966.

Bensman, David: "On Radicalizing Our Students," *Dissent,* vol. 19, pp. 653–654, Fall 1972.

Berg, Ivar: *Education and Jobs: The Great Training Robbery,* Frederick A. Praeger, Inc., New York, 1970.

Berger, Bennett M.: "The Identity Myth," in Bennett M. Berger, *Looking for America,* Prentice-Hall, Inc., Englewood Cliffs, N. J., 1971, pp. 87–98.

Blackmer, Allen: *Andover to Harvard: A Study of Role Transition,* undergraduate honors thesis, Harvard College, Cambridge, Mass., 1960.

Bundy, McGeorge: "Were Those the Days?" *Daedalus,* vol. 99, pp. 531–567, Summer 1970.

Cantarow, Ellen: "The Radicalizing of a Teacher of Literature," *Change,* vol. 4, pp. 50–61, May 1972.

Carnegie Commission on Higher Education: *Less Time, More Options: Education beyond the High School,* McGraw-Hill Book Company, New York, 1971.

Carnegie Commission on Higher Education: *Reform on Campus: Changing Students, Changing Academic Programs,* McGraw-Hill Book Company, New York, 1972.

Cass, James, and Max Birnbaum: *Comparative Guide to American Colleges,* 4th ed., Harper and Row, Publishers, Incorporated, New York, 1971.

Cass, James, and Max Birnbaum: *Comparative Guide to American Colleges,* 5th ed., Harper and Row, Publishers, Incorporated, New York, 1972.

Clark, Burton R.: *The Distinctive College: Antioch, Reed and Swarthmore,* Aldine Publishing Company, Chicago, 1970.

Cohen, Rob, and Michael Williams: *Experience,* a film, joint senior thesis, Harvard College, Cambridge, Mass., 1971.

Committee on Graduate Education: unpublished report, Harvard University, Cambridge, Mass., June 8, 1973.

Cottle, Thomas: "Pains of Permanence," in Bardwell L. Smith and associates, *The Tenure Debate,* Jossey-Bass Inc., Publishers, San Francisco, 1973, pp. 9–33.

"The Crimson Predicts: 1972," Harvard *Crimson,* p. 2, Jan. 3, 1972.

Davis, James A.: "The Campus as a Frog Pond: An Application of the Theory of Relative Deprivation to Career Decisions of College Men," *American Journal of Sociology,* vol. 72, no. 1, pp. 17–31, July 1966.

Davis, Robert Gorham: "The Professors' Lie," *Columbia Forum,* vol. 1, pp. 6–15, Fall 1972.

DeMott, Benjamin: "Letter to an Unhappy Alumnus," *Change,* vol. 4, pp. 24–29, Summer 1972.

Deutsch, Karl W., and Thomas Edsal: "The Meritocracy Scare," *Society* (formerly *Trans-action*), vol. 9, pp. 71–79, September–October 1972.

Doermann, Humphrey: "Lack of Money: A Barrier to Higher Education," in College Entrance Examination Board, *Barriers to Higher Education,* New York, 1971, pp. 130–147.

Donald, Cleveland, Jr.: "Cornell: Confrontation in Black and White," in Cushing Strout and David I. Grossvogel (eds.), *Divided We Stand: Reflections on the Crisis at Cornell,* Doubleday & Company, Inc., Garden City, N. Y., 1970, pp. 153–204.

Duberman, Martin: *Black Mountain: An Exploration in Community,* E. P. Dutton & Co., Inc., New York, 1972.

Elbow, Peter: "The Pedagogy of the Bamboozled," *Soundings: An Interdisciplinary Journal,* vol. 61, pp. 247–258, Summer 1973.

Epps, Garrett: Valedictory column, Harvard *Crimson,* Harvard University, Cambridge, Mass., Feb. 2, 1972, p. 2.

Faltermayer, Edmund: "Let's Break the Go-to-College Lock Step," *Fortune,* vol. 82, pp. 98–103, November 1970.

The First Three Years of the Afro-American Studies Department, 1969–1972, Report to the Faculty of Arts and Sciences, Harvard University, Cambridge, Mass., Oct. 16, 1972.

Fleming, Donald: *William H. Welch and the Rise of Modern Medicine*, Little, Brown and Company, Boston, 1954.

Flexner, Abraham: *Universities: American, English, and German*, Teachers College Press, Columbia University, New York, 1967.

Ford, Franklin: "Roles and the Critique of Learning," *Daedalus*, vol. 99, pp. 661–675, Summer 1970.

Fulton, Oliver, and Martin Trow: "Research Activities in American Higher Education," University of Edinburgh, Centre for Research in Educational Sciences, May 1972.

Funkenstein, Daniel H.: "The Learning and Personal Development of Medical Students and the Recent Changes in Universities and Medical Schools," *The Journal of Medical Education*, vol. 43, pp. 883–897, August 1968.

Glazer, Nathan: "Remembering the Answers," in Nathan Glazer, *Remembering the Answers: Essays on the American Student Revolt*, Basic Books, Inc., Publishers, New York, 1970, chapter 13.

Glazer, Nathan: "City College," in David Riesman and Verne A. Stadtman (eds.), *Academic Transformation: Seventeen Institutions Under Pressure*, McGraw-Hill Book Company, New York, 1973, pp. 71–98.

Glazer, Nathan: "Conflicts in Schools for the Minor Professions," *Harvard Graduate School of Education Association Bulletin*, vol. 18, pp. 18–24, Spring–Summer 1974a.

Glazer, Nathan: "The Schools of the Minor Professions," *Minerva: A Review of Science, Learning, and Policy*, forthcoming, 1974b.

Goldsmith, Jeff: "Youth and the Public Sector: Institutional Paths to Social Membership," unpublished doctoral dissertation for Department of Sociology, University of Chicago, 1973.

Gordon, Robert W.: "Thoughts from an Army Camp in Germany," *The Harvard Review*, vol. 3, pp. 54–65, Winter 1965.

Grant, Gerald: "A Network of Antiochs," in David Riesman and Verne A. Stadtman (eds.), *Academic Transformation: Seventeen Institutions Under Pressure*, McGraw-Hill Book Company, New York, 1973, pp. 13–50.

Grant, Gerald, and David Riesman: "The Ecology of Academic Reform," *Daedalus*, forthcoming.

Harvard Committee: *General Education in a Free Society*, Harvard University Press, Cambridge, Mass., 1946.

Harvard Student Council: "Report of 1926," unpublished, Harvard College, Cambridge, Mass., 1926.

Harvard Student Council Committee on Education: "Report of June 12, 1939," unpublished, Harvard College, Cambridge, Mass., 1939.

Hawkins, Hugh: *Between Harvard and America: The Educational Leadership of Charles W. Eliot,* Oxford University Press, New York, 1972.

Heath, Roy: *The Reasonable Adventurer,* University of Pittsburgh Press, Pittsburgh, 1964.

Hughes, H. Stuart: "The Need Now Is to De-Politicize the University," *Harvard Alumni Bulletin,* vol. 72, pp. 35–38, Sept. 15, 1969.

Huntington, Samuel P.: "The Changing Cultures of Harvard," *Harvard Alumni Bulletin,* vol. 72, pp. 51–54, Sept. 15, 1969.

An Informal Discussion of Advanced Standing at Harvard and Radcliffe Colleges, Office of Advanced Standing, Harvard University, Cambridge, Mass., n.d.

Jencks, Christopher, and David Riesman: "Patterns of Residential Education: A Case Study of Harvard," in Nevitt Sanford (ed.), *The American College: A Psychological and Social Interpretation of Higher Learning,* John Wiley & Sons, Inc., New York, 1962, pp. 731–773.

Jencks, Christopher, and David Riesman: *The Academic Revolution,* Doubleday & Company, Inc., Garden City, N. Y., 1968.

Jencks, Christopher, et al.: *Inequality: A Reassessment of the Effect of Family and Schooling in America,* Basic Books, Inc., Publishers, New York, 1972.

Keniston, Kenneth: *The Uncommitted: Alienated Youth in American Society,* Harcourt, Brace & World, Inc., New York, 1965.

Lipset, Seymour Martin: *Rebellion in the University,* Little, Brown and Company, Boston, 1972.

Livingston, John C.: "Tenure Everyone?" in Bardwell L. Smith and associates, *The Tenure Debate,* Jossey-Bass Inc., Publishers, San Francisco, 1972, pp. 54–73.

Mangelsdorf, Paul: "Swarthmore Knocks on Wood," in David Riesman and Verne A. Stadtman (eds.), *Academic Transformation: Seventeen Institutions Under Pressure,* McGraw-Hill Book Company, New York, 1973, pp. 323–342.

May, Ernest: "Report to the Faculty," unpublished, Harvard University, Cambridge, Mass., Feb. 15, 1972.

McCarley, Robert: "A Walk Around the Yard," senior honors thesis, Department of Social Relations, Harvard University, Cambridge, Mass., 1959.

McCaughey, Robert A.: "The Transformation of American Academic Life: Harvard University (1821–1892)," *Perspectives in American History,* vol. 8, 1974.

Meyer, Marshall W.: "After the Bust: Student Politics at Harvard, 1969–1972," in David Riesman and Verne A. Stadtman, (eds.), *Academic Transformation: Seventeen Institutions Under Pressure,* McGraw-Hill Book Commpany, New York, 1973, pp. 127–153.

Miller, Lilian D., Frederick Voss, and Jeannette M. Husse: *The Lazzaroni: Science and Scientists in Mid-Nineteenth Century America,* The Smithsonian Institution, Washington, D. C., 1972.

Mills, C. Wright: *The Sociological Imagination,* Oxford University Press, New York, 1959.

Monroe, Sylvester: "Guest in a Strange House," *Saturday Review of Education,* vol. 1, pp. 45–48, Jan. 13, 1973.

Morimoto, Kiyo: "On Trying to Understand the Frustrations of Students," unpublished, 1972.

Morison, Samuel Eliot: *Three Centuries of Harvard: 1636–1936,* Harvard University Press, Cambridge, Mass., 1936.

Morris, Willie: *North Toward Home,* Houghton Mifflin Company, Boston, 1967.

Moynihan, Daniel P.: " 'Peace'—Some Thoughts on the 1960's and 1970's," *The Public Interest,* no. 32, pp. 3–12, Summer 1973.

Nagai, Michio: "The Problem of Indoctrination: As Viewed from Sociological and Philosophical Bases," Ph.D. thesis, Department of Sociology, Ohio State University, Columbus, Ohio, 1952. Quoted and discussed in Seymour M. Lipset, *Rebellion in the University,* Little, Brown and Company, Boston, 1972, pp. 225 – 226.

Parsons, Talcott, and Gerald M. Platt: *The American Academic System: A National Survey of Faculty,* Harvard University Press, Cambridge, Mass., 1972.

Parsons, Talcott, Gerald M. Platt, and Neil Smelser: *The American Academic System: A Sociological Point of View,* Harvard University Press, Cambridge, Mass., 1973.

Pattullo, Edward L.: "The Case for a Different Kind of Harvard," *Harvard Alumni Bulletin,* vol. 75, pp. 20–26, December 1972.

Perry, William C., Jr.: *Forms of Intellectual and Ethical Development in the College Years,* Holt, Rinehart and Winston, Inc., New York, 1970.

Petrie, Asenath: *Individuality in Pain and Suffering,* The University of Chicago Press, Chicago, 1967.

Price, Derek J.: *Science since Babylon,* Yale University Press, New Haven, Conn., 1961.

Report of the Committee to Review the Department of Afro-American Studies, Harvard University, Cambridge, Mass., October 1972.

Report of the Committee on the Role of Phi Beta Kappa, Bentley Glass, chairman, April 17, 1973. Unpublished report.

Richter, Melvin (ed.): *Essays in Theory and History: An Approach to the Social Sciences,* Harvard University Press, Cambridge, Mass., 1970.

Ricks, David: "Tests and Scholarships: A Cautioning Tale," *Financial Aid News,* no. 3, March 1961.

Ricks, David, and Robert McCarley: "Identity at Harvard and Harvard's Identity," *The Harvard Review*, vol. 3, pp. 39–53, Winter 1965.

Riesman, David: "Scientists Versus Captains of Erudition," in David Riesman, *Thorstein Veblen: A Critical Interpretation*, Charles Scribner's Sons, New York, 1953, pp. 99–113.

Riesman, David: "Values in Context," *American Scholar*, vol. 22, pp. 29–39, 1952. Reprinted in David Riesman, *Individualism Reconsidered*, The Free Press of Glencoe, Ill., Chicago, 1954, pp. 17–25.

Riesman, David: *Constraint and Variety in American Education*, University of Nebraska Press, Lincoln, 1956.

Riesman, David: "The Uncertain Freshman," *The Current: A Review of Catholicism in Contemporary Culture*, vol. 2, pp. 117–125, October 1961.

Riesman, David: "The Impact of Examinations," in Leon Bramson (ed.), *Examining in Harvard College: A Collection of Essays by Members of the Harvard Faculty*, Faculty of Arts and Sciences, Harvard University, Cambridge, Mass., November 1963, pp. 71–87.

Riesman, David: "Two Generations," *Daedalus*, vol. 93, pp. 711–735, Spring 1964.

Riesman, David: "Notes on Meritocracy," *Daedalus*, vol. 96, pp. 897–908, Summer 1967.

Riesman, David: "Return to Hiroshima," *Dissent*, pp. 265–269, May–June 1968.

Riesman, David: "Notes on Educational Reform," *Journal of General Education*, vol. 23, no. 12, pp. 81–110, July 1971.

Riesman, David: "The Business of 'Business as Usual,'" *Change*, vol. 2, pp. 6–8, September–October 1970. Reprinted in *Inside Academe: Culture in Crisis*, Change Magazine Books, New Rochelle, N. Y., 1972*a*.

Riesman, David: "The Validity of Traditional Disciplinary Boundaries," in *Higher Education and Changing Population Patterns*, Council for International Studies, University of Florida, Gainesville, 1972*b*.

Riesman, David, and Reuel Denney: "Football: A Study in Culture Diffusion," *American Quarterly*, vol. 3, pp. 309–325, Winter, 1951. Reprinted in David Riesman, *Individualism Reconsidered*, The Free Press of Glencoe, Ill., Chicago, 1954.

Riesman, David, Joseph Gusfield, and Zelda Gamson: *Academic Values and Mass Education*, Doubleday & Company, Inc., Garden City, N. Y., 1970.

Riesman, David, and Verne A. Stadtman (eds.): *Academic Transformation: Seventeen Institutions Under Pressure*, McGraw-Hill Book Company, New York, 1973.

Riesman, David, and Jeanne Watson: "The Sociability Project: A Chronicle of Frustration and Achievement," in Phillip E. Hammond (ed.), *Sociologists at Work*, Basic Books, Inc., Publishers, New York, 1964, pp. 235–321.

Rosovsky, Henry: "Black Studies at Harvard," *The American Scholar,* vol. 38, p. 568, Autumn 1969.

Schendel, William B.: *A Guide to Law and Law-Related Fields,* Office of Career Services and Off-Campus Learning, Harvard University, Cambridge, Mass., September 1973.

Schudson, Michael S.: "Organizing the 'Meritocracy': A History of the College Entrance Examination Board," *Harvard Educational Review,* vol. 42, pp. 54–69, February 1972.

Schumpeter, Joseph: *Capitalism, Socialism, and Democracy,* Harper & Brothers, New York, 1942.

Searle, John R.: *The Campus War: A Sympathetic Look at a University in Agony,* World Publishing Company, New York, 1971.

Sennett, Richard, and Jonathan Cobb: *The Hidden Injuries of Class,* Alfred A. Knopf, Inc., New York, 1972.

Shils, Edward: "Plenitude and Scarcity: The Anatomy of an International Cultural Crisis," *Encounter,* vol. 32, pp. 37–43, May 1969.

Slaughter, Thomas F., Jr.: "The Status of Black Studies Programs in American Colleges and Universities," with Rhoda L. Goldstein and June Albert, paper prepared for presentation at the American Sociological Association meetings, Aug. 29, 1972.

Smelser, Neil J.: "Berkeley in Crisis and Change," in David Riesman and Verne A. Stadtman (eds.), *Academic Transformation: Seventeen Institutions Under Pressure,* McGraw-Hill Book Company, New York, 1973, pp. 51–69.

Spady, William G.: "Peer Integration and Academic Success: The Dropout Process among Chicago Freshmen," unpublished Ph.D. dissertation, University of Chicago, 1967.

Spady, William G.: "Dropouts from Higher Education: Toward an Empirical Model," *Interchange,* vol. 2, no. 3, pp. 38–62, Summer 1971.

Starr, Kevin: "What Is an Allston Burr Senior Tutorship and Why Are They Saying Such Terrible Things about It?" *Harvard Alumni Bulletin,* vol. 75, pp. 21–26, September 1972.

Stookey, Byron: *An Analysis of the Harvard Freshman Seminar Program: Report to the Faculty of Arts and Sciences,* Harvard University, Cambridge, Mass., February 1963.

Teaching Fellowships in Harvard College, a survey by the Committee on Teaching as a Career, Harvard University, Cambridge, Mass., October 1960.

"Ten Harvard Professors Answer a Question . . . ," *Harvard Alumni Bulletin,* vol. 72, pp. 43–50, Sept. 15, 1969.

Thelin, John: "Images of the Ivy League 1890–1960: The Collegiate Ideal and the Education of Elites in American Culture," Ph.D. dissertation, University of California, Berkeley, 1972.

Tomasson, Richard F.: "Report of the Department of Sociology, 1971–1972," University of New Mexico, Albuquerque, 1973. (Mimeographed.)

Trilling, Lionel: *Sincerity and Authenticity*, Harvard University Press, Cambridge, Mass., 1972.

Trow, Martin: "Notes on Undergraduate Teaching at Large State Universities," unpublished paper, Berkeley, Calif., 1966.

Trow, Martin: "The Public and Private Lives of Higher Education," paper read at the Second National Forum on New Planning and Management Practices in Post-Secondary Education, Education Commission of the States, Chicago, Nov. 16, 1973.

Trow, Martin (ed.) : *Teachers and Students: Aspects of American Higher Education*, McGraw-Hill Book Company, New York, forthcoming.

Turner, Ralph H.: "Sponsored and Contest Mobility and the School System," *American Sociological Review*, vol. 25, pp. 855–867, December 1960.

Tussman, Joseph: *Experiment at Berkeley*, Oxford University Press, New York, 1969.

Ulam, Adam B.: "The University Should Mind Its Own Business," *Harvard Alumni Bulletin*, vol. 72, pp. 29–34, Sept. 15, 1969.

Ulam, Adam B.: *The Fall of the American University*, Harvard University Press, Cambridge, Mass., 1972.

Vogel, Ezra: "The Gateway to Salary: The Informal Entrance Examinations," in Ezra Vogel (ed.), *Japan's New Middle Class: The Salaryman and His Family in a Tokyo Suburb*, University of California Press, Berkeley, 1963, chapter 3.

von Wittich, Barbara: "The Impact of the Pass-Fail System upon Achievement of College Students," *Journal of Higher Education*, vol. 43, pp. 499–508, May 1972.

Vreeland, Rebecca S.: "Is It True What They Say about Harvard Boys?" *Psychology Today*, vol. 5, pp. 65–69, January 1972.

Vreeland, Rebecca S., and Charles E. Bidwell: "Organizational Effects upon Student Attitudes: A Study of the Harvard Houses," *Sociology of Education*, vol. 38, pp. 233–250, Spring 1965.

Vreeland, Rebecca S., and Charles E. Bidwell: "Classifying University Departments: An Approach to the Analysis of Their Effects upon Undergraduates' Values and Attitudes," *Sociology of Education*, vol. 39, pp. 237–254, Summer 1966.

Wagoner, Jennings L., Jr.: "The American Compromise: Charles W. Eliot and the Solution to the 'Southern Problem,'" paper presented to the Southern History of Education Society, Atlanta, Nov. 16, 1973.

Weiss, Robert S., Edwin Harwood, and David Riesman: "Work and Automation: Problems and Prospects," in Robert K. Merton and Robert Nisbet (eds.), *Comtemporary Social Problems,* 3d ed., Harcourt Brace Jovanovich, New York, 1971, pp. 545–600.

Weller, George Anthony: *Not to Eat, Not for Love,* H. Smith and R. Haas, New York, 1933.

Whitla, Dean: "Some Notes on Grading," Harvard University, Cambridge, Mass., Nov. 30, 1966. (Mimeographed.)

Wickenden, James W., Jr.: *The Harvard College Class of 1971,* Office of Graduate and Career Plans, Harvard University, Cambridge, Mass., January 1972.

Wilcox, Edward T.: "Memorandum to Faculty Council," unpublished report, March 3, 1973.

Young, Michael: *The Rise of the Meritocracy, 1870–2033: An Essay on Education and Equality,* Random House, Inc., New York, 1959.

Index

AAUP (American Association of University Professors), 169
Abolitionist movement:
 Follen's sympathies with, 69
 Harvard as center of opposition to, 84
 scholars in, 4
Absenteeism, rules governing (1870s), 96
Academic achievement:
 competing for, 324
 Crimson's editors and, 323
 expected by Committee on Social Studies, 327
 of high-risk students, 319
 meritocracy and pressures for, 308
 self-confidence and, 320
 (*See also* Graduation with honors)
Academic careers, attitudes toward, 362
Academic culture, 190–191, 274
 anti-intellectual counterculture and, 255
 intellectuality and, 248
Academic excellence (*see* Scholarship)
Academic freedom:
 Bowen case, 79, 99–100, 108
 classroom privacy as component of, 388
 in Colonial period, 31–35
  first battle for, 27
 under Eliot, 99–102, 108–110, 117–118, 187–188
 Lowell and, 138–142, 185, 186
 political control and, 8
 in post-Civil War era, 91
 in post-Revolutionary era, 55, 62–63
 post-World War I threats to, 138–142
 in post-World War II era, 169, 185–187, 193, 233
  (*See also* Communists, in Cold War era)
 traditional faculty struggles for, 12
 Walsh-Sweezy case, 164–167, 169, 173
 during World War I, 136–138

"Academic Freedom" (speech), 117
Academic Legion of Vienna, 4, 8
Academic nepotism, 168, 309
Academic standing, remaining in good (1920s), 297–298
Acheson, Dean, 193
Achievement:
 academic culture and, 190
 intellectual, under Eliot, 118, 126–128
 meritocracy and, 290
 (*See also* Academic achievement)
Achievement orientation, 6, 307–308
Ad Hoc Committee, 302, 354
Ad Hoc Committee system, 308–314
ADA (Americans for Democratic Action), 181
Adams, Abigail, 36
Adams, Brooks, 27, 85
Adams, Charles Francis, 85–86, 129, 287n.
Adams, Comfort Avery, 121, 122
Adams, Henry, 50, 53, 85, 100
 attempts to enlarge *lern freiheit* principle, 95
 slavery issue and, 82, 83
Adams, John, 3, 40, 44, 48, 57
Adams, John Quincy, 50, 57, 70, 143
Adams, John Quincy (son), 70
Addams, Jane, 135
Administrative Board of Graduate School, 219, 285
Admissions Committee, 320, 366
Admissions policies:
 changes in: effect on black student enrollment, 222
 meritocracy and, 305–308, 317–319, 333, 355, 380
 under Conant, 180, 190
 under Eliot, 106, 247
 for Freshman Seminar Program, 283

Admissions policies:
under Lowell, 145–150, 179, 246
open admissions, 330
in post-Civil War era, 92
in post-Revolutionary era, 60, 75, 77
in pre-Civil War era, 86
sex-blind admissions advocated,
366–367
Admonitions to students involved in antiwar protests (1960s), 214
Advanced Management and Business
School Students, 350
Advanced Standing, Program of, 285,
317–318
Advising, 384–385
Advisory Committee on Sacco-Vanzetti
trial, 151
AEC (Atomic Energy Commission), 202
Affectively oriented education, 365
African and Afro-American Studies, Facul-
ty Committee on (Rosovsky Commit-
tee), 222–223, 340, 369–370
Afro-American Studies (program),
222–224, 340, 341
Afro-American Studies, Department of,
231, 240–241, 243, 340, 342, 369
Agassiz, Louis, 86
Agassiz Theater, 323
Aldrich, Winthrop W., 193
Alexis, Lucien V., Jr., 177
Alger, Frederick M., Jr., 193
Allmendinger, David, 91, 93
Allport, Gordon, 315
Alumni:
children of, given admission preference,
180, 333
Communist party members barred from
teaching and, 186
under Eliot Presidency: attack academic
freedom, 108–110
control Board of Overseers, 100, 103
reactions to Eliot's policies, 102–103
responses to Lowell Committee, 130
number of ambassadorships held by
(1950s), 193
Overseers elected by (in Civil War era),
88–89
post-World War I liberalism and,
139–140
reactions of, to racism, 143
withhold financial support (1930s), 170
Alumni Association, Economics Department attacked by (1960s), 209

Ambassadorships, number of, held by
Harvard alumni (1950s), 193
America First Committee, 175
American Academy of Arts and Sciences, 52
American Association of University Ad-
ministrators, 186
American Association of University Pro-
fessors (AAUP), 169
American Conservative Party, call for (late
1950s), 203
American Council on Education, 234
American Defense Committee, 174
American Defense League, 175
American Federation of Teachers, 163
American Independence League, 174
American Jewish Committee, 149
American Men of Science, 126
American neutrality laws, repeal of, advocated (1930s), 171
American Peace Mobilization, 175, 177
American Revolution (1776), 9, 174
changes brought about by, 39, 44, 45
literary societies formed after, 52
radicalism spurred on by, 47
religious liberalism spread by, 49
and revolutionary politics, 3, 35–39
students who played major roles in, 35
American Student Union (ASU), 162–165,
241, 249
in 1930s: Communist control of,
171–172
fails to build wide following, 173
invasion of Finland condemned by,
174
support Nazi-Soviet pact, 172
Walsh-Sweezy case and, 164–165
in World War II era, 171, 177
"American Students and the 'Political Revival'" (Keniston), 208
American Youth for Democracy (AYD),
181, 182
Americans for Democratic Action (ADA),
181
Ames, James Barr, 108
Amnesty:
for participants in 1969 strike, 224–225
vis-à-vis grades and examinations
(1970), 374–375
Anarchist groups, 122, 135
Andover (prep school), 294*n.*, 317
Angell, Norman, 123
Annan, Noel, 99
Annual Spring Riot as tradition, 210–211

Anthropology Department, 354
Antielitism, burgeoning, 38
  (*See also* Meritocracy)
Antifascist alliance, ASU advocates, 171
Anti-Imperialism (end of nineteenth century), 116–117, 124, 192
Anti-intellectual counterculture, 255
Antijaywalking law (Cambridge, 1966), riot against, 211
Antimilitarism (*see* Antiwar movement; Pacifism)
Antimonarchial sentiments in pre-Revolutionary period, 38, 43, 47
Antioch College, 286, 365
Anti-Semitism:
  Cambridge Union of University Teachers refuses to deal with, 164
  drop in, following World War II, 180
  under Lowell, 139, 144–150, 301
  in Russia, 185
Antiwar movement:
  under Eliot, 115–117
  in 1960s, 202, 331
    demonstrations and protests, 206, 212–216
    faculty members in, 374
    SDS in, 210
  pre-World War II, 159
  World War I, 136
  World War II, 174–177
Apolitical students, number of, in 1959 *Crimson* poll, 203
Appleton, Nathan, 24, 99
Appointments, 109
  Ad Hoc Committee system in, 308–310, 314
  to chairs, 353–354
  under Conant, 164
  to Economics Department (post-World War II), 183–184
  of first Jewish dean (1973), 243–244
  in post-Revolutionary era, faculty involvement in, 58, 62–66
  role of departments in, 313
  student participation in, 340, 341
  to University Professorships, 352
April Peace Demonstration (1938), 172
Architectural Sciences Department, 342
"Are the People the Sole Judges of their Rights and Liberties?" (Hunt), 35
Area-focused centers, 314–315
Aristocratic meritocracy, 293
  Eliot and, 287–289

Aristocratic meritocracy:
  Lowell and, 288
  at Oxford and Cambridge universities, 310
Aristotle, 8
Arrests:
  in Hanfstaengl incident, 160
  in *Karlsruhe* incident, 159
Arrow, Kenneth, 242
Arts, the, state of (1920s), 297
Arts and Sciences, Faculty of:
  Ad Hoc Committee system and, 310
  Bundy as Dean of, 316–317, 333, 354–355
  created, 101
  Freshman Seminars and, 350
  in 1940 straw vote, 176
  tenure in, 389
    number of women and blacks as tenured professors in (1974), 244
    tenured members (as of March 1974), 371
Ascription, meritocracy vs., 293, 294
Ashbrook, John, 201
Ashley, William James, 109, 118
ASU (*see* American Student Union)
Atheism in late eighteenth century, 47
Athletes, 321–322, 333
Athletic activities:
  intercollegiate, 122
  managed through Houses, 347
Atlantic Monthly (magazine), 90, 116, 237
Atomic Energy Commission (AEC), 202
Atomic testing, support for suspension of (late 1950s), 203, 206
Authenticity, student view of, 361
Avukah (Zionist organization), 172, 245
AYD (American Youth for Democracy), 181, 182

Babbitt, Irving, 361
Bachelors' degrees (B.A.'s):
  curtailed requirements for, in World War I, 136
  in Latin, 211
  number of faculty members having received, at Harvard (1936), 300
  obtaining, in three years, 129, 130, 284, 379
  as proof of competence, 380–381
  residence requirements for, 18*n*.
Bailyn, Bernard, 297*n*., 371*n*.

Baker, George Pierce, 297
Baldwin, Roger, 299
Bancroft, George, 66, 73–75
Banfield, Edward, 231
Bank tax as source of financial support in post-Revolutionary era, 58
Baptism, popular views on, opposed, 17, 123
Bassett, Mr., 87
Beer, Samuel, 337
Bell, Daniel, 7, 289n.
Bender, Wilbur, 306
Bender, William, 182
Berg, Ivar, 380n.
Berger, Bennett M., 380n.
Bergson, Abram, 163
Berkeley Free Speech Movement (FSM), 119
Berkeley Revolt (1964), 225, 240, 248
  effects of, 233
  origins of, 331
  police action in, 220
  reasons for, 227, 228, 248–249
  strategy followed in, 217
Berlin Blockade (1948), 185
Bicameral form of government, 15, 16
Bidwell, Charles, 372n.
Big-Man-on-Campus types, frowned upon, 350
Birkhoff, George, 165
Birnbaum, Max, 308, 318n.
Birney, James, 83
Black power, 252
Black professors:
  nondepartmental teaching and, 355
  tenure for, 244
Black separatism, 372
Black student organizations:
  Afro-American studies and, 222
  SDS backs, 230
  (*See also* Civil rights movement)
Black students, 142, 290
  average preparation of, 334
  colonialism opposed by, 230, 231, 237, 238, 241
  creation of Afro-American Studies Department and, 231, 240–241, 340–341, 369
  Eliot and, 106
  first admitted to Harvard (1850), 83
  guidance needed by, 334–336
  under Lowell, 295n.
    enrollment, 144, 145, 180, 222

Black students:
  Oberlin College recruits, 333
  occupy Massachusetts Hall (1972), 237, 241
  proletarian style of, 307
Blackmer, Allan, 294n.
Blaine, James G., 111
Blasphemy, punishment for, 20
Board of Overseers (*see* Overseers)
Board of Visitors (William and Mary College), 43
Boer Relief Fund, 117
Boer War (1899–1902), 117
Bohemianism, 124
Bohlen, Charles E., 193
Bok, Derek, 235–240, 284, 316n., 346n.
  becomes President, 235–236
  characteristics and background of, 237
  conciliatory policies of, 237–238, 240
  praised, 239
  Rosovsky appointed by, 244
  sex-blind admissions and, 367
  student participation and, 365
  training in teaching and, 390
Bolshevism, 138, 141
Bonbright, James C. H., 193
Bonfires, students building (1870s), 94
Book thieves, 146
Boston Athenaeum, 98
Boston elite:
  American culture dominated by (end of nineteenth century), 99
  in Colonial period, governance of Harvard and, 42
  conservatism of, 73
  financial support from, 98–99
  Jews compared with, 307
  in post-Revolutionary era, 59
    ties between faculty members and, 52–53
  religious prejudices of, 301
Boston Massacre (1770), 37, 38
Bourne, Randolph S., 105, 120–121
Boutwell, George, 77
Boutwell Committee, 77–78
Bowdoin, James, 42
Bowen, Francis, 79, 99–100, 108
Boxing as form of punishment, 18
Boycotts:
  to desegregate bars (1946), 198
  of Harvard Square merchants (1940s), 181
Boyle, Robert, 18
Boylston Oratorical Contest, 106

Brady, William C., 199
Brandeis, Louis, 152
Bread and Butter Rebellion (1766), 32, 35–36, 53
Brewster, Kingman, Jr., 175, 236
Briggs, LeBaron, 102
Brinton, Crane, 163, 298
Bristed, C. A., 9
Britt, George, 149
Bronx High School of Science, 317
Brooks, Van Wyck, 104, 125, 129–130
Broun, Heywood, 119, 143, 149
Browder, Earl, 174, 176
Brower, Reuben A., 337
Brown University, 113
Bryan, William Jennings, 111, 112, 117
Bryn Mawr College, 286
Buck, Paul, 180, 190, 286, 295*n.*
Buckley, William F., 205
Bundy, McGeorge, 197, 207, 256, 289, 302
  balance issue in Economics Department and, 183–84
  as Dean of Faculty of Arts and Sciences, 316–317, 333, 354–355
  nondepartmental teaching and, 353
  on personnel policies, 234
Bureaucracy, meritocracy and, 290, 332
Bureaucratic society, 332
Burney, Evelina, 116
Burns, Anthony, 84
Business community:
  attacks Economics Department, 108–109
  criticizes leftist faculty, 171
  slavery issue and, 81
Butler, Nicholas Murray, 136, 137

Cable, Theodore, 178
Cabot, George, 36
Cabot, John M., 193
Caffey, C. G., 111
California at Berkeley, University of, 370
  centers and institutes at, 315
  loyalty oath crisis at (1950s), 187
  1964 scholarly status of, 234
  Tussman College of, 281
  (*See also* Berkeley Revolt)
California at Los Angeles, University of (UCLA), 179, 187
California Institute of Technology (Cal Tech), 333, 343, 379
Calvinism:
  elitism and, 81

Calvinism:
  five points of, challenged, 34–35
  in post-Revolutionary era, 72
  slavery issue and, 84
  Unitarianism triumphs over, 51–53
  (*See also* Puritans)
Cambodian invasion (1970), 240, 251, 374, 375
Cambridge Electron Accelerator (joint venture of MIT and Harvard), 314, 350
Cambridge School Board, 187
Cambridge Union of University Teachers, 163–166
Cambridge University, 25, 40, 43, 45, 301
  appointments at, 310
  faculty struggles at, 12
  governance of, 15
  prize system used in, 131
Campus rebellion (*see* Student unrest)
"Can the new Prohibitary Duties which make it useless for the People to engage in Commerce, be evaded by them as Faithful Subjects?" (Gerry), 35
Capitalist society:
  egalitarian ethos in, 282
  undoing of, 332*n.*
Careers:
  attitudes toward: in 1940s, 188
    in 1970s, 359–363
  meritocracy and, 332, 381–382
  mixed feelings about, 356
Carleton College, 337
Carnegie Corporation, 125, 184
Cass, James, 308, 318*n.*
Catholic student organizations, 113
Catholic students, 142
  enrollment of (1810), 52
  under Lowell, 144, 145
  Irish, 307
Cattell, J. McKeen, 126
CCNY (City College of New York), 299*n.*
Center for International Affairs, 314, 366
  bombed (1970), 231
  trashed (1972), 211, 230
Center for International Affairs Fellows, 350
Center for Middle Eastern Studies, 314
Chafee, Zechariah, Jr., 140, 186
Chairs, 353–354
Channing, Edward T., 54
Channing, William Ellery, 47–50
Chapel attendance, compulsory, 31, 32, 55, 85

Chapel attendance, compulsory:
  Eliot abolishes, 113
  protests against, 10, 49, 50
Character development, 5
Charles Eliot Norton Lectures, 362
Charles Warren Center for Studies in
  American History, 353
Chauncy, Charles, 17, 18n., 123
Checks and balances, system of, 16
Chemistry Department:
  backgrounds of faculty members of
    (1930s), 300
  student evaluation of courses in,
    284–285, 385n.
Chicago, University of, 226, 227, 248, 371
  academic culture at, 191
  advanced standing at, 317n., 318n.
  Communist organization at, 181
  lack of social integration at, 312n.
  social and academic prestige at, 302
  top position of, in 1925 survey, 153, 154
Child, Francis, 108, 127
Child Labor Amendment (1938), 152, 165
China, support for recognition of (late
    1950s), 201, 203
Chinese bureaucracy, meritocracy in, 287
Chinese students, 142
Church of England, 25, 29
Civil disobedience (1966–1967), 212–213
Civil liberties:
  of Communists in Cold War era,
    180–183
  in 1930s, 138, 174
Civil rights movement, 202, 252
  activism revives around, 207–209
  Berkeley Revolt originates in, 331
  early, 206
  SDS in, 210
Civil Service System, meritocracy in, 287
Civil War (1861–1865), 85, 89
Clark, Grenville, 186
Clark University, 302
Clarke, Dr. John, 34
Class elections, social-class differences
  and, 105
Classroom privacy as component of aca-
  demic freedom, 388
Classroom recitation, demonstrations
  against, 36
Clergy on Board of Overseers, 15
  influence undermined (end of eigh-
    teenth century), 40, 42, 43, 45, 51
Clerk, Sir Philip Jennings, 116

Cleveland, Grover, 107, 111, 115, 162
Clinic to Improve University Teaching,
  388n.
"Clubby" culture, 190, 247, 255
Cobb, Jonathan, 382n.
Coe, Robert D., 193
Cogswell, Joseph, 66
Cohen, Rob, 342n.
Cold War era, 179–204
College of the City of New York (CCNY),
  299n.
College degrees:
  attacked, 365
  held by faculty members (1930s), 301n.
  importance of, in securing jobs, 380
  "pass," 333
  (*See also* Bachelor's degrees; Master's
    degrees; Ph.D's)
"College Discipline" (editorial), 104
College Entrance Examination Board, 287,
  305
College Preachers, Board of, 244
College presidents:
  power and functions of, 12
  toppled: at Columbia University, 233
    end of nineteenth century, 104
  (*See also* Presidents of Harvard)
Collegiate Anti-Militarism League, 135
Colman, Benjamin (Fellow), 24
Colonial period, 15–45
Colonialism, black students' concern with,
  230, 231, 237, 238, 241
Columbia University, 119, 136, 149, 154,
  216, 281
  Gulf stock owned by, 237
  loses its elite (1920s and 1930s), 295
  1968 crisis at, 220, 225–227, 248, 370
    change in administration following, 233
    confrontation tactics in, 249–250
    sources of, 215
Columbian Centinel (newspaper), 49
Combined University Students' Commit-
  tee on Academic Freedom, 197
Commencement ceremonies, disruption of
  (1969 and 1970), 230–231
Comment Book (of *Harvard Crimson*), 323
Commentary (magazine), 238
Commercial careers, views on, 360
Committee assignments, 102, 391
Communism, international, McCarthy's
  first speech against (1950), 192
Communist China, support for recognition
  of (1950s), 201, 203

Communists:
  in Cold War era: barred from teaching,
    185 — 188, 193 — 194, 199, 203
  civil rights of, 180 — 183
  McCarthy's crusade against, 192, 195
  in 1930s, 158, 163, 169
    control ASU, 171 — 172
    isolationism and, 171
    support Roosevelt (1936), 171 — 172
  and World War II, 175
Community control in Colonial period, 15,
  16, 41, 42, 45
Community service, careers involving, 363
Commuter students, 295 — 296
Compulsory chapel attendance, 31, 32, 55,
  85
  Eliot abolishes, 113
  protests against, 10, 49, 50
Conant, James B., 150, 193, 305
  becomes Ambassador, 191, 195
  favors intervention in World War II, 175,
    176
  presidency of, 154 — 155, 302
    achievement orientation of Jewish stu-
      dents and, 307 — 308
    Browder barred from public appear-
      ance and, 174
    changes in admissions policy and, 180,
      190
    Communists barred from teaching
      and, 185 — 186
    concern for faculty quality under,
      167 — 169
    external pressures on, 171
    Galbraith's nomination supported by,
      183
    honorary degree for Hanfstaengl and
      160 — 161
    honorary degree for Wallace and, 162
    personnel policies under, 167 — 169
    teachers' oath bill opposed by, 162
    Walsh and Sweezy case and, 164,
      166 — 167
  Pusey compared with, 192
Concentrations:
  Afro-American Studies as, 341
  honors system combined with, 134, 293
  linking fields of, 344
  overenrolled fields of, 283, 328
  students designing their own fields of,
    344
  switching, 325
Concord (1776), 38

Conformism in 1950s, 248
Confrontation tactics, 212, 249 — 251
  opposed, 228
  SDS and, 250
Congregationalism, 29, 30, 51, 52
Conscientious objection in early history of
  Harvard, 17
Conscientious objector status, number of
  students having applied for
  (1966 — 1967), 213
Conscription (*see* Draft)
Conscription law (1863), 85
Conservatism:
  colleges as allies of, 82
  of Governing Boards (1930s), 161 — 162
  growth of (1960s), 205 — 206
  of Lowell, 152 — 153
  of post-Revolutionary Corporation and
    faculty, 73
  of post-Revolutionary New England
    elite, 49
  revival of (1950s), 202
  (*See also* Religious orthodoxy)
Conservative caucus of faculty members,
  214, 225
Conservative Club, 206, 208
Conservative League, 198
Conservatives:
  alumni as: in 1930s, 170
    in post-World War I era, 140
  backlash from (1970s), 370
  Boston elite as, 73
  early 1960s, 205 — 206
  Economics Department criticized by
    (1970s), 243
  number of, in 1959 *Crimson* poll, 203
Constitution Convention (Mass.), 40, 42
Constitutional Unionists, 85
Consumer's League of Boston, 110
Continental Army, 38
Conventional thought, church-controlled
  universities as centers of, 6
Conviction, sacrificing comfort for, in
  choice of careers, 363
Coolidge, Albert Sprague, 150
Coolidge, Calvin, 140, 144, 150
Coolidge, Shepley, Bulfinch and Abbott
  (architectural firm), 298
Copeland, Charles Townsend (Copey), 297
Coresidential living, 286, 336 — 337, 352,
  366
Cornell University, 149, 179, 223, 224, 233,
  248

Corporal punishment, trials for use of,
16 – 17
Corporation, the:
in Civil War era: end of state control and,
88 – 89
struggle between Overseers and,
86 – 88
in Colonial period: Bread and Butter riot
and, 36
changes in governance of Harvard
and, 41 – 43
demonstrations against classroom recitations and, 36
discipline and, 32
faculty members as Fellows, 15 – 16,
24, 25
under Hoar, 18
under Leverett, 22, 23
under I. Mather, 21
original composition of, 15
power of, 16
ranking system and, 24, 25
resident vs. nonresident government
issue and, 26, 27
resolution of 1659 passed by, 19 – 20
Revolutionary politics and, 37, 39
under Eliot: academic freedom and,
99 – 100
approves Eliot's reorganization, 101
dissatisfaction with Eliot, 131
Eliot candidacy and, 90
Socialist students and, 123
under Lowell: basis for selecting Lowell,
133
freedom of speech and, 135
racism and, 143
in 1930s, 154
academic freedom and, 141
honorary degree for Hanfstaengl and,
161
New Deal opposed by, 162
Walsh-Sweezy case and, 167
in 1940s, racism in athletic activities and,
178
in 1960s: 1969 crisis and, 225, 251
ROTC issue and, 219 – 220
in 1970s, 233, 244
black student occupation of President's office and, 237
choosing of successor to Pusey,
234 – 236
in post-Revolutionary era: bill to elect
Fellows and, 78

Corporation, the, in post-Revolutionary era:
conservatism of, 73
efforts at reforms, 59 – 66
opposes War of 1812, 56
partisan conflicts and, 55, 79 – 80
Quincy's hard-line discipline and, 69
religious liberalism and, 72
in Webber nomination, 51
in post-World War II era: McCarthyism
and, 195 – 197
non-Communist hiring policy and,
194
in World War I, academic freedom and,
136 – 137
Correspondence, Committees of, 38, 206
Cottle, Tom, 217
Counterculture, 360
anti-intellectual, 255
New Left caucus view of, 217
Courses:
black student organizations demand
control of, 222
lottery allocation system for overenrolled, 282 – 283, 328
1902 survey on quality of, 128
offered by General Education Program,
348 – 349
offered by Houses, 345 – 347
in post-Revolutionary era, 67, 73
reduction in, providing more time for
senior thesis, 343
SDS obtains approval of radical,
217 – 218, 225, 339
in Sociology Department, 376
student evaluation of (1970s), 254,
284 – 285
of Visual and Environmental Studies
Department, 342
(*See also* Concentrations; Credits; Elective system)
Cox, Archibald, 226, 231
Crawford, T. J., 249
Creativity, 13
political views and, 5 – 7, 246, 247
rejection of established order and, 6
scientific, Puritans and, 28 – 29
as source of change, 256
(*See also* Scholarship)
Credentialing function, 379 – 381
Credits:
without examinations (following
student protest, 1969 – 1970), 374
in Freshman Seminars, 338

Credits:
  for Social Relations, 148 – 149, 218
  in Visual and Environmental Studies, 342
Crimson's Confidential Guide to Courses, 285,
  286, 319, 325
Critic, The (newspaper), 104, 105
Critical thought, universities as centers of,
  4 – 5, 10
Croly, Herbert, 143
CRR (Committee on Rights and Responsi-
  bilities), 233, 237, 241
Cuban missile crisis (1962), 207, 209
CUE (Committee on Undergraduate Education), 281, 283, 285, 344
Culture:
  New England dominates, 99
  transmitters of traditional, 12
  (*See also* Academic culture; "Clubby"
  culture; Counterculture)
Curiosity, stimulating, in students, 386
Curriculum:
  affected by Socialist Club, 122
  changes in (1960s – 1970s), 342 – 345
    basis for, 379
    student reformers and, 365
  control of: black student organizations
    want control, 222
    faculty struggle for, 12
  demonstrations against (end of nine-
    teenth century), 104
  faculty-student relationship in matters
    of, 10, 12
  Freshman Seminars moderating rigors
    of, 328
  hegemony of, waning (1970s), 356
  in post-Revolutionary era, 64, 77
  in Scientific School, 86
  student influence on (1920s), 284
  (*See also* Courses)
Currier House, 352
Cutler, Eliot, 160
Cynicism among faculty members, 391

Dana, Richard Henry, Jr., 54, 68, 221
DARs (Damned Average Raisers), women
  as, 306
Dartmouth College, 112, 179, 294, 346
Darwin, Charles, 99
Davis, James A., 312*n.*
Davis, Norman H., 151
Davis, Robert G., 163
Deans, Council of, 235

Dearborn *Independent* (newspaper), 144
Debs, Eugene Victor, 138
Decision making, student participation in
  231 – 232, 240
Declaration of Independence (1776), 42
Defend America by Aiding the Allies,
  Committee to, 175
Deism, 49
Democratic Campaign Club, 111
Democratic meritocracy:
  criticized, 289 – 290
  Houses undercutting, 346
  issues around, 291
  Lowell and, 288, 289
  represented by Harvard National Schol-
    arships, 305
  "wonks" admitted under, 318
Democratic National Convention:
  of 1924, 144
  of 1968, 215
Democratic Party, 48, 205
Democrats:
  under Eliot, 108, 110 – 111
  involved in election campaigns (1877,
    1880, and 1890), 108
  in 1920s, 138
  number of: in 1860, 85
    in 1974, 254
  in post-Revolutionary era, governance of
    Harvard and, 77 – 79
  slavery issue and, 84
  support for (1912 – 1960), 245 – 246
Demonstrations:
  in Colonial period, against classroom
    recitations, 36
  under Eliot, against lack of due process
    in discipline, 104
  against food quality: in 1805, 53
    in 1818, 58
  in 1930s: April Peace Demonstration
    (1938), 172
    Karlsruhe incident (1934), 158 – 159,
    173
  in 1960s, 206 – 107, 249
Departmental chairmen, increasing power
  of, 59
Departments:
  attitudes toward Freshman Seminars of,
    350 – 351
  Bundy as Dean of Arts and Sciences Fac-
    ulty and, 354 – 355
  effects of 1960s – 1970s curriculum
    changes on, 344

Departments:
  established, 101
  General Education Program as viewed
    by, 348—349
  House offerings and, 345
  nominations by (1890s), 102
  role of, in making appointments, 313
  size of, 315
  University Professorships and, 353
Depression era, 157—178
  lack of social consciousness during,
    298—299
Design, School of, student participation in,
  231
DeVoto, Bernard, 153—154
Dewey, John, 286
Dewey, Thomas, 188
Dexter, Franklin, 38
Dillon, C. Douglas, 193, 354
Disarmament, Committee to Study, 206
Disarmament, groups favoring, 206
Discharges of faculty members over loyalty
  issue, 136, 138
Discipline, 10
  of faculty members: in Colonial period,
    32
    suspensions and discharges (World
      War I era), 136, 138
    (*See also* Dismissals, of faculty
      members)
  (*See also* Student discipline)
Discrimination (*see* Anti-Semitism; Hous-
  ing discrimination; Job discrimi-
  nation; Racism)
Dismissals:
  of faculty members: for conflict of inter-
    est, 141
    of Hicks, 169
    of Waterhouse, 54—55
  of students: for disrespect, 32
    during 1807—1824, 58—59
    in Great Rebellion (1823), 57
    of 1969 strike participants, 225
    in Rotten Cabbage Rebellion, 54
Dissent, universities as traditional centers
  of, 3—5
  (*See also* Student unrest)
Dissertations (*see* Theses)
Divinity, School of, 113
  Pusey attempts to revive, 197
  religious liberalism in, 113
  student participation in, 231
Doctorates (*see* Ph.D.'s)

Dodd, E. M., 166
Dodge, Mabel, 125
Domestic orientation of academic and in-
  tellectual life, 382
Dow Chemical incident (1967), 214, 215,
  219
Draft (conscription), 85, 227, 240
  effects of disappearance of, 356
  sanctuary from, 360
Draper, Hal, 119
Dress:
  in counterculture, 217
  nonconformity to: in 1920s, 157
    in post-Revolutionary era, 72
Drinan, Father Robert, 375
Drinking, dismissals for, 32
Dropping out, 359
Drugs, 217
DuBois, W. E. B., 106, 127
Dudley House, 372*n.*
Due process, demonstrations against lack
  of (end of nineteenth century), 104
Dunbar, Asa, 35
Dunbar, Charles, 127
Dunlop, John, 225, 233*n.*, 353
  as potential successor to Pusey, 235—236
  resigns, 243
Dunster, Henry, 17, 81, 123
Dunster House, 298

Earnest, Ernst, 47, 190
East Asian Studies (research center), 314
Eaton, Nathaniel, 16—17
Echols Scholar Program, 328*n.*
Economic development, universities and, 7
Economics Department, 118, 233
  attacks on academic freedom of,
    108—109
  Committee on Social Studies and, 326
  in 1930s: procapitalist bias of, 170
    Walsh and Sweezy reappointment to,
    164—166
  in 1960s, attacks on, 208—209
  in 1970s, radicals demand Marxist pro-
    fessors in, 241—243
  in post-World War II era, threats to,
    183—184
  self-evaluation by (1912—1913), 134
  student participation and, 232
Economics of Harvard, The (Harris), 170
Edinburgh, Scotland, 16
Editors of college newspapers, 322—323
Edsall, John T., 139

Education:
  affectively oriented, 365
  decline in quality of (1969), 227, 228
  federal aid to private and public, sup-
    ported (1950s), 263
  free thought and, emphasis on, 28
  as producer's and consumer's good, 381
  Puritan commitment to, 13, 28
  state of, in pre-Civil War era, 85 – 88
Education, School of, student participation
    in, 231
Education of American Leaders (Pierson),
    256*n.*
Educational institutions, occupational vs.,
    meritocracy and, 291
Educational Policies Commission, 186
Educational Policy, Faculty Committee on,
    225, 337 – 338, 344
Educational reforms:
  curricular (1960s and 1970s), 342 – 345
    basis for, 379
    student reformers and, 365
  interest in (1920s), 299
  Jacksonian attempts at, 73 – 74
  under Kirkland, 58 – 66
  in 1970s: factors limiting possibilities of
    (1973), 284
  in General Education Program,
    281 – 285
    (*See also* General Education Pro-
      gram)
  in post-World War II era, 190
    student body composition affected by,
      180
  responsibility for, 357
  as tokenism, 356
  (*See also specific programs*)
Eight, Committee of, 166 – 167, 173
1812, War of, 55, 56
1848, Revolution of, 4, 8
1850, Compromise of, 79, 81, 83
Eisenhower, Dwight D., 188, 200 – 202,
    245
Eisler, Gerhard, 182
Elections:
  class, 105
  to Final Clubs, 294
  gubernatorial, 1890, 103
  of Harvard presidents: in Colonial
    period, 27
  plans for reforms under Eliot, 102
  senatorial, in 1962, 207
  (*See also* Presidential elections)

Elective system:
  Democrats support, 77
  under Eliot, 100 – 103
    effects on student unrest, 94
    followed by other universities, 103
    reactions to, 102
  opposition to, 129 – 130, 134, 142, 283,
    293
Eleven Resident Instructors, 59 – 60
Eliot, Amory, 287*n.*
Eliot, Andrew, 36
Eliot, Charles, 76, 133, 142, 285
  bicameral form of government and, 16
  curriculum of Scientific School and, 86
  and meritocracy, 295
    aristocratic meritocracy, 287 – 289
    Eliot's belief in, 106
  presidency of, 88 – 131, 154, 155, 180, 216,
    247, 302
    academic freedom under, 99 – 102
      108 – 110, 117 – 118, 187 – 188
    antiwar activity under, 115 – 117
    becomes President, 88, 89
    dissatisfaction with, 128 – 131
    ethnic and social heterogeneity under,
      294
    intellectual achievements under,
      126 – 128
    Lowell presidency compared with, 147
    political activity under, 107 – 108
    racism under, 142 – 144
    reactions to policies of, 93 – 99,
      102 – 105
    religious liberalism under, 112 – 114
    and scholarship, 96, 113, 133, 287 – 288
    social-class differences among stu-
      dents and, 105 – 107
    sources of nonconformism under,
      124 – 126
    three-year requirement for baccalau-
      reate degree and, 129, 130, 284
  Pusey compared with, 192
  slavery issue and, 84, 85
  student politics under, 107, 108
    political views and activities,
      110 – 112, 115 – 117
    socialism, 119 – 124
    two-party system and, 105
  and World War I, 135
Eliot, Rev. John, 51
Eliot, Samuel, 42, 74, 99
Eliot, Samuel (son), 99
Eliot, T. S., 299

Eliot House, 352

Elite:
Columbia University loses its (1920s and 1930s), 295
dropping out as way of rejecting, 359
Harvard faculty and students as members of, 5
identifies with Federalism, 47
influence of, in Colonial period, 36
merit defined in self-serving way by, 290
Protestant Ethic rejected by, 331
Unitarianism appeals to, 30
(*See also* Boston elite; Business community; Upper-class students)

Elitism:
attempts to establish a General Education Program and, 282
Calvinism and, 81
in Committee on Social Studies, 326 – 329
in Freshman Seminars, 328 – 329
Jacksonians attack, 73 – 75
(*See also* Meritocracy)

Emergency Relief Administration, 162

Emerson, Ralph Waldo, 57, 72, 83, 84, 113, 124

Emerson, Rupert, 163

Employment examination, 381

Encounter groups, 365

End-of-year examinations, protests against (1791), 50

Endowments (*see* Grants)

English Department, 342

English Revolution (1642), 3

Enrollment:
in Afro-American Studies (1973 – 1974), 241
of black students: under Lowell, 144, 145
in 1960s, 180, 222
of Catholic students: in 1810, 52
under Lowell, 144, 145
in Colonial period, 27
during 1870 – 1900, 98
in Freshman Seminars, 350
in General Education, 337
of Jewish students: in 1810, 52
under Lowell, 144 – 150, 179
lottery allocation system for, 282 – 283, 328
after Peace of Utrecht, 24
in post-Revolutionary era, 66, 67, 78
in pre-Civil War era, 83
religious liberalism affects, 114

Enrollment:
in specialized courses, 348*n.*
(*See also* Admissions policies)

Entrance examinations:
Japanese, 381
proposal to waive, 147 – 148

Epps, Archie, 208

Equality of opportunity:
admission quotas and, 147
freedom and, 106
functional specificity and, 6 – 7
meritocracy and, 289*n.*
(*see also* Meritocracy)

Erikson, Erik, 3, 354

Established order:
rejection of, 6
intellectuality and, 246 – 248
and universities as centers of dissent, 3 – 4

Ethics, attitudes of liberals toward (late 1950s), 202

European students, political activity of (end of nineteenth century), 107

Evans, David, 336*n.*

Evans, M. Stanton, 202

Everett, Edward, 80
Compromise of 1850 supported by, 83
Jackson attacked by, 73
resigns, 66 – 67

Evergreen State College, 365

Examinations:
as alternate system of discipline, 93
alternative to, in General Education (1958), 337 – 338
amnesty vis-à-vis, following student protest (1969 – 1970), 374 – 375
employment, 381
entrance: Japanese, 381
as learning experience, 339*n.*
proposal to waive, 147 – 148
protests against end- of-year (1791), 50
(*See also* Grades; Grading system)

Exeter Academy, 143, 296

Exiles in McCarthy era, 195

Expulsions:
at Chicago University, 226
for failure to attend chapel, 32
following Great Rebellion (1823), 70
number of (1807 – 1824), 58 – 59

Extension Program for Adults, 350

Extracurricular activities:
academic achievement and, 323
upper-class students in, 152, 246

Fabian Socialism, 109, 121, 249
Faculty:
  achievement orientation of Jewish
    members of, 307–308
  Ad Hoc Committee system of appoint-
    ments and, 308–312
  in Civil War era: Eliot's candidacy and,
    90
    Hill presidency and, 87
  in Colonial period: antagonistic to Hoar,
    18, 19
    authority of, 31, 43, 44
    clerical influence undermined (end of
      eighteenth century), 40
    control on, 16
    demonstrations against, 36
    enforcing religious orthodoxy among
      members of, 33
    as Fellows of the Corporation, 15–16,
      24, 25
    under I. Mather, 21
    ranking system and, 23, 24
    resident vs. nonresident government
      issue and, 25–26
    and Revolutionary politics, 38
  creativity of, as source of radicalism, 246
  under Eliot, 96–97
    antiwar activity and, 115–117
    average age of, 91–92
    faculty participation, 101–102
    members listed, 127
    politics and, 119, 120, 122
    reactions to Eliot's policies, 102–104,
      131
    religious liberalism and, 113–114
  in Freshman Seminars, 350, 351n., 352
  function of, 5
  General Education Program and,
    348–349, 352
  House offerings and, 345–347
  under Lowell: decline of scholarship, 153
    Jewish faculty members, 149
    meritocracy and, 296
    racism and, 143
    scholarship encouraged by elective
      system, 293
  in 1930s, 171, 299
    concern for quality of, 167–169
    European faculty members, 300–301,
      305
    political activity of, 163–167
    socioeconomic backgrounds of, 299
    teachers' oath bill and, 162–163

Faculty, in 1930s:
    Walsh-Sweezy case and, 167
    where faculty members received their
      degrees, 301n.
  in 1950s: Advanced Standing Program
    and, 317–318
    Bundy on, 316
    liberalism of, 204
  in 1960s, 211
    Advanced Standing Program and,
      317–318
    Afro-American Studies and, 223, 224,
      340–341
    militancy of, 213–215, 370, 373–374
    1969 crisis, 220–221, 224, 251
    political positions of, 253
    Princeton Plan turned down by,
      375–376
    Rosovsky Report on Afro-American
      Studies and, 369–370
    ROTC issue and, 221
    in Tocsin demonstration, 206
    value of success doubted by, 331
  in 1970s: anti-intellectual counterculture
    and, 255
    appointment of Wilson and, 243–244
    choosing a successor to Pusey and,
      234–237
    cynicism among, 391–392
    harassment of, 231
    minority group members on, 244
    number of Jewish members, 307
    political positions of, 253
    student participation and, 232
  nondepartmental offerings and, 344
  in post-Revolutionary era: efforts at re-
    form and, 59–66
    elective system and, 76
    Federalism and, 47, 48
    Jacksonian views of, 73, 74
    Quincy assesses role of, 75–76
    Quincy's hard-line discipline and, 69
    reducing power of, 58
    size of (1820s), 67
    student discipline and, 49, 53–54
    ties between Boston elite and, 52–53
  in post-World War II era: academic cul-
    ture and, 191
    barring Communists from teaching
      and, 187
    involved in religious disputation,
      197–198
    Jewish members of, 179

Faculty, in post-World War II era:
McCarthyism and, 190, 194—197
political activity of, 200—202
rights of Communists and, 182—183
working on government research projects and, 201
of pre-Civil War era, 84, 86
professionalism of, 287—288
status quo accepted by, 5
of Visual and Environmental Studies
Department, 342
in World War I, pressures to fire antiwar
faculty members, 136
in World War II, intervention supported,
174—176
(*See also* Discipline, of faculty members;
Faculty-student relations; Personnel
policies; Scholars; Scholarship;
Teaching)
Faculty Advisory Committee, 195
Faculty Club, 372
Faculty Council (1939), 169—170, 233
Faculty Council (1970), 233, 236—238
candidates for vacancies on, 236—237
student participation and, 232
Faculty-student relations, 10—12
contemporary: advising in, 384—385
departmental variations in, 377
emphasis on scholarship affecting, 378
as factor in 1969 crisis, 227, 228
in General Education Program,
337—338
in Houses, 298, 372—373
in Meyer's 1972 survey, 356n.
in 1974 survey, 254—255
positive effects of, 378—379
problems in, 383
trying to establish personal and egalitarian relations, 360—361, 365
under Eliot, 93—94, 103—104, 129
in post-Civil War era, 93
in post-Revolutionary era, 50, 53, 68
in pre-Civil War era, 85—86
Failures, rarity of, 319
Fainsod, Merle, 353
Fairbank, John K., 174
Faltermayer, Edmund, 380n.
Farrar, John, 69
Fascism, 158, 175
refugees from, as faculty members
(1930s), 300—301
Fast, Howard, 182

Federal aid to public and private educa-
tion, student support for (late 1950s),
263
Federalism, 47, 48
Federalist party, 49, 73
Federalists:
in post-Revolutionary era: attempts to
control Board of Overseers, 54—55
attitudes toward student discipline,
53—54
Massachusetts Legislature controlled
by, 67
Whigs succeed, in state politics, 70
Fellows of the Corporation (*see* Corporation, the)
Ferguson, W. S., 166
Feuer, Lewis, 163
Fifteen, Committee of, 225, 227, 250
Fifth Amendment (1791) in McCarthy investigations, 185, 195—197
Final Clubs, 294, 295, 298, 329, 342n.
Financial support:
from Boston elite, 98—99
for classified research, 201
in Colonial period, 15, 28, 40—42
in Depression era, 164
from Douglas Dillon, 354
in 1848 and 1849, 80
from Ford Foundation, 354
for Freshman Seminars, 351
in 1930s, 170
conservative alumni withhold,
170
for impoverished students, 161—162
in 1970s, shrinking, 391
for Oxford and Cambridge universities,
47
political disputation and, 12
in post-Revolutionary era, 58
private and public, in post-World War II
era, 302
state, 57, 67, 80
(*See also* Grants)
Fine Arts courses, selected on pass/fail
basis, 343
Finland, Soviet Union invades (1939), 172,
174
Finley, John, 286, 348, 352
First Church of Cambridge, 30—31
First World War (World War I, 1914—1918),
135—138
Fischer, Louis, 164

Fisk University, 179, 189
Fiske, John, 100
Flexner, Abraham, 305*n*.
Flogging, proposed revival of, 57
Follen, Charles, 84
Follen, Karl, 69
Follen, Mrs. Karl, 69
Food quality:
  demonstrations against: in 1805, 53
    in 1818, 58
  riots against, 11, 32, 35−36
Football, politics rivaling (1924), 150
Ford, Franklin, 225, 226, 381*n*.
Ford, Henry, 144, 145
Ford Foundation, 354
Foreign aid, attitudes toward (late 1950s),
  203
Foreign policy:
  attitudes toward, in post-World War II
    era, 189
  of Cleveland, opposed, 115
  Korean War, 185, 188, 189, 198
  Mexican War, 116
  recognition of China (late 1950s), sup-
    ported, 201, 203
  Spanish-American War, 115−118
  Vietnam War (*see* Vietnam War)
  World War I, 135−138
  World War II, 172−177
  Young Democrats and, 201
Foster, William Z., 157
14, Committee of (Temporary Student
    Committee on Instruction in the
    Social Sciences), 165
Fraenkel, Osmond, 119
France, fall of (1940), 175
Francis, Alexander, 120
Frankfurter, Felix, 140, 146, 149, 151, 166,
    330*n*.
Fraternities, 306
  effects of Houses on, 294
  emergence of, 105
  Houses compared with coed, 346
  outlawing, in state institutions, 105
  student attitudes toward (post-World
    War II era), 189
  working-class students attracted to,
    306*n*.
Frazier, Benjamin West, III, 298
Free schools, 364
Free society, guiding values of scholarship
  in, 6

Free Soilers, 78, 83, 84
Free thought:
  emphasis on education and, 28
  inherent consequences of, 4−5
  triumph of Unitarianism and, 51
Free trade, 108
"Freedom at Harvard" (article), 186
Freedom of speech:
  banquet for (1920), 140
  Bok and, 238
  for Communists, 182−183, 187
  under Lowell, 135
  in 1930s, 161
  in 1970s, 243−244
  in post-Revolutionary era, 48
  for students, 12
Freeman (magazine), 192
Freethinking, 113
French Revolution (1789), 4, 47, 48
Freshman Advisers, Board of, 334
Freshman Seminar Program, 282−283,
  328−329
  atmosphere of, 351
  departmental attitudes towards,
    350−351
  grading system in, 338, 351
  teaching in, 388*n*.
Freshman Union, 342
Freund, Paul, 353
Friedrich, Carl J., 297, 298, 301*n*.
Friendly, Henry, 227
Friendly Committee, 227
Friends of New Germany, 160
FSM (Berkeley Free Speech Movement), 119
Fugitive Slave Law, 78, 83
Fuller, Alvin Tufts, 151
Fuller, Martha, 301*n*.
Fundamentalism, 30
Funkenstein, Daniel, 363*n*.
Furry, Wendell, 195−196

Gadfly, The (magazine), 139, 148, 150, 199
Galbraith, John Kenneth, 163, 183
Gay, Edwin F., 122
General Education, Committee on, 348
General Education Program, 285, 321, 337,
  353
  attempts to reform (1973), 281−282
  basis for creating, 347
  chair appointees in, 354
  courses of, 345, 348−349

General Education Program:
  diluted requirements of, 376
  faculty attitudes towards, 352
  Houses offering courses in, 347
  philosophy of, 385–386
  proposed innovations for (1958),
    337–338
  University Professors in, 353
General Studies, honors in, 375, 378
Generational conflicts:
  in Colonial period, 19
  in 1960s, 250, 368n.
Genetic theory of intelligence, 231, 237,
  238, 243
Geneva, Switzerland, Calvinist-dominated
  universities in, 16
Geology Department, 391
Georgetown University, 307
Georgia, University of, 301
German faculties (end of nineteenth centu-
  ry), 105
German Jews, 295, 307
German students (end of nineteenth centu-
  ry), 104
German universities (nineteenth century),
  4
Germanic Languages and Literatures, De-
  partment of, 377
Gerry, Elbridge, 55
GI Bill of Rights, 306
Gibbs, Wolcott, 86, 288n.
Glass, Bentley, 328n.
Glazer, Nathan, 364
Glimp, Fred, 225, 227
Goddard College, 365
Godkin, E. L., 97n., 99
Gold Coast residences, 92–93, 106, 293
Goldberg, Arthur, 213
Goldwater, Barry, 205, 210
Goodwin, William, 127
Gordon, Robert A., 163
Göttingen, University of, 67
Governing Boards (*see* Corporation, the;
  Overseers, Board of)
Government, Department of, 327, 344
Government research projects, 201
Government-supported universities, 4
Grades:
  amnesty for, following student protest
    (1969–1970), 374–375
  of black students, 335
  Crimson's editors' attitudes towards,
    322–323

Grades:
  importance of, 288
  low or failing, given in cases of plagia-
    rism, 340
  relations between success and,
    380
  spread of, in different fields, 297
Grading system:
  abandoning, 380–381
  as alternate system of discipline, 93
  in Freshman Seminars, 338, 351
  meritocracy and, 288, 380
  protests against, 11
  recruiting of nonwhite students and
    changes in (1970s), 333
  standards of performance and, 338–339
Graduate Department, established, 101
Graduate Student and Teaching Fellows
  Union, 355, 371
Graduate-student assistants, complaints
  about (1902), 128, 134
Graduation with honors:
  from General Studies, 375, 378
  number of students, 318
  from 1934 and 1935 classes, 297–298
  sense of self-confidence derived from,
    320
Graduation requirements:
  Advanced Standing Program accelera-
    ting, 317
  in 1902, 130
Grant, Gerald, 366n.
Grant, Robert, 93–94
Grants:
  ability to influence appointments
    through, 109
  between 1870 and 1900, 98
  in post-Revolutionary era, 58, 73
  to study in Germany, 160–161
Gray, Asa, 76, 86
Gray, John, 74
Great American Universities (survey),
  103
Great Awakening, the, 34
Great Rebellion (1823), 57, 58, 70
Great Rebellion (1834), 68–70, 227
Great Rebellion (1969), 212, 220, 222–224
  changes following, 230–233
  in administration, 233–237
  police action in, 220–222, 229, 246, 254,
    340
  opposed, 235
  rationale for, 226–227

Great Rebellion (1969):
restoring authority after, 224—230
sit-in at University Hall in, 69, 211, 212, 215, 220, 221, 321, 340, 372*n.*, 374
Great Tradition, The (Hicks), 169
Green, Beriah, 84
Green, Martin, 98
Greenwood, Isaac, 32, 33
Gregariousness, frowned upon, 350
Grenfell Mission, 299
Griswold, Dean, 195
Gropius, Walter, 298
Gross, Charles, 113
Groton (prep school), 288*n.*, 320
Gruening, Ernest, 143
Gubernatorial elections, 1890, 103
"Gunpowder Plot" (1842), 71

Halifax, Lord (Edward Frederick Lindley Wood, Earl of Halifax), 177
Hallowell, Robert, 125
Hancock, John, 35, 41
Hand, Learned, 162
Handlin, Oscar, 353
Hanfstaengl, Ernst F. S., 160—161
Hapgood, Norman, 127
Harding, Warren G., 138, 144
Harkness, Edward, 149
Harris, Seymour, 170, 180, 184, 299
Harrison, Benjamin, 111
Hart, Henry, 163
Harvard Class Fund, 321
Harvard Alumni Bulletin, 170, 186, 193, 215
Harvard Anti-War Committee, 174
Harvard Athletic Association, 177, 178
Harvard Crimson (newspaper), 115, 198, 238, 286, 361
academic freedom and, 138
Afro-American Studies and, 222, 223
antiwar position of (World War II), 174—177
antiwar protests and (1960s), 215
on Bok, 239
civil rights of Communists and, 180—182
critics of Economics Department and, 243
editors of, 117, 317, 364
attitudes toward grades, 322—323
government research projects and, 201
on KKK, 145
in 1930s: ASU criticizes, 172
on Hicks' appointment, 169
Karlsruhe incident and, 159

Harvard Crimson (newspaper), in 1930s:
on lack of student militancy, 173
Nazism supported, 160, 161
on Walsh-Sweezy case, 165
in 1950s:
1956 poll taken by, 200
1959 poll taken by, 202—204
opinion on political groups, 199—200
on political activity, 202
as SDS organ, 246
straw polls of: in 1936, 162
in 1940, 176
supports admission quotas, 146
and World War I, 135, 136
Harvard Democratic Club, 150
Harvard *Gazette* (newspaper), 366
Harvard Graduate School of Business Administration, 361, 385, 388
Harvard Graduate's Magazine (magazine), 123, 148, 154
Harvard *Guardian* (newspaper), 175
Harvard *Independent* (newspaper), 246
Harvard Lampoon, The (magazine), 140, 176
Harvard Law Review (magazine), 140, 195
Harvard Law School:
attention paid to teaching in, 388
competitive atmosphere of, 296, 330—331
Jews as professors in, 149
Harvard Liberal Club, 139, 148, 245
in 1920s, radicalism of, 249
in 1930s: activities of, 158
in Harvard Student Union, 171
opposes building of Memorial Church, 150
Harvard Liberal Union:
in 1950s, 198—199
declining liberalism of, 188—189
rights of Communists and, 180, 181
in 1960s, 208
supports intervention in World War II, 177
"Harvard man," 350
Harvard Medical School, founded, 55
Harvard Men's League for Women's Suffrage, 122
Harvard National Scholarships, 305
Harvard Progressive (newspaper), 177
Harvard-Radcliffe Policy Committee, 285, 343
"Harvard Rallies for Tomorrow" (article), 172
Harvard Republican Club, 111, 112, 150

Harvard Socialist Club, 118, 171, 241
  curriculum affected by (1900s), 122
  Lowell opposed by, 151
  membership of: brilliancy of members,
    123
    in 1905, 119
    pre-World War I, 245
  in 1960s, 208, 209
  pre-World War I: membership of, 245
    political sympathies of, 249
  Reed, John, 121–122
  revival of (1930s), 158
  World War I and, 135, 136
Harvard Society of Individualists, 208
Harvard Student Council, 134, 197, 337
  Conant's personnel policies and, 168
  Phillips' political activities and, 205
  Walsh-Sweezy case and, 165–166
Harvard Student Union, 181, 212
  in 1930s: developments in, 171–173
    membership of, 245
    radicalism of, 249
  World War II and, 174, 175
Harvard Traveling Fellowships, 327
Harvard Undergraduate Council, 232
Harvard University:
  founded, 15
  future of, 392
  1972 scholarly status of, 234
  preeminence, of, 13, 26, 91, 247, 256
  tercentenary celebration of, 162
  as world center of research (early twen-
    tieth century), 126
Haverford College, 346
Hawkins, Hugh, 286n., 288n.
Heimert, Alan, 223
Henderson, Gerard, 123
Henderson, Lawrence J., 296
Heresies, 17, 52
Herrnstein, Richard, 231, 237–239, 243,
  373
Herter, Christian A., 196
Hicks, Granville, 163, 168–169
High-risk students, 318, 334
High school preparation, Advanced Stand-
  ing Program and, 317
Hill, Thomas, 49, 86–89
Hillel exemption, 375n.
Himmelhoch, Jerome, 171
History and Literature (program), 283
History and Literature, Committee on, 377
History of Massachusetts Bay (Hutchinson),
  37

History Department, 325
  background of faculty members of
    (1930s), 300
  Committee on Social Studies and, 326
Hitler, Adolf, 159–161, 177
Hoar, Ebenezer Rockwood, 69
Hoar, Leonard, 17, 18
Hobbes, Thomas, 3, 373
Hocking, William Ernest, 159
Hoff, Philip, 375
Hoffman, John Maynard, 33
Hofstadter, Richard, 51–52
Holcombe, Arthur N., 119, 159
Holmes, Abiel, 56
Holmes, Oliver Wendell, Jr., 56, 116
Holt, Hamilton, 299n.
Holton, Gerald, 351n.
Holy Cross, College of the, 307
Holyoke, Edward, 31, 34–37
Honorary degrees:
  to Bok, 237
  to Halifax, 177
  to Hanfstaengl, proposed, 160
  to Jackson, 70
  to Monroe, 70
  to F. D. Roosevelt, 177
  to H. Wallace, 162
Honors programs:
  course reduction for those in, 343
  elitism and, 282
  interdisciplinary, 344
  without theses, 376
Honors students:
  allowed to design their fields of concen-
    tration, 344
  in Independent Study, 344
Honors system:
  based on grades, 131
  combined with concentrations, 134, 293
Hoover, Herbert, 144, 151, 157, 158, 298
Houses, 92, 149, 215, 293, 301
  athletes in, 321
  atmosphere of, 349–350
  coresidential, 286, 336–337, 352, 366
  course offerings by, 345–347
  defended, 286
  difference between, 283
  effects of, on Final Clubs, 294
  elections for CRR opposed by, 232
  faculty-student relations in, 298,
    345–346
  General Education courses in, 372
  inadequacy of (1969), 227

Houses:
    physical quality of, 153–154
    Student Council report on, 284
    used as student centers, 342
Housing discrimination, civil rights move-
        ment fights, 207
Hughes, Everett, 382*n.*
Hughes, H. Stuart, 184–185, 206, 207, 256,
    372
Humphrey, Hubert H., 212–213
Hunt, Edward Eyre, 125
Huntington, Samuel P., 190, 191, 317*n.*
    on academic culture, 247
    anti-intellectual counterculture and, 255
    as government consultant, 231
    1969 crisis and, 225
Hutchinson, Thomas, 37

Immediate Government, 58
Immigration restrictions(1920s), 144
Imperialism, opposed, 116–117, 124, 192
"Imperialism and the University" (course),
    218
"In the Colleges" (speech), 135
Independent Study (program), 336, 343, 384
Independents, number of students regis-
        tered as (1974), 254
In loco parentis, doctrine of, demonstrations
        against (end of nineteenth century), 104
Innis, Roy, 243
Innovative teaching, research compared
        with, 303
Institute of Politics, 213, 251, 366
Intellectual achievement under Eliot, 118,
    126–128
    (*See also* Scholarship)
"Intellectual Aristocracy, The" (Annan), 99
Intellectuality:
    creativity and, 6
    socially critical outlook and, 246–248
Intellectuals:
    defined, 6
    McCarthy's view of, 192
    as newly born concept (end of nine-
        teenth century), 118
    pre-Civil War, 7–8
    reactions of, to McCarthyism, 190
    rights of Communists and, 185
    (*See also* Scholars)
Intelligence:
    genetic theory of, 231, 237, 238, 243
    trained, rewards and, 7

Intelligentsia, scientific-technological, 7
    (*See also* Elite; Elitism, Intellectuals;
        Scholars; Scholarship)
Intercollegiate athletics, socialist students
        attack, 122
Intercollegiate Liberal League, 138–139,
    245
Intercollegiate Socialist Society (ISS), 119,
    138, 209, 245
Interdisciplinary honors programs, 344
Interdisciplinary teaching, University pro-
        fessorship and, 352–353
Internal Security, Senate Committee on,
    195, 197
International Communism, McCarthy's
        first speech against (1950), 192
International Gallup Poll (1971), 256
International Polity Club, 122
International Relations Club, 208
Intervention in World War II, supporters
        and opponents of, 173–177
"Introduction" (Holcombe, Perry, and
        Hocking), 159
"Introduction to Literature" (course), 337
Irish Catholic students, 307
"Is an Absolute and Arbitrary Monarchy
        contrary to Right Reason?" (Suman),
    35
"Is Harvard's Liberalism Myth or Reali-
        ty?" (statement of Cambridge
        Union of University Teachers), 166
"Is it Lawful to resist the Supreme Magis-
        trate, if the Commonwealth cannot
        otherwise be preserved?" 35
"Is unlimited obedience to rulers taught by
        Christ and His Apostles?" (Greene), 35
"Is the Voice of the People the Voice of
        God?" (Whittaker), 35
Isolationism, 171, 174, 175
ISS (Intercollegiate Socialist Society, later
        League for Industrial Democracy),
    119, 138, 209, 245

Jackson, Andrew, 70, 162
Jackson State University shootings (1970),
    374
Jacksonians, 73–75, 147
James, William, 127, 209, 289, 301
    academic freedom and, 118
    on committee work, 102
    opposes Spanish-American War,
        116–117

James, William:
  right to dissent and, 115
  as Mugwump, 108
  Socialist Club supported by, 121, 123
Japan, 4, 5, 381
Jefferson, Thomas, 44, 48, 55
"Jefferson Davis as a Representative of
    Civilization" (speech), 106
Jeffersonians, 47, 53 – 55, 67, 147
Jenner, William E., 191, 195, 197
Jensen, Arthur, 238
Jewish professors:
  achievement orientation of, 307 – 308
  first Jewish dean (1973), 244
  hiring of (in post-World War II era), 179
  under Lowell, 149
  number of (1970s), 307
Jewish student organizations, 113
Jewish students, 142
  achievement orientation of, 307 – 308
  admission quotas lifted for, 179
  Eliot and, 106
  enrollment of: in 1810, 52
    under Lowell, 144 – 150, 179
  number of (1970s), 307
  Saturday examination exemptions for,
    375n.
Jewish War Veterans, 176
Jews:
  commitment to education of, 28
  German, 295, 307
Job discrimination, protests against, 207,
    230
"Jocks," defined, 318
John Reed Club, 181, 182
Johns Hopkins University, 149, 288n., 302
Johnson, Lewis J., 122
Johnson, Lyndon B., 210
Johnson, S. B., 121
Joint Center for Urban Studies (MIT and
    Harvard), 314
Journal of Afro-American Affairs (formerly
    Journal of Negro Affairs), 340
Journal of 1832 (Dana), 68, 221
Journal of Negro Affairs (later *Journal of
    Afro-American Affairs*), 340
Junior faculty (*see* Faculty)
Junior Fellows, 289n., 353, 354
Juvenile court work, 364

Kagan Committee, 286
Kahn, E. J., Jr., 211, 212, 234

Kaltenborn, Rolf, 165
Karlsruhe incident (1934), 158 – 159, 173
Kaysen, Carl, 207, 316n.
Keep America Out of War Committee,
    174 – 175
Keep America Out of War Congress, 177
Kelley, Nicholas, 119
Kelman, Steven, 212, 218, 230, 250
Keniston, Kenneth, 208, 213, 359
Kennedy, John F., 204, 206, 207, 245 – 246
Kennedy, Robert F., 215, 246
Kennedy Fellows, 350
Kent State University shootings (1970), 374
Keppel, Frederick, 153
Kerr, Clark, 300n.
Keynes, John Maynard, 183
*Keynes at Harvard: Economic Deception as a
    Political Credo*, 208
Khrushchev, Nikita, 248
Kiely, Robert, 281, 285, 346n., 365
Kilson, Martin, 240, 369 – 370
King, Martin Luther, Jr., 210
Kirk, Grayson L., 216
Kirkland, John, 51, 56 – 67
  efforts at reform under, 58 – 66
  resigns, 67
  War of 1812 opposed by, 56
Kissinger, Henry, 230, 372
Kistiakowsky, George, 300
Klaw, Spenser, 175
Kluckhohn, Clyde, 184, 315
Kneeland, William, 39
Knowledge-creating centers, universities
    as, 5
Koch, Adolph, 52
Kohler, Elmer, 166n.
Kopit, Arthur, 323
Korean War (1949 – 1953), 185, 188, 189, 198
Kozol, Jonathan, 364
Kramer, Joel, 215 – 216, 220
Ku Klux Klan (KKK), 143, 144, 145
Kuttner, Alfred, 125

Labor unions, 152
Labor Youth League, 182
LaFollette, Robert, 150, 151, 246
LaFollette-Wheeler Club, 150
Lamont, Corliss, 152, 298
Land, Edwin, 231, 360n.
Landon, Alfred, 162
Lane, Robert, 171, 177
Langdon, Samuel, 39

Langmuir, Alexander, 298
Lash, Joseph, 177
Laski, Harold, 140, 157, 186, 187
Latin diplomas, issuance of, 211
Law Students Association, 175
Lawrence Scientific School, 86, 101
Laws and Liberties of Massachusetts, The, 28
Lazarsfeld, Paul, 190
League for a Declared War for National
    Self-Respect, 177
League for Industrial Democracy (LID, for-
    merly Intercollegiate Socialist Soci-
    ety), 138, 209
  growth of, 157–158
  in protest against ROTC oath, 181
League for Woman Suffrage, 135
Leave policies, 389
Lectures, 362
  deprecated, 385
  discussions following, 387
  hierarchical nature of, 360–361
  "Legal Process, The" (course), 353
Legal professions, attraction to, 363, 364
Legal rights of students in Colonial period,
    19–20
Leman, Christopher, 390
Lenin, Vladimir Illych, 140
  "Leninism" (course), 218
Leontief, Wassily, 224
Lern freiheit principle, 12, 27
  attempts to enlarge, 95
  under Eliot, 102
Lerner, Max, 163
Leverett, John, 20–26
  power relations under, 23
  as radical, 123–124
  resident vs. nonresident government
    and, 24–26
  successor to, 31
Leverett, Governor John, 24
Leverett House, 372
Levi, Edward H., 226
Levin, Harry, 389n.
Lexington, Massachusetts (1776), 38
Liberal caucus of faculty, 214, 220, 232, 233
  restoring authority after 1969 crisis and,
    224–225
Liberalism:
  as dominant climate at Harvard, 204
  in 1950s, 204
  in 1972, 252
  as dominant ideology since World War
    II, 246

Liberalism:
  post-World War I, 138–140
    in social sciences opposed (1930s), 166
  as threat to conservatives, 206
  (*See also* Religious liberalism)
Liberals:
  in Cold War era, 188–190
  under Lowell: activities of, 150
    admission quotas opposed by,
      146–147
  in 1930s: in ASU, 172
    isolationism opposed by, 171
  1950 attitudes of, 202–204
  in 1969 crisis, 228
  in post-World War I era, 139–140
  Soviet totalitarianism opposed by, 185
Liberation movements, support for, 217
Liberty tree (Rebellion Tree), 36, 39, 57
Library facilities:
  under Eliot, 98
  library size in pre-Civil War era, 86
LID (*see* League for Industrial Democracy)
Lifestyle, importance of finding one's, 363
Lincoln, Abraham, 85
Lincoln, Levi, 53
Lincoln Report (1805), 54
Lineage, meritocracy and, 320–321
Lippmann, Walter, 119, 121–122, 209
  intellectual rebellion of, 125
  on 1920s generation, 157
  racism opposed by, 143
  World War I supported by, 136
Literary societies, 52
Little, Clarence Cook, 299n.
Lodge, Henry Cabot, 95
Lodge, John D., 193
Loeb Theater, 297n., 323
Long hair as an issue in Colonial period, 19
Longfellow, Henry Wadsworth, 76, 83, 99
Longloissorie, Mr., 33
Look Back in Anger, 321
Loring, Edward O., 83, 84
Lottery allocation system for overenrolled
    courses, 282–283, 328
Lovett, Robert Morss, 127, 143
Low Countries, invasion of (1940), 175
Lowell, James, (judge), 42, 55
Lowell, A. Lawrence, 124, 128–155, 247,
    284, 297n., 305, 312
  academic freedom and, 138–142, 185, 186
  anti-Semitism under, 144–150
  appointments to University Profes-
    sorships by, 353

Lowell, A. Lawrence:
  Conant compared with, 167
  decline of scholarship under, 153–155,
    234
  Eliot compared with, 285, 286
  meritocracy and, 293–296, 298, 301
    aristocratic, 288
    democratic, 288, 289
  in 1902 Faculty Committee, 129
  Pusey compared with, 192
  racism under, 142–145
  recruitment of Masters under, 352
  F. D. Roosevelt opposed by, 162
  social-class differences among students
    under, 152, 293, 294
    on-campus residence to offset, 134, 142
    (*See also* Houses)
  student politics under, 150–153
  Walsh criticizes, 165
  and World War I, 135
Lowell, Augustus, 99
Lowell, James Russell, 42, 86, 99
Lowell, John, 56, 86–87
Lowell Committee, 130–131
Lowell House, 372n.
Lowell Institute, 98
Lower-middle-class students, attracted to
  fraternities, 306n.
Loyalty issue in World War I, 138
  suspensions and discharges resulting
    from, 136, 138
Loyalty oath (1950s), 187
Luther, Martin, 3
Lyell, Charles, 53

McCarley, Robert, 308n.
McCarthy, Eugene, 215, 246, 252, 311
McCarthy, Joseph, 190–194, 247
  Corporation denounced by, 196
  Harvard as target of, 192–193
  support for, 198
McCarthy Committee (Senate permanent
    investigations subcommittee), 190
McCarthyism, 189–190, 194–197, 233
McCaughey, Robert A., 288n., 293n.
McCloskey, Robert, 214
McGovern, George, 246, 251, 252, 311
Macgowan, Kenneth, 119
McIlwain, Charles, 297
McKean, Henry, 69
McKinley, William, 107, 111, 112, 115
McNamara, Robert S., 213

Maisel, Sherman, 172
Maistre, Joseph de, 3
Majors (*see* Concentrations)
Malraux, André, 164
Mancall, Mark, 281
Mann, Horace, 83, 84
Manners, 10
  nonconformity to: in Colonial period, 19
    in 1920s, 157
Manuel, Frank, 163
Maoists, 220, 230, 249–251
  goals of, 217
  in MSM, 210, 245, 249–250
  socioeconomic background of, 250–251
March on the Pentagon (1967), 214
Marches:
  antiwar (1917), 136
  March on the Pentagon (1967), 214
  against price controls (1940s), 181
  Selma-Montgomery (1964), 210
Marching and Chowder Club, 159
Marcuse, Herbert, 165, 359, 370n.
Marking system, 68
  (*See also* Grading system)
Marks, Harry, 158
Marshall Scholarships, 327
Marxist professors in Economics Depart-
    ment, 242–243
Maryland Commission on Subversive Ac-
    tivities, 186
Massachusetts at Amherst, University of,
    113, 337, 388n.
Massachusetts Bar Association, 195
Massachusetts General Court, 37–39, 77,
    78, 80, 88
  Board of Overseers responsible to, 21
  financial support and, 41
  founding of Harvard and, 15
  ranking issue and, 24, 25
  resident government vs. nonresident
    government issue and, 26
Massachusetts Institute of Technology
    (MIT), 86, 159, 314, 343
Massachusetts Legislature, 25, 37
  Child Labor Amendment and, 165
  control of (1820s), 67
  Free Soilers and Democrats control
    (1850), 78
  political control and, 40
  in post-Revolutionary era, Board of
    Overseers and, 65
  teachers' oath bill and, 162
Massachusetts Youth for Nixon, 205

Masters:
  characterized, 348
  demands placed on, 352
  functions of, 372
  House offerings and, 345, 346
  prestige of, 310
  recruitment of, 352
  visitors to Houses and, 366
Master's degrees:
  first given to Jewish scholar, 30
  in teaching, 363
Mathematics Department, 309
Mather, Cotton, 12, 18−19, 28, 29, 124
Mather, Increase, 17, 20−21, 23, 28, 29, 124
Mather, Kirtley F., 163
Mather, Richard, 17, 28, 29, 124
Matthew, Joseph, 33
Matthews, William C., 178
Matthiessen, F. O., 163
May, Ernest, 225, 348n., 365
May, Henry, 125, 246, 247
May Second Movement (MSM), 210, 245, 249−250
Mayer, Arno, 370n.
Mayo, Elton, 296
Medical careers to serve the community, 363, 364
Medicine, support for socialization of (late 1950s), 203
Meiklejohn, Alexander, 299n.
Melon (antislavery enthusiast), 84
Mellon, Matthew T., 161
Memoirs (Channing), 48
Memorial Church, 150
Meritocracy, 7
  academic culture and, 190
  in appointments, 62−64
  aristocratic, 293
    Eliot and, 287−289
    Lowell and, 288
    at Oxford and Cambridge universities, 310
  democratic: criticized, 289−290
    Houses undercutting, 306
    issues around, 291
    Lowell and, 288, 289
    represented by Harvard National Scholarship, 305
    "wonks" admitted under, 318
  edging toward (1920s), 293−303
  Eliot and, 295
    aristocratic meritocracy, 287−289

Meritocracy:
  Eliot's belief in, 106
  increased under Conant, 247
  Lowell and, 293−296, 298, 301
    aristocratic meritocracy, 288
    democratic meritocracy, 288, 289
  moderating, 333−357
  origin of term, 287
  politics and, 73−77
  status vs., in ranking system, 23−25
  students and, in 1920s and early 1930s, 301−302
  triumph of, 305−332
Merton, Robert K., 6, 28, 163
Messenger (newspaper), 143
Mexican War (1846−1848), 116
Meyer, Marshall, 227−229, 240n., 254−255, 316n., 356n.
Michigan State University, 113, 179, 248, 289n., 319
Military training:
  demonstrations against (end of nineteenth century), 104
  in World War I, 135, 136
Milton (prep school), 296
MIT (Massachusetts Institute of Technology), 86, 159, 314, 343
Moderate caucus of faculty, 232
Monis, Judah, 30−31
Monro, John, 213
Monroe, James, 70
Moore, Barrington, Jr., 185, 200, 255, 374
Moore, Kathryn McDaniel, 19
Morgan, Arthur, 286
Morgan, Clement, 106
Morgan, Edmund, 106
Mori, Arinori, 4−5, 10
Morison, Samuel Eliot, 19, 101, 221, 297n.
  on conservatism, 73
  on decline of scholarship under Lowell, 153
  on 1825 reforms, 66
  on faculty-student relations (1870s), 94
  racism opposed by, 143
  ranking system and, 24
  religious orthodoxy and liberalism and, 22−23
  on 1790s students, 47
  teachers' oath bill and, 162
  Walsh-Sweezy case and, 166n.
Mormons, 113
Morse, John T., 109
"Mother of Radicals, The" (Thayer), 123

Mount Holyoke College, 337
MSM (May Second Movement), 210, 245, 249–250
Mugwumps, 107–108, 111, 117, 124, 192
Mullins, Michael, 159, 161
Munitz, Barry, 359*n*.
Munro, William Benet, 135
Münsterberg, Hugo, 114, 137, 186
Murdock, Kenneth, 166
Murray, Henry A., 315
Music courses, selected on pass/fail basis, 343
Music Department, 342

NAACP (National Association for the Advancement of Colored People), 198, 207
Nagai, Michio, 360*n*.
Namier, Lewis, 4
Narcissism, interfering with curiosity, 386
Nation, The (magazine), 97*n*., 127
National Association for the Advancement of Colored People (NAACP), 198, 207
National Defense Act (1916), 136
National Educational Association, 186
National Merit Scholars, number of, at Harvard, 319
National Review (magazine), 205
National Science Foundation, 202
National Student Forum, 139
National Student League (NSL), 158, 159, 161, 171, 245
National Youth Administration, 162
Natural Sciences, departments of, 309
Navy ROTC oath, 181
Nazi-Soviet Pact (1939), 172
Nazism, 158–161, 202
Negro students (*see* Black students)
Nepotism, academic, 168, 309
Netherlands, the, Calvinist-dominated universities in, 16
Neutrality Council, 172
New American Movement, 251
New College, (Sarasota), 365
New Conservative Club, 198
New Deal policies, opposed, 161–162
New England College, The, 114
New England Convention Movement, 56
New England dominates American high culture (end of nineteenth century), 93–99
New England's First Fruits, 15

New Jersey, College of, 30
(*See also* Princeton University)
New Left, the, 201
anti-intellectualism of, 255
origins of, 194
(*See also specific manifestations*)
New Left caucus (later November Action Committee), 217, 220, 230, 249, 250
New Masses (magazine), 169
New Republic, The (magazine), 120, 125, 146
New Student, The (magazine), 157
New York Call (newspaper), 136
New York Post (newspaper), 127
New York Times (newspaper), 144, 223
New York Tribune (newspaper), 4
Newsweek (magazine), 181
"Newsweek Surveys Communism in the Colleges" (article), 181
Niebuhr, Chris, 198–200
Niebuhr, Reinhold, 198
Nieman Fellows, 350
Nisbet, Robert, 194
Nixon, Richard M., 201, 228
Nock, Arthur Darby, 305*n*.
Nonconformism:
to dress: in 1920s, 157
in post-Revolutionary era, 72
under Eliot, sources of, 124–126
to manners: in Colonial period, 19
in 1920s, 157
Nondepartmental teaching, 352–355
chair appointments and, 354
student participation and, 355
University Professorships and, 352–353
Non-Partisan League, 139
Nonpolitical spring riots (1960, 1963, and 1966), 211
Nonresident government issue vs. resident:
in Colonial period, 21, 23–27
in post-Revolutionary era, 59–61, 63–64
shift from resident government, 41–44
North Carolina, University of, 179, 181
North Vietnam, resuming bombing of (1972), 251
Northwestern University, 149
Norton, Andrews, 62, 99
Norton, Charles Eliot, 99, 108, 116–117, 127
Norway, invasion of (1940), 175
Not to Eat, Not for Love (Weller), 295*n*.
Notre Dame University, 307

November Action Committee (formerly New Left caucus), 217, 220, 230, 249, 250
Noyes, George Rapall, 86
NSL (National Student League), 158, 159, 161, 171, 245
Nurturance needs, performance needs vs., 291

Oakes, Urian, 17–19
Oath bill (Mass., 1934–1935), 162
Ober, Frank P., 186
Oberlin College, 113, 333, 337
O'Connell, Barry, 326n.
Occupational, recruitment to:
    ascription in, 380
    educational tests in, 291
Ohio State University, 181
Open admissions, 330
Oppenheimer, J. Robert, 139, 199, 202
"Oppression and Tyranny" (speech), 37
Oregon, University of, 181
Organizers, students as, 324
Otis, Harrison Gray, 56, 73
Outward Bound (physical program), 282
Overenrollment:
    in General Education, 337
    lottery allocation system for, 282–283, 328
Overseers:
    in Civil War era: alumni elected, 88–89
        struggle between Corporation and, 86–88
    in Cold War era: Fifth Amendment issue in McCarthyite investigations and, 196–197
        Galbraith nomination and, 183
    in Colonial period, 21
        Bread and Butter riot and, 35–36
        clerical influence undermined, 40, 42, 43, 45, 51
        discipline and, 31, 32
        enforcing religious orthodoxy and, 33
        under Leverett, 22
        long-hair issue and, 19
        members of clergy in, 15
        original composition of, 15
        power of, 16
        ranking system and, 24
        in resident and nonresident government issue, 27
        Revolutionary politics and, 38–39
    under Eliot, 130

Overseers, under Eliot:
    academic freedom and, 100
    alumni-controlled, 100, 103
    approve Eliot's reorganization, 101
    chapel attendance requirements and, 113
    dissatisfaction with Eliot, 131
    Eliot candidacy and, 90
    student discipline and, 96
    under Lowell: academic freedom and, 140
        admission restrictions and, 147
        in 1930s, honorary degree for H. Wallace and, 162
        in 1960s, Great Rebellion (1969) and, 227
        in 1970s, election of Bok to presidency and, 236
        in post-Revolutionary era: Federalists and Jeffersonians struggle to gain control of, 54–55
        Jacksonians on, 73
        partisan conflicts in application of discipline, 53–54
        partisan conflicts in governance of Harvard and, 78–81
        reforms and, 59, 65, 66
        Unitarian triumph and, 51
        Whigs control, 70
    in pre-Civil War era, slavery issue and, 83
Overseers' Visiting Committee, 108–109, 171, 183–184, 209
Oxbridge, educational style of, 133, 134, 149
Oxford Oath, 161, 171
Oxford University, 25, 43, 45, 301
    appointments at, 310
    faculty struggles in, 12
    goverance of, 15
    system of prizes used in, 131

Pacifism:
    in 1930s, 159
    in post-World War I era, 139
    in War of 1812, 115
    in World War I, 136
    (*See also* Antiwar movement)
Pacifist League, 175
Palfrey, John Gorham, 81
Palmer, George, 127
Pankhurst, Mrs. Emmeline, 135
Pareto, Vilfredo, 296
Parker, Isaac, 56
Parker, Theodore, 84

Parsons, Talcott, 193, 291, 315
"Pass" degrees, 333
Patterson, Orlando, 240
Pattullo, Edward L., 378, 379
Peabody, Rev. Andrew, 76, 113
Peabody, Francis, 127
Peace-day strike (1935), 159, 161
Peace movement (1960s), 206
  (*See also* Antiwar movement)
Peace Society, 171
Pearl Harbor, bombed (1941), 177
Peer group solidarity in Great Rebellion
  (1969), 221
Peirce, Benjamin, 25, 31, 76, 86
Pennsylvania, University of, 295
Pension system established under Eliot, 96
People's Republic of China, support for
  recognition of (1950s), 201, 203
Performance needs, nurturance needs vs.,
  291
Perkins Institute for the Blind, 98
Permissiveness in 1950s, 202
"Pernicious Practice of Drinking, The"
  (speech), 37
Perry, Bliss, 116
Perry, Ralph Barton, 159, 166
Personal religion, search for, 368
Personality development, 5
Personnel policies, 309–310
  under Conant, 164, 166–169
  in Pusey era, 234
  sabbatical year's leaves in, 96
  (*See also* Appointments; Discipline, of
    faculty members; Salaries; Selection
    process; Tenure)
Petrie, Asenath, 390
Ph.D.'s:
  James' view of, 289
  number of faculty members having re-
    ceived, at Harvard (1936), 300
  pursuing research after receiving, 303
  in Social Relations, demand for, 315
Phelps, William Lyon, 118
Philippine Insurrection (1898), 116, 118
Phillips, Howard, 205
Phillips Brooks House, 115, 172, 175, 299
Philosophical Club, 127
Pierce, Edward, 83
Pierson, George W., 256n.
Plagiarism, 338–340
PLP (Progressive Labor Party), 210, 217
Polaroid Corporation, 231

Police action:
  at Columbia University, 215–216, 220
  in Hanfstaengl incident, 160
  in Harvard crisis (1969) [*see* Great Rebel-
    lion (1969)]
  in *Karlsruhe* incident, 159
  under Quincy, 69, 72
Political views:
  creativity and, 5–7, 246, 247
  factors affecting (late 1950s), 204
Pomona College, 346
Poor students:
  opening Harvard to: under Eliot, 110
    in post-Revolutionary era, 75, 78–79
  residences of, 92–93
  (*See also* Working-class students)
Popular Front approach of ASU, 171–172
Populists, 81, 105
Port Huron convention (1962), 209
Portsmouth Priory (prep school), 307
Potter, Samuel, 189
Pound, Roscoe, 140
Powell, Thomas Reid, 330n.
Prague International Students Congress
  (1946), 180
Prall, David, 163
Prayer requirements, 85, 94
  (*See also* Chapel attendance)
Preferment struggles, 12, 18–19
Premedical students:
  competitiveness of, 321, 367
  Freshman Seminars turned down by, 351
  Science departments and, 295–296
Presidential elections (national):
  1868, 1872, and 1876, 110
  1884, 1888, and 1892, 111
  1896, 111–112
  1924, 150–151
  1928, 157, 298
  1932, 298
  1936, 171
  1952, 200
  1964, 210
  straw votes on: 1888, 111
    1912, 242
    1920, 138
    1924, 246
    1928, 151
    1932, 157, 245, 246
    1936, 162
    1940, 176
    1948, 188, 246

Presidential elections (national), straw
    votes on:
  1952, 188, 245
  1956, 200, 245
  1960, 205−206
Presidents of Harvard:
  average age of, 92
  in Colonial period: elections of, 27
    as Fellows of the Corporation, 15
    power of, 16, 31
  under Eliot: Eliot's plan for election, 102
    emphasis on power of, 101
  in post-Revolutionary era, 50
    increasing power of, 58, 59, 65
Price controls, opposed, 181
Prince, Nathan, 32
Princeton Plan, 375−376
Princeton University, 30, 315, 317n., 370, 371
  athletes at, 322n.
  religious liberalism at, 113
  secret societies of, 105
  social class differences at, 106
  as target of McCarthy, 193
Private education, federal aid to, supported
    (1950s), 263
Probations:
  for academic deficiences, 319
  antiwar protesters placed on (1967), 214
  for students involved in ROTC issue, 219
Professional careers, 360
Progressive (newspaper), 172
Progressive Labor Party (PLP), 210, 217
Progressivism, 107
Promotions (*see* Personnel policies)
Prospect Union (night school), 115
Protest committee (1934), 159
Protestant Ethic, 331
Psychology Department, 315, 349
Public education, federal aid to, supported
    (1950s), 263
Published works:
  as evidence of scholarly capacity, 166,
    168
  Quincy emphasizes, 75−76
  by students in Committee on Social
    Studies, 327
  teaching and, 390
Purcell, Edward Mills, 353
Purges, Soviet (1940s), 185
Puritans:
  attack universities, 17−18
  commitment of, to education, 13, 28

Puritans:
  denominational split among, 51
  division among (end of seventeenth cen-
    tury), 29
  in founding of Harvard, 15−16
  long-hair issue and, 19
  political control by, 16−17, 21−23
Pusey, Nathan, 195, 217, 225, 315, 316n., 369
  academic freedom and, 193
  accomplishments of, 233−234
  achievement orientation of Jews and,
    307−308
  antiwar protests and, 214, 215
  attacks on Economics Department and, 209
  Bok compared with, 237, 239
  Bundy's appointment and, 316n., 354
  characteristics of, 191−192
  civil rights movement and, 208
  Communists barred from teaching and,
    193−194
  Fifth Amendment in McCarthyite inves-
    tigations and, 196−197
  involved in religious disputation, 197
  nondepartmental teaching and, 353
  police called in by (1969), 221
    [*See also* Great Rebellion (1969)]
  resigns, 233
  theater opened under, 297n.
Putnam, Hillary, 219

Quincy, Josiah, 19, 22, 29, 57, 369, 372n.
  awarding honorary degrees for Jackson
    and, 70−71
  discipline and, 33
  elected President, 67
  emphasis on research and publications
    under, 75−76
  problems faced by, 69−72
  reduced tuition costs and, 75
  religious liberalism and, 29
  revolutionary politics and, 35
  slavery issue and, 81
Quincy, Mrs. Josiah, 69
Quincy, Josiah, Jr., 57
Quincy House, 372

Racism, 106, 124
  under Eliot, 142−144
  in Harvard Athletic Association,
    177−178

Racism:
  charges against Herrnstein, 237
  under Lowell, 142—145
  meritocracy and, 331
  in 1920s and 1930s, 246
    F. D. Roosevelt opposes, 143
  in 1960s, 370
    SDS opposes, 237—238
Radcliffe College, 182, 286
Radcliffe House, 285—286, 372
Radcliffe Student Council, 182
Radcliffe students, 296
  black students compared with, 336
  in Houses, 286, 336—337, 352, 366
  medical careers of, 363
  social status and, 321
  taught jointly with men, 306
  in teaching professions, 364
"Radical perspective" (course), 217
Radicalism:
  at Harvard: Harvard as center of (1960s),
    208—209
    as reason for withholding financial
      support (1930s), 170
    reviewed, 245—251
    sources of, 246—247
  intellectuality and, 247
  of scholars, 4
  spurred on by American Revolution, 47
Radicals:
  cooptation and, 359
  influence of, 366
  intellectual leadership of, 4
  in 1930s, 163
    Conant's personnel policies not affect-
      ing, 168—169
    denounce procapitalist bias of Eco-
      nomics Department (1930s), 170
  in 1950s, 201-203
    number of, in 1959 *Crimson* poll, 203
  in 1960s, in antiwar movement, 213
  in 1970s: Bok's policies undercut, 239
    demands for Marxist economics pro-
      fessors, 241—243
    freedom of speech and, 243
  in post-World War I era: civil rights of,
    138
    repression of, 140
  restricting enrollment of, 145
  Thayer defines, 123—124
  upper-class, 251
  (*See also specific kinds of radicals*)
Randall, Clarence, 184

Randolph, A. Philip, 143
Ranking system, 68
  merit vs. status in, 23-25
  unrest caused by, 37—38
Rationing system in admissions policies,
    283, 328
Rebellion Tree (Liberty tree), 36, 39, 57
Recession, effects of, on educational re-
    forms, 284
"Reds vs. Academic Freedom" (article), 181
Reed, John, 121—122, 125, 135, 169
Reforms (*see* Educational reforms)
Reid, Whitelaw, 4
Reischauer, Edwin O., 353
Religion:
  attitudes toward, 202
    in late 1950s, 197—198, 204
    in post-World War II era, 189
  early universities upholding, 5
  innovative intellectual activity and rejec-
    tion of, 6
  search for personal, 368
  (*See also* Religious disputations; Re-
    ligious liberalism; Religious ortho-
    doxy)
Religion (course), in House programs, 344
Religious disputations:
  in Colonial period, 17, 20—21
  in 1950s, 197—198
  in 1970s, 244
  in post-Revolutionary era, 51—53
  universities as main arena of, 3
Religious liberalism:
  in Colonial period, 13
    battles resulting in triumph of, 20, 21,
      29—30
  under Eliot, 112—114
  of New England elite, 49
  in post-Revolutionary era, 72—73
  scholarship and, 10, 52
  (*See also* Congregationalism; Uni-
    tarianism)
Religious orthodoxy:
  in Colonial period: battle against, 20
    enforcing it among faculty, 33
    openness to new ideas vs., 28
    purity and, 21
  shift from, to scholarly innovation, 10
  (*See also* Calvinism; Puritans)
Religious prejudices:
  in 1920s and early 1930s, 301
  of students (late 1950s), 204
Religious tests in Colonial period, 21

"Report upon the Illegal Practices of the United States Department of Justice", 140
"Report to the Overseers" (Pusey, 1968), 214
Reporter (magazine), 199
Republican National Convention of 1924, 144
Republican Party, 205—206
Republicans:
  in Cold War era, 189
  in 1890 gubernatorial election, 108
  under Eliot, 110—111
    academic freedom and, 108—109
    faculty members as, 107
  on Governing Boards (1930s), 161
  under Lowell, 150
  in 1920s, 138
  number of: in 1860, 85
    from 1860 to 1868, 110
    number of registered (1974), 254
  student support for (from 1912 to 1960), 245—246
Research:
  area-focused centers of, 314—315
  in Civil War era, increased concern for, 87
  under Conant, 155
  under Eliot: emphasis on, 103
    Eliot anticipates research professorships, 97
    facilities for, 98
  German emphasis on, 91, 105, 300
  Harvard as world center of (early twentieth century), 126
  as main objective, 378
  Quincy and, 75—76
  teaching vs., 5, 302—303
  (*See also* Scholarship)
Resident government issue vs. nonresident (*see* Nonresident government issue vs. resident)
Residential-college system, 153
  under Eliot, 92—93
  Lowell and, 134, 142, 149
  (*See also* Houses)
Revolutionary movements:
  eighteenth-century European, enthusiasm for, 47
  student-based, as goal of New Left caucus, 217
  students as traditionally in, 9
Revolutionary politics, 3, 35—39

Rhodes scholars, 327
  selection of, 289
Rice, John Andrew, 299*n.*
Richards, Theodore, 96—97
Ricks, David, 306*n.*, 308*n.*
Rights and Responsibilities, Committee on (CRR), 232, 237, 241
Robbins, Herbert, 158
Robeson, Paul, 182
Romance Languages and Literatures, Department of, 354
Ronin (Japanese students), 381
Roosevelt, Franklin D., 117, 157, 206, 246
  Communist support for (1936), 171—172
  interventionist policies of, opposed, 174—177
  Lowell opposes, 152—153
  in 1940 straw vote, 176
  at Tercentenary celebration of Harvard, 162
Roosevelt, Theodore, 115, 245
Rosovsky, Henry, 223, 224, 243—244
Rosovsky Committee (Faculty Committee on African and Afro-American Studies), 222—223, 340, 369—370
Ross, Irwin, 171, 177
ROTC issue (1968—1969), 219, 221, 228
ROTC training, 136
Rotten Cabbage Rebellion (1805), 54
Rousseau, Jean-Jacques, 373
Royal Governor, powers of, 21, 22
Royal Society, 28, 33
Royce, Josiah, 127
Rudd, Mark, 217
Russell, Bertrand, 286
Russell, William, 108
Russia (*see* Soviet Union)
Russian Research Center, 184, 185, 314
Russian Revolution (Feb. 1917), 136
Russian universities, eighteenth-century, 3
Rustications (*see* Suspensions)

Sabbatical year's leaves, 96
Sacco, Nicola, 93, 151, 152, 157
Sachs, Paul, 295
St. Louis Country Day School (prep school), 296
St. Paul (prep school), 287*n.*
Salaries:
  ceilings on, 282
  in Civil War era, struggle over control of, 86
  in Colonial period, 16
  in 1870s, 96, 97

Salaries:
  under Lowell, 154
  in post-Revolutionary era, 58, 77–78
  in 1970s, 311*n.*
Saltonstall, Leverett, 74
Salvemini, Gaetano, 300
Sane Nuclear Policy, Committee for a
    (SANE), 206
Santayana, George, 97–98, 107, 118, 127,
    301
SAT scores:
  of black students, 334*n.*
  at CalTech, 333
  of Radcliffe students, 367*n.*
Schirmer, D. B., 117
Schlesinger, Arthur, Jr., 166, 182, 200, 207,
    289
Scholar-teachers, 389–390
Scholars:
  academic freedom and, 8
  relationship of, to politics, 4
  (*See also* Intellectuals; Scholarship)
Scholarship:
  Cold War pressures on, 184–188
  Conant's concern for, 167
  conditions necessary for fertile and free,
    295
  creative: increased importance of, 7
    relationship between faculty's political
      views and, 5–6
  decline of, under Lowell, 153–155, 234
  Eliot's concern for, 96, 113, 133, 287–288
  encouraged by elective system, 293
  German emphasis on, 300
  guiding values of, 6
  Harvard's commitment to, 256
  published works as evidence of, 166, 168
  religious liberalism and, 10, 52
  trained intelligence, rewards and, 7
Scholarship aid (financial aid), 75,
    161–162, 305, 307
School teaching, 363–364
Schudson, Michael S., 306*n.*
Schumpeter, Joseph, 301*n.*, 332*n.*
Scientific-technological intelligentsia, 7
Scientific truth, nonenduring quality of,
    as guiding value of scholarship, 6
SDS (*see* Students for a Democratic Soci-
    ety)
Searle, John R., 370*n.*
Sears, Mr., 87
Second-chance country, U. S. as, 382

Second World War (World War II,
    1939–1945), 172–177
Secret societies, 105, 294*n.*
Secularization of universities, 6
Seeger, Pete, 171
Segregation (*see* Racism)
Selection process in post-Revolutionary
    era, 62–66
Self-correction mechanisms, 302
Selma-Montgomery march (1964), 210
Seltzer, Daniel, 297*n.*
Senatorial elections (national) in 1962,
    207
Sennett, Richard, 382*n.*
Settlement movement, 114–115, 120, 299
Seven Arts, 125
1720, Petition of, 24
1780, Constitution of (Massachusetts),
    40–41, 44, 51
Sever, Nicholas, 23–24, 27
Sex-blind admissions, 366–367
Sex relations, debates on, in Colonial
    period, 22
Sexual behavior:
  adhering to conventional morality on
    (under Eliot), 114
  changes in (1920s), 157
  in counterculture, 217
SFAC (Student-Faculty Advisory Council),
    214
Shaler, Nathaniel S., 96, 127
Shannon, David, 119
Shapley, Harlow, 166
Shaw, Robert Gould, 143
Shepherd (Evangelical writer), 34
Shipton, Clifford K., 24
Shockley, William, 238, 243
Signet Society, 298, 342*n.*
Sigourney, David, 175
Simmons, Ernest J., 163
Simonson, Lee, 125
Single Tax Club, 122
Sit-ins:
  as antiwar protests (1968), 214–215
  by black students (1972), 237, 241
  at Columbia University (*see* Columbia
    University, 1968 crisis at)
  over ROTC issue (1968–1969), 219
  at University Hall (1969), 69, 211, 212,
    215, 220, 221, 321, 340, 372*n.*, 374
  [*see also* Great Rebellion (1969)]
1647, law of (Mass. law), 28

1650, Charter of, 15, 16, 21
1667, Act of, 16
Skepticism as guiding value of scholarship, 6
Slavery issue, 81–85, 124
SLID (*see* Student League for Industrial Democracy)
Slosson, E., E., 127
Smelser, Neil, 370*n.*
Smith, Al, 151
Smith, Elizabeth, 36
Smith, Gerit, 83
Smith, Wilson, 82
Smith College, 346
SNCC (Student Non-Violent Coordinating Committee), 207, 210
Social action groups, 365
Social change, universities as dynamic force for, 7
"Social Change in America" (course), 217
Social-class differences:
 under Eliot, 105–107, 110
 under Lowell, 152, 293, 294
 on-campus residence to offset, 134, 142
 (*See also* Houses)
 (*See also* Elite; Lower-middle-class satudents; Poor students; Upper-class students; Workers; Working-class students)
Social consciousness, lack of, in Depression era, 298–299
Social criticism, intellectuality and, 247
Social Darwinism, 331
Social development, universities and, 7
Social Ethics, Department of, established, 115
Social mobility, meritocracy and, 291
Social Politics Club, 122, 123
Social problems:
 faculty concern for (1930s), 163
 Lowell's conservative approach to, 142
 settlement movement to help alleviate, 114–115, 120, 299
Social Relations Department, 286, 314, 354
 attractiveness of, 344
 critics and supporters of, 349
 student participation in, 231
Social Relations 148–149 (course), 217, 225, 339
Social sciences:
 liberalism in, opposed (1930s), 166

Social sciences:
 as new science in post-World War I era, 140
 tone of (1920s), 301
Social Studies, Committee on, 232, 326–328, 336
Social Studies Program, 283, 344, 377
 Faculty Committee on the, 285
Social Union (night school), 115
Social welfare, Young Democrats' view of, 201
Social work, 114–115, 120, 299, 364
Socialism:
 cooperative doctrines of, 330
 under Eliot, 119–124
 Fabian, 109, 121, 249
Socialists:
 in Cold War era: Communists barred from teaching and, 188
 in Economics Department, 183
 Soviet totalitarianism opposed by, 185
 under Lowell, 150
 in 1930s: faculty members as, 163
 1932 presidential election and, 157
 oppose American involvement in World War I, 135
 and World War II, 174
Socialization of industries and medicine, support for (late 1950s), 203
Socialization process, 6
Society:
 authority system of, legitimated by universities, 5
 bureaucratic, 332
 capitalist: egalitarian ethos in, 282
 undoing of, 332*n.*
 (*See also* Established order)
Society of Fellows, 289, 305
Society of Minority Rights, 207
Socioeconomic status:
 of faculty members (1930s), 299, 300
 of Maoist students, 250–251
 of 1960s black students, 222
 of post-World War II Harvard students, 179–180
 of Radcliffe students, 367*n.*
Sociology Department, 314
 course requirements in, 376
 established, 286
 student participation in, 231
Sorokin, Pitirim, 300

Sound Money Campaign Club, 112
South Africa, black students protest U.S. investments in, 230, 231, 238
Soviet Union, 5
    effects of post-World War II behavior of, 190
    invaded (1941), 177
    in social sciences courses (1920s), 301
    totalitarianism of, opposed, 185
Soviet-U.S. alliance, Student Union advocates (1935), 171
Space Nuclear Weapons Development, Committee on, 208
Spady, William G., 312*n*.
Spanish-American War (1898), 115–118
Spanish Civil War (1936–1939), 164, 171
Spanish Loyalists, support for, 171
Spanish-speaking students, SAT scores of, 334*n*.
Spargo, John, 135
Sparks, Jared, 66, 76, 85
Spaulding, Charles, 84
Speaking Club, 37
Special Studies, Committee on, 344
Specialized courses, enrollment in, 348*n*.
Spontaneity, 361–362
Spring riots, political and nonpolitical (1960s), 210–212
SPU (Student Peace Union), 206–207, 209, 243, 249
Sputnik (1957), 201, 317
Stalin, Joseph, 177
Stalinism, 248
Stanford University, 124, 281, 370, 371
State control, end of, 88–90
State funds, 58, 67, 80
Statism, attitudes of liberals towards (late 1950s), 202
Status, meritocracy vs., in ranking system, 23–25
    (*See also* Socioeconomic status)
Status of Women, Committee on, 314*n*.
Status quo, acceptance of, 5
Stauder, Jack, 217, 225
Stearns, Harold, 125
Stephen, Leslie, 99
Stevenson, Adlai, 188, 200, 201, 245
Stewart, Zeph, 223
Stoddard (Evangelical writer), 34
Story, Joseph, 48, 50, 59
Story Committee, 59–64, 211
Stowe, Harriet Beecher, 83
Strikebreakers, students as (1920), 140

Strikes:
    Boston policemen (1920), 140, 142
    miners' (1930s), 158
    (*See also* Student strikes)
Strong, Caleb, 57
Student activism, contemporary, reasons for, 10–11
    (*See also* Student unrest; *and specific forms of activism*)
Student-based revolutionary movement, as goal of SDS New Left caucus, 217
Student body:
    composition of: as homogeneous, 350
        under Lowell, 142
        political (1860), 85
        in post-Revolutionary era, 73
        post-World War II admission policies affecting, 190
        religious (by 1820), 52
        by social class (end of nineteenth century), 110
        socioeconomic background (post-World War II), 179–180
        under Eliot, average age, 91–92
    in 1970s: number of Jewish students, 307
        self-confidence of, 311
        as truly national, 308
    Story Committee findings on, 60
Student centers associated with Midwestern gregarious Philistinism, 341–342
Student Committee to Save Harvard Education, 168
Student Council Committee on Education (1939), 148–149, 283–284
Student discipline:
    in cases of plagiarism, 340
    under Eliot, 91, 92, 96, 103
    faculty struggle for control of, 12
    under Hoar, 18
    lack of due process in, 11
    under Leverett, 23
    in 1960s, 213, 214
    in post-Revolutionary era, 49–51
    partisan conflicts in, 53–54
    Quincy's hard line, 69
    reforming, 58–60
    in pre-Civil War era, 85
    student participation in, 232
    (*See also* Admonitions; Boxing; Corporal punishment; Dismissals, of students; Expulsions; Flogging; Probations; Suspended sentences; Suspensions,

Student discipline:
of students; Warnings; Whipping)
Student-Faculty Advisory Council (SFAC),
214
Student housing, Gold Coast residences as,
92–93, 293
(*See also* Houses)
Student League for Industrial Democracy
(SLID), 122, 138
membership of (1950s), 198
in 1930s, 245
antiwar strike called by, 159
growth of, 158
in Harvard Student Union, 171
peace-day strike organized by, 161
tour of mining regions sponsored by
SLID and NSL, 158
Student movement:
ASU fails to build (1930s), 173
as twentieth-century phenomenon, 245
Student Non-Violent Coordinating Committee (SNCC), 207, 210
Student participation, 255–256, 344
in appointments, 340, 341
in Chemistry Department, 284–285,
385*n*.
in curricular reforms, 365
in Department of Afro-American Studies, 231–232, 240
in faculty meetings and departmental
committees, 355
Student Peace Union (SPU), 206–207, 209,
243, 249
Student-police relations in Colonial
period, 19–20
(*See also* Police action)
Student politics:
characterization of, 8–9
under Eliot, 107, 108
political views and activities,
110–112, 115–117
socialism, 119–124
two-party system and, 105
under Lowell, 144–145, 150–153
in 1930s, 157–163, 167, 299
in 1950s, 197–204, 247
barring Communists from teaching
and, 187
civil rights of Communists and,
182–183
effects of McCarthyism on, 195
1960s protest wave originating in, 248
opinions of, 188–190

Student politics:
in 1970s, 251–252, 254
old-fashioned meaning of, 324
in post-Revolutionary era, 55–58
radicalism in: intellectuality and, 247
unorthodox students as source of radicalism, 246
(*See also* Radicalism; Radicals)
slavery issue and, 82–85
status quo accepted by students, 5
survey of 1969 and 1974, 227–230, 253
in World War II: oppose racism in athletic activities (1941), 178
politics of intervention and, 173–174
(*See also student politics under specific denominations and political groups*)
Student riots:
Annual Spring Riot as tradition,
210–211
as cyclical events, 369
against food quality, 11
"Bread and Butter" riot (1766), 32,
35–36
Rotten Cabbage Rebellion (1805), 54
Great Rebellion (1823), 57–58, 70
Great Rebellion (1834), 68–70, 227
Great Rebellion (1969) [*see* Great Rebellion (1969)]
against Navy ROTC oath, 181
in 1960s: against 1966 antijaywalking
law, 211
spring riots, 210–212
(*See also* Berkeley Revolt; Columbia University, 1968 crisis at)
Student self-government, 11–12, 104,
135
Student senates, 134
Student strikes:
at Columbia University (*see* Columbia
University, 1968 crisis at)
at Harvard [*see* Great Rebellion (1969)]
in 1970s, 230, 355, 371
for peace (1934), 159, 161
Student unrest:
in Colonial period: against classroom
recitations, 36
under Langdon, 39
mass resignation of students, 18
against ranking system, 37–38
records of, 31
as cyclical, 369
dealing with compulsory chapel attendance, 10, 49, 50

Student unrest:
  under Eliot, 93–99, 104
    effects of elective system on, 94–95
    students blow up a university build-
      ing (1870), 93
  grading system as source of, 11
  "Gun powder Plot" (1842), 71
  in McCarthy era, 197
  in 1930s, 157–163
  in 1960s, 3, 13, 47
    fear of, 369–370
    origins of, 248
  in 1970s, 237, 241, 254
  post-Civil War, 91–93
  in post-Revolutionary era, 47–49, 57,
    66–72
  (*See also* Demonstrations; Marches; Stu-
    dent riots; Student strikes)
"Student Vagabond, The" (column), 286
Student Volunteer Committee, 115
Student work program (1934), 161
Students:
  academic culture and, 191
  antagonistic to Hoar, 18, 19
  Conant's concern for faculty quality and,
    168
  under Eliot: reactions to Eliot, 93–99,
    103
    religious liberalism and, 112, 113
    in settlement movement, 114–115,
      120, 299
    social-class differences among,
      105–107
  meritocracy and, 295–297, 301–302
    (*See also* Meritocracy)
  in 1970s: attitudes towards careers,
    362-364
    choosing a successor to Pusey and,
      234–235
    educational reforms and, 284, 365
    lineage as embarassing to, 320–321
    reasons for staying at Harvard,
      365–366
    spiritual search of, 368
  as organizers, 324
  of Revolutionary generation, character-
    ized, 39
  who played major roles in American
    Revolution, 35
  (*See also specific types of students*)
Students for a Democratic Society (SDS),
  69, 119, 181, 209–215, 245

Students for a Democratic Society (SDS):
  in antiwar movement: organizes civil
    disobedience protests, 212–213
  organizes sit-ins, 214–215
  in civil rights movement, 210
  direct lineal parent of, 198
  founded, 209–210
  Herrnstein opposed by, 237–238
  Meyer's 1969 survey and, 228*n.*
  New Left caucus of, 217, 220, 249, 250
  1969 split of, 230
  1970 activities of, 230–231
  plans for action of (1968–1969), 216–220
  radical course obtained by, 217, 225,
    339*n.*
  radicalism of, 249–250
  rejected (1970s), 375
  socioeconomic background of members
    of (1969), 230
  WSA as faction of, 217, 220, 230, 249
Study Counsel, Bureau of, 334, 338*n.*
"Subversion of the Pretensions and
    Scheme of the Memoralists" (Le-
    verett), 25
Success:
  relation between grades and, 380
  upper-class students and: fear of success,
    330–331
  viewed as undesirable, 364–365
Sumner, Charles, 83, 84, 143
Suspended sentences for black students
    having occupied Massachusetts Hall
    (1972), 241
Suspensions (rustications):
  of faculty members in World War I loyal-
    ty issue, 136
  of students: at Chicago University, 226
    in Colonial period, 36
    in 1805 riots, 53
    from 1807 to 1824, 58–59
    of Emerson and Quincy, Jr. (1818), 57
    involved in Dow Chemical incident,
      219
    in 1969 crisis, 225
    in 1970s, 231
    in post-Revolutionary era, 68–69
Swarthmore College, 282, 317*n.*, 337
Swarthmore Honors Program, 328*n.*, 339*n.*
Sweezy, Alan, 163–167
Sweezy, Paul, 163, 286
Sycamore trees, riots caused by cutting of
    (1963), 211

Taft, William Howard, 245
Taussig, Frank, 108, 127
Tax-supported schools, law laying down principles of, 28
Tea, abstaining from consuming, as political act (1768), 37
Teachers, training of, 5
Teachers colleges, 5
Teaching:
  assessing quality of, 388
  Communists barred from (Cold War era), 185 – 188, 193 – 194, 199, 203
  dilemmas of, 387
  dispassionateness in, 386
  disregard for ability in, in Conant's personnel policies, 168
  grade school, 363 – 364
  nondepartmental, 352 – 355
    chair appointments and, 354
    student participation in, 355
    University Professorships and, 352 – 353
  quality of, as factor in obtaining tenure, 389
  research vs., 5, 302 – 303
  training in, 390 – 391
Teaching Fellows, 313*n.*, 371, 390
Teaching loads, 391
  Eliot reduces, 97, 98
  emphasis on research and light, 76
  Jacksonians want to increase, 74
Teach-ins on Vietnam War, 231
Tell Tale, The (newspaper), 22
Temporary Student Committee on Instruction in the Social Sciences (Committee of 14), 165
Tenure:
  of assistant professors, 310
  under Conant, 164
  concern for faculty quality and, 167 – 168
  in Economics Department, for radical faculty, 241, 242
  under Eliot, 96
  in Faculty of Arts and Sciences, 389
  number of women and blacks as tenured members (1974), 244
  tenured members (as of March 1974), 371
  under Leverett, 23, 26
  for Teaching Fellows and Assistant Professors, 371

Tercentenary Drive, 170, 171
Texas, University of, 179
Thayer, W. R., 123, 124
Theater, absence of, in 1920s, 297
Theoretical knowledge as principal source of social and economic development, 7
Theses:
  course reduction providing more time for writing, 343
  graduations without, 376
  as most valuable experience, 325
Thielens, Wagner, 190
Third World movements, support for, 217
Thomas, Norman, 152, 162, 176, 188, 245, 248
Thoreau, Henry David, 35, 124
Thurmond, Strom, 188
Ticknor, George, 58 – 59, 65 – 67, 76, 99
Tilghman, William, 57
Tillich, Paul, 353
Tillotson, John, 34
Time (magazine), 205
Titoists, purged (1940s), 185
Tobin, James, 283
Tocqueville, Alexis de, 7
Tocsin (group), 206 – 209, 247, 249, 324, 372
Tocsin Forum (magazine), 206
Tomasson, Richard F., 339*n.*
Tonis, Robert, 216, 220
Trade Union Fellows, 350
Trade Unions, 152, 164
Transfer policies, 319 – 320
Trilling, Lionel, 362
Trinitarian doctrine, 51
Trotsky, Leon, 140
Trow, Martin, 284, 315*n.*
Trowbridge, John, 127
Truman, Harry S., 188, 193
Tuition costs, 67, 73 – 75, 78 – 79
Tutors:
  in Colonial period: Hoar and, 18
    Leverett and, 23 – 26
    as members of Corporation, 15
    ranking system and, 24
    religious instruction by, 33 – 34
  House, 153
    approval of student's design of his own field of concentration, 344
    burden of, 384
    Conant's personnel policies affecting, 167

Tutors, House:
  grading system and, 339
  House offerings and, 345, 346
  in post-Revolutionary era, reforms and,
    58, 64
Twentieth Party Congress (Soviet Union,
  1956), 248
Two-party system:
  emergence of, 47
  in student politics under Eliot, 105
  students' view of (late 1950s), 203
Two Years Before the Mast (Dana), 68

UCLA (University of California at Los
  Angeles), 179, 187
Ulam, Adam, 212, 386*n.*
Undergraduate Education, Committee on
  (CUE), 281, 283, 285, 344
Unemployment in 1920s, 299
Union College, 302
Unitarianism, 73, 124
  admissions and curriculum policies and,
    77
  Eliot presses for propagation of, 113
  leaders of, 47
  religious liberalism as source of, 30
  triumph of, 51–53
United Nations (UN), admission of Com-
  munist China to, supported (late
  1950s), 203
U. S. Naval Academy, 177
Universalism as guiding value of scholar-
  ship, 6
Universities:
  as educational institutions, 5
  increased political importance of, 7–8
  as traditional centers of dissent, 3–5
  as transmitters of traditional culture, 12
University Committee on Governance,
  233*n.*
University Hall, sit-in at, (1969), 69, 211,
  212, 215, 220, 221, 321, 340, 372*n.*, 374
University Memorial Church, 197
University Professorships, appointments
  to, 352
Upper class (*see* Elite)
Upper-class radicals, problems facing, 251
Upper-class students:
  Civil War conscription of, 85
  dilemmas facing 329
  discontent among, in post-Revolu-
    tionary era, 51

Upper-class students:
  dropping out, 359
  in extracurricular activities, 152, 246
  in Gold Coast residences, 92–93, 293
  Harvard serving, 74
  of 1920s compared with 1970s, 321
  success and: fear of success, 330–331
    viewed as undesirable, 364–365
Urban problems, 114–115, 120
Urban Research Corporation, 212, 226
U.S.S.R. (*see* Soviet Union)
Utrecht, Peace of (1713), 24

Vaccination introduced, 55
Values, indoctrination of accepted, 5, 6
Vanzetti, Bartolomeo, 93, 151, 152, 158
Veblen, Thorstein, 386
Velde, Harold H., 191
Velde Committee, 190
Venezuelan-British Guiana boundary dis-
  pute (1895), 115
Veterans as students, 306
Veto power of Harvard Presidents, 65
Veysey, Laurence, 11, 93, 107, 246, 247
  nonconformism and, 124, 125
  and racism under Lowell, 142
  on religious liberalism under Eliot, 112
Vienna, Austria, 4
"Vietnam Summer" (project), 213
Vietnam War, 174
  Goldwater favors bombing in, 210
  opposition to, 8, 247, 252, 254, 370
    faculty members as early critics of, 373
    1960s student unrest and, 212
    1969 poll on, 228
    1970 protest of Cambodian invasion,
      240, 241, 251, 374–375
    1972 protest against resumed bomb-
      ing, 251
Village in the Vaucluse (Wylie), 354
Villard, Oswald Garrison, 127, 143
Violent tactics, rejected (1970s), 254
Virginia, University of, 75, 328*n.*
Virginia House of Burgesses, 43
Virtuoso students, faculty members as
  models for, 317
Visual and Environmental Studies, Depart-
  ment of, 342
Vogel, Ezra, 371*n.*
Volunteers for Adlai Stevenson, 360*n.*
Voting rights for eighteen-year-olds, 254
Vreeland, Rebecca, 372*n.*

Wadsworth, Benjamin, 24, 31
Wage and price control, support for (late 1950s), 203
Wagoner, Jennings, Jr., 287*n.*, 288*n.*, 294
Walker, James, 82
Wallace, Henry, 162, 181, 182, 184, 188, 246
Walsh, J. Raymond, 163–167
Walsh-Sweezy case (1937), 164–167, 169, 173
Walzer, Michael L., 313*n.*, 327
Ware, Henry, 51
Warren, George Washington, 79
Washington, George, 38
Washington, University of, 181
Washington Action Project (Feb. 1962), 206–207
Watergate scandal (1972), 254, 255
Waterhouse, Benjamin, 54
Watson, James D., 318
Wayne State University, 179, 189
"We won't go" statement, signees of, 213
Weatherman organization, 230
Webber, Samuel, 51
Webster, Daniel, 79, 84
Wechsler, James, 163
Weld, Theodore, 83
Welfare State project, support for (late 1950s), 203
Weller, George Anthony, 295*n.*
Welsteed, 24
Wendell, Barrett, 94, 101, 108, 127
"Were Those the Days?" (Bundy), 316
Wesleyan University, 113, 119, 179
West European Studies (research center), 314, 366
Western Reserve Academy (prep school), 113, 296
"Western Thought and Institutions" (course), 337
"What Makes a College Good?" (speech), 208
Whigs, 70, 81, 83
Whipping, 18
White, Daniel Appleton, 47, 74, 77
White, William Allen, 175
Whitefield, George, 33–35
Whitla, Dean K., 286, 297*n.*, 350, 368
WHRB (Cambridge radio station), 212, 218, 223
"Why Don't Your Young Men Care?" (Laski), 157
Widener Library (Harvard), 302
Wiener, George, 137
Wigglesworth, Edward, 34–35

Wilcox, Edward T., 346*n.*
Willard, Samuel, 21
Willard, Sidney, 53
William and Mary College, 43–45, 302
Williams, Col. Isaac, 38
Williams, Michael, 317*n.*, 342*n.*
Williams College, 113, 294
Willkie, Wendell, 176
Wilson, James Q., 238, 243
Wilson, Woodrow, 188, 245, 293
Winsor, Justin, 127
Winthrop, John, 33
Winthrop House, 372
Wisconsin, University of, 154, 248
Wittenberg, University of, 3
Woman suffrage, 135
"Women and Sex-Role Oppression" (course), 218
Women professors:
    nondepartmental teaching and, 355
    tenure for, 244
        number tenured in Faculty of Arts and Sciences (1974), 244
Women students, 372
    at Chicago University, 312*n.*
    as DARs (Damned Average Raisers), 306
    number of, graduating with honors, 318
    "work over life" choice by, 327*n.*
    (*See also* Radcliffe students)
Women's Liberation, 370
"Wonks," defined, 318
Wood, Gen. Leonard, 135, 136
Woolf, Virginia, 99
Woolsey, Theodore D., 88
Work ethic, 332
"Work over life" choice, 327
Worker-Student Alliance (WSA), 217, 220, 230, 249
Workers:
    coalition between Democrats and (1890s), 108
    movement for education of (1920s), 139
    socialists fail to make contact with, 120–121
    students fight (1833 and 1843), 71
Working-class students:
    attracted to fraternities, 306*n.*
    number of, in 1952 survey, 179–180
    as Republicans, 189
    as YAF members, 230
World Federalists, 208
World War I (First World War, 1914–1918), 135–138

World War II (Second World War, 1939–1945), 172–177
WSA (Worker-Student Alliance), 217, 220, 230, 249
Wylie, Laurence, 354

YAF (Young Americans for Freedom), 205, 206, 230, 231
Yale Daily News (newspaper), 175
Yale University, 97, 191, 315, 317*n*., 345, 371
    admissions restrictions against Jews at, 149
    athletes at, 322*n*.
    celebrities visiting, 366*n*.
    faculty-student relations at, 346
    Gulf stock owned by, 237
    Jewish enrollment at (post-World War 11), 179
    1952 survey of students at, 189
    religious liberalism at, 112–113
    secret societies of, 105, 294*n*.
    social-class differences at, 106
    socialism at, 119

Yale University:
    as target of McCarthy, 193
    tuition fees at, 79
Yarmolinsky, Adam, 171
Yeats, William Butler, 327
Young, Michael, 287, 290, 331
Young Americans for Freedom (YAF), 205, 206, 230, 231
Young Democrats, 198, 201, 208
Young Intellectuals, 125
Young People's Socialist League (YPSL), 212, 218, 250
Young Progressives of America (YPA), 181, 182
Young Republicans, 181, 198, 201, 208, 252
Youth for Goldwater, 205
Youth Committee Against War, 174
YPA (Young Progressives of America), 181, 182
YPSL (Young People's Socialist League), 212, 218, 250

Zorza, Richard, 212

About the Authors

SEYMOUR MARTIN LIPSET is the George D. Markham Professor of Government and Sociology at Harvard University, where he has been since 1965. He was born in New York City, attended City College, and earned his Ph.D. from Columbia University. He has taught at the University of Toronto, Columbia, and, prior to his appointment to Harvard, was Professor of Sociology at the University of California at Berkeley and Director of its Institute of International Studies. Professor Lipset is on the Executive Committee of the Center for International Affairs at Harvard and Vice-President for the Social Sciences of the American Academy of Arts and Sciences.

Two of his books have received awards, *Political Man* (the MacIver Award) and *The Politics of Unreason* (the Myrdal Prize). His work *The First New Nation* was a National Book Award finalist. Various of his books have been translated into 18 languages including all those of Western Europe, Polish, Serbo-Croatian, Turkish, Arabic, and Japanese.

Professor Lipset is Chairman of the Section on the Social and Economic Sciences of the American Association for the Advancement of Science, and he has held fellowships from the Center for Advanced Study in the Behavioral Sciences, the Ford Foundation, the Guggenheim Foundation, and the Social Science Research Council. He has been elected to membership in the National Academy of Sciences and the National Academy of Education. He has served on the Councils of the American Political Science and American Sociological Associations.

DAVID RIESMAN attended Harvard College where he majored in biochemical sciences and was one of the editors of the *Crimson*, graduating in 1931. Thereafter he attended Harvard Law School. His law career included a year as Law Clerk to Mr. Justice Brandeis of the U.S. Supreme Court, a year in the practice of law, and four years as professor of law at the University of Buffalo Law School. He also was Deputy Assistant District Attorney of New York County. After World War II he joined the sociology department at the University of Chicago. It was during leaves of absence from Chicago to Yale that the two books he is best known for were written, *The Lonely Crowd* and *Faces in the Crowd*.

Since 1958, Mr. Riesman has been Henry Ford II Professor of the

Social Sciences at Harvard. His research has been primarily concerned with the development and present state of American higher education. With Christopher Jencks he is the author of *The Academic Revolution*, an account of the development of a great variety of American colleges and universities up to the present era. With Joseph Gusfield and Zelda Gamson he is the author of *Academic Values and Mass Education*.

Mr. Riesman served in the past as a member of the National Advisory Council of the Peace Corps and on the Carnegie Commission on Higher Education. Presently, he is a member of the Editorial Board of *Universities Quarterly, Sociology of Education, Change in Higher Education, Reviews in Education*, and *Communication*. Professional societies in which he is a member include the American Academy of Arts and Sciences, the American Philosophical Society, the Century Association, and the National Academy of Education.

Carnegie Commission on Higher Education

Sponsored Research Studies

EDUCATION AND POLITICS
AT HARVARD
*Seymour Martin Lipset and
David Riesman*

HIGHER EDUCATION AND EARNINGS:
COLLEGE AS AN INVESTMENT AND A
SCREENING DEVICE
Paul Taubman and Terence Wales

EDUCATION, INCOME, AND HUMAN
BEHAVIOR
F. Thomas Juster (ed.)

AMERICAN LEARNED SOCIETIES
IN TRANSITION:
THE IMPACT OF DISSENT
AND RECESSION
*Harland G. Bloland and
Sue M. Bloland*

ANTIBIAS REGULATION OF UNIVERSITIES:
FACULTY PROBLEMS AND THEIR SOLUTIONS
Richard A. Lester

CHANGES IN UNIVERSITY
ORGANIZATION, 1964–1971
Edward Gross and Paul V. Grambsch

ESCAPE FROM THE DOLL'S HOUSE:
WOMEN IN GRADUATE AND PROFESSIONAL
SCHOOL EDUCATION
Saul D. Feldman

HIGHER EDUCATION AND
THE LABOR MARKET
Margaret S. Gordon (ed.)

THE ACADEMIC MELTING POT:
CATHOLICS AND JEWS IN
AMERICAN HIGHER EDUCATION
Stephen Steinberg

LEADERSHIP AND AMBIGUITY:
THE AMERICAN COLLEGE
PRESIDENT
*Michael D. Cohen and
James G. March*

THE ACADEMIC SYSTEM IN
AMERICAN SOCIETY
Alain Touraine

EDUCATION FOR THE PROFESSIONS
OF MEDICINE, LAW, THEOLOGY,
AND SOCIAL WELFARE
*Everett C. Hughes, Barrie Thorne,
Agostino DeBaggis, Arnold Gurin,
and David Williams*

THE FUTURE OF HIGHER
EDUCATION:
SOME SPECULATIONS AND
SUGGESTIONS
Alexander M. Mood

CONTENT AND CONTEXT:
ESSAYS ON COLLEGE EDUCATION
Carl Kaysen (ed.)

THE RISE OF THE ARTS ON THE AMERICAN
CAMPUS
Jack Morrison

THE UNIVERSITY AND THE CITY:
EIGHT CASES OF INVOLVEMENT
*George Nash, Dan Waldorf, and Robert E.
Price*

THE BEGINNING OF THE FUTURE:
A HISTORICAL APPROACH TO GRADUATE
EDUCATION IN THE ARTS AND SCIENCES
Richard J. Storr

ACADEMIC TRANSFORMATION:
SEVENTEEN INSTITUTIONS UNDER PRESSURE
David Riesman and Verne A. Stadtman (eds.)

WHERE COLLEGES ARE AND WHO ATTENDS:
EFFECTS OF ACCESSIBILITY ON COLLEGE
ATTENDANCE
*C. Arnold Anderson, Mary Jean Bowman, and
Vincent Tinto*

NEW DIRECTIONS IN LEGAL EDUCATION
*Herbert L. Packer and Thomas Ehrlich
abridged and unabridged editions*

THE UNIVERSITY AS AN ORGANIZATION
James A. Perkins (ed.)

THE EMERGING TECHNOLOGY:
INSTRUCTIONAL USES OF THE COMPUTER
IN HIGHER EDUCATION
Roger E. Levien

A STATISTICAL PORTRAIT OF HIGHER
EDUCATION
Seymour E. Harris

THE HOME OF SCIENCE:
THE ROLE OF THE UNIVERSITY
Dael Wolfle

EDUCATION AND EVANGELISM:
A PROFILE OF PROTESTANT COLLEGES
C. Robert Pace

PROFESSIONAL EDUCATION:
SOME NEW DIRECTIONS
Edgar H. Schein

THE NONPROFIT RESEARCH INSTITUTE:
ITS ORIGIN, OPERATION, PROBLEMS, AND
PROSPECTS
Harold Orlans

THE INVISIBLE COLLEGES:
A PROFILE OF SMALL, PRIVATE COLLEGES
WITH LIMITED RESOURCES
Alexander W. Astin and Calvin B. T. Lee

AMERICAN HIGHER EDUCATION:
DIRECTIONS OLD AND NEW
Joseph Ben-David

A DEGREE AND WHAT ELSE?
CORRELATES AND CONSEQUENCES OF A
COLLEGE EDUCATION
*Stephen B. Withey, Jo Anne Coble, Gerald
Gurin, John P. Robinson, Burkhard Strumpel,
Elizabeth Keogh Taylor, and Arthur C. Wolfe*

THE MULTICAMPUS UNIVERSITY:
A STUDY OF ACADEMIC GOVERNANCE
Eugene C. Lee and Frank M. Bowen

INSTITUTIONS IN TRANSITION:
A PROFILE OF CHANGE IN HIGHER
EDUCATION
(INCORPORATING THE 1970 STATISTICAL
REPORT)
Harold L. Hodgkinson

EFFICIENCY IN LIBERAL EDUCATION:
A STUDY OF COMPARATIVE INSTRUCTIONAL
COSTS FOR DIFFERENT WAYS OF ORGANIZ-
ING TEACHING-LEARNING IN A LIBERAL
ARTS COLLEGE
Howard R. Bowen and Gordon K. Douglass

CREDIT FOR COLLEGE:
PUBLIC POLICY FOR STUDENT LOANS
Robert W. Hartman

MODELS AND MAVERICKS:
A PROFILE OF PRIVATE LIBERAL ARTS
COLLEGES
Morris T. Keeton

BETWEEN TWO WORLDS:
A PROFILE OF NEGRO HIGHER EDUCATION
Frank Bowles and Frank A. DeCosta

BREAKING THE ACCESS BARRIERS:
A PROFILE OF TWO-YEAR COLLEGES
Leland L. Medsker and Dale Tillery

ANY PERSON, ANY STUDY:
AN ESSAY ON HIGHER EDUCATION IN THE
UNITED STATES
Eric Ashby

THE NEW DEPRESSION IN HIGHER
EDUCATION:
A STUDY OF FINANCIAL CONDITIONS AT 41
COLLEGES AND UNIVERSITIES
Earl F. Cheit

FINANCING MEDICAL EDUCATION:
AN ANALYSIS OF ALTERNATIVE POLICIES
AND MECHANISMS
Rashi Fein and Gerald I. Weber

HIGHER EDUCATION IN NINE COUNTRIES:
A COMPARATIVE STUDY OF COLLEGES AND
UNIVERSITIES ABROAD
*Barbara B. Burn, Philip G. Altbach, Clark Kerr,
and James A. Perkins*

BRIDGES TO UNDERSTANDING:
INTERNATIONAL PROGRAMS OF AMERICAN
COLLEGES AND UNIVERSITIES
Irwin T. Sanders and Jennifer C. Ward

GRADUATE AND PROFESSIONAL EDUCATION,
1980:
A SURVEY OF INSTITUTIONAL PLANS
Lewis B. Mayhew
(Out of print, but available from University Microfilms.)

THE AMERICAN COLLEGE AND AMERICAN
CULTURE:
SOCIALIZATION AS A FUNCTION OF HIGHER
EDUCATION
Oscar Handlin and Mary F. Handlin

RECENT ALUMNI AND HIGHER EDUCATION:
A SURVEY OF COLLEGE GRADUATES
Joe L. Spaeth and Andrew M. Greeley
(Out of print, but available from University Microfilms.)

CHANGE IN EDUCATIONAL POLICY:
SELF-STUDIES IN SELECTED COLLEGES AND
UNIVERSITIES
Dwight R. Ladd

STATE OFFICIALS AND HIGHER EDUCATION:
A SURVEY OF THE OPINIONS AND
EXPECTATIONS OF POLICY MAKERS IN NINE
STATES
Heinz Eulau and Harold Quinley
(Out of print, but available from University Microfilms.)

ACADEMIC DEGREE STRUCTURES,
INNOVATIVE APPROACHES:
PRINCIPLES OF REFORM IN DEGREE
STRUCTURES IN THE UNITED STATES
Stephen H. Spurr

COLLEGES OF THE FORGOTTEN AMERICANS:
A PROFILE OF STATE COLLEGES AND
REGIONAL UNIVERSITIES
E. Alden Dunham

FROM BACKWATER TO MAINSTREAM:
A PROFILE OF CATHOLIC HIGHER
EDUCATION
Andrew M. Greeley

THE ECONOMICS OF THE MAJOR PRIVATE
UNIVERSITIES
William G. Bowen
(Out of print, but available from University Microfilms.)

THE FINANCE OF HIGHER EDUCATION
Howard R. Bowen
(Out of print, but available from University Microfilms.)

ALTERNATIVE METHODS OF FEDERAL
FUNDING FOR HIGHER EDUCATION
Ron Wolk
(Out of print, but available from University Microfilms.)

INVENTORY OF CURRENT RESEARCH ON
HIGHER EDUCATION 1968
Dale M. Heckman and Warren Bryan Martin
(Out of print, but available from University Microfilms.)

The following technical reports are available from the Carnegie Commission on Higher Education, 2150 Shattuck Ave., Berkeley, California 94704.

RESOURCE USE IN HIGHER EDUCATION:
TRENDS IN OUTPUT AND INPUTS, 1930–1967
June O'Neill

THE NEW DEPRESSION IN HIGHER
EDUCATION—TWO YEARS LATER
Earl F. Cheit

MAY 1970:
THE CAMPUS AFTERMATH OF CAMBODIA
AND KENT STATE
Richard E. Peterson and John A. Bilorusky

PROFESSORS, UNIONS, AND AMERICAN
HIGHER EDUCATION
Everett Carll Ladd, Jr. and
Seymour Martin Lipset

MENTAL ABILITY AND HIGHER EDUCATIONAL
ATTAINMENT IN THE 20TH CENTURY
Paul Taubman and Terence Wales

A CLASSIFICATION OF INSTITUTIONS
OF HIGHER EDUCATION

AMERICAN COLLEGE AND UNIVERSITY
ENROLLMENT TRENDS IN 1971
Richard E. Peterson

POLITICAL IDEOLOGIES OF
GRADUATE STUDENTS:
CRYSTALLIZATION, CONSISTENCY, AND
CONTEXTUAL EFFECT
Margaret Fay and Jeff Weintraub

PAPERS ON EFFICIENCY IN THE
MANAGEMENT OF HIGHER EDUCATION
Alexander M. Mood, Colin Bell, Lawrence
Bogard, Helen Brownlee, and Joseph McCloskey

FLYING A LEARNING CENTER:
DESIGN AND COSTS OF AN OFF-CAMPUS
SPACE FOR LEARNING
Thomas J. Karwin

AN INVENTORY OF ACADEMIC INNOVATION
AND REFORM
Ann Heiss

THE DEMISE OF DIVERSITY?:
A COMPARATIVE PROFILE OF EIGHT
TYPES OF INSTITUTIONS
C. Robert Pace

ESTIMATING THE RETURNS TO EDUCATION:
A DISAGGREGATED APPROACH
Richard S. Eckaus

SOURCES OF FUNDS TO COLLEGES AND
UNIVERSITIES
June O'Neill

TUITION: A SUPPLEMENTAL
STATEMENT TO THE REPORT
OF THE CARNEGIE COMMISSION
ON HIGHER EDUCATION ON
"WHO PAYS? WHO BENEFITS?
WHO SHOULD PAY?"

TRENDS AND PROJECTIONS OF PHYSICIANS
IN THE UNITED STATES 1967–2002
Mark S. Blumberg

THE GREAT AMERICAN DEGREE
MACHINE
Douglas L. Adkins

The following reprints are available from the Carnegie Commission on Higher Education, 2150 Shattuck Ave., Berkeley, California 94704.

ACCELERATED PROGRAMS OF MEDICAL EDUCATION, by Mark S. Blumberg, reprinted from JOURNAL OF MEDICAL EDUCATION, vol. 46, no. 8, August 1971.*

*The Commission's stock of this reprint has been exhausted.

SCIENTIFIC MANPOWER FOR 1970–1985, by *Allan M. Cartter, reprinted from* SCIENCE, *vol. 172, no. 3979, pp. 132–140, April 9, 1971.**

A NEW METHOD OF MEASURING STATES' HIGHER EDUCATION BURDEN, by *Neil Timm, reprinted from* THE JOURNAL OF HIGHER EDUCATION, *vol. 42, no. 1, pp. 27–33, January 1971.**

REGENT WATCHING, by *Earl F. Cheit, reprinted from* AGB REPORTS, *vol. 13, no. 6, pp. 4–13, March 1971.**

COLLEGE GENERATIONS—FROM THE 1930S TO THE 1960S, by *Seymour M. Lipset and Everett C. Ladd, Jr., reprinted from* THE PUBLIC INTEREST, *no. 25, Summer 1971.**

WHAT'S BUGGING THE STUDENTS?, by *Kenneth Keniston, reprinted from* EDUCATIONAL RECORD, *American Council on Education, Washington, D.C., Spring 1970.**

THE POLITICS OF ACADEMIA, by *Seymour Martin Lipset, reprinted from David C. Nichols (ed.),* PERSPECTIVES ON CAMPUS TENSIONS: PAPERS PREPARED FOR THE SPECIAL COMMITTEE ON CAMPUS TENSIONS, *American Council on Education, Washington, D.C., September 1970.**

INTERNATIONAL PROGRAMS OF U.S. COLLEGES AND UNIVERSITIES: PRIORITIES FOR THE SEVENTIES, by *James A. Perkins, reprinted by permission of the International Council for Educational Development, Occasional Paper no. 1, July 1971.**

FACULTY UNIONISM: FROM THEORY TO PRACTICE, by *Joseph W. Garbarino, reprinted from* INDUSTRIAL RELATIONS, *vol. 11, no. 1, pp. 1–17, February 1972.**

MORE FOR LESS: HIGHER EDUCATION'S NEW PRIORITY, by *Virginia B. Smith, reprinted from* UNIVERSAL HIGHER EDUCATION: COSTS AND BENEFITS, *American Council on Education, Washington, D.C., 1971.**

ACADEMIA AND POLITICS IN AMERICA, by *Seymour M. Lipset, reprinted from Thomas J. Nossiter (ed.),* IMAGINATION AND PRECISION IN THE SOCIAL SCIENCES, *pp. 211–289, Faber and Faber, London, 1972.**

POLITICS OF ACADEMIC NATURAL SCIENTISTS AND ENGINEERS, by *Everett C. Ladd, Jr., and Seymour M. Lipset, reprinted from* SCIENCE, *vol. 176, no. 4039, pp. 1091–1100, June 9, 1972.*

THE INTELLECTUAL AS CRITIC AND REBEL, WITH SPECIAL REFERENCE TO THE UNITED STATES AND THE SOVIET UNION, by *Seymour M. Lipset and Richard B. Dobson, reprinted from* DAEDALUS, *vol. 101, no. 3, pp. 137–198, Summer 1972.*

THE POLITICS OF AMERICAN SOCIOLOGISTS, by *Seymour M. Lipset and Everett C. Ladd, Jr., reprinted from* THE AMERICAN JOURNAL OF SOCIOLOGY, *vol. 78, no. 1, July 1972.*

*The Commission's stock of this reprint has been exhausted.

THE DISTRIBUTION OF ACADEMIC TENURE IN AMERICAN HIGHER EDUCATION, *by Martin Trow, reprinted from* THE TENURE DEBATE, *Bardwell Smith (ed.), Jossey-Bass, San Francisco, 1972.*

THE NATURE AND ORIGINS OF THE CARNEGIE COMMISSION ON HIGHER EDUCATION, *by Alan Pifer, based on a speech delivered to the Pennsylvania Association of Colleges and Universities, Oct. 16, 1972, reprinted by permission of the Carnegie Foundation for the Advancement of Teaching.*

AMERICAN SOCIAL SCIENTISTS AND THE GROWTH OF CAMPUS POLITICAL ACTIVISM IN THE 1960s, *by Everett C. Ladd, Jr., and Seymour M. Lipset, reprinted from* SOCIAL SCIENCES INFORMATION, *vol. 10, no. 2, April 1971.**

THE POLITICS OF AMERICAN POLITICAL SCIENTISTS, *by Everett C. Ladd, Jr., and Seymour M. Lipset, reprinted from* PS, *vol. 4, no. 2, Spring 1971.**

THE DIVIDED PROFESSORIATE, *by Seymour M. Lipset and Everett C. Ladd, Jr., reprinted from* CHANGE, *vol. 3, no. 3, pp. 54–60, May 1971.**

JEWISH ACADEMICS IN THE UNITED STATES: THEIR ACHIEVEMENTS, CULTURE AND POLITICS, *by Seymour M. Lipset and Everett C. Ladd, Jr., reprinted from* AMERICAN JEWISH YEAR BOOK, *1971.**

THE UNHOLY ALLIANCE AGAINST THE CAMPUS, *by Kenneth Keniston and Michael Lerner, reprinted from* NEW YORK TIMES MAGAZINE, *November 8, 1970.**

PRECARIOUS PROFESSORS: NEW PATTERNS OF REPRESENTATION, *by Joseph W. Garbarino, reprinted from* INDUSTRIAL RELATIONS, *vol. 10, no. 1, February 1971.**

. . . AND WHAT PROFESSORS THINK: ABOUT STUDENT PROTEST AND MANNERS, MORALS, POLITICS, AND CHAOS ON THE CAMPUS, *by Seymour Martin Lipset and Everett C. Ladd, Jr., reprinted from* PSYCHOLOGY TODAY, *November 1970.**

DEMAND AND SUPPLY IN U.S. HIGHER EDUCATION: A PROGRESS REPORT, *by Roy Radner and Leonard S. Miller, reprinted from* AMERICAN ECONOMIC REVIEW, *May 1970.**

RESOURCES FOR HIGHER EDUCATION: AN ECONOMIST'S VIEW, *by Theodore W. Schultz, reprinted from* JOURNAL OF POLITICAL ECONOMY, *vol. 76, no. 3, University of Chicago, May/June 1968.**

INDUSTRIAL RELATIONS AND UNIVERSITY RELATIONS, *by Clark Kerr, reprinted from* PROCEEDINGS OF THE 21ST ANNUAL WINTER MEETING OF THE INDUSTRIAL RELATIONS RESEARCH ASSOCIATION, *pp. 15–25.**

*The Commission's stock of this reprint has been exhausted.

NEW CHALLENGES TO THE COLLEGE AND UNIVERSITY, *by Clark Kerr, reprinted from Kermit Gordon (ed.),* AGENDA FOR THE NATION, *The Brookings Institution, Washington, D.C., 1968.**

PRESIDENTIAL DISCONTENT, *by Clark Kerr, reprinted from David C. Nichols (ed.),* PERSPECTIVES ON CAMPUS TENSIONS: PAPERS PREPARED FOR THE SPECIAL COMMITTEE ON CAMPUS TENSIONS, *American Council on Education, Washington, D.C., September 1970.**

STUDENT PROTEST—AN INSTITUTIONAL AND NATIONAL PROFILE, *by Harold Hodgkinson, reprinted from* THE RECORD, *vol. 71, no. 4, May 1970.**

COMING OF MIDDLE AGE IN HIGHER EDUCATION, *by Earl F. Cheit, address delivered to American Association of State Colleges and Universities and National Association of State Universities and Land-Grant Colleges, Nov. 13, 1972.*

MEASURING FACULTY UNIONISM: QUANTITY AND QUALITY, *by Bill Aussieker and J. W. Garbarino, reprinted from* INDUSTRIAL RELATIONS, *vol. 12, no. 2, May 1973.*

PROBLEMS IN THE TRANSITION FROM ELITE TO MASS HIGHER EDUCATION, *by Martin Trow, paper prepared for a conference on mass higher education sponsored by the Organization for Economic Co-operation and Development, June 1973.**